THE BOOK OF
POSITIVE
QUOTATIONS

*Compiled and Arranged
by John Cook*

Fairview Press
Minneapolis

Library of Congress Cataloging-in-Publication Data
Rubicon dictionary of positive & motivational quotations.
    The book of positive quotations / compiled and arranged by John Cook.
        p.   cm.
    The 1996 ed. published under title: The Fairview guide to positive quotations was originally published: The Rubicon dictionary of positive and motivational quotations. Newington, Conn. : Rubicon Press, © 1993.
    Includes index.
    ISBN 1-57749-053-3 (pbk. : alk. paper)
    1. Quotations. 2. Motivation (Psychology)--Quotations, maxims, etc. 3. Inspiration--Quotations, maxims, etc. I. Cook, John, 1939– . II Title.
[PN6081.R83   1997]
082--dc21   97-15078
                                                          CIP

First Printing: September 1997
05   04   16   15   14

Cover: Cover design by Laurie Ingram Duren, inc.

Printed in the United States of America

Fairview Press, a division of Fairview Health Services, publishes books and related materials that educate families and individuals about their physical, emotional, and spiritual health and motivate them to seek positive changes in themselves and their communities. For a free current catalog of Fairview Press titles, call toll-free 1-800-544-8207, or visit our website at www.fairviewpress.org.

for Freddi, Blake, Brian, and Timmy

CONTENTS

Part 3: Preparing for Success

Part 4: Knowing What to Do

Part 5: Overcoming Negatives and Uncertainties

PART 6: MAKING DREAMS COME TRUE

INTRODUCTION

There are many excellent collections of quotations. My hope is that this volume may prove a worthy companion to them, in two main ways.

First, in its size and scope. *The Book of Positive Quotations* is the largest collection of its kind, containing 7,340 quotations on 62 subjects. And, within those subjects, the quotations are arranged according to 703 concepts. (Similar, if less comprehensive, collections include Frank S. Mead's *Encyclopedia of Religious Quotations,* Margaret Pepper's *The Harper Religious and Inspirational Quotation Companion*, and Albert M. Well, Jr.'s *Inspiring Quotations, Contemporary and Classical*, all of which are wonderful resources.)

Second, in its practicality and ease of use. Special steps have been taken to make this dictionary as friendly to users as possible.

To begin with, the quotations are arranged not just by individual subjects or concepts—such as "Acceptance" or "Self-Reliance"—but by specific aspects of, or approaches to, those concepts.

For example, the chapter "Acceptance" consists of eighteen sections, such as "Acceptance Isn't Resignation" (six quotes), "Tension, Trouble, and Adversity Are Normal Parts of Life" (twenty-two quotes), and "Paradox: Acceptance Can Lead to Change" (seven quotes). And "Self-Reliance" features eleven sections, such as "We Must Rely on What's Inside Us" (nineteen quotes), "We're Responsible for Our Own Happiness" (thirty quotes), and "Accepting Responsibility for Our Errors and Mistakes" (fifteen quotes).

And, to provide readers with a wide selection of styles and tones, the collection includes many different ways of expressing each concept. Including many expressions of a concept lends that concept more credibility. Further, it shows how smart, sensitive men and women throughout history have agreed about certain basic approaches to life. They have expressed these ideas in very different ways, of course. But whether expressed in the language of the schools or the language of the streets, there must be truth in concepts that so many different people have believed in and lived by—and, in some cases, died for.

The Book of Positive Quotations is one of the few, if not the only, collection to include the same quotation in more than one category; this brings the total number of entries to more than 8,500. One reason for this approach is that, because of their subject matter, insight, or eloquence, many quotations and concepts virtually demand to appear in more than one category. (Does it not make sense to include the twenty-four quotations in the section entitled "Doing Our Duty and Pursuing Goals Leads to Happiness" in two chapters, "Goals" and "Happiness"? And shouldn't the thirty-seven quotations found in "Having Realistic Expectations of Ourselves" be included in the chapters on "Realistic Expectations" and "Self-Acceptance"?)

Equally important, however, making each chapter self-sufficient gives readers—quickly and easily, with minimal cross-checking of other chapters—the greatest range of quotations about a particular topic. (It's a shame to miss a wonderful quotation because it doesn't appear exactly where one is looking.)

• • •

Numerous questions and concerns about accuracy confront anyone who compiles quotations. Take, for example, differences in the spelling of sources' names. The same famous Russian novelist has had his name spelled "Dostoevski," "Dostoievski," and "Dostoyevsky."

The formality required to identify sources is another issue. The Spanish Jesuit writer Baltasar Gracian Y Morales, for example, is more commonly referred to as "Baltasar Gracian," or simply "Gracian." And some sources are almost universally referred to by only one name, usually in the interest of brevity, and because it would be difficult to confuse them with anyone else. "Crebillion," for example, is used for Prosper Jolyot de Crebillion, the French dramatic poet.

And, of course, through the years many exact quotations—and even more that are very similar—have been attributed to more than one source.

I have made every effort to present each quotation as accurately as possible, and to recognize and honor the appropriate source. In particularly demanding situations, the language and sources cited are those most often used by other compilers and editors. Where it was impossible to verify the accuracy or source of a quotation, I have included it anyway if I believed that the usefulness of the quotation outweighed the demands of scholarly rigor.

• • •

This book originated as a selection of life-affirming quotations I compiled for my nephews and niece for Christmas 1989.

Because I was concerned that one of them was too young for it, I wrote in a letter that accompanied the collection, "just put it away in a safe place until you're ready for it." To address the question of how someone would know they were "ready," I wrote:

"You'll be ready the first time things don't go the way you want them to, the first time you doubt your ability to do something, the first time you're tempted to quit or give up, the first time you actually fail at something.

"You'll be ready the first time you doubt a friend, or think you can't trust anyone.

"You'll be ready the first time you have to make an important decision, or choice.

"You'll be ready the first time you're afraid of something, or worried.

"You'll know when you're ready. When you are, these thoughts should give you the courage and confidence and spirit you need ... and they'll remind you of the wonder and the joy of life, regardless of how dark things seem at the moment.

"I know they will.... They always have for me."

So, in addition to being a resource for researchers, writers, students, and professionals, I hope this collection will provide comfort and inspiration for the casual browser or reader.

PART I

Peace of Mind

Peace of Mind

We All Seek Peace of Mind

I take it that what all men are really after is some form of, perhaps only some formula of, peace.

—James Conrad

The mind is never right but when it is at peace within itself.

—Lucius Annaeus Seneca

I am searching for that which every man seeks—peace and rest.

—Dante Alighieri

Primary Sources of Peace of Mind

[In] back of tranquility lies always conquered unhappiness.

—David Grayson

Order your soul; reduce your wants; live in charity; associate in Christian community; obey the laws; trust in Providence.   —Saint Augustine

Thinking about interior peace destroys interior peace. The patient who constantly feels his pulse is not getting any better.

—Hubert van Zeller

To be glad of life, because it gives you the chance to love and to work and to play and to look up at the stars; to be satisfied with your possessions, but not contented with yourself until you have made the best of them; to despise nothing in the world except falsehood and meanness, and to fear nothing except cowardice; to be governed by your admirations rather than by your disgusts; to covet nothing that is your neighbor's except his kindness of heart and gentleness of manners; to think seldom of your enemies, often of your friends, and every day of Christ; and to spend as much time as you can, with body and with spirit, in God's out-of-doors—these are little guideposts on the footpath to peace.   —Henry Van Dyke

Forgiving those who hurt us is the key to personal peace.

—G. Weatherly

The first rule is to keep an untroubled spirit. The second is to look things in the face and know them for what they are.   —Marcus Aurelius

It takes time, love, and support to find peace with the restless one.
—Deidra Sarault

The only peace, the only security, is in fulfillment. —Henry Miller

Peace of mind is that mental condition in which you have accepted the worst. —Lin Yutang

In truth, to attain to interior peace, one must be willing to pass through the contrary to peace.
—Swami Brahmananda

When at night you cannot sleep, talk to the Shepherd and stop counting sheep. —Anon.

We Must Find Peace within Ourselves

When we are unable to find tranquility within ourselves, it is useless to seek it elsewhere.
—Francois de La Rochefoucauld

If you do not find peace in yourself, you will never find it anywhere else.
—Paula A. Bendry

If there is to be any peace it will come through being, not having.
—Henry Miller

Nowhere can man find a quieter or more untroubled retreat than in his own soul. —Marcus Aurelius

Peace does not dwell in outward things, but within the soul; we may preserve it in the midst of the bitterest pain, if our will remains firm and submissive. Peace in this life springs from acquiescence to, not in an exemption from, suffering.
—Francois de Fenelon

Nothing can bring you peace but yourself.
—Ralph Waldo Emerson

Peace and a Higher Power

In a world filled with causes for worry and anxiety ... we need the peace of God standing guard over our hearts and minds.
—Jerry W. McCant

Peace is not the absence of conflict, but the presence of God no matter what the conflict. —Anon.

There may be those on earth who dress better or eat better, but those who enjoy the peace of God sleep better. —L. Thomas Holdcroft

This is a sane, wholesome, practical, working faith: That it is a man's business to do the will of God; second, that God himself takes on the care of that man; and third, that therefore that man ought never to be afraid of anything.
—George MacDonald

When we believe that God is Father, we also believe that such a father's hand will never cause his child a needless tear. We may not understand life any better, but we will not resent life any longer.
—William Barclay

The peace is won by accompanying God into the battle.
—Eivind Josef Berggrav

GENERAL QUOTATIONS ABOUT PEACE OF MIND

It takes more distress and poison to kill someone who has peace of mind and loves life.

—Bernie S. Siegel, M.D.

Happiness

The Importance of Happiness

When a man has lost all happiness, he's not alive. Call him a breathing corpse.　　　　　　—Sophocles

Happiness is the meaning and the purpose of life, the whole aim and end of human existence.　—Aristotle

Happiness is the only sanction in life; where happiness fails, existence remains a mad and lamentable experiment.　　—George Santayana

The pursuit of happiness ... is the greatest feat man has to accomplish.
　　　　　　—Robert Henri

Make us happy and you make us good.　　　—Robert Browning

The joyfulness of a man prolongeth his days.　　　　　—Psalms

Everyone, without exception, is searching for happiness.
　　　　　　—Blaise Pascal

Living Fully and Enjoying Life

Live all you can; it's a mistake not to. It doesn't so much matter what you do in particular, so long as you have your life. If you haven't had that, what *have* you had?
　　　　　　—Henry James

There is no cure for birth and death save to enjoy the interval.
　　　　　　—George Santayana

Men are made for happiness, and anyone who is completely happy has a right to say to himself: "I am doing God's will on earth."
　　　　　　—Anton Chekhov

Without pleasure man would live like a fool and soon die.
　　　　—Pierre de Beaumarchais

All animals except man know that the principle business of life is to enjoy it.　　　—Samuel Butler

To live as fully, as completely as possible, to be happy ... is the true aim and end to life.　—Llewelyn Powers

Living well and beautifully and justly are all one thing.　　—Socrates

This is life! It can harden and it can exalt! —Henrik Ibsen

All I can say about life is, Oh God, enjoy it! —Bob Newhart

It is in his pleasure that a man really lives. —Agnes Repplier

Happiness hates the timid!
—Eugene O'Neill

I have smelt all the aromas there are in the fragrant kitchen they call Earth; and what we can enjoy in this life, I surely have enjoyed just like a lord! —Heinrich Heine

Man is that he might have joy.
—Joseph Smith

It is better to be happy for a moment and be burned up with beauty than to live a long time and be bored all the while. —Don Marquis

If you want to die happily, learn to live; if you would live happily, learn to die. —Celio Calcagnini

Happiness comes more from loving than being loved; and often when our affection seems wounded it is only our vanity bleeding. To love, and to be hurt often, and to love again—this is the brave and happy life. —J.E. Buchrose

The true object of all human life is play. —G.K. Chesterton

The right to happiness is fundamental. —Anna Pavlova

We Have a Duty to Be Happy

Not only is there a right to be happy, there is a duty to be happy. So much sadness exists in the world that we are all under obligation to contribute as much joy as lies within our powers. —John Sutherland Bonnell

There is no duty so much underrated as the duty of being happy.
—Robert Louis Stevenson

Pleasure is the object, duty and the goal of all rational creatures.
—Voltaire

There Are Different Forms of Happiness for Different People

Different men seek ... happiness in different ways and by different means. —Aristotle

What's joy to one is a nightmare to the other. —Bertolt Brecht

Happiness ... leads none of us by the same route.
—Charles Caleb Colton

Even the lowliest, provided he is whole, can be happy, and in his own way, perfect.
—Johann von Goethe

Happiness, to some, is elation; to others it is mere stagnation.
—Amy Lowell

No sooner is it a little calmer with me than it is almost too calm, as though I have the true feeling of myself only when I am unbearably unhappy. —Franz Kafka

Your readiest desire is your path to joy ... even if it destroys you.
—Holbrook Jackson

All men have happiness as their object: there are no exceptions. However different the means they employ, they aim at the same end.
—Blaise Pascal

We all live with the objective of being happy; our lives are all different and yet the same.
—Anne Frank

The world is so full of a number of things, I'm sure we should all be as happy as kings.
—Robert Louis Stevenson

BEWARE FALSE HAPPINESS

Real happiness is cheap enough, yet how dearly we pay for its counterfeit.
—Hosea Ballou

False happiness renders men stern and proud, and that happiness is never communicated. True happiness renders kind and sensible, and that happiness is always shared.
—Charles de Montesquieu

Don't mistake pleasures for happiness. They are a different breed of dog.
—Josh Billings

Mirth is better than fun, and happiness is better than mirth.
—William Blake

Amusement is the happiness of those who cannot think.
—Alexander Pope

Happiness is a small and unworthy goal for something as big and fancy as a whole lifetime, and should be taken in small doses.
—Russell Baker

False happiness is like false money; it passes for a long time as well as the true, and serves some ordinary occasions; but when it is brought to the touch, we find the lightness and alloy, and feel the loss.
—Alexander Pope

There is more to life than just existing and having a pleasant time.
—J.C.F. von Schiller

The test of enjoyment is the remembrance which it leaves behind.
—Logan Pearsall Smith

WE'RE RESPONSIBLE FOR OUR OWN HAPPINESS

When I have been unhappy, I have heard an opera ... and it seemed the shrieking of winds; when I am happy, a sparrow's chirp is delicious to me. But it is not the chirp that makes me happy, but I that make it sweet.
—John Ruskin

Happiness depends upon ourselves.
—Aristotle

The U.S. Constitution doesn't guarantee happiness, only the pursuit of it. Your have to catch up with it yourself.
—Benjamin Franklin

Happiness belongs to those who are sufficient unto themselves. For all external sources of happiness and pleasure are, by their very nature, highly uncertain, precarious, ephemeral and subject to chance.
—Arthur Schopenhauer

Most folks are about as happy as they make up their minds to be.
—Abraham Lincoln

One is happy as a result of one's own efforts—once one knows the necessary ingredients of happiness—simple tastes, a certain degree of courage, self-denial to a point, love of work, and, above all, a clear conscience. —George Sand

Discontent is want of self-reliance; it is infirmity of will.
—Ralph Waldo Emerson

I'm happier.... I guess I made up my mind to be that way.
—Merle Haggard

The essence of philosophy is that a man should so live that his happiness shall depend as little as possible on external things. —Epictetus

Nothing can bring you peace but yourself.
—Ralph Waldo Emerson

No one gives joy or sorrow.... We gather the consequences of our own deeds. —Garuda Purana

Happiness, happiness ... the flavor is with you—with you alone, and you can make it as intoxicating as you please. —Joseph Conrad

Few are they who have never had the chance to achieve happiness ... and fewer those who have taken that chance. —André Maurois

To win one's joy through struggle is better than to yield to melancholy.
—André Gide

Life is a romantic business, but you have to make the romance.
—Oliver Wendell Holmes

To be obliged to beg our daily happiness from others bespeaks a more lamentable poverty than that of him who begs his daily bread.
—Charles Caleb Colton

Some pursue happiness, others create it. —Anon .

The man who makes everything that leads to happiness depend upon himself, and not upon other men, has adopted the very best plan for living happily. —Plato

Man is the artificer of his own happiness. —Henry David Thoreau

It is not the level of prosperity that makes for happiness but the kinship of heart to heart and the way we look at the world. Both attitudes are within our power, so that a man is happy so long as he chooses to be happy, and no one can stop him.
—Aleksandr Solzhenitsyn

Happy is he that chastens himself.
—Anon.

How unhappy is he who cannot forgive himself. —Publilius Syrus

WE CAN LEARN HOW TO BE HAPPY

Like swimming, riding, writing or playing golf, happiness can be learned. —Dr. Boris Sokoloff

Being happy is something you have to learn. I often surprise myself by saying, "Wow, this is it. I guess I'm happy. I've got a home that I love. A career that I love. I'm even feeling more and more at peace with myself." If there's something else to happiness, let me know. I'm ambitious for that, too.   —Harrison Ford

Learn how to feel joy.   —Seneca

PRESCRIPTIONS FOR TOTAL HAPPINESS

Nine requisites for contented living: Health enough to make work a pleasure. Wealth enough to support your needs. Strength to battle with difficulties and overcome them. Grace enough to confess your sins and forsake them. Patience enough to toil until some good is accomplished. Charity enough to see some good in your neighbor. Love enough to move you to be useful and helpful to others. Faith enough to make real the things of God. Hope enough to remove all anxious fears concerning the future.   —Johann von Goethe

Happiness comes of the capacity to feel deeply, to enjoy simply, to think freely, to risk life, to be needed.
                —Storm Jameson

Do not worry; eat three square meals a day; say your prayers; be courteous to your creditors; keep your digestion good; exercise; go slow and easy. Maybe there are other things your special case requires to make you happy; but, my friend, these I reckon will give you a good lift.
                —Abraham Lincoln

Have a variety of interests.... These interests relax the mind and lessen tension on the nervous system. People with many interests live, not only longest, but happiest.
          —George Matthew Allen

This is wisdom: to love wine, beauty, and the heavenly spring. That's sufficient—the rest is worthless.
            —Theodore De Banville

If a man has important work, and enough leisure and income to enable him to do it properly, he is in possession of as much happiness as is good for any of the children of Adam.
                —R.H. Tawney

The secret of happiness ... is to be in harmony with existence, to be always calm, always lucid, always willing "to be joined to the universe without being more conscious of it than an idiot," to let each wave of life wash us a little farther up the shore.   —Cyril Connolly

Good friends, good books and a sleepy conscience: this is the ideal life.   —Mark Twain

The best philosophy is to do one's duties, to take the world as it comes, submit respectfully to one's lot, and bless the goodness that has given us so much happiness with it, whatever it is.   —Horace Walpole

The grand essentials to happiness in this life are something to do, something to love and something to hope for.   —Joseph Addison

One is happy as a result of one's own efforts—once one knows the necessary ingredients of happiness— simple tastes, a certain degree of courage, self-denial to a point, love of work, and, above all, a clear conscience.   —George Sand

In order to be utterly happy the only

thing necessary is to refrain from comparing this moment with other moments in the past, which I often did not fully enjoy because I was comparing them with other moments of the future. —André Gide

To make a man happy, fill his hands with work, his heart with affection, his mind with purpose, his memory with useful knowledge, his future with hope, and his stomach with food. —Frederick E. Crane

For me, happiness came from prayer to a kindly God, faith in a kindly God, love for my fellow man, and doing the very best I could every day of my life. I had looked for happiness in fast living, but it was not there. I tried to find it in money, but it was not there, either. But when I placed myself in tune with what I believe to be fundamental truths of life, when I began to develop my limited ability, to rid my mind of all kinds of tangled thoughts and fill it with zeal and courage and love, when I gave myself a chance by treating myself decently and sensibly, I began to feel the stimulating, warm glow of happiness. —Edward Young

There are three ingredients in the good life: learning, earning and yearning.
—Christopher Morley

Work and love—these are the basics. Without them there is neurosis.
—Theodor Reik

If thou workest at that which is before thee ... expecting nothing, fearing nothing, but satisfied with thy present activity according to

Nature, and with heroic truth in every word and sound which thou utterest, thou wilt live happy. And there is no man who is able to prevent this. —Marcus Aurelius

Our greatest happiness does not depend on the condition of life in which chance has placed us, but is always the result of a good conscience, good health, occupation and freedom in all just pursuits.
—Thomas Jefferson

I believe the recipe for happiness to be just enough money to pay the monthly bills you acquire, a little surplus to give you confidence, a little too much work each day, enthusiasm for your work, a substantial share of good health, a couple of real friends and a wife and children to share life's beauty with you.
—J. Kenfield Morley

If we could learn how to balance rest against effort, calmness against strain, quiet against turmoil, we would assure ourselves of joy in living and psychological health for life.
—Josephine Rathbone

Five great enemies to peace inhabit us: avarice, ambition, envy, anger and pride. If those enemies were to be banished, we should infallibly enjoy perpetual peace.
—Ralph Waldo Emerson

True happiness ... arises, in the first place, from the enjoyment of one's self, and in the next, from the friendship and conversation of a few select companions. —Joseph Addison

May you have warmth in your igloo,

oil in your lamp, and peace in your heart.   —Eskimo proverb

What can be added to the happiness of man who is in health, out of debt, and has a clear conscience?
                        —Adam Smith

Do you prefer that you be right, or that you be happy?
                —*A Course In Miracles*

To do the useful thing, to say the courageous thing, to contemplate the beautiful thing: that is enough for one man's life.   —T.S. Eliot

To be glad of life, because it gives you the chance to love and to work and to play and to look up at the stars; to be satisfied with your possessions, but not contented with yourself until you have made the best of them; to despise nothing in the world except falsehood and meanness, and to fear nothing except cowardice; to be governed by your admirations rather than by your disgusts; to covet nothing that is your neighbor's except his kindness of heart and gentleness of manners; to think seldom of your enemies, often of your friends, and every day of Christ; and to spend as much time as you can, with body and with spirit, in God's out-of-doors—these are little guideposts on the footpath to peace.   —Henry Van Dyke

Let your boat of life be light, packed only with what you need—a homely home and simple pleasures, one or two friends worth the name, someone to love and to love you, a cat, a dog, enough to eat and enough to wear, and a little more than enough

to drink, for thirst is a dangerous thing.   —Jerome K. Jerome

Order your soul; reduce your wants; live in charity; associate in Christian community; obey the laws; trust in Providence.   —Saint Augustine

Simplicity, clarity, singleness: these are the attributes that give our lives power and vividness and joy.
                —Richard Halloway

Manifest plainness,
Embrace simplicity,
Reduce selfishness,
Have few desires.   —Lao-tzu

Happiness comes of the capacity to feel deeply, to enjoy simply, to think freely, to risk life, to be needed.
                —Storm Jameson

Fear less, hope more; eat less, chew more; whine less, breathe more; talk less, say more; love more, and all good things will be yours.
                —Swedish proverb

Practice easing your way along. Don't get het up or in a dither. Do your best; take it as it comes. You can handle anything if you think you can. Just keep your cool and your sense of humor.
                —Smiley Blanton, M.D.

To live content with small means; to seek elegance rather than luxury, and refinement rather than fashion; to be worthy, not respectable, and wealthy, not rich; to study hard, think quietly, talk gently, act frankly; to listen to the stars and birds, to babes and sages, with open heart; to bear on cheerfully, do all

bravely, awaiting occasions, worry never; in a word to, like the spiritual, unbidden and unconscious, grow up through the common.
—William Ellery Channing

To live and let live, without clamor for distinction or recognition; to wait on divine Love; to write truth first on the tablet of one's own heart—this is the sanity and perfection of living, and my human ideal.
—Mary Baker Eddy

Do all the good you can,
By all the means you can,
In all the ways you can,
In all the places you can,
At all the times you can.   —Anon.

Go placidly amid the noise and the haste, and remember what peace there may be in silence. As far as possible without surrender, be on good terms with all persons. Speak your truth quietly and clearly, and listen to others, even the dull and ignorant; they too have their story.... Be yourself. Especially do not feign affection. Neither be cynical about love; for in the face of all aridity and disenchantment it is as perennial as the grass. Take kindly the counsel of the years, gracefully surrendering the things of youth. Nurture strength of spirit to shield you in sudden misfortune. But do not distress yourself with imaginings. Many fears are born of fatigue and loneliness. Beyond a wholesome discipline, be gentle with yourself. You are a child of the universe no less than the trees and the stars; you have a right to be here. And whether or not it is clear to you, no doubt the universe is unfolding as it should. Therefore be

at peace with God, whatever you conceive Him to be, and whatever your labours and aspirations, in the noisy confusion of life keep peace with your soul. With all its sham, drudgery and broken dreams, it is still a beautiful world.
—Max Ehrmann

Accept the pain, cherish the joys, resolve the regrets; then can come the best of benedictions—"If I had my life to live over, I'd do it all the same."   —Joan McIntosh

The way of a superior man is three-fold: Virtuous, he is free from anxieties; wise, he is free from perplexities; bold, he is free from fear.
—Confucius

The first rule is to keep an untroubled spirit. The second is to look things in the face and know them for what they are.   —Marcus Aurelius

Happiness Comes from Who and What We Are, and Our Inner Life

It is not easy to find happiness in ourselves, and it is not possible to find it elsewhere.   —Agnes Repplier

To live happily is an inward power of the soul.   —Marcus Aurelius

All times are beautiful for those who maintain joy within them; but there is no happy or favorable time for those with disconsolate or orphaned souls.   —Rosalia Castro

If an Arab in the desert were suddenly to discover a spring in his tent, and so would always be able to have water in abundance, how fortunate he would consider himself; so too, when a man who ... is always turned toward the outside, thinking that his happiness lies outside him, finally turns inward and discovers that the source is within him.

—Søren Kierkegaard

Happiness is not in our circumstances, but in ourselves. It is not something we see, like a rainbow, or feel, like the heat of a fire. Happiness is something we *are*.

—John B. Sheerin

If we have not peace within ourselves, it is in vain to seek it from outward sources.

—Francois de La Rochefoucauld

Most true happiness comes from one's inner life, from the disposition of the mind and soul. Admittedly, a good inner life is difficult to achieve, especially in these trying times. It takes reflection and contemplation and self-discipline. —W.L. Shirer

The happiest people seem to be those who have no particular cause for being happy except that they are so.

—William Ralph Inge

I don't think that ... one gets a flash of happiness once, and never again; it is there within you, and it will come as certainly as death.

—Isak Dinesen

A happy life is one which is in accordance with its own nature.

—Marcus Annaeus Seneca

It Doesn't Pay to Seek Happiness Directly

Happiness is a butterfly which, when

pursued, is always beyond our grasp, but, if you will sit down quietly, may alight upon you.

—Nathaniel Hawthorne

Perfect happiness is the absence of striving for happiness. —Chuang-Tse

Pleasure is very seldom found where it is sought. Our brightest blazes are commonly kindled by unexpected sparks. —Samuel Johnson

Those who seek happiness miss it, and those who discuss it, lack it.

—Holbrook Jackson

Nothing is more hopeless than a scheme of merriment.

—Samuel Johnson

Now and then it's good to pause in our pursuit of happiness and just be happy. —*The Cockle Bur*

Happiness is never stopping to think if you are. —Palmer Sondreal

It is the paradox of life that the way to miss pleasure is to seek it first. The very first condition of lasting happiness is that a life should be full of purpose, aiming at something outside self. —Hugh Black

If you pursue happiness you'll never find it. —C.P. Snow

Some of us might find happiness if we quit struggling so desperately for it. —William Feather

Seek not happiness too greedily, and be not fearful of unhappiness.

—Lao-tzu

13

The man of pleasure, by a vain attempt to be more happy than any man can be, is often more miserable than most men.
—Charles Caleb Colton

The bird of paradise alights only on the hand that does not grasp.
—John Berry

The only way to happiness is never to give happiness a thought.
—Elton Trueblood

Everyone chases after happiness, not noticing that happiness is at their heels.   —Bertolt Brecht

Deliberately to pursue happiness is not the surest way of achieving it. Seek it for its own sake and I doubt whether you will find it.
—Robert J. McCracken

Seek to do good, and you will find that happiness will run after you.
—James Freeman Clarke

Happiness must not be sought for; when what disturbs passes away, happiness comes of itself.
—*The Gospel According To Zen*

Enjoyment is not a goal, it is a feeling that accompanies important ongoing activity.   —Paul Goodman

If only we'd stop trying to be happy we'd have a pretty good time.
—Edith Wharton

Most men pursue pleasure with such breathless haste that they hurry past it.   —Søren Kierkegaard

Happiness comes most to persons who seek it least, and think least about it. It is not an object to be sought, it is a state to be induced. It must follow and not lead. It must overtake you, and not you overtake it.   —John Burroughs

Happiness sneaks in through a door you didn't know you left open.
—John Barrymore

Happiness is like a cat. If you try to coax it or call it, it will avoid you. It will never come. But if you pay no attention to it and go about your business, you'll find it rubbing against your legs and jumping into your lap.   —William Bennett

They seemed to come suddenly upon happiness as if they had surprised a butterfly in the winter woods.
—Edith Wharton

One must never look for happiness: one meets it by the way.
—Isabelle Eberhardt

Happiness in this world, when it comes, comes incidentally. Make it the object of pursuit, and it leads us on a wild-goose chase, and is never attained. Follow some other object, and very possibly we may find that we have caught happiness without dreaming of it.
—Nathaniel Hawthorne

Happiness and beauty are by-products. Folly is the direct pursuit of happiness and beauty.
—George Bernard Shaw

It is the very pursuit of happiness that thwarts happiness.
—Viktor Frankel

If you ever find happiness by hunting for it, you will find it, as the old woman did her lost spectacles, safe on her nose all the time.
—Josh Billings

Happiness is not a goal, it is a by-product.
—Eleanor Roosevelt

Happiness is mostly a by-product of doing what makes us feel fulfilled.
—Dr. Benjamin Spock

Happiness is something you get as a by-product in the process of making something else.
—Aldous Huxley

Happiness is not a horse, you cannot harness it.
—Chinese proverb

To Be Happy, We Must Be True to Ourselves

The principles we live by, in business and in social life, are the most important part of happiness.
—Harry Harrison

Happiness is when what you think, what you say, and what you do are in harmony.
—Mahatma Gandhi

There can be no happiness if the things we believe in are different from the things we do.
—Freya Stark

Happy is the man who ventures boldly to defend what he holds dear.
—Ovid

It is necessary to the happiness of man that he be mentally faithful to himself.
—Thomas Paine

It is the chiefest point of happiness that a man is willing to be what he is.
—Erasmus

Resolve to be thyself; and know that who finds himself, loses his misery.
—Matthew Arnold

But what is happiness except the simple harmony between a man and the life he leads?
—Albert Camus

That kind of life is most happy which affords us most opportunities of gaining our own esteem.
—Samuel Johnson

Keeping Busy Is a Key to Happiness

Happiness is action.
—David Thomas

Action may not always bring happiness, but there is no happiness without action.
—William James

Happiness is often the result of being too busy to be miserable.
—Anon.

To attain happiness in another world we need only to believe something; to secure it in this world, we must do something.
—Charlotte Perkins Gilman

To fill the hour, and leave no crevice ... that is happiness.
—Ralph Waldo Emerson

If you observe a really happy man, you will find ... that he is happy in the course of living life twenty-four crowded hours of each day.
—W. Beran Wolfe

I find my joy of living in the fierce and ruthless battles of life.
—August Strindberg

15

Happiness is an expression of the soul in considered actions.
—Aristotle

We must be doing something to be happy.
—William Hazlitt

Happiness lies in the fulfillment of the spirit through the body.
—Cyrol Connolly

We must not seek happiness in peace, but in conflict.
—Paul Claudel

Happiness walks on busy feet.
—Kitte Turmell

Our actions are the springs of our happiness or misery.
—Philip Skelton

The formula for complete happiness is to be very busy.
—A. Edward Newton

The busiest man is the happiest man.
—Sir Theodore Martin

To be busy is man's only happiness.
—Mark Twain

The only way to avoid being miserable is not to have enough leisure to wonder whether you are happy or not.
—George Bernard Shaw

The happiest people are those who are too busy to notice whether they are or not.
—William Feather

ACCEPTING THE INEVITABLE IS CRITICAL TO OUR HAPPINESS

Happiness ... can exist only in acceptance.
—Denis De Rougemont

Knowledge of what is possible is the beginning of happiness.
—George Santayana

There is only one way to happiness, and that is to cease worrying about things which are beyond the power of our will.
—Epictetus

Happiness comes from ... some curious adjustment to life.
—Hugh Walpole

Happy is he who learns to bear what he cannot change!
—J.C.F. von Schiller

The secret of happiness is not in doing what one likes, but in liking what one has to do.
—Sir James M. Barrie

He is happy whose circumstances suit his temper; but he is more excellent who suits his temper to any circumstances.
—David Hume

Happiness is experienced when your life gives you what you are willing to accept.
—Ken Keyes, Jr.

Life is not always what one wants it to be, but to make the best of it as it is, is the only way of being happy.
—Jennie Jerome Churchill

We deem those happy who from the experience of life have learned to bear its ills, without being overcome by them.
—Juvenal

Peace of mind is that mental condition in which you have accepted the worst.
—Lin Yutang

Doing Our Duty and Pursuing Goals Leads to Happiness

This is true joy of life—being used for a purpose that is recognized by yourself as a mighty one ... instead of being a feverish, selfish little clod of ailments and grievances, complaining that the world will not devote itself to making you happy.
—George Bernard Shaw

Never mind your happiness; do your duty. —Will Durant

Human happiness and moral duty are inseparably connected.
—George Washington

When we ... devote ourselves to the strict and unsparing performance of duty, then happiness comes of itself.
—Wilhelm von Humboldt

Seek happiness for its own sake, and you will not find it; seek for duty, and happiness will follow as the shadow comes with the sunshine.
—Tyron Edwards

True happiness ... is not attained through self-gratification, but through fidelity to a worthy purpose.
—Helen Keller

The only true happiness comes from squandering ourselves for a purpose.
—William Cowper

Happiness is the natural flower of duty. —Phillips Brooks

The happiest excitement in life is to be convinced that one is fighting for all one is worth on behalf of some clearly seen and deeply felt good.
—Ruth Benedict

True happiness, we are told, consists in getting out of one's self. But the point is not only to get out, you must stay out. And to stay out, you must have some absorbing errand.
—Henry James

The secret of living is to find ... the pivot of a concept on which you can make your stand. —Luigi Pirandello

A man's happiness: to do the things proper to man. —Marcus Aurelius

Happy [is] the man who knows his duties!—Christian Furchtegott Gellert

The only ones among you who will be really happy are those who will have sought and found how to serve.
—Albert Schweitzer

He who never sacrificed a present to a future good, or a personal to a general one, can speak of happiness only as the blind speak of color.
—Horace Mann

There is no happiness except in the realization that we have accomplished something. —Henry Ford

I believe half the unhappiness in life comes from people being afraid to go straight at things.
—William J. Locke

The full-grown modern human being ... is conscious of touching the highest pinnacle of fulfillment ... when he is consumed in the service of an idea, in the conquest of the goal pursued.
—R. Briffault

Happiness is essentially a state of going somewhere, wholeheartedly, one-directionally, without regret or reservation.   —William H. Sheldon

Happiness is the overcoming of not unknown obstacles toward a known goal.   —L. Ron Hubbard

Give a man health and a course to steer, and he'll never stop to trouble about whether he's happy or not.
    —George Bernard Shaw

Having a goal is a state of happiness.
    —E.J. Bartek

Happiness lies in the joy of achievement and the thrill of creative effort.
    —Franklin Delano Roosevelt

Without duty, life is soft and boneless.   —Joseph Joubert

True Happiness Comes from Little Things—Not Big Ones

Man is meant for happiness and this happiness is in him, in the satisfaction of the daily needs of his existence.   —Leo Tolstoy

A multitude of small delights constitute happiness.
    —Charles Baudelaire

The happiness of life is made up of minute fractions—the little, soon-forgotten charities of a kiss or smile, a kind look, a heart-felt compliment, and the countless infinitesimals of pleasurable and genial feeling.
    —Samuel Taylor Coleridge

For me it is sufficient to have a corner by my hearth, a book and a friend, and a nap undisturbed by creditors or grief.
    —Fernandez de Andrada

A happy life is made up of little things ... a gift sent, a letter written, a call made, a recommendation given, transportation provided, a cake made, a book lent, a check sent.
    —Carol Holmes

Yes, there is a Nirvanah; it is in leading your sheep to a green pasture, and in putting your child to sleep, and in writing the last line of your poem.   —Kahlil Gibran

I know well that happiness is in little things.   —John Ruskin

It is by studying little things that we attain the great knowledge of having as little misery and as much happiness as possible.   —Samuel Johnson

The happiest people I have known in this world have been the Saints—and, after these, the men and women who get immediate and conscious enjoyment from little things.
    —Hugh Walpole

First health, then wealth, then pleasure, and do not owe anything to anybody.   —Catherine the Great

The little things are infinitely the most important. —Sir Arthur Conan Doyle

Happiness consists more in small conveniences or pleasures that occur every day, than in great pieces of good fortune that happen but seldom.   —Benjamin Franklin

The happiness of most people is not ruined by great catastrophes or fatal errors, but by the repetition of slowly destructive little things.
    —Ernest Dimnet

Enjoy the little things, for one day you may look back and realize they were the big things. —Robert Brault

Why not learn to enjoy the little things—there are so many of them.
—Anon.

The best things are nearest: breath in your nostrils, light in your eyes, flowers at your feet, duties at your hand, the path of God just before you. Then do not grasp at the stars, but do life's plain, common work as it comes, certain that daily duties and daily bread are the sweetest things of life.
—Robert Louis Stevenson

For most of life, nothing wonderful happens. If you don't enjoy getting up and working and finishing your work and sitting down to a meal with family or friends, then the chances are you're not going to be very happy. If someone bases his happiness or unhappiness on major events like a great new job, huge amounts of money, a flawlessly happy marriage or a trip to Paris, that person isn't going to be happy much of the time. If, on the other hand, happiness depends on a good breakfast, flowers in the yard, a drink or a nap, then we are more likely to live with quite a bit of hap-piness. —Andy Rooney

The mere sense of living is joy enough. —Emily Dickinson

OUR HAPPINESS INCREASES WHEN WE HELP OTHER PEOPLE

The true way to soften one's troubles is to solace those of others.
—Madame De Maintenon

To complain that life has no joys while there is a single creature whom we can relieve by our bounty, assist by our counsels or enliven by our presence, is ... just as rational as to die of thirst with the cup in our hands. —Thomas Fitzosborne

No man is more cheated than the selfish man. —Henry Ward Beecher

In about the same degree as you are helpful, you will be happy.
—Karl Reiland

You cannot always *have* happiness, but you can always *give* happiness.
—Anon.

No one can sincerely try to help another without helping himself.
—Charles Dudley Warner

Happiness is a by-product of helping others. —Denny Miller

The most exquisite pleasure is giving pleasure to others.
—Jean de La Bruyere

No man can live happily who regards himself alone, who turns everything to his own advantage. Thou must live for another if thou wishest to live for thyself.
—Marcus Annaeus Seneca

The habit of being uniformly consid-erate toward others will bring increased happiness to you.
—Grenville Kleiser

If you have not often felt the joy of doing a kind act, you have neglected much, and most of all yourself.
—A. Neilen

We cannot hold a torch to light another's path without brightening our own. —Ben Sweetland

Life becomes harder for us when we live for others, but it also becomes richer and happier.
—Albert Schweitzer

Happiness ... consists in giving, and in serving others.
—Henry Drummond

Pleasure is a reciprocal; no one feels it who does not at the same time give it. To be pleased, one must please.
—Lord Chesterfield

He that despiseth his neighbor sinneth; but he that hath mercy on the poor, happy is he.
—Proverbs

If all our happiness is bound up entirely in our personal circumstances, it is difficult not to demand of life more than it has to give.
—Bertrand Russell

Scatter seeds of kindness everywhere
    you go;
Scatter bits of courtesy—watch them
    grow and grow.
Gather buds of friendship, keep
    them till full-blown;
You will find more happiness than
    you have ever known.
—Amy R. Raabe

Instinct teaches us to look for happiness outside ourselves.
—Blaise Pascal

A bit of fragrance always clings to the hand that gives you roses.
—Chinese proverb

One thing I know: the only ones among you who will be really happy are those who will have sought and found how to serve.
—Albert Schweitzer

Caring about others, running the risk of feeling, and leaving an impact on people, brings happiness.
—Rabbi Harold Kushner

The entire sum of existence is the magic of being needed by just one person. —Vi Putnam

One of the things I keep learning is that the secret of being happy is doing things for other people.
—Dick Gregory

Make one person happy each day and in forty years you will have made 14,600 human beings happy for a little time, at least.
—Charley Willey

When you dig another out of their troubles, you find a place to bury your own. —Anon.

The most satisfying thing in life is to have been able to give a large part of oneself to others.
—Pierre Teilhard de Chardin

To be kind to all, to like many and love a few, to be needed and wanted by those we love, is certainly the nearest we can come to happiness.
—Mary Roberts Rinehart

Seldom can the heart be lonely,
If it seeks a lonelier still;
Self-forgetting, seeking only
Emptier cups of love to fill.
—Frances Ridley Havergal

The older you get, the more you realize that kindness is synonymous with happiness. —Lionel Barrymore

There is no happiness in having or in getting, but only in giving.
—Henry Drummond

Make happy those who are near, and those who are far will come.
—Chinese proverb

True happiness consists in making others happy. —Hindu proverb

HAPPINESS IS MEANT TO BE SHARED

All who would win joy, must share it; happiness was born a twin.
—Lord Byron

Happiness is not so much in having as sharing. We make a living by what we get, but we make a life by what we give. —Norman MacEwan

Happiness quite unshared can scarcely be called happiness; it has no taste. —Brone

Unshared joy is an unlighted candle.
—Spanish proverb

A joy that's shared is a joy made double. —English proverb

Happiness is the cheapest thing in the world ... when we buy it for someone else. —Paul Flemming

To get the full value of a joy you must have somebody to divide it with. —Mark Twain

We have no more right to consume happiness without producing it than to consume wealth without producing it. —George Bernard Shaw

When someone does something good, applaud! You will make two people happy. —Samuel Goldwyn

Happiness is not perfected until it is shared. —Jane Porter

Happiness ... is achieved only by making others happy.
—Stuart Cloete

OUR THOUGHTS DETERMINE OUR HAPPINESS

The happiness of your life depends upon the quality of your thoughts.
—Marcus Aurelius

I am happy and content because I think I am. —Alain-Rene Lesage

All happiness is in the mind.
—Anon.

Happiness is not a matter of events; it depends upon the tides of the mind. —Alice Meynell

A happy life consists in tranquility of mind. —Cicero

A man's as miserable as he thinks he is. —Marcus Annaeus Seneca

The happiest person is the person who thinks the most interesting thoughts. —William Lyon Phelps

Unhappiness indicates wrong thinking, just as ill health indicates a bad regimen. —Paul Bourge

He is happy that knoweth not himself to be otherwise. —Thomas Fuller

The greater part of our happiness or misery depends on our dispositions, and not our circumstances.
—Martha Washington

Happiness does not depend on outward things, but on the way we see them. —Leo Tolstoy

Happiness will never be any greater than the idea we have of it.
—Maurice Maeterlinck

We are never so happy or so unhappy as we think.
—Francois de La Rochefoucauld

Misery is almost always the result of thinking. —Joseph Joubert

A great obstacle to happiness is to expect too much happiness.
—Bernard de Fontenelle

It isn't our position, but our disposition, that makes us happy.
—Anon.

A man's happiness or unhappiness depends as much on his temperament as on his destiny.
—Francois de La Rochefoucauld

WORK IS ESSENTIAL TO MOST PEOPLE'S HAPPINESS

The high prize of life, the crowning fortune of man, is to be born with a bias to some pursuit which finds him in employment and happiness.
—Ralph Waldo Emerson

The road to happiness lies in two simple principles: find what it is that interests you and that you can do well, and when you find it put your whole soul into it—every bit of energy and ambition and natural ability you have. —John D. Rockefeller III

They are happy men whose natures sort with their vocations.
—Francis Bacon

The happy people are those who are producing something.
—William Ralph Inge

Congenial labor is the secret of happiness.
—Arthur Christopher Benson

To find out what one is fitted to do, and to secure an opportunity to do it, is the key to happiness.
—John Dewey

If I were to suggest a general rule for happiness, I would say "Work a little harder; Work a little longer; Work!" —Frederick H. Ecker

To make a man happy, fill his hands with work. —Frederick E. Crane

Work is the true elixir of life. The busiest man is the happiest man.
—Sir Theodore Martin

Happiness ... loves to see men work. She loves sweat, weariness, self-sacrifice. She will not be found in the palaces, but lurking in cornfields and factories, and hovering over littered desks. —David Grayson

Every job has drudgery.... The first secret of happiness is the recognition of this fundamental fact.
—M.C. McIntosh

There is work that is work and there is play that is play; there is play that

22

is work and work that is play. And in only one of these lie happiness.

—Gelett Burgess

Employment ... is so essential to human happiness that indolence is justly considered the mother of misery. —Burton

Happiness comes only when we push our brains and hearts to the farthest reaches of which we are capable.

—Leo C. Rosten

A man is relieved and gay when he has put his heart into his work and done his best.

—Ralph Waldo Emerson

All happiness depends on courage and work. —Honore de Balzac

Man is happy only as he finds a work worth doing—and does it well.

—E. Merrill Root

Life without absorbing occupation is hell. —Elbert Hubbard

There is certainly no greater happiness than to be able to look back on a life usefully and virtuously employed, to trace our own progress in existence by such tokens as excite neither shame nor sorrow.

—Samuel Johnson

Continuity of purpose is one of the most essential ingredients of happiness in the long run, and for most men this comes chiefly through their work. —Bertrand Russell

Blessed is he who has found his work; let him ask no other blessedness. He has a work, a life-pur-

pose.... Get your happiness out of your work or you will never know what real happiness is.... Even in the meanest sorts of labor, the whole soul of a man is composed into a kind of real harmony the instant he sets himself to work.

—Thomas Carlyle

Few persons realize how much of their happiness, such as it is, is dependent upon their work.

—John Burroughs

Joy is the will which labours, which overcomes obstacles, which knows triumph. —William Butler Yeats

Get happiness out of your work or you may never know what happiness is. —Elbert Hubbard

When men are rightly occupied, their amusement grows out of their work, as the color-petals out of a fruitful flower. —John Ruskin

HOME AND FAMILY LIFE CAN BE A PRIME SOURCE OF HAPPINESS

He is happiest, be he king or peasant, who finds peace in his home.

—Johann von Goethe

Family life is the source of the greatest human happiness.

—Robert J. Havighurst

If this world affords true happiness, it is to be found in a home where love and confidence increase with the years, where the necessities of life come without severe strain, where luxuries enter only after their cost has been carefully considered.

—A. Edward Newton

Happiness grows at our own firesides, and is not to be picked in
strangers' gardens.

        —Douglas Jerrold

If solid happiness we prize,
within our breast this jewel lies,
And they are fools who roam;
the world has nothing to bestow,
From our own selves our bliss must
    flow,
And that dear hut—our home.

        —Nathaniel Cotton

He who would be happy should stay
at home.   —Greek proverb

He who leaves his house in search of
happiness pursues a shadow.

        —Anon.

HAPPINESS AND HEALTH

In the Orient people believed that
the basis of all disease was unhappiness. Thus to make a patient happy
again was to restore him to health.

        —Donald Law

The simple truth is that happy people generally don't get sick.

        —Bernie S. Siegel, M.D.

Happiness is good health and a bad
memory.   —Ingrid Bergman

Laughter is the best medicine.

        —Anon.

Happiness is not being pained in
body nor troubled in mind.

        —Thomas Jefferson

Being asked one day what was the
surest way of remaining happy in
this world, the Emperor Sigismund
of Germany replied: "Only do in

health what you have promised to
do when you were sick."   —Anon.

HAPPINESS AND MONEY AND
SUCCESS

I have now reigned above fifty years
in victory or peace, beloved by my
subjects, dreaded by my enemies,
respected by my allies. Riches and
honors, power and pleasure, have
awaited my call, nor does any earthly blessing seem to have been wanting.... I have diligently numbered the
days of pure and genuine happiness
that have fallen to my lot; they
amount to fourteen.

        —Abd-Al-Rahman

It's pretty hard to tell what does
bring happiness; poverty and wealth
have both failed.   —Kin Hubbard

It is neither wealth nor splendor, but
tranquility and occupation, which
give happiness.   —Thomas Jefferson

Joy has nothing to do with material
things, or with a man's outward circumstance ... a man living in the lap
of luxury can be wretched, and a
man in the depths of poverty can
overflow with joy. —William Barclay

Money, or even power, can never
yield happiness unless it be accompanied by the goodwill of others.

        —B.C. Forbes

The secret of happiness is to admire
without desiring.   —F.H. Bradley

Success can also cause misery. The
trick is not to be surprised when you
discover it doesn't bring you all the
happiness and answers you thought
it would.   —Prince

No social system will bring us happiness, health and prosperity unless it is inspired by something greater than materialism.　　—Clement R. Attlee

Happiness seems to require a modicum of external prosperity.
　　　　　　　　　　—Aristotle

The essence of philosophy is that a man should so live that his happiness shall depend as little as possible on external things.　　—Epictetus

Happiness depends, as Nature shows, less on exterior things than most suppose.　　—William Cowper

There are two things to aim at in life: first, to get what you want; and, after that, to enjoy it. Only the wisest of mankind achieve the second.
　　　　　　—Logan Pearsall Smith

In this world there are only two tragedies. One is not getting what one wants, and the other is getting it.
　　　　　　　　　—Oscar Wilde

A life of frustration is inevitable for any coach whose main enjoyment is winning.　　　　—Chuck Noll

Money is human happiness in the abstract; he, then, who is no longer capable of enjoying human happiness in the concrete devotes himself utterly to money.
　　　　　—Arthur Schopenhauer

Those who have easy, cheerful attitudes tend to be happier than those with less pleasant temperaments regardless of money, "making it" or success.　　—Dr. Joyce Brothers

Money, or even power, can never yield happiness unless it be accompanied by the goodwill of others.
　　　　　　　　　—B.C. Forbes

Few rich men own their own property. Their property owns them.
　　　　　—Robert G. Ingersoll

HAPPINESS AND WISDOM

Our happiness depends on wisdom all the way.　　　　—Sophocles

Wisdom is the most important part of happiness.　　—Sophocles

Better be happy than wise.
　　　　　　　　　　—Anon.

Be happy. It's one way of being wise.
　　　　　　　　　—Colette

With happiness comes intelligence to the heart.　　—Chinese proverb

Best trust the happy moments.... The days that make us happy make us wise.　　—John Masefield

OTHER SOURCES OF HAPPINESS

It is an aspect of all happiness to suppose that we deserve it.
　　　　　　　　—Joseph Joubert

A reasonable man needs only to practice moderation to find happiness.　　—Johann von Goethe

To forget oneself is to be happy.
　　　　　—Robert Louis Stevenson

Happiness is a resultant of the relative strengths of positive and negative feelings rather than an absolute amount of one or the other.
　　　　　　　—Norman Bradburn

25

The first recipe for happiness is:
Avoid too lengthy meditations on
the past.   —André Maurois

Man needs, for his happiness, not
only the enjoyment of this or that,
but hope and enterprise and change.
                          —Bertrand Russell

Happy is the man who can do only
one thing; in doing it, he fulfills his
destiny.   —Joseph Joubert

And may I live the remainder of my
life ... for myself; may there be plenty of books and many years' store of
the fruits of the earth!   —Horace

Behold, we count them happy which
endure.   —Jas. 5:11

The will of man is his happiness.
                      —J.C.F. von Schiller

Happiness to a dog is what lies on
the other side of the door.
                    —Charlton Ogburn, Jr.

The supreme happiness of life is the
conviction that we are loved.
                          —Victor Hugo

The happiness of a man in this life
does not consist in the absence, but
in the mastery, of his passions.
                    —Alfred, Lord Tennyson

It is comparison that makes men
happy or miserable.   —Anon.

Let him that would be happy for a
day, go to the barber; for a week,
marry a wife; for a month, buy him
a new horse; for a year, build him a
new house; for all his lifetime, be an
honest man.   —Anon.

Who will present pleasure refrain,
shall in time to come the more pleasure obtain.   —Anon.

No man can be merry unless he is
serious.   —G.K. Chesterton

A happy life must be to a great
extent a quiet life, for it is only in an
atmosphere of quiet that true joy can
live.   —Bertrand Russell

To live we must conquer incessantly,
we must have the courage to be
happy.   —Frederic Amiel

Happiness has many roots, but none
more important than security.
                      —E.R. Stettinius, Jr.

It is in virtue that happiness consists,
for virtue is the state of mind which
tends to make the whole of life harmonious.   —Zeno

Happy [is] the man who has learned
the cause of things and has put
under his feet all fear, inexorable
fate, and the noisy strife of the hell
of greed.   —Virgil

The happiest man is he who learns
from nature the lesson of worship.
                    —Ralph Waldo Emerson

It takes great wit and interest and
energy to be happy. The pursuit of
happiness is a great activity. One
must be open and alive. It is the
greatest feat man has to accomplish.
                          —Robert Henri

Talk happiness. The world is sad
enough without your woe. No path
is wholly rough.
                    —Ella Wheeler Wilcox

We act as though comfort and luxury were the chief requirements of life, when all that we need to make us really happy is something to be enthusiastic about.
—Charles Kingsley

What we call happiness is what we do not know. —Anatole France

For the happiest life, days should be rigorously planned, nights left open to chance. —Mignon McLaughlin

If you want *others* to be happy, practice compassion. If *you* want to be happy, practice compassion.
—The Dalai Lama

It is neither wealth nor splendor, but tranquility and occupation, which give happiness. —Thomas Jefferson

The best way for a person to have happy thoughts is to count his blessings and not his cash. —Anon.

Happy people plan actions, they don't plan results. —Dennis Wholey

All happiness depends on a leisurely breakfast. —John Gunther

Happy is he who still loves something he loved in the nursery: He has not been broken in two by time; he is not two men, but one, and he has saved not only his soul, but his life.
—G.K. Chesterton

To be happy means to be free, not from pain or fear, but from care or anxiety. —W.H. Auden

THE SOURCES OF OUR HAPPINESS CHANGE

The art of living does not consist in preserving and clinging to a particular mode of happiness, but in allowing happiness to change its form without being disappointed by the change; happiness, like a child, must be allowed to grow up.
—Charles L. Morgan

When one door of happiness closes, another opens; but often we look so long at the closed door that we do not see the one which has been opened for us. —Helen Keller

Just as a cautious businessman avoids investing all his capital in one concern, so wisdom would probably admonish us also not to anticipate all our happiness from one quarter alone. —Sigmund Freud

We live in an ascending scale when we live happily, one thing leading to another in an endless series.
—Robert Louis Stevenson

HAPPINESS IS A JOURNEY

Happiness is not a station to arrive at, but a manner of traveling.
—Margaret Lee Runbeck

Everyone only goes around the track once in life, and if you don't enjoy that trip, it's pretty pathetic.
—Gary Rogers

The really happy man is one who can enjoy the scenery on a detour.
—Anon.

Happiness is to be found along the way, not at the end of the road, for then the journey is over and it is too late. —Robert R. Updegraff

Happiness is a way station between too little and too much.
—Channing Pollock

DON'T EXAMINE HAPPINESS ... JUST ENJOY IT

Enjoy your happiness while you have it, and while you have it do not too closely scrutinize its foundation.
—Joseph Farrall

My advice to you is not to inquire why or whither, but just enjoy your ice cream while it's on your plate.
—Thornton Wilder

Most people ask for happiness on condition. Happiness can only be felt if you don't set any condition.
—Arthur Rubinstein

Suspicion of happiness is in our blood. —E.V. Lucas

Ask yourself whether you are happy, and you will cease to be so.
—John Stuart Mill

Best to live lightly, unthinkingly.
—Sophocles

The secret of being miserable is to have leisure to bother about whether you are happy or not.
—George Bernard Shaw

My life has no purpose, no direction, no aim, no meaning, and yet I'm happy. I can't figure it out. What am I doing right? —Charles M. Schulz

To describe happiness is to diminish it. —Stendhal

DON'T POSTPONE HAPPINESS

People who postpone happiness are like children who try chasing rainbows in an effort to find the pot of gold at the rainbow's end.... Your life will never be fulfilled until you are happy here and now.
—Ken Keyes, Jr.

Happiness consists of living each day as if it were the first day of your honeymoon and the last day of your vacation. —Anon.

Every minute your mouth is turned down you lose sixty seconds of happiness. —Tom Walsh

Why not seize the pleasure at once? How often is happiness destroyed by preparation, foolish preparation?
—Jane Austen

Enjoy yourself. These are the "good old days" you're going to miss in the years ahead. —Anon.

UNHAPPINESS

Is anyone in all the world safe from unhappiness? —Sophocles

Unhappiness is the ultimate form of self-indulgence. —Tom Robbins

Sadness is a state of sin.
—André Gide

Unhappiness indicates wrong thinking, just as ill health indicates a bad regimen. —Paul Bourge

Unhappiness is best defined as the difference between our talents and our expectations.
—Dr. Edward De Bono

By becoming more unhappy, we sometimes learn how to be less so.
—Madame Swetchine

Men are the only animals that devote themselves, day in and day out, to making one another unhappy.　　—H.L. Mencken

The worst sin—perhaps the only sin—passion can commit is to be joyless.　　—Dorothy Sayers

O Lord! Unhappy is the man whom man can make unhappy.
—Ralph Waldo Emerson

Those who are unhappy have no need for anything in this world but people capable of giving them their attention.　　—Simone Weil

Irresolution on the schemes of life which offer themselves to our choice, and inconstancy in pursuing them, are the greatest causes of all unhappiness.　　—Joseph Addison

Unhappiness is not knowing what we want and killing ourselves to get it.　　—Don Herold

All mankind's unhappiness derives from one thing: his inability to know how to remain in repose in one room.　　—Blaise Pascal

None think the great unhappy but the great.　　—Edward Young

The primary cause of unhappiness in the world today is ... lack of faith.
—Carl Jung

Fate often puts all the material for happiness and prosperity into a man's hands just to see how miserable he can make himself with them.
—Don Marquis

Whenever one finds oneself inclined to bitterness, it is a sign of emotional failure.　　—Bertrand Russell

CHEERFULNESS

I'm not happy, I'm cheerful. There's a difference. A happy woman has no cares at all. A cheerful woman has cares but has learned how to deal with them.　　—Beverly Sills

Cheerfulness is as natural to the heart of man in strong health as color to his cheek; and wherever there is habitual gloom there must be either bad air, unwholesome food, improperly severe labor or erring habits of life.　　—John Ruskin

The clearest sign of wisdom is continued cheerfulness.
—Michel de Montaigne

A man of gladness seldom falls into madness.　　—Anon.

Gaiety alone, as it were, is the hard cash of happiness; everything else is just a promissory note.
—Arthur Schopenhauer

HAPPINESS CAN COME FROM UNHAPPINESS

No pleasure without pain.
—Anon.

Pleasure is not pleasant unless it cost dear.　　—Anon.

So they speak soothingly about progress and the greatest possible happiness, forgetting that happiness

is itself poisoned if the measure of suffering has not been fulfilled.
—Carl Jung

Life begins on the other side of despair.   —Jean-Paul Sartre

Sadness and gladness succeed each other.   —Anon.

THE HAPPINESS OF NOT NEEDING HAPPINESS

The greatest happiness you can have is knowing that you do not necessarily require happiness.
—William Saroyan

Happiness comes fleetingly now and then to those who have learned to do without it, and to them only.
—Don Marquis

Unquestionably, it is possible to do without happiness; it is done involuntarily by nineteen-twentieths of mankind.   —John Stuart Mill

Perfect happiness is the absence of striving for happiness.
—Chuang-Tse

WE'RE HAPPIER THAN WE THINK

There are men who are happy without knowing it.   —Vauvenargues

Why is it that so many people are afraid to admit that they are happy?
—William Lyon Phelps

Man's real life is happy, chiefly because he is ever expecting that it soon will be so.   —Edgar Allan Poe

Those who are the most happy appear to know it the least; happiness is something that for the most part seems to mainly consist in not knowing it.   —Dr. Joyce Brothers

We are all happy, if we only knew it.
—Fyodor Dostoyevsky

What a wonderful life I've had! I only wish I'd realized it sooner.
—Colette

Eden is that old-fashioned house we dwell in every day Without suspecting our abode until we drive away.
—Emily Dickinson

Happiness is a Swedish sunset; it is there for all, but most of us look the other way and lose it. —Mark Twain

Happiness always looks small while you hold it in your hands, but let it go, and you learn at once how big and precious it is.   —Maxim Gorky

HAPPINESS AND CONTENTMENT

Contentment is not happiness. An oyster may be contented. Happiness is compounded of richer elements.
—Christian Bovee

The world is full of people looking for spectacular happiness while they snub contentment.   —Doug Larson

If all were gentle and contented as sheep, all would be as feeble and helpless. —John Lancaster Spalding

GENERAL QUOTATIONS ABOUT HAPPINESS

The world of those who are happy is different from the world of those who are not. —Ludwig Wittgenstein

If happiness truly consisted in physical ease and freedom from care, then

the happiest individual ... would be,
I think, an American cow.
—William Lyon Phelps

When unhappy, one doubts everything; when happy, one doubts nothing.
—Joseph Roux

There is a courage of happiness as well as a courage of sorrow.
—Maurice Maeterlinck

Who is the happiest of men? He who values the merits of others, And in their pleasure takes joy, even as though t'were his own.
—Johann von Goethe

Only man clogs his happiness with care, destroying what is, with thoughts of what may be.
—John Dryden

We never enjoy perfect happiness; our most fortunate successes are mingled with sadness; some anxieties always perplex the reality of our satisfaction.
—Pierre Corneille

Happiness is not the end of life; character is.
—Henry Ward Beecher

Human life is basically a comedy. Even its tragedies often seem comic to the spectator, and not infrequently they actually have comic touches to the victim. Happiness probably consists largely in the capacity to detect and relish them.
—H.L. Mencken

We may fail of our happiness, strive we ever so bravely; but we are less likely to fail if we measure with judgement our chances and our capabilities.
—Agnes Repplier

We always have enough to be happy if we are enjoying what we do have—and not worrying about what we don't have.
—Ken Keyes, Jr.

That sanguine expectation of happiness which is happiness itself.
—Jane Austen

No man is happy unless he believes he is.
—Publilius Syrus

A great obstacle to happiness is to expect too much happiness.
—Bernard de Fontenelle

If you always do what interests you, at least one person is pleased.
—Katharine Hepburn

If you obey all the rules you miss all the fun.
—Katharine Hepburn

Suffering is not a prerequisite for happiness.
—Judy Tatelbaum

He is happy that knoweth not himself to be otherwise.
—Thomas Fuller

That man is happiest who lives from day to day and asks no more, garnering the simple goodness of a life.
—Euripides

Change is an easy panacea. It takes character to stay in one place and be happy there.
—Elizabeth Clarke Dunn

Such is the state of life that none are happy but by the anticipation of change. The change itself is nothing; when we have made it the next wish is to change again.
—Samuel Johnson

Life delights in life. —William Blake

I look at what I have not and think myself unhappy; others look at what I have and think me happy.

—Joseph Roux

Part of the happiness of life consists not in fighting battles, but in avoiding them. A masterly retreat is in itself a victory.

—Norman Vincent Peale

ACCEPTANCE

ACCEPTANCE ISN'T RESIGNATION

Some people confuse acceptance with apathy, but there's all the difference in the world. Apathy fails to distinguish between what can and what cannot be helped; acceptance makes that distinction. Apathy paralyzes the will-to-action; acceptance frees it by relieving it of impossible burdens. —Arthur Gordon

God, grant me the serenity to accept the things I cannot change, the courage to change the things I can, and the wisdom to know the difference. —Reinhold Niebuhr

We must accept finite disappointment, but we must never lose infinite hope. —Martin Luther King, Jr.

Acceptance is not submission; it is acknowledgement of the facts of a situation. Then deciding what you're going to do about it.
—Kathleen Casey Theisen

You have to take it as it happens, but you should try to make it happen the way you want to take it.
—Old German proverb

Never deny a diagnosis, but do deny the negative verdict that may go with it. —Norman Cousins

TENSION, TROUBLE, AND ADVERSITY ARE NORMAL PARTS OF LIFE

All that is necessary is to accept the impossible, do without the indispensable, and bear the intolerable.
—Kathleen Norris

The happy and efficient people in this world are those who accept trouble as a normal detail of human life and resolve to capitalize it when it comes along. —H. Bertram Lewis

Who except the gods can live without any pain? —Aeschylus

Misfortune comes to all men.
—Chinese proverb

Life has no smooth road for any of us; and in the bracing atmosphere of a high aim the very roughness stimulates the climber to steadier steps 'til the legend, "over steep ways to the stars," fulfills self.
—William C. Doane

Maturity is achieved when a person accepts life as full of tension.
—Joshua L. Liebman

Yet man is born unto trouble, as the sparks fly upward.   —Jb. 5:7

Into each life some rain must fall, some days must be dark and dreary.
—Henry Wadsworth Longfellow

There is no man in this world without some manner of tribulation or anguish, though he be king or pope.
—Thomas a'Kempis

There is no armor against fate; death lays his icy hands on kings.
—James Shirley

There is no easy path leading out of life, and few are the easy ones that lie within it.
—Walter Savage Landor

A man shares his days with hunger, thirst, and cold, with the good times and the bad, and the first part of being a man is to understand that.
—Louis L'Amour

The mass of men lead lives of quiet desperation.
—Henry David Thoreau

The real world is not easy to live in. It is rough; it is slippery. Without the most clear-eyed adjustments we fall and get crushed.   —Clarence Day

It is arrogance to expect that life will always be music.... Harmony, like a following breeze at sea, is the exception. In a world where most things wind up broken or lost, our lot is to tack and tune.   —Harvey Oxenhorn

One cannot get through life without pain ... What we can do is choose how to use the pain life presents to us.   —Bernie S. Siegel, M.D.

If you have arthritis, calmly say, I was always complaining about the ruts in the road until I realized that the ruts *are* the road.   —Anon.

"Okay, I have arthritis, and this is the way arthritis is." Take pain as it comes and you can better master it.
—Charles Clifford Peale

It is right it should be so,
Man was made for joy and woe;
And when this we rightly know,
Through the world we safely go.
—William Blake

Anyone who proposes to do good must not expect people to roll stones out of his way, but must accept his lot calmly, even if they roll a few more upon it.   —Albert Schweitzer

Free man is by necessity insecure; thinking man by necessity uncertain.
—Erich Fromm

You have come into a hard world. I know of only one easy place in it, and that is the grave.
—Henry Ward Beecher

ACCEPTANCE AND NECESSITY

Against necessity, against its strength, no one can fight and win.
—Aeschylus

A wise man never refuses anything to necessity.   —Publilius Syrus

When necessity speaks, it demands.
—Russian proverb

34

How base a thing it is when a man will struggle with necessity! We have to die.   —Euripides

ACCEPTING THIS WORLD

The reasonable man adapts himself to the world; the unreasonable one persists in trying to adapt the world to himself.   —George Bernard Shaw

We win half the battle when we make up our minds to take the world as we find it, including the thorns.   —Orison S. Marden

A man must live in the world and make the best of it, such as it is.
          —Michel de Montaigne

The world is not to be put in order, the world is order incarnate. It is for us to put ourselves in unison with this order.   —Henry Miller

God asks no man whether he will accept life. This is not the choice. You must take it. The only question is how.   —Henry Ward Beecher

There is no cure for birth or death save to enjoy the interval.
          —George Santayana

No man can have society upon his own terms. —Ralph Waldo Emerson

The most popular persons are those who take the world as it is, who find the least fault.
          —Charles Dudley Warner

GOING WITH THE FLOW

If you bear the cross unwillingly, you make it a burden, and load yourself more heavily; but you must bear it.
          —Thomas a'Kempis

To repel one's cross is to make it heavier.   —Henri Frederic Amiel

There are two ways of meeting difficulties: you alter the difficulties, or you alter yourself to meet them.
          —Phyllis Bottome

The art of life lies in a constant readjustment to our surroundings.
          —Okakura Kakuzo

I find that it is not the circumstances in which we are placed, but the spirit in which we face them, that constitutes our comfort.
          —Elizabeth T. King

It is almost more important how a person takes his fate than what it is.
          —Wilhelm von Humboldt

The individual who is best prepared for any occupation is the one ... able to adapt himself to any situation.
          —Mortimer Smith

To act with common sense, according to the moment, is the best wisdom; and the best philosophy is to do one's duties, to take the world as it comes, submit respectfully to one's lot, and bless the goodness that has given us so much happiness with it, whatever it is.   —Horace Walpole

Ask not that events should happen as you will, but let your will be that events should happen as they do, and you shall have peace.
          —Epictetus

The survival of the fittest is the ageless law of nature, but the fittest are rarely the strong. The fittest are those endowed with the qualifications for adaptation, the ability to accept the inevitable and conform to the unavoidable, to harmonize with existing or changing conditions.

—Dave E. Smalley

The ideal man bears the accidents of life with dignity and grace, making the best of circumstances. —Aristotle

He is happy whose circumstances suit his temper; but he is more excellent who can suit his temper to any circumstances.   —David Hume

Life is 10 percent what you make it, and 90 percent how you take it.

—Irving Berlin

A mountain man tries to live with the country instead of against it.

—Louis L'Amour

Today I know that I cannot control the ocean tides. I can only go with the flow.... When I struggle and try to organize the Atlantic to my specifications, I sink. If I flail and thrash and growl and grumble, I go under. But if I let go and float, I am borne aloft.   —Marie Stilkind

If you can't fight, and you can't flee, flow.   —Robert Eliot

You can't fight the desert ... you have to ride with it.

—Louis L'Amour

One learns to adapt to the land in which one lives.   —Louis L'Amour

She had believed the land was her enemy, and she struggled against it, but you could not make war against

a land any more than you could against the sea. One had to learn to live with it, to belong to it, to fit into its seasons and its ways.

—Louis L'Amour

Flow with whatever may happen and let your mind be free. Stay centered by accepting whatever you are doing. This is the ultimate.

—Chuang-tzu

Vex not thy spirit at the course of things; they heed not thy vexation. How ludicrous and outlandish is astonishment at anything that may happen in life.   —Marcus Aurelius

When you have got an elephant by the hind legs and he is trying to run away, it is best to let him run.

—Abraham Lincoln

Learn to drink the cup of life as it comes.   —Agnes Turnbull

Arrange whatever pieces come your way.   —Virginia Woolf

Everything in life that we really accept undergoes a change. So suffering must become love. That is the mystery.   —Katherine Mansfield

All I can do is play the game the way the cards fall.   —James A. Michener

Don't be sad, don't be angry, if life deceives you! Submit to your grief; your time for joy will come, believe me.   —Aleksandr Pushkin

When we see ourselves in a situation which must be endured and gone through, it is best to meet it with firmness, and accommodate everything to it in the best way practicable. This lessens the evil, while fretting and fuming only increase your own torments. —Thomas Jefferson

Always fall in with what you're asked to accept.... My aim in life has always been to hold my own with whatever's going. Not against: with.
—Robert Frost

There is no quality of human nature so nearly royal as the ability to yield gracefully. —Charles Conrad

The best thing we can do is to make wherever we're lost look as much like home as we can.
—Christopher Fry

Make a virtue of necessity.
—Geoffrey Chaucer

Cooperation is doing with a smile what you have to do anyhow.
—Anon.

We must make the best of those ills which cannot be avoided.
—Alexander Hamilton

For so must it be, and help me do my part. —A Tibetan master

ADAPTING TO NEW CONDITIONS

There are no conditions to which a man cannot become accustomed.
—Leo Tolstoy

Man adapts himself to everything, to the best and the worst.
—José Ortega y Gasset

Being unready and ill-equipped is what you have to expect in life. It is the universal predicament. It is your lot as a human being to lack what it takes. Circumstances are seldom right. You never have the capacities, the strength, the wisdom, the virtue you ought to have. You must always do with less than you need in a situation vastly different from what you would have chosen as appropriate for your special endowments.
—Charlton Ogburn, Jr.

To exist is to adapt, and if one could not adapt, one died and made room for those who could.
—Louis L'Amour

In the face of an obstacle which is impossible to overcome, stubbornness is stupid. —Simone de Beauvoir

Very few live by choice. Every man is placed in his present condition by causes which acted without his foresight, and with which he did not always willingly cooperate; and therefore you will rarely meet one who does not think the lot of his neighbor better than his own.
—Samuel Johnson

ACCEPTING THE SPREAD BETWEEN WISHES AND REALITIES

Happy the man who early learns the wide chasm that lies between his wishes and his powers.
—Johann von Goethe

Real life is, to most men ... a perpetual compromise between the ideal and the possible. —Bertrand Russell

People are lucky and unlucky ... according to the ratio between what they get and what they have been led to expect. —Samuel Butler

He who cannot do what he wants must make do with what he can.
—Terence

What has always made a hell on earth has been that man has tried to make it his heaven.
—Friedrich Holderlin

Good is not good, where better is expected.
—Thomas Fuller

Nobody has things just as he would like them. The thing to do is to make a success with what material I have. It is a sheer waste of time and soul-power to imagine what I would do if things were different. They are not different.
—Dr. Frank Crane

We must like what we have when we don't have what we like.
—Roger De Bussy-Rabutin

Better is the enemy of the good.
—Voltaire

If you aspire to the highest place, it is no disgrace to stop at the second, or even the third, place.
—Cicero

Genius does what it must, talent does what it can.
—Edward Bulwer-Lytton

Nature is what you may do. There is much you may not do.
—Ralph Waldo Emerson

Results are what you expect; consequences are what you get.
—Anon.

To expect life to be tailored to our specifications is to invite frustration.
—Anon.

A hero is a man who does what he can.
—Romain Rolland

The resistance to the unpleasant situation is the root of suffering.
—Ram Dass and Paul Gorman

The chief pang of most trials is not so much the actual suffering itself as our own spirit of resistance to it.
—Jean Nicholas Grou

Each of us does, in effect, strike a series of "deals" or compromises between the wants and longings of the inner self, and an outer environment that offers certain possibilities and sets certain limitations.
—Maggie Scarf

Man is the only animal that laughs and weeps; for he is the only animal that is struck with the difference between what things are and what they might have been.
—William Hazlitt

Every creator painfully experiences the chasm between his inner vision and its ultimate expression. The chasm is never completely bridged. We all have the conviction, perhaps illusory, that we have much more to say than appears on the paper.
—Isaac Bashevis Singer

The greatest and most important problems in life are all in a certain sense insoluble. They can never be solved, but only outgrown.
—Carl Jung

Unhappiness is best defined as the difference between our talents and our expectations.
—Dr. Edward De Bono

We do not write as we want, but as we can. —W. Somerset Maugham

The art of living lies less in eliminating our troubles than in growing with them. —Bernard M. Baruch

A body shouldn't heed what might be. He's got to do with what is. —Louis L'Amour

The greatest evil which fortune can inflict on men is to endow them with small talents and great ambitions. —Vauvenargues

We may fail of our happiness, strive we ever so bravely; but we are less likely to fail if we measure with judgment our chances and our capabilities. —Agnes Repplier

One of the signs of maturity is a healthy respect for reality—a respect that manifests itself in the level of one's aspirations and in the accuracy of one's assessment of the difficulties which separate the facts of today from the bright hopes of tomorrow. —Robert H. Davies

Is life so wretched? Isn't it rather your hands which are too small, your vision which is muddled? You are the one who must grow up. —Dag Hammarskjold

Nothing you write, if you hope to be any good, will ever come out as you first hoped. —Lillian Hellman

The trouble with most people is that they think with their hopes or fears or wishes rather than with their minds. —Will Durant

There is a mortal breed most full of futility. In contempt of what is at hand, they strain into the future, hunting impossibilities on the wings of ineffectual hopes. —Pindar

Anxiety is that range of distress which attends willing what cannot be willed. —Leslie H. Farber

A life of frustration is inevitable for any coach whose man enjoyment is winning. —Chuck Noll

No traveler e'er reached that blest abode who found not thorns and briers in his road. —William Cowper

Life's under no obligation to give us what we expect. —Margaret Mitchell

It is a common observation that those who dwell continually upon their expectations are apt to become oblivious to the requirements of their actual situation. —Charles Sanders Peirce

Buddha's doctrine: Man suffers because of his craving to possess and keep forever things which are essentially impermanent ... this frustration of the desire to possess is the immediate cause of suffering. —Alan Watts

It Is Wise to Seek Out the Best Things in Whatever We Must Accept

The point ... is to dwell upon the brightest parts in every prospect, to call off the thoughts when turning upon disagreeable objects, and strive to be pleased with the present circumstances. —Abraham Tucker

Everything has its wonders, even darkness and silence, and I learn, whatever state I may be in, therein to be content.   —Helen Keller

Life is not always what one wants it to be, but to make the best of it, as it is, is the only way of being happy.
                    —Jennie Jerome Churchill

The English know how to make the best of things. Their so-called muddling through is simply skill at dealing with the inevitable.
                    —Sir Winston Churchill

I make the most of all that comes and the least of all that goes.
                    —Sara Teasdale

It's Best to Accept Things Enthusiastically

If one has to submit, it is wasteful not to do so with the best grace possible.   —Sir Winston Churchill

We cannot conquer fate and necessity, yet we can yield to them in such a manner as to be greater than if we could.   —Walter Savage Landor

Here is a rule to remember when anything tempts you to feel bitter: not, "This is a misfortune," but "To bear this worthily is good fortune."
                    —Marcus Aurelius

There is no good in arguing with the inevitable. The only argument available with an east wind is to put on your overcoat.
                    —James Russell Lowell

Trouble will come soon enough, and when he does come receive him as pleasantly as possible ... the more

amiably you greet him, the sooner he will go away.   —Artemus Ward

Adapt yourself to the things among which your lot has been cast and love sincerely the fellow creatures with whom destiny has ordained that you shall live.
                    —Marcus Aurelius

When we accept tough jobs as a challenge to our ability and wade into them with joy and enthusiasm, miracles can happen.
                    —Arland Gilbert

Love only what befalls you and is spun for you by fate.
                    —Marcus Aurelius

What you can't get out of, get into wholeheartedly.
                    —Mignon McLaughlin

Let us train our minds to desire what the situation demands.
                    —Marcus Annaeus Seneca

When a dog runs at you, whistle for him.   —Henry David Thoreau

Ride the horse in the direction that it's going.   —Werner Erhard

Since God has been pleased to give us the Papacy, let us enjoy it.
                    —Pope Leo X

It is no use to grumble and complain;
It's just as cheap and easy to rejoice;
When God sorts out the weather and sends rain —
Why, rain's my choice.
                    —James Whitcomb Riley

Nature Shows That It's Better to Bend Than to Break

An oak and a reed were arguing about their strength. When a strong wind came up, the reed avoided being uprooted by bending and leaning with the gusts of wind. But the oak stood firm and was torn up by the roots. —Aesop

He who attempts to resist the wave is swept away, but he who bends before it abides.
—Leviticus

The grass must bend when the wind blows across it. —Confucius

Adapt or perish, now as ever, is nature's inexorable imperative.
—H.G. Wells

One does not have to stand again the gale.
One yields and becomes part of the wind. —Emmanuel

I like trees because they seem more resigned to the way they have to live than other things do. —Willa Cather

Nature magically suits a man to his fortunes, by making them the fruit of his character.
—Ralph Waldo Emerson

Better bend than break.
—Scottish proverb

Acceptance and Happiness

The secret of success is to be in harmony with existence, to be always calm ... to let each wave of life wash us a little farther up the shore.
—Cyril Connolly

There is only one way to happiness, and that is to cease worrying about things which are beyond the power of our will. —Epictetus

Happiness comes from within a man, from some curious adjustment to life. —Hugh Walpole

Happy he who learns to bear what he cannot change!
—J.C.F. von Schiller

Happiness ... can exist only in acceptance. —Denis De Rougemont

Contentment, and indeed usefulness, comes as the infallible result of great acceptances, great humilities—of not trying to conform to some dramatized version of ourselves.
—David Grayson

My advice to you is not to inquire why or whither, but just enjoy your ice cream while it's on your plate.
—Thornton Wilder

It is not necessarily those lands which are the most fertile or most favored in climate that seem to me the happiest, but those in which a long struggle of adaptation between man and his environment has brought out the best qualities of both. —T.S. Eliot

Life is not always what one wants it to be, but to make the best of it, as it is, is the only way of being happy.
—Jennie Jerome Churchill

Everything has its wonders, even darkness and silence, and I learn, whatever state I may be in, therein to be content. —Helen Keller

41

I accept life unconditionally ... Most people ask for happiness on condition. Happiness can only be felt if you don't set any condition.
—Arthur Rubenstein

Happiness is a function of accepting what is.   —Werner Erhard

ACCEPTANCE AND WISDOM

One's first step in wisdom is to question everything; one's last is to come to terms with everything.
—Georg Christoph Lichtenberg

If you are wise, live as you can; if you cannot, live as you would.
—Baltasar Gracian

Wisdom never kicks at the iron walls it can't bring down.
—Olive Schreiner

For this is wisdom: to live, to take what fate, or the Gods, may give.
—Laurence Hope

ACCEPTANCE AND WORK

If you have a job without aggravations, you don't have a job.
—Malcolm Forbes

When I decided to go into politics I weighed the costs. I would get criticism. But I went ahead. So when virulent criticism came I wasn't surprised. I was better able to handle it.
—Herbert Hoover

Every job has drudgery.... The first secret of happiness is the recognition of this fundamental fact.
—M.C. McIntosh

The fishermen know that the sea is dangerous and the storm terrible, but they have never found these dangers sufficient reason for remaining ashore.   —Vincent van Gogh

ACCEPTANCE AND THE SOUL

He who doesn't accept the conditions of life sells his soul.
—Charles Baudelaire

Greatness of soul consists not so much in soaring high and in pressing forward, as in knowing how to adapt and limit oneself.
—Michel de Montaigne

The beauty of the soul shines out when a man bears with composure one heavy mischance after another, not because he does not feel them, but because he is a man of high and heroic temper.   —Aristotle

The great soul surrenders itself to fate.   —Marcus Annaeus Seneca

THE BENEFITS OF ACCEPTING THE INEVITABLE

The mind which renounces, once and forever, a futile hope, has its compensations in ever-growing calm.
—George R. Gissing

I not only bow to the inevitable, I am fortified by it.
—Thornton Wilder

I have accepted all and I am free. The inner chains are broken, as well as those outside.   —C.F. Ramuz

We cannot change anything unless we accept it.   —Carl Jung

Peace of mind is that mental condition in which you have accepted the worst.   —Lin Yutang

Acceptance of what has happened is the first step to overcoming the consequence of any misfortune.
—William James

Almost any event will put on a new face when received with cheerful acceptance. —Henry S. Haskins

What it is forbidden to be put right becomes lighter by acceptance.
—Horace

One completely overcomes only what one assimilates. —André Gide

If you cast away one cross, you will certainly find another, and perhaps a heavier. —Thomas a'Kempis

To repel one's cross is to make it heavier. —Henri Frederic Amiel

Science says: "We must live," and seeks the means of prolonging, increasing, facilitating and amplifying life, of making it tolerable and acceptable; wisdom says: "We must die," and seeks how to make us die well. —Miguel De Unamuno

Things turn out best for people who make the best of the way things turn out. —Anon.

As the soft yield of water cleaves obstinate stone,
So to yield with life solves the insolvable:
To yield, I have learned, is to come back again. —Lao-tzu

And acceptance is the answer to all my problems today.... I can find no serenity until I accept that person, place, thing, or situation as being exactly the way it is supposed to be at this moment.
—Alcoholics Anonymous

True freedom lies in the realization and calm acceptance of the fact that there may very well be no perfect answer. —Allen Reid McGinnis

Resistance causes pain and lethargy. It is when we practice acceptance that new possibilities appear.
—Anon.

To oppose something is to maintain it. —Ursula K. LeGuin

No life is so hard that you can't make it easier by the way you take it. —Ellen Glasgow

Anything in life that we don't accept will simply make trouble for us until we make peace with it.
—Shakti Gawain

Often the prudent, far from making their destinies, succumb to them.
—Voltaire

Things past redress are now with me past care. —William Shakespeare

What we call reality is an agreement that people have arrived at to make life more livable. —Louise Nevelson

He who has calmly reconciled his life to fate ... can look fortune in the face. —Boethius

TO GET WHAT WE WANT, WE MUST ACCEPT SOME THINGS WE DON'T WANT

No rose without a thorn.
—French proverb

If you want a place in the sun, you've got to put up with a few blisters. —Abigail Van Buren

Those who aim at great deeds must also suffer greatly. —Plutarch

PARADOX: ACCEPTANCE CAN LEAD TO CHANGE

Nature, to be commanded, must be obeyed. —Francis Bacon

The first step toward change is acceptance. Once you accept yourself, you open the door to change. That's all you have to do. Change is not something you do, it's something you allow.
—Will Garcia, person with AIDS

Our very first problem is to accept our present circumstances as they are, ourselves as we are, and the people about us as they are. This is to adopt a realistic humility without which no genuine advance can even begin.... Provided we strenuously avoid turning these realistic surveys of the facts of life into unrealistic alibis for apathy or defeatism, they can be the sure foundation upon which increased emotional health and therefore spiritual progress can be built. —*As Bill Sees It*

We cannot change anything unless we accept it. Condemnation does not liberate, it oppresses. —Carl Jung

When you make your peace with authority, you become authority.
—Jim Morrison

Keep doing what you're doing and you'll keep getting what you're getting. —Anon.

Everything in life that we really accept undergoes a change. So suffering must become love. That is the mystery. —Katherine Mansfield

GENERAL QUOTATIONS ABOUT ACCEPTANCE

Ours must be the first age whose great goal, on a nonmaterial plane, is not fulfillment but adjustment.
—Louis Kronenberger

We have fought this fight as long, and as well, as we know how. We have been defeated. There is now but one course to pursue. We must accept the situation. —Robert E. Lee

It is so. It cannot be otherwise.
—Cathedral inscription, Amsterdam

Teach me neither to cry for the moon nor over spilt milk.
—On the library wall of George V of England

Better to accept whatever happens.
—Horace

If we cannot do what we will, we must will what we can.
—Yiddish proverb

Every man must be content with that glory which he may have at home.
—Boethius

Every new adjustment is a crisis in self-esteem. —Eric Hoffer

What cannot be avoided, t'were childish weakness to lament or fear.
—William Shakespeare

I will not meddle with that which I cannot mend. —Thomas Fuller

I have learned to live with it all ... whatever happens ... all of it.

—Edelgard

There is no such thing as pure pleasure; some anxiety always goes with it.

—Ovid

If a ship has been sunk, I can't bring it up. If it is going to be sunk, I can't stop it. I can use my time much better working on tomorrow's problem than by fretting about yesterday's. Besides, if I let those things get me, I wouldn't last long.

—Admiral Ernest J. King

One of the many lessons that one learns in prison is that things are what they are and will be what they will be.

—Oscar Wilde

Part of the happiness of life consists not in fighting battles, but in avoiding them. A masterly retreat is in itself a victory.

—Norman Vincent Peale

A flower falls even though we love it. A weed grows even though we don't love it.

—Dogen

Acceptance says, True, this is my situation at the moment. I'll look unblinkingly at the reality of it. But I'll also open my hands to accept willingly whatever a loving Father sends me.

—Catherine Marshall

Man is a pliant animal, a being who gets accustomed to anything.

—Fyodor Dostoyevsky

The unknown is what it is. And to be frightened of it is what sends everybody scurrying around chasing dreams, illusions, wars, peace, love, hate, all that. Unknown is what it is. Accept that it's unknown, and it's plain sailing.

—John Lennon

Happiness is experienced when your life gives you what you are willing to accept.

—Ken Keyes, Jr.

Acceptance is the truest kinship with humanity.

—G.K. Chesterton

Acceptance makes any event put on a new face.

—Henry S. Haskins

There is no sense in the struggle, but there is no choice but to struggle.

—Ernie Pyle

What must be shall be; and that which is a necessity to him that struggles, is little more than choice to him that is willing.

—Marcus Annaeus Seneca

Boys, this is only a game. But it's like life in that you will be dealt some bad hands. Take each hand, good or bad, and don't whine and complain, but play it out. If you're men enough to do that, God will help and you will come out well.

—Dwight D. Eisenhower's mother

Practice easing your way along. Don't get het up or in a dither. Do your best; take it as it comes. You can handle anything if you think you can. Just keep your cool and your sense of humor.

—Smiley Blanton, M.D.

Accept that all of us can be hurt, that all of us can—and surely will at times—fail. Other vulnerabilities, like being embarrassed or risking

love, can be terrifying too. I think we should follow a simple rule: if we can take the worst, take the risk.
—Dr. Joyce Brothers

Do not weep; do not wax indignant. Understand.   —Baruch Spinoza

We must learn to accept life and to accept ourselves ... with a shrug and a smile ... because it's all we've got.
—Harvey Mindess

I have accepted fear as a part of life —specifically the fear of change ... I have gone ahead despite the pounding in the heart that says: turn back....   —Erica Jong

There are things I can't force. I must adjust.   —C.M. Ward

Let a man accept his destiny. No pity and no tears.   —Euripides

Wood may remain ten years in the water, but it will never become a crocodile.   —Congolese proverb

No matter how much you feed a wolf, he will always return to the forest.   —Russian proverb

Can the Ethiopian change his skin, or the leopard his spots?
—Jer. 13:23

FORGIVENESS

FORGIVING AND FORGETTING— REALLY LETTING GO

The stupid neither forgive nor forget; the naive forgive and forget; the wise forgive, but do not forget.

— Thomas Szasz

"I can forgive, but I cannot forget" is only another way of saying, "I will not forgive." Forgiveness ought to be like a canceled note—torn in two and burned up so that it never can be shown against one.

— Henry Ward Beecher

Forgiveness means letting go of the past.

— Gerald Jampolsky

Nobody ever forgets where he buried a hatchet.

— Kin Hubbard

There's no point in burying a hatchet if you're going to put up a marker on the site.

— Sydney Harris

Not the power to remember, but its very opposite, the power to forget, is a necessary condition for our existence.

— Sholem Asch

Once a woman has forgiven a man, she must not reheat his sins for breakfast.

— Marlene Dietrich

Keeping score of old scores and scars, getting even and one-upping, always make you less than you are.

— Malcolm Forbes

To be wronged is nothing unless you continue to remember it.

— Confucius

WE RARELY KNOW EVERYTHING ABOUT A SITUATION

Know all and you will pardon all.

— Thomas a'Kempis

The secret of forgiving everything is to understand nothing.

— George Bernard Shaw

To understand is to forgive, even oneself.

— Alexander Chase

To what extent is any given man morally responsible for any given act? We do not know.

— Dr. Alexis Carrel

ONLY THE STRONG CAN FORGIVE

The weak can never forgive.
Forgiveness is the attribute of the
strong.   —Mahatma Ghandi

Only the brave know how to forgive.... A coward never forgave; it is
not in his nature. —Laurence Sterne

Any man can seek revenge; it takes a
king or prince to grant a pardon.
                    —Arthur J. Rehrat

To be angry about trifles is mean
and childish; to rage and be furious
is brutish; and to maintain perpetual
wrath is akin to the practice and
temper of devils; but to prevent and
suppress rising resentment is wise
and glorious, is manly and divine.
                    —Isaac Watts

RESENTMENTS AND HATRED

Resentment is the "number one"
offender. It destroys more alcoholics
than anything else. From it stem all
forms of spiritual disease, for we
have been not only mentally and
physically ill, we have been spiritually sick.   —Alcoholics Anonymous

To carry a grudge is like being stung
to death by one bee.
                    —William H. Walton

Resentments are burdens we don't
need to carry.   —Anon.

Without forgiveness life is governed
... by an endless cycle of resentment
and retaliation. —Robert Assaglioli

Malice drinks one-half of its own
poison.   —Marcus Annaeus Seneca

Hate would destroy him who hated.
                    —Louis L'Amour

Hate is a prolonged form of suicide.
                    —Douglas V. Steere

Bitterness imprisons life; love releases it.   —Harry Emerson Fosdick

If the will remains in protest, it stays
dependent on that which it is
protesting against.   —Rollo May

If you hate a person, you hate something in him that is part of yourself.
                    —Herman Hesse

Whom they have injured, they also
hate.   —Marcus Annaeus Seneca

ANGER

Anger is a short madness. —Horace

The angry people are those people
who are most afraid.
                    —Dr. Robert Anthony

Anger as soon as fed is dead, 'tis
starving makes it fat.
                    —Emily Dickinson

Anger dwells only in the bosom of
fools.   —Albert Einstein

Holding on to anger is like grasping
a hot coal with the intent of throwing it at someone else; you are the
one who gets burned.   —Buddha

Anger is a killing thing: it kills the
man who angers, for each rage
leaves him less than he had been
before—it takes something from
him.   —Louis L'Amour

REVENGE

Revenge could steal a man's life until there was nothing left but emptiness.
—Louis L'Amour

The human heart in its perversity finds it hard to escape hatred and revenge.
—Moses Luzzatto

A man can lose sight of everything else when he's bent on revenge, and it ain't worth it.
—Louis L'Amour

Forgiveness is the sweetest revenge.
—Isaac Friedmann

FORGIVENESS AND LOVE

One forgives to the degree that one loves.
—Francois de La Rochefoucauld

One is as one is, and the love that can't encompass both is a poor sort of love.
—Marya Mannes

Forgiveness is the final form of love.
—Reinhold Niebuhr

Forgiveness is the most tender part of love.
—John Sheffield

Love is an act of endless forgiveness, a tender look which becomes a habit.
—Peter Ustinov

Today I forgive all those who have ever offended me. I give my love to all thirsty hearts, both to those who love me and to those who do not love me.
—Paramahansa Yogananda

FORGIVENESS AND GOD

We never ask God to forgive anybody except when *we* haven't.
—Elbert Hubbard

Forgiveness is God's command.
—Martin Luther

God will forgive me, that is His business.
—Heinrich Heine

God will forgive me the foolish remarks I have made about Him just as I will forgive my opponents the foolish things they have written about me, even though they are spiritually as inferior to me as I to thee, O God!
—Heinrich Heine

Let all bitterness, and wrath, and anger, and clamour, and evil speaking, be put away from you, with all malice; and be ye kind to one another, tenderhearted, forgiving one another, even as God, for Christ's sake, hath forgiven you.
—Eph. 4:31–32

I have looked on a lot of women with lust. I've committed adultery in my heart many times. God recognizes I will do this and forgives me.
—Jimmy Carter

HOW FORGIVENESS HELPS US

Forgiveness is the answer to the child's dream of a miracle by which what is broken is made whole again, what is soiled is again made clean.
—Dag Hammarskjold

Forgiveness is all-powerful. Forgiveness heals all ills.
—Catherine Ponder

Those who are free of resentful thoughts surely find peace. —Buddha

I can have peace of mind only when I forgive rather than judge.
—Gerald Jampolsky

The forgiving state of mind is a magnetic power for attracting good.
—Catherine Ponder

Judge not, that ye be not judged.
—Mt. 7:1

It is in pardoning that we are pardoned.   —Saint Francis of Assisi

Forgiving those who hurt us is the key to personal peace.
—G. Weatherly

Forgive all who have offended you, not for them, but for yourself.
—Harriet Uts Nelson

To forgive is the highest, most beautiful form of love. In return, you will receive untold peace and happiness.
—Robert Muller

Forgiveness is the key to action and freedom.   —Hannah Arendt

Forgiveness is the way to true health and happiness.   —Gerald Jampolsky

Humanity is never so beautiful as when praying for forgiveness, or else forgiving another.
—Jean Paul Richter

Those who can't forget are worse off than those who can't remember.
—Anon.

Forgiveness is the remission of sins. For it is by this that what has been lost, and was found, is saved from being lost again.   —Saint Augustine

WE MUST FORGIVE OURSELVES, TOO

I can pardon everybody's mistakes except my own.
—Marcus Cato the Elder

If you haven't forgiven yourself something, how can you forgive others?   —Dolores Huerta

The moment an individual can accept and forgive himself, even a little, is the moment in which he becomes to some degree lovable.
—Eugene Kennedy

They may not deserve forgiveness, but I do.   —Anon.

I forgive myself for having believed for so long that ... I was never good enough to have, get, be what I wanted.   —Ceanne DeRohan

How unhappy is he who cannot forgive himself.   —Publilius Syrus

Every man treats himself as society treats the criminal.
—Harvey Fergusson

To understand is to forgive, even oneself.   —Alexander Chase

Give us this day our daily bread. And forgive us our debts, as we forgive our debtors.
—Mt. 6:11–12

He that cannot forgive others breaks the bridge over which he must pass himself; for every man has need to be forgiven.   —Thomas Fuller

FORGIVENESS DOESN'T ALWAYS PLEASE THOSE WE FORGIVE

Always forgive your enemies; nothing annoys them so much.
—Oscar Wilde

Forgiveness is the noblest vengeance.
—H.G. Bohn

There is no revenge so complete as forgiveness.   —Josh Billings

Many promising reconciliations have broken down because while both parties came prepared to forgive, neither party came prepared to be forgiven.   —Charles William

GENERAL QUOTATIONS ABOUT FORGIVENESS

Forgiveness is man's deepest need and highest achievement.
—Horace Bushnell

Abandon your animosities and make your sons Americans!
—Robert E. Lee

Her breasts and arms ached with the beauty of her own forgiveness.
—Meridel Le Sueur

Dream of your brother's kindnesses instead of dwelling in your dreams on his mistakes. Select his thoughtfulness to dream about instead of counting up the hurts he gave.
—*A Course In Miracles*

Life is an adventure in forgiveness.
—Norman Cousins

Forgiveness is the highest and most difficult of all moral lessons.
—Joseph Jacobs

The cut worm forgives the plow.
—William Blake

The fragrance of the violet sheds on the heel that has crushed it.
—Mark Twain

How shall I love the sin, yet keep the sense,
And love the offender, yet detest the offence?   —Alexander Pope

Forgiveness is the giving, and so the receiving, of life.
—George Macdonald

Who would care to question the ground of forgiveness or compassion?   —Joseph Conrad

O friends, I pray tonight,
Keep not your kisses for my dead cold brow.
The way is lonely; let me feel them now.
Think gently of me; I am travelworn,
My faltering feet are pierced with many a   thorn.
Forgive! O hearts estranged, forgive, I plead!
When ceaseless bliss is mine I shall not need
The tenderness for which I long tonight.   —Belle Eugenia Smith

Let us forget and forgive injuries.
—Miguel de Cervantes

Even a stopped clock is right twice a day. —Marie von Ebner-Eschenbach

It is easier to forgive an enemy than a friend.
—Madame Dorothee Deluzy

51

It is very easy to forgive others their mistakes; it takes more grit and gumption to forgive them for having witnessed your own.

—Jessamyn West

When you pray for anyone you tend to modify your personal attitude toward him.

—Norman Vincent Peale

Forgiving means to pardon the unpardonable, faith means believing the unbelievable, and hoping means to hope when things are hopeless.

—G.K. Chesterton

To err is human; to forgive, divine.

—Alexander Pope

COUNTING OUR BLESSINGS

WE SHOULD BE AWARE OF THE BLESSINGS OF OUR EVERYDAY LIVES

Normal day, let me be aware of the treasure you are. Let me learn from you, love you, bless you before you depart. Let me not pass you by in quest of some rare and perfect tomorrow. Let me hold you while I may, for it may not always be so. One day I shall dig my nails into the earth, or bury my face in the pillow, or stretch myself taut, or raise my hands to the sky and want, more than all the world, your return.

— Mary Jean Iron

The unthankful heart ... discovers no mercies; but let the thankful heart sweep through the day and, as the magnet finds the iron, so it will find, in every hour, some heavenly blessings! — Henry Ward Beecher

Good heavens, of what uncostly material is our earthly happiness composed ... if we only knew it. What incomes have we not had from a flower, and how unfailing are the dividends of the seasons.

— James Russell Lowell

Be on the lookout for mercies. The more we look for them, the more of them we will see.... Better to loose count while naming your blessings than to lose your blessings to counting your troubles.

— Maltbie D. Babcock

The man who thinks his wife, his baby, his house, his horse, his dog, and himself severely unequalled, is almost sure to be a good-humored person. — Oliver Wendell Holmes

There is nothing so bitter that a patient mind cannot find some solace for it.

— Marcus Annaeus Seneca

I thank You God for this most amazing day; for the leaping greenly spirits of trees and a blue true dream of sky; and for everything which is natural which is infinite which is yes.

— e.e. cummings

Yes, there is a Nirvanah: it is in leading your sheep to a green pasture, and in putting your child to sleep, and in writing the last line of your poem. — Kahlil Gibran

53

That daily life is really good one appreciates when one wakes from a horrible dream, or when one takes the first outing after a sickness. Why not realize it now?
—William Lyon Phelps

Thank God every morning when you get up that you have something to do which must be done, whether you like it or not. —Charles Kingsley

When I first open my eyes upon the morning meadows and look out upon the beautiful world, I thank God I am alive.
—Ralph Waldo Emerson

Each day comes bearing its own gifts. Untie the ribbons.
—Ruth Ann Schabacker

We can be thankful to a friend for a few acres or a little money; and yet for the freedom and command of the whole earth, and for the great benefits of our being, our life, health, and reason, we look upon ourselves as under no obligation.
—Marcus Annaeus Seneca

When something does not insist on being noticed, when we aren't grabbed by the collar or struck on the skull by a presence or an event, we take for granted the very things that most deserve our gratitude.
—Cynthia Ozick

The best things are nearest: breath in your nostrils, light in your eyes, flowers at your feet, duties at your hand, the path of God just before you. Then do not grasp at the stars, but do life's plain, common work as it comes, certain that daily duties and daily bread are the sweetest things of life.
—Robert Louis Stevenson

Why do some people always see beautiful skies and grass and lovely flowers and incredible human beings, while others are hard-pressed to find anything or any place that is beautiful? —Leo Buscaglia

Most human beings have an almost infinite capacity for taking things for granted. —Aldous Huxley

My country ... gave me schooling, independence of action and opportunity for service.... I am indebted to my country beyond any human power to repay. —Herbert Hoover

Dwell upon the brightest parts in every prospect ... and strive to be pleased with the present circumstances. —Abraham Tucker

We are never either so wretched or so happy as we say we are.
—Honore de Balzac

Is life so wretched? Isn't it rather your hands which are too small, your vision which is muddled? You are the one who must grow up.
—Dag Hammarskjold

LOOKING FOR SILVER LININGS

Our real blessings often appear to us in the shape of pains, losses and disappointments. —Joseph Addison

Most of my major disappointments have turned out to be blessings in disguise. So whenever anything bad does happen to me, I kind of sit back and feel, well, if I give this enough time, it'll turn out that this was good, so I shan't worry about it too much. —William Gaines

Sometimes the best deals are the ones you don't make. —Bill Veeck

The advantages of a losing team: (1) There is everything to hope for and nothing to fear. (2) Defeats do not disturb one's sleep. (3) An occasional victory is a surprise and a delight. (4) There is no danger of any club passing you. (5) You are not asked fifty times a day, "What was the score?"; people take it for granted that you lost. —Elmer E. Bates

That which does not kill me makes me stronger. —Friedrich Nietzsche

Not being beautiful was the true blessing.... Not being beautiful forced me to develop my inner resources. The pretty girl has a handicap to overcome. —Golda Meir

The difficulties, hardships and trials of life, the obstacles ... are positive blessings. They knit the muscles more firmly, and teach self-reliance. —William Matthews

Many a man curses the rain that falls upon his head, and knows not that it brings abundance to drive away hunger. —Saint Basil

Trouble is only opportunity in work clothes. —Henry J. Kaiser

Adversity has the same effect on a man that severe training has on the pugilist: it reduces him to his fighting weight. —Josh Billings

You will never be the person you can be if pressure, tension and discipline are taken out of your life. —Dr. James G. Bilkey

God brings men into deep waters not to drown them, but to cleanse them. —Aughey

Some troubles, like a protested note of a solvent debtor, bear interest. —Honore de Balzac

Failure changes for the better, success for the worse. —Marcus Annaeus Seneca

The basis of optimism is sheer terror. —Oscar Wilde

No evil is without its compensation ... it is not the loss itself, but the estimate of the loss, that troubles us. —Marcus Annaeus Seneca

Let me embrace thee, sour adversity, for wise men say it is the wisest course. —William Shakespeare

Give thanks for sorrow that teaches you pity; for pain that teaches you courage—and give exceeding thanks for the mystery which remains a mystery still—the veil that hides you from the infinite, which makes it possible for you to believe in what you cannot see. —Robert Nathan

A Christian could even give thanks for Hell, because Hell was a threat and a warning to keep him in the right way. —Anon.

To every disadvantage there is a corresponding advantage. —W. Clement Stone

Too many people miss the silver lining because they're expecting gold.
—Maurice Setter

If you count all your assets, you always show a profit.
—Robert Quillen

Too happy would you be, did ye but know your own advantages! —Virgil

Much unhappiness results from our inability to remember the nice things that happen to us. —W.N. Rieger

If we go down into ourselves, we find that we possess exactly what we desire. —Simone Weil

LIFE ITSELF IS A BLESSING

Be grateful for yourself ... be thankful. —William Saroyan

There is no wealth but life.
—John Ruskin

Just to be is a blessing. Just to live is holy. —Abraham Heschel

Life may be hard, but it's also wonderful. —*Small Change*

I like living. I have sometimes been wildly, despairingly, acutely miserable, racked with sorrow, but through it all I still know quite certainly that just to *be alive* is a grand thing. —Agatha Christie

Be glad of life because it gives you the chance to love, and to work, and to play and to look up at the stars.
—Henry Van Dyke

To be alive, to be able to see, to walk ... it's all a miracle. I have

adapted the technique of living life from miracle to miracle.
—Arthur Rubinstein

Life is the first gift, love is the second, and understanding the third.
—Marge Piercy

This is another day! Are its eyes
    blurred
With maudlin grief for any wasted
    past?
A thousand thousand failures shall
    not daunt!
Let dust clasp dust, death, death; I
    am alive! —Don Marquis

The mere sense of living is joy enough. —Emily Dickinson

However mean your life is, meet it and live it; do not shun it and call it hard names. It is not so bad as you are. It looks poorest when you are richest. The fault-finder will find faults even in Paradise. Love your life. —Henry David Thoreau

THE SIMPLEST THINGS ARE BLESSINGS

To have a full stomach and fixed income are no small things .
—Elbert Hubbard

How can they say my life is not a success? Have I not for more than sixty years gotten enough to eat and escaped being eaten?
—Logan Pearsall Smith

Sunshine is delicious, rain is refreshing, wind braces us up, snow is exhilarating; there is really no such thing as bad weather, only different kinds of good weather.
—John Ruskin

Is it so small a thing to have enjoyed the sun, to have lived light in the spring, to have loved, to have thought, to have done?
—Matthew Arnold

Only a stomach that rarely feels hungry scorns common things. —Horace

You say grace before meals. All right. But I say grace before the concert and the opera, and grace before the play and pantomime, and grace before I open a book, and grace before sketching, painting, swimming, fencing, boxing, walking, playing, dancing and grace before I dip the pen in the ink.
—G.K. Chesterton

Thank God for dirty dishes; they have a tale to tell.
While other folks go hungry, we're eating pretty well.
With home, and health, and happiness, we shouldn't want to fuss;
For by this stack of evidence, God's very good to us.   —Anon.

An easy thing, O Power Divine,
To thank thee for these gifts of Thine,
For summer's sunshine, winter's snow,
For hearts that kindle, thoughts that glow;
But when shall I attain to this—
To thank Thee for the things I miss?
—Thomas Wentworth Higginson

I thank Thee, Lord, for blessings, big and small;
For spring's warm glow and songbird's welcome call;
For autumn's hue and winter's white snow shawl.

I thank Thee for the harvest rich with grain;
For tall trees and the quiet shadowed lane;
For rushing stream, for birds that love to fly;
My country's land, the mountains and the plain.
I thank Thee for each sunset in the sky.
For sleepy nights, the bed in which I lie;
A life of truth and peace; a woman's hand,
Her hand in mine until the day I die.
I thank Thee, Lord for all these things above;
But most of all I thank Thee for Thy Love.
—Ralph Gaither (written while a POW in North Vietnam)

People call me an optimist, but I'm really an appreciator ... years ago, I was cured of a badly infected finger with antibiotics when once my doctor could have recommended only a hot water soak or, eventually, surgery.... When I was six years old and had scarlet fever, the first of the miracle drugs, sulfanilamide, saved my life. I'm grateful for computers and photocopiers ... I appreciate where we've come from.
—Julian Simon

If only the people who worry about their liabilities would think about the riches they do possess, they would stop worrying. Would you sell both your eyes for a million dollars ... or your two legs ... or your hands ... or your hearing? Add up what you do have, and you'll find that you won't sell them for all the gold in the world. The best things in life are yours, if you can appreciate yourself. —Dale Carnegie

It is strange what a contempt men have for the joys that are offered them freely. —Georges Duhamel

Grateful! for the blessing lent of simple tastes and mind content!
—Oliver Wendell Holmes

Most of us miss out on life's big prizes. The Pulitzer. The Nobel. Oscars. Tonys. Emmys. But we're all eligible for life's small pleasures. A pat on the back. A kiss behind the ear. A four-pound bass. A full moon. An empty parking space. A crackling fire. A great meal. A glorious sunset. Hot soup. Cold beer. Don't fret about copping life's grand awards. Enjoy its tiny delights. There are plenty for all of us.
—United Technologies Corporation advertisement

We can be thankful to a friend for a few acres or a little money; and yet for the freedom and command of the whole earth, and for the great benefits of our being, our life, health, and reason, we look upon ourselves as under no obligation.
—Marcus Annaeus Seneca

HEALTH IS A GIFT
Health is ... a blessing that money cannot buy. —Izaak Walton

Happiness lies, first of all, in health.
—George William Curtis

A sound mind in a sound body is a short but full description of a happy state in this world. —John Locke

Health is the vital principle of bliss.
—James Thomson

THINK OF ALL THE PROBLEMS WE'VE BEEN SPARED, OF HOW MUCH TOUGHER THINGS COULD BE
If you can't be thankful for what you receive, be thankful for what you escape. —Anon.

Even though we can't have all we want, we ought to be thankful we don't get all we deserve. —Anon.

Happy the man who can count his sufferings. —Ovid

Happiness is composed of misfortunes avoided. —Alphonse Karr

Considering the fortune you might have lost, you'll have to admit you're rich already. —John Rothchild

I thank Thee first because I was never robbed before; second, because although they took my purse they did not take my life; third, because although they took my all, it was not much; and fourth because it was I who was robbed, and not I who robbed. —Matthew Henry

Think of the ills from which you are exempt. —Joseph Joubert

A man should always consider ... how much more unhappy he might be than he is. —Joseph Addison

The happiness of any given life is to be measured not by its joys and pleasures, but by the extent to which it has been free from suffering, from positive evil. —Arthur Schopenhauer

Better to suffer than to die.
—Francois de La Fontaine

For grief unsuffered, tears unshed,
for clouds that scattered overhead;
For pestilence that came not high,
for dangers great that passed me by;
For sharp suspicion smoothed,
allayed, for doubt dispelled that
made afraid;
For fierce temptation well withstood,
for evil plot that brought forth good;
For weakened links in friendship's
chain that, sorely tested, stood the
strain;
For harmless blows with malice
dealt, for base ingratitude unfelt;
For hatred's sharp unuttered word,
for bitter jest unknown, unheard;
For every evil turned away, unmea-
sured thanks I give today.
—Anon.

Better a little fire to warm us than a
great one to burn us.
—Thomas Fuller

It isn't important to come out on
top. What matters is to come out
alive.   —Bertolt Brecht

He who limps still walks.
—Stanislaw Lec

I have gout, asthma, and seven other
maladies, but am otherwise very
well.   —Sydney Smith

The Absence of Pain Is a Blessing

Luckily, I never feel at one time
more than half my pains.
—Joseph Joubert

We are content to forgo joy when
pain is also lost.   —Latin proverb

The happiest is he who suffers the
least pain; the most miserable, he
who enjoys the least pleasure.
—Jean-Jacques Rousseau

Happiness is not being pained in
body, or troubled in mind.
—Thomas Jefferson

The end of pain we take as happiness.   —Giacomo Leopardi

You can be happy indeed if you have
breathing space from pain.
—Giacomo Leopardi

The summit of pleasure is the elimination of all that gives pain.
—Epicurus

I seek the utmost pleasure and the
least pain.   —Plautus

We Should Be Thankful for What We've Got, Not Unhappy over What We Don't Have

A prudent man will think more
important what fate has conceded to
him, than what it has denied.
—Baltasar Gracian

He is a man of sense who does not
grieve for what he has not, but
rejoices in what he has.   —Epictetus

For everything you have missed, you
have gained something else.
—Ralph Waldo Emerson

Few love what they may have.
—Ovid

The knowledge that something
remains yet unenjoyed impairs our
enjoyment of the good before us.
—Samuel Johnson

May we never let the things we can't have, or don't have, spoil our enjoyment of the things we do have and can have.   —Richard L. Evans

The talent for being happy is appreciating and liking what you have, instead of what you don't have.
                    —Woody Allen

It is not customary to love what one has.   —Anatole France

Happy thou art not; for what thou hast not, still thou striv'est to get; and what thou hast, forget'est.
          —William Shakespeare

Men ... always think that something they are going to get is better than what they have got.
          —John Oliver Hobbes

When we cannot get what we love, we must love what is within our reach.   —French proverb

Take full account of the excellencies which you possess, and in gratitude remember how you would hanker after them, if you had them not.
          —Marcus Aurelius

A wise man cares not for what he cannot have.   —Anon.

A man can refrain from wanting what he has not, and cheerfully make the best of a bird in the hand.
          —Marcus Annaeus Seneca

Long only for what you have.
                    —André Gide

The tulip is, among flowers, what the peacock is among birds. A tulip lacks scent, a peacock has an unpleasant voice. The one takes pride in its garb, the other in its tail.
                    —French proverb

Slight not what is near though aiming at what is far.   —Euripides

Greediness of getting more, deprives ... the enjoyment of what it had got.
                    —Thomas Sprat

There is a mortal breed most full of futility. In contempt of what is at hand, they strain into the future, hunting impossibilities on the wings of ineffectual hopes.   —Pindar

What you really value is what you miss, not what you have.
                    —Jorge Luis Borges

While you fear missing a meal, you aren't fully aware of the meals you do eat.   —Dan Millman

To be upset over what you don't have is to waste what you do have.
                    —Ken Keyes, Jr.

If there's no bread, cakes are very good.   —Spanish proverb

Not what we have, but what we enjoy, constitutes our abundance.
                    —J. Petit-Senn

Not what we have, but what we use, not what we see, but what we choose—these are the things that mar or bless human happiness.
                    —Joseph Fort Newton

The happiness which is lacking makes one think even the happiness one has unbearable.   —Joseph Roux

We always have enough to be happy if we are enjoying what we do have—and not worrying about what we don't have.   —Ken Keyes, Jr.

If there is a sin against life, it consists perhaps not so much in despairing of life as in hoping for another, and in eluding the implacable grandeur of this life.   —Albert Camus

Welcome everything that comes to you, but do not long for anything else.   —André Gide

The superiority of the distant over the present is only due to the mass and variety of the pleasures that can be suggested, compared with the poverty of those that can at any time be felt.   —George Santayana

WE OFTEN DON'T VALUE THINGS AFTER WE GET THEM

Mankind, by the perverse depravity of their nature, esteem that which they have most desired as of no value the moment it is possessed, and torment themselves with fruitless wishes for that which is beyond their reach.   —Francois de Fenelon

Do not spoil what you have by desiring what you have not; remember that what you now have was once among the things only hoped for.   —Epicurus

It ain't so much trouble to get rich as it is to tell when we have got rich.   —Josh Billings

No man can be satisfied with his attainment, although he may be satisfied with his circumstances.   —Frank Swinnerton

Life is a progress from want to want, not from enjoyment to enjoyment.   —Samuel Johnson

We spend our time searching for security and hate it when we get it.   —John Steinbeck

There must be more to life than having everything.   —Maurice Sendak

Is there no end to this escalation of desire?   —Marya Mannes

Ambition has its disappointments to sour us, but never the good fortune to satisfy us.   —Benjamin Franklin

There is no banquet but some dislike something in it.   —Thomas Fuller

If we get everything that we want, we will soon want nothing that we get.   —Vernon Luchies

It matters very little whether a man is discontented in the name of pessimism or progress, if his discontent does in fact paralyse his power of appreciating what he has got.   —G.K. Chesterton

WE OFTEN DON'T APPRECIATE WHAT WE HAVE UNTIL WE LOSE IT

So long as we can lose any happiness, we possess some.   —Booth Tarkington

Happiness always looks small while you hold it in your hands, but let it go, and you learn at once how big and precious it is.   —Maxim Gorky

We never know the worth of water till the well is dry.   —English proverb

The way to love anything is to realize that it may be lost.
—G.K. Chesterton

Jesus, please teach me to appreciate
what I have before time forces me to
appreciate what I had.
—Susan L. Lenzkes

Eden is that old-fashioned house we
dwell in every day
Without suspecting our abode, until
we drive away.
—Emily Dickinson

Generally the man with a good wife,
or the woman with a good husband,
or the children with good parents
discover too late the goodness they
overlooked while it was in full
bloom. —James Douglas

The best things in life are appreciated most after they have been lost.
—Roy L. Smith

Only with a new ruler do you realize
the value of the old.
—Burmese proverb

I remember those happy days and
often wish I could speak into the
ears of the dead the gratitude which
was due to them in life and so ill-
returned. —Gwyn Thomas

You can't appreciate home until
you've left it, money till it's spent,
your wife till she's joined a woman's
club, nor Old Glory till you see it
hanging on a broomstick on the
shanty of a consul in a foreign town.
—O. Henry

What Counts Is What's Left
Birds sing after a storm; why

shouldn't people feel as free to
delight in whatever remains to
them? —Rose Fitzgerald Kennedy

Think of all the beauty still left
around you and be happy.
—Anne Frank

Oh, my friend, it's not what they
take away from you that counts—it's
what you do with what you have
left. —Hubert H. Humphrey,
after cancer surgery

Giving Thanks
God gave you a gift of 86,400 seconds today. Have you used one to
say "thank you"? —William A. Ward

The Pilgrims made seven times more
graves than huts. No Americans
have been more impoverished than
these who, nevertheless, set aside a
day of thanksgiving.
—H.U. Westermayer

The greatest saint in the world is not
he who prays most or fasts most; it
is not he who gives alms, or is most
eminent for temperance, chastity or
justice. It is he who is most thankful
to God. —William Law

Not what we say about our blessings, but how we use them, is the
true measure of our thanksgiving.
—W.T. Purkiser

The unthankful heart ... discovers no
mercies; but the thankful heart ...
will find, in every hour, some heavenly blessings.
—Henry Ward Beecher

Thanksgiving is a sure index of spiritual health. —Maurice Dametz

If the only prayer you say in your whole life is "Thank you," that would suffice.   —Meister Eckhart

Who does not thank for little will not thank for much.

—Estonian proverb

The beginning of men's rebellion against God was, and is, the lack of a thankful heart. —Francis Schaeffer

A thankful heart is not only the greatest virtue, but the parent of all other virtues.   —Cicero

Seeds of discouragement will not grow in the thankful heart.

—Anon.

The private and personal blessings we enjoy—the blessings of immunity, safeguard, liberty and integrity—deserve the thanksgiving of a whole life.   —Jeremy Taylor

One of life's gifts is that each of us, no matter how tired and downtrodden, finds reasons for thankfulness.

—J. Robert Maskin

GRATITUDE

Joy is the simplest form of gratitude.
—Karl Barth

He who receives a benefit with gratitude repays the first installment on his debt.   —Marcus Annaeus Seneca

Gratitude is the memory of the heart.   —Massieu

Happiness is itself a kind of gratitude.   —Joseph Wood Krutch

WHAT IS ENOUGH?

What is the proper limit for wealth? It is, first, to have what is necessary; and, second, to have what is enough.
—Marcus Annaeus Seneca

He has enough who is contented with little.   —Anon.

More than enough is too much.
—Anon.

Nothing is enough to the man for whom enough is too little.
—Epicurus

Let him who has enough wish for nothing more.   —Horace

Sufficiency's enough for men of sense.   —Euripides

You never know what is enough unless you know what is more than enough.   —William Blake

Enough is as good as a feast.
—John Heywood

There is satiety in all things, in sleep, and love-making, in the loveliness of singing and the innocent dance.
—Homer

The average man is rich enough when he has a little more than he has got.   —William Ralph Inge

A wise man will desire no more than what he may get justly, use soberly, distribute cheerfully, and leave contently.   —Benjamin Franklin

Money and time are the heaviest burdens of life, and the unhappiest of all mortals are those who have more of either than they know how to use.　　　　—Samuel Johnson

Whoever is not in his coffin and the dark grave, let him know he has enough.　　　　—Walt Whitman

Too much is unwholesome.
　　　—Georg Christoph Lichtenberg

This only grant me, that my means may lie too low for envy, for contempt too high.　—Abraham Cowley

Moderation is the key to lasting enjoyment.　　　　—Hosea Ballou

Nothing in excess.　　　　—Solon

Ask the gods nothing excessive.
　　　　—Aeschylus

Avarice is as destitute of what it has as poverty is of what it has not.
　　　　—Publilius Syrus

Philosophy ... should not pretend to increase our present stock, but make us economists of what we are possessed of.　　　—Oliver Goldsmith

The use we make of our fortune determines as to its sufficiency. A little is enough if used wisely, and too much is not enough if expended foolishly.　　　　—Christian Bovee

It is possible to own too much. A man with one watch knows what time it is; a man with two watches is never quite sure.　　—Lee Segall

Happiness is a way station between too much and too little.
　　　　—Channing Pollock

GREED

He who is greedy is always in want.
　　　　—Horace

No gain satisfies a greedy mind.
　　　　—Latin proverb

Greed lessens what is gathered.
　　　　—Arab proverb

We risk all in being too greedy.
　　　　—Jean de La Fontaine

Greed is a bottomless pit which exhausts the person in an endless effort to satisfy the need without ever reaching satisfaction.
　　　　—Erich Fromm

Greed, like the love of comfort, is a kind of fear.　　—Cyril Connolly

The greedy man is incontent with a whole world set before him.　—Sa'Di

For greed, all nature is too little.
　　　—Marcus Annaeus Seneca

Greed's worst point is its ingratitude.
　　　—Marcus Annaeus Seneca

CONTROLLING WANTS

We don't need to increase our goods nearly as much as we need to scale down our wants. Not wanting something is as good as possessing it.
　　　　—Donald Horban

To be able to dispense with good things is tantamount to possessing them.　　—Jean Francois Regnard

The hardest thing is to take less when you can get more.
　　　　—Kin Hubbard

Whoever does not regard what he has as most ample wealth is unhappy, though he is master of the world.
—Epicurus

I have learned to seek my happiness by limiting my desires, rather than in attempting to satisfy them.
—John Stuart Mill

How few are our real wants, and how easy is it to satisfy them! Our imaginary ones are boundless and insatiable.
—Julius Charles Hare

Of all the people in the world, those who want the most are those who have the most.
—David Grayson

Who covets more is evermore a slave.
—Robert Herrick

If you desire many things, many things will seem but a few.
—Benjamin Franklin

The heart is great which shows moderation in the midst of prosperity.
—Marcus Annaeus Seneca

Want is a growing giant whom the coat of Have was never large enough to cover.
—Ralph Waldo Emerson

How many things there are which I do not want.
—Socrates

Moderate desires constitute a character fitted to acquire all the good which the world can yield. He who has this character is prepared, in whatever situation he is, therewith to be content and has learned the science of being happy.
—Timothy Dwight

Freedom is not procured by a full enjoyment of what is desired, but by controlling the desire.
—Epictetus

Were a man to order his life by the rules of true reason, a frugal substance joined to a contented mind is for him great riches.
—Lucretius

One is never fortunate or as unfortunate as one imagines.
—Francois de La Rochefoucauld

Man needs so little ... yet he begins wanting so much.
—Louis L'Amour

Man never has what he wants, because what he wants is everything.
—C.F. Ramuz

If your desires be endless, your cares and fears will be so, too.
—Thomas Fuller

We are no longer happy so soon as we wish to be happier.
—Walter Savage Landor

He is not rich that possesses much, but he that covets no more; and he is not poor that enjoys little, but he that wants too much.
—Beaumont

Independence may be found in comparative as well as in absolute abundance; I mean where a person contracts his desires within the limits of his fortune.
—William Shenstone

There Are Always Others Worse Off Than Us

One never hugs one's good luck so affectionately as when listening to the relation of some horrible misfortunes which has overtaken others.
—Alexander Smith

If you would but exchange places with the other fellow, how much more you could appreciate your own position. —Victor E. Gardner

We should learn, by reflection on the misfortunes of others, that there is nothing singular in those which befall ourselves. —Thomas Fitzosborne

Double—no, triple—our troubles and we'd still be better off than any other people on earth. —Ronald Reagan

I wept because I had no shoes, until I saw a man who had no feet. —Ancient Persian saying

When life's problems seem overwhelming, look around and see what other people are coping with. You may consider yourself fortunate. —Ann Landers

If all misfortunes were laid in one common heap whence everyone must take an equal portion, most people would be contented to take their own and depart. —Socrates

Who Is Really Poor?

Not he who has little, but he who wishes more, is poor. —Marcus Annaeus Seneca

The covetous man is always poor. —Claudian

He is not poor that hath not much, but he that craves much. —Thomas Fuller

He is poor who does not feel content. —Japanese proverb

Who Is Really Rich?

He who curbs his desires will always be rich enough. —French proverb

That man is richest whose pleasures are the cheapest. —Henry David Thoreau

True affluence is not needing anything. —Gary Snyder

To be satisfied with what one has; that is wealth. As long as one sorely needs a certain additional amount, that man isn't rich. —Mark Twain

I have the greatest of all riches: that of not desiring them. —Eleonora Duse

A man is rich in proportion to the things he can afford to let alone. —Henry David Thoreau

He is rich that is satisfied. —Thomas Fuller

He is well paid that is well satisfied. —William Shakespeare

He who is content in his poverty is wonderfully rich. —Anon.

He who is contented is rich. —Lao-tzu

All fortune belongs to him who has a contented mind. —The Panchatantra

Poor and content is rich, and rich enough. —William Shakespeare

The greatest wealth is contentment with a little. —Anon.

He is not rich that possesses much,

but he that is content with what he has. —Anon.

BEING THANKFUL FOR OUR ABILITIES AND TALENTS

One well-cultivated talent, deepened and enlarged, is worth one hundred shallow faculties.
—William Matthews

If only every man would make proper use of his strength and do his utmost, he need never regret his limited ability. —Cicero

I knew I had no lyrical quality, a small vocabulary, little gift of metaphor. The original and striking simile never occurred to me. Poetic flights ... were beyond my powers. On the other hand, I had an acute power of observation, and it seemed to me that I could see a great many things that other people missed. I could put down in clear terms what I saw.... I knew that I should never write as well as I could wish, but I thought, with pains, that I could arrive at writing as well as my natural defects allowed.
—W. Somerset Maugham

Anyone is to be pitied who has just sense enough to perceive his deficiencies. —William Hazlitt

What strange perversity is it that induces a man to set his heart on doing those things which he has not succeeded in, and makes him slight those in which his achievement has been respectable.
—Gamaliel Bradford

I may not amount to much, but at least I am unique.
—Jean-Jacques Rousseau

Happy is the man who can do only one thing: in doing it, he fulfills his destiny. —Joseph Joubert

The real tragedy of life is not being limited to one talent, but in failing to use that one talent.
—Edgar Watson Howe

Too many people overvalue what they are not and undervalue what they are. —Malcolm Forbes

CONTENTMENT

Nothing will content him who is not content with a little.
—Greek proverb

Contentment is worth more than riches. —German proverb

I figure if I have my health, can pay the rent and I have my friends, I call it "content." —Lauren Bacall

Be content with what thou hast received, and smooth thy frowning forehead. —Hafez

He is poor who does not feel content. —Japanese proverb

If thou covetest riches, ask not but for contentment, which is an immense treasure. —Sa'Di

Who is content with nothing possesses all things. —Nicolas Boileau

My crown is called content, a crown that seldom kings enjoy.
—William Shakespeare

It is right to be contented with what we have, never with what we are.
—Mackintosh

Be content with your lot; one cannot be first in everything.　　—Aesop

Content may dwell in all stations. To be low, but above contempt, may be high enough to be happy.
　　　　　　—Sir Thomas Browne

True contentment ... is the power of getting out of any situation all that there is in it. It is arduous, and it is rare.　　　　—G.K. Chesterton

Poor and content is rich, and rich enough.　　—William Shakespeare

The greatest wealth is contentment with a little.　　　　—Anon.

And be content with such things as ye have.　　　　—Heb. 13:5

Everything has its wonders, even darkness and silence, and I learn, whatever state I may be in, therein to be content.　　　　—Helen Keller

Try to live the life of the good man who is more than content with what is allocated to him.
　　　　　　—Marcus Aurelius

He is not rich that possesses much, but he that is content with what he has.　　　　—Anon.

The world is full of people looking for spectacular happiness while they snub contentment.　—Doug Larson

We are never content with our lot.
　　　　　　—Jean de La Fontaine

Until you make peace with who you are, you'll never be content with what you have.　—Doris Mortman

True contentment depends not upon what we have; a tub was large enough for Diogenes, but a world was too little for Alexander.
　　　　　—Charles Caleb Colton

To be content with little is difficult; to be content with much, impossible.
　　　　　　—Anon.

HAPPINESS

To be without some of the things you want is an indispensable part of happiness.　　—Bertrand Russell

Man is fond of counting his troubles, but he does not count his joys. If he counted them up as he ought to, he would see that every lot has enough happiness provided for it.
　　　　　—Fyodor Dostoyevsky

Happiness is itself a kind of gratitude.　　　—Joseph Wood Krutch

I am happy and content because I think I am.　—Alain-Rene Lesage

Unhappy is the man, though he rule the world, who doesn't consider himself supremely blessed.
　　　　—Marcus Annaeus Seneca

The happiness which is lacking makes one think even the happiness one has unbearable.　—Joseph Roux

Happiness is a result of the relative strengths of positive and negative feelings, rather than an absolute amount of one or the other.
　　　　　—Norman Bradburn

The best way for a person to have happy thoughts is to count his blessings and not his cash.　　—Anon.

Surfeits of happiness are fatal.
—Baltasar Gracian

If thou wouldst be happy ... have an indifference for more than what is sufficient. —William Penn

You will live wisely if you are happy in your lot. —Horace

We always have enough to be happy if we are enjoying what we do have—and not worrying about what we don't have. —Ken Keyes, Jr.

Talk happiness. The world is sad enough without your woe. No path is wholly rough.
—Ella Wheeler Wilcox

COUNT TODAY'S BLESSINGS, RATHER THAN LONGING FOR YESTERDAY'S

Reflect upon your present blessings, of which every man has many; not on your past misfortunes, of which all men have some.
—Charles Dickens

No longer forward nor behind
I look in hope or fear;
But, grateful, take the good I find,
The best of now and here.
—John Greenleaf Whittier

WE'RE BETTER OFF, AND HAPPIER, THAN WE REALIZE OR ADMIT

What a wonderful life I've had! I only wish I'd realized it sooner.
—Colette

Was it always my nature to take a bad time and block out the good times, until any success became an accident and failure seemed the only truth? —Lillian Hellman

Most human beings have an almost infinite capacity for taking things for granted. —Aldous Huxley

There are men who are happy without knowing it. —Vauvenargues

We are all of us richer than we think we are. —Michel de Montaigne

What a miserable thing life is: you're living in clover, only the clover isn't good enough. —Bertolt Brecht

I am convinced, the longer I live, that life and its blessings are not so entirely unjustly distributed as when we are suffering greatly we are inclined to suppose.
—Mary Todd Lincoln

GENERAL QUOTATIONS ABOUT OUR BLESSINGS

Life is hard. Next to what?
—Anon.

Over a period of time it's been driven home to me that I'm not going to be the most popular writer in the world, so I'm always happy when anything in any way is accepted.
—Stephen Sondheim

In the country of the blind, the one-eyed man is king.
—Michael Apostolius

We give thanks for unknown blessings already on their way.
—Sacred ritual chant

A man with ambition and love for his blessings here on earth is ever so alive. Having been alive, it won't be so hard in the end to lie down and rest. —Pearl Bailey

69

Be satisfied, and pleased with what
    thou art,
Act cheerfully and well thou allotted
    part;
Enjoy the present hour, be thankful
    for the past,
And neither fear, nor wish, the
    approaches of the last. —Martial

No one is satisfied with his fortune,
or dissatisfied with his intellect.
           —Antoinette Deshouliere

'Tis better to have loved and lost
than never to have loved at all.
           —Alfred, Lord Tennyson

THE GRASS IS ALWAYS GREENER ON THE OTHER SIDE OF THE FENCE

PEOPLE THINK THE GRASS IS GREENER ON THE OTHER SIDE OF THE FENCE

What you can't get is just what suits you. —French proverb

Every stage of life has its troubles, and no man is content with his own age. —Ausonius

No one is content with his own lot. —Horace

We love in others what we lack ourselves, and would be everything but what we are. —R.H. Stoddard

When you don't have any money, the problem is food. When you have money, it's sex. When you have both, it's health. If everything is simply jake, then you're frightened of death. —J.P. Donleavy

Diogenes was asked what wine he liked best, and he answered, "Somebody else's." —Michel de Montaigne

The apples on the other side of the wall are the sweetest. —Anon.

Happiness is ... usually attributed by adults to children, and by children to adults. —Thomas Szasz

Acorns were good till bread was found. —Anon.

None of us is ever satisfied with what we are. —Terence

We always long for forbidden things, and desire what is denied us. —Francois Rabelais

Man's heart is never satisfied; the snake would swallow the elephant. —Chinese proverb

We all envy other people's luck. —Latin proverb

When every blessed thing you have is made of silver, or of gold, you long for simple pewter. —W.S. Gilbert

I'd rather have written "Cheers" than anything I've written. —Kurt Vonnegut

To most of us the real life is the life we do not lead. —Oscar Wilde

When a man's busy, leisure strikes him as a wonderful pleasure; and at leisure once is he? Straightway he wants to be busy.
— Robert Browning

Happiness to a dog is what lies on the other side of the door.
— Charlton Ogburn, Jr.

Man would be otherwise. That is the essence of the specifically human.
— Antonio Machado

He who would be happy should stay at home. — Greek proverb

He who leaves his house in search of happiness pursues a shadow.
— Anon.

DISTANT PLACES AND THINGS

It is not irritating to be where one is. It is only irritating to think one would like to be somewhere else.
— John Cage

He that is discontented in one place will seldom be happy in another.
— Aesop

We are under the spell always of what is distant from us. It is not in our nature to desire passionately what is near at hand. — Alec Waugh

In all climates, under all skies, man's happiness is always somewhere else.
— Giacomo Leopardi

In Rome you long for the country. In the country you praise to the skies the distant town. — Horace

He who would be happy should stay at home. — Greek proverb

Life is a hospital in which every patient is possessed by the desire of changing his bed. One would prefer to suffer near the fire, and another is certain he would get well if he were by the window.
— Charles Baudelaire

It is common to overlook what is near by keeping the eye fixed on something remote.
— Samuel Johnson

There are three wants which can never be satisfied: that of the rich, who want something more; that of the sick, who want something different; and that of the traveler, who says, "Anywhere but here."
— Ralph Waldo Emerson

Happiness grows at our firesides, and is not to be picked in strangers' gardens. — Douglas Jerrold

Men run away to other countries because they are not good in their own, and run back to their own because they pass for nothing in the new places. — Ralph Waldo Emerson

The proper means of increasing the love we bear our native country is to reside some time in a foreign one.
— William Shenstone

If solid happiness we prize, within
  our breast this jewel lies,
And they are fools who roam; the
  world has nothing to bestow,
From our own selves our bliss must
  flow,
And that dear hut—our home.
— Nathaniel Cotton

A child on a farm sees a plane fly

overhead and dreams of a faraway place. A traveler on the plane sees the farmhouse and dreams of home.
—Carl Burns

Everyone Has Problems and Difficulties

Life has no smooth road for any of us; and in the bracing atmosphere of a high aim the very roughness stimulates the climber to steadier steps till the legend, "over steep ways to the stars," fulfills itself.   —W.C. Doane

The only normal people are the ones you don't know very well.
—Foe Ancis

Before we set our hearts too much upon anything, let us examine how happy they are who already possess it.   —Francois de La Rochefoucauld

What makes us discontented with our condition is the absurdly exaggerated idea we have of the happiness of others.   —Anon.

Nobody's problem is ideal. Nobody has things just as he would like them.   —Dr. Frank Crane

We are convinced that happiness is never to be found, and each believes it possessed by others, to keep alive the hope of obtaining it for himself.
—Samuel Johnson

Men would be angels; angels would be gods.   —Alexander Pope

If every man's internal care
Were written on his brow,
How many would our pity share
Who raise our envy now?
—Pietro Metastasio

Misfortunes come to all men.
—Chinese proverb

You have no idea how big the other fellow's troubles are.   —B.C. Forbes

The Powerful, Famous and Rich All Have Their Troubles

I have now reigned above fifty years in victory or peace, beloved by my subjects, dreaded by my enemies, respected by my allies. Riches and honors, power and pleasure, have awaited my call, nor does any earthly blessing seem to have been wanting.... I have diligently numbered the days of pure and genuine happiness that have fallen to my lot; they amount to fourteen.
—Abd-Al-Rahman

Great and small suffer the same mishaps.   —Blaise Pascal

None think the great unhappy but the great.   —Edward Young

I thought I had reached a point in life where everything would be smooth. But it is not. It just gets more jagged and pitted and filled with turns that take you into the dark recesses of your mind. It never seems to get easy.
—Sylvester Stallone

If I were given a change of life, I'd like to see how it would be to live as a mere six-footer.
—Wilt Chamberlain

Oh God, don't envy me, I have my own pains.   —Barbra Streisand

I just want to be an ordinary girl.
—Princess Stephanie of Monaco

73

Money is another pressure. I'm not complaining, I'm just saying that there's a certain luxury in having no money. I spent ten years in New York not having it, not worrying about it. Suddenly you have it, then you worry, where is it going? Am I doing the right thing with it?
—Dustin Hoffman

On the outside one is a star. But in reality, one is completely alone, doubting everything. To experience this loneliness of soul is the hardest thing in the world. —Brigitte Bardot

There is no man in this world without some manner of tribulation or anguish, though he be king or pope.
—Thomas a'Kempis

The only incurable troubles of the rich are the troubles that money can't cure.   —Ogden Nash

There is no man in any rank who is always at liberty to act as he would incline; in some quarter or other he is limited by circumstances.   —Blair

None of us can be free of conflict and woe. Even the greatest men have had to accept disappointments as their daily bread.... The art of living lies less in eliminating our troubles than in growing with them.
—Bernard M. Baruch

Renown is a source of toil and sorrow; obscurity is a source of happiness.   —Johann L. von Mosheim

My crown is called content; a crown it is that seldom kings enjoy.
—William Shakespeare

If I had my life to live over, I wish I could be a great pianist or something.   —Woody Allen

There is no armour against fate; death lays his icy hands on kings.
—James Shirley

Pale death with impartial tread beats at the poor man's cottage door and at the palaces of kings.   —Horace

I want to be able to live without a crowded calendar. I want to be able to read a book without feeling guilty, or go to a concert when I like.
—Golda Meir

I'd like to be a truck driver. I think you could run your life that way. It wouldn't be such a bad way of doing it. It would offer a chance to be alone.   —Princess Anne of England

There is as much confusion in the world of the gods as in ours.
—Euripides

Pray the gods do not envy your happiness!   —Euripides

The suffering of the rich is among the sweetest pleasures of the poor.
—R.M. Huber

SUCCESS ISN'T ALWAYS THE ANSWER

Success is counted sweetest by those who never succeed.
—Emily Dickinson

I have known no man of genius who had not to pay, in some affliction or defect either physical or spiritual, for what the gods had given him.
—Max Beerbohm

Men are all the same. They always think that something they are going to get is better than what they have got.   —John Oliver Hobbes

Success is not greedy, as people think, but insignificant. That's why it satisfies nobody.
          —Marcus Annaeus Seneca

Beggars do not envy millionaires, though of course they will envy other beggars who are more success-ful.   —Bertrand Russell

Ambition, having reached the sum-mit, longs to descend.
          —Pierre Corneille

What we call progress is the exchange of one nuisance for anoth-er nuisance. —Henry Havelock Ellis

The superpowers often behave like two heavily armed blind men feeling their way around a room, each believing himself in mortal peril from the other, who he assumes to have perfect vision.
          —Henry Kissinger

Wanting to change, to improve, a person's situation means offering him, for difficulties in which he is practiced and experienced, other dif-ficulties that will find him perhaps even more bewildered.
          —Rainer Maria Rilke

BEING BETTER LOOKING WOULDN'T SOLVE OUR PROBLEMS

Being considered beautiful at a young age sends confusing signals. You think people only like you because of your beauty.
          —Priscilla Presley

I am desperate and vulnerable.... I am always terrified.... Beauty can sometimes be so very troublesome.
          —Faye Dunaway

I hate myself on the screen. I want to die ... my voice is either too high or too gravelly. I want to dive under the carpet.... I'd love to be tall and wil-lowy ... I'm short. —ElizabethTaylor

I don't like my voice. I don't like the way I look. I don't like the way I move. I don't like the way I act. I mean, period. So, you know, I don't like myself.   —Elizabeth Taylor

I look forward to being older, when what you look like becomes less and less an issue and what you are is the point.   —Susan Sarandon

Beauty can get a woman what she wants: love and money. But when beauty leaves you, so can the things it brought.   —Paulina Porizkova

If you're considered a beauty, it's hard to be accepted doing anything but standing around.
          —Cybil Shepherd

Just because you're beautiful, they think you can't act.... I've got a lot more to prove.   —Carol Alt

I intimidate men ... People look a lot, but there's no line outside my door.
          —Joan Severance

People see you as an object, not as a person, and they project a set of expectations onto you. People who don't have it think beauty is a bless-ing, but actually it sets you apart.
          —Candice Bergen

Each time I get off a plane in Hollywood, I don't think I'm pretty enough.   —Christine Lahti

I can count the number of dates I've had on one hand. I wish that guys would approach me, but they don't.
                                —LaToya Jackson

When you step on the first tee it doesn't matter what you look like.... It doesn't help your 5-iron if you're pretty.   —Laura Baugh

For years I stopped reading beauty magazines because I couldn't look at one without wanting to blow my brains out. How can those women look so good?   —Jamie Lee Curtis

Frankly, I like the fact that I no longer fit the young beauty type— people take me more seriously now.
                                —Cybil Shepherd

You know how many stunning women told me they can't stand a good-looking man? ... Women feel secure with an ugly guy because a man in bad shape isn't gonna cheat.
                                —Jackie Mason

Outstanding beauty, like outstanding gifts of any kind, tends to get in the way of normal emotional development, and thus of that particular success in life which we call happiness.   —Milton R. Sapirstein

A full bosom is actually a millstone around a woman's neck.... [Breasts] are not parts of a person but lures slung around her neck, to be kneaded and twisted like magic putty, or mumbled and mouthed like lolly ices.   —Germaine Greer

Plain women know more about men than beautiful ones do.
                                —Katharine Hepburn

Not many people ask me out.
                                —Marina Sirtis

People are crying up the rich and variegated plumage of the peacock, and he is himself blushing at the sight of his ugly feet.   —Sa'Di

I'm walking insecurity. Without all this makeup, I look like a refugee when I get up in the morning.... I generally look like one major bow-wow. I mean arf.   —Connie Chung

You start out happy that you have no hips or boobs. All of a sudden you get them, and it feels sloppy. Then just when you start liking them, they start dropping.
                                —Cindy Crawford

The problem with beauty is that it's like being born rich and getting poorer.   —Joan Collins

Guys think that if a girl is pretty, she's automatically going to say no. Most of the guy's I've gone out with, I've had to make it completely obvious that I'd like them to ask me out. Or, I've had to ask them.
                                —Brooke Shields

I think if I weren't so beautiful, maybe I'd have more character.
                                —Jerry Hall

BE CAREFUL IN MAKING COMPARISONS

Comparison, more than reality, makes men happy or wretched.
                                —Thomas Fuller

Instead of comparing our lot with that of those who are more fortunate than we are, we should compare it with the lot of the great majority of our fellow men. It then appears that we are among the privileged.
—Helen Keller

I murmured because I had no shoes, until I met man who had no feet.
—Persian proverb

The man with a toothache thinks everyone happy whose teeth are sound. The poverty-stricken man makes the same mistake about the rich man. —George Bernard Shaw

If you compare yourself with others, you may become vain or bitter, for always there will be greater and lesser persons than yourself.
—Max Ehrmann

I look at what I have not and think myself unhappy; others look at what I have and think me happy.
—Joseph Roux

Enjoy your own life without comparing it with that of another.
—*The Condorcet*

If we only wanted to be happy it would be easy; but we want to be happier than other people, which is almost always difficult, since we think them happier than they are.
—Charles de Montesquieu

I never admired another's fortune so much that I became dissatisfied with my own. —Cicero

Every horse thinks his own pack heaviest. —Thomas Fuller

Comparisons of one's lot with others' teaches us nothing and enfeebles the will. —Thornton Wilder

To think well of every other man's condition, and to dislike our own, is one of the misfortunes of human nature. —Burton

Other people's eggs have two yolks.
—Hungarian proverb

No story ever looks as bad as the story you've just bought; no story ever looks as good as the story the other fellow just bought.
—Irving Thalberg

If all our misfortunes were laid in one common heap, whence every one must take an equal portion, most people would be content to take their own and depart. —Solon

Money, it turned out, was exactly like sex; you thought of nothing else if you didn't have it and thought of other things if you did.
—James Baldwin

WE CAN'T LET OURSELVES BE WARPED BY JEALOUSY AND ENVY

Envy is an insult to oneself.
—Yevgeny Yevtushenko

Envy has the ugliness of a trapped rat that has gnawed its own foot in its effort to escape. —Angus Wilson

Envy eats nothing but its own heart.
—German proverb

Jealousy would be far less torturous if we understood that love is a passion entirely unrelated to our merits.
—Paul Eldridges

In jealousy there is more of self-love than love.
—Francois de La Rochefoucauld

Jealousy is an inner consciousness of one's own inferiority. It is a mental cancer. —B.C. Forbes

Jealousy, that dragon which slays love under the pretense of keeping it alive. —Havelock Ellis

There is no greater glory than love, nor any greater punishment than jealousy. —Lope de Vega

You can't be envious and happy at the same time. —Frank Tyger

As a moth gnaws a garment, so doth envy consume a man.
—Saint John Chrysostom

Envy is the most stupid of vices, for there is no single advantage to be gained from it. —Honore de Balzac

The jealous are troublesome to others, but torment to themselves.
—William Penn

Envy and fear are the only passions to which no pleasure is attached.
—John Churton Collins

If malice or envy were tangible and had a shape, it would be the shape of a boomerang. —Charley Reese

Jealousy is all the fun you think they had. —Erica Jong

Envy is a kind of praise. —John Gay

Envy, among other ingredients, has a mixture of the love of justice in it. We are more angry at undeserved than at deserved good fortune.
—William Hazlitt

Envy comes from people's ignorance of, or lack of belief in, their own gifts. —Jean Vanier

To cure jealousy is to see it for what it is, a dissatisfaction with self.
—Joan Didion

If envy were a fever, all the world would be ill. —Danish proverb

Jealousy is not a barometer by which the depth of love can be read. It merely records the degree of the lover's insecurity. —Margaret Mead

The heaven of the envied is hell for the envious. —Baltasar Gracian

HELPING OTHER PEOPLE

WE CAN'T LIVE JUST FOR OURSELVES

The entire population of the universe, with one trifling exception, is composed of others.
—John Andrew Holmes

You don't live in a world all your own. Your brothers are here, too.
—Albert Schweitzer

Everyone needs help from everyone.
—Bertolt Brecht

What do we live for if not to make life less difficult for each other?
—George Eliot

The service we render others is the rent we pay for our room on earth.
—Wilfred Grenfell

A man is called selfish not for pursuing his own good, but for neglecting his neighbor's.
—Richard Whately

In this world we must help one another.
—Jean de La Fontaine

Man absolutely cannot live by himself.
—Erich Fromm

We cannot live only for ourselves. A thousand fibers connect us with our fellow men.
—Herman Melville

We have no more right to consume happiness without producing it than to consume wealth without producing it.
—George Bernard Shaw

In the time we have it is surely our duty to do all the good we can to all the people we can in all the ways we can.
—William Barclay

There ain't nothing but one thing wrong with every one of us, and that's selfishness.
—Will Rogers

He who lives only for himself is truly dead to others.
—Publilius Syrus

Provision for others is a fundamental responsibility of human life.
—Woodrow Wilson

Everything that lives, lives not alone, nor for itself.
—William Blake

A man wrapped up in himself makes a very small bundle.
—Benjamin Franklin

Maturity begins to grow when you can sense your concern for others outweighing your concern for yourself.　　　—John MacNaughton

NOTHING IS MORE IMPORTANT THAN KINDNESS

Three things in human life are important: The first is to be kind. The second is to be kind. And the third is to be kind.　　—Henry James

Be kind, for everyone you meet is fighting a hard battle.　　—Philo

Kindness in words creates confidence. Kindness in thinking creates profoundness. Kindness in giving creates love.　　　—Lao-tzu

Kindness is the language which the deaf can hear and the blind can see.
　　　—Mark Twain

Wherever there is a human being, there is an opportunity for a kindness.　　—Marcus Annaeus Seneca

Kindness is the golden chain by which society is bound together.
　　　—Johann von Goethe

I expect to pass through life but once. If, therefore, there be any kindness I can show, or any good thing I can do for any fellow being, let me do it now ... as I shall not pass this way again.　　　—William Penn

I wonder why it is that we are not all kinder to each other.... How much the world needs it! How easily it is done!　　　—Henry Drummond

We are made kind by being kind.
　　　—Eric Hoffer

Kindness causes us to learn, and to forget, many things.
　　　—Madame Swetchine

Knowing sorrow well, I learn to succor the distressed.　　　—Virgil

There is nothing in life but refraining from hurting others, and comforting those that are sad.　—Olive Schreiner

Without kindness, there can be no true joy.　　　—Thomas Carlyle

Wise sayings often fall on barren ground, but a kind word is never thrown away.　　—Sir Arthur Helps

A word of kindness is seldom spoken in vain, while witty sayings are as easily lost as the pearls slipping from a broken string.　　—George Prentice

A kind word is like a Spring day.
　　　—Russian proverb

Kindness is in our power, even when fondness is not.　—Samuel Johnson

Kindness affects more than severity.
　　　—Aesop

Always be a little kinder than necessary.　　　—Sir James M. Barrie

Kindness is the ability to love people more than they deserve. —Anon.

The sense that someone else cares always helps because it is the sense of love.　　—George E. Woodberry

Today I bent the truth to be kind, and I have no regret, for I am far surer of what is kind that I am of what is true.　　—Robert Brault

Kindness, I've discovered, is everything in life. —Isaac Bashevis Singer

What wisdom can you find that is greater than kindness?
—Jean-Jacques Rousseau

Have you had a kindness shown?
    Pass it on!
'Twas not given for thee alone,
    Pass it on!
Let it travel down the years,
Let it wipe another's tears,
Till in Heaven the deed appears—
    Pass it on!   —Henry Burton

Goodwill ... is an immeasurable and tremendous energy, the atomic energy of the spirit.   —Eleanor B. Stock

Goodwill is the mightiest practical force in the universe.
—Charles F. Dole

Compassion is the basis of all morality.   —Arthur Schopenhauer

Success has nothing to do with what you gain in life or accomplish for yourself. It's what you do for others.
—Danny Thomas

RIGHT NOW IS THE TIME TO BE KIND

You cannot do a kindness too soon, for you never know how soon it will be too late. —Ralph Waldo Emerson

There's no use in doing a kindness if you do it a day too late.
—Charles Kingsley

He who sees a need and waits to be asked for help is as unkind as if he had refused it.   —Dante Alighieri

The golden rule is of no use whatsoever unless you realize that it is *your* move.   —Dr. Frank Crane

He gives twice who gives promptly.
—Publilius Syrus

WE MUSTN'T JUDGE BEFORE WE HELP

Charity looks at the need, not at the cause.   —German proverb

People who won't help others in trouble "because they got into trouble through their own fault" would probably not throw a lifeline to a drowning man until they learned whether he fell in through his own fault or not.   —Sydney J. Harris

If you judge people, you have no time to love them. —Mother Teresa

IF WE WANT TO HELP SOMEONE, WE SHOULD GIVE THEM PRACTICAL HELP

A little help is worth a great deal of pity.   —Anon.

Generosity gives assistance, rather than advice.   —Vauvenargues

Our worth is determined by the good deeds we *do*, rather than by the fine emotions we *feel*.
—Elias L. Magoon

When a person is down in the world, an ounce of help is better than a pound of preaching.
—Edward Bulwer-Lytton

Live and let live is not enough; live and help live is not too much.
—Orison Swett Marden

81

To give pleasure to a single heart by a single kind act is better than a thousand head-bowings in prayer.
—Sa'Di

Pity costs nothing and ain't worth nothing.　　　　—Josh Billings

To feel sorry for the needy is not the mark of a Christian—to help them is.　　　　—Frank A. Clark

'Tis not enough to help the feeble up, but to support him after.
—William Shakespeare

Where *our* bread is concerned, it is a material matter. Where our *neighbor's* bread is concerned, it is a spiritual matter.　　　—I.D. Douglas

HELPING OTHERS TO HELP THEMSELVES

The greatest good you can do for another is not just to share your riches, but to reveal to him his own.
—Benjamin Disraeli

The truest help we can render an afflicted man is not to take his burden from him, but to call out his best energy, that he may be able to bear the burden.　　　—Phillips Brooks

Time and money spent in helping men to do more for themselves is far better than mere giving.
—Henry Ford

SHARING

Find out how much God has given you and from it take what you need; the remainder is needed by others.
—Saint Augustine

For we must share, if we would keep, that blessing from above; Ceasing to give, we cease to have; such is the law of love.
—Richard C. Trench

An unshared life is not living. He who shares does not lessen, but greatens, his life.　—Stephen S. Wise

Sharing what you have is more important than what you have.
—Albert M. Wells, Jr.

GIVING

You cannot always have happiness, but you can always give happiness.
—Anon.

Be charitable and indulgent to every one but thyself.　　—Joseph Joubert

Real unselfishness consists in sharing the interests of others.
—George Santayana

Whoever in trouble and sorrow needs your help, give it to him. Whoever in anxiety or fear needs your friendship, give it to him. It isn't important whether he likes you. It isn't important whether you approve of his conduct. It isn't important what his creed or nationality may be.　　　　—E.N. West

I was hungered, and ye gave me meat: I was thirsty, and ye gave me drink: I was a stranger, and ye took me in: I was naked, and ye clothed me: I was sick, and ye visited me: I was in prison, and ye came unto me.
—Anon.

To give and then not feel that one has given is the very best of all ways of giving.　　—Max Beerbohm

It is more blessed to give than to receive. —Acts 20:35

God loveth a cheerful giver. —2 Cor. 9:7

CHARITY

In necessary things, unity; in doubtful things, liberty; in all things, charity. —Richard Baxter

Did universal charity prevail, earth would be a heaven, and hell a fable. —Charles Caleb Colton

He that has no charity deserves no mercy. —English proverb

I as little fear that God will damn a man that has charity as I hope that the priests can save one who has not. —Alexander Pope

In faith and hope the world will disagree, but all mankind's concern is charity. —Alexander Pope

There is no real religious experience that does not express itself in charity. —C.H. Dodd

Charity begins at home, and usually stays there. —Elbert Hubbard

Charity begins at home, but should not end there. —Thomas Fuller

He is rich who hath enough to be charitable. —Sir Thomas Browne

WE NEEDN'T BE CONCERNED THAT WE CAN'T GIVE "ENOUGH"

Give what you have. To someone else it may be better than you dare to think.
—Henry Wadsworth Longfellow

Even if it's a little thing, do something for those who have need of help, something for which you get no pay but the privilege of doing it. —Albert Schweitzer

Give, if thou can, an alms; if not, a sweet and gentle word. —Robert Herrick

It was only a sunny smile,
And little it cost in the giving.
But like morning light, it scattered the night,
And made the day worth living. —Anon.

Two thirds of help is to give courage. —Irish proverb

WE SHOULDN'T BE CONCERNED THAT WE MIGHT GIVE "TOO MUCH"

What boundary ever set limits to the service of mankind? —Claudian

I hate the giving of the hand unless the whole man accompanies it. —Ralph Waldo Emerson

You can never expect too much of yourself in the matter of giving yourself to others. —Theodore C. Speers

Isn't it better to have men be ungrateful, than to miss a chance to do good? —Denis Diderot

Better to expose ourselves to ingratitude than fail in assisting the unfortunate. —Du Coeur

THE BEST GIFT IS OURSELVES

Behold! I do not give lectures on a little charity. When I give, I give myself. —Walt Whitman

83

Simply give others a bit of yourself; a thoughtful act, a helpful idea, a word of appreciation, a lift over a rough spot, a sense of understanding, a timely suggestion. You take something out of your mind, garnished in kindness out of your heart, and put it into the other fellow's mind and heart.   —Charles H. Burr

The only gift is a portion of thyself.
　　　　—Ralph Waldo Emerson

There is no greater loan than a sympathetic ear.   —Frank Tyger

Do not inflict your will. Just give love. The soul will take that love and put it where it can best be used.
　　　　—Emmanuel

You give but little when you give of your possessions. It is when you give of yourself that you truly give.
　　　　—Kahlil Gibran

WHAT NOT HELPING OTHERS INDICATES

We are cold to others only when we are dull in ourselves.
　　　　—William Hazlitt

The mortal sickness of a mind too unhappy to be kind.
　　　　—A.E. Housman

Where there is no capacity to affirm another as a person in his own right, there is no love. There is only masked fear.   —Bonaro Overstreet

WHAT'S IN IT FOR US

The habit of being uniformly considerate toward others will bring increased happiness to you.
　　　　—Grenville Kleiser

He who does not live in some degree for others, hardly lives for himself.
　　　　—Michel de Montaigne

We cannot hold a torch to light another's path without brightening our own.   —Ben Sweetland

An act of goodness is of itself an act of happiness. —Maurice Maeterlinck

Happiness ... is achieved only by making others happy.
　　　　—Stuart Cloete

The most infectiously joyous men and women are those who forget themselves in thinking about others and serving others.
　　　　—Robert J. McCracken

He that will not permit his wealth to do any good for others ... cuts himself off from the truest pleasure here and the highest happiness later.
　　　　—Charles Caleb Colton

True religion ... is giving and finding one's happiness by bringing happiness into the lives of others.
　　　　—William J.H. Boetcker

Pleasure is a reciprocal; no one feels it who does not at the same time give it. To be pleased, one must please.
　　　　—Lord Chesterfield

If we had no regard for others' feelings or fortune, we would grow cold and indifferent to life itself.
　　　　—George Matthew Adams

To devote a portion of one's leisure to doing something for someone else is one of the highest forms of recreation.   —Gerald B. Fitzgerald

Live for thy neighbor if thou wouldst live for thyself.
—Marcus Annaeus Seneca

The true way to soften one's troubles is to solace those of others.
—Madame de Maintenon

Anything done for another is done for oneself. —Boniface VIII

What we frankly give, forever is our own. —Granville

As the purse is emptied, the heart is filled. —Victor Hugo

Every charitable act is a stepping stone toward heaven.
—Henry Ward Beecher

The human being who lives only for himself finally reaps nothing but unhappiness. Selfishness corrodes. Unselfishness ennobles, satisfies. Don't put off the joy derivable from doing helpful, kindly things for others. —B.C. Forbes

There is no exercise better for the heart than reaching down and lifting people up. —John Andrew Holmes

Goodness is the only investment that never fails. —Henry David Thoreau

Help your brother's boat across, and your own will reach the shore.
—Hindu proverb

Be unselfish.... If you think of yourself only, you cannot develop because you are choking the source of development, which is spiritual expansion through thought for others. —Charles W. Eliot

An effort made for the happiness of others lifts us above ourselves.
—Lydia M. Child

Happiness ... consists in giving, and in serving others.
—Henry Drummond

Try to forget yourself in the service of others. For when we think too much of ourselves and our own interests, we easily become despondent. But when we work for others, our efforts return to bless us.
—Sidney Powell

Doing good is the only certainly happy action of a man's life.
—Sir Philip Sidney

The greatest happiness in the world is to make others happy.
—Luther Burbank

We make a living by what we get, but we make a life by what we give.
—Norman MacEwan

You may not have saved a lot of money in your life, but if you have saved a lot of heartaches for other folks, you are a pretty rich man.
—Seth Parker

Unless we give part of ourselves away, unless we can live with other people and understand them and help them, we are missing the most essential part of our own lives.
—Harold Taylor

To complain that life has no joys while there is a single creature whom we can relieve by our bounty, assist by our counsels or enliven by our presence, is to lament the loss of that

which we possess, and is just as rational as to die of thirst with the cup in our hands.
—Thomas Fitzosborne

The world has cares enough to plague us; but he who meditates on others' woes shall, in that meditation, lose his own.   —Cumberland

If you have not often felt the joy of doing a kind act, you have neglected much, and most of all yourself.
—A. Neilen

Goodwill to others ... helps build you up. It is good for your body. It makes your blood purer, your muscles stronger, and your whole form more symmetrical in shape. It is the real elixir of life. —Prentice Mulford

Set about doing good to somebody. Put on your hat and go and visit the sick and poor of your neighborhood; inquire into their circumstances and minister to their wants. Seek out the desolate and afflicted and oppressed ... I have often tried this method, and have always found it the best medicine for a heavy heart.   —Howard

We grow by love ... others are our nutriment.
—William Ellery Channing

When you learn to live for others, they will live for you.
—Paramahansa Yogananda

Only a life lived for others is a life worth while.   —Albert Einstein

No man is more cheated than the selfish man. —Henry Ward Beecher

In about the same degree as you are helpful, you will be happy.
—Karl Reiland

He that despiseth his neighbor sinneth; but he that hath mercy on the poor, happy is he.
—Prv. 14:21

The most exquisite pleasure is giving pleasure to others.
—Jean de La Bruyere

Happiness is a by-product of an effort to make someone else happy.
—Gretta Brooker Palmer

The fragrance of what you give away stays with you.   —Earl Allen

Life becomes harder for us when we live for others, but it also becomes richer and happier.
—Albert Schweitzer

Sow good services; sweet remembrances will grow from them.
—Madame de Stael

We all of us need assistance. Those who sustain others themselves want to be sustained.   —Maurice Hulst

To help all created things, that is the measure of our responsibility; to be helped by all, that is the measure of our hope.   —Gerald Vann

When you cease to make a contribution, you begin to die.
—Eleanor Roosevelt

Those who bring sunshine to the lives of others cannot keep it from themselves.   —Sir James M. Barrie

When one's own problems are unsolvable and all best efforts are frustrated, it is lifesaving to listen to other people's problems.

—Suzanne Massie

The best way to cheer yourself is to try to cheer somebody else up.

—Mark Twain

There is no happiness in having or in getting, but only in giving.

—Henry Drummond

There remain times when one can only endure. One lives on, one doesn't die, and the only thing that one can do, is to fill one's mind and time as far as possible with the concerns of other people. It doesn't bring immediate peace, but it brings the dawn nearer.

—Arthur Christopher Benson

Avarice hoards itself poor; charity gives itself rich.   —German proverb

Do things for others and you'll find your self-consciousness evaporating like morning dew.   —Dale Carnegie

ASKING FOR AND ACCEPTING HELP FROM OTHERS

Be brave enough to accept the help of others.   —Melba Colgrove, Harold H. Bloomfield, Peter McWilliams

The smartest thing I ever said was, "Help Me!"   —Anon.

Like the body that is made up of different limbs and organs, all mortal creatures exist depending upon one another.   —Hindu proverb

We not only need to be willing to give, but also to be open to receiving from others.   —*On Hope*

It seems sometimes as if one were powerless to do any more from within to overcome troubles, and that help must come from without.

—Arthur Christopher Benson

The healthy and strong individual is the one who asks for help when he needs it. Whether he's got an abscess on his knee, or in his soul.

—Rona Barrett

I've discovered I'm a strong and capable person. I can handle almost anything except being alone with this.

—Keith Gann, person with AIDS

GENERAL QUOTATIONS ABOUT HELPING OTHER PEOPLE

Make yourself necessary to somebody.   —Ralph Waldo Emerson

All altruism springs from putting yourself in the other person's place.

—Harry Emerson Fosdick

A helping word to one in trouble is often like a switch on a railroad track ... an inch between wreck and smooth, rolling prosperity.

—Henry Ward Beecher

Often we can help each other most by leaving each other alone; at other times we need the hand-grasp and the word of cheer. —Elbert Hubbard

If I can stop one heart from breaking, I shall not live in vain.

—Emily Dickinson

87

It takes wisdom and discernment to minister to people in need. We must look beyond the apparent and seek to meet the needs of the whole person. —Richard C. Chewning

If I am not for myself, who will be for me? If I am not for others, who am I for? And if not now, when? —Talmud

Believe, when you are most unhappy, that there is something for you to do in the world. So long as you can sweeten another's pain, life is not in vain. —Helen Keller

Much misconstruction and bitterness are spared to him who thinks naturally upon what he owes to others, rather than on what he ought to expect from them. —Elizabeth de Meulan Guizot

It is enough that I am of value to somebody today. —Hugh Prather

If we could all hear one another's prayers, God might be relieved of some of his burden. —Ashleigh Brilliant

I know some good marriages—marriages where both people are just trying to get through their days by helping each other, being good to each other. —Erica Jong

The entire sum of existence is the magic of being needed by just one person. —Vi Putnam

Happiness is the cheapest thing in the world when we buy it for someone else. —Paul Flemming

Who is the happiest of men? He who values the merits of others, and in their pleasure takes joy, even as though it were his own. —Johann von Goethe

The race of mankind would perish did they cease to aid each other. We cannot exist without mutual help. All therefore that need aid have a right to ask it from their fellow man; and no one who has the power of granting can refuse it without guilt. —Sir Walter Scott

It is the individual who is not interested in his fellow men who has the greatest difficulties in life and provides the greatest injury to others. It is from among such individuals that all human failures spring. —Alfred Adler

And they said one to another, We are verily guilty concerning our brother, in that we saw the anguish of his soul, when he besought us, and we would not hear. —Gen. 42:21

FRIENDSHIP

FRIENDSHIP IS ONE OF THE MOST IMPORTANT THINGS IN LIFE

Life without a friend is death without a witness.   —Spanish proverb

Without friends no one would choose to live, though he had all other goods.   —Aristotle

We call that person who has lost his father, an orphan; and a widower, that man who has lost his wife. But that man who has known that immense unhappiness of losing a friend, by what name do we call him? Here every language holds its peace in impotence.   —Joseph Roux

There is no hope or joy except in human relations.
     —Antoine de Saint-Exupery

I feel the need of relations and friendship, of affection, of friendly intercourse.... I cannot miss these things without feeling, as does any other intelligent man, a void and a deep need.   —Vincent van Gogh

Your wealth is where your friends are.   —Plautus

Can you understand how cruelly I feel the lack of friends who will believe in me a bit?
     —D.H. Lawrence

To have a good friend is one of the highest delights of life; to be a good friend is one of the noblest and most difficult undertakings.   —Anon.

The two most important things in life are good friends and a strong bull pen.   —Bob Lemon

There is no wilderness like a life without friends; friendship multiplies blessings and minimizes misfortunes; it is a unique remedy against adversity, and it soothes the soul.
     —Baltasar Gracian

There is nothing on this earth more to be prized than true friendship.
     —Saint Thomas Aquinas

Man's best support is a very dear friend.   —Cicero

I know what things are good: friendship and work and conversation.
     —Rupert Brooke

Friendship is the source of the greatest pleasures, and without friends even the most agreeable pursuits become tedious.
—Saint Thomas Aquinas

No medicine is more valuable, none more efficacious, none better suited to the cure of all our temporal ills than a friend to whom we may turn for consolation in time of trouble, and with whom we may share our happiness in time of joy.
—Saint Ailred of Rievaulx

Brotherhood is the very price and condition of man's survival.
—Carlos P. Romulo

One thing everybody in the world wants and needs is friendliness.
—William E. Holler

A man cannot be said to succeed in this life who does not satisfy one friend.
—Henry David Thoreau

We take care of our health, we lay up money, we make our roof tight and our clothing sufficient, but who provides wisely that he shall not be wanting in the best property of all—friends?
—Ralph Waldo Emerson

There is no physician like a true friend.
—Anon.

There is nothing meritorious but virtue and friendship.
—Alexander Pope

The bird, a nest; the spider, a web; man, friendship.
—William Blake

True happiness ... arises, in the first place, from the enjoyment of one's self, and in the next from the friendship and conversation of a few select companions.
—Joseph Addison

It was such a joy to see thee. I wish I could tell how much thee is to my life. I always turn to thee as a sort of rest.
—Lady Henry Somerset

Today a man discovered gold and
  fame,
Another flew the stormy seas;
Another set an unarmed world
  aflame,
One found the germ of a disease.
But what high fates my path attend:
For I—today—I found a friend.
—Helen Barker Parker

Good friends, good books and a sleepy conscience: this is the ideal life.
—Mark Twain

Man is a knot, a web, a mesh into which relationships are tied. Only those relationships matter.
—Antoine de Saint-Exupery

Friendship is the only cement that will ever hold the world together.
—Woodrow Wilson

Friends are an aid to the young, to guard them from error; to the elderly, to attend to their wants and to supplement their failing power of action; to those in the prime of life, to assist them to noble deeds.
—Aristotle

Friendship is the allay of our sorrows, the ease of our passions, the discharge of our oppression, the sanctuary of our calamities, the counselor of our doubts, the clarity of our minds, the emission of our

thoughts, the exercise and improvement of what we dedicate.
—Jeremy Taylor

Of all the things which wisdom provides to make life entirely happy, much the greatest is the possession of friendship.   —Epicurus

Friends are the sunshine of life.
—John Hay

There's nothing worth the wear of winning but laughter, and the love of friends.   —Hilaire Belloc

Each friend represents a world in us, a world possibly not born until they arrive, and it is only by this meeting that a new world is born.
—Anaïs Nin

The feeling of friendship is like that of being comfortably filled with roast beef, love, like being enlivened with champagne. —Samuel Johnson

One is taught by experience to put a premium on those few people who can appreciate you for what you are.
—Gail Godwin

Oh Dear! How unfortunate I am not to have anyone to weep with!
—Madame de Sevigne

The worst solitude is to be destitute of sincere friendship.
—Francis Bacon

If you want an accounting of your worth, count your friends.
—Merry Browne

A man with few friends is only half-developed; there are whole sides of

his nature which are locked up and have never been expressed. He cannot unlock them himself, he cannot even discover them; friends alone can stimulate him and open him.
—Randolph Bourne

'Tis the human touch in the world
    that counts—the touch of your
    hand and mine—
Which means far more to the sinking
    heart than shelter or bread or
    wine
For shelter is gone when the night is
    o'er, and bread lasts only a day
But the touch of the hand and the
    sound of the voice
Live on in the soul always.
—Spencer M. Free

Good company and good discourse are the very sinews of virtue.
—Izaak Walton

My friends have made the story of my life. In a thousand ways they have turned my limitations into beautiful privileges, and enabled me to walk serene and happy in the shadow cast by my deprivation.
—Helen Keller

The support of one's personality is friends. A part of one's self and a real foundation and existence.
—Katharine Butler Hathaway

No greater burden can be born by an individual than to know none who cares or understands.
—Arthur H. Stainback

My life seems to have become suddenly hollow, and I do not know what is hanging over me. I cannot even put the shadow that has fallen on me into words. At least into written words. I would give a great deal for a friend's voice.

—John Addington Symonds

A true friend is the best possession.

—Anon.

It is not so much our friends' help that helps us, as the confidence of their help.　　—Epicurus

HOW WE CAN BE A BETTER FRIEND

Friendship is an art, and very few persons are born with a natural gift for it.　　—Kathleen Norris

The art of friendship has been little cultivated in our society.

—Robert J. Havighurst

Good friendships are fragile things and require as much care as any other fragile and precious thing.

—Randolph Bourne

Human beings are born into this little span of life of which the best thing is its friendships and intimacies ... and yet they leave their friendships and intimacies with no cultivation, to grow as they will by the roadside, expecting them to "keep" by force of mere inertia.

—William James

The only way to have a friend is to be one.　　—Ralph Waldo Emerson

To accept a favor from a friend is to confer one.　—John Churton Collins

There is a magnet in your heart that will attract true friends. That magnet is unselfishness, thinking of others

first ... when you learn to live for others, they will live for you.

—Paramahansa Yogananda

Blessed are they who have the gift of making friends, for it is one of God's best gifts. It involves many things, but above all, the power of getting out of one's self, and appreciating whatever is noble and loving in another.　　—Thomas Hughes

Don't ask of your friends what you yourself can do.　—Quintus Ennius

Half the secret of getting along with people is consideration of their values; the other half is tolerance in one's own views.　—Daniel Frohman

A true friend unbosoms freely, advises justly, assists readily, adventures boldly, takes all patiently, defends courageously, and continues a friend unchangeably.　　—William Penn

Friendships, like marriages, are dependent on avoiding the unforgivable.　　—John D. MacDonald

Confidence is the foundation of friendship. If we give it, we will receive it. —Harry E. Humphreys, Jr.

Loyalty is what we seek in friendship.　　—Cicero

There is a definite process by which one made people into friends, and it involved talking to them and listening to them for hours at a time.

—Rebecca West

Actions, not words, are the true criterion of the attachment of friends.

—George Washington

92

Any man will usually get from other men what he is expecting from them. If he is looking for friendship, he will likely receive it. If his attitude is that of indifference, it will beget indifference. And if a man is looking for a fight, he will in all likelihood be accommodated in that.

—John Richelsen

One who knows how to show and to accept kindness will be a friend better than any possession. —Sophocles

There is nothing we like to see so much as the gleam of pleasure in a person's eye when he feels that we have sympathized with him, understood him, interested ourself in his welfare. At these moments something fine and spiritual passes between two friends. These moments are the moments worth living.

—Don Marquis

He does good to himself who does good to his friend.   Erasmus

A sense of duty is useful in work, but offensive in personal relations.
People wish to be liked, not endured with patient resignation.

—Bertrand Russell

When a friend is in trouble, don't annoy him by asking if there is anything you can do. Think up something appropriate and do it.

—Edgar Watson Howe

If two friends ask you to judge a dispute, don't accept, because you will lose one friend; on the other hand, if two strangers come with the same request, accept, because you will gain one friend.   —Saint Augustine

Perhaps the most delightful friendships are those in which there is much agreement, much disputation, and yet more personal liking.

—George Eliot

Friendship requires great communication.   —Saint Francis de Sales

True friendship comes when silence between two people is comfortable.

—Dave Tyson Gentry

There can be no friendship when there is no freedom. Friendship loves the free air, and will not be fenced up in straight and narrow enclosures.   —William Penn

You will find yourself refreshed by the presence of cheerful people. Why not make earnest effort to confer that pleasure on others?...Half the battle is gained if you never allow yourself to say anything gloomy.

—Lydia M. Child

Wear a smile and have friends; wear a scowl and have wrinkles.

—George Eliot

Lead the life that will make you kindly and friendly to everyone about you, and you will be surprised what a happy life you will live.

—Charles M. Schwab

Those who cannot give friendship will rarely receive it, and never hold it.   —Dagobert D. Runes

It is not the services we render them, but the services they render us, that attaches people to us.

—Labiche et Martin

We cherish our friends not for their ability to amuse us, but for ours to amuse them. —Evelyn Waugh

It is foolish to make experiments upon the constancy of a friend, as upon the chastity of a wife.
                          —Samuel Johnson

Give and take makes good friends.
                          —Scottish proverb

A quarrel between friends, when made up, adds a new tie to friendship, as ... the callosity formed 'round a broken bone makes it stronger than before.
                          —Saint Francis de Sales

No real friendship is ever made without an initial clashing which discloses the metal of each to each.
                          —David Grayson

Nothing wounds a friend like a want of confidence.
                          —Jean Baptiste LaCordaire

Friendship is a plant which must be often watered.   —Anon.

The first thing to learn in intercourse with others is non-interference with their own peculiar ways of being happy, provided those ways do not assume to interfere with ours.
                          —William James

No man can have society upon his own terms. If he seeks it, he must serve it too.
                          —Ralph Waldo Emerson

We cannot tell the precise moment when friendship is formed. As in filling a vessel drop by drop, there is at last a drop which makes it run over. So in a series of kindnesses there is, at last, one which makes the heart run over.   —James Boswell

A friend should bear his friend's infirmities.   —William Shakespeare

No man is much pleased with a companion who does not increase, in some respect, his fondness of himself.   —Samuel Johnson

You win the victory when you yield to friends.   —Sophocles

The condition which high friendship demands is the ability to do without it.   —Ralph Waldo Emerson

Women can form a friendship with a man very well; but to preserve it, a slight physical antipathy most probably helps.   —Friedrich Nietzsche

Love your friends as if they would some day hate you.   —Bias

Friendship is a strong and habitual inclination in two persons to promote the good and happiness of one another.   —Eustace Budgell

Friendship is the pleasing game of interchanging praise.
                          —Oliver Wendell Holmes

The hardest of all is learning to be a well of affection, and not a fountain, to show them that we love them, not when we feel like it, but when *they* do.   —Nan Fairbrother

If you want to be listened to, you should put in time listening.
                          —Marge Piercy

"Stay" is a charming word in a friend's vocabulary. —Louisa May Alcott

The only service a friend can really render is to keep up your courage by holding up to you a mirror in which you can see a noble image of yourself. —George Bernard Shaw

The way to make a true friend is to be one. Friendship implies loyalty, esteem, cordiality, sympathy, affection, readiness to aid, to help, to stick, to fight for, if need be.... Radiate friendship and it will return sevenfold. —B.C. Forbes

The most called-upon prerequisite of a friend is an accessible ear. —Maya Angelou

A loyal friend laughs at your jokes when they're not so good, and sympathizes with your problems when they're not so bad. —Arnold H. Glasow

Politeness is an inexpensive way of making friends. —William Feather

The secret of success in society is a certain heartiness and sympathy. —Ralph Waldo Emerson

Sometimes we owe a friend to the lucky circumstance that we give him no cause for envy. —Friedrich Nietzsche

Friendship requires more time than poor busy men can usually command. —Ralph Waldo Emerson

You can make more friends in two months by becoming more interested in other people than you can in two years by trying to get people interested in you. —Anon.

We should behave to our friends as we would wish our friends to behave to us. —Aristotle

We secure our friends not by accepting favors but by doing them. —Thucydides

Friendship multiplies the good of life and divides the evil. 'Tis the sole remedy against misfortune, the very ventilation of the soul. —Baltasar Gracian

FREQUENCY OF INTERACTION

It is easier to visit friends than to live with them. —Chinese proverb

The chain of friendship, however bright, does not stand the attrition of constant close contact. —Sir Walter Scott

Friendship increases in visiting friends, but not in visiting them too often. —Anon.

I am quite sure that no friendship yields its true pleasure and nobility of nature without frequent communication, sympathy and service. —George E. Woodberry

Go oft to the house of thy friend, for weeds choke the unused path. —Ralph Waldo Emerson

I am learning to live close to the lives of my friends without ever seeing them. No miles of any measurement can separate your soul from mine. —John Muir

The most beautiful discovery true friends make is that they can grow separately without growing apart.
—Elizabeth Foley

Friends are lost by calling often and calling seldom.   —Scottish proverb

A hedge between keeps friendships green.   —Anon.

WE MUST MAKE ALLOWANCES FOR OUR FRIENDS, AND OVERLOOK THEIR LITTLE FAILINGS

When my friends lack an eye, I look at them in profile.   —Joseph Joubert

You can always tell a real friend; when you've made a fool of yourself he doesn't feel you've done a permanent job.   —Laurence J. Peter

The best rule of friendship is to keep your heart a little softer than your head.   —Anon.

Who seeks a faultless friend remains friendless.   —Turkish proverb

Unless you bear with the faults of a friend you betray your own.
—Publilius Syrus

Probably no man ever had a friend he did not dislike a little; we are all so constituted by nature that no one can possibly entirely approve of us.
—Edgar Watson Howe

Love your friend with his fault.
—Anon.

It is well, when judging a friend, to remember that he is judging you with the same godlike and superior impartiality.   —Arnold Bennett

Two persons cannot long be friends if they cannot forgive each other's little failings.   —Jean de La Bruyere

To find a friend one must close one eye. To keep him ... two.
—Norman Douglas

Sooner or later you've heard all your best friends have to say. Then comes the tolerance of real love.
—Ned Rorem

We shall never have friends if we expect to find them without fault.
—Thomas Fuller

It is well there is no one without fault; for he would not have a friend in the world. He would seem to belong to a different species.
—William Hazlitt

The essence of true friendship is to make allowance for another's little lapses.   —David Storey

To be social is to be forgiving.
—Robert Frost

It is easier to forgive an enemy than a friend.
—Madame Dorothee Deluzy

It is more shameful to distrust our friends than to be deceived by them.
—Francois de La Rochefoucauld

It is better to be deceived by one's friends than to deceive them.
—Johann von Goethe

The man who trusts other men will make fewer mistakes than he who distrusts them.
—Camillo Di Cavour

A friend who cannot at a pinch remember a thing or two that never happened is as bad as one who does not know how to forget.
—Samuel Butler

It should be part of our private ritual to devote a quarter of an hour every day to the enumeration of the good qualities of our friends. When we are not active we fall back idly upon defects, even of those whom we most love. —Mark Rutherford

Friendship admits of difference of character, as love does that of sex.
—Joseph Roux

Between friends there is no need of justice. —Aristotle

Treat your fiends as you do your picture, and place them in their best light. —Jennie Jerome Churchill

What I cannot love, I overlook.
—Anaïs Nin

Friendships aren't perfect and yet they are very precious. For me, not expecting perfection all in one place was a great release.
—Letty Cottin Pogrebin

COURTESY AND FRIENDSHIP

Nothing is ever lost by courtesy. It is the cheapest of pleasures, costs nothing, and conveys much. It pleases him who gives and receives and thus, like mercy, is twice blessed.
—Erastus Wiman

Don't flatter yourself that friendship authorizes to say disagreeable things to your intimates. The nearer you come into relation with a per-

son, the more necessary do tact and courtesy become.
—Oliver Wendell Holmes

Friendship cannot live with ceremony, nor without civility.
—Lord Halifax

There are limits to the indulgence which friendship allows. —Cicero

Friends are like a pleasant park where you wish to go; while you may enjoy the flowers, you may not eat them. —Edgar Watson Howe

Friendship is honey, but don't eat it all. —Moroccan proverb

CANDOR ABOUT FRIENDS

Except in cases of necessity, which are rare, leave your friend to learn unpleasant things from his enemies; they are ready enough to tell him.
—Oliver Wendell Holmes

Don't tell your friends their social faults; they will cure the fault and never forgive you.
—Logan Pearsall Smith

Flattery makes friends, truth enemies. —Spanish proverb

If we all told what we know of one another, there would not be four friends in the world. —Blaise Pascal

If we were all given by magic the power to read each other's thoughts, I suppose the first effect would be to dissolve all friendships. —Anon.

The truth that is suppressed by friends is the readiest weapon of the enemy. —Robert Louis Stevenson

Give me the avowed, the erect and
manly foe,
Bold I can meet, perhaps may turn
the blow;
But of all plagues, good Heaven, thy
wrath can send,
Save, oh save me from the candid
friend!   —George Canning

A good friend can tell you what is
the matter with you in a minute. He
may not seem such a good friend
after telling.   —Arthur Brisbane

Do not remove a fly from your
friend's forehead with a hatchet.
                    —Chinese proverb

Friendship will not stand the strain
of very much good advice for very
long.   —Robert Lynd

There is not so good an understanding between any two, but the exposure by the one of a serious fault in
the other will produce a misunderstanding in proportion to its
heinousness.
          —Henry David Thoreau

It's important to our friends to
believe that we are unreservedly
frank with them, and important to
our friendship that we are not.
          —Mignon McLaughlin

Flatterers look like friends, as wolves
like dogs.   —George Chapman

Friendship may sometimes step a few
paces in advance of truth.
          —Walter Savage Landor

A friend should be a master at guess-
ing and keeping still.
          —Friedrich Nietzsche

A cheerful friend is like a sunny day,
which sheds its brightness on all
around.   —John Lubbock

The more we love our friends, the
less we flatter them; it is by excusing
nothing that pure love shows itself.
          —Moliere

What a wonderful thing it is to have
a good friend. He identifies your
innermost desires, and spares you
the embarrassment of disclosing
them to him yourself.
          —Jean de La Fontaine

I always felt that the great high privilege, relief and comfort of friendship
was that one had to explain nothing.
          —Katherine Mansfield

Nobody who is afraid of laughing,
and heartily too, at his friend can be
said to have a true and thorough
love for him.   —Julius Charles Hare

Don't believe your friends when they
ask you to be honest with them. All
they really want is to be maintained
in the good opinion they have of
themselves.   —Albert Camus

It is the weak and confused who
worship the pseudo-simplicities of
brutal directness.
          —Marshall McLuhan

Only friends will tell you the truths
you need to hear to make ... your life
bearable.
          —Francine Du Plessix Gray

Keep the other person's well-being in
mind when you feel an attack of
soul-purging truth coming on.
          —Betty White

If it's very painful for you to criticize your friends—you're safe in doing it. But if you take the slightest pleasure in it, that's the time to hold your tongue.   —Alice Duer Miller

CANDOR ABOUT OURSELVES

A friend is a person with whom I may be sincere. Before him, I may think aloud.
          —Ralph Waldo Emerson

Oh, the comfort, the inexpressible comfort of feeling safe with a person, having neither to weigh thoughts nor measure words, but pouring them all out, just as they are, chaff and grain together, certain that a faithful hand will take and sift them, keep what is worth keeping, and with a breath of kindness blow the rest away.
          —Dinah Maria Mulock Craik

One's friends are that part of the human race with which one can be human.   —George Santayana

I should like to tell you again of my bitter troubles so that mutually, by recounting our grief, we can lighten each other's sorrow.
          —*The Kanteletar*

'Tis the privilege of friendship to talk nonsense, and have her nonsense respected.   —Charles Lamb

There are only two people who can tell you the truth about yourself—an enemy who has lost his temper and a friend who loves you dearly.
          —Antisthenes

Since we are mortal, friendships are best kept to a moderate level, rather than sharing the very depths of our souls.   —Hippolytus

Those that lack friends to open themselves unto are cannibals of their own hearts.   —Francis Bacon

BUT WE MUST NOT OVER-BURDEN OUR FRIENDS WITH OUR TROUBLES

Laugh, and the world laughs with you; weep and you weep alone.
          —Ella Wheeler Wilcox

Forget your woes when you see your friend.   —Priscian

We have no more right to put our discordant states of mind into the lives of those around us and rob them of their sunshine and brightness than we have to enter their houses and steal their silverware.
          —Julia Seton

When good cheer is lacking, our friends will be packing.   —Anon.

FRIENDS AND MONEY

The richest man in the world is not the one who still has the first dollar he ever earned. It's the man who still has his best friend. —Martha Mason

They are rich who have true friends.
          —Thomas Fuller

Friendship is like money, easier made than kept.   —Samuel Butler

The rich know not who is his friend.
          —Anon.

Prosperity makes few friends.
          —Vauvenargues

It is a good thing to be rich, it is a good thing to be strong, but it is a better thing to be beloved of many friends. —Euripides

Better the friend we can see than the money we cannot. —Greek proverb

It is better in times of need to have a friend rather than money.
—Greek proverb

The richer your friends, the more they will cost you.
—Elizabeth Marbury

Never have a friend that's poorer than yourself. —Douglas Jerrold

Wealth maketh many friends.
—Prv. 17:4

FRIENDSHIP IN BAD TIMES

It's the friends you can call up at 4 A.M. that matter. —Marlene Dietrich

In time of great anxiety we can draw power from our friends. We should at such times, however, avoid friends who sympathize too deeply, who give us pity rather than strength.
—D. Lupton

The firmest friendships have been formed in mutual adversity, as iron is most strongly united by the fiercest flame.
—Charles Caleb Colton

Adversity not only draws people together, but brings forth that beautiful inward friendship.
—Søren Kierkegaard

A friend in need is a friend indeed.
—Richard Graves

In times of difficulty friendship is on trial. —Greek proverb

A friend is never known till a man has need. —Anon.

As the yellow gold is tried in fire, so the faith of friendship must be seen in adversity. —Ovid

Friendship, of itself a holy tie, is made more sacred by adversity.
—John Dryden

He who endures penance and hardships for another delights in that person's company.
—Malik Muhammad Jayasi

A cheer, then, for the noble breast
    that fears not danger's post;
And like the lifeboat, proves a
    friend,
When friends are wanted most.
—Eliza Cook

There are moments in life when all that we can bear is the sense that our friend is near us; our wounds would wince at consoling words that would reveal the depths of our pain.
—Honore de Balzac

FRIENDSHIP IN GOOD TIMES— AND BAD TIMES

Grief can take care of itself, but to get the full value of a joy you must have somebody to divide it with.
—Mark Twain

Prosperity makes friends, adversity tries them. —Publilius Syrus

Prosperity is not just scale; adversity is the only balance to weigh friends.
—Plutarch

There is no man that imparteth his joys to his friends, but he joyeth the more; and no man that imparteth his griefs to his friends, but he grieveth the less. —Francis Bacon

I am treating you as my friend, asking you to share my present minuses in the hope I can ask you to share my future pluses.
—Katherine Mansfield

No man can be happy without a friend, nor be sure of his friend till he is unhappy. —Thomas Fuller

Friendship makes prosperity more brilliant, and lightens adversity by dividing and sharing it. —Cicero

Real friendship is shown in times of trouble; prosperity is full of friends.
—Euripides

The friend of my adversity I shall always cherish most. I can better trust those who helped to relieve the gloom of my dark hours than those who are so ready to enjoy with me the sunshine of my prosperity.
—Ulysses S. Grant

In prosperity our friends know us; in adversity we know our friends.
—John Churton Collins

O summer friendship, whose flattering leaves shadowed us in our prosperity,
With the least gust, drop off in the autumn of adversity.
—Philip Massinger

I loathe a friend ... who takes his friend's prosperity but will not voyage with him in his grief. —Euripides

In prosperity friends do not leave you unless desired, whereas in adversity they stay away of their own accord. —Demetrius

Friendship was given by nature to be an assistant to virtue, not a companion in vice. —Cicero

We are fonder of visiting our friends in health than in sickness. We judge less favorably of their characters when any misfortune happens to them; and a lucky hit, either in business or reputation, improves even their personal appearance in our eyes. —William Hazlitt

The shifts of fortune test the reliability of friends. —Cicero

Never befriend the oppressed unless you are prepared to take on the oppressor. —Ogden Nash

Trouble shared is trouble halved.
—Dorothy Sayers

Friends and Family

A sympathetic friend can be quite dear as a brother. —Homer

One loyal friend is worth ten thousand relatives. —Euripides

Friends are relatives you make for yourself. —Eustache Deschamps

Chance makes our parents, but choice makes our friends.
—Jacques Delille

God gave us our relatives; thank God we can choose our friends.
—Ethel Watts Mumford

A good friend is my nearest relation.
—Thomas Fuller

ENEMIES

Instead of loving your enemies, treat your friends a little better.
—Edgar Watson Howe

Friends come and go, enemies linger.
—Anon.

One enemy is too many; a hundred friends too few.
—Anon.

Faithful are the wounds of a friend, but the kisses of an enemy are deceitful.
—Prv. 27:6

SOMETIMES A FRIEND WILL SUPPORT US EVEN WHEN WE'RE WRONG

The proper office of a friend is to side with you when you are in the wrong. Nearly everybody will side with you when you are in the right.
—Mark Twain

I like a highland friend who will stand by me not only when I am in the right, but when I am a little in the wrong.
—Sir Walter Scott

I don't care a damn for your loyal service when you think I am right; when I really want it most is when you think I am wrong.
—General Sir John Monash

WE NEED SEVERAL KINDS OF FRIENDS

Fortify yourself with a flock of friends! You can select them at random, write to one, dine with one, visit one, or take your problems to one. There is always at least one who will understand, inspire, and give you the lift you may need at the time.
—George Matthew Adams

A man with few friends is only half-developed; there are whole sides of his nature which are locked up and have never been expressed. He cannot unlock them himself, he cannot even discover them; friends alone can stimulate him and open him.
—Randolph Bourne

Many a person has held close, throughout their entire lives, two friends that always remained strange to one another, because one of them attracted by virtue of similarity, the other by difference.
—Emil Ludwig

Nothing is more limiting than a closed circle of acquaintanceship where every avenue of conversation has been explored and social exchanges are fixed in a known routine.
—A.J. Cronin

Friendship is almost always the union of a part of one mind with a part of another; people are friends in spots.
—George Santayana

The wise man's ... friendship is capable of going to extremes with many people, evoked as it is by many qualities.
—Charles Dudley Warner

I cannot concentrate all my friendship on any single one of my friends because no one is complete enough in himself.
—Anaïs Nin

No one person can possibly combine all the elements supposed to make up what everyone means by friendship.
—Francis Marion Crawford

102

We need two kinds of acquaintances, one to complain to, while we boast to the others.—Logan Pearsall Smith

Every organism requires an environment of friends, partly to shield it from violent changes, and partly to supply it with its wants.
—Alfred North Whitehead

Without wearing any mask we are conscious of, we have a special face for each friend.
—Oliver Wendell Holmes

SOME THOUGHTS ABOUT OLD FRIENDS

An old friend never can be found, and nature has provided that he cannot easily be lost. —Samuel Johnson

Years and years of happiness only make us realize how lucky we are to have friends that have shared and made that happiness a reality.
—Robert E. Frederick

Ah, how good it feels! The hand of an old friend.
—Henry Wadsworth Longfellow

It is one of the blessings of old friends that you can afford to be stupid with them.
—Ralph Waldo Emerson

Old friends are the great blessing of one's later years.... They have a memory of the same events and have the same mode of thinking.
—Horace Walpole

As in the case of wines that improve with age, the oldest friendships ought to be the most delightful.
—Cicero

Friends and wine should be old.
—Spanish proverb

There is a magic in the memory of a schoolboy friendship. It softens the heart, and even affects the nervous system of those who have no heart.
—Benjamin Disraeli

The best mirror is an old friend.
—Anon.

It is great to have friends when one is young, but indeed it is still more so when you are getting old. When we are young, friends are, like everything else, a matter of course. In the old days we know what it means to have them.   —Edvard Grieg

When you are young and without success, you have only a few friends. Then, later on, when you are rich and famous, you still have a few ... if you are lucky.   —Pablo Picasso

Old friends, we say, are best, when some sudden disillusionment shakes our faith in a new comrade.
—Gelett Burgess

Forsake not an old friend, for the new is not comparable to him; a new friend is as new wine.
—Ecclesiastes

To be capable of steady friendship or lasting love are the two greatest proofs, not only of goodness of heart, but of strength of mind.
—William Hazlitt

WE MUST NOT LOSE OR DISCARD OUR FRIENDS

I keep my friends as misers do their treasure because, of all the things

granted us by wisdom, none is greater or better than friendship.
—Pietro Aretino

There is only one thing better than making a new friend, and that is keeping an old one.
—Elmer G. Leterman

To throw away an honest friend is, as it were, to throw your life away.
—Sophocles

Hold a true friend with both your hands.　　　—Nigerian proverb

None is so rich as to throw away a friend.　　　—Turkish proverb

Those friends thou hast, and their adoption tried, grapple them to thy soul with hoops of steel.
—William Shakespeare

True friendship is like sound health; the value of it is seldom known until it be lost.　—Charles Caleb Colton

Affinities are rare. They come but a few times in a life. It is awful to risk losing one when it arrives.
—Florence H. Winterburn

Rather throw away that which is dearest to you, your own life, than turn away a good friend.
—Sophocles

Thine own friend, and thy father's friend, forsake not.
—Prv. 27:10

The best way to keep your friends is not to give them away.
—Wilson Mizner

We die as often as we lose a friend.
—Publilius Syrus

Some Thoughts about New Friends

I never enter a new company without the hope that I may discover a friend, perhaps the friend, sitting there with an expectant smile. That hope survives a thousand disappointments.

—Arthur Christopher Benson

Since there is nothing so well worth having as friends, never lose a chance to make them.
—Francesco Guicciardini

If a man does not make new acquaintances as he advances through life, he will soon find himself left alone.　—Samuel Johnson

A man's growth is seen in the successive choirs of his friends.
—Ralph Waldo Emerson

Five years from now you will be pretty much the same as you are today except for two things: the books you read and the people you get close to.　　—Charles Jones

What causes us to like new acquaintances is not so much weariness of our old ones, or the pleasure of change, as disgust at not being sufficiently admired by those who know us too well, and the hope of being admired more by those who do not know so much about us.
—Francois de La Rochefoucauld

Every man passes his life in the search after friendship.
—Ralph Waldo Emerson

A new acquaintance is like a new book. I prefer it, even if bad, to a classic. —Benjamin Disraeli

To cement a new friendship, especially between foreigners or persons of a different social world, a spark with which both were secretly charged must fly from person to person, and cut across the accidents of place and time. —George Santayana

A new friend is like new wine; when it has aged you will drink it with pleasure. —Apocrypha

He alone has lost the art to live who cannot win new friends.
—S. Weir Mitchell

I want no men around me who have not the knack of making friends.
—Frank A. Vanderlip

Yes'm, old friends is always best, 'less you can catch a new one that's fit to make an old one out of.
—Sarah Orne Jewett

Many a friendship—long, loyal, and self-sacrificing—rested at first upon no thicker a foundation than a kind word. —Frederick W. Faber

Accident counts for much in companionship, as in marriage.
—Henry Adams

A home-made friend wears longer than one you buy in the market.
—Austin O'Malley

The best time to make friends is before you need them.
—Ethel Barrymore

We need new friends. Some of us are cannibals who have eaten their old friends up; others must have ever-renewed audiences before whom to re-enact an ideal version of their lives. —Logan Pearsall Smith

WE SHOULD BE CAREFUL IN MAKING NEW FRIENDS

A true friend is the greatest of all blessings, and that which we take the least care of all to acquire.
—Francois de La Rochefoucauld

A man must eat a peck of salt with his friend before he knows him.
—Miguel de Cervantes

One who's our friend is fond of us; one who's fond of us isn't necessarily our friend.
—Marcus Annaeus Seneca

Make all good men your well-wishers, and then, in the years' steady sifting, some of them will turn into friends. —John Hay

Distrust all those who love you extremely upon a very slight acquaintance and without any viable reason. —Lord Chesterfield

We often choose a friend as we do a mistress, for no particular excellence in themselves, but merely from some circumstance that flatters our self-love. —William Hazlitt

How casually and unobservedly we make all our most valued acquaintances. —Ralph Waldo Emerson

Be courteous to all, but intimate with few; and let those few be well

tried before you give them your confidence. —George Washington

Be slow to fall into friendship; but
when thou art in, continue firm and
constant. —Socrates

How often we find ourselves turning
our backs on our actual friends, that
we may go and meet their ideal
cousins. —Henry David Thoreau

Let him have the key of thy heart,
who hath the lock of his own.
  —Sir Thomas Browne

Be slow in choosing a friend, slower
in changing. —Benjamin Franklin

Have but few friends, though many
acquaintances. —Anon.

Books and friends should be few but
good. —Anon.

Sudden friendship, sure repentance.
  —Anon.

As there are some flowers which you
should smell but slightly to extract
all that is pleasant in them ... so
there are some men with whom a
slight acquaintance is quite sufficient
to draw out all that is agreeable; a
more intimate one would be unsafe
and unsatisfactory.
  —Walter Savage Landor

Friendship that flames goes out in a
flash. —Thomas Fuller

Acquaintance I would have, but
when it depends not on the number,
but the choice of friends.
  —Abraham Cowley

Always set high value on spontaneous kindness. He whose inclination prompts him to cultivate your
friendship of his own accord will
love you more than one whom you
have been at pains to attach to you.
  —Samuel Johnson

Trouble is a sieve through which we
sift our acquaintances. Those too big
to pass through are our friends.
  —Arlene Francis

Wishing to be friends is quick work,
but friendship is a slow-ripening
fruit. —Aristotle

WHO WE ASSOCIATE WITH IS CRITICAL, BECAUSE WE MAY BECOME LIKE THEM

Every man is like the company he is
wont to keep. —Euripides

Go to the place where the thing you
wish to know is native; your best
teacher is there.... You acquire a language most readily in the country
where it is spoken, you study miner-
alogy best among miners, and so
with everything else.
  —Johann von Goethe

If I wanted to become a tramp, I
would seek information and advice
from the most successful tramp I
could find. If I wanted to become a
failure, I would seek advice from
men who have never succeeded. If I
wanted to succeed in all things, I
would look around me for those
who are succeeding, and do as they
have done. —Joseph Marshall Wade

Better fare hard with good men than
feast with bad. —Thomas Fuller

He that lies down with dogs shall rise up with fleas. —Anon.

By associating with good and evil persons a man acquires the virtues and vices which they possess, even as the wind blowing over different places takes along good and bad odors. —The Panchatantra

I would prefer as a friend a good man who is ignorant than one more clever who is evil, too. —Euripides

Associate yourself with men of good quality if you esteem your own reputation, for 'tis better to be alone than in bad company. —George Washington

Tell me whom you frequent, and I will tell you who you are. —French proverb

Tell me thy company, and I'll tell thee what thou art. —Miguel de Cervantes

Who friendship with a knave hath made, is judged a partner in the trade. —John Gay

The lion is ashamed, it's true, when he hunts with the fox. —Gotthold Ephraim Lessing

Life is partly what we make it, and partly what it is made by the friends we choose. —Tehyi Hsieh

If you always live with those who are lame, you will yourself learn to limp. —Latin proverb

He that walketh with wise men shall be wise. —Solomon

Keep good men company, and you shall be of their number. —Anon.

A man is known by the company he keeps. —Anon.

A man becomes like those whose society he loves. —Hindu proverb

A wise man associating with the vicious becomes an idiot; a dog traveling with good men becomes a rational being. —Arabic proverb

It is better to weep with wise men than to laugh with fools. —Spanish proverb

A wise man may look ridiculous in the company of fools. —Thomas Fuller

Ill company is like a dog, who dirts those most whom he loves best. —Jonathan Swift

Satan's friendship reaches to the prison door. —Turkish proverb

Have no friends not equal to yourself. —Confucius

Friendship is seldom lasting but between equals, or where the superiority on one side is reduced by some equivalent advantage on the other. —Samuel Johnson

Friendship neither finds nor makes equals. —Publilius Syrus

You cannot be friends upon any other terms than upon the terms of equality. —Woodrow Wilson

The Importance of Similar Values and Interests

Friendship is nothing else than an accord in all things, human and divine, conjoined with mutual goodwill and affection. —Cicero

Friendship is a union of spirits, a marriage of hearts, and the bond there of virtue. —Samuel Johnson

To associate with other like-minded people in small purposeful groups is for the great majority of men and women a source of profound psychological satisfaction. —Aldous Huxley

Shared joys make a friend, not shared sufferings. —Friedrich Nietzsche

Men only become friends by community of pleasures. —Samuel Johnson

Seek those who find your road agreeable, your personality and mind stimulating, your philosophy acceptable, and your experiences helpful. Let those who do not, seek their own kind. —Jean-Henri Fabre

To like and dislike the same things, this is what makes a solid friendship. —Sallust

Friendship is only a reciprocal conciliation of interests. —Francois de La Rochefoucauld

Friendship needs a certain parallelism of life, a community of thought, a rivalry of aim. —Henry Adams

True friends ... face in the same direction, toward common projects, interests, goals. —C.S. Lewis

That friendship may be at once fond and lasting, there must not only be equal virtue on each part, but virtue of the same kind; not only the same end must be proposed, but the same means must be approved by both. —Samuel Johnson

It is characteristic of spontaneous friendship to take on, without enquiry and almost at first sight, the unseen doings and unspoken sentiments of our friends; the part known gives us evidence enough that the unknown part cannot be much amiss. —George Santayana

We Should Have No Ulterior Motive in Making Friends

He who looks for advantage out of friendship strips it all of its nobility. —Marcus Annaeus Seneca

The reward of friendship is itself. The man who hopes for anything else does not understand what true friendship is. —Saint Alfred of Rievaulx

That friendship will not continue to the end which is begun for an end. —Francis Quarles

The friendships which last are those wherein each friend respects the other's dignity to the point of not really wanting anything from him. —Cyril Connolly

My best friend is the man who in wishing me well wishes it for my sake. —Aristotle

I have always differentiated between two types of friends; those who want proofs of friendship, and those who do not. One kind loves me for myself, and the others for themselves. —Gerard de Nerval

Friendship, like credit, is highest where it is not used.
—Elbert Hubbard

Friendship without self-interest is one of the rare and beautiful things of life. —James Francis Byrnes

I have learned that to have a good friend is the purest of all God's gifts, for it is a love that has no exchange of payment. —Frances Farmer

Friendship is always a sweet responsibility, never an opportunity.
—Kahlil Gibran

I have friends in overalls whose friendship I would not swap for the favor of the kings of the world.
—Thomas A. Edison

If you press me to say why I loved him, I can say no more than because he was he, and I was I.
—Michel de Montaigne

OURSELVES AS FRIENDS

Friendship with oneself is all-important, because without it one cannot be friends with anyone else.
—Eleanor Roosevelt

I desire so to conduct the affairs of this administration that if at the end ... I have lost every other friend on earth, I shall at least have one friend left, and that friend shall be down inside of me. —Abraham Lincoln

Be a friend to thyself, and others will be so too. —Thomas Fuller

Of my friends, I am the only one I have left. —Terence

OTHER DEFINITIONS OF FRIENDSHIP

Friendship is neither a formality nor a mode: it is rather a life.
—David Grayson

Friendship is one mind in two bodies. —Menclus

A friend is, as it were, a second self.
—Cicero

Friend: One who knows all about you and loves you just the same.
—Elbert Hubbard

A friend is like a poem.
—Persian proverb

A friend is a present you give to yourself. —Robert Louis Stevenson

A friend is someone you can do nothing with, and enjoy it.
—The Optimist

Friendship needs no words—it is solitude delivered from the anguish of loneliness. —Dag Hammarskjold

A friend may well be reckoned the masterpiece of nature.
—Ralph Waldo Emerson

Two friends—two bodies with one soul inspired. —Homer

In poverty and other misfortunes of life, true friends are a sure refuge.
—Aristotle

Friendship is a single soul dwelling in two bodies. —Aristotle

A faithful friend is the medicine of life. —Apocrypha

Friends are a second existence. —Baltasar Gracian

A real friend helps us think our best thoughts, do our noblest deeds, be our finest selves. —Anon.

Friendship is a furrow in the sand. —Tongan proverb

Friendship is love without his wings! —Lord Byron

True friendship is self-love at second hand. —William Hazlitt

The real friend is he or she who can share all our sorrow and double our joys. —B.C. Forbes

GENERAL QUOTATIONS ABOUT FRIENDSHIP

Friendship is a word the very sight of which in print makes the heart warm. —Augustine Birrell

The feeling of friendship is like that of being comfortably filled with roast beef. —Samuel Johnson

Most men's friendships are too inarticulate. —William James

The language of friendship is not words, but meanings. —Henry David Thoreau

Iron sharpeneth iron; so a man sharpeneth the countenance of his friend. —Prv. 27:17

Love demands infinitely less than friendship. —George Jean Nathan

The company makes the feast. —Anon.

Good company upon the road is the shortest cut. —Anon.

The best preservative to keep the mind in health is the faithful admonition of a friend. —Francis Bacon

What is thine is mine, and all mine is thine. —Plautus

Do not protect yourself by a fence, but rather by your friends. —Czech proverb

If our friends' idealizations of us need the corrective of our own experience, it may be true also that our own sordid view of our lives needs the corrective of our friends' idealizations. —Oscar W. Firkins

The thicker one gets with some people, the thinner they become. —Puzant Thomain

If a man is worth knowing at all, he is worth knowing well. —Alexander Smith

When our friends are alive, we see the good qualities they lack; dead, we remember only those they possessed. —J. Petit-Senn

When one friend washes another, both become clean. —Dutch proverb

I observed once to Goethe ... that when a friend is with us we do not think the same of him as when he is

110

away. He replied, "Yes! because the absent friend is yourself, and he exists only in your head; whereas the friend who is present has an individuality of his own, and moves according to laws of his own, which cannot always be in accordance with those which you form for yourself."
—Arthur Schopenhauer

In reality, we are still children. We want to find a playmate for our thoughts and feelings.
—Dr. Wilhelm Stekhel

Love me, please; I love you; I can bear to be your friend. So ask of me anything ... I am not a tentative person. Whatever I do, I give up my whole self to it.
—Edna Saint Vincent Millay

Most of our misfortunes are comments of our friends upon them.
—Charles Caleb Colton

Greater love hath no man than this, that a man lay down his life for his friends.   — 1 Jn. 15:13

Animals are such agreeable friends— they ask no questions, they pass no criticisms.   —George Eliot

Great friendship is never without anxiety.   —Marquise de Sevigne

It is good to have friends, even in hell.   —Spanish proverb

One of the signs of passing youth is the birth of a sense of fellowship with other human beings as we take our place among them.
—Virginia Woolf

Silences make the real conversations between friends.
—Margaret Lee Runbeck

Live so that your friends can defend you, but never have to.
—Arnold Glasow

Intimacies between women often go backwards, beginning in revelations and ending in small talk.
—Elizabeth Bowen

There is space within sisterhood for likeness and difference, for the subtle differences that challenge and delight; there is space for disappointment—and surprise.
—Christine Downing

Friendship ought to be a gratuitous joy, like the joys afforded by art.
—Simone Weil

We challenge one another to be funnier and smarter.... It's the way friends make love to one another.
—Annie Gottlieb

Four be the things I am wiser to know: Idleness, sorrow, a friend and a foe.   —Anon.

Our Higher Power, or God

We Can't, Don't Need, and Aren't Expected to Understand God

It is the heart which experiences God, not the reason.   —Blaise Pascal

I believe in the incomprehensibility of God.   —Honore de Balzac

Every conjecture we can form with regard to the works of God has as little probability as the conjectures of a child with regard to the works of a man.   —Thomas Reid

No statement about God is simply, literally true. God is far more than can be measured, described, defined in ordinary language, or pinned down to any particular happening.
—David Jenkins

Who fathoms the Eternal Thought?
Who talks of scheme and plan?
The Lord is God! He needeth not
The poor device of man.
—John Greenleaf Whittier

Some people want to see God with their eyes as they see a cow, and to love Him as they love their cow—for the milk and cheese and profit it brings them. This is how it is with people who love God for the sake of outward wealth or inward comfort.
—Meister Eckhart

Your mind cannot possibly understand God. Your heart already knows. Minds were designed for carrying out the orders of the heart.
—Emmanuel

A comprehended God is no God at all.   —Gerhard Tersteegen

"What do you think of God," the teacher asked. After a pause, the young pupil replied, "He's not a think, he's a feel."   —Paul Frost

To them that ask, where have you seen the Gods, or how do you know for certain there are Gods, that you are so devout in their worship? I answer: Neither have I ever seen my own soul, and yet I respect and honor it.   —Marcus Aurelius

God May Be Different to Each of Us

God is like a mirror. The mirror

never changes, but everybody who looks at it sees something different.
—Rabbi Harold Kushner

God is to me that creative Force, behind and in the universe, who manifests Himself as energy, as life, as order, as beauty, as thought, as conscience, as love.
—Henry Sloane Coffin

God is incorporeal, divine, supreme, infinite. Mind, Spirit, Soul, Principle, Life, Truth, Love.
—Mary Baker Eddy

The God of many men is little more than their court of appeal against the damnatory judgement passed on their failures by the opinion of the world.
—William James

God, to be God, must transcend what is. He must be the maker of what ought to be.
—Rufus M. Jones

God is an unutterable sigh, planted in the depths of the soul.
—Jean Paul Richter

God is a verb, not a noun.
—R. Buckminster Fuller

The most beautiful of all emblems is that of God, whom Timaeus of Locris describes under the image of "A circle whose centre is everywhere and whose circumference is nowhere."
—Voltaire

God is what man finds that is divine in himself. God is the best way man can behave in the ordinary occasions of life, and the farthest point to which man can stretch himself.
—Max Lerner

The deep emotional conviction of the presence of a superior reasoning power, which is revealed in the incomprehensible universe, forms my idea of God.
—Albert Einstein

God has many names, though He is only one Being.
—Aristotle

There is but one ultimate Power. This Power is to each one what he is to it.
—Ernest Holmes

God, that dumping ground of our dreams.
—Jean Rostand

How to Find and Reach God

When we lose God, it is not God who is lost.
—Anon.

God enters by a private door into every individual.
—Ralph Waldo Emerson

A humble knowledge of oneself is a surer road to God than a deep searching of the sciences.
—Thomas a'Kempis

By learning to contact, listen to, and act on our intuition, we can directly connect to the higher power of the universe and allow it to become our guiding force.
—Shakti Gawain

When a man takes one step toward God, God takes more steps toward that man than there are sands in the worlds of time.
—*The Work of the Chariot*

Some people talk about finding God, as if He could get lost.
—Anon.

Hunting God is a great adventure.
—Marie DeFloris

113

In the faces of men and women I see God. —Walt Whitman

To Be is to live with God.
—Ralph Waldo Emerson

Nothing hath separated us from God but our own will, or rather our own will is our separation from God.
—William Law

The kingdom of God is within you.
—Lk. 17:21

Not only then has each man his individual relation to God, but each man has his *peculiar* relation to God.
—George MacDonald

Because you cannot see him, God is everywhere. —Yasunari Kawabata

It's only by forgetting yourself that you draw near to God.
—Henry David Thoreau

All who call on God in true faith, earnestly from the heart, will certainly be heard, and will receive what they have asked and desired.
—Martin Luther

The light of God surrounds me,
The love of God enfolds me,
The power of God protects me,
The Presence of God watches over me,
Wherever I am, God is.
—*Prayer Card*

To think you are separate from God is to remain separate from your own being. —D.M. Street

God knows no distance.
—Charleszetta Waddles

God Will Help Us

Without the assistance of the Divine Being ... I cannot succeed. With that assistance, I cannot fail.
—Abraham Lincoln

Whoever falls from God's right hand Is caught into His left.
—Edwin Markham

Pardon, not wrath, is God's best attribute. —Bayard Taylor

In God We Trust. —Motto of the United States, adopted by Congress for use on coins and one-dollar bills

I will not fear, for you are ever with me, and you will never leave me to face my perils alone.
—Thomas Merton

Walk boldly and wisely.... There is a hand above that will help you on.
—Philip James Bailey

The things which are impossible with men are possible with God.
—Lk. 18:27

For the multitude of worldly friends profiteth not, nor may strong helpers anything avail, nor wise counselors give profitable counsel, nor the cunning of doctors give consolation, nor riches deliver in time of need, nor a secret place to defend, if Thou, Lord, do not assist, help, comfort, counsel, inform, and defend.
—Thomas a'Kempis

Some Ways That God Makes Wishes Known to Us

Trust in the Lord with all thine heart, and lean not unto thine own

understanding. In all thy ways acknowledge Him, and He shall direct thy paths.
—Prv. 3:5–6

God speaks to all individuals through what happens to them moment by moment.
—J.P. DeCaussade

God uses lust to impel men to marry, ambition to office, avarice to earning, and fear to faith. God led me like an old blind goat.
—Martin Luther

An act of God was defined as "something which no reasonable man could have expected."
—A.P. Herbert

GOD AND LOVE
Let God love you through others and let God love others through you.
—D.M. Street

One unquestioned text we read,
All doubt beyond, all fear above;
Nor crackling pile nor cursing creed
Can burn or blot it: God is Love.
—Oliver Wendell Holmes

A true love of God must begin with a delight in his holiness.
—Jonathan Edwards

No man hates God without first hating himself.
—Fulton J. Sheen

GENERAL QUOTATIONS ABOUT A HIGHER POWER, OR GOD
I have never understood why it should be considered derogatory to the Creator to suppose that He has a sense of humor.
—William Ralph Inge

Every law of matter or the body, supposed to govern man, is rendered null and void by the law of Life, God.
—Mary Baker Eddy

Whom the heart of man shuts out, Sometimes the heart of God takes in.
—James Russell Lowell

I would rather walk with God in the dark than go alone in the light.
—Mary Gardiner Brainard

What we are is God's gift to us. What we become is our gift to God.
—Anon.

Gawd knows, and 'E won't split on a pal.
—Rudyard Kipling

"You are accepted!" ... accepted by that which is greater than you and the name of which you do not know. Do not ask the name now, perhaps you will know it later. Do not try to do anything, perhaps later you will do much. Do not seek for anything, do not perform anything, do not intend anything. Simply accept the fact that you are accepted.
—Paul Tillich

God delays, but doesn't forget.
—Spanish proverb

How is it, Lord, that we are cowards in everything save in opposing Thee?
—Saint Teresa of Avila

God is clever, but not dishonest.
—Albert Einstein

What is there in man so worthy of honor and reverence as this, that he is capable of contemplating something higher than his own reason, more sublime than the whole universe—that Spirit which alone is self-subsistent, from which all truth proceeds, without which there is no truth?   —Friedrich Jacobi

Yet, in the maddening maze of
    things,
And tossed by storm and flood,
To one fixed trust my spirit clings;
I know that God is good!
            —John Greenleaf Whittier

A consciousness of God releases the greatest power of all.
                    —*Science of Mind*

Above all am I convinced of the need, irrevocable and inescapable, of every human heart, for God. No matter how we try to escape, to lose ourselves in restless seeking, we cannot separate ourselves from our divine source. There is no substitute for God.   —A.J. Cronin

Talking about God is not at all the same thing as experiencing God, or acting out God through our lives.
            —Phillip Hewett

The person who has a firm trust in the Supreme Being is powerful in his power, wise by his wisdom, happy by his happiness.   —Joseph Addison

God has not promised skies always
    blue,
flower-strewn pathways all our lives
    through;
God has not promised sun without
    rain,
joy without sorrow, peace without
    pain.
But God has promised strength for
    the day,

rest for the labor, light for the way,
Grace for the trials, help from above,
unfailing sympathy, undying love.
                        —Kristone

Courage is not afraid to weep, and she is not afraid to pray, even when she is not sure who she is praying to.
                    —J. Ruth Gendler

God is no enemy to you. He asks no more than that He hear you call Him "Friend."   —*A Course in Miracles*

Deep down in every man, woman and child, is the fundamental idea of God. It may be obscured by calamity, by pomp, by worship of other things, but in some form or other it is there. For faith in a Power greater than ourselves, and miraculous demonstrations of that power in human lives, are facts as old as man himself.   —Alcoholics Anonymous

Our human resources, as marshalled by the will, were not sufficient; they failed utterly.... Every day is a day when we must carry the vision of God's will into all our activities.
            —Alcoholics Anonymous

Then comes the insight that All is God. One still realizes that the world is as it was, but it does not matter, it does not affect one's faith.
                    —Abraham Heschel

The experience of God, or in any case the possibility of experiencing God, is innate.   —Alice Walker

Before me, even as behind, God is, and all is well.
            —John Greenleaf Whittier

Forgetfulness of self is remembrance of God. —Bayazid Al-Bistami

Every morning I spend fifteen minutes filling my mind full of God, and so there's no room left for worry thoughts.
—Howard Chandler Christy

Darkness is strong, and so is Sin,
But surely God endures forever!
—James Russell Lowell

We have grasped the mystery of the atom and rejected the Sermon on the Mount. —General Omar N. Bradley

Faith and Belief

We Must Have Faith in What We Can't See

I believe in the sun even if it isn't shining. I believe in love even when I am alone. I believe in God even when He is silent.
— World War II refugee

Faith is the daring of the soul to go farther than it can see.
— William Newton Clark

Faith is the substance of things hoped for, the evidence of things not seen. — Heb. 11:1

All I have seen teaches me to trust the Creator for all I have not seen.
— Ralph Waldo Emerson

Some things have to be believed to be seen. — Ralph Hodgson

Faith is like radar that sees through the fog—the reality of things at a distance that the human eye cannot see. — Corrie Ten Boom

Faith sees the invisible, believes the incredible and receives the impossible. — Anon.

A believer, a mind whose faith is consciousness, is never disturbed because other persons do not yet see the fact which he sees.
— Ralph Waldo Emerson

We walk by faith, not by sight.
— 2 Cor. 5:7

Faith is to believe what we do not see; the reward of this faith is to see what we believe. — Saint Augustine

Because you cannot see him, God is everywhere. — Yasunari Kawabata

Sorrow looks back, worry looks around, faith looks up.
— *Guideposts*

You have to believe in gods to see them. — Hopi Indian saying

Faith declares what the senses do not see, but not the contrary of what they see. — Blaise Pascal

Faith has to do with things that are not seen, and hope with things that are not in hand.
— Saint Thomas Aquinas

118

Faith is the capacity of the soul to perceive the abiding ... the invisible in the visible. —Leo Baeck

WE MUST HAVE FAITH IN OTHER PEOPLE

We must have infinite faith in each other. —Henry David Thoreau

Faith in our associates is part of our faith in God.
　　　　—Charles Horton Cooley

He who has no faith in others shall find no faith in them. —Lao-tzu

Don't lose faith in humanity: think of all the people in the United States who have never played you a single nasty trick. —Elbert Hubbard

WE MUST HAVE FAITH IN OURSELVES

Only the person who has faith in himself is able to be faithful to others. —Erich Fromm

Faith in oneself ... is the best and safest course. —Michelangelo

FAITH OR BELIEF: REASON, KNOWLEDGE, AND UNDERSTANDING

Faith doesn't wait until it understands; in that case it wouldn't be faith. —Vance Havner

Your faith is what you believe, not what you know.
　　　　—John Lancaster Spalding

It is faith, and not reason, which impels men to action.... Intelligence is content to point out the road, but never drives us along it.
　　　　—Dr. Alexis Carrel

Faith consists, not in ignorance, but in knowledge, and that, not only of God, but also of the divine will.
　　　　—John Calvin

All the scholastic scaffolding falls, as a ruined edifice, before a single word: faith. —Napoleon Bonaparte

Some like to understand what they believe in. Others like to believe in what they understand. —Stanislaus

Seek not to understand that thou mayest believe, but believe that thou mayest understand.
　　　　—Saint Augustine

Faith is a sounder guide than reason. Reason can go only so far, but faith has no limits. —Blaise Pascal

It is the heart which experiences God, and not the reason.
　　　　—Blaise Pascal

Faith is the continuation of reason.
　　　　—William Adams

Faith is a higher faculty than reason.
　　　　—Bailey

If we were logical, the future would be bleak indeed. But we are more than logical. We are human beings, and we have faith, and we have hope. —Jacques Cousteau

Faith is the art of holding on to things your reason has once accepted, in spite of your changing moods.
　　　　—C.S. Lewis

Reason is the triumph of the intellect, faith of the heart.
　　　　—James Schouler

Reason is our soul's left hand, Faith her right. By this we reach divinity.
—John Donne

It is as absurd to argue men, as to torture them, into believing.
—John Henry Cardinal Newman

Reason's voice and God's, Nature's and Duty's, never are at odds.
—John Greenleaf Whittier

The way to see by Faith is to shut the eye of Reason.
—Benjamin Franklin

Faith is believing what we cannot prove.   —Alfred, Lord Tennyson

Faith is to believe what you do not yet see; the reward for this faith is to see what you believe.
—Saint Augustine

Faith is believing when it is beyond the power of reason to believe.
—Voltaire

Faith is reason grown courageous.
—Sherwood Eddy

Faith is the result of the act of the will, following upon a conviction that to believe is a duty.
—John Henry Cardinal Newman

So often we have a kind of vague, wistful longing that the promises of Jesus should be true. The only way really to enter into them is to believe them with the clutching intensity of a drowning man.   —William Barclay

Man makes holy what he believes, as he makes beautiful what he loves.
—Ernest Renan

If life is a comedy to him who thinks, and a tragedy to him who feels, it is a victory to him who believes.   —Anon.

You're not free until you've been made captive by supreme belief.
—Marianne Moore

It is by believing in roses that one brings them to bloom.
—French proverb

If you wish to strive for peace of soul and pleasure, then believe.
—Heinrich Heine

Loving is half of believing.
—Victor Hugo

A faith that sets bounds to itself, that will believe so much and no more, that will trust so far and no further, is none.   —Julius Charles Hare

FAITH AND DOUBT

Doubt is a pain too lonely to know that faith is his twin brother.
—Kahlil Gibran

Faith which does not doubt is dead faith.   —Miguel de Unamuno

To believe with certainty we must begin with doubting.   —Stanislaus I

O thou of little faith, why didst thou doubt?
—Mt. 14:31

In the midst of your doubts, don't forget how many of the important questions God *does* answer.
—Verne Becker

The only limit to our realization of tomorrow will be our doubts of today. Let us move forward with strong and active faith.
—Franklin Delano Roosevelt

It is impossible on reasonable grounds to disbelieve miracles.
—Blaise Pascal

FAITH AND FEAR
Deep faith eliminates fear.
—Lech Walesa

Our faith triumphant o'er our fears.
—Henry Wadsworth Longfellow

Fear imprisons, faith liberates; fear paralyzes, faith empowers; fear disheartens, faith encourages; fear sickens, faith heals; fear makes useless, faith makes serviceable.
—Harry Emerson Fosdick

Fear knocked at the door. Faith answered. And lo, no one was there.
—Anon.

TRUSTING AND DARING
Faith is kind of like jumping out of an airplane at ten thousand feet. If God doesn't catch you, you splatter. But how do you know whether or not He is going to catch you unless you jump out?   —Ann Kiemel

Faith ... acts promptly and boldly on the occasion, on slender evidence.
—John Henry Cardinal Newman

The will of God will not take you where the grace of God cannot keep you.   —Anon.

Without risk, faith is an impossibility.   —Søren Kierkegaard

If it wasn't for faith, there would be no living in this world; we couldn't even eat hash with any safety.
—Josh Billings

Living is a form of not being sure, not knowing what next, or how. The moment you know how, you begin to die a little. The artist never entirely knows. We guess. We may be wrong, but we take leap after leap in the dark.   —Agnes de Mille

Let us move on, and step out boldly, though it be into the night, and we can scarcely see the way. A Higher Intelligence than the mortal sees the road before us.
—Charles B. Newcomb

Faith is an assent of the mind and a consent of the heart, consisting mainly of belief and trust.
—E.T. Hiscox

WE EACH HAVE OUR OWN FAITH
The relation of faith between subject and object is unique in every case. Hundreds may believe, but each has to believe by himself.
—W.H. Auden

We cannot hand our faith to one another.... Even in the Middle Ages, when faith was theoretically uniform, it was always practically individual.   —John Jay Chapman

HOW TO DEVELOP FAITH
Every human being is born without faith. Faith comes only through the process of making decisions to change before we can be sure it's the right move. —Dr. Robert H. Schuller

To believe in God is to yearn for His

existence, and furthermore, it is to act as if He did exist.
—Miguel de Unamuno

The principle part of faith is patience.   —George MacDonald

FAITH REQUIRES WORK AND EFFORT

Can a faith that does nothing be called sincere?   —Jean Racine

Faith without works is dead.
—Jas. 2:26

He does not believe who does not live according to his belief.
—Thomas Fuller

All effort is in the last analysis sustained by faith that it is worth making.   —Ordway Tweed

I have fought a good fight, I have finished my course, I have kept the faith.   —2 Tm. 4:7

Faith is not something to grasp, it is a state to grow into.
—Mahatma Gandhi

To disbelieve is easy; to scoff is simple; to have faith is harder.
—Louis L'Amour

No faith is our own that we have not arduously won.   —Havelock Ellis

OTHER DEFINITIONS OF FAITH AND BELIEF

Faith is a living and unshakable confidence, a belief in the grace of God so assured that a man would die a thousand deaths for its sake.
—Martin Luther

Faith, to my mind, is a stiffening process, a sort of mental starch.
—E.M. Forster

Faith is love taking the form of aspiration.   —William Ellery Channing

Faith is hidden household capital.
—Johann von Goethe

Faith is the soul riding at anchor.
—Josh Billings

Faith is ... knowing with your heart.
—N. Richard Nash

Faith is the only known cure for fear.   —Lena K. Sadler

Faith is an attitude of the person. It means you are prepared to stake yourself on something being so.
—Arthur M. Ramsey

Faith, as an intellectual state, is self-reliance.   —Oliver Wendell Holmes

Faith is the subtle chain which binds us to the infinite.
—Elizabeth O. Smith

Faith is nothing but obedience and piety.   —Baruch Spinoza

Faith is a theological virtue that inclines the mind, under the influence of the will and grace, to yield firm assent to revealed truths, because of the authority of God.
—Adolphe Tanqueray

What's up is faith, what's down is heresy.   —Alfred, Lord Tennyson

Faith is spiritualized imagination.
—Henry Ward Beecher

Faith is the final triumph over incongruity, the final assertion of the meaningfulness of existence.
—Reinhold Niebuhr

Faith is an encounter in which God takes and keeps the initiative.
—Eugene Joly

Faith is that which is woven of conviction and set with the sharp mordant of experience.
—James Russell Lowell

Faith is a practical attitude of the will.
—John MacMurray

Faith is a total attitude of the self.
—John Macquarrie

Faith is nothing else than trust in the divine mercy promised in Christ.
—Philipp Melanchthon

Faith is the divine evidence whereby the spiritual man discerneth God, and the things of God.
—John Wesley

Faith is a passionate intuition.
—William Wordsworth

Faith is a bridge across the gulf of death.
—Edward Young

Faith is verification by the heart; confession by the tongue; action by the limbs.
—Anon.

Faith is a certitude without proofs ... a sentiment, for it is a hope; it is an instinct, for it precedes all outward instruction.
—Henry Frederic Amiel

Faith is the proper name of religious experience.
—John Baillie

Faith is an outward and visible sign of an inward and spiritual grace.
—Book of Common Prayer

Faith is the soul's adventure.
—William Bridges

Faith is obedience, nothing else.
—Emil Brunner

Faith is a kind of betting, or speculation.
—Samuel Butler

Faith is the response of our spirits to beckonings of the eternal.
—George A. Buttrick

Faith is a knowledge of the benevolence of God toward us, and a certain persuasion of His veracity.
—John Calvin

Faith is loyalty to some inspired teacher, some spiritual hero.
—Thomas Carlyle

Faith is God's work within us.
—Saint Thomas Aquinas

To me, faith means not worrying.
—John Dewey

Faith is building on what you know is here, so you can reach what you know is there.
—Cullen Hightower

Faith is a gift of God which man can neither give nor take away by promise of rewards, or menaces of torture.
—Thomas Hobbes

Faith is primarily a process of identification; the process by which the individual ceases to be himself and becomes part of something eternal.
—Eric Hoffer

Faith is the function of the heart.
—Mahatma Gandhi

Faith implies the disbelief of a lesser fact in favor of a greater.
—Oliver Wendell Holmes

The great act of faith is when a man decides that he is not God.
—Oliver Wendell Holmes

Faith is the little night-light that burns in a sick-room; as long as it is there, the obscurity is not complete, we turn towards it and await the daylight.   —Abbé Henri Huvelin

Faith is the summit of the Torah.
—Solomon Ibn Gabirol

Faith is an act of self-consecration, in which the will, the intellect, and the affections all have their place.
—William Ralph Inge

Faith is courage; it is creative, while despair is always destructive.
—David S. Muzzey

Faith is to believe in something not yet proved and to underwrite it with our lives: it is the only way we can leave the future open.
—Lillian Smith

Faith begins as an experiment and ends as an experience.
—William Ralph Inge

Faith is an act of a finite being who is grasped by, and turned to, the infinite.   —Paul Tillich

Faith is not a storm cellar to which men and women can flee for refuge from the storms of life. It is, instead, an inner force that gives them the strength to face those storms and their consequences with serenity of spirit.   —Sam J. Ervin, Jr.

Faith is putting all your eggs in God's basket, then counting your blessings before they hatch.
—Ramona C. Carroll

Faith is the force of life.
—Leo Tolstoy

GENERAL QUOTATIONS ABOUT FAITH AND BELIEF

You can do very little with faith, but you can do nothing without it.
—Samuel Butler

The opposite of having faith is having self-pity.   —Og Guinness

Faith is necessary to victory.
—William Hazlitt

Every tomorrow has two handles. We can take hold of it by the handle of anxiety, or by the handle of faith.
—Anon.

Faith is a gift of God. —Blaise Pascal

Faith assuages, guides, restores.
—Arthur Rimbaud

Far graver is it to corrupt the faith that is the life of the soul than to counterfeit the money that sustains temporal life.
—Saint Thomas Aquinas

I would rather live in a world where my life is surrounded by mystery than live in a world so small that my mind could comprehend it.
—Henry Emerson Fosdick

I am living on hope and faith ... a pretty good diet when the mind will receive them.
—Edwin Arlington Robinson

Faith is the sturdiest, the most manly of the virtues. It lies behind our pluckiest ... strivings. It is the virtue of the storm, just as happiness is the virtue of the sunshine.
—Ruth Benedict

There is one inevitable criterion of judgment touching religious faith ... Can you reduce it to practice? If not, have none of it.   —Hosea Ballou

Strike from mankind the principle of faith, and men would have no more history than a flock of sheep.
—Edward Bulwer-Lytton

Be thou faithful unto death.
—Rev. 2:10

Faith is one of the forces by which men live; the total absence of it means collapse.   —William James

Pity the human being who is not able to connect faith within himself with the infinite.... He who has faith has ... an inward reservoir of courage, hope, confidence, calmness, and assuring trust that all will come out well—even though to the world it may appear to come out most badly.
—B.C. Forbes

Through the dark and stormy night
Faith beholds a feeble light
Up the blackness streaking;
Knowing God's own time is best,
In a patient hope I rest
For the full day-breaking!
—John Greenleaf Whittier

To win true peace, a man needs to feel himself directed, pardoned and sustained by a supreme power, to feel himself in the right road, at the point where God would have him be—in order with God and the universe. This faith gives strength and calm.   —Henri Frederic Amiel

Faith may be relied upon to produce sustained action and, more rarely, sustained contemplation.
—Aldous Huxley

The person who has a firm trust in the Supreme Being is powerful in his power, wise by his wisdom, happy by his happiness.   —Joseph Addison

Something will turn up.
—Benjamin Disraeli

The disease with which the human mind now labors is want of faith.
—Ralph Waldo Emerson

As your faith is strengthened you will find that there is no longer the need to have a sense of control, that things will flow as they will, and that you will flow with them, to your great delight and benefit.
—Emmanuel

The historic glory of America lies in the fact that it is the one nation that was founded like a church. That is, it was founded on a faith that was not merely summed up after it had exited, but was defined before it existed.
—G.K. Chesterton

The only faith that wears well and holds its color in all weather is that which is woven of conviction.
—James Russell Lowell

The primary cause of unhappiness in the world today is ... lack of faith.
—Carl Jung

You do build in darkness if you have faith. When the light returns you have made of yourself a fortress which is impregnable to certain kinds of trouble; you may even find yourself needed and sought by others as a beacon in *their* dark.
—Olga Rosmanith

It is by faith that poetry, as well as devotion, soars above this dull earth; that imagination breaks through its clouds, breathes a purer air, and lives in a softer light.
—Henry Giles

Religious faith, indeed, relates to that which is above us, but it must arise from that which is within us.
—Josiah Royce

Faith enables persons to be persons because it lets God be God.
—Carter Lindberg

Faith makes the discords of the present the harmonies of the future.
—Robert Collyer

A person consists of his faith. Whatever is his faith, even so is he.
—Hindu proverb

In Israel, in order to be a realist, you must believe in miracles.
—David Ben-Gurion

For the believer, there is no question; for the non-believer, there is no answer.
—Anon.

Life without faith in something is too narrow a space in which to live.
—George Lancaster Spalding

PRAYER

WHY PRAY

I pray on the principle that wine
knocks the cork out of a bottle.
There is an inward fermentation,
and there must be a vent.
—Henry Ward Beecher

They who have steeped their soul in
prayer can every anguish calmly
bear.   —Richard M. Milnes

Unless I had the spirit of prayer, I
could do nothing.
—Charles G. Finney

Prayer is an end to isolation. It is living our daily life with someone; with
him who alone can deliver us from
solitude.   —Georges Lefevre

Prayer moves the hand that moves
the world.   —John Aikman Wallace

Prayer changes things.   —Anon.

Prayer does not change God, but it
changes him who prays.
—Søren Kierkegaard

There is no hope but in prayer.
—Andrew Bonar

We can do nothing without prayer.
All things can be done by importu-
nate prayer. It surmounts or removes
all obstacles, overcomes every resist-
ing force and gains its ends in the
face of invincible hindrances.
—E.M. Bounds

By prayer we couple the powers of
heaven to our helplessness, the powers which can capture strongholds
and make the impossible possible.
—O. Hallesby

Faith, and hope, and patience and all
the strong, beautiful, vital forces of
piety are withered and dead in a
prayerless life. The life of the individual believer, his personal salvation, and personal Christian graces
have their being, bloom, and fruitage
in prayer.   —E.M. Bounds

Every chain that spirits wear crum-
bles in the breadth of prayer.
—John Greenleaf Whittier

Though we cannot by our prayers
give God any information, yet we
must by our prayers give him honor.
—Matthew Henry

In the war upon the powers of darkness, prayer is the primary and mightiest weapon, both in aggressive war upon them and their works; in the deliverance of men from their power; and against them as a hierarchy of powers opposed to Christ and His Church.   —Jessie Penn-Lewis

God shapes the world by prayer. Prayers are deathless. They outlive the lives of those who uttered them.
                —E.M. Bounds

Men of God are always men of prayer.   —Henry T. Mahan

Religion is no more possible without prayer than poetry without language or music without atmosphere.
                —James Martineau

All who have walked with God have viewed prayer as the main business of their lives.   —Delma Jackson

To have a curable illness and to leave it untreated except for prayer is like sticking your hand in a fire and asking God to remove the flame.
                —Sandra L. Douglas

Oh, what a cause of thankfulness it is that we have a gracious God to go to on all occasions! Use and enjoy this privilege and you can never be miserable. Oh, what an unspeakable privilege is prayer! —Lady Maxwell

What is the life of a Christian but a life of prayer!   —David Brown

Even if no command to pray had existed, our very weakness would have suggested it.
                —Francois de Fenelon

He who ceases to pray ceases to prosper.   —Sir William Gurney Benham

By prayer, the ability is secured to feel the law of love, to speak according to the law of love, and to do everything in harmony with the law of love.   —E.M. Bounds

Time spent on the knees in prayer will do more to remedy heart strain and nerve worry than anything else.
                —George David Stewart

A man's state before God may always be measured by his prayers.
                —J.C. Ryle

No one is a firmer believer in the power of prayer than the devil; not that he practices it, but he suffers from it.   —Guy H. King

The one concern of the devil is to keep Christians from praying. He fears nothing from prayerless studies, prayerless work, and prayerless religion. He laughs at our toil, mocks at our wisdom, but trembles when we pray.   —Samuel Chadwick

Prayer is the great engine to overthrow and rout my spiritual enemies, the great means to procure the graces of which I stand in hourly need.   —John Newton

No heart thrives without much secret converse with God and nothing will make amends for the want of it.   —John Berridge

Trouble and perplexity drive me to prayer and prayer drives away perplexity and trouble.
                —Philipp Melanchthon

Prayer covers the whole of man's life. There is no thought, feeling, yearning, or desire, however low, trifling, or vulgar we may deem it, which, if it affects our real interest or happiness, we may not lay before God and be sure of sympathy. His nature is such that our often coming does not tire him. The whole burden of the whole life of every man may be rolled on to God and not weary him, though it has wearied the man.
　　　　—Henry Ward Beecher

The first purpose of prayer is to know God.　　—Charles L. Allen

We, one and all of us, have an instinct to pray; and this fact constitutes an invitation from God to pray.
　　　　—Charles Sanders Peirce

Teach us to pray that we may cause
The enemy to flee,
That we his evil power may bind,
His prisoners to free.
　　　　—Watchman Nee

No matter what may be the test,
God will take care of you;
Lean, weary one, upon His breast,
God will take care of you.
　　　　—C.D. Martin

He who has learned to pray has learned the greatest secret of a holy and a happy life.　　—William Law

Non-praying is lawlessness, discord, anarchy.　　—E.M. Bounds

We look upon prayer as a means of getting things for ourselves; The Bible idea of prayer is that we may get to know God Himself.
　　　　—Oswald Chambers

Pray, always pray; when sickness wastes thy frame,
Prayer brings the healing power of Jesus' name.　　—A.B. Simpson

The purpose of prayer is to reveal the presence of God equally present, all the time, in every condition.
　　　　—Oswald Chambers

Prayer is of transcendent importance. Prayer is the mightiest agent to advance God's work. Praying hearts and hands only can do God's work. Prayer succeeds when all else fails.　　—E.M. Bounds

The goal of prayer is the ear of God, a goal that can only be reached by patient and continued and continuous waiting upon Him, pouring out our heart to Him and permitting Him to speak to us. Only by so doing can we expect to know Him, and as we come to know Him better we shall spend more time in His presence and find that presence a constant and ever-increasing delight.
　　　　—E.M. Bounds

The value of consistent prayer is not that He will hear us, but that we will hear Him.　　—William McGill

Prayer honors God, acknowledges His being, exalts His power, adores His providence, secures His aid.
　　　　—E.M. Bounds

The whole meaning of prayer is that we may know God.
　　　　—Oswald Chambers

Prayer crowns God with the honor and glory due to His name, and God crowns prayer with assurance and comfort. The most praying souls are the most assured souls.

—Thomas B. Brooks

PRAYER IS PRACTICAL

The influence of prayer on the human mind and body ... can be measured in terms of increased physical buoyancy, greater intellectual vigor, moral stamina, and a deeper understanding of the realities underlying human relationships.

—Dr. Alexis Carrel

Prayer is the force as real as terrestrial gravity. As a physician, I have seen men, after all other therapy had failed, lifted out of disease and melancholy by the serene effort of prayer. Only in prayer do we achieve that complete and harmonious assembly of body, mind and spirit which gives the frail human reed its unshakable strength.

—Dr. Alexis Carrel

Prayer is not an old woman's idle amusement. Properly understood and applied, it is the most potent instrument of action.

—Mahatma Gandhi

Today any successful and competent businessman will employ the latest and best-tested methods in production, distribution, and administration, and many are discovering that one of the greatest of all efficiency methods is prayer power.

—Norman Vincent Peale

To have a curable illness and to leave it untreated except for prayer is like sticking your hand in a fire and asking God to remove the flame.

—Sandra L. Douglas

PRAYER CHANGES US

One night alone in prayer might make us new men, changed from poverty of soul to spiritual wealth, from trembling to triumphing.

—Charles Haddon Spurgeon

Every time we pray our horizon is altered, our attitude to things is altered, not sometimes but every time, and the amazing thing is that we don't pray more.

—Oswald Chambers

It is not so true that "prayer changes things" as that prayer changes me and I change things. God has so constituted things that prayer on the basis of Redemption alters the way in which a man looks at things. Prayer is not a question of altering things externally, but of working wonders in a man's disposition.

—Oswald Chambers

Prayer may not change things for you, but it for sure changes you for things.   —Samuel M. Shoemaker

HOW TO PRAY

When you cannot pray as you would, pray as you can.

—Edward M. Goulburn

If you can't pray as you want to, pray as you can. God knows what you mean.   —Vance Havner

The main lesson about prayer is just this: Do it! Do it! Do it! You want to be taught to pray? My answer is: pray.   —John Laidlaw

Praying is learned by praying.

—L.A.T. van Dooren

The only way to pray is to pray, and the way to pray well is to pray much.   —Anon.

The less I pray, the harder it gets; the more I pray, the better it goes.
                    —Martin Luther

Pray till you pray. —D.M. McIntyre

It has been well said that almost the only scoffers at prayer are those who never tried it enough.
                    —*Twelve Steps and Twelve Traditions*

Prayer is a trade to be learned. We must be apprentices and serve our time at it. Painstaking care, much thought, practice and labour are required to be a skillful tradesman in praying. Practice in this, as well as in all other trades, makes perfect.
                    —E.M. Bounds

If we are willing to spend hours on end to learn to play the piano, operate a computer, or fly an airplane, it is sheer nonsense for us to imagine that we can learn the high art of getting guidance through communion with the Lord without being willing to set aside time for it.   —Paul Rees

He that will learn to pray, let him to sea.   —George Herbert

The great thing in prayer is to feel that we are putting our supplications into the bosom of omnipotent love.
                    —Andrew Murray

All the prayers in the Scripture you will find to be reasoning with God, not a multitude of words heaped together.   —Stephen Charnock

Scream at God if that's the only thing that will get results.
                    —Brendan Francis

You need not cry very loud; he is nearer to us than we think.
                    —Brother Lawrence

Rejoice always, pray constantly, and in all circumstances give thanks.
                    —The Desert Fathers

God tells us to burden him with whatever burdens us.   —Anon.

Do I want to pray or only to think about my human problems? Do I want to pray or simply kneel there contemplating my sorrow? Do I want to direct my prayer toward God or let it direct itself towards me?   —Hubert Van Zeller

O thou, by whom we come to God,
The Life, the Truth, the Way,
The path of prayer Thyself hast
    trod—
Lord teach us how to pray.
                    —James Montgomery

Dealing in generalities is the death of prayer.   —J.H. Evans

Don't try to reach God with your understanding; that is impossible. Reach him in love; that is possible.
                    —Carlo Carretto

The right way to pray, then, is any way that allows us to communicate with God.
                    —Colleen Townsend Evans

Grant us grace, Almighty Father, so to pray as to deserve to be heard.
                    —Jane Austen

He prayeth well, who loveth well
Both man and bird and beast.
He prayeth best, who loveth best
All things both great and small;
For the dear God who loveth us,
He made and loveth all.
—Samuel Taylor Coleridge

Confess your faults one to another,
and pray one for another, that ye
may be healed. The effectual, fervent
prayer of a righteous man availeth
much.
—Jas. 5:16

Incense is prayer
That drives no bargain.
Child, learn from incense
How best to pray.   —Alfred Barrett

When we go to our meeting with
God, we should go like a patient to
his doctor, first to be thoroughly
examined and afterwards to be treated for our ailment. Then something
will happen when you pray.
—O. Hallesby

Natural ability and educational
advantages do not figure as factors
in this matter of prayer; but a capacity for faith, the power of a thorough
consecration, the ability of self-
littleness, an absolute losing of one's
self in God's glory and an ever present and insatiable yearning and
seeking after all the fullness of God.
—E.M. Bounds

We have to pray with our eyes on
God, not on the difficulties.
—Oswald Chambers

If our petitions are in accordance
with His will, and if we seek His
glory in the asking, the answers will
come in ways that will astonish us
and fill our hearts with songs of
thanksgiving.   —J.K. Maclean

Pray if thou canst with hope, but
ever pray, though hope be weak or
sick with long delay; pray in the
darkness if there be no light; and if
for any wish thou dare not pray,
then pray to God to cast that wish
away.   —Anon.

Prayer can assume very different
forms, from quiet, blessed contemplation of God, in which eye meets
eye in restful meditation, to deep
sighs or sudden exclamations of
wonder, joy, gratitude or adoration.
—O. Hallesby

To pray is nothing more involved
than to open the door, giving Jesus
access to our needs and permitting
Him to exercise His own power in
dealing with them.   —O. Hallesby

He prays best who does not know
that he is praying.
—Saint Anthony of Padua

DAILY PRAYER

A day without prayer is a boast
against God.   —Owen Carr

Prayer should be the key of the day
and the lock of the night.
—Thomas Fuller

I care not what black spiritual crisis
we may come through or what
delightful spiritual Canaan we may
enter, no blessing of the Christian
life becomes continually possessed
unless we are men and women of
regular, daily, unhurried, secret lin-
gerings in prayer. —J. Sidlow Baxter

In the morning, prayer is the key that opens to us the treasures of God's mercies and blessings; in the evening, it is the key that shuts us up under His protection and safeguard.
—Anon.

Prayer is a kind of calling home every day. And there can come to you a serenity, a feeling of at-homeness in God's universe, a peace that the world can neither give nor disturb, a fresh courage, a new insight, a holy boldness that you'll never, never get any other way. —Earl G. Hunt, Jr.

O God, if in the day of battle I forget Thee, do not Thou forget me.
—Anon.

Seven days without prayer makes one weak. —Allen E. Bartlett

Lord, you know how busy I must be this day. If I forget you, do not you forget me. —Jacob Astley

We read of preaching the Word out of season, but we do not read of praying out of season, for that is never out of season.
—Matthew Henry

Let prayer be the key of the morning and the bolt at night. —Philip Henry

Evening, and morning, and at noon, will I pray. —PS. 55:17

Prayer should be the means by which I, at all times, receive all that I need, and, for this reason, be my daily refuge, my daily consolation, my daily joy, my source of rich and inexhaustible joy in life.
—Saint John Chrysostom

CONTINUAL PRAYER

As impossible as it is for us to take a breath in the morning large enough to last us until noon, so impossible is it to pray in the morning in such a way as to last us until noon. Let your prayers ascend to Him constantly, audibly or silently, as circumstances throughout the day permit. —O. Hallesby

To God your every Want
In instant Prayer display,
Pray always; Pray, and never faint;
Pray, without ceasing, Pray.
—Charles Wesely

Constant prayer quickly straightens out our thoughts.
—The Desert Fathers

Teach us to pray often, that we may pray oftener. —Jeremy Taylor

Abiding fully means praying much.
—Andrew Murray

Pray, always pray; beneath sins
heaviest load,
Prayer claims the blood from Jesus'
side that flowed.
Pray, always pray; though weary,
faint, and lone,
Prayer nestles by the Father's shelter-
ing throne. —A.B. Simpson

When the knees are not often bent, the feet soon slide. —Anon.

The more praying there is in the world, the better the world will be; the mightier the forces against evil everywhere. —E.M. Bounds

Those who always pray are necessary to those who never pray.
—Victor Hugo

133

WE MUST MAKE TIME TO PRAY

When it becomes clear to us that prayer is a part of our daily program of work, it will also become clear to us that we must arrange our daily program in such a way that there is time also for this work, just as we set aside time for other necessary things, such as eating and dressing.
—O. Hallesby

Tomorrow I plan to work, work, from early until late. In fact I have so much to do that I shall spend the first three hours in prayer.
—Martin Luther

Begin to realize more and more that prayer is the most important thing you do. You can use your time to no better advantage than to pray whenever you have an opportunity to do so, either alone or with others; while at work, while at rest, or while walking down the street. Anywhere!
—O. Hallesby

Sometimes we think we are too busy to pray. That is a great mistake, for praying is a saving of time.
—Charles Haddon Spurgeon

Prayer time must be kept up as duly as meal-time.   —Matthew Henry

The minds of people are so cluttered up with every-day living these days that they don't, or won't, take time out for a little prayer—for mental cleansing, just as they take a bath for physical, outer cleansing. Both are necessary.   —Jo Ann Carlson

The Christian will find his parentheses for prayer even in the busiest hours of life.   —Richard Cecil

Time spent in prayer is never wasted.
—Francois de Fenelon

I have to hurry all day to get time to pray.   —Martin Luther

No time is so well spent in every day as that which we spend upon our knees.   —J.C. Ryle

Other duties become pressing and absorbing and crowd our prayer. "Choked to death" would be the coroner's verdict in many cases of dead praying if an inquest could be secured on this dire, spiritual calamity.   —E.M. Bounds

It is impossible to conduct your life as a disciple without definite times of secret prayer.   —Oswald Chambers

MORNING PRAYER

While others still slept, He went away to pray and to renew His strength in communion with His Father. He had need of this, otherwise He would not have been ready for the new day. The holy work of delivering souls demands constant renewal through fellowship with God.   —Andrew Murray

And in the morning, rising up a great while before day, he went out, and departed into a solitary place, and there prayed.   —Mk. 1:35

Get into the habit of dealing with God about everything. Unless in the first waking moment of the day you learn to fling the door wide back and let God in, you will work on a wrong level all day; but swing the door wide open and pray to your Father in secret, and every public

134

thing will be stamped with the presence of God.   —Oswald Chambers

Temptations which accompany the working day will be conquered on the basis of the morning breakthrough to God. Decisions, demanded by work, become easier and simpler where they are made not in the fear of men, but only in the sight of God. He wants to give us today the power which we need for our work.
     —Dietrich Bonhoeffer

It is by no haphazard chance that in every age men have risen early to pray. The first thing that marks decline in spiritual life is our relationship to the early morning.
     —Oswald Chambers

The entire day receives order and discipline when it acquires unity. This unity must be sought and found in morning prayer. The morning prayer determines the day.
     —Dietrich Bonhoeffer

Cause me to hear thy loving kindness in the morning.
     —Psalms

In the morning will I direct my prayer unto thee.
     —Ps. 5:3

If you have ever prayed in the dawn you will ask yourself why you were so foolish as not to do it always: it is difficult to get into communion with God in the midst of the hurly-burly of the day.   —Oswald Chambers

I feel it is far better to begin with God, to see His face first, to get my soul near Him before it is near

another. In general it is best to have at least one hour alone with God before engaging in anything else.
     —E.M. Bounds

Lord, if any have to die this day, let it be me, for I am ready. —Billy Bray

EVENING PRAYER

The man who says his prayers in the evening is a captain posting his sentries. After that, he can sleep.
     —Charles Baudelaire

I did this night promise my wife never to go to bed without calling upon God, upon my knees, in prayer.   —Samuel Pepys

When at night you cannot sleep, talk to the Shepherd and stop counting sheep.   —Anon.

PRAYING WHEN WE BOTTOM OUT

I have been driven many times to my knees by the overwhelming conviction that I had nowhere else to go. My own wisdom and that of all about me seemed insufficient for the day.   —Abraham Lincoln

Ordinarily when a man in difficulty turns to prayer, he has already tried every other means of escape.
     —Austin O'Malley

Now I am past all comforts here, but prayer.   —William Shakespeare

Prayer begins where human capacity ends.   —Marian Anderson

"Oh, God, if I were sure I were to die tonight I would repent at once." It is the commonest prayer in all languages.   —Sir James M. Barrie

135

If you are swept off your feet, it's time to get on your knees.

—Fred Beck

When I am weak, then am I strong.

—2 Cor. 12:10

To pray is to open the door unto Jesus and admit Him into your distress. Your helplessness is the very thing which opens wide the door unto Him and gives Him access to all your needs.

—O. Hallesby

My helpless friend, your helplessness is the most powerful plea which rises up to the tender father-heart of God. You think that everything is closed to you because you cannot pray. My friend, your helplessness is the very essence of prayer.

—O. Hallesby

Listen, my friend! Your helplessness is your best prayer. It calls from your heart to the heart of God with greater effect than all your uttered pleas. He hears it from the very moment that you are seized with helplessness, and He becomes actively engaged at once in hearing and answering the prayer of your helplessness.

—O. Hallesby

Helplessness is unquestionably the first and the surest indication of a praying heart.... Prayer and helplessness are inseparable. Only he who is helpless can truly pray.

—O. Hallesby

When we pray for the Spirit's help ... we will simply fall down at the Lord's feet in our weakness. There we will find the victory and power that comes from His love.

—Andrew Murray

The more helpless you are, the better you are fitted to pray, and the more answers to prayer you will experience.

—O. Hallesby

Being in an agony, he prayed more earnestly.

—Lk. 22:44

When a man is at his wits' end it is not a cowardly thing to pray, it is the only way he can get in touch with Reality.

—Oswald Chambers

When my soul fainted within me ... my prayer came in unto thee.

—Jon. 2:7

He will regard the prayer of the destitute.

—Ps. 102:17

My strength is made perfect in weakness.

—2 Cor. 12:9

God listens to our weeping when the occasion itself is beyond our knowledge, but still within His love and power.

—Daniel A. Poling

Trouble and prayer are closely related.... Trouble often drives men to God in prayer, while prayer is but the voice of men in trouble.

—E.M. Bounds

Trouble and perplexity drive me to prayer and prayer drives away perplexity and trouble.

—Philipp Melanchthon

BUT WE CAN'T PRAY JUST WHEN WE'RE IN TROUBLE

You pray in your distress and in your need; would that you might also pray in the fullness of your joy and in your days of abundance.

—Kahlil Gibran

Many people pray as if God were a big aspirin pill; they come only when they hurt. —B. Graham Dienert

An agnostic found himself in trouble, and a friend suggested he pray. "How can I pray when I do not know whether or not there is a God?" he asked. "If you are lost in the forest," his friend replied, "you do not wait until you find someone before shouting for help."
—Dan Plies

Don't pray when it rains if you don't pray when the sun shines.
—Satchel Paige

He who cannot pray when the sun is shining will not know how to pray when the clouds come. —Anon.

All those football coaches who hold dressing-room prayers before a game should be forced to attend church once a week. —Duffy Daugherty

Prayer is not merely an occasional impulse to which we respond when we are in trouble: prayer is a life attitude. —Walter A. Mueller

A SPECIAL PLACE FOR PRAYER

Do not have as your motive the desire to be known as a praying man. Get an inner chamber in which to pray where no one knows you are praying, shut the door, and talk to God in secret. —Oswald Chambers

Of all things, guard against neglecting God in the secret place of prayer.
—William Wilberforce

Private place and plenty of time are the life of prayer. —E.M. Bounds

Nowhere can we get to know the holiness of God, and come under His influence and power, except in the inner chamber. It has been well said: "No man can expect to make progress in holiness who is not often and long alone with God."
—Andrew Murray

But thou, when thou prayest, enter into thy room, and when thou hast shut thy door, pray to thy Father who is in secret; and thy Father who seeth in secret, shall reward thee openly. —Mt. 6:6

When you enter your secret chamber, take plenty of time before you begin to speak. Let quietude wield its influence upon you. Let the fact that you are alone assert itself. Give your soul time to get released from the many outward things. Give God time to play the prelude to prayer for the benefit of your distracted soul.
—O. Hallesby

There is no need to get to a place of prayer; pray wherever you are.
—Oswald Chambers

OUR PRAYERS SHOULD BE SINCERE, AND JIBE WITH HOW WE LIVE DAY TO DAY

Prayer, to the patriarchs and prophets, was more than the recital of well-known and well-worn phrases—it was the outpouring of the heart. —Herbert Lockyer

Do not pray by heart, but with the heart. —Anon.

Heaven is never deaf but when man's heart is dumb.
—Francis Quarles

Sincerity is the prime requisite in every approach to the God who ... hates all hypocrisy, falsehood, and deceit. —Geoffrey B. Wilson

The Lord's Prayer may be committed to memory quickly, but it is slowly learnt by heart.
—Frederick Denison Maurice

God hears no more than the heart speaks; and if the heart be dumb, God will certainly be dumb.
—Thomas B. Brooks

Without the incense of heartfelt prayer, even the greatest of cathedrals is dead. —Anon.

Deep down in me I knowed it was a lie, and He knowed it. You can't pray a lie—I found that out.
—Mark Twain

Prayers not felt by us are seldom heard by God. —Philip Henry

Many pray with their lips for that for which their hearts have no desire.
—Jonathan Edwards

God may turn his ears from prattling prayers, or preaching prayers, but never from penitent, believing prayers. —William S. Plumer

Two went to pray? Better to say one went to brag, the other to pray.
—Richard Crashaw

I pray like a robber asking alms at the door of a farmhouse to which he is ready to set fire. —Leon Bloy

God's ear lies close to the believer's lip. —Anon.

Our prayers must mean something to us if they are to mean anything to God. —Maltbie D. Babcock

Our prayers must spring from the indigenous soil of our own personal confrontation with the Spirit of God in our lives. —Malcolm Boyd

God eagerly awaits the chance to bless the person whose heart is turned toward Him. —Anon.

We must lay before him what *is* in us, not what *ought* to be in us.
—C.S. Lewis

In prayer the lips ne'er act the winning part, without the sweet concurrence of the heart. —Robert Herrick

The cry of a young raven is nothing but the natural cry of a creature, but your cry, if it be sincere, is the result of a work of grace in your heart.
—Charles Haddon Spurgeon

Every time you pray, if your prayer is sincere, there will be new feeling and new meaning in it which will give you fresh courage, and you will understand that prayer is an education. —Fyodor Dostoyevsky

When you pray, rather let your heart be without words than your words without heart. —John Bunyan

He offered a prayer so deeply devout that he seemed kneeling and praying at the bottom of the sea.
—Herman Melville

Prayer is a serious thing. We may be taken at our words.
—Dwight L. Moody

Prayer at its best is the expression of the total life, for all things else being equal, our prayers are only as powerful as our lives.   —A.W. Tozer

And help us, this and every day, to live more nearly as we pray.
                              —John Keble

My words fly up, my thoughts
    remain below;
Words without thoughts never to
    heaven go.
                              —William Shakespeare

It is not well for a man to pray cream and live skim milk.
                              —Henry Ward Beecher

She heard the snuffle of hypocrisy in her prayer. She had to cease to pray.
                              —George Meredith

Prayer is the soul's sincere desire.
                              —James Montgomery

None can pray well but he that lives well.   —Thomas Fuller

Straight praying is never born of crooked conduct.   —E.M. Bounds

A wicked man in prayer may lift up his hands, but he cannot lift up his face.   —Thomas Watson

He who prays as he ought, will endeavor to live as he prays.
                              —John Owen

We pray pious blether, our will is not in it, and then we say God does not answer; we never *asked* Him for anything. Asking means that our wills are in what we ask.
                              —Oswald Chambers

It is good for us to keep some account of our prayers, that we may not unsay them in our practice.
                              —Matthew Henry

Be not hot in prayer and cold in praise.   —Anon.

Praying which does not result in pure conduct is a delusion. We have missed the whole office and virtue of praying if it does not rectify conduct. It is in the very nature of things that we must quit praying, or quit bad conduct.   —E.M. Bounds

Our praying, to be strong, must be buttressed by holy living. The life of faith perfects the prayer of faith.
                              —E.M. Bounds

Search me, O God, and know my heart: try me, and know my thoughts: and see if there be any wicked way in me.
                              —Ps. 139:23–24

When our will wholeheartedly enters into the prayer of Christ, then we pray correctly.
                              —Dietrich Bonhoeffer

We cannot talk to God strongly when we have not lived for God strongly. The closet cannot be made holy to God when the life has not been holy to God.   —E.M. Bounds

If we would have God in the closet, God must have us out of the closet. There is no way of praying to God, but by living to God.
                              —E.M. Bounds

Men would pray better if they lived better. They would get more from

God if they lived more obedient and well-pleasing to God.

—E.M. Bounds

Though smooth be the heartless prayer, no ear in heaven will mind it; And the finest phrase falls dead, if there is no feeling behind it.

—Ella Wheeler Wilcox

Our Prayers Needn't Be Eloquent

Prayer is not eloquence, but earnestness; not the definition of helplessness, but the feeling of it; not figures of speech, but earnestness of soul.

—Hannah More

Prayer is something deeper than words. It is present in the soul before it has been formulated in words. And it abides in the soul after the last words of prayer have passed over our lips.

—O. Hallesby

If we rely on the Holy Spirit, we shall find that our prayers become more and more inarticulate; and when they are inarticulate, reverence grows deeper and deeper.

—Oswald Chambers

God prefers bad verses recited with a pure heart to the finest verses chanted by the wicked.

—Voltaire

We cannot all argue, but we can all pray; we cannot all be leaders, but we can all be pleaders; we cannot all be mighty in rhetoric, but we can all be prevalent in prayer.

—Charles Haddon Spurgeon

In prayer it is better to have a heart without words than words without a heart.

—John Bunyan

We ought to act with God in the greatest simplicity, speak to Him frankly and plainly, and implore His assistance in our affairs.

—Brother Lawrence

The best prayers have often more groans than words.

—John Bunyan

Prayer is not artful monologue Of voice uplifted from the son; It is Love's tender dialogue Between the soul and God.

—John Richard Moreland

God can pick sense out of a confused prayer.

—Richard Sibbes

They tell about a fifteen-year-old boy in an orphans' home who had an incurable stutter. One Sunday the minister was detained and the boy volunteered to say the prayer in his stead. He did it perfectly, too, without a single stutter. Later he explained, "I don't stutter when I talk to God. He loves me."

—Bennett Cerf

Prayer is a fine, delicate instrument. To use it right is a great art, a holy art. There is perhaps no greater art than the art of prayer. Yet the least gifted, the uneducated and the poor can cultivate the holy art of prayer.

—O. Hallesby

Our groanings, which cannot be uttered, rise to Him and tell Him better than words how dependent we are upon Him.

—O. Hallesby

When prayer is a struggle, do not worry about the prayers that you cannot pray. You yourself are a prayer to God at that moment. All that is within you cries out to Him. And He hears all the pleas that your suffering soul and body are making to Him with groanings which cannot be uttered.   —O. Hallesby

Prayer requires more of the heart than of the tongue.   —Adam Clarke

Productive prayer requires earnestness, not eloquence.   —Anon.

THE BEST PRAYERS ARE OFTEN BRIEF

Short prayers pierceth Heaven.
                    —*The Cloud of Unknowing*

The fewer the words, the better the prayer.   —Martin Luther

Prayer should be short, without giving God Almighty reasons why He should grant this or that; He knows best what is good for us.
                    —John Selden

God is in heaven, and thou upon earth: therefore let thy words be few.
                    —Eccl. 5:2

Many words do not a good prayer make; what counts is the heartfelt desire to commune with God, and the faith to back it up.   —Anon.

A little lifting of the heart suffices; a little remembrance of God, one act of inward worship are prayers which, however short, are nevertheless acceptable to God.
                    —Brother Lawrence

There come times when I have nothing more to tell God. If I were to continue to pray in words, I would have to repeat what I have already

said. At such times it is wonderful to say to God, "May I be in Thy presence, Lord? I have nothing more to say to Thee, but I do love to be in Thy presence."   —O. Hallesby

ASKING FOR THINGS THROUGH PRAYER

You are coming to a King,
Large petitions with you bring
For his grace and power are such
None can ever ask too much.
                    —John Newton

Most Christians expect little from God, ask little, and therefore receive little and are content with little.
                    —A.W. Pink

Ye have not, because ye ask not.
                    —Js. 4:2

Ye ask, and receive not, because ye ask amiss.   —Js. 4:3

Ask, and it shall be given you; seek, and ye shall find; knock, and it shall be opened unto you.
                    —Mt. 7:7

God never denied that soul anything that went as far as heaven to ask it.
                    —John Trapp

Whether we like it or not, asking is the rule of the Kingdom.
                    —Charles Haddon Spurgeon

The simple heart that freely asks in love, obtains.
                    —John Greenleaf Whittier

Our immediate temptation will be to ask for specific solutions to specific problems, and for the ability to help other people as we have already thought they should be helped. In that case, we are asking God to do it our way. —Bill W.

It is the will of our heavenly Father that we should come to Him freely and confidently and make known our desires to Him, just as we would have our children come freely and of their own accord and speak to us about the things they would like to have. —O. Hallesby

My praying friend, continue to make known your desires to God in all things.... Let Him decide whether you are to receive what you ask for or not. —O. Hallesby

Let your requests be made known unto God. —Phil. 4:6

Pray for whatsoever you will. In the name of Jesus you have permission, not only to stand in the presence of God, but also to pray for everything you need. —O. Hallesby

And whatever ye shall ask in my name, that will I do. —1 Jn. 14:13

We should not be afraid, when praying to God, to give expression to a definite desire, even though we are in doubt at the time we are praying whether it is really the right thing to pray for or not. —O. Hallesby

We can never know God as it is our privilege to know Him by brief repetitions that are requests for personal favors, and nothing more. —E.M. Bounds

O Lord, attend unto my cry. —Psalms

Prayer is not only asking, it is an attitude of heart that produces an atmosphere in which asking is perfectly natural, and Jesus says, "every one that asketh receiveth." —Oswald Chambers

Helplessness becomes prayer the moment that you go to Jesus and speak candidly and confidently with him about your needs. This is to believe. —O. Hallesby

Ask in faith. —Jas. 1:6

The clue is not to ask in a miserly way—the key is to ask in a grand manner. —Ann Wigmore

To avail yourself of His certain wisdom, ask of Him whatever questions you have. But do not entreat Him, for that will never be necessary. —Hugh Prather

We pray pious blether, our will is not in it, and then we say God does not answer; we never asked Him for anything. Asking means that our wills are in what we ask. —Oswald Chambers

Ask the gods nothing excessive. —Aeschylus

When praying for healing, ask great things of God and expect great things from God. But let us seek for that healing that really matters, the healing of the heart, enabling us to trust God simply, face God honestly, and live triumphantly. —Arlo F. Newell

Most people do not pray; they only beg. —Bernard Shaw

Prayer is not asking. It is a longing of the soul.   —Mahatma Gandhi

Prayer in the sense of petition, asking for things, is a small part of it; confession and penitence are its threshold, adoration its sanctuary, the presence and vision and enjoyment of God its bread and wine.
—C.S. Lewis

SELFISHNESS AND PRAYER

If your prayer is selfish, the answer will be something that will rebuke your selfishness. You may not recognize it as having come at all, but it is sure to be there.   —William Temple

Selfishness is never so exquisitely selfish as when it is on its knees.... Self turns what would otherwise be a pure and powerful prayer into a weak and ineffective one.
—A.W. Tozer

I seldom made an errand to God for another but I got something for myself.   —Samuel Rutherford

When we make self the end of prayer, it is not worship but self-seeking.   —Thomas Manton

We look upon prayer as a means of getting things for ourselves; The Bible idea of prayer is that we may get to know God Himself.
—Oswald Chambers

WE SHOULD PRAY FOR OTHERS

Pray for one another.
—Jas. 5:16

Intercessory prayer for one who is sinning prevails. God says so! The will of the man prayed for does not come into question at all, he is connected with God by prayer, and prayer on the basis of the Redemption sets the connection working and God gives life.
—Oswald Chambers

We should say to God as we mingle with our dear ones each day, "God, give them each Thy blessing. They need it, because they live with me, and I am very selfish and unwilling to sacrifice very much for them, although I do love them."
—O. Hallesby

See to it, night and day, that you pray for your children. Then you will leave them a great legacy of answers to prayer, which will follow them all the days of their life. Then you may calmly and with a good conscience depart from them, even though you may not leave them a great deal of material wealth.
—O. Hallesby

God bless all those that I love; God bless all those that love me; God bless all those that love those that I love and all those that love those that love me.
—*A New England Sampler*

He who prays for his neighbors will be heard for himself.   —Talmud

No one who has had a unique experience with prayer has a right to withhold it from others.
—Soong Mel-Ling

GRATITUDE

Thou who has given so much to me, give one thing more: a grateful heart.
—George Herbert

If the only prayer you say in your whole life is "Thank you," that would suffice.   —Meister Eckhart

Fear of trouble, present and future, often blinds us to the numerous small blessings we enjoy, silencing our prayers of praise and thanksgiving.   —Anon.

For food, for raiment, for life and opportunity, for sun and rain, for water and the portage trails, we give you thanks, O Lord.
   —*A Prayer from the North Woods*

God deserves far more praise than any of us could ever give Him.
   —Anon.

Our Father, let the spirit of gratitude so prevail in our hearts that we may manifest thy Spirit in our lives.
   —W.B. Slack

A sensible thanksgiving for mercies received is a mighty prayer in the Spirit of God. It prevails with Him unspeakably.   —John Bunyan

Pray without ceasing. In everything give thanks.
   —1 Th. 5:17

God receives little thanks, even for his greatest gifts.   —Anon.

It is not only blessed to give thanks; it is also of vital importance to our prayer life in general. If we have noted the Lord's answers to our prayers and thanked Him for what we have received of Him, then it becomes easier for us, and we get more courage, to pray for more.
   —O. Hallesby

To stand on one leg and prove God's existence is a very different thing from going down on one's knees and thanking him.   —Søren Kierkegaard

Our thanks to God should always precede our requests.   —Anon.

Jesus is moved to happiness every time He sees that you appreciate what He has done for you. Grip His pierced hand and say to Him, "I thank Thee, Savior, because Thou hast died for me." Thank Him likewise for all the other blessings He has showered upon you from day to day. It brings joy to Jesus.
   —O. Hallesby

Let us thank God heartily as often as we pray that we have His Spirit in us to teach us to pray. Thanksgiving will draw our hearts out to God and keep us engaged with Him; it will take our attention from ourselves and give the Spirit room in our hearts.   —Andrew Murray

Let us come before his presence with thanksgiving.   —Ps. 95:2

When we succeed in truly thanking God, we feel good at heart. The reason is that we have been created to give glory to God, now and forevermore. And every time we do so, we feel that we are in harmony with His plans and purposes for our lives. Then we are truly in our element. That is why it is so blessed.
   —O. Hallesby

ENTHUSIASTIC PRAYING

Don't be timid when you pray; rather, batter the very gates of heaven with storms of prayer.   —Anon.

How those holy men of old could storm the battlements above! When there was no way to look but up, they lifted up their eyes to God who made the hills, with unshakable confidence. —Herbert Lockyer

We must wrestle earnestly in prayer, like men contending with a deadly enemy for life. —J.C. Ryle

We may as well not pray at all as offer our prayers in a lifeless manner. —William S. Plumer

Look, as a painted man is no man, and as painted fire is no fire, so a cold prayer is no prayer.
—Thomas B. Brooks

Productive prayer requires earnestness, not eloquence. —Anon.

There must be fired affections before our prayers will go up.
—William Jenkyn

Cold prayers shall never have any warm answers. —Thomas B. Brooks

There is neither encouragement nor room in Bible religion for feeble desires, listless efforts, lazy attitudes; all must be strenuous, urgent, ardent. Flamed desires, impassioned, unwearied insistence delight heaven. God would have His children incorrigibly in earnest and persistently bold in their efforts. Heaven is too busy to listen to half-hearted prayers or to respond to pop-calls. Our whole being must be in our praying.
—E.M. Bounds

To say prayers in a decent, delicate way is not heavy work. But to pray really, to pray till hell feels the ponderous stroke, to pray till the iron gates of difficulty are opened, till the mountains of obstacles are removed, till the mists are exhaled and the clouds are lifted, and the sunshine of a cloudless day brightens—this is hard work, but it is God's work, and man's best labor. —E.M. Bounds

Importunity is a condition of prayer. We are to press the matter, not with vain repetitions, but with urgent repetitions. We repeat, not to count the times, but to gain the prayer. We cannot quit praying because heart and soul are in it. We pray "with all perseverance." We hang to our prayers because by them we live. We press our pleas because we must have them, or die. —E.M. Bounds

It is only when the whole heart is gripped with the passion of prayer that the life-giving fire descends, for none but the earnest man gets access to the ear of God. —E.M. Bounds

The effectual, fervent prayer of a righteous man availeth much.
—Jas. 5:16

From silly devotions and from sour-faced saints, good Lord, deliver us.
—Saint Teresa of Avila

Let me burn out for God ... prayer is the great thing. Oh, that I may be a man of prayer! —Henry Martyn

Bear up the hands that hang down, by faith and prayer; support the tottering knees. Storm the throne of grace and persevere therein, and mercy will come down.
—John Wesley

Do not work so hard for Christ that you have no strength to pray, for prayer requires strength.
——J. Hudson Taylor

Jesus taught that perseverance is the essential element of prayer. Men must be in earnest when they kneel at God's footstool. Too often we get faint-hearted and quit praying at the point where we ought to begin. We let go at the very point where we should hold on strongest. Our prayers are weak because they are not impassioned by an unfailing and resistless will.　——E.M. Bounds

In Fellowship; alone
To God, with Faith, draw near,
Approach His Courts, besiege His
　　Throne
With all the power of Prayer.
　　　　——Charles Wesley

Things to Pray For

We must move from asking God to take care of the things that are breaking our hearts, to praying about the things that are breaking *His* heart.　——Margaret Gibb

We cannot ask in behalf of Christ what Christ would not ask Himself if He were praying.　——A.B. Simpson

Thou who has given so much to me, give one thing more: a grateful heart.
　　　　——George Herbert

We should pray for a sane mind in a sound body.　——Juvenal

We do pray for mercy, and that same prayer doth teach us all to render the deeds of mercy.
　　　　——William Shakespeare

Our prayers should be for blessings in general, for God knows best what is good for us.　——Socrates

Not what we wish, but what we
　need,
Oh! let your grace supply,
The good unasked, in mercy grant;
The ill, though asked, deny.
　　　　——James Merrik

For we know not what we should pray for.　——Rom. 8:26

If we are to pray aright, perhaps it is quite necessary that we pray contrary to our own heart. Not what we want to pray is important, but what God wants us to pray. The richness of the Word of God ought to determine our prayer, not the poverty of our heart.　——Dietrich Bonhoeffer

O Lord, help me not to despise or oppose what I do not understand.
　　　　——William Penn

We are going home to many who cannot read. So, Lord, make us to be Bibles so that those who cannot read the Book can read it in us.
　　　　——Anonymous Chinese woman

Lord, take my lips and speak through them; take my mind and think through it; take my heart and set it on fire.　——W.H. Aitken

God's promises are to be our pleas in prayer.　——Matthew Henry

Help me to work and pray,
Help me to live each day,
That all I do may say,
Thy kingdom come.
　　　　——A.B. Simpson

We must pray for more prayer, for it is the world's mightiest healing force.   —Frank C. Laubach

Just pray for a tough hide and a tender heart.   —Ruth Graham

O Lord, let me not live to be useless!
               —Bishop John de Stratford

Humbly asked Him to remove our shortcomings.   —*Twelve Steps and Twelve Traditions*

God give me work, till my life shall end
And life, till my work is done.
               —Winifred Holtby's epitaph

The whole meaning of prayer is that we may know God.
               —Oswald Chambers

Watch your motive before God; have no other motive in prayer than to know Him.   —Oswald Chambers

Pray a little each day in a childlike way for the Spirit of prayer. If you feel that you know, as yet, very little concerning the deep things of prayer and what prayer really is, then pray for the Spirit of prayer. There is nothing He would rather do than unveil to you the grace of prayer.
               —O. Hallesby

God does not exist to answer our prayers, but by our prayers we come to discern the mind of God.
               —Oswald Chambers

I sit beside my lonely fire and pray for wisdom yet: for calmness to remember or courage to forget.
               —Charles Hamilton Aide

Give us Lord, a bit o'sun,
A bit o'work, and a bit o'fun;
Give us all, in the struggle and sputter
Our daily bread and a bit o'butter.
               —On an old inn, Lancaster, England

When we in prayer seek only the glorification of the name of God, then we are in complete harmony with the spirit of prayer. Then our hearts are at rest both while we pray and after we have prayed. Then we can wait for the Lord.   —O. Hallesby

Grant that we may not so much seek to be understood as to understand.
               —Saint Francis of Assisi

The first petition that we are to make to Almighty God is for a good conscience, the next for health of mind, and then of body.
               —Lucius Annaeius Seneca

Grant me the courage not to give up, even though I think it is hopeless.
               —Admiral Chester W. Nimitz

Prayer for worldly goods is worse than fruitless, but prayer for strength of soul is that passion of the soul which catches the gift it seeks.
               —George Meredith

WE SHOULD PRAY TO DO GOD'S WILL

The purpose of prayer is not to inform God of our needs, but to invite Him to rule our lives.
               —Clarence Bauman

[P]raying only for knowledge of His will for us and the power to carry that out.   —*Twelve Steps and Twelve Traditions*

147

Don't pray to escape trouble. Don't pray to be comfortable in your emotions. Pray to do the will of God in every situation. Nothing else is worth praying for.
—Samuel M. Shoemaker

O Lord, forgive what I have been, sanctify what I am, and order what I shall be. —Anon.

We had not even prayed rightly. We had always said, "Grant me my wishes" instead of "Thy will be done." —*Twelve Steps and Twelve Traditions*

O Lord, you know what is best for me. Let this or that be done, as you please. Give what you will, how much you will, and when you will.
—Thomas a'Kempis

Spread out your petition before God, and then say, "Thy will, not mine, be done." The sweetest lesson I have learned in God's school is to let the Lord choose for me.
—Dwight L. Moody

Show me your ways, O Lord, teach me your paths; guide me in your truth and teach me, for you are God my Savior, and my hope is in you all day long. —Psalms

The possibilities of prayer are found in its allying itself with the purposes of God, for God's purposes and man's praying are the combination of all potent and omnipotent forces.
—E.M. Bounds

If we ask anything according to his will, he heareth us.
—1 Jn. 5:14

I would have no desire other than to accomplish thy will. Teach me to pray; pray thyself in me.
—Francois de Fenelon

True prayer brings a person's will into accordance with God's will, not the other way around. —Anon.

Do not forget that prayer is ordained for the purpose of glorifying the name of God. Therefore, whether you pray for big things or for little things, say to God, "If it will glorify Thy name, then grant my prayer and help me." —O. Hallesby

It is only when we pray for something according to the will of God that we have the promise of being heard and answered. —O. Hallesby

I used to pray that God would do this or that; now I pray that God will make His will known to me.
—Madame Chiang Kai-Shek

PRAYING FOR HELP IN BECOMING BETTER PEOPLE

How many of us will ever sit ... bow our heads, and pray "Lord, show me where I'm wrong"? —Anon.

A Chinese Christian prayed every day ... "Lord, reform Thy world, beginning with me."
—Franklin Delano Roosevelt

Create in me a clean heart, O God.
—Ps. 51:10

WE SHOULDN'T PRAY FOR THE END OF PROBLEMS, BUT FOR THE ABILITY TO HANDLE THEM

Do not pray for easy lives, pray to be

stronger men. Do not pray for tasks equal to your powers, pray for powers equal to your tasks.
—Phillips Brooks

Pray not for lighter burdens, but for stronger backs.
—Theodore Roosevelt

The wise man in the storm prays God not for safety from danger, but for deliverance from fear.
—Ralph Waldo Emerson

It is quite useless knocking at the door of heaven for earthly comfort. It's not the sort of comfort they supply there.
—C.S. Lewis

TURNING THINGS OVER THROUGH PRAYER

We lie to God in prayer if we do not rely on him afterwards.
—Robert Leighton

Prayer covers the whole of man's life. There is no thought, feeling, yearning, or desire, however low, trifling, or vulgar we may deem it, which if it affects our real interest or happiness, we may not lay before God and be sure of sympathy. His nature is such that our often coming does not tire him. The whole burden of the whole life of every man may be rolled on to God and not weary him, though it has wearied man.
—Henry Ward Beecher

What a friend we have in Jesus,
All our sins and griefs to bear!
What a privilege to carry
Everything to God in Prayer!

Have we trials and temptations?
Is there trouble anywhere?

We should never be discouraged,
Take it to the Lord in prayer.

Are we weak and heavy laden,
Cumbered with a load of care?
Precious Savior, still our refuge,
Take it to the Lord in prayer.

O what peace we often forfeit,
O what needless pain we bear,
All because we do not carry
Everything to God in prayer!
—Joseph Scriven

Take my will, and make it Thine,
It shall be no longer mine;
Take my heart, it is Thine own;
It shall be Thy royal throne.
—Frances Ridley Havergal

And since He bids me seek His face,
Believe His word and trust His grace,
I'll cast on Him my every care,
And wait for thee, sweet hour of prayer.
—W.W. Walford

Prayer puts God's work in his hands—and keeps it there.
—E.M. Bounds

I know not by what methods rare,
But this I know: God answers prayer.
I know not if the blessing sought
Will come in just the guise I thought.
I leave my prayer to Him alone
Whose will is wiser than my own.
—Eliza M. Hickok

Do not want things to turn out as they seem best to you, but as God pleases. Then you will be free from confusion, and thankful in prayer.
—The Desert Fathers

O Lord, you know what is best for

me. Let this or that be done, as you please. Give what you will, how much you will, and when you will.
—Thomas a'Kempis

Spread out your petition before God, and then say, "Thy will, not mine, be done." The sweetest lesson I have learned in God's school is to let the Lord choose for me.
—Dwight L. Moody

Do not strive in your own strength; cast yourself at the feet of the Lord Jesus, and wait upon Him in the sure confidence that He is with you, and works in you. Strive in prayer; let faith fill your heart—so will you be strong in the Lord, and in the power of His might.   —Andrew Murray

A humble and contrite heart knows that it can merit nothing before God, and that all that is necessary is to be reconciled to one's helplessness and let our holy and almighty God care for us, just as an infant surrenders himself to his mother's care.
—O. Hallesby

We need to learn to know Him so well that we feel safe when we have left our difficulties with Him. To know Jesus in that way is a prerequisite of all true prayer. —O. Hallesby

The only prayer which a well-meaning man can pray is, O ye gods, give me whatever is fitting unto me!
—Appollonius of Tyana

Our prayer life will become restful when it really dawns upon us that we have done all we are supposed to do when we have spoken to Him about it. From the moment we have

left it with Him, it is His responsibility.   —O. Hallesby

Cast thy burden upon the Lord, and he shall sustain thee.
—Ps. 55:22

Casting all your care upon Him; for he careth for you.
—1 Pt. 5:7

This is what I found out about religion: It gives you courage to make decisions you must make in a crisis, and then the confidence to leave the result to a Higher Power. Only by trust in God can a man carrying responsibility find repose.
—Dwight D. Eisenhower

God tells us to burden him with whatever burdens us.   —Anon.

Do what you can and pray for what you cannot yet do.
—Saint Augustine

Before we can pray, "Lord, Thy Kingdom come," we must be willing to pray, "My Kingdom go."
—Alan Redpath

PRAYER AND FORGIVENESS
No prayers can be heard which do not come from a forgiving heart.
—J.C. Ryle

I firmly believe a great many prayers are not answered because we are not willing to forgive someone.
—Dwight L. Moody

When you pray for anyone, you tend to modify your personal attitude toward him.
—Norman Vincent Peale

When my children do wrong, I ache to hear their stumbling requests for forgiveness. I'm sure our heavenly Father aches even more deeply to hear from us. —Anon.

There is nothing that makes us love a man so much as praying for him. —William Law

WE MUST PRAY, BUT WE MUST ALSO WORK, AND HELP OURSELVES

Ask God's blessing on your work, but don't ask him to do it for you. —Dame Flora Robson

Prayer indeed is good, but while calling on the gods, a man should himself lend a hand. —Hippocrates

Prayer, among sane people, has never superseded practical efforts to secure the desired end. —George Santayana

It is vain to expect our prayers to be heard if we do not strive as well as pray. —Aesop

He who labors as he prays lifts his heart to God with his hands. —Bernard of Clairvaux

Pray as if everything depended on God, and work as if everything depended upon man. —Archbishop Francis J. Spellman

Work as if everything depended upon work and pray as if everything depended upon prayer. —William Booth

Help yourself and heaven will help you. —Jean de La Fontaine

Work as if you were to live one hundred years; pray as if you were to die tomorrow. —Benjamin Franklin

God helps those who help themselves. —German proverb

God help those who do not help themselves. —Wilson Mizner

God gives the nuts, but he does not crack them. —German proverb

God gives every bird its food, but he does not throw it into the nest. —Josiah Holland

Pray devoutly, but hammer stoutly. —Sir William Gurney Benham

The Ancient Mariner said to Neptune during a great storm, "O God, you will save me if you wish, but I am going to go on holding my tiller straight." —Michel de Montaigne

Pray to God, but keep rowing to shore. —Russian proverb

Trust in Allah, but tie your camel first. —Arabic proverb

Call on God, but row away from the rocks. —Indian proverb

To the man who himself strives earnestly, God also lends a helping hand. —Aeschylus

It is vain to ask of the gods what man is capable of supplying for himself. —Epicurus

Heaven ne'er helps the men who will not act. —Sophocles

To give pleasure to a single heart by a single kind act is better than a thousand head-bowings in prayer.
—Sa'Di

Always look for ways to act upon the faith you display in your prayers.
—Anon.

You can do more than pray after you have prayed, but you cannot do more than pray *until* you have prayed.   —A.J. Gordon

There is a time for all things; a time to preach and a time to pray, but those times have passed away; there is a time to fight, *and that time has come!* —General Peter Muhlenberg

Prayer is often a temptation to bank on a miracle of God instead of on a moral issue, i.e., it is much easier to ask God to do my work than it is to do it myself. Until we are disciplined properly, we will always be inclined to bank on God's miracles and refuse to do the moral thing ourselves. It is our job, and it will never be done unless we do it.
—Oswald Chambers

Visualize, "prayerize," "actionize," and your wishes will come true.
—Charles L. Allen

Some Responses to, and Rewards of, Praying

Some people think that prayer just means asking for things, and if they fail to receive exactly what they asked for, they think the whole thing is a fraud.   —Gerald Vann

Real prayer seeks an audience and an answer.   —William S. Plumer

There are three answers to prayer: yes, no, and wait awhile. It must be recognized that no is an answer.
—Ruth Stafford Peale

There are four ways God answers prayer: No, not yet; No, I love you too much; Yes, I thought you'd never ask; Yes, and here's more.
—Anne Lewis

No answer to prayer is an indication of our merit; every answer to prayer is an indication of God's mercy.
—John Blanchard

God answers all true prayer, either in kind or in kindness.
—Adoniram Judson

God is not a cosmic bellboy for whom we can press a button to get things. —Harry Emerson Fosdick

More things are wrought by prayer than this world dreams of.
—Alfred, Lord Tennyson

When I have a problem I pray about it, and what comes to mind and stays there I assume to be my answer. And this has been right so often that I know it is God's answer.
—J.L. Kraft

Whenever the insistence is on the point that God answers prayer, we are off the track. The meaning of prayer is that we get hold of God, not of the answer.
—Oswald Chambers

I think Christians fail so often to get answers to their prayers because they do not wait long enough on God. They just drop down and say a few words, and then jump up and forget it and expect God to answer them. Such praying always reminds me of the small boy ringing his neighbor's door-bell, and then running away as fast as he can go.   —E.M. Bounds

Our understanding of God is the answer to prayer; getting things from God is God's indulgence of us. When God stops giving us things, He brings us into the place where we can begin to understand Him.
—Oswald Chambers

If God sees that my spiritual life will be furthered by giving the things for which I ask, then He will give them, but that is not the end of prayer. The end of prayer is that I come to know God Himself.   —Oswald Chambers

You say, "But He has not answered." He has, He is so near to you that His silence is the answer. His silence is big with terrific meaning that you cannot understand yet, but presently you will.
—Oswald Chambers

When we pray "in the Name of Jesus" the answers are in accordance with His nature, and if we think our prayers are unanswered it is because we are not interpreting the answer along this line.   —Oswald Chambers

God's silences are His answers. If we only take as answers those that are visible to our senses, we are in a very elementary condition of grace.
—Oswald Chambers

When I pray, coincidences happen, and when I don't, they don't.
—William Temple

Who rises from prayer a better man, his prayer is answered.
—George Meredith

The great tragedy of life is not unanswered prayer, but *unoffered* prayer.
—F.B. Meyer

God has editing rights over our prayers. He will ... edit them, correct them, bring them in line with His will and then hand them back to us to be resubmitted.   —Stephen Crotts

My prayers, my God, flow from what I am not; I think Thy answers make me what I am.
—George MacDonald

The greatest blessing of prayer is not receiving the answer, but being the kind of person God can trust with His answer.   —Anon.

God answers prayer with certainty. Wish fulfillment is something else.
—Anon.

A generous prayer is never presented in vain; the petition may be refused, but the petitioner is always, I believe, rewarded by some gracious visitation.   —Robert Louis Stevenson

Our prayers are often filled with self-ish "wants"; God always answers with what we need.   —Anon.

We ought not to tolerate for a minute the ghastly and grievous thought that God will not answer prayer. —Charles Haddon Spurgeon

I tremble for my country when I reflect that God is just.
—Thomas Jefferson

The answer of our prayers is secured by the fact that in rejecting them God would in a certain sense deny His own nature.　　—John Calvin

There are two main pitfalls on the road to mastery of the art of prayer. If a person gets what he asks for, his humility is in danger. If he fails to get what he asks for, he is apt to lose confidence. Indeed, no matter whether prayer seems to be succeeding or failing, humility and confidence are two virtues which are absolutely essential.
　　　　　　—A Trappist Monk

If we be empty and poor, it is not because God's hand is straitened, but ours is not opened.
　　　　　　—Thomas Manton

I firmly believe a great many prayers are not answered because we are not willing to forgive someone.
　　　　　　—Dwight L. Moody

I know not by what methods rare,
But this I know: God answers
　　prayer.
I know not if the blessing sought
Will come in just the guise I thought.
I leave my prayer to Him alone
Whose will is wiser than my own.
　　　　　　—Eliza M. Hickok

God delays, but doesn't forget.
　　　　　　—Spanish proverb

Though I am weak, yet God, when
　　prayed,
Cannot withhold his conquering aid.
　　　　—Ralph Waldo Emerson

Beyond our utmost wants
His love and power can bless;

To praying souls he always grants
More than they can express.
　　　　　　—John Newton

Whatever things ye desire, when ye pray, believe that you receive them, and ye shall have them.
　　　　　　—Mk. 11:24

Never was a faithful prayer lost. Some prayers have a longer voyage than others, but then they return with their richer lading at last, so that the praying soul is a gainer by waiting for an answer.
　　　　　　—William Gurnall

In Gethsemane the holiest of all petitioners prayed three times that a certain cup might pass from Him. It did not. After that the idea that prayer is recommended to us as a sort of infallible gimmick may be dismissed.
　　　　　　—C.S. Lewis

Sometimes ... God answers our prayers in the way our parents do, who reply to the pleas of their children with "Not just now" or "I'll have to think about that for a little while."　　　　—Roy M. Pearson

The firmament of the Bible is ablaze with answers to prayer.
　　　　　　—T.L. Cuyler

Answered prayers cover the field of providential history as flowers cover western prairies.　　—T.L. Cuyler

God answers sharp and sudden on
　　some prayers,
And thrusts the thing we have
　　prayed for in our face.
A gauntlet with a gift in't.
　　　—Elizabeth Barrett Browning

154

Our prayers run along one road and God's answers by another, and by and by they meet.

—Adoniram Judson

Asking for anything is allowed with the understanding that God's answers come from God's perspective. They are not always in harmony with our expectations, for only He knows the whole story.

—Anon.

May the Lord answer you when you are in distress; May the name of the God of Jacob protect you, May he send you help from the sanctuary and grant you support from Zion.

—Psalms

Just when I need Him, He is my all, Answering when upon Him I call; Tenderly watching lest I should fall.

—William Poole

The king shall joy in thy strength, O Lord; and in thy salvation how greatly shall he rejoice! Thou hast given him his heart's desire, and hast not withheld the request of his lips.

—Ps. 21:1–2

In seasons of distress and grief, My soul has often found relief, And oft escaped the tempter's snare, By thy return, sweet hour of prayer.

—W.W. Walford

Those who trade with heaven by prayer grow rich by quick returns.

—William S. Plumer

The great thing in prayer is to feel that we are putting our supplications into the bosom of omnipotent love.

—Andrew Murray

God's chief gift to those who seek him is Himself.   —E.B. Pusey

Amazing things start happening when we start praying!   —Anon.

When you go to your knees, God will help you stand up to anything.

—Anon.

It is impossible to lose your footing while on your knees.   —Anon.

Prayer has marked the trees across the wilderness of a skeptical world to direct the traveler in distress, and all paths lead to a single light.

—Douglas Meador

Prayer enlarges the heart until it is capable of containing God's gift of Himself.   —Mother Teresa

The man who prays grows, and the muscles of the soul swell from this whipcord to iron bands.

—F.B. Meyer

Prayer opens our eyes that we may see ourselves and others as God sees us.   —Clara Palmer

The essence of prayer, even of a mystical experience, is the way we are altered to see everything from its life-filled dimension.   —Matthew Fox

The exercise of prayer, in those who habitually exert it, must be regarded by us doctors as the most adequate and normal of all the pacifiers of the mind and calmers of the nerves.

—William James

The influence of prayer on the human mind and body ... can be

measured in terms of increased physical buoyancy, greater intellectual vigor, moral stamina, and a deeper understanding of the realities underlying human relationships.
—Dr. Alexis Carrel

Prayer puts God's work in His hands—and keeps it there.
—E.M. Bounds

Prayer is a kind of calling home every day. And there can come to you a serenity, a feeling of at-homeness in God's universe, a peace that the world can neither give nor disturb, a fresh courage, a new insight, a holy boldness that you'll never, never get any other way.
—Earl G. Hunt, Jr.

Pray because you have a Father, not because it quietens you, and give Him time to answer.
—Oswald Chambers

Perhaps one of the greatest rewards of meditation and prayer is the sense of belonging that comes to us.
—Bill W.

We impoverish God in our minds when we say there must be answers to our prayers on the material plane; the biggest answers to our prayers are in the realm of the unseen.
—Oswald Chambers

If a door slams shut it means that God is pointing to an open door further on down. —Anna Delaney Peale

Our Lord never referred to unanswered prayer; he taught that prayers are always answered. He ever implied that prayers were answered rightly because of the Heavenly Father's wisdom.
—Oswald Chambers

As white snow flakes fall quietly and thickly on a winter day, answers to prayer will settle down upon you at every step you take, even to your dying day. The story of your life will be the story of prayer and answers to prayer.
—O. Hallesby

God is a rich and bountiful Father, and He does not forget His children, nor withhold from them anything which it would be to their advantage to receive.
—J.K. Maclean

Just as an earthly father knows what is best for his children's welfare, so does God take into consideration the particular needs of His human family, and meets them out of His wonderful storehouse.
—J.K. Maclean

Prayer brings a good spirit in our homes. For God hears prayer. Heaven itself would come down to our homes. And even though we who constitute the home all have our imperfections and our failings, our home would, through God's answer to prayer, become a little paradise.
—O. Hallesby

God's willingness to answer our prayers exceeds our willingness to give good and necessary things to our children, just as far as God's ability, goodness and perfection exceed our infirmities and evil.
—E.M. Bounds

It is hard to wait and press and pray, and hear no voice, but stay till God answers.
—E.M. Bounds

The greatest answer to prayer is that I am brought into a perfect understanding with God, and that alters my view of actual things.
—Oswald Chambers

God's "nothings" are His most positive answers. We have to stay on God and wait. Never try to help God to fulfill His word.
—Oswald Chambers

The shower of answers to your prayers will continue to your dying hour. Nor will it cease then. When you pass out from beneath the shower, your dear ones will step into it. Every prayer and every sigh which you have uttered for them and their future welfare will, in God's time, descend upon them as a gentle rain of answers to prayer. —O. Hallesby

If we will make use of prayer to call down upon ourselves and others those things which will glorify the name of God, then we shall see the strongest and boldest promises of the Bible about prayer fulfilled. Then we shall see such answers to prayer as we had never thought were possible.
—O. Hallesby

Let it be your business every day, in the secrecy of the inner chamber, to meet the holy God. You will be repaid for the trouble it may cost you. The reward will be sure and rich. —Andrew Murray

One great effect of prayer is that it enables the soul to command the body. By obedience I make my body submissive to my soul, but prayer puts my soul in command of my body. —Oswald Chambers

Prayer, like faith, obtains promises, enlarges their operation, and adds to the measure of their results.
—E.M. Bounds

Prayer is the easiest and hardest of all things; the simplest and the sublimest; the weakest and the most powerful; its results lie outside the range of human possibilities—they are limited only by the omnipotence of God. —E.M. Bounds

If we pray for anything according to the will of God, we already have what we pray for the moment we ask it. We do not know exactly when it will arrive; but we have learned to know God through the Spirit of God, and have learned to leave this in His hands, and to live just as happily whether the answer arrives immediately or later.
—O. Hallesby

It is God's will not only to hear our prayer, but to give us the best and the richest answer which He, the almighty and omniscient God, can devise. He will send us the answer when it will benefit us and His cause the most. —O. Hallesby

If God does not give you something you ask for, wait on Him. He will speak with you tenderly and sympathetically about the matter until you yourself understand that He cannot grant your prayer. —O. Hallesby

Be sure to remember that nothing in your daily life is so insignificant and so inconsequential that the Lord will not help you by answering your prayer. —O. Hallesby

The potency of prayer hath subdued the strength of fire; it hath bridled the rage of lions, hushed anarchy to rest, extinguished wars, appeased the elements, expelled demons, burst the chains of death, expanded the gates of heaven, assuaged diseases, repelled frauds, rescued cities from destruction, stayed the sun in its course, and arrested the progress of the thunderbolt.

—Saint John Chrysostom

It's Often a Blessing That We Don't Get What We Pray for

More tears are shed over answered prayers than unanswered ones.

—Saint Teresa of Avila

True prayer always receives what it asks for—or something better.

—Bryon Edwards

Be thankful that God's answers are wiser than your answers.

—William Culbertson

God punishes us mildly by ignoring our prayers, and severely by answering them.   —Richard J. Needham

When the gods wish to punish us, they answer our prayers.

—Oscar Wilde

When the gods are angry with a man, they give him what he asks for.

—Greek proverb

We, ignorant of ourselves, beg often our own harms, which the wise powers deny us for our good.

—William Shakespeare

God alone fully understands what each one of us needs; we make mistakes continually and pray for things which would be harmful to us if we received them. Afterwards we see our mistakes and realize that God is good and wise in not giving us these things, even though we plead ever so earnestly for them.   —O. Hallesby

I have lived to thank God that all my prayers have not been answered.

—Jean Ingelow

Prayer and Faith

Prayer is the supreme activity of all that is noblest in our personality, and the essential nature of prayer is faith.   —Oswald Chambers

Prayer is the voice of faith. —Horne

The prayer that is faithless is fruitless.   —Thomas Watson

A saint is to put forth his faith in prayer, and afterwards follow his prayer with faith. —Vavasor Powell

The prayer of faith is the only power in the universe to which the great Jehovah yields.   —Robert Hall

Prayers are heard in heaven very much in proportion to your faith. Little faith will get very great mercies, but great faith still greater.

—Charles Haddon Spurgeon

The beginning of anxiety is the end of faith, and the beginning of true faith is the end of anxiety.

—George Mueller

Teach me, O God, not to torture myself, not to make a martyr out of myself through stifling reflection, but rather teach me to breathe deeply in faith.   —Søren Kierkegaard

Faith is the fountain of prayer, and prayer should be nothing else but faith exercised.   —Thomas Manton

Without faith it is impossible to please God, for he that cometh to God must believe that He is.
—Heb. 11:6

Connecting to God through Prayer

Jesus Christ is a God whom we approach without pride, and before whom we humble ourselves without despair.   —Blaise Pascal

It is in recognizing the actual presence of God that we find prayer no longer a chore, but a supreme delight.   —Gordon Lindsay

Essentially prayer is based on a relationship. We don't converse freely with someone we don't know. We bare our souls and disclose our hidden secrets only to someone we trust.   —Dean Register

I who still pray at morning and at
   eve
Thrice in my life perhaps have truly
   prayed,
Thrice stirred below conscious self
Have felt that perfect disenthrall-
   ment which is God.
   —James Russell Lowell

When we pray we link ourselves with an inexhaustible motive power.
   —Dr. Alexis Carrel

Because God is the living God, he can hear; because he is a loving God, he will hear; because he is our covenant God, he has bound himself to hear. —Charles Haddon Spurgeon

Nothing is so blessed as quiet, unbroken communication with our Lord. The sense of the Lord's nearness, which then fills our souls, is greater than any other peace, joy, inner satisfaction, or security which we have known.   —O. Hallesby

We look upon prayer as a means of getting things for ourselves; The Bible idea of prayer is that we may get to know God Himself.
   —Oswald Chambers

A person must recognize his need for God before he can request divine aid and give God due thanks.
   —Anon.

Meditation

Prayer is when you talk to God; meditation is when you listen to God.   —Diana Robinson

When one devotes oneself to meditation, mental burdens, unnecessary worries, and wandering thoughts drop off one by one; life seems to run smoothly and pleasantly.
   —Nyogen Senzaki

But first of all we shall want sunlight; nothing much can grow in the dark. Meditation is our step out into the sun.   —*As Bill Sees It*

We must hear Jesus speak if we expect him to hear us speak.
   —Charles Haddon Spurgeon

You are used to listening to the buzz of the world, but now is the time to develop the inner ear that listens to the inner world. It is time to have a foot in each world, and it can be done.   —Saint Bartholomew

Meditation is a mental discipline that enables us to do one thing at a time. —Max Picard

The very best and utmost of attainment in this life is to remain still and let God act and speak in thee.
—Meister Eckhart

All the troubles of life come upon us because we refuse to sit quietly for awhile each day in our rooms.
—Blaise Pascal

It is necessary for us to withdraw at regular intervals and enable our souls to attain that quietude and inward composure which are essential if we would hear the voice of God. —O. Hallesby

The quiet hour of prayer is one of the most favorable opportunities He has in which to speak to us seriously. In quietude and solitude before the face of God our souls can hear better than at any other time.
—O. Hallesby

OTHER DEFINITIONS OF PRAYER

Prayer is man's greatest means of trapping the infinite resources of God. —J. Edgar Hoover

Prayer is the simplest form of speech
That infant lips can try;
Prayer the sublimest strains that reach
The Majesty on high.
—James Montgomery

Prayer is the soul's sincere desire,
Uttered, or unexpressed;
The motion of a hidden fire
That trembles in the breast.
—James Montgomery

Prayer is the heavenly telephone that brings the distant near, till heaven to earth comes down. —A.B. Simpson

Prayer is conversation with God.
—Clement of Alexandria

Prayer is invoking the impossible.
—Jack W. Hayford

Prayer is the golden key that opens heaven. —Thomas Watson

Prayer is the key that opens the door to all that is good in life.
—Anon.

Prayer is and remains always a native and deepest impulse of the soul of man. —Thomas Carlyle

Prayer is essentially man standing before his God in wonder, awe, and humility; man, made in the image of God, responding to his maker.
—George Appleton

Prayer is the language of a man burdened with a sense of need.
—E.M. Bounds

Prayer is the incense of a holy heart
Rising to God from bruised and broken things,
When kindled by the Spirit's burning breath
And upward borne by faith's ascending wings. —A.B. Simpson

Prayer is a strong wall and fortress of the church; it is a goodly Christian's weapon.
—Martin Luther

Prayer is a sincere, sensible, affectionate pouring out of the soul to

God, through Christ, in the strength and assistance of the Spirit, for such things as God has promised.
—John Bunyan

For prayer is not a ritual; it is the soul's inherent response to a relationship with a loving Father.
—Colleen Townsend Evans

Prayer is the sovereign remedy.
—Robert Hall

Prayer, even more than sheer thought, is the firmest anchor.
—Jeremiah A. Denton, Jr.

Prayer is our humble answer to the inconceivable surprise of living.
—Abraham Heschel

Prayer is not conquering God's reluctance, but taking hold of God's willingness. —Phillips Brooks

Prayers are the leeches of care.
—Anon.

Prayer is the soul's breathing itself into the bosom of its heavenly Father. —Thomas Watson

Prayer is a shield to the soul, a sacrifice to God, and a scourge for Satan.
—John Bunyan

Prayer is the spiritual gymnasium in which we exercise and practice godliness. —V.L. Crawford

Prayer is exhaling the spirit of man and inhaling the spirit of God.
—Edwin Keith

Prayer is the spirit speaking truth to Truth. —Philip James Bailey

Prayer is communion with God, usually comprising petition, adoration, praise, confession, and thanksgiving.
—International Standard Bible Encyclopedia

Prayer serves as an edge and border to preserve the web of life from unraveling. —Robert Hall

Prayer is the ascending vapor which supplies
The showers of blessing, and the stream that flows
Through earth's dry places, till on every side
"The wilderness shall blossom as the rose." —A.B. Simpson

Prayer is the acid test of devotion.
—Samuel Chadwick

Prayer is a rising up and a drawing near to God in mind and in heart, and in spirit. —Alexander Whyte

Prayer means that we have come boldly into the throne room and we are standing in His presence.
—E.W. Kenyon

Prayer is the pillow of religion.
—Arab proverb

To labor is to pray. —Motto of the Benedictine Order

Prayer is the contemplation of the facts of life from the highest point of view. —Ralph Waldo Emerson

Prayer does not mean simply to pour out one's heart. It means rather to find the way to God and to speak with him, whether the heart is full or empty. —Dietrich Bonhoeffer

161

Prayer is our most formidable weapon, the thing which makes all else we do efficient.   —E.M. Bounds

Prayer is not logical, it is a mysterious moral working of the Holy Spirit.   —Oswald Chambers

Prayer should be the means by which I, at all times, receive all that I need, and, for this reason, be my daily refuge, my daily consolation, my daily joy, my source of rich and inexhaustible joy in life.
          —Saint John Chrysostom

Prayer is a cry of distress, a demand for help, a hymn of love.
          —Dr. Alexis Carrel

Prayer, in its simplest definition, is merely a wish turned God-ward.
          —Phillips Brooks

Prayer is the evidence that I am spiritually concentrated on God.
          —Oswald Chambers

Prayer is God's answer to our poverty, not a power we exercise to obtain an answer.   —Oswald Chambers

Prayer is a condition of mind, an attitude of heart, which God recognizes as prayer whether it manifests itself in quiet thinking, in sighing or in audible words.   —O. Hallesby

Prayer is an all-efficient panoply, a treasure undiminished, a mine which is never exhausted, a sky unobscured by clouds, a heaven unruffled by the storm. It is the root, the fountain, the mother of a thousand blessings.
          —Saint John Chrystostom

Prayer is not an exercise, it is the life.
          —Oswald Chambers

GENERAL QUOTATIONS ABOUT PRAYER

The prayers of the Christian are secret, but their effect cannot be hidden.   —Howard Chandler Robbins

Man is the only creature which rises by bowing, for he finds elevation in his subjection to his Maker.
          —Anon.

Lord, till I reach that blissful shore,
No privilege so dear shall be
As thus my inmost soul to pour
In prayer to thee. —Charlotte Elliott

If we could all hear one another's prayers, God might be relieved of some of his burden.
          —Ashleigh Brilliant

What I dislike least in my former self are the moments of prayer.
          —André Gide

Revival fires flame where hearts are praying.   —Dick Eastman

Our rages, daughters of despair, creep and squirm like worms. Prayer is the only form of revolt which remains upright.
          —Georges Bernanos

Prayer reaches out in love to a dying world and says, "I care."
          —Dick Eastman

To pray together, in whatever tongue or ritual, is the most tender brotherhood of hope and sympathy that man can contract in this life.
          —Anne Germain De Stael

The deepest wishes of the heart find expression in secret prayer.
—George E. Rees

We are never more like Christ than in prayers of intercession.
—Austin Phelps

The spirit of prayer is the fruit and token of the Spirit of adoption.
—John Newton

If we do not love one another, we certainly shall not have much power with God in prayer.
—Dwight L. Moody

Keep us, Lord, so awake in the duties of our calling that we may sleep in thy peace and wake in thy glory.
—John Donne

I find in the Psalms much the same range of mood and expression as I perceive within my own life of prayer.
—Malcolm Boyd

I am used to praying when I am alone, thank God. But when I come together with other people, when I need more than ever to pray, I still cannot get used to it.
—Leo Tolstoy

I always love to begin a journey on Sundays, because I shall have the prayers of the church to preserve all that travel by land, or by water.
—Jonathan Swift

Nor it is an objection to say that we must understand a prayer if it is to have its true effect. That simply is not the case. Who understands the wisdom of a flower? Yet we can take pleasure in it.
—Rudolph Steiner

At church, with meek and unaffected grace,
His looks adorn'd the venerable place;
Truth from his lips prevail'd with double sway,
And fools who came to scoff, remain'd to pray.
—Oliver Goldsmith

I would rather stand against the cannons of the wicked than against the prayers of the righteous.
—Thomas Lye

Restraining prayer, we cease to fight;
Prayer keeps the Christian's armor bright;
And Satan trembles when he sees
The weakest saint upon his knees.
—William Cowper

Nothing is discussed more and practiced less than prayer.
—Anon.

God dwells where we let God in.
—Menachem Mendel

Saints of the early church reaped great harvests in the field of prayer and found the mercy seat to be a mine of untold treasures.
—Charles Haddon Spurgeon

The wings of prayer carry high and far.
—Anon.

In the calm of sweet communion
Let thy daily work be done;
In the peace of soul-outpouring
Care be banished, patience won;
And if earth with its enchantments
Seek thy spirit to enthrall,
Ere thou listen, ere thou answer,
Turn to Jesus, tell Him all.
—G.M. Taylor

Courage is not afraid to weep, and she is not afraid to pray, even when she is not sure who she is praying to.
—J. Ruth Gendler

God warms his hands at man's heart when he prays. —Masefield

Turn your doubts to question; turn your question to prayers; turn your prayers to God. —Mark R. Litteton

Prayer, like radium, is a luminous and self-generating form of energy.
—Dr. Alexis Carrel

Whatever you do in revenge against your brother will appear all at once in your heart at the time of payer.
—The Desert Fathers

Any concern too small to be turned into a prayer is too small to be made into a burden. —Corrie ten Boom

Never say you will pray about a thing; *pray* about it.
—Oswald Chambers

Doubt not but God who sits on high,
Thy secret prayers can hear;
When a dead wall thus cunningly
Conveys soft whispers to the ear.
—Anon.

The granting of prayer, when offered in the name of Jesus, reveals the Father's love to him, and the honor which he has put upon him.
—Charles Haddon Spurgeon

164

SELF-KNOWLEDGE

THE IMPORTANCE OF KNOWING OURSELVES

Ninety percent of the world's woe comes from people not knowing themselves, their abilities, their frailties, and even their real virtues. Most of us go almost all the way through life as complete strangers to ourselves. —Sydney J. Harris

A man who knows he is a fool is not a great fool. —Chuang-Tse

We should know what our convictions are, and stand for them. Upon one's own philosophy, conscious or unconscious, depends one's ultimate interpretation of facts. Therefore it is wise to be as clear as possible about one's subjective principles. As the man is, so will be his ultimate truth. —Carl Jung

Resolve to be thyself; and know that he who finds himself, loses his misery. —Matthew Arnold

Many men go fishing all of their lives without knowing that it is not fish they are after.
—Henry David Thoreau

It is the individual who knows how little he knows about himself who stands a reasonable chance of finding out something about himself.
—S.I. Hayakawa

To understand is to forgive, even oneself. —Alexander Chase

Knowing others is wisdom, knowing yourself is Enlightenment. —Lao-tzu

The life which is unexamined is not worth living. —Plato

WE CAN'T START TO IMPROVE UNTIL WE KNOW WHO WE ARE

Self-knowledge is the beginning of self-improvement. —Spanish proverb

When a man begins to understand himself, he begins to live.
—Norvin G. McGranahan

A humble knowledge of oneself is a surer road to God than a deep searching of the sciences.
—Thomas a'Kempis

If you do not ask yourself what it is you know, you will go on listening to others and change will not come because you will not hear your own truth.   —Saint Bartholomew

No man remains quite what he was when he recognizes himself.
                              —Thomas Mann

Awakening begins when a man realizes that he is going nowhere and does not know where to go.
                          —Georges Gurdjieff

Self-searching is the means by which we bring new vision, action, and grace to bear upon the dark and negative side of our natures. With it comes the development of that kind of humility that makes it possible for us to receive God's help.... We find that bit by bit we can discard the old life—the one that did not work—for a new life that can and does work under conditions whatever.
                              —As Bill Sees It

It's Not Easy to Know Ourselves

The most difficult thing in life is to know yourself.   —Thales

It is not only the most difficult thing to know oneself, but the most inconvenient, too.   —Josh Billings

He knows the universe and does not know himself. —Jean de La Fontaine

No man ever understands quite his own artful dodges to escape from the grim shadow of self-knowledge.
                          —Joseph Conrad

Nothing is easier than self-deceit.
                          —Demosthenes

One may understand the cosmos, but never the ego; the self is more distant than any star.
                      —G.K. Chesterton

You can live a lifetime and, at the end of it, know more about other people than you know about yourself.   —Beryl Markham

We Must Know Both Our Possibilities and Our Limitations

Learn what you are, and be such.
                              —Pindar

The happy man is he who knows his limitations, yet bows to no false gods.   —Robert W. Service

Sometimes it is more important to discover what one cannot do, than what one can.   —Lin Yutang

Somehow we learn who we really are and then live with that decision.
                      —Eleanor Roosevelt

Self-understanding rather than self-condemnation is the way to inner peace and mature conscience.
                      —Joshua Loth Liebman

It's not our disadvantages or shortcomings that are ridiculous, but rather the studious way we try to hide them, and our desire to act as if they did not exist.
                      —Giacomo Leopardi

Of all the idiots I have met in my life, and the Lord knows that they have not been few or little, I think that I have been the biggest.
                          —Isak Dinesen

The precept, "Know yourself," was not solely intended to obviate the pride of mankind; but likewise that we might understand our own worth. —Cicero

I'm a salami writer. I try to write good salami, but salami is salami.
—Stephen King

GENERAL QUOTATIONS ABOUT SELF-KNOWLEDGE

To know oneself, one should assert oneself. —Albert Camus

Rebellion against your handicaps gets you nowhere. Self-pity gets you nowhere. One must have the adventurous daring to accept oneself as a bundle of possibilities and undertake the most interesting game in the world—making the most of one's best. —Harry Emerson Fosdick

In other living creatures the ignorance of themselves is nature, but in men it is a vice. —Boethius

It is doubtless a vice to turn one's eyes inward too much, but I am my own comedy and tragedy.
—Ralph Waldo Emerson

Many people today don't want honest answers insofar as honest means unpleasant or disturbing. They want a soft answer that turneth away anxiety. —Louis Kronenberger

A single event can awaken within us a stranger totally unknown to us.
—Antoine de Saint-Exupery

There is no disappointment we endure one-half so great as what we are to ourselves.
—Philip James Bailey

167

Self-Acceptance

How We Feel about Ourselves Is More Important Than How Others Feel about Us

I care not so much what I am to others as what I am to myself. I will be rich by myself, and not by borrowing. —Michel de Montaigne

You can succeed if nobody else believes it, but you will never succeed if you don't believe in yourself. —William J.H. Boetcker

Do not attempt to do a thing unless you are sure of yourself, but do not relinquish it simply because someone else is not sure of you. —Stewart E. White

No one can make you feel inferior without your consent. —Eleanor Roosevelt

Every man stamps his value on himself ... man is made great or small by his own will. —J.C.F. von Schiller

Let a man's talents or virtues be what they may, he will only feel satisfaction as he is satisfied in himself. —William Hazlitt

It is not the eyes of others that I am wary of, but my own. —Noel Coward

I ... know what I do, and am unmoved by men's blame, or their praise either. —Robert Browning

Do not let your peace depend on the hearts of men; whatever they say about you, good or bad, you are not because of it another man, for as you are, you are. —Thomas a'Kempis

A man cannot be comfortable without his own approval. —Mark Twain

The worst loneliness is not to be comfortable with yourself. —Mark Twain

Perhaps the most important thing we can undertake toward the reduction of fear is to make it easier for people to accept themselves, to like themselves. —Bonaro Overstreet

I have had more trouble with myself than with any other man. —Dwight L. Moody

What you think about yourself is much more important than what others think of you.
—Marcus Annaeus Seneca

What a man thinks of himself, that is what determines, or rather indicates, his fate.   —Henry David Thoreau

As soon as you trust yourself, you will know how to live.
—Johann von Goethe

WE ARE OUR OWN MOST IMPORTANT SOURCE OF RECOGNITION AND APPRECIATION

He who seeks for applause only from without has all his happiness in another's keeping.
—Oliver Goldsmith

From self alone expect applause.
—Marion L. Burton

You can *enjoy* encouragement coming from outside, but you cannot *need* for it to come from outside.
—Vladimir Zworykin

Do not look for approval except for the consciousness of doing your best.
—Bernard M. Baruch

I was always willing to take a great deal of the burden of getting along in life on my own shoulders, but I wasn't willing to give myself a pat on the back. I was always looking to somebody else to give me that.... That was all wrong.   —Raquel Welch

She lacks confidence, she craves admiration insatiably. She lives on the reflections of herself in the eyes of others. She does not dare to be herself.   —Anaïs Nin

Blessed is he who expects no gratitude, for he shall not be disappointed.   —William Bennett

When you know you are doing your very best within the circumstances of your existence, applaud yourself!
—Rusty Berkus

To accept ourselves as we are means to value our imperfections as much as our perfections.   —Sandra Bierig

I exist as I am, that is enough,
If no other in the world be aware, I sit content,
And if each and all be aware, I sit content.   —Walt Whitman

Not in the shouts and plaudits of the throng, but in ourselves, are triumph and defeat.
—Henry Wadsworth Longfellow

If there are two hundred people in a room and one of them doesn't like me, I've got to get out.
—Marlon Brando

I care not what others think of what I do, but I care very much about what I think of what I do. That is character!   —Theodore Roosevelt

I am somebody. I am me. I like being me. And I need nobody to make me somebody.   —Louis L'Amour

Life, I fancy, would very often be insupportable, but for the luxury of self-compassion.
—George R. Gissing

Spirituality is ... the awareness that survival is the savage fight between you and yourself.   —Anon.

The work praises the man.
                    —Irish proverb

Of all afflictions, the worst is self-contempt.   —Berthold Auerbach

If you must love your neighbor as yourself, it is at least as fair to love yourself as your neighbor.
                    —Nicolas de Chamfort

Believing in our hearts that who we are is enough is the key to a more satisfying and balanced life.
                    —Ellen Sue Stern

WE ARE WHO WE ARE

If God had wanted me otherwise, He would have created me otherwise.
                    —Johann von Goethe

I am what I am, so take me as I am!
                    —Johann von Goethe

Be content with what you are, and wish not change; nor dread your last day, nor long for it.   —Martial

It is the chiefest point of happiness that a man is willing to be what he is.   —Erasmus

Learn what you are and be such.
                    —Pindar

What thou art, that thou art.
                    —Thomas a'Kempis

I is who I is.   —Tom Peterson

People remain what they are, even when their faces fall to pieces.
                    —Bertolt Brecht

You have to deal with the fact that your life is your life.   —Alex Hailey

The search for a new personality is futile; what is fruitful is the interest the old personality can take in new activities.   —Cesare Pavese

IT'S OK TO BE WHOMEVER WE ARE

The courage to be is the courage to accept oneself, in spite of being unacceptable.   —Paul Tillich

Contentment, and indeed usefulness, comes as the infallible result of great acceptances, great humilities—of not trying to conform to some drama-tized version of ourselves.
                    —David Grayson

A man should not strive to eliminate his complexes but to get into accord with them, for they are legitimately what directs his conduct in the world.   —Sigmund Freud

Resolve to be thyself ... he who finds himself loses his misery!
                    —Matthew Arnold

There's a period of life when we swallow a knowledge of ourselves and it becomes either good or sour inside.   —Pearl Bailey

There is always a certain peace in being what one is, in being that com-pletely.   —Ugo Betti

I'm not OK, you're not OK—and that's OK.   —William Sloane Coffin

We will discover the nature of our particular genius when we stop try-ing to conform to our own or to other people's models, learn to be ourselves, and allow our natural channel to open.   —Shakti Gawain

All the discontented people I know are trying to be something they are not, to do something they cannot do.
—David Grayson

It is better to be hated for what you are than loved for what you are not.
—André Gide

Do not wish to be anything but what you are.   —Saint Francis de Sales

Every man must at last accept himself for his portion, and learn to do his work with the tools and talents with which he has been endowed.
—Charles A. Hawley

Of all our infirmities, the most savage is to despise our being.
—Michel de Montaigne

Our entire life ... consists ultimately in accepting ourselves as we are.
—Jean Anouilh

The secret of my success is that at an early age I discovered I was not God.
—Oliver Wendell Holmes, Jr.

To find the good life you must become yourself.   —Dr. Bill Jackson

Man has to live with the body and soul which have fallen to him by chance.   —José Ortega y Gasset

Be content with what you are, and wish not change; nor dread your last day, nor long for it.   —Martial

Change occurs when one becomes what she is, not when she tries to become what she is not.
—Ruth P. Freedman

A man can stand a lot as long as he can stand himself.   —Axel Munthe

HAVING REALISTIC EXPECTATIONS OF OURSELVES

We expect more of ourselves than we have any right to.
—Oliver Wendell Holmes, Jr.

Try as hard as we may for perfection, the net result of our labors is an amazing variety of imperfectness. We are surprised at our own versatility in being able to fail in so many different ways.
—Samuel McChord Crothers

Do not lose courage in considering your own imperfections.
—Saint Francis de Sales

We set up harsh and unkind rules against ourselves. No one is born without faults. That man is best who has fewest.   —Horace

One must not hope to be more than one can be.   —Nicolas de Chamfort

I can't write a book commensurate with Shakespeare, but I can write a book by me.   —Sir Walter Raleigh

I have done what I could do in life, and if I could not do better, I did not deserve it. In vain I have tried to step beyond what bound me.
—Maurice Maeterlinck

The man with insight enough to admit his limitations comes nearest to perfection.   —Johann von Goethe

The one important thing I have learned over the years is the difference between taking one's work seriously and taking one's self seriously. The first is imperative and the second is disastrous. —Margaret Fontey

Growth begins when we start to accept our own weakness.
—Jean Vanier

To dream of the person you would like to be is to waste the person you are. —Anon.

Shall a man go and hang himself because he belongs to the race of pygmies, and not be the biggest pygmy that he can?
—Henry David Thoreau

Of all the young men in America only a few hundred can get into major league baseball, and of these only a handful in a decade can get into the Hall of Fame. So it goes in all human activity.... Some become multimillionaires and chairmen of the board, and some of us must be content to play baseball at company picnics or manage a credit union without pay. —William Feather

At thirty a man should know himself like the palm of his hand, know the exact number of his defects and qualities.... And above all, accept these things. —Albert Camus

You can't make the Duchess of Windsor into Rebecca of Sunnybrook Farm. The facts of life are very stubborn things.
—Cleveland Amory

Learn to ... be what you are, and learn to resign with a good grace all that you are not.
—Henri Frederic Amiel

We cannot all be masters.
—William Shakespeare

No man can climb out beyond the limitations of his own character.
—John Morley

Sometimes it is more important to discover what one cannot do, than what one can do. —Lin Yutang

To do all that one is able to do is to be a man; to do all that one would like to do is to be a god.
—Napoleon Bonaparte

No one is expected to achieve the impossible. —French proverb

A hero is a man who does what he can. —Romain Rolland

It is only fools who keep straining at high C all their lives.
—Charles Dudley Warner

May God ... let me strive for attainable things. —Pindar

Despair is the price one pays for setting himself an impossible aim.
—Graham Greene

We would have to settle for the elegant goal of becoming ourselves.
—William Styron

A great obstacle to happiness is to expect too much happiness.
—Bernard de Fontenelle

I cannot do everything, but still I can do something; and because I cannot do everything, I will not refuse to do something I *can* do.
—Edward Everett Hale

I hope to work, support my children and die quietly without pain.
—Sean Connery

As we advance in life, we learn the limits of our abilities. —J.A. Froud

Striving for excellence motivates you; striving for perfection is demoralizing. —Dr. Harriet Braiker

There is a proper balance between not asking enough of oneself and asking or expecting too much.
—May Sarton

It is enough that I am of value to somebody today. —Hugh Prather

A tomb now suffices him for whom the whole world was not sufficient.
—Epitaph of Alexander the Great

To wish to act like angels while we are still in this world is nothing but folly. —Saint Teresa of Avila

It isn't important to come out on top, what matters is to be the one who comes out alive.
—Bertolt Brecht

I long to accomplish a great and noble task, but it my chief duty to accomplish small tasks as if they were great and noble. —Helen Keller

SELF-ACCEPTANCE IS CRITICAL TO OUR RELATIONS WITH OTHER PEOPLE

Those people who are uncomfortable in themselves are disagreeable to others. —William Hazlitt

To love others, we must first learn to love ourselves. —Anon.

Friendship with oneself is all-important, because without it one cannot be friends with anyone else.
—Eleanor Roosevelt

How I relate to my inner self influences my relationships with all others. My satisfaction with myself and my satisfaction with other people are directly proportional.
—Sue Atchley Ebaugh

If you want to be respected by others, the great thing is to respect yourself. —Fyodor Dostoyevsky

If one is cruel to himself, how can we expect him to be compassionate with others? —Hasdai Ibn Shaprut

There is overwhelming evidence that the higher the level of self-esteem, the more likely one will treat others with respect, kindness, and generosity. People who do not experience self-love have little or no capacity to love others. —Nathaniel Branden

Let a man's talents or virtues be what they may, he will only feel satisfaction in his society as he is satisfied in himself. —William Hazlitt

Interest in the lives of others, the high evaluation of these lives, what are they but the overflow of the interest a man finds in himself, the value he attributes to his own being?
—Sherwood Anderson

Nobody holds a good opinion of a man who has a low opinion of himself. —Anthony Trollope

Self-love is not opposed to the love of other people. You cannot really

love yourself and do yourself a favor without doing other people a favor, and vice versa.
—Dr. Karl Menninger

Healthy personalities accept themselves not in any self-idolizing way, but in the sense that they see themselves as persons who are worth giving to another and worthy to receive from another.   —William Klassen

A man needs self-acceptance or he can't live with himself; he needs self-criticism or others can't live with him.   —James A. Pike

SELF-ACCEPTANCE AND HUMOR

You grow up the day you have your first real laugh at yourself.
—Ethel Barrymore

Imagination was given to us to compensate for what we are not; a sense of humor was provided to console us for what we are.   —Mack McGinnis

GENERAL QUOTATIONS ABOUT SELF-ACCEPTANCE

Accept the place the divine providence has found for you.
—Ralph Waldo Emerson

A true man never frets about his place in the world, but just slides into it by the gravitation of his nature, and swings there as easily as a star.   —Edwin H. Chapin

My recipe for life is not being afraid of myself, afraid of what I think or of my opinions.   —Eartha Kitt

Every man must be content with that glory which he may have at home.
—Boethius

Each of us has a day ... when he has to accept, finally, the fact that he is a man.   —Jean Anouilh

I needed to find my way to write. I need about six hours of uninterrupted time in order to produce about two hours of writing, and when I accepted that and found the way to do it, then I was able to write.
—Robert B. Parker

Life is a very sad piece of buffoonery, because we have ... the need to fool ourselves continuously by the spontaneous creation of a reality ... which, from time to time, reveals itself to be vain and illusory.
—Luigi Pirandello

The deepest principle in human nature is the craving to be appreciated.   —William James

It's OK if you mess up. You should give yourself a break.   —Billy Joel

Accept your humanness as well as your divinity, totally and without reserve.   —Emmanuel

The things we hate about ourselves aren't more real than things we like about ourselves.   —Ellen Goodman

Until you make peace with who you are, you'll never be content with what you have.   —Doris Mortman

If you make friends with yourself you will never be alone.
—Maxwell Maltz

It is a sign of strength, not of weakness, to admit that you don't know all the answers. —John P. Lougbrane

174

The fundamental problem most patients have is an inability to love themselves, having been unloved by others during some crucial part of their lives.   —Bernie S. Siegel, M.D.

Who you are is a necessary step to being who you will be. —Emmanuel

Ultimately, love is self approval.
—Sondra Ray

Unless I accept my faults, I will most certainly doubt my virtues.
—Hugh Prather

Too many people overvalue what they are not and undervalue what they are.   —Malcolm Forbes

If I am not for myself, who is for me? And if I am only for myself, what am I? And if not now, when?
—Hillel

Accept your defeats
With your head up and your eyes
    open
With the grace of woman, not the
    grief of a child ...
—Kara DiGiovanna

He who despises himself esteems himself as a self-despiser.
—Susan Sontag

Your problem is you're ... too busy holding onto your unworthiness.
—Ram Dass

Self-Control

DEVELOPING SELF-CONTROL

When the fight begins within himself, a man's worth something.
—Robert Browning

Self-command is the main elegance.
—Ralph Waldo Emerson

I will write of him who fights and vanquishes his sins, who struggles on through weary years against himself ... and wins.
—Caroline Begelow LeRow

The man who masters his own soul will forever be called conqueror of conquerors.
—Plautus

There is little that can withstand a man who can conquer himself.
—Louis XIV

What we do upon some great occasion will probably depend on what we already are; and what we are will be the result of previous years of self-discipline.
—H.P. Liddon

Man who man would be, must rule the empire of himself.
—Percy Bysshe Shelley

He that hath no rule over his own spirit is like a city that is broken down, and without walls.
—Proverbs

Most powerful is he who has himself in his own power.
—Marcus Annaeus Seneca

I am, indeed, a king, because I know how to rule myself.
—Pietro Aretino

He who conquers others is strong; he who conquers himself is mighty.
—Lao-tzu

What lies in our power to do, it lies in our power not to do.
—Aristotle

It isn't until you come to a spiritual understanding of who you are—not necessarily a religious feeling, but deep down, the spirit within—that you can begin to take control.
—Oprah Winfrey

Anger is only one letter short of danger.
—Anon.

Without discipline, there's no life at all.
—Katharine Hepburn

Self-control is the quality that distinguishes the fittest to survive.
—George Bernard Shaw

Many people have the ambition to succeed; they may even have a special aptitude for their job. And yet they do not move ahead. Why? Perhaps they think that since they can master the job, there is no need to master themselves.
—John Stevenson

The Only Thing We Can Control Is Ourselves

There is only one corner of the universe you can be certain of improving, and that's your own self.
—Aldous Huxley

Not being able to govern events, I govern myself.
—Michel de Montaigne

He that would govern others should first be the master of himself.
—Philip Massinger

Self-Control and Freedom

No man is free who is not master of himself.
—Epictetus

Freedom is not procured by a full enjoyment of what is desired, but by controlling that desire.
—Epictetus

Self-Control and Passion

The happiness of a man in this life does not consist in the absence, but in the mastery, of his passions.
—Alfred, Lord Tennyson

I count him braver who overcomes his desires than him who conquers his enemies; the hardest victory is the victory over self.
—Aristotle

The strong man is the one who is able to intercept at will the communication between the senses and the mind.
—Napoleon Bonaparte

He that would be superior to external influences must first become superior to his own passions.
—Samuel Johnson

He who reigns within himself and rules his passions, desires, and fears is more than a king.
—John Milton

SELF-CONFIDENCE

SELF-CONFIDENCE ISN'T CONCEIT OR EGOMANIA

Calm self-confidence is as far from conceit as the desire to earn a decent living is remote from greed.
—Channing Pollock

Self-love, my liege, is not so vile a sin as self-neglecting.
—William Shakespeare

It is as proper to have pride in oneself as it is ridiculous to show it to others.
—Francois de La Rochefoucauld

If a man doesn't delight in himself and the force in him and feel that he and it are wonders, how is all life to become important to him?
—Sherwood Anderson

Pride ... is the direct appreciation of oneself.   —Arthur Schopenhauer

WITHOUT SELF-CONFIDENCE, WE'RE DONE FOR

As soon as you trust yourself, you will know how to live.
—Johann von Goethe

He who has lost confidence can lose nothing more.   —Boiste

To have that sense of one's intrinsic worth which constitutes self-respect is potentially to have everything.
—Joan Didion

It is best to act with confidence, no matter how little right you have to it.
—Lillian Hellman

I've always seen myself as a winner, even as a kid. If I hadn't, I just might have gone down the drain a couple of times. I've got something inside of me, peasantlike and stubborn, and I'm in it 'til the end of the race.
—Truman Capote

Self-respect will keep a man from being abject when he is in the power of enemies, and will enable him to feel that he may be in the right when the world is against him.
—Bertrand Russell

There's one blessing only, the source and cornerstone of beatitude: confidence in self.
—Marcus Annaeus Seneca

As is our confidence, so is our capacity. —William Hazlitt

Only so far as a man believes strongly, mightily, can he act cheerfully, or do anything worth doing.
—Frederick W. Robertson

Experience tells you what to do; confidence allows you to do it.
—Stan Smith

Your success depends mainly upon what you think of yourself and whether you believe in yourself.
—William J.H. Boetcker

The man who cannot believe in himself cannot believe in anything else.
—Roy L. Smith

A man cannot be comfortable without his own approval.
—Mark Twain

Believe that you can whip the enemy, and you have won half the battle.
—General J.E.B. Stuart

WE CAN'T AFFORD TO DOUBT OURSELVES

Our doubts are traitors, and make us lose the good we oft might win, by fearing to attempt.
—William Shakespeare

A man's doubts and fears are his worst enemies.
—William Wrigley, Jr.

Doubt whom you will, but never yourself. —Christian Bovee

Our self-conceit sustains, and always must sustain us. —Samuel Butler

Self-distrust is the cause of most of our failures ... they are the weakest, however strong, who have no faith in themselves or their own powers.
—Christian Bovee

Faith in oneself ... is the best and safest course. —Michelangelo

SELF-CONFIDENCE IS ESSENTIAL TO SUCCESS

Self-trust is the first secret of success.
—Ralph Waldo Emerson

Self-confidence is the first requisite to great undertakings.
—Samuel Johnson

They are able because they think they are able. —Virgil

Nothing splendid has ever been achieved except by those who dared believe that something inside them was superior to circumstances.
—Bruce Barton

Confidence is that feeling by which the mind embarks on great and honorable courses with a sure hope and trust in itself. —Cicero

One's self-image is very important because if that's in good shape, then you can do anything, or practically anything. —Sir John Gielgud

If one advances confidently in the direction of his dreams, and endeavors to live the life which he has imagined, he will meet with a success unexpected in common hours.
—Henry David Thoreau

They conquer who believe they can.
—John Dryden

It's so important to believe in yourself. Believe that you can do it, under
any circumstances. Because if you
believe you can, then you really will.
That belief just keeps you searching
for the answers, and then pretty
soon you get it.
—Wally "Famous" Amos

Search and you will find that at the
base and birth of every great business organization was an enthusiast,
a man consumed with earnestness of
purpose, with confidence in his powers, with faith in the worthwhileness
of his endeavors.   —B.C. Forbes

Immense power is acquired by assuring yourself in your secret reveries
that you were born to control
affairs.   —Andrew Carnegie

Self-reverence, self-knowledge, self-
control. These three alone lead to
sovereign power.
—Alfred, Lord Tennyson

The big gap between the ability of
actors is confidence.
—Kathleen Turner

Optimism is the faith that leads to
achievement. Nothing can be done
without hope and confidence.
—Helen Keller

Confidence imparts a wonderful
inspiration to its possessor.
—John Milton

Great poetry is always written by
somebody straining to go beyond
what he can do.   —Stephen Spender

SELF-CONFIDENCE IS CRITICAL TO OUR RELATIONS WITH OTHER PEOPLE

The confidence which we have in
ourselves gives birth to much of that
which we have in others.
—Francois de La Rochefoucauld

The way in which we think of ourselves has everything to do with how
our world sees us.   —Arlene Raven

Once you get rid of the idea that you
must please other people before you
please yourself, and you begin to follow your own instincts—only then
can you be successful. You become
more satisfied, and when you are
other people tend to be satisfied by
what you do.   —Raquel Welch

Nothing is a greater impediment to
being on good terms with others
than being ill at ease with yourself.
—Honore de Balzac

Nobody holds a good opinion of a
man who has a low opinion of himself.   —Anthony Trollope

There is overwhelming evidence that
the higher the level of self-esteem,
the more likely one will treat others
with respect, kindness, and generosity. People who do not experience
self-love have little or no capacity to
love others.   —Nathaniel Branden

Only the person who has faith in
himself is able to be faithful to others.   —Erich Fromm

He can inspire a group only if he
himself is filled with confidence and
hope of success.   —Floyd V. Filson

A good sweat, with the blood pounding through my body, makes me feel alive, revitalized. I gain a sense of mastery and assurance. I feel good about myself. Then I can feel good about others. —Arthur Dobrin

SOME SOURCES OF SELF-CONFIDENCE

Confidence ... is directness and courage in meeting the facts of life.
—John Dewey

Measure yourself by your best moments, not by your worst. We are too prone to judge ourselves by our moments of despondency and depression.   —Robert Johnson

The way to develop self-confidence is to do the thing you fear and get a record of successful experiences behind you.
—William Jennings Bryan

Oftentimes nothing profits more than self-esteem, grounded on what is just and right and well-managed.
—John Milton

Believe that with your feelings and your work you are taking part in the greatest; the more strongly you culti-vate this belief, the more will reality and the world go forth from it.
—Rainer Maria Rilke

Class is an aura of confidence that is being sure without being cocky. Class has nothing to do with money. Class never runs scared. It is self-discipline and self-knowledge. It's the sure-footedness that comes with having proved you can meet life.
—Ann Landers

In forty hours I shall be in battle, with little information, and on the spur of the moment will have to make the most momentous deci-sions, but I believe that one's spirit enlarges with responsibility and that, with God's help, I shall make them and make them right.
—General George S. Patton

Be always sure you're right, then go ahead.   —Davy Crockett

The gain in self-confidence of having accomplished a tiresome labour is immense.   —Arnold Bennett

GENERAL QUOTATIONS ABOUT SELF-CONFIDENCE

I always thought I should be treated like a star.   —Madonna

Perhaps I am stronger than I think.
—Thomas Merton

Confidence is contagious. So is lack of confidence.   —Vince Lombardi

"Glamour" is assurance. It is a kind of knowing that you are all right in every way, mentally and physically and in appearance, and that, whatev-er the occasion or the situation, you are equal to it.   —Marlene Dietrich

Never bend your head. Hold it high. Look the world straight in the eye.
—Helen Keller

To be confident is to act in faith.
—Bernard Bynion

Skill and confidence are an uncon-quered army.   —George Herbert

Self-Reliance

The Importance of Self-Reliance

Your future depends on many things, but mostly on you.
—Frank Tyger

Don't ask of your friends what you yourself can do.   —Quintus Ennius

A man who finds no satisfaction in himself, seeks for it in vain elsewhere.
—Francois de La Rochefoucauld

The wise don't expect to find life worth living; they make it that way.
—Anon.

To be a man is, precisely, to be responsible.
—Antoine de Saint-Exupery

Real adulthood is the result of two qualities: self-discipline and self-reliance. The process of developing them together in balance is called maturing.   —J.W. Jepson

He who would be well taken care of must take care of himself.
—William Graham Sumner

The best bet is to bet on yourself.
—Arnold Glasow

Do for yourself or do without.
—Gaylord Perry

For the great benefits of our being— our life, health, and reason—we look upon ourselves.
—Marcus Annaeus Seneca

I have always regarded myself as the pillar of my life.   —Meryl Streep

A secure individual ... knows that the responsibility for anything concerning his life remains with himself—and he accepts that responsibility.   —Harry Browne

An axe at home saves hiring a carpenter.   —J.C.F. von Schiller

We're all in this together ... alone.
—Lily Tomlin

No one can really pull you up very high—you lose your grip on the rope. But on your own two feet you can climb mountains.
—Louis Brandeis

There is no dependence that can be sure but a dependence upon one's self. —John Gay

The future is not in the hands of fate, but in ours. —Jules Jusserano

Men are made stronger on realization that the helping hand they need is at the end of their own arm. —Sidney J. Phil

The best place to find a helping hand is at the end of your own arm. —Swedish proverb

Every tub must stand on its own bottom. —Thomas Fuller

You've got to do your own growing, no matter how tall your grandfather was. —Irish proverb

Do not rely completely on any other human being, however dear. We meet all of life's greatest tests alone. —Agnes MacPhail

Only those means of security are good, are certain, are lasting, that depend on yourself and your own vigor. —Niccolo Machiavelli

Every man paddles his own canoe. —Frederick Marryat

If you would have a faithful servant, and one that you like, serve yourself. —Benjamin Franklin

If you want a thing done, go; if not, send. —Benjamin Franklin

I am not afraid of storms, for I am learning how to sail my ship. —Louisa May Alcott

Our remedies oft in ourselves do lie. —William Shakespeare

If it is to be, it is up to me. —Anon.

There are three types of baseball players—those who make it happen, those who watch it happen, and those who wonder what happened. —Tommy Lasorda

Rogers sees daylight. Campbell *makes* daylight. —Bum Phillips

The only discipline that lasts is self-discipline. —Bum Phillips

The destiny of man is in his own soul. —Herodotus

My future is one I must make myself. —Louis L'Amour

Faced with crisis, the man of character falls back on himself. —Charles de Gaulle

If there is no wind, row. —Latin proverb

No bird soars too high if he soars on his own wings. —William Blake

WE MUST RELY ON WHAT'S INSIDE US

We carry with us the wonders we seek without us. —Sir Thomas Browne

The best things in life must come by effort from within, not by gifts from the outside. —Fred Corson

Ruin and recovery are both from within. —Epictetus

He who is plenteously provided for from within needs but little from without. —Johann von Goethe

What pulls the strings is the force hidden within; there lies ... the real man. —Marcus Aurelius

The foundations which we would dig about and find are within us, like the Kingdom of Heaven, rather than without. —Samuel Butler

No external advantages can supply self-reliance. The force of one's being ... must come from within. —R.W. Clark

Every time I start a picture ... I feel the same fear, the same self-doubts ... and I have only one source on which I can draw, because it comes from within me. —Federico Fellini

There is no man so low down that the cure for his condition does not lie strictly within himself. —Thomas L. Masson

It is what you are inside that matters. You, yourself, are your only real capital. —Vladimir Zworykin

Look well into thyself; there is a source which will always spring up if thou wilt always search there. —Marcus Aurelius

I've never met a person, I don't care what his condition, in whom I could not see possibilities. I don't care how much a man may consider himself a failure, I believe in him, for he can change the thing that is wrong in his life anytime he is prepared and ready to do it. Whenever he develops the desire, he can take away from his life the thing that is defeating it. The capacity for reformation and change lies within. —Preston Bradley

You will not find poetry anywhere unless you bring some of it with you. —Joseph Joubert

God, why do I storm heaven for answers that are already in my heart? Every grace I need has already been given me. Oh, lead me to the Beyond within. —Macrina Wieherkehr

The only Zen you find on the tops of mountains is the Zen you bring up there. —Robert M. Pirsig

There ain't nothing from the outside can lick any of us. —Margaret Mitchell

Man must be arched and buttressed from within, else the temple wavers to dust. —Marcus Aurelius

There is no reality except the one contained within us. —Herman Hesse

Religious faith, indeed, relates to that which is above us, but it must arise from that which is within us. —Josiah Royce

CREATING OURSELVES

God creates the animals, man creates himself. —Georg Christoph Lichtenberg

Man cannot remake himself without suffering, for he is both the marble and the sculptor. —Dr. Alexis Carrel

Every man is his own ancestor, and
every man his own heir. He devises
his own future, and he inherits his
own past. —H.F. Hedge

In the long run we shape our lives
and we shape ourselves. The process
never ends until we die. And the
choices we make are ultimately our
own responsibility.
—Eleanor Roosevelt

Up to a point a man's life is shaped
by environment, heredity, and move-
ments and changes in the world
about him; then there comes a time
when it lies within his grasp to shape
the clay of his life into the sort of
thing he wishes to be.... Everyone
has it within his power to say, this I
am today, that I shall be tomorrow.
—Louis L'Amour

We either make ourselves miserable,
or we make ourselves strong. The
amount of work is the same.
—Carlos Castaneda

There's only one corner of the universe you can be certain of improving, and that's your own self.
—Aldous Huxley

Parents can only give good advice or
put them on the right paths, but the
final forming of a person's character
lies in their own hands.
—Anne Frank

CREATING AND USING OUR CIRCUMSTANCES

I would not sit waiting for some value
tomorrow, nor for something to happen. One could wait a lifetime.... I
would *make* something happen.
—Louis L'Amour

Circumstances are the rulers of the
weak; they are but the instruments
of the wise. —Samuel Lover

Circumstances—what are circumstances? I *make* circumstances.
—Napoleon Bonaparte

Man is not the creature of circumstances, circumstances are the creature of man. We are free agents, and
man is more powerful than matter.
—Benjamin Disraeli

It is our relation to circumstances
that determines their influence over
us. The same wind that carries one
vessel into port may blow another
off shore. —Christian Bovee

We will either find a way, or make
one. —Hannibal

People are always blaming their circumstances for what they are. The
people who get on in this world are
they who get up and look for the circumstances they want, and, if they
can't find them, make them.
—George Bernard Shaw

Choice of attention—to pay attention to this and ignore that—is to the
inner life what choice of action is to
the outer. In both cases, a man is
responsible for his choice and must
accept the consequences.
—W.H. Auden

Heaven and hell is right now.... You
make it heaven or you make it hell
by your actions. —George Harrison

Freedom means choosing your burden. —Hephzibah Menuhin

We create our fate every day ... most of the ills we suffer from are directly traceable to our own behavior.
—Henry Miller

You have to take it as it happens, but you should try to make it happen the way you want to take it.
—Old German proverb

The winds and waves are always on the side of the ablest navigators.
—Edward Gibbon

A life of reaction is a life of slavery, intellectually and spiritually. One must fight for a life of action, not reaction.
—Rita Mae Brown

Life is raw material. We are artisans. We can sculpt our existence into something beautiful, or debase it into ugliness. It's in our hands.
—Cathy Better

The proverb warns that "You should not bite that hand that feeds you." But maybe you should, if it prevents you from feeding yourself.
—Thomas Szasz

If we live good lives, the times are also good. As we are, such are the times.
—Saint Augustine

Change and growth take place when a person has risked himself and dares to become involved with experimenting with his own life.
—Herbert Otto

They have rights who dare defend them.
—Roger Baldwin

Make good use of bad rubbish.
—Elizabeth Beresford

Things alter for the worse spontaneously, if they be not altered for the better designedly.
—Francis Bacon

Things don't turn up in this world until somebody turns them up.
—James A. Garfield

Is life so wretched? Isn't it rather your hands which are too small, your vision which is muddied? You are the one who must grow up.
—Dag Hammarskjold

Be thine own palace, or the world's thy jail.
—John Donne

A filly who wants to run will always find a rider.
—Jacques Audiberti

Each of us makes his own weather, determines the color of the skies in the emotional universe which he inhabits.
—Fulton J. Sheen

RELYING ON OUR OWN THINKING

Thinking is like loving and dying. Each of us must do it for himself.
—Josiah Royce

Be yourself and think for yourself; and while your conclusions may not be infallible, they will be nearer right than the conclusions forced upon you.
—Elbert Hubbard

Though reading and conversation may furnish us with many ideas of men and things, our own meditation must form our judgement.
—Isaac Watts

He who has no opinion of his own, but depends upon the opinion and taste of others, is a slave.
—Friedrich Klopstock

How much time he gains who does not look to see what his neighbor says or does or thinks, but only at what he does himself, to make it just and holy. —Marcus Aurelius

The efficient man is the man who thinks for himself.
—Charles W. Eliot

Learn to depend upon yourself by doing things in accordance with your own way of thinking.
—Grenville Kleiser

If we are not responsible for the thoughts that pass our doors, we are at least responsible for those we admit and entertain.
—Charles B. Newcomb

Think wrongly, if you please, but in all cases think for yourself.
—Doris Lessing

Let me listen to me and not to them.
—Gertrude Stein

Each man must for himself alone decide what is right and what is wrong, which course is patriotic and which isn't. You cannot shirk this and be a man. To decide against your conviction is to be an unqualified and excusable traitor, both to yourself and to your country, let men label you as they may.
—Mark Twain

WE'RE RESPONSIBLE FOR OUR OWN HAPPINESS

The man who makes everything that leads to happiness depend upon himself, and not upon other men, has adopted the very best plan for living happily. —Plato

Happiness depends upon ourselves.
—Aristotle

We are taught you must blame your father, your sisters, your brothers, the school, the teachers—you can blame anyone, but never blame yourself. It's never your fault. But it's *always* your fault, because if you want to change, you're the one who has got to change. It's as simple as that, isn't it? —Katharine Hepburn

Discontent is want of self-discipline; it is infirmity of will.
—Ralph Waldo Emerson

The essence of philosophy is that a man should so live that his happiness shall depend as little as possible on external things. —Epictetus

Most folks are about as happy as they make up their minds to be.
—Abraham Lincoln

Happiness is not in our circumstances, but in ourselves. It is not something we see, like a rainbow, or feel, like the heat of a fire. Happiness is something we are.
—John B. Sheerin

When I have been unhappy, I have heard an opera ... and it seemed the shrieking of winds; when I am happy, a sparrow's chirp is delicious to me. But it is not the chirp that makes me happy, but I that make it sweet. —John Ruskin

To believe that if only we had this or that we would be happy, or to pursue any excessive desire, diverts us from seeing that happiness depends on an adequate self. —Eric Hoffer

187

Nothing can bring you peace but yourself.   —Ralph Waldo Emerson

No-one *gives* joy or sorrow.... We gather the consequences of our own deeds.   —Garuda Purana

The U.S. Constitution doesn't guarantee happiness, only the pursuit of it. You have to catch up with it yourself.   —Benjamin Franklin

Happiness belongs to those who are sufficient unto themselves. For all external sources of happiness and pleasure are, by their very nature, highly uncertain, precarious, ephemeral, and subject to chance.
            —Arthur Schopenhauer

All times are beautiful for those who maintain joy within them; but there is no happy or favorable time for those with disconsolate or orphaned souls.   —Rosalia Castro

I am my own heaven and hell!
            —J.C.F. von Schiller

Felicity, felicity ... is quaffed out of a golden cup ... the flavour is with you alone, and you can make it as intoxicating as you please.
            —Joseph Conrad

Some pursue happiness—others create it.   —Anon.

To be obliged to beg our daily happiness from others bespeaks a more lamentable poverty than that of him who begs his daily bread.
            —Charles Caleb Colton

Man is the artificer of his own happiness.   —Henry David Thoreau

To wait for someone else, or to expect someone else to make my life richer, or fuller, or more satisfying, puts me in a constant state of suspension. —Kathleen Tierney Andrus

It is not easy to find happiness in ourselves, and it is not possible to find it elsewhere.   —Agnes Repplier

I am responsible for my own well-being, my own happiness. The choices and decisions I make regarding my life directly influence the quality of my days.   —Kathleen Andrus

If you do not find peace in yourself you will never find it anywhere else.
            —Paula A. Bendry

To know what you prefer, instead of humbly saying Amen to what the world tells you that you ought to prefer, is to have kept your soul alive.   —Robert Louis Stevenson

If people are suffering, then they must look within themselves.... Happiness is not something ready-made [Buddha] can give you. It comes from your own actions.
            —The Dalai Lama

Blame yourself if you have no branches or leaves; don't accuse the sun of partiality.   —Chinese proverb

The opportunities for enjoyment in your life are limitless. If you feel you are not experiencing enough joy, you have only yourself to blame.
            —David E. Bresler

Happiness is like time and space— we make and measure it ourselves; it is as fancy, as big, as little, as you please, just a thing of contrasts and comparisons.   —George du Marier

The greatest griefs are those we cause ourselves.   —Sophocles

No human being can really understand another, and no one can arrange another's happiness.
—Graham Greene

It's Up to Us to Defeat Boredom

The amount of satisfaction you get from life depends largely on your own ingenuity, self-sufficiency, and resourcefulness. People who wait around for life to supply their satisfaction usually find boredom instead.   —Dr. William Menninger

Somebody's boring me; I think it's me.   —Dylan Thomas

Being bored is an insult to oneself.
—Jules Renard

When people are bored, it is primarily with their own selves that they are bored.   —Jules Renard

If your daily life seems poor, do not blame it; blame yourself, tell yourself that you are not poet enough to call forth its riches.
—Rainer Maria Rilke

Self-Reliance and Success

If you want to succeed, you must make your own opportunities as you go.   —John B. Gough

If, after all, men cannot always make history have a meaning, they can always act so that their own lives have one.   —Albert Camus

Every man is the architect of his own fortune.   —Sallust

A wise man will make more opportunities than he finds.
—Francis Bacon

Man is still responsible.... His success lies not with the stars, but with himself. He must carry on the fight of self-correction and discipline.
—Frank Curtis Williams

No one can help you in holding a good job except Old Man You.
—Edgar Watson Howe

Under normal periods, any man's success hinges about 5 percent on what others do for him and 95 percent on what he does.
—James A. Worsham

No man will succeed unless he is ready to face and overcome difficulties and prepared to assume responsibilities.   —William J.H. Boetcker

The brave man carves out his fortune, and every man is the sum of his own works.   —Miguel de Cervantes

If a man wants his dreams to come true, he must wake up.   —Anon.

Pa, he always said a man had to look spry for himself, because nobody would do it for him; your opportunities didn't come knocking around, you had to hunt them down and hog-tie them.   —Louis L'Amour

Destiny is not a matter of chance, it is a matter of choice; it is not a thing to be waited for, it is a thing to be achieved.   —William Jennings Bryan

Men at some time are masters of
their fates.   —William Shakespeare

The people who get on in this world
are the people who get up and look
for the circumstances they want,
and, if they can't find them, make
them.   —George Bernard Shaw

ACCEPTING RESPONSIBILITY FOR OUR ERRORS AND MISTAKES

We have not passed that subtle line
between childhood and adulthood
until ... we have stopped saying "It
got lost," and say "I lost it."
—Sydney J. Harris

Do not blame anybody for your mistakes and failures.
—Bernard M. Baruch

Mistakes fail in their mission of
helping the person who blames them
on the other fellow.
—Henry S. Haskins

The day you take complete responsibility for yourself, the day you stop
making excuses, that's the day you
start your move to the top.
—O.J. Simpson

It is a painful thing to look at your
own trouble and know that you
yourself, and no one else, has made
it.   —Sophocles

The greatest griefs are those we
cause ourselves.   —Sophocles

When you blame others, you give up
your power to change.   —Anon.

Take your life in your own hands,
and what happens? A terrible thing:
no one to blame.   —Erica Jong

What fate can be worse than to
know we have no one but ourselves
to blame for our misfortunes!
—Sophocles

Fair play with others is primarily not
blaming them for anything that is
wrong with us.   —Eric Hoffer

How we love to blame others for our
misfortunes! Almost every individual
who has lost money in stock speculation has on the tip of his tongue an
explanation which he trots out to
show that it wasn't his own fault at
all.... Hardly one loser has the manli-
ness to say frankly, "I was wrong."
—B.C. Forbes

Man must cease attributing his problems to his environment and learn
again to exercise ... his personal
responsibility in the realm of faith
and morals.   —Albert Schweitzer

The fault, dear Brutus, is not in our
stars, but in ourselves.
—William Shakespeare

A chief is a man who assumes
responsibility. He does not say, "My
men were beaten," he says, "I was
beaten." —Antoine de Saint-Exupery

Debt is a trap which man sets and
baits himself, and then deliberately
gets into.   —Josh Billings

WE SHOULD RELY ON GOD ... UP TO A POINT

God helps those who help themselves.   —German proverb

It is vain to ask of the gods what
man is capable of supplying for himself.   —Epicurus

The gods help those who help them-selves.　　—Marcus Terentius Varro

Ask God's blessing on your work, but don't ask him to do it for you.
　　—Dame Flora Robson

He who prays and labours lifts his heart to God with his hands.
　　—Saint Bernard

God gives every bird its food, but he does not throw it into the nest.
　　—Josiah Holland

God gives the nuts, but he does not crack them.　　—German proverb

Trust in Allah, but tie your camel first.　　—Arabic proverb

Put your trust in God, my boys, and keep your powder dry!
　　—Valentine Blacker

God loves to help him who strives to help himself.　　—Aeschylus

Religious faith, indeed, relates to that which is above us, but it must arise from that which is within us.
　　—Josiah Royce

Even God lends a hand to honest boldness.　　—Menander

Help yourself and heaven will help you.　　—Jean de La Fontaine

God has entrusted me with myself.
　　—Epictetus

The Ancient Mariner said to Neptune during a great storm, "O God, you will save me if you wish, but I am going to go on holding my tiller straight."
　　—Michel de Montaigne

If your ship doesn't come in, swim out to it.　　—Jonathan Winters

To character and success, two things, contradictory as they may seem, must go together—humble dependence and manly indepen-dence; humble dependence on God and manly reliance on self.
　　—William Wordsworth

GENERAL QUOTATIONS ABOUT SELF-RELIANCE

Never grow a wishbone, daughter, where your backbone ought to be.
　　—Clementine Paddleford

You are the handicap you must face. *You* are the one who must choose your place.　　—James Lane Allen

The best and most efficient pharma-cy is within your own system.
　　—Robert C. Peale, M.D.

I am the master of my fate; I am the captain of my soul.
　　—William Ernest Henley

Champions take responsibility. When the ball is coming over the net, you can be sure I *want* the ball.
　　—Billie Jean King

SIMPLICITY

THE IMPORTANCE OF KEEPING THINGS SIMPLE

Simplicity is the ultimate sophistication. —Leonardo da Vinci

To be simple is to be great. —Ralph Waldo Emerson

A man must be able to cut a knot, for everything cannot be untied; he must know how to disengage what is essential from the detail in which it is enwrapped, for everything cannot be equally considered; in a word, he must be able to simplify his duties, his business and his life. —Henri Frederic Amiel

Simplicity is an exact medium between too little and too much. —Sir Joshua Reynolds

Simplicity and naturalness are the truest marks of distinction. —W. Somerset Maugham

The trouble about man is twofold. He cannot learn truths which are too complicated; he forgets truths which are too simple. —Dame Rebecca West

Everything should be made as simple as possible ... but not simpler. —Albert Einstein

To be simple is the best thing in the world. —G.K. Chesterton

SIMPLICITY AND LIVING

If we live, we live; if we die, we die; if we suffer, we suffer; if we are terrified, we are terrified. There is no problem about it. —Alan Watts

I go about looking at horses and cattle. They eat grass, make love, work when they have to, bear their young. I am sick with envy of them. —Sherwood Anderson

What you do not want done to yourself, do not do to others. —Confucius

I know only that what is moral is what you feel good after and what is immoral is what you feel bad after. —Ernest Hemingway

There is no cure for birth or death save to enjoy the interval. —George Santayana

192

My formula for living is quite simple. I get up in the morning and I go to bed at night. In between I occupy myself as best I can.   —Cary Grant

There is only one meaning of life, the act of living itself.   —Erich Fromm

Keep doing what you're doing and you'll keep getting what you're getting.   —Anon.

I believe that a simple and unassuming manner of life is best for everyone, best both for the body and the mind.   —Albert Einstein

Is nothing in life ever straight and clear, the way children see it?
          —Rosie Thomas

We cannot solve life's problems except by solving them.
          —M. Scott Peck

If it's working, keep doing it. If it's not working, stop doing it. If you don't know what to do, don't do anything.   —Dr. Melvin Konner

If you don't like something about yourself, change it. If you can't change it, accept it.
          —Ted Shackelford

The great business of life is to be, to do, to do without, and to depart.
          —John, Viscount Morley
          of Blackburn

Love, and do what you like.
          —Saint Augustine

Eat when you're hungry. Drink when you're thirsty. Sleep when you're tired.   —Buddhist proverb

When you are at sea, keep clear of the land.   —Publilius Syrus

I have a simple philosophy. Fill what's empty. Empty what's full. Scratch where it itches.
          —Alice Roosevelt Longworth

Reduce the complexity of life by eliminating the needless wants of life, and the labors of life reduce themselves.   —Edwin Way Teale

Simplicity is making the journey of this life with just baggage enough.
          —Anon.

I take a simple view of living. It is, keep your eyes open and get on with it.   —Sir Laurence Olivier

The boy and girl going hand in hand through a meadow; the mother washing her baby; the sweet simple things in life. We have almost lost track of them. On the one side, we overintellectualize everything; on the other hand, we are over-mechanized. We can understand the danger of the atomic bomb, but the danger of our misunderstanding the meaning of life is much more serious.
          —Edward Steichen

Fear less, hope more; eat less, chew more; whine less, breathe more; talk less, say more; love more, and all good things will be yours.
          —Swedish proverb

Manifest plainness,
Embrace simplicity,
Reduce selfishness,
Have few desires.   —Lao-tzu

Keep breathing.   —Sophie Tucker

Simplicity, clarity, singleness: these are the attributes that give our lives power and vividness and joy.
—Richard Halloway

I searched through rebellion, drugs, diet, mysticism, religion, intellectualism and much more, only to find that truth is basically simple and feels good, clear and right.
—Chick Corea

If you walk, just walk. If you sit, just sit. But whatever you do, don't wobble.
—Anon.

To keep a lamp burning, we have to keep putting oil in it.
—Mother Teresa

If a Plant's Roots Are Too Tight, Repot.
—Gardening headline, *The New York Times*

WE COMPLICATE LIFE

Life is not complex. *We* are complex. Life is simple, and the simple thing is the right thing.
—Oscar Wilde

God made man simple, but how he changed and got complicated is hard to say.
—Johann von Goethe

Making the simple complicated is commonplace; making the complicated simple, awesomely simple, that's creativity.
—Charles Mingus

The man of fixed ingrained principles who has mapped out a straight course, and has the courage and self-control to adhere to it, does not find life complex. Complexities are all of our own making.
—B.C. Forbes

The whole is simpler than the sum of its parts.
—Willard Gibbs

At times almost all of us envy the animals. They suffer and die, but do not seem to make a "problem" of it.
—Alan Watts

The course of every intellectual, if he pursues his journey long and unflinchingly enough, ends in the obvious, from which the non-intellectuals have never stirred.
—Aldous Huxley

Any intelligent fool can make things bigger, more complex, and more violent. It takes a touch of genius—and a lot of courage—to move in the opposite direction.
—E.F. Schumacher

FIRST THINGS FIRST

First say to yourself what you would be, and then do what you have to do.
—Epictetus

Do what you can, with what you have, where you are.
—Theodore Roosevelt

Do the duty which lies nearest thee.... Thy second duty will already have become clearer.
—Thomas Carlyle

Start by doing what's necessary, then what's possible and suddenly you are doing the impossible.
—Saint Francis of Assisi

When you see a rattlesnake poised to strike, you do not wait until he has struck before you crush him.
—Franklin Delano Roosevelt

If a madman were to come into this room with a stick in his hand, no doubt we should pity the state of his mind; but our primary consideration would be to take care of ourselves. We should knock him down first, and pity him afterwards.

—Samuel Johnson

You decide what it is you want to accomplish and then you lay out your plans to get there, and then you just do it. It's pretty straightforward.

—Nancy Ditz

There is a point at which everything becomes simple and there is no longer any question of choice, because all you have staked will be lost if you look back. Life's point of no return.   —Dag Hammarskjold

ELIMINATING NON-ESSENTIALS

The wisdom of life consists in the elimination of nonessentials.

—Lin Yutang

The ability to simplify means to eliminate the unnecessary so that the necessary may speak.

—Hans Hofmann

The sculptor produces the beautiful statue by chipping away such parts of the marble block as are not need-ed—it is a process of elimination.

—Elbert Hubbard

A great man is one who seizes the vital issue in a complex question, what we might call the jugular vein of the whole organism, and spends his energies upon that.

—Joseph Rickaby

The more we reduce the size of our world, the more we shall be its mas-ter.   —Jacinto Benavente

Simplicity, simplicity, simplicity! I say, let your affairs be as two or three, and not a hundred or a thou-sand.... Simplify, simplify.

—Henry David Thoreau

There is no greatness where there is not simplicity.   —Leo Tolstoy

SIMPLICITY AND HAPPINESS

All animals except man know that the ultimate of life is to enjoy it.

—Samuel Butler

I finally figured out the only reason to be alive is to enjoy it.

—Rita Mae Brown

Happiness comes of the capacity to feel deeply, to enjoy simply, to think freely, to risk life, to be needed.

—Storm Jameson

The main obligation is to amuse yourself.   —S.J. Perelman

There is no cure for birth or death save to enjoy the interval.

—George Santayana

SIMPLICITY AND SUCCESS

Success is simple. Do what's right, the right way, at the right time.

—Arnold Glasow

There is a master key to success with which no man can fail. Its name is simplicity ... reducing to the simplest possible terms every problem.

—Henri Deterding

If you want to be found, stand where the seeker seeks.   —Sidney Lanier

If you aren't going all the way, why go at all?   —Joe Namath

195

Many things are lost for want of asking. —English proverb

What I do, I do very well, and what I don't do well, I don't do at all. —Anon.

SIMPLICITY IN SPORTS

Players have two things to do: Play and keep their mouths shut. —Sparky Anderson

Hitting is timing. Pitching is upsetting timing. —Warren Spahn

All I had to do was keep turning left. —George Robson, after winning the Indianapolis 500

The rules of soccer are very simple. Basically it's this: If it moves, kick it; if it doesn't move, kick it until it does. —Phil Woosnam

I just take my three swings and go sit on the bench. I don't ever want to mess up my swing. —Dick Allen

You've got a lot of cute stuff. But son, there's only one thing we're looking for, and that's a pitcher who can tear the catcher's head off with a fastball. You get one of those, come on back. —Baseball scout, quoted by Tom Wolfe

It's a round ball and a round bat, and you got to hit it square. —Pete Rose

There are only five things you can do in baseball: run, throw, catch, hit, and hit with power. —Leo Durocher

If you don't throw it, they can't hit it. —Lefty Gomez

Football is blocking and tackling. Everything else is mythology. —Vince Lombardi

Losers have tons of variety. Champions take pride in just learning to hit the same old boring winners. —Vic Braden

The way you get better at playing football is to play football. —Gene Brodie

SIMPLICITY IN ACTING

Just learn your lines and don't bump into the furniture. —Spencer Tracy

My advice about acting? Speak clearly, don't bump into people, and if you must have motivation, think of your pay packet on Friday. —Noel Coward

Just sit out there and have them go through the moves. When you see something you don't like, change it. —Joshua Logan's advice to directors

Don't let go of the vine. —John Weissmuller, who played Tarzan, giving advice to acting students

Stay out of jail. —Alfred Hitchcock's advice to directors

SIMPLICITY AND WARFARE

Putting aside all the fancy words and academic doubletalk, the basic reason for having a military is to do two jobs—to kill people and to destroy the works of man. —Thomas S. Power

The object of war is to survive it. —John Irving

The first law of war is to preserve ourselves and destroy the enemy.
—Mao Tse-Tung

In combat, life is short, nasty and brutish. The issues of national policy which brought him into war are irrelevant to the combat soldier; he is concerned with his literal life chances.   —Charles E. Moskos, Jr.

You don't hurt 'em if you don't hit 'em.
—General Lewis "Chesty" Puller

There is nothing certain about war except that one side won't win.
—Sir Ian Hamilton

I can always make it a rule to get there first with the most men.
—Nathan Bedford Forrest

The object of war is not to die for your country, but to make the other bastard die for his.
—General George S. Patton

Simplicity and Writing

When ideas come, I write them; when they don't come, I don't.
—William Faulkner

The idea is to get the pencil moving quickly.   —Bernard Malamud

I never thought of myself as a writer, but the simplest thing seemed to be to put a piece of paper in the roller and start typing. —Cynthia Friedman

The niftiest turn of phrase, the most elegant flight of rhetorical fancy, isn't worth beans next to a clear thought clearly expressed.
—Jeff Greenfield

Get black on white.
—Guy de Maupassant

Art, it seems to me, should simplify.
—Willa Cather

It's a simple formula; do your best and somebody might like it.
—Dorothy Baker

Simplicity, carried to an extreme, becomes elegance.   —Jon Franklin

The Simplest Ideas and Sayings Are Often the Best and Most Profound

All the great things are simple, and many can be expressed in a single word: freedom; justice; honor; duty; mercy; hope.
—Sir Winston Churchill

It is the essence of genius to make use of the simplest ideas.
—Charles Peguy

Genius is the ability to reduce the complicated to the simple.
—C.W. Ceram

If you can't write your idea on the back of my calling card, you don't have a clear idea.   —David Belasco

It is proof of high culture to say the greatest matters in the simplest way.
—Ralph Waldo Emerson

The greatest truths are the simplest, and so are the greatest men.
—Julius Charles Hare

The art of art, the glory of expression and the sunshine of the light of letters is simplicity: nothing is better than simplicity.   —Walt Whitman

The great artist and thinker are the simplifiers.   —Henri Frederic Amiel

True eloquence consists of saying all that should be said, and that only.
   —Francois de La Rochefoucauld

Simplicity of character is no hindrance to subtlety of intellect.
                  —John Morley

Simplicity of character is the natural result of profound thought.
                  —William Hazlitt

The obvious is that which is never seen until someone expresses it simply.   —Kahlil Gibran

The simplest things give me ideas.
                  —Joan Miro

Simple style is like white light. It is complex, but its complexity is not obvious.   —Anatole France

When an idea is too weak to support a simple statement, it is a sign that it should be rejected.   —Vauvenargues

When thought is too weak to be simply expressed, it's clear proof that it should be rejected. —Luc de Claplers

Simple truths are a relief from grand speculations.   —Vauvenargues

PART 2

Living One Day at a Time

One Day

It's Impossible to Overstate the Value of One Day

No one can confidently say that he will still be living tomorrow.
—Euripides

Nothing is worth more than this day.
—Johann von Goethe

What a folly to dread the thought of throwing away life at once, and yet have no regard to throwing it away by parcels and piecemeal.
—John Howe

Not a day passes over this earth but men and women of note do great deeds, speak great words and suffer noble sorrows.
—Charles Reed

We create our fate every day we live.
—Henry Miller

Who loses a day loses life.
—Ralph Waldo Emerson

May you live all the days of your life.
—Jonathan Swift

If we only knew the real value of a day.
—Joseph Farrell

We are involved in a life that passes understanding: our highest business is our daily life.
—John Cage

We die daily. Happy those who daily come to life as well.
—George MacDonald

He who has lived a day has lived an age.
—Jean de La Bruyere

Life, we learn too late, is in the living, in the tissue of every day and hour.
—Stephen Leacock

To sensible men, every day is a day of reckoning.
—John W. Gardner

A day's impact is better than a month of dead pull.
—Oliver Wendell Holmes

They deem me mad because I will not sell my days for gold; and I deem them mad because they think my days have a price.
—Kahlil Gibran

The proper function of man is to live, not to exist. I shall not waste my days in trying to prolong them.
—Jack London

A day, an hour, of virtuous liberty is worth a whole eternity in bondage.
—Joseph Addison

Live mindful of how brief your life is.　　　　　—Horace

Gladly accept the gifts of the present hour.　　　　　—Horace

There is but a step between me and death.　　　　—1 Sm. 20:3

Everyone once, once only. Just once and no more. And we also once. Never again.　—Rainer Maria Rilke

Most of us spend our lives as if we had another one in the bank.
—Ben Irwin

It's better to be a lion for a day than a sheep all your life.
—Sister Elizabeth Kenny

While we live, let us live.
—D.H. Lawrence

No objects of value ... are worth risking the priceless experience of waking up one more day.
—Jack Smith

Every possession and every happiness is but lent by chance for an uncertain time, and may therefore be demanded back the next hour.
—Arthur Schopenhauer

Some days you tame the tiger. And some days the tiger has you for lunch.　　　　—Tug McGraw

So teach us to number our days, that we may apply our hearts unto wisdom.　　　　　—Ps. 90:12

You have got to own your days and live them, each one of them, every one of them, or else the years go right by and none of them belong to you.　　　　—Herb Gardner

The ideal never comes. Today is ideal for him who makes it so.
—Horatio W. Dresser

True wisdom lies in gathering the precious things out of each day as it goes by.　　　　—E.S. Bouton

The most important thing in our lives is what we are doing now.
—Anon.

Write it on your heart that every day is the best day in the year.
—Ralph Waldo Emerson

He possesses dominion over himself, and is happy, who can every day say, "I have lived." Tomorrow the heavenly Father may either involve the world in dark clouds, or cheer it with clear sunshine; he will not, however, render ineffectual the things which have already taken place.　　　　　—Horace

The days come and go like muffled and veiled figures sent from a distant friendly party, but they say nothing, and if we do not use the gifts they bring, they carry them as silently away.　—Ralph Waldo Emerson

Your daily life is your temple and your religion.　—Kahlil Gibran

He is only rich who owns the day. There is no king, rich man, fairy, or demon who possesses such power as that.　—Ralph Waldo Emerson

Life is now ... this day, this hour ...
and is probably the only experience
of the kind one is to have.
—Charles Macomb Flandrau

Each day, each hour, an entire life.
—Juan Ramon Jimenel

Gather ye rose-buds while ye may,
Old time is still a-flying.
And this same flower that smiles
today, Tomorrow will be dying.
—Henry David Thoreau

Seize the hour.   —Sophocles

THE VALUE OF TIME

Nothing is ours except time.
—Marcus Annaeus Seneca

Our costliest expenditure is time.
—Theophrastus

Nothing in business is so valuable as
time.   —John H. Patterson

Many people take no care of their
money till they come nearly to the
end of it, and others do just the same
with their time.
—Johann von Goethe

Possessions dwindle: I mourn their
loss. But I mourn the loss of time
much more, for anyone can save his
purse, but none can win back lost
time.   —Latin proverb

Riches are chiefly good because they
give us time.   —Charles Lamb

One realizes the full importance of
time only when there is little of it
left. Every man's greatest capital
asset is his unexpired years of productive life.   —Paul W. Litchfield

Know the true value of time; snatch,
seize, and enjoy every moment of it.
No idleness, no laziness, no procrastination: never put off till tomorrow
what you can do today.
—Lord Chesterfield

A sense of the value of time ... is an
essential preliminary to efficient
work; it is the only method of avoiding hurry.   —Arnold Bennett

All my possessions for a moment of
time.   —Queen Elizabeth I

Let me tell thee, time is a very precious gift of God; so precious that
it's only given to us moment by
moment.   —Amelia Barr

Pick my left pocket of its silver dime,
but spare the right—it holds my
golden time!
—Oliver Wendell Holmes

We work not only to produce, but to
give value to time.
—Eugene Delacroix

As every thread of gold is valuable,
so is every moment of time.
—John Mason

Minutes are worth more than
money. Spend them wisely.
—Thomas P. Murphy

Time is the coin of your life. It is the
only coin you have, and only you
can determine how it will be spent.
Be careful lest you let other people
spend it for you.   —Carl Sandburg

Every minute of life carries with it its
miraculous value, and its face of
eternal youth.   —Albert Camus

202

Dollars cannot buy yesterday.
—Admiral Harold R. Stark

Lost time is never found again.
—Benjamin Franklin

If a person gives you his time, he can give you no more precious gift.
—Frank Tyger

You may ask me for anything you like except time.
—Napoleon Bonaparte

The laboring man and the artificer knows what every hour of his time is worth, and parts not with it but for the full value.　—Lord Clarendon

Time isn't a commodity, something you pass around like cake. Time is the substance of life. When anyone asks you to give your time, they're really asking for a chunk of your life.
—Antoinette Bosco

Love and time—those are the only two things in all the world and all of life that cannot be bought, but only spent.　—Gary Jennings

There is nothing good in this world which time does not improve.
—Alexander Smith

Time is the most valuable thing a man can spend.　—Laertius Diogenes

The great rule of moral conduct is, next to God, to respect Time.
—Johann Kaspar Lavater

It is the time you have wasted for your rose that makes your rose so important.
—Antoine de Saint-Exupery

One hour of life, crowded to the full with glorious action and filled with noble risks, is worth whole years of those mean observances of paltry decorum.　—Sir Walter Scott

Don't be fooled by the calendar. There are only as many days in the year as you make use of. One man gets only a week's value out of a year while another man gets a full year's value out of a week.
—Charles Richards

THE IMPORTANCE OF USING TIME WELL

I must govern the clock, not be governed by it.　—Golda Meir

The organized person ... makes the most of his time and goes to his bed for the night perfectly relaxed for rest and renewal.
—George Matthew Adams

He who every morning plans the transactions of the day and follows out that plan carries a thread that will guide him through the labyrinth of the most busy life.... If the disposal of time is surrendered merely to the chance of incident, chaos will soon reign.　—Victor Hugo

Have a time and place for everything, and do everything in its time and place, and you will not only accomplish more, but have far more leisure than those who are always hurrying.　—Tyron Edwards

During a very busy life I have often been asked, "How did you manage to it all?" The answer is very simple: it is because I did everything promptly.　—Sir Richard Tangye

Time cannot be expanded, accumulated, mortgaged, hastened, or retarded. —Anon.

Seize time by the forelock.
—Pittacus of Mitylene

Time is a tyranny to be abolished.
—Eugene Jolus

The time which we have at our disposal every day is elastic; the passions that we feel expand it, those that we inspire contract it; and habit fills up the rest. —Marcel Proust

The ability to concentrate and to use time well is everything.
—Lee Iacocca

Time is an equal opportunity employer. Each human being has exactly the same number of hours and minutes every day. Rich people can't buy more hours. Scientists can't invent new minutes. And you can't save time to spend it on another day. Even so, time is amazingly fair and forgiving. No matter how much time you've wasted in the past, you still have an entire tomorrow. Success depends upon using it wisely—by planning and setting priorities. —Denis Waitely

An Italian philosopher said that "time was his estate"; an estate indeed which will produce nothing without cultivation, but will always abundantly repay the labors of industry, and generally satisfy the most extensive desires, if no part of it be suffered to lie in waste by negligence, to be overrun with noxious plants, or laid out for show rather than for use. —Samuel Johnson

Timely service, like timely gifts, is doubled in value.
—George MacDonald

Time is the one thing that can never be retrieved. —C.R. Lawton

We must use time as a tool, not as a crutch. —John F. Kennedy

Make use of time, let not advantage slip. —William Shakespeare

O, for an engine to keep back all clocks! —Ben Johnson

You may delay, but time will not.
—Benjamin Franklin

He who would make serious use of his life must always act as though he had a long time to live and schedule his time as though he were about to die. —Emile Littre

The highest value in life is found in the stewardship of time.
—Robert M. Fine

WASTING TIME

I wish I could stand on a busy corner, hat in hand, and beg people to throw me all their wasted hours.
—Bernard Berenson

Wasted time means wasted lives.
—R. Shannon

Regret for time wasted can become a power for good in the time that remains, if we will only stop the waste and the idle, useless regretting.
—Arthur Brisbane

I wasted time, and now doth time waste me. —William Shakespeare

All that time is lost which might be better employed.
—Jean-Jacques Rousseau

Lost, yesterday, somewhere between sunrise and sunset, two golden hours, each set with sixty diamond minutes. No reward is offered, for they are gone forever.
—Horace Mann

Thrift of time will repay you in after-life, with a usury of profit beyond your most sanguine dreams; waste of it will make you dwindle, alike in intellectual and moral stature, beyond your darkest reckoning.
—William Gladstone

The clock upbraids me with the waste of time.
—William Shakespeare

Time is lost when we have not lived a full human life, time unenriched by experience, creative endeavor, enjoyment, and suffering.
—Dietrich Bonhoeffer

Does't thou love life? Then do not squander time, for that is the stuff life is made of.   —Benjamin Franklin

Time wasted is a theft from God.
—Henri Frederic Amiel

Lost time is like a run in a stocking. It always gets worse.
—Ann Morrow Lindbergh

As if you could kill time without injuring eternity.
—Henry David Thoreau

Killing time is the chief end of our society.   —Ugo Betti

No person will have occasion to complain of the want of time who never loses any. —Thomas Jefferson

Time is that which man is always trying to kill, but which ends in killing him.   —Herbert Spencer

Men talk of killing time, while time quietly kills them. —Dion Boucicault

Modern man thinks he loses something—time—when he does not do things quickly. Yet he does not know what to do with the time he gains—except kill it.   —Erich Fromm

If you want to kill time, try working it to death.   —Sam Levenson

A man who dares to waste one hour of life has not discovered the value of life.   —Charles Darwin

If time be of all things most precious, wasting time must be the greatest prodigality, since lost time is never found again.   —Benjamin Franklin

THERE'S NEVER ENOUGH TIME

Curse ruthless time! Curse our mortality. How cruelly short is the allotted span for all we must cram into it!
—Sir Winston Churchill

There is a time for work. And a time for love. That leaves no other time.
—Coco Chanel

You will never "find" time for anything. If you want time you must make it.   —Charles Buxton

Ah! the clock is always slow; it is later than you think.
—Robert W. Service

205

The forty-four-hour week has no charm for me. I'm looking for a forty-hour day.
—Nicholas Murray Butler

Those who make the worst use of their time most complain of its brevity.
—Jean de La Bruyere

I still find each day too short for all the thoughts I want to think, all the walks I want to take, all the books I want to read, and all the friends I want to see.
—John Burroughs

HAVING ENOUGH TIME

What we love to do we find time to do.
—John Lancaster Spalding

Time stays long enough for anyone who will use it.
—Anon.

There is time for everything.
—Thomas A. Edison

We all find time to do what we really want to do.
—William Feather

It is nonsense to say there is not enough time to be fully informed.... Time given to thought is the greatest timesaver of all.
—Norman Cousins

Time is a fixed income and, as with any income, the real problem facing most of us is how to live successfully within our daily allotment.
—Margaret B. Johnstone

We shall never have more time. We have, and have always had, all the time there is. No object is served in waiting until next week or even until to-morrow. Keep going.... Concentrate on something useful.
—Arnold Bennett

There is time enough for everything in the course of the day if you do but one thing at once; but there is not time enough in the year if you will do two things at a time.
—Lord Chesterfield

USING SMALL PIECES OF TIME

Much may be done in those little shreds and patches of time which every day produces, and which most men throw away.
—Charles Caleb Colton

Learn to use ten minutes intelligently. It will pay you huge dividends.
—William A. Irwin

It is better to do the most trifling thing in the world than to regard half an hour as trifle.
—Johann von Goethe

I recommend you to take care of the minutes, for the hours will take care of themselves.
—Lord Chesterfield

The real secret of how to use time is to pack it as you would a portmanteau, filling up the small spaces with small things.
—Sir Henry Haddow

One must learn a different ... sense of time, one that depends more on small amounts than big ones.
—Sister Mary Paul

An earnest purpose finds time, or makes it. It seizes on spare moments, and turns fragments to golden account.
—William Ellery Channing

Guard well your spare moments. They are like uncut diamonds. Discard them and their value will never be known. Improve them and they will become the brightest gems in a useful life.

—Ralph Waldo Emerson

The butterfly counts not months but moments, and has time enough.

—Rabindranath Tagore

LIVING ONE DAY AT A TIME IS A KEY TO HAPPINESS

That man is happiest who lives from day to day and asks no more, garnering the simple goodness of life.

—Euripides

It is only possible to live happily-ever-after on a day-to-day basis.

—Margaret Bonnano

Happiness is produced not so much by great pieces of good fortune that seldom happen, as by little advantages that occur every day.

—Benjamin Franklin

The best way to secure future happiness is to be as happy as is rightfully possible today. —Charles W. Eliot

Happiness is to be found along the way, not at the end of the road, for then the journey is over and it is too late. Today, this hour, this minute is the day, the hour, the minute for each of us to sense the fact that life is good, with all of its trials and troubles, and perhaps more interesting because of them.

—Robert R. Updegraff

Each day provides its own gifts.

—Martial

Let us savour the swift delights of the most beautiful of our days!

—Alphonse de Lamartine

Death accompanies us at every step and enables us to use those moments when life smiles at us to feel more deeply the sweetness of life. The more certain the end, the more tempting the minute.

—Theodore Fontane

Happiness is not a state to arrive at, but a manner of traveling.

—Margaret Lee Runback

My advice to you is not to inquire why or whither, but just to enjoy your ice cream while it's on your plate. —Thornton Wilder

Those who face that which is actually before them, unburdened by the past, undistracted by the future, these are they who live, who make the best use of their lives; these are those who have found the secret of contentment. —Alban Goodier

And that was victory. The freedom to sprawl loosely upon a city street, heat his coffee and eat a can of beans ... with no enemy bullets forcing him to toss the can aside while diving behind another wall for momentary survival. —David Douglas Duncan

Taking time to live is taking time to appreciate simple silence as better than any kind of talk, or watching a flower, or watching a guy wash the windows on a skyscraper and wondering what he is thinking.

—Gersi Douchan

If you observe a really happy man, you will find ... that he is happy in the course of living life twenty-four crowded hours each day.

—W. Beran Wolfe

207

To fill the hour, that is happiness; to fill the hour, and leave no crevice for a repentance or an approval.
—Ralph Waldo Emerson

Live your life each day as you would climb a mountain. An occasional glance toward the summit keeps the goal in mind, but many beautiful scenes are to be observed from each new vantage point. Climb slowly, steadily, enjoying each passing moment; and the view from the summit will serve as a fitting climax for the journey.   —Harold B. Melchart

One day of pleasure is worth two of sorrow.   —Anon.

Present joys are more to flesh and
    blood
Than the dull prospect of a distant
    good.   —John Dryden

In order to be utterly happy the only thing necessary is to refrain from comparing this moment with other moments in the past, which I often did not fully enjoy because I was comparing them with other moments of the future.   —André Gide

Live in day-tight compartments.
—Dale Carnegie

If you are not happy here and now, you never will be.
—Taisen Deshimaru

People who postpone happiness are like children who try chasing rainbows in an effort to find the pot of gold at the rainbow's end.... Your life will never be fulfilled until you are happy here and now.
—Ken Keyes, Jr.

He's one of those Christmas Eve guys. There are people like that ... every day in their lives is Christmas Eve.   —Joe Garagiola,
talking about Yogi Berri

SOME BASIC THINGS
TO DO EACH DAY

There is no other solution to man's progress but the day's honest work, the day's honest decisions, the day's generous utterances and the day's good deed.   —Clare Boothe Luce

A man should hear a little music, read a little poetry, and see a fine picture every day of his life, in order that worldly cares may not obliterate the sense of the beautiful which God has implanted in the human soul.
—Johann von Goethe

I have resolved that from this day on, I will do all the business I can honestly, have all the fun I can reasonably, do all the good I can willingly, and save my digestion by thinking pleasantly.
—Robert Louis Stevenson

Make the most of today. Translate your good intentions into actual deeds.   —Grenville Kleiser

Today is the day in which to express your noblest qualities of mind and heart, to do at least one worthy thing which you have long postponed.   —Grenville Kleiser

Do what you can, with what you have, where you are.
—Theodore Roosevelt

Our grand business undoubtedly is not to see what lies dimly at a distance but to do what lies clearly at hand. —Thomas Carlyle

My formula for living is quite simple. I get up in the morning and I go to bed at night. In between I occupy myself as best I can. —Cary Grant

What you are afraid to do is a clear indicator of the next thing you need to do. —Anon.

If we cannot meet our everyday surroundings with equanimity and pleasure and grow each day in some useful direction, then ... life is on the road toward misfortune, misery and destruction. —Luther Burbank

A day's work is a day's work, neither more nor less, and the man who does it needs a day's sustenance, a night's repose and due leisure, whether he be painter or ploughman. —George Bernard Shaw

Add each day something to fortify you against poverty and death. —Marcus Annaeus Seneca

It isn't hard to be good from time to time in sports. What's tough is being good every day. —Willie Mays

Make it a point to do something every day that you don't want to do. This is the golden rule for acquiring the habit of doing your duty without pain. —Mark Twain

A homer a day will boost my pay. —Josh Gibson

Realize life as an end in itself. Functioning is all there is. —Oliver Wendell Holmes, Jr.

He has not learned the first lesson of life who does not every day surmount a fear. —Ralph Waldo Emerson

Act well at the moment, and you have performed a good action to all eternity. —Johann Kaspar Lavater

If I had my life to live over, I would start barefoot earlier in the spring and stay that way later in the fall. I would go to more dances. I would ride more merry-go-rounds. I would pick more daisies. —Nadine Stair

Nothing determines who we will become so much as those things we choose to ignore. —Sandor Minab

Love, and do what you like. —Saint Augustine

Take the time to come home to yourself everyday. —Robin Casarjean

The power of a man's virtue should not be measured by his special efforts, but by his ordinary doing. —Blaise Pascal

The great business of life is to be, to do, to do without, and to depart. —John, Viscount Morley of Blackburn

Resolve to perform what you ought. Perform without fail what you resolve. —Benjamin Franklin

Know what you want to do, hold the thought firmly, and do every day what should be done, and every sunset will see you that much nearer the goal. —Elbert Hubbard

It is no easy thing for a principle to become a man's own unless each day he maintains it and works it out in his life. —Epictetus

Showing up is 80 percent of life.
—Woody Allen

Follow your bliss.
—Joseph Campbell

Resolve to edge in a little reading every day, if it is but a single sentence. If you gain fifteen minutes a day, it will make itself felt at the end of the year. —Horace Mann

I work every day—or at least I force myself into my office or room. I may get nothing done, but you don't earn bonuses without putting in time. Nothing may come for three months, but you don't get the fourth without it. —Mordecai Richler

Take short views, hope for the best, and trust in God. —Sydney Smith

Each day can be one of triumph if you keep up your interests.
—George Matthew Adams

If you always do what interests you, at least one person is pleased.
—Katharine Hepburn's mother

When action grows unprofitable, gather information; when information grows unprofitable, sleep.
—Ursula K. LeGuin

I long to accomplish a great and noble task, but it is my chief duty to accomplish small tasks as if they were great and noble.
—Helen Keller

To do the useful thing, to say the courageous thing, to contemplate the beautiful thing: that is enough for one man's life. —T.S. Eliot

Do you know that disease and death must needs overtake us, no matter what we are doing?... What do you wish to be doing when it overtakes you? If you have anything better to be doing when you are so overtaken, get to work on that. —Epictetus

Have patience with all things, but chiefly have patience with yourself. Do not lose courage in considering your own imperfections, but instantly set about remedying them—every day begin the task anew.
—Saint Francis de Sales

Without duty, life is soft and boneless. —Joseph Joubert

A man may fulfill the object of his existence by asking a question he cannot answer, and attempting a task he cannot achieve.
—Oliver Wendell Holmes

And each man stands with his face in the light of his own drawn sword. Ready to do what a hero can.
—Elizabeth Barrett Browning

Be strong!
We are not here to play, to dream, to
   drift;
We have hard work to do and loads
   to lift;
Shun not the struggle—face it; 'tis
   God's gift. —Maltbie D. Babcock

Man goeth forth unto his work and to his labor until the evening.
—Ps. 104:23

Every day give yourself a good mental shampoo.　—Sara Jordan, M.D.

To look up and not down,
To look forward and not back,
To look out and not in, and
To lend a hand.
　　　　　—Edward Everett Hale

Do all the good you can,
By all the means you can,
In all the ways you can,
In all the places you can,
At all the times you can.　—Anon.

I like the man who faces what he
　　must,
With steps triumphant and a heart of
　　cheer;
Who fights the daily battle without
　　fear.　—Sarah Knowles Bolton

To accomplish our destiny ... [w]e
must cover before nightfall the distance assigned to each of us.
　　　　　—Dr. Alexis Carrel

Fulfill your works, your daily tasks.
　　　　　—Ex. 5:13

Man goeth forth unto his work and
to his labor until the evening.
　　　　　—Ps. 104:23

Living Each Day as Though It Were Our Last

Each day should be passed as though
it were our last.　—Publilius Syrus

To live each day as though one's
last, never flustered, never apathetic,
never attitudinizing—here is perfection of character.　—Marcus Aurelius

One should count each day a separate life.　—Marcus Annaeus Seneca

Every day is a little life ... live every
day as if it would be the last. Those
that dare lose a day are dangerously
prodigal; those that dare misspend it
are desperate.　　　—Joseph Hall

Learn as if you were going to live
forever. Live as if you were going to
die tomorrow.　　　　—Anon.

You have to count on living every
single day in a way you believe will
make you feel good about your
life—so that if it were over tomorrow, you'd be content with yourself.
　　　　　—Jane Seymour

No one can confidently say that he
will still be living tomorrow.
　　　　　—Euripides

Happy the man, and happy he alone
He who can call today his own
He who, secure within, can say
"Tomorrow, do thy worst
For I have lived today."
　　　　　—Henry Fielding

Doing Our Best Every Day

Do your best every day and your life
will gradually expand into satisfying
fullness.　—Horatio W. Dresser

Any man's life will be filled with
constant and unexpected encouragement if he makes up his mind to do
his level best each day.
　　　　　—Booker T. Washington

Do each daily task the best we can;
act as though the eye of opportunity
were always upon us.
　　　　　—William Feather

So get a few laughs and do the best
you can.　　　　—Will Rogers

What a man accomplishes in a day depends upon the way in which he approaches his tasks. When we accept tough jobs as a challenge to our ability and wade into them with joy and enthusiasm, miracles can happen. —Arland Gilbert

I come to the office each morning and stay for long hours doing what has to be done to the best of my ability. And when you've done the best you can, you can't do any better. So when I go to sleep I turn everything over to the Lord and forget it.
—Harry S. Truman

That man is blest who does his best and leaves the rest.
—Charles F. Deems

DO SOMETHING FOR SOMEONE ELSE, EVERY DAY

When you rise in the morning, form a resolution to make the day a happy one for a fellow creature.
—Sydney Smith

He who allows his day to pass by without practicing generosity and enjoying life's pleasures is like a blacksmith's bellows; he breathes, but does not live. —Sanskrit proverb

You have not lived a perfect day, even though you have earned your money, unless you have done something for someone who will never be able to repay you. —Ruth Smeltzer

Think that day lost whose descending sun, views from thy hand no noble action done. —Joseph Joubert

I expect to pass through life but once. If, therefore, there can be any kindness I can show, or any good thing I can do to any fellow human being, let me do it now.
—William Penn

Be ashamed to die until you have won some victory for humanity.
—Horace Mann

HAVE SOME FUN, SOME RELAXATION, EACH DAY

The most thoroughly wasted of all days is that on which one has not laughed. —Nicolas de Chamfort

Each day, and the living of it, has to be a conscious creation in which discipline and order are relieved with some play and pure foolishness.
—May Sarton

Friends, I beg you do not shirk your daily task of indolence.
—Don Marquis

We should consider every day lost on which we have not danced at least once. —Friedrich Nietzsche

He who does not get fun and enjoyment out of every day ... needs to reorganize his life.
—George Matthew Adams

Unless each day can be looked back upon by an individual as one in which he has had some fun, some joy, some real satisfaction, that day is a loss. —Anon.

Take time every day to do something silly. —Philipa Walker

I finally figured out the only reason to be alive is to enjoy it.
—Rita Mae Brown

It's fun to get together and have something good to eat at least once a day. That's what human life is all about—enjoying things.
—Julia Child

Come, let us give a little time to folly ... and even in a melancholy day let us find time for an hour of pleasure.
—Saint Bonaventura

No matter what looms ahead, if you can eat today, enjoy the sunlight today, mix good cheer with friends today, enjoy it and bless God for it.
—Henry Ward Beecher

BE SATISFIED WITH A GOOD DAY'S WORK

There are hundreds of tasks we feel we must accomplish in the day, but if we do not take them one at a time ... we are bound to break our own physical or mental structure.
—Ted Bengermino

A man can do only what he can do. But if he does that each day he can sleep at night and do it again the next day.
—Albert Schweitzer

We cannot do everything at once, but we can do something at once.
—Calvin Coolidge

Always do one thing less than you think you can do.
—Bernard Baruch

I come to the office each morning and stay for long hours doing what has to be done to the best of my ability. And when you've done the best you can, you can't do any better. So when I go to sleep I turn everything over to the Lord and forget it.
—Harry S. Truman

A day's work is a day's work, neither more nor less, and the man who does it needs a day's sustenance, a night's repose and due leisure, whether he be painter or ploughman.
—George Bernard Shaw

Sufficient to each day are the duties to be done and the trials to be endured.
—T.L. Gayler

I have fought a good fight, I have finished my course, I have kept the faith.
—2 Tm. 4:7

I look back on my life like a good day's work; it is done, and I am satisfied with it.
—Grandma Moses

GOOD HABITS MAKE OUR DAILY LIVES EASIER

The moment we pass out of our habits we lose all sense of permanency and routine.
—George Moore

It is too bad if you have to do everything upon reflection and can't do anything from early habit.
—Georg Christoph Lichtenberg

Most of life is routine—dull and grubby, but routine is the mountain that keeps a man going. If you wait for inspiration you'll be standing on the corner after the parade is a mile down the street.
—Ben Nicholas

Good habits, which bring our lower passions and appetites under automatic control, leave our natures free to explore the larger experiences of life.
—Ralph W. Sockman, D.D.

Motivation is what gets you started. Habit is what keeps you going.
—Jim Ryuh

Without the aid of prejudice and custom, I should not be able to find my way across the room.
—William Hazlitt

Habits are safer than rules; you don't have to watch them. And you don't have to keep them, either; they keep you.   —Dr. Frank Crane

Habit is not mere subjugation, it is a tender tie; when one remembers habit it seems to have been happiness.   —Elizabeth Bowen

To learn new habits is everything, for it is to reach the substance of life. Life is but a tissue of habits.
—Henri Frederic Amiel

Choose always the way that seems the best, however rough it may be; custom will soon render it easy and agreeable.   —Pythagoras

Quality is not an act. It is a habit.
—Aristotle

It is not in novelty but in habit that we find the greatest pleasure.
—Raymond Radiguet

Habit is stronger than reason.
—George Santayana

Character is simply habit long enough continued.   —Plutarch

Nothing is more powerful than habit.   —Ovid

If you do the same thing every day at the same time for the same length of time, you'll save yourself from many a sink. Routine is a condition of survival.   —Flannery O'Connor

Have a time and place for everything, and do everything in its time and place, and you will not only accomplish more, but have far more leisure than those who are always hurrying.   —Tyron Edwards

SOMETIMES, THE BEST WE CAN DO IS JUST MAKE IT THROUGH THE DAY

Anyone can carry his burden, however hard, until nightfall. Anyone can do his work, however hard, for one day. Anyone can live sweetly, patiently, lovingly, purely, till the sun goes down. And this is all life really means.
—Robert Louis Stevenson

Come what may, time and the hour runs through the roughest day.
—William Shakespeare

At any rate, you can bear it for a quarter of an hour!
—Theodore Haecker

The longest day is soon ended.
—Pliny, the Younger

The secret of my success is that I always managed to live to fly another day.   —Chuck Yeager

HOW LONG IS A DAY?

A day is a miniature eternity.
—Ralph Waldo Emerson

A day is a span of time no one is wealthy enough to waste.
—Anon.

One day, with life and heart, is more than time enough to find a world.
—James Russell Lowell

The time which we have at our disposal every day is elastic; the passions that we feel expand it, those that we inspire contract it; and habit fills up what remains.
—Marcel Proust

Time Is Relative

When a man sits with a pretty girl for an hour, it seems like a minute. But let him sit on a hot stove for a minute, and it's longer than any hour. That's relativity.
—Albert Einstein

Time is
Too slow for those who wait,
Too swift for those who fear,
Too long for those who grieve,
Too short for those who rejoice.
But for those who love, time is not.
—Henry van Dyke

The less one has to do, the less time one finds to do it in. One yawns, one procrastinates, one can do it when one will, and, therefore, one seldom does it at all; whereas those who have a great deal of business must buckle to it; and then they always find time enough to do it.
—Lord Chesterfield

Time is nothing absolute; its duration depends on the rate of thought and feeling.
—John Draper

Time is a fluid condition which has no existence except in the momentary avatars of individual people.
—William Faulkner

What then is time? If no one asks me, I know what it is. If I wish to explain it to him who asks, I do not know.
—Saint Augustine

Time is the product of changing realities, beings, existences.
—Nicholas Berdyaev

Time is the relationship between events.
—Yakima Indian Nation

Time is the arbitrary division of eternity.
—Anon.

Time is a part of eternity, and of the same piece with it.
—Moses Mendelssohn

Time is eternity begun.
—James Montgomery

Time is not a line, but a series of now-points.
—Taisen Deshimaru

You can't measure time in days the way you can money in dollars, because each day is different.
—Phillip Hewett

An hour of pain is as long as a day of pleasure.
—Anon.

The value of life lies not in the length of days, but in the use we make of them; a man may live long yet live very little.
—Michel de Montaigne

Reality is a staircase going neither up nor down, we don't move; today is today, always is today.
—Octavio Paz

Other Definitions of One Day

What runs through a person like water through a sieve.
—Samuel Butler

Scrolls: write on them what you want to be remembered for.
—Joseph Ibn Pakuda

Every day is a messenger of God.
—Russian proverb

Each day is a little life; every waking
and rising a little birth; every fresh
morning a little youth; every going
to rest and sleep a little death.
—Arthur Schopenhauer

A little space of time before time
expires; a little way of breath.
—Algernon Swinburne

OTHER DEFINITIONS OF TIME

Time is an avid gambler who has no
need to cheat to win every time.
—Charles Baudelaire

Time is the only critic without ambition.   —John Steinbeck

Time is the most valuable thing a
man can spend.   —Theophrastus

Time is a storm in which we are all
lost.   —William C. Williams

Time is the tyrant of the body.
—Anon.

Time is the wisest counsellor of all.
—Pericles

Time is the moving image of eternity.   —Plato

Time is the soul of this world.
—Plutarch

Time is a sandpile we run our fingers
in.   —Carl Sandburg

Time is one kind of robber whom
the law does not strike at, and who
steals what is most precious to men.
—Napoleon Bonaparte

Time is that in which all things pass
away.   —Arthur Schopenhauer

Time is a file that wears and makes
no noise.   —English proverb

Time is what we want most, but ...
what we use worst.   —William Penn

Time is the king of men.
—William Shakespeare

Time ... is the life of the soul.
—Henry Wadsworth Longfellow

Time is the dressing room for eternity.   —Anon.

Time is an available instrument for
reaching the eternal.
—John W. Lynch

Time itself is an element.
—Johann von Goethe

Time is the devourer of all things.
—Ovid

Time is a very shadow that passeth
away.   —Apocrypha

Time is the subtle thief of youth.
—John Milton

Time is the rider that breaks youth.
—George Herbert

Time is an eternal guest that ban-
quets on our ideals and bodies.
—Elbert Hubbard

Time is an illusion—to orators.
—Elbert Hubbard

The surest poison is time.
—Ralph Waldo Emerson

Time is a great manager: it arranges things well. —Pierre Corneille

Time is the greatest and longest-established spinner of all.... His factory is a secret place, his work noiseless, and his hands are mutes.
—Charles Dickens

Time is the stuff life's made of.
—David Belasco

Time is my estate: to Time I'm heir.
—Johann von Goethe

Time is change, transformation, evolution. —Isaac L. Peretz

Time is a circus always packing up and moving away. —Ben Hecht

Time is a dressmaker specializing in alterations. —Faith Baldwin

Time is the greatest innovator.
—Francis Bacon

Time is a wealth of change, but the clock in its parody makes it mere change and no wealth.
—Rabindranath Tagore

Time is the author of authors.
—Francis Bacon

Time is but the stream I go a-fishing in. —Henry David Thoreau

Time is a river without banks.
—Marc Chagall

Time is the silent, never-resting thing ... rolling, rushing on, swift, silent, like an all-embracing oceantide, on which we and all the universe swim.
—Thomas Carlyle

Time is a flowing river. Happy those who allow themselves to be carried, unresisting, with the current. They float through easy days. They live, unquestioning, in the moment.
—Christopher Morley

Time is a stream which glides smoothly on and is past before we know. —Ovid

Time is a sort of river of passing events, and strong is its current; no sooner is a thing brought to sight than it is swept by and another takes its place, and this too will be swept away. —Marcus Aurelius

Time is the sea in which men grow, are born, or die. —Freya Stark

Time is the longest distance between two places. —Tennessee Williams

YESTERDAY: THE PAST

WE REMEMBER MORE OF THE GOOD THAN OF THE BAD OR THE DIFFICULT

Vanity plays lurid tricks with our memory.   —Joseph Conrad

Nostalgia is a seductive liar.
                    —George W. Ball

Nostalgia: A device that removes the ruts and potholes from memory lane.
                    —Doug Larson

What was hard to bear is sweet to remember.   —Portuguese proverb

The heart's memory eliminates the bad and magnifies the good; and thanks to this artifice we manage to endure the burdens of the past.
        —Gabriel Garcia Marquez

A man's memory may almost become the art of continually varying and misrepresenting his past, according to his interest in the present.   —George Santayana

Praising what is lost makes the remembrance dear.
            —William Shakespeare

Some folks never exaggerate—they just remember big.   —Audrey Snead

God gave us memory that we might have roses in December.
            —Sir James M. Barrie

PEOPLE HAVE ALWAYS THOUGHT "THE GOOD OLD DAYS" WERE BETTER

Children today are tyrants. They contradict their parents, gobble their food, and tyrannize their teachers.
        —Socrates (470–399 B.C.)

Only sick music makes money today.
        —Friedrich Nietzsche (in 1888)

Let others praise ancient times; I am glad I was born in these.
                —Ovid (81 B.C.)

Posterity will say as usual: "In the past things were better, the present is worse than the past."
        —Anton Chekhov (1860–1904)

Our ignorance of history makes us libel to our own times. People have always been like this.
        —Gustave Flaubert (1821–1880)

Oh, this age! How tasteless and ill-bred it is!   —Catullus (87–54 B.C.)

This strange disease of modern life, with its sick hurry, its divided aims.
    —Matthew Arnold (1822–1888)

The illusion that times that were are better than those that are has probably pervaded all ages.
    —Horace Greeley (1811–1872)

There has never been an age that did not applaud the past and lament the present.   —Lillian Eichler Watson

Oh, what times! Oh, what standards!   —Cicero (106–43 B.C.)

Probably no one alive hasn't at one time or another brooded over the possibility of going back to an earlier, ideal age in his existence and living a different kind of life.
    —Hal Boyle

The Golden Age was never the present Age.
    —Thomas Fuller (1608–1661)

The worst time is always the present.
    —Jean de La Fontaine (1621–1695)

The "good old times"—all times, when old, are good.
    —Lord Byron (1788–1824)

REGRETS

If you have behaved badly, repent, make what amends you can and address yourself to the task of behaving better next time. On no account brood over your wrongdoing. Rolling in the muck is not the best way of getting clean.
    —Aldous Huxley

When one door closes another opens. But we often look so long and so regretfully upon the closed door that we fail to see the one that has opened for us.
    —Alexander Graham Bell

Regret for the things we did can be tempered by time; it is regret for the things we did not do that is inconsolable.   —Sydney J. Harris

Always repenting of wrongs done will never bring my heart to rest.
    —Chi K'ang

The error of the past is the success of the future. A mistake is evidence that someone tried to do something.
    —Anon.

Regret is an appalling waste of energy; you can't build on it; it is good only for wallowing.
    —Katherine Mansfield

I have always found that each step we take in life is to be regretted—if we once begin to wonder how many other steps might have been possible.
    —John Oliver Hobbes

Let the dead Past bury its dead!
    —Henry Wadsworth Longfellow

"The horror of that moment," the King went on, "I shall never forget." "You will, though," the Queen said, "if you don't make a memorandum of it."   —Lewis Carroll

Reflect upon your present blessings, of which every man has many—not on your past misfortunes, of which all men have some.
    —Charles Dickens

They say you should not suffer through the past. You should be able to wear it like a loose garment, take it off and let it drop.   —Eva Jessye

Your past is always going to be the way it was. Stop trying to change it.
                                        —Anon.

If you cannot get rid of the family skeleton, you may as well make it dance.   —George Bernard Shaw

The only thing I regret about my past is the length of it. If I had to live my life again, I'd make the same mistakes, only sooner.
                            —Tallulah Bankhead

Hindsight is always 20/20.
                                —Billy Wilder

There is no greater sorrow than to recall a happy time in the midst of wretchedness.   —Dante Alighieri

We should have no regrets.... The past is finished. There is nothing to be gained by going over it. Whatever it gave us in the experiences it brought us was something we had to know.   —Rebecca Beard

This is another day! Are its eyes blurred with maudlin grief for any wasted past? A thousand thousand failures shall not daunt! Let dust clasp dust, death, death; I am alive!
                            —Don Marquis

Yesterday's errors let yesterday cover.   —Susan Coolidge

Whatever with the past has gone, the best is always yet to come.
                                —Lucy Larcom

One must never lose time in vainly regretting the past or in complaining against the changes which cause us discomfort, for change is the essence of life.   —Anatole France

LEARNING FROM THE PAST

Recognizing what we have done in the past is a recognition of ourselves. By conducting a dialogue with our past, we are searching how to go forward.   —Kiyoko Takeda

I know of no way of judging the future but by the past.
                                —Patrick Henry

Those who cannot remember the past are condemned to repeat it.
                            —George Santayana

The past is never dead—it is not even past.   —William Faulkner

The past is the best way to suppose what may come.   —Lord Halifax

Past: Our cradle, not our prison, and there is danger as well as appeal in its glamour. The past is for inspiration, not imitation; for continuation, not repetition.   —Israel Zangwill

Life can only be understood backwards, but it must be lived forward.
                            —Søren Kierkegaard

When I want to understand what is happening today or try to decide what will happen tomorrow, I look back.   —Oliver Wendell Holmes

We live in the present, we dream of the future, but we learn eternal truths from the past.
                        —Madame Chiang Kai-shek

The past is the best prophet of the future. —Lord Byron

The past will not tell us what we ought to do, but ... what we ought to avoid. —José Ortega y Gasset

Tomorrow hopes we have learned something from yesterday.
—John Wayne

Judgement comes from experience, and great judgement comes from bad experience. —Robert Packwood

The only use of a knowledge of the past is to equip us for the present.
—Alfred North Whitehead

When the past has taught us that we have more within us than we have ever used, our prayer is a cry to the divine to come to us and fill us with its power. —Rudolph Steiner

IT'S IMPORTANT TO BURY THE PAST, TO LET IT GO— TO MOVE ON

Here lies my past,
Goodbye I have kissed it;
Thank you kids,
I wouldn't have missed it.
—Ogden Nash

Living in the past is a dull and lonely business; looking back strains the neck muscles, causes you to bump into people not going your way.
—Edna Ferber

I demolish my bridges behind me ... then there is no choice but forward.
—Firdtjof Nansen

Let the past drift away with the water. —Japanese saying

Not the power to remember, but its very opposite, the power to forget, is a necessary condition for our existence. —Sholem Asch

You cannot step twice into the same river, for other waters are continually flowing on. —Heraclitus

Better by far you should forget and smile, than that you should remember and be sad. —Christina Rosetti

The past should be culled like a box of fresh strawberries, rinsed of debris, sweetened judiciously and served in small portions, not very often. —Laura Palmer

May I forget what ought to be forgotten; and recall, unfailing, all that ought to be recalled, each kindly thing, forgetting what might sting.
—Maty Caroline Davies

Here's to the past. Thank God it's past! —Anon.

One must be thrust out of a finished cycle in life, and that leap is the most difficult to make—to part with one's faith, one's love, when one would prefer to renew the faith and recreate the passion. —Anaïs Nin

The biggest thing in today's sorrow is the memory of yesterday's joy.
—Kahlil Gibran

The worst thing you can do is to try to cling to something that's gone, or to recreate it. —Johnette Napolitano

Ne'er look for the birds of this year in the nests of the last.
—Miguel de Cervantes

Don't look back. Something may be
gaining on you.   —Satchel Paige

Anyone who limits her vision to
memories of yesterday is already
dead.   —Lily Langtry

I like the dreams for the future better
than the history of the past.
                —Thomas Jefferson

The first recipe for happiness is:
Avoid too lengthy meditations on
the past.   —André Maurois

The past is a funeral gone by.
                —Edmund Gosse

How the past perishes is how the
future becomes.
            —Alfred North Whitehead

Never let yesterday use up today.
            —Richard H. Nelson

The dogmas of the quiet past are
inadequate to the stormy present.
                —Abraham Lincoln

THE PAST AS PROLOGUE—
A BEGINNING

The past is but the beginning of a
beginning, and all that is and has
been is but the twilight of the dawn.
                —H. G. Wells

Nor deem the irrevocable Past
As wholly wasted, wholly vain,
If, rising on its wrecks, at last
To something nobler we attain.
            —Henry Wadsworth Longfellow

Nothing is predestined: The obstacles of your past can become the
gateways that lead to new beginnings.   —Ralph Blum

What's past is prologue.
                —William Shakespeare

Visualize yourself standing before a
gateway on a hilltop. Your entire life
lies out before you and below. Before
you step through, pause and review
the past; the learning and the joys,
the victories and the sorrows—everything it took to bring you here.
                —*The Book of Runes*

The good old days were never that
good, believe me. The good new
days are today, and better days are
coming tomorrow. Our greatest
songs are still unsung.
            —Hubert H. Humphrey

The past is never completely lost,
however extensive the devastation.
Your sorrows are the bricks and
mortar of a magnificent temple.
What you are today and what you
will be tomorrow are because of
what you have been.
                —Gordon Wright

YESTERDAY AND TOMORROW

Fear not for the future, weep not for
the past.   —Percy Bysshe Shelley

There are two days about which
nobody should ever worry, and these
are yesterday and tomorrow.
            —Robert Jones Burdette

We crucify ourselves between two
thieves: regret for yesterday and fear
of tomorrow.   —Fulton Oursler

Every saint has a past, and every sin-
ner has a future.   —Oscar Wilde

When I am anxious it is because I
am living in the future. When I am

222

depressed it is because I am living in the past. —Anon.

MANY THINGS REMAIN THE SAME

I'm not convinced that the world is in any worse shape than it ever was. It's just that in this age of almost instantaneous communication, we bear the weight of problems our forefathers only read about after they were solved. —Burton Hillis

The world's history is constant, like the laws of nature, and simple, like the souls of men.
—J.C.F. von Schiller

This time, like all times, is a very good one if we but know what to do with it. —Ralph Waldo Emerson

In times like these, it helps to recall that there have *always* been times like these. —Paul Harvey

Our ignorance of history makes us libel our own times. People have always been like this.
—Gustave Flaubert

The good old days are neither better nor worse than the ones we're living through right now. —Artie Shaw

GENERAL QUOTATIONS ABOUT THE PAST

Respect the past in the full measure of its deserts, but do not make the mistake of confusing it with the present, nor seek in it the ideals of the future. —José Ingenieros

The best compliment we can pay our past is to prophetically and bravely face today and tomorrow.
—Bernie Wiebe

We have to do with the past only as we can make it useful to the present and the future. —Frederick Douglass

The past is a guidepost, not a hitching post. —L. Thomas Holdcroft

The past in retrospect holds manifold disenchantments, failures and even tragedies; and yet the worse may be forgotten and the best held fast. —W. Robertson Neicoll

No yesterdays are ever wasted for those who give themselves to today.
—Brendan Francis

Yesterday I lived, today I suffer, tomorrow I die; but I still think fondly, today and tomorrow, of yesterday. —Gotthold Ephraim Lessing

Each has his past shut in him like the leaves of a book shown to him by heart, and his friends can only read the title. —Virginia Woolf

We are well advised to keep on nodding terms with the people we used to be, whether we find them attractive company or not.... We forget all too soon the things we thought we could never forget. —Joan Didion

The past is a work of art, free of irrelevancies and loose ends.
—Max Beerbohm

The past is a foreign country; they do things differently there.
—Leslie Poles Hartley

The past with its pleasures, its rewards, its foolishness, its punishments, is there for each of us forever, and it should be. —Lillian Hellman

223

The past is that which we possess fully and in whole.   —Isidor Eliashev

Our deeds still travel with us from afar, and what we have been makes us what we are.   —George Eliot

The past is the tomorrow that got away.   —Leonard L. Levinson

Our life is like some vast lake that is slowly filling with the stream of our years. As the waters creep surely upward the landmarks of the past are one by one submerged. But there shall always be memory to lift its head above the tide until the lake is overflowing.
—Alexandre Charles Auguste Bisson

Why should we grope among the dry bones of the past, or put the living generation into masquerade out of its faded wardrobe?
           —Ralph Waldo Emerson

No past is dead for us, but only sleeping, love. —Helen Hunt Jackson

I look back on my life like a good day's work; it is done and I am satisfied with it.   —Grandma Moses

Of all sad words of tongue or pen, the saddest are these: It might have been.   —John Greenleaf Whittier

That sign of old age, extolling the past at the expense of the present.
                —Sydney Smith

The past is one evil less and one memory more.   —Elbert Hubbard

Then is then. Now is now. We must grow to learn the difference.
                      —Anon.

Say not thou, what is the cause that the former days were better than these, for thou dost not inquire wisely concerning this.
                    —Eccl. 7:10

The past not merely is not fugitive, it remains present.   —Marcel Proust

The past which is so presumptuously brought forward as a precedent for the present was itself founded on some past that went before it.
               —Madame de Stael

"Old times" never come back and I suppose it's just as well. What comes back is a new morning every day in the year, and that's better.
             —George E. Woodberry

We have inherited new difficulties because we have inherited more privileges.   —Dr. Abram Sacher

People are always asking about the good old days. I say, why don't you say the good "now" days? Isn't "now" the only time you're living?
                 —Robert M. Young

Life in the twentieth century undeniably has ... such richness, joy and adventure as were unknown to our ancestors except in their dreams.
              —Arthur H. Campton

Enjoy yourself. These are the "good old days" you're going to miss in the years ahead.   —Anon.

The past is our very being.
                —David Ben-Gurion

To disdain today is to prove that yesterday has been misunderstood.
              —Maurice Maeterlinck

TODAY: THE PRESENT

THE IMPORTANCE OF TODAY

This is not a dress rehearsal. This is
It. —Tom Cunningham

Seize the day, and put the least possible trust in tomorrow. —Horace

Tomorrow's life is too late. Live
today. —Martial

One today is worth two tomorrows.
—Benjamin Franklin

Half of today is better than all of
tomorrow. —Jean de La Fontaine

Never put off until tomorrow what
you can do today, because if you
enjoy it today, you can do it again,
tomorrow. —Anon.

The present moment is significant,
not as the bridge between past and
future, but by reason of its contents,
which can fill our emptiness and
become ours, if we are capable of
receiving them
—Dag Hammarskjold

Today is the first day of the rest of
your life. —Abbie Hoffman

All of us tend to put off living. We
are all dreaming of some magical
rose garden over the horizon instead
of enjoying the roses that are bloom-
ing outside our windows today.
—Dale Carnegie

It's not that "today is the first day of
the rest of my life," but that now is
all there is of my life.
—Hugh Prather

We want to live in the present, and
the only history that is worth a tinker's damn is the history we make
today. —Henry Ford

Now is the only time we own; give,
love, toil with a will.
And place no faith in tomorrow, for
the clock may then be still.
—Anon.

Enjoy yourself, drink, call the life
you live today your own—but only
that; the rest belongs to chance.
—Euripides

You are younger today than you
ever will be again. Make use of it for
the sake of tomorrow. —Anon.

If we are ever to enjoy life, now is the time, not tomorrow or next year.... Today should always be our most wonderful day.
—Thomas Dreier

Live now, believe me, wait not till tomorrow, gather the roses of life today. —Pierre de Ronsard

So often we rob tomorrow's memories by today's economies.
—John Mason Brown

You had better live your best and act your best and think your best today; for today is the sure preparation for tomorrow and all the other tomorrows that follow.
—Harriet Martineau

Happy the man, and happy he alone
He can call today his own.
He who, secure within can say,
"Tomorrow, do thy worst, for I have lived today." —Henry Fielding

Forget mistakes. Forget failures. Forget everything except what you're going to do now and do it. Today is your lucky day. —Will Durant

Yesterday is ashes; tomorrow wood. Only today does the fire burn brightly. —Old Eskimo proverb

One of these days is none of these days. —H.G. Bohn

Look lovingly upon the present, for it holds the only things that are forever true. —A Course In Miracles

This is the day which the Lord has made. Let us rejoice and be glad in it. —Ps. 118:24

He growled at morning, noon, and
night,
And trouble sought to borrow;
Although today the sky was bright,
He knew t'would storm tomorrow;
A thought of joy he could not stand,
And struggled to resist it;
Though sunshine dappled all the
land
This sorry pessimist it.
—Nixon Waterman

To those leaning on the sustaining infinite, to-day is big with blessings.
—Mary Baker Eddy

The here-and-now is no mere filling of time, but a filling of time with God. —John Foster

In the present, every day is a miracle.
—James Gould Cozzens

Life is only this place, this time, and these people right here and now.
—Vincent Collins

I believe that only one person in a thousand knows the trick of really living in the present.
—Storm Jameson

There is one thing we can do, and the happiest people are those who do it to the limit of their ability. We can be completely present. We can be all here. We can ... give all our attention to the opportunity before us.
—Mark Van Doren

The more I give myself permission to live in the moment and enjoy it without feeling guilty or judgmental about any other time, the better I feel about the quality of my work.
—Wayne Dyer

226

Act—act in the living Present!
   —Henry Wadsworth Longfellow

Are not my days few? Cease then, and let me alone, that I may take comfort a little, Before I go to the place from which I shall not return.
   —Jb. 10:21–22

Now or never was the time.
   —Laurence Sterne

And now, Lord, what wait I for?
   —Psalms

The future belongs to those who live intensely in the present.   —Anon.

The present is elastic to embrace infinity.   —Louis Anspacher

The present is the living sum-total of the whole past.   —Thomas Carlyle

The present is an eternal now.
   —Abraham Cowley

The present is all the ready money Fate can give.   —Abraham Cowley

The present is an edifice which God cannot rebuild.
   —Ralph Waldo Emerson

The present is the blocks with which we build. —Henry W. Longfellow

The present is the symbol and vehicle of the future. —Joseph McSorely

The present is all you have for your certain possession.   —Anon.

We are here and it is now. Further than that, all knowledge is moonshine.   —H.L. Mencken

Having spent the better part of my life trying either to relive the past or experience the future before it arrives, I have come to believe that in between these two extremes is peace.   —Anon.

This time, like all times, is a very good one if we but know what to do with it.   —Ralph Waldo Emerson

The time is always right to do what is right.   —Martin Luther King, Jr.

One realm we have never conquered: the pure present.   —D.H. Lawrence

He who lives in the present lives in eternity.   —Ludwig Wittgenstein

I am in the present. I cannot know what tomorrow will bring forth. I can know only what the truth is for me today. That is what I am called upon to serve.   —Igor Stravinsky

The present offers itself to our touch for only an instant of time and then eludes the senses.   —Plutarch

A life uncommanded now is uncommanded; a life unenjoyed now is unenjoyed; a life not lived wisely now is not lived wisely.   —David Grayson

The word "now" is like a bomb thrown through the window, and it ticks.   —Arthur Miller

Whether it's the best of times or the worst of times, it's the only time we've got.   —Art Buchwald

It is now, and in this world, that we must live.   —André Gide

227

Who cares about great marks left behind? We have one life ... Just one. Our life. We have nothing else.
—Ugo Betti

This—the immediate, everyday, and present experience—is *IT,* the entire and ultimate point for the existence of a universe.　　　—Alan Watts

Let us live today.
—J.C.F. von Schiller

Work accomplished means little. It is in the past. What we all want is the glorious and living present.
—Sherwood Anderson

Yesterday is a cancelled check. Tomorrow is a promissory note. Today is cash in hand. *Spend It!*
—John W. Newbern

TODAY RELATIVE TO YESTERDAY AND TOMORROW

Yesterday is but a dream, tomorrow is only a vision. But today, well lived, makes every yesterday a dream of happiness, and every tomorrow a vision of hope. Look well, therefore, to this day, for it is life, the very life of life.　　　—*The Sanskrit*

Do not look back on happiness, or dream of it in the future. You are only sure of today; do not let yourself be cheated out of it.
—Henry Ward Beecher

I am not afraid of tomorrow, for I have seen yesterday and I love today.
—William Allen White

The past, the present and the future are really one: they are today.
—Harriet Beecher Stowe

The present contains all that there is. It is holy ground; for it is the past, and it is the future.
—Alfred North Whitehead

With the past, I have nothing to do; nor with the future. I live now.
—Ralph Waldo Emerson

Children have neither a past nor a future. Thus they enjoy the present, which seldom happens to us.
—Jean de La Bruyere

The past is a bucket of ashes, so live not in your yesterdays, nor just for tomorrow, but in the here and now.
—Carl Sandburg

It is not the weight of the future or the past that is pressing upon you, but ever that of the present alone. Even this burden, too, can be lessened if you confine it strictly to its own limits.　　　—Marcus Aurelius

We can easily manage if we will only take, each day, the burden appointed to it. But the load will be too heavy for us if we carry yesterday's burden over again today, and then add the burden of the morrow before we are required to bear it.　　—John Newton

Take in the ideas of the day, drain off those of yesterday. As to the morrow, time enough to consider it when it becomes today.
—Edward Bulwer-Lytton

Tomorrow I will live, the fool does say; today itself's too late, the wise lived yesterday.　　　　—Martial

The cares of today are seldom those of tomorrow.　　—William Cowper

Yesterday is a cancelled check; tomorrow is a promissory note; today is the only cash you have—so spend it wisely.   —Kay Lyons

Everyman's life lies within the present, for the past is spent and done with, and the future is uncertain.
                    —Marcus Aurelius

The flesh endures the storms of the present alone, the mind those of the past and future as well.   —Epicurus

I try to learn from the past, but I plan for the future by focusing exclusively on the present. That's where the fun is.   —Donald Trump

No mind is much employed upon the present; recollection and anticipation fill up almost all our moments.
                    —Samuel Johnson

The only living life is in the past and future—the present is an interlude—strange interlude in which we call on past and future to bear witness that we are living.   —Eugene O'Neill

Past, and to come, seems best; things present, worst.
                    —William Shakespeare

The past cannot be regained, although we can learn from it; the future is not yet ours even though we must plan for it.... Time is now. We have only today. —Charles Hummell

Look not mournfully into the past, it comes not back again. Wisely improve the present, it is thine. Go forth to meet the shadowy future without fear and with a manly heart.
                    —Henry Wadsworth Longfellow

No longer forward nor behind I look in hope or fear; but grateful, take the good I find, the best of now and here.   —John Greenleaf Whittier

The present, like a note in music, is nothing but as it appertains to what is past and what is to come.
                    —Walter Savage Landor

We can see well into the past; we can guess shrewdly in to the future; but that which is rolled up and muffled in impenetrable folds is today.
                    —Ralph Waldo Emerson

The present time is seldom able to fill desire or imagination with immediate enjoyment, and we are forced to supply its deficiencies by recollection or anticipation.
                    —Samuel Johnson

Be satisfied, and pleased with what
    thou art,
Act cheerfully and well thy allotted
    part;
Enjoy the present hour, be thankful
    for the past,
And neither fear, nor wish, the
    approaches of the last. —Martial

It is difficult to live in the present, ridiculous to live in the future and impossible to live in the past.
                    —Jim Bishop

If you have one eye on yesterday, and one eye on tomorrow, you're going to be cockeyed today.
                    —Anon.

Yesterday has gone. Tomorrow may never come. There is only the miracle of this moment. Savor it. It is a gift.   —Anon.

Don't waste today regretting yesterday instead of making a memory for tomorrow. —Laura Palmer

I just take one day. Yesterday is gone. Tomorrow has not come. We have only today to love Jesus. —Mother Teresa

Patterns of the past echo in the present and resound through the future. —Dhyani Ywahoo

Who controls the past controls the future; who controls the present controls the past. —George Orwell

If we spend our time with regrets over yesterday, and worries over what might happen tomorrow, we have no today in which to live. —Anon.

Now is all we have. Everything that has ever happened to you, and anything that is ever going to happen to you, is just a thought. —Wayne Dyer

The present is the necessary product of all the past, the necessary cause of all the future. —Robert G. Ingersoll

The present is the now, the here, through which all future plunges to the past. —James Joyce

If we open a quarrel between the past and the present, we shall find we have lost the future. —Sir Winston Churchill

Few of us ever live in the present, we are forever anticipating what is to come or remembering what has gone. —Louis L'Amour

The secret of health for both mind and body is not to mourn for the past, not to worry about the future, nor to anticipate troubles, but to live the present moment wisely and earnestly. —Buddha

When we have a world of only now, with no shadows of yesterdays or clouds of tomorrow, then saying what we can do will work. —Goldie Ivener

I can feel guilty about the past, apprehensive about the future, but only in the present can I act. The ability to be in the present moment is a major component of mental wellness. —Abraham Maslow

The idea of "twenty-four-hour living" applies primarily to the emotional life of the individual. Emotionally speaking, we must not live in yesterday, nor in tomorrow. —As Bill Sees It

I have realized that the past and the future are real illusions, that they exist only in the present, which is what there is and all that there is. —Alan Watts

There is no present or future, only the past, happening over and over again, now. —Eugene O'Neill

Today was once the future from which you expected so much in the past. —Anon.

Today is yesterday's pupil. —Benjamin Franklin

Today is yesterday's effect and tomorrow's cause. —Phillip Gribble

230

Through loyalty to the past, our mind refuses to realize that tomorrow's joy is possible only if today's makes way for it; that each wave owes the beauty of its line only to the withdrawal of the preceding one.
—André Gide

I have everything I need to enjoy my here and now—unless I am letting my consciousness be dominated by demands and expectations based on the dead past or the imagined future.
—Ken Keyes, Jr.

Today is the blocks with which we build.
—Henry Wadsworth Longfellow

In order to be utterly happy, the only thing necessary is to refrain from comparing this moment with other moments in the past, which I often did not fully enjoy because I was comparing them with other moments of the future.
—André Gide

Don't Waste Today Preparing for Tomorrow

Seize from every moment its unique novelty, and do not prepare your joys.
—André Gide

Do not manage as if you had ten thousand years before you. Look you, death stands at your elbow; make the most of your minute, and be good for something while it is in your power.
—Charles Palmer

And if not now, when?
—Talmud

As we are always preparing to be happy, it is inevitable that we should never be so.
—Blaise Pascal

Why not seize the pleasure at once? How often is happiness destroyed by preparation, foolish preparation!
—Jane Austen

When shall we live if not now?
—M.F.K. Fisher

We cannot put off living until we are ready. The most salient characteristic of life is its coerciveness: it is always urgent, "here and now," without any possible postponement. Life is fired at us point-blank.
—José Ortega y Gasset

Very few men, properly speaking, live at present, but are providing to live another time.   —Jonathan Swift

Real generosity toward the future lies in giving all to the present.
—Albert Camus

Freedom from worries and surcease from strain are illusions that always inhabit the distance.
—Edwin Way Teale

Study as if you were to live forever. Live as if you were to die tomorrow.
—Isidore of Seville

The best preparation for a better life next year is a full, complete, harmonious, joyous life this year.
—Thomas Dreier

If you spend your whole life waiting for the storm, you'll never enjoy the sunshine.   —Morris West

Some people are making such thorough preparation for rainy days that they aren't enjoying today's sunshine.   —William Feather

231

The greater part of our lives is spent
in dreaming over the morrow, and
when it comes, it, too, is consumed
in the anticipation of a brighter morrow, and so the cheat is prolonged,
even to the grave.
—Mark Rutherford

It is cheap generosity which promises
the future in compensation for the
present.   —J.A. Spender

Who knows if the gods above will
add tomorrow's span to this day's
sum?   —Horace

Defer not till tomorrow to be wise,
tomorrow's sun to thee may never
rise.   —William Congreve

My head is buried in the sands of
tomorrow, while my tail feathers are
singed by the hot sun of today.
—John Barrymore

Today, well lived, will prepare me
for both the pleasure and the pain of
tomorrow.   —Anon.

The future belongs to those who live
intensely in the present.   —Anon.

Every moment that I am centered in
the future, I suffer a temporary loss
of this life.   —Hugh Prather

We know nothing of tomorrow; our
business is to be good and happy
today.   —Sydney Smith

We are always beginning to live, but
are never living.   —Manilius

Live wastes itself while we are
preparing to live.
—Ralph Waldo Emerson

I have always been waiting for something better—sometimes to see the
best I had snatched from me.
—Dorothy Reed Mendenhall

Men spend their lives in anticipation,
in determining to be vastly happy at
some period when they have time.
But the present time has one advantage over every other—it is our
own.... We may lay in a stock of
pleasures, as we would lay in a stock
of wine; but if we defer the tasting of
them too long, we shall find that
both are soured by age.
—Charles Caleb Colton

You do well to have visions of a better life than of every day, but it is the
life of every day from which the elements of a better life must come.
—Maurice Maeterlinck

The most effective way to ensure the
value of the future is to confront the
present courageously and construc-
tively.   —Rollo May

The habit of looking into the future
and thinking that the whole meaning
of the present lies in what it will
bring forth is a pernicious one. There
can be no value in the whole unless
there is value in the parts.
—Bertrand Russell

Very strange is this quality of our
human nature which decrees that
unless we feel a future before us we
do not live completely in the present.
—Phillips Brooks

Just do your best today and tomorrow will come ... tomorrow's going
to be a busy day, a happy day.
—Helen Boehm

232

Do today's duty, fight today's temptation; do not weaken and distract yourself by looking forward to things you cannot see, and could not understand if you saw them.
—Charles Kingsley

The best preparation for good work tomorrow is to do good work today.
—Elbert Hubbard

Live for today. Multitudes of people have failed to live for today.... What they have had within their grasp today they have missed entirely, because only the future has intrigued them.   —William Allen White

Present opportunities are neglected, and attainable good is slighted, by minds busied in extensive ranges and intent upon future advantages.
—Samuel Johnson

You don't save a pitcher for tomorrow. Tomorrow it may rain.
—Leo Durocher

Light tomorrow with today.
—Elizabeth Barrett Browning

A preoccupation with the future not only prevents us from seeing the present as it is, but often prompts us to rearrange the past.   —Eric Hoffer

The man least dependent upon the morrow goes to meet the morrow most cheerfully.   —Epicurus

Today's egg is better than tomorrow's hen.   —Turkish proverb

T'were too absurd to slight for the hereafter, the day's delight!
—Robert Browning

The best part of our lives we pass in counting on what is to come.
—William Hazlitt

It seems to be the fate of man to seek all his consolations in futurity.
—Samuel Johnson

The prospect of being pleased tomorrow will never console me for the boredom of today.
—Francois de La Rochefoucauld

To live only for some future goal is shallow. It's the sides of the mountain that sustain life, not the top.
—Robert M. Pirsig

We steal if we touch tomorrow. It is God's.   —Henry Ward Beecher

The past and present are only our means; the future is always our end. Thus we never really live, but only hope to live.   —Blaise Pascal

233

THIS MOMENT

THE PRECIOUSNESS OF EACH MOMENT

Every second is of infinite value.
—Johann von Goethe

Let me tell thee, time is a very precious gift of God; so precious that it's only given to us moment by moment.
—Amelia Barr

This—this was what made life: a moment of quiet, the water falling in the fountain, the girl's voice ... a moment of captured beauty. He who is truly wise will never permit such moments to escape.
—Louis L'Amour

The span of life is waning fast;
Beware, unthinking youth, beware!
Thy soul's eternity depends
Upon the record moments bear!
—Eliza Cook

Florence Farr once said to me, "If we could say to ourselves, with sincerity, 'this passing moment is as good as any I shall ever know,' we could die upon the instant and be united with God." —William Butler Yeats

Sometimes I would almost rather have people take away years of my life than take away a moment.
—Pearl Bailey

We do not remember days, we remember moments.
—Cesare Pavese

Life is a succession of moments. To live each one is to succeed.
—Corita Kent

Life is not lost by dying; life is lost minute by minute, day by day, in all the thousand small, uncaring ways.
—Stephen Saint Vincent Benet

I have the happiness of the passing moment, and what more can mortal ask?
—George R. Gissing

The sole life which a man can lose is that which he is living at the moment.
—Marcus Aurelius

I always say to myself, what is the most important thing we can think about at this extraordinary moment.
—Francois de La Rochefoucauld

Fill the unforgiving minute with
sixty seconds worth of distance run.
—Rudyard Kipling

The present moment is creative, creating with an unheard-of intensity.
—Le Corbusier

The only way to live is to accept
each minute as an unrepeatable miracle, which is exactly what it is: a
miracle and unrepeatable.
—Storm Jameson

Who makes quick use of the moment
is a genius of prudence.
—Johann Kaspar Lavater

I live now and only now, and I will
do what I want to do *this* moment
and not what I decided was best for
me yesterday.   —Hugh Prather

But what minutes! Count them by
sensation, and not by calendars, and
each moment is a day.
—Benjamin Disraeli

It may be life is only worthwhile at
moments. Perhaps that is all we
ought to expect.
—Sherwood Anderson

To finish the moment, to find the
journey's end in every step of the
road, to live the greatest number of
good hours, is wisdom.
—Ralph Waldo Emerson

Our latest moment is always our
supreme moment. Five minutes delay
in dinner now is more important
than a great sorrow ten years gone.
—Samuel Butler

God speaks to all individuals
through what happens to them
moment by moment.
—J.P. DeCaussade

Be always resolute with the present
hour. Every moment is of infinite
value.   —Boethe

A player's effectiveness is directly
related to his ability to be right
there, doing that thing, in the
moment.... He can't be worrying
about the past or the future or the
crowd or some other extraneous
event. He must be able to respond in
the here and now.   —John Brodie

OUR MOMENTS PASS TOO QUICKLY

Life is all memory except for the one
present moment that goes by so
quick you can hardly catch it going.
—Tennessee Williams

We have only this moment,
sparkling like a star in our hand ...
and melting like a snowflake. Let us
use it before it is too late.
—Marie Beynon Ray

It is privilege of living to be ... acutely, agonizingly conscious of the
moment that is always present and
always passing.   —Marya Mannes

The passing moment is all we can be
sure of; it is only common sense to
extract its utmost value from it.
—W. Somerset Maugham

He is blessed over all mortals who
loses no moment of the passing life.
—Henry David Thoreau

General Quotations about Moments

We must not wish anything other than what happens from moment to moment, all the while, however, exercising ourselves in goodness.
—Saint Catherine of Genoa

The only courage that matters is the kind that gets you from one moment to the next.   —Mignon McLaughlin

The moment of change is the only poem.   —Adrienne Rich

If it weren't for the last minute, nothing would get done.
—Anon.

Once to every man and nation comes the moment to decide....
And the choice goes by forever t'wixt that darkness and that light.
—James Russell Lowell

Love the moment and the energy of the moment will spread beyond all boundaries.   —Corita Kent

Mornings

No Matter How Bad Things Look at Night, They Usually Look Better in the Morning

Weeping may endure for a night, but joy cometh in the morning.

— Ps. 30:5

Sadness flies on the wings of the morning, and out of the heart of darkness comes the light.

—Jean Giraudoux

Out of the scabbard of the night,
By God's hand drawn,
Flashes his shining sword of light,
And lo, the dawn!

—Frank Dempster Sherman

For what human ill does not dawn seem to be an alleviation?

—Thornton Wilder

The weariest night, the longest day, sooner or later must perforce come to an end.　　—Baroness Orczy

Beware of desp'rate steps; the darkest day lived till tomorrow will have pass'd away.　—William Cowper

Have hope. Though clouds environs now,
And gladness hides her face in scorn,
Put thou the shadow from thy brow—
No night but hath its morn.

—J.C.F. von Schiller

Snow endures but for a season, and joy comes with the morning.

—Marcus Aurelius

The morning is wiser than the evening.　　—Russian proverb

For the mind disturbed, the still beauty of dawn is nature's finest balm.　　—Edwin Way Teale

Hold your head high, stick your chest out. You can make it. It gets dark sometimes, but morning comes.... Keep hope alive.

—Jesse Jackson

It is a common experience that a problem difficult at night is resolved in the morning after the committee of sleep has worked on it.

—John Steinbeck

WE'RE REBORN EACH MORNING

Each day is a new life. Seize it. Live it. —David Guy Powers

Always begin anew with the day, just as nature does. It is one of the sensible things that nature does.
—George E. Woodberry

With each sunrise, we start anew.
—Anon.

We are new every day.
—Irene Claremont de Castillego

I have always been delighted at the prospect of a new day, a fresh try, one more start, with perhaps a bit of magic waiting somewhere behind the morning. —J.B. Priestly

Each day the world is born anew for him who takes it rightly.
—James Russell Lowell

Relying on God has to begin all over again every day as if nothing had yet been done. —C.S. Lewis

Have patience with all things, but chiefly have patience with yourself. Do not lose courage in considering your own imperfections, but instantly set about remedying them—every day begin the task anew.
—Saint Francis de Sales

Each day is a little life; every waking and rising a little birth; every fresh morning a little youth; every going to rest and sleep a little death.
—Arthur Schopenhauer

I love the challenge of starting at zero every day and seeing how much I can accomplish. —Martha Stewart

Whether one is twenty, forty, or sixty; whether one has succeeded, failed or just muddled along; whether yesterday was full of sun or storm, or one of those dull days with no weather at all, life begins each morning!... Each morning is the open door to a new world—new vistas, new aims, new tryings.
—Leigh Mitchell Hodges

To be seeing the world made new every morning, as if it were the morning of the first day, and then to make the most of it for the individual soul as if each were the last day, is the daily curriculum of the mind's desire. —John H. Finley

Do not say, "It is morning," and dismiss it with a name of yesterday. See it for the first time as a newborn child that has no name.
—Rabindranath Tagore

God had infinite time to give us.... He cut it up into a near succession of new mornings, and, with each, therefore, a new idea, new inventions, and new applications.
—Ralph Waldo Emerson

GET UP QUICKLY

No matter how big or soft or warm your bed is, you still have to get out of it. —Grace Slick

Spill not the morning (the quintessence of the day!) in recreations, for sleep is a recreation. Add not, therefore, sauce to sauce.... Pastime, like wine, is poison in the morning. It is then good husbandry to sow the head, which hath lain fallow all night, with some serious work.
—Thomas Fuller

238

Do not shorten the morning by getting up late; look upon it as the quintessence of life, and to a certain extent sacred.

—Arthur Schopenhauer

Let us then be up and doing, with a heart for any fate.

—Henry Wadsworth Longfellow

He'd jolt up in bed every morning, sit quietly for a moment, and you could feel those wheels spinning in his mind as he planned his day. Then he'd hit the floor almost on the run.

—Sasha Stallone, describing Sylvester's early Hollywood days

Clay lies still, but blood's a rover
Breath's a ware that will not keep.
Up lad: when the journey's over
There'll be time enough to sleep.

—A.E. Housman

Even if a farmer intends to loaf, he gets up in time to get an early start.

—Edgar Watson Howe

GIVE THANKS

I thank You God for this most amazing day; for the leaping greenly spirits of trees and a blue true dream of sky; and for everything which is natural which is infinite which is yes.

—e.e. cummings

I get up and I bless the light thin clouds and the first twittering of birds, and the breathing air and smiling face of the hills.

—Giacomo Leopardi

I'm a most lucky and thankful woman. Lucky and thankful for each morning I wake up. For three wonderful daughters and one son. For an understanding and very loving husband with whom I've shared fifty-two blessed years, all in good health.

—Thelma Elliott

If God adds another day to our life, let us receive it gladly.

—Marcus Annaeus Seneca

Wake at dawn with a winged heart and give thanks for another day of loving.

—Kahlil Gibran

CHOOSING HOW OUR DAY WILL BE

Here we stand between two eternities of darkness. What are we to do with this glory while it is still ours?

—Gilbert Murray

Your morning thoughts may determine your conduct for the day. Optimistic thoughts will make your day bright and productive, while pessimistic thinking will make it dull and wasteful. Face each day cheerfully, smilingly and courageously, and it will naturally follow that your work will be a real pleasure and progress will be a delightful accomplishment.

—William M. Peck

The first thing each morning, and the last thing each night, suggest to yourself specific ideas that you wish to embody in your character and personality. Address such suggestions to yourself, silently or aloud, until they are deeply impressed upon your mind.

—Grenville Kleiser

Everyday ask yourself the question, "Do I want to experience Peace of Mind or do I want to experience Conflict?"

—Gerald Jampolsky

Be pleasant until ten o'clock in the morning and the rest of the day will take care of itself. —Elbert Hubbard

It was only a sunny smile,
And little it cost in the giving.
But like morning light, it scattered the night,
And made the day worth living.
　　　　　　　　　　　—Anon.

To get up each morning with the resolve to be happy ... is to set our own conditions to the events of each day. To do this is to condition circumstances instead of being conditioned by them.
　　　　　　—Ralph Waldo Trine

Today is a new day. You will get out of it just what you put into it.... If you have made mistakes, even serious mistakes, there is always another chance for you. And supposing you have tried and failed again and again, you may have a fresh start any moment you choose, for this thing that we call "failure" is not the falling down, but the staying down.
　　　　　　　　—Mary Pickford

When you rise in the morning, form a resolution to make the day a happy one for a fellow creature.
　　　　　　　　—Sydney Smith

As soon as you open your eyes in the morning, you can square away for a happy and successful day. It's the mood and the purpose at the inception of each day that are the important facts in charting your course for the day. We can always square away for a fresh start, no matter what the past has been.
　　　　—George Matthew Adams

This is the beginning of a new day. God has given me this day to use as I will. I can waste it or use it for good, but what I do today is important, because I am exchanging a day of my life for it! When tomorrow comes, this day will be gone forever, leaving in its place something that I have traded for it. I want it to be gain, and not loss; good, and not evil; success, and not failure; in order that I shall not regret the price I have paid for it. 　　　　　—Anon.

I think in terms of the day's resolutions, not the year's. —Henry Moore

Every new day begins with possibilities. It's up to us to fill it with the things that move us toward progress and peace. 　　　—Ronald Reagan

Here hath been dawning another blue day: think, wilt thou let it slip useless away? 　　—Thomas Carlyle

Today a thousand doors of enterprise are open to you, inviting you to useful work. To live at this time is an inestimable privilege, and a sacred obligation devolves upon you to make right use of your opportunities. Today is the day in which to attempt and achieve something worthwhile. 　　—Grenville Kleiser

Get out of bed forcing a smile. You may not smile because you are cheerful; but if you will force yourself to smile you'll ... be cheerful because you smile. Repeated experiments prove that when man assumes the facial expression of a given mental mood, any given mood, then that mental mood itself will follow.
　　　　　　　—Kenneth Goode

He who every morning plans the transactions of the day and follows that plan carries thread that will guide him through the labyrinth of the most busy life.　　—Victor Hugo

A man without a plan for the day is lost before he starts.
　　　　　　—Lewis K. Bendele

My credo is etched on my mirror in my bathroom and I see it when I brush my teeth in the morning. It says, "Don't worry, Be Happy, Feel Good." When you see that first thing, and you reflect on it, the rest of the day seems to glide by pretty well.　　　　　—Larry Hagman

Only that day dawns to which we are awake.　—Henry David Thoreau

The day returns and brings us the petty round of irritating concerns and duties. Help us to play the man, help us to perform them with laughter and kind faces; let cheerfulness abound with industry. Give us to go blithely on our business all this day, bring us to our resting beds weary and content and undishonored, and grant us in the end the gift of sleep.
　　　　—Robert Louis Stevenson

REMAINING OPEN TO UNFORESEEN OPPORTUNITIES AND GIFTS

A day dawns, quite like other days; in it, a single hour comes, quite like other hours; but in that day and in that hour the chance of a lifetime faces us.　　　—Maltbie Babcock

One never knows what each day is going to bring. The important thing is to be open and ready for it.
　　　　　　—Henry Moore

Great opportunities come to all, but many do not know they have met them. The only preparation to take advantage of them is ... to watch what each day brings.
　　　　　　—Albert E. Dunning

There will be something, anguish or elation, that is peculiar to this day alone. I rise from sleep and say: Hail to the morning! Come down to me, my beautiful unknown.
　　　　　　—Jessica Powers

THE MORNING SUN

The sun is new each day.
　　　　　　—Heraclitus

With every rising of the sun, think of your life as just begun.　—Anon.

I feel very happy to see the sun come up every day. I feel happy to be around.... I like to take this day—any day—and go to town with it.
　　　　　　—James Dickey

Each golden sunrise ushers in new opportunities for those who retain faith in themselves, and keep their chins up.... Meet the sunrise with confidence. Fill every golden minute with right thinking and worthwhile endeavor. Do this and there will be joy for you in each golden sunset.
　　　　　　—Alonzo Newton Benn

Today a new sun rises for me; everything lives, everything is animated, everything seems to speak to me of my passion, everything invites me to cherish it.　—Anne De Lenclos

What humbugs we are, who pretend to live for Beauty, and never see the Dawn!　—Logan Pearsall Smith

241

Sunrise: day's great progenitor.
—Emily Dickinson

GENERAL QUOTATIONS ABOUT MORNINGS

Put yourself in competition with yourself each day. Each morning look back upon your work of yesterday and then try to beat it.
—Charles M. Sheldon

The morning has gold in its mouth.
—German proverb

Do you know what the greatest test is? Do you still get excited about what you do when you get up in the morning?   —David Halberstam

Oft when the white, still dawn lifted the skies and pushed the hills apart, I have felt it like a glory in my heart.
—Edwin Markham

Sometimes I have believed as many as six impossible things before breakfast.   —Lewis Carroll

The mind is found most acute and most uneasy in the morning. Uneasiness is, indeed, a species of sagacity—a passive sagacity. Fools are never uneasy.
—Johann von Goethe

Day's sweetest moments are at dawn.   —Ella Wheeler Wilcox

EVENINGS

NIGHTLY ASSESSMENTS

We should every night call ourselves to an account: What infirmity have I mastered today? What passions opposed! What temptation resisted? What virtue acquired?
　　　　—Marcus Annaeus Seneca

Each morning puts man on trial and each evening passes judgement.
　　　　—Roy L. Smith

I think, what has this day brought me, and what have I given it?
　　　　—Henry Moore

Every night before I turn out the lights to sleep, I ask myself this question: Have I done everything that I can.... Have I done enough?
　　　　—Lyndon B. Johnson

Each morning sees some task begin, each evening sees it close;
Something attempted, something done, has earned a night's repose.
　　　　—Henry Wadsworth Longfellow

Judge each day not by it's harvest, but by the seeds you plant.
　　　　—Anon.

Sum up at night what thou has done by day.
　　　　—Lord Herbert

TAKING OFF OUR CARES AND NEGATIVE EMOTIONS WITH OUR CLOTHING

Shed, as you do your garments, your daily sins, whether of omission or commission, and you will wake a free man, with a new life.
　　　　—Sir William Osler

Put off thy cares with thy clothes; so shall thy rest strengthen thy labor, and so thy labor sweeten thy rest.
　　　　—Francis Quarles

One of the secrets of a long and fruitful life is to forgive everybody everything every night before you go to bed.
　　　　—Anon.

The camel, at the close of day,
Kneels down upon the sandy plain
To have his burden lifted off
And rest again.
My soul, thou too should to thy knees
When daylight draweth to a close,
And let thy Master lift the load
And grant repose.
　　　　—Anon.

To carry care to bed is to sleep with
a pack on your back.
      —Thomas C. Haliburton

Let not the sun go down upon your
wrath.   —Eph. 14:26

Don't fight with the pillow, but lay
  down your head
And kick every worriment out of the
  bed.   —Edmund Vance Cooke

SLEEP

Thou driftest gently down the tides
of sleep.
    —Henry Wadsworth Longfellow

Go to bed early, get up early—this is
wise.   —Mark Twain

Come Sleep! Oh Sleep, the certain
  knot of peace,
The baiting-place of wit, the balm of
  woe,
The poor man's wealth, the prison-
  er's release,
The indifferent judge between the
  high and low. —Sir Philip Sidney

Blessings on him that invented sleep!
It covers a man, thoughts and all,
like a cloak; it is meat for the hungry, drink for the thirsty, heat for the
cold, and cold for the hot. It is the
currency with which everything may
be purchased, and the balance that
sets even king and shepherd, simple-
ton and sage. —Miguel de Cervantes

Health is the first muse, and sleep is
the condition to produce it.
    —Ralph Waldo Emerson

O bed! O bed! Delicious bed! That
heaven on earth to the weary head!
      —Thomas Hood

Fatigue is the best pillow.
      —Benjamin Franklin

A well-spent day brings happy sleep.
      —Leonardo da Vinci

It is a delicious moment, certainly,
that of being well-nestled in bed and
feeling that you shall drop gently to
sleep. The good is to come, not past;
the limbs are tired enough to render
the remaining in one posture delightful; the labor of the day is gone.
      —Leigh Hunt

Sleep, Silence's child, sweet father of
  soft rest,
Prince whose approach peace to all
  mortals brings,
Indifferent host to shepherds and
  kings,
Sole comforter to minds with grief
  oppressed. —William Drummond

Sleep, that knits up the ravell'd slave
  of care,
The death of each day's life, sore
  labour's bath,
Balm of hurt minds, great nature's
  second course,
Chief nourisher in life's feast.
      —William Shakespeare

There is only one thing people like
that is good for them; a good night's
sleep.   —Edgar Watson Howe

Sleep is the most blessed and blessing
of all natural graces.
      —Aldous Huxley

It is a common experience that a
problem difficult at night is resolved
in the morning after the committee
of sleep has worked on it.
      —John Steinbeck

Sleep: The golden chain that ties
health and our bodies together.
—Thomas Dekker

Thank God for sleep! And when you
cannot sleep, still thank Him that
you live to lie awake.
—John Oxenham

Sleep ... peace of the soul, who
puttest care to flight.
—Ovid

Now I lay me down to sleep, I pray
the Lord my soul to keep.
—Anon.

There may be those on earth who
dress better or eat better, but those
who enjoy the peace of God sleep
better.
—L. Thomas Holdcroft

GENERAL QUOTATIONS ABOUT EVENINGS

Let us add this one more night to
our lives.
—Suetonius

Fools look to tomorrow; wise men
use tonight.
—Scottish proverb

Tomorrow: the Future

We're Not Supposed to See Too Far Ahead

It is a mistake to look too far ahead. Only one link in the chain of destiny can be handled at a time.
—Sir Winston Churchill

Neither in the life of the individual nor in that of mankind is it desirable to know the future.
—Jakob Burckhardt

God made the world round so we would never be able to see too far down the road.   —Isak Dinesen

The future comes one day at a time.
—Dean Acheson

There is a case, and a strong case, for that particular form of indolence that allows us to move through life knowing only what immediately concerns us.   —Alec Waugh

Cease to inquire what the future has in store, and take as a gift whatever the day brings forth.   —Horace

There is no data on the future.
—Laurel Cutler

The best thing about the future is that it comes only one day at a time.
—Abraham Lincoln

Hardly anyone knows how much is gained by ignoring the future.
—Bernard de Fontenelle

The future is hidden even from those who make it.   —Anatole France

Tomorrow's Always Another Day

They who lose today may win tomorrow.   —Miguel de Cervantes

Be of good cheer. Do not think of today's failures, but of the success that may come tomorrow. You have set yourselves a difficult task, but you will succeed if you persevere; and you will find a joy in overcoming obstacles. Remember, no effort that we make to attain something beautiful is ever lost.   —Helen Keller

When all else is lost, the future still remains.   —Christian Bovee

I have been nothing ... but there is tomorrow.   —Louis L'Amour

After all, tomorrow is another day.
                    —Scarlett O'Hara,
Gone With The Wind

Everyone has it within his power to say, this I am today, that I shall be tomorrow.   —Louis L'Amour

WE CAN'T BE AFRAID
OF THE FUTURE

He who foresees calamities suffers them twice over.   —Beilby Porteous

Only man clogs his happiness with care, destroying what is with thoughts of what may be.
                    —John Dryden

If you are afraid for your future, you don't have a present.
                    —James Petersen

He that fears not the future may enjoy the present.   —Thomas Fuller

Cowards die many times before their deaths; the valiant never taste of death but once.
                    —William Shakespeare

The future is called "perhaps," which is the only possible thing to call the future. And the important thing is not to allow that to scare you.   —Tennessee Williams

To relinquish a present good through apprehension of a future evil is in most instances unwise ... from a fear which may afterwards turn out groundless, you lost the good that lay within your grasp.
                    —Francesco Guicciardini

It is never safe to look into the future with eyes of fear.   —E.H. Harriman

Nothing in life is more remarkable than the unnecessary anxiety which we endure, and generally create ourselves.   —Benjamin Disraeli

Every man, through fear, mugs his aspirations a dozen times a day.
                    —Brendan Francis

The mere apprehension of a coming evil has put many into a situation of the utmost danger.   —Lucan

We need not be afraid of the future, for the future will be in our own hands.   —Thomas E. Dewey

I am not afraid of tomorrow, for I have seen yesterday and I love today.
                    —William Allen White

Go forth to meet the shadowy Future without fear and with a manly heart.
                    —Henry Wadsworth Longfellow

WE MUST LEARN TO TRUST
THE FUTURE

We grow in time to trust the future for our answers.   —Ruth Benedict

Every tomorrow has two handles. We can take hold of it with the handle of anxiety or the handle of faith.
                    —Henry Ward Beecher

Put aside the need to know some future design and simply leave your life open to what is needed of it by the Divine forces.   —Emmanuel

The only limit to our realization of tomorrow will be our doubts of today. Let us move forward with strong and active faith.
                    —Franklin Delano Roosevelt

It is not the cares of today, but the cares of tomorrow, that weigh a man down. For the needs of today we have corresponding strength given. For the morrow we are told to trust. It is not ours yet.
—George MacDonald

Take therefore no thought of the morrow; for the morrow shall take thought for the things of itself.
— Mt. 6:34

OTHER DEFINITIONS OF TOMORROW AND THE FUTURE

Tomorrow is the day when idlers work, and fools reform, and mortal men lay hold on heaven.
—Edward Young

Tomorrow is the mysterious, unknown guest.
—Henry Wadsworth Longfellow

Tomorrow is the only day in the year that appeals to a lazy man.
—Jimmy Lyons

The future is something which everyone reaches at the rate of sixty minutes an hour, whatever he does, whoever he is.   —C.S. Lewis

The future is a world limited by ourselves—in it we discover only what concerns us.   —Maurice Maeterlinck

The future is only the past again, entered through another gate.
—Arthur Wing Pinero

The future is the most expensive luxury in the world. —Thornton Wilder

The future is the shape of things to come.   —H. G. Wells

The future is the past in preparation.
—Pierre Dac

To the being of fully alive, the future is not ominous but a promise; it surrounds the present like a halo.
—John Dewey

The future is hope!   —John Fiske

The future is a great land.
—Anon.

The future is wider than vision, and has no end.   —Donald G. Mitchell

GENERAL QUOTATIONS ABOUT TOMORROW AND THE FUTURE

Grow old along with me! The best is yet to be.   —Robert Browning

He who lives in the future lives in a featureless blank; he lives in impersonality; he lives in Nirvana. The past is democratic, because it is a people. The future is despotic, because it is a caprice. Every man is alone in his prediction, just as each man is alone in a dream.
—G.K. Chesterton

The future belongs to those who believe in the beauty of their dreams.
—Eleanor Roosevelt

I like the dreams of the future better than the history of the past.
—Thomas Jefferson

You cannot plan the future by the past.   —Edmund Burke

It is when tomorrow's burden is added to the burden of today that the weight is more than a man can bear.   —George MacDonald

248

My interest is in the future because I am going to spend the rest of my life there.　　—Charles F. Kettering

I never think of the future. It comes soon enough.　　—Albert Einstein

Yesterday is not ours to recover, but tomorrow is ours to win or lose.
　　—Lyndon B. Johnson

The possibilities for tomorrow are usually beyond our expectations.
　　—Anon.

Where will I be five years from now? I delight in not knowing. That's one of the greatest things about life—its wonderful surprises.
　　—Marlo Thomas

When I look at the future, it's so bright, it burns my eyes.
　　—Oprah Winfrey

Everyone's future is, in reality, uncertain and full of unknown treasures from which all may draw unguessed prizes.　　—Lord Dunsany

The future is made of the same stuff as the present.　　—Simone Weil

The future is much like the present, only longer.　　—Dan Quisenberry

The bridges you cross before you come to them are over rivers that aren't there.　　—Gene Brown

Strike when thou wilt, the hour of rest, but let my last days be my best.
　　—Robert Browning

By-and-by never comes.
　　—Saint Augustine

For you and me, today is all we have; tomorrow is a mirage that may never become reality.
　　—Louis L'Amour

I fear there will be no future for those who do not change.
　　—Louis L'Amour

If a man carefully examines his thoughts he will be surprised to find how much he lives in the future. His well-being is always ahead.
　　—Ralph Waldo Emerson

I got the blues thinking of the future, so I left off and made some marmalade. It's amazing how it cheers one up to shred oranges and scrub the floor.　　—D.H. Lawrence

You learn to build your roads on today, because tomorrow's ground is too uncertain for plans, and futures have a way of falling down in midflight.　　—Veronica Shoffstal

Fortunately for children, the uncertainties of the present always give way to the enchanted possibilities of the future.　　—Gelsey Kirkland

Average, "Boring" Days

Average Days

Normal day, let me be aware of the treasure you are. Let me learn from you, love you, bless you before you depart. Let me not pass you by in quest of some rare and perfect tomorrow. Let me hold you while I may, for it may not always be so. One day I shall dig my nails into the earth, or bury my face in the pillow, or stretch myself taut, or raise my hands to the sky and want, more than all the world, your return.
— Mary Jean Iron

Either you reach a higher point today, or you exercise your strength in order to be able to climb higher tomorrow. — Friedrich Nietzsche

One appreciates that daily life is really good when one wakes from a horrible dream, or when one takes the first outing after a sickness. Why not realize it now?
— William Lyon Phelps

That man is happiest who lives from day to day and asks no more, garnering the simple goodness of a life.
— Euripides

Write it on your heart that every day is the best day in the year.
— Ralph Waldo Emerson

Sunshine is delicious, rain is refreshing, wind braces us, snow is exhilarating; there is no such thing as bad weather, only different kinds of good weather. — John Ruskin

This is the day which the Lord hath made; we will rejoice and be glad.
— Ps. 118:24

Day-to-Day Living Is Harder Than an Emergency

A man can stand almost anything except a succession of ordinary days.
— Johann von Goethe

We look wishfully to emergencies, to eventful, revolutionary times ... and think how easy to have taken our part when the drum was rolling and the house was burning over our heads. — Ralph Waldo Emerson

Poets are like baseball pitchers. Both have their moments. The intervals are the tough things.
— Robert Frost

Any idiot can face a crisis—it's day to day living that wears you out.
—Anton Chekhov

They sicken of the calm that know the storm.   —Ralph Waldo Emerson

Peace is not only better than war, but infinitely more arduous.
—George Bernard Shaw

Peace hath higher tests of manhood Than battle ever knew.
—John Greenleaf Whittier

Man lives by habits indeed, but what he lives for is thrill and excitements.... From time immemorial war has been ... the supremely thrilling excitement.   —William James

It is not merely cruelty that leads men to love war, it is excitement.
—Henry Ward Beecher

The statistics of suicide show that, for non-combatants at least, life is more interesting in war than in peace.   —William Ralph Inge

The Problems and Dangers of Boredom

Boredom is rage spread thin.
—Paul Tillich

Boredom is the most horrible of wolves.   —Jean Giono

Ennui has made more gamblers than avarice, more drunkards than thirst, and perhaps as many suicides as despair.   —Charles Caleb Colton

Boredom ... causes us to neglect more duties than does interest.
—Francois de La Rochefoucauld

Boredom is a vital problem for the moralist, since at least half of the sins of mankind are caused by the fear of it.   —Bertrand Russell

Boredom slays more of existence than war.   —Norman Mailer

One of the worst forms of mental suffering is boredom, not knowing what to do with oneself and one's life. Even if man had no monetary, or any other reward, he would be eager to spend his energy in some meaningful way because he could not stand the boredom which inactivity produces.   —Erich Fromm

Monotony is the awful reward of the careful.   —A.G. Buckham

We Bore Ourselves, and It's Up to Us to Overcome Boredom

If your daily life seems poor, do not blame it; blame yourself, tell yourself that you are not poet enough to call forth its riches.
—Rainer Maria Rilke

Somebody's boring me; I think it's me.   —Dylan Thomas

Being bored is an insult to oneself.
—Jules Renard

The amount of satisfaction you get from life depends largely on your own ingenuity, self-sufficiency, and resourcefulness. People who wait around for life to supply their satisfaction usually find boredom instead.   —Dr. William Menninger

When people are bored, it is primarily with their own selves that they are bored.   —Eric Hoffer

Is not life a hundred times too short for us to bore ourselves?
—Friedrich Nietzsche

Nothing is interesting if you're not interested.   —Helen MacInness

Boredom is a sickness of the soul.
—Anon.

Boredom is simply the lack of imagination.   —Julie O. Smith

Perhaps the world's second worst crime is boredom. The first is being a bore.   —Cecil Beaton

SOME REMEDIES FOR BOREDOM

In the ancient recipe, the three antidotes for dullness or boredom are sleep, drink, and travel. It is rather feeble. From sleep you wake up, from drink you become sober, and from travel you come home again. And then where are you? No, the two sovereign remedies for dullness are love or a crusade.
—D.H. Lawrence

As for boredom ... I notice that it leaves me as soon as I am doing something that has got to be done.
—John Jay Chapman

Uncertainty and mystery are energies of life. Don't let them scare you unduly, for they keep boredom at bay and spark creativity.
—R.I. Fitzbenry

If something is boring after two minutes, try it for four. If still boring, try it for eight, sixteen, thirty-two, and so on. Eventually, one discovers that it is not boring, but very interesting.
—Zen saying

Nobody is bored when he is trying to make something that is beautiful, or to discover something that is true.
—William Ralph Inge

The one sure means of dealing with boredom is to care for someone else, to do something kind and good.
—Theodore Haecker

Everything considered, work is less boring than amusing oneself.
—Charles Baudelaire

GENERAL QUOTATIONS ABOUT BOREDOM

Man is the only animal that can be bored.   —Erich Fromm

The only unhappiness is a life of boredom.   —Stendhal

One can be bored until boredom becomes a mystical experience.
—Logan Pearsall Smith

One must choose in life between boredom and suffering.
—Madame de Stael

We often forgive those who bore us, but can't forgive those whom we bore.
—Francois de La Rochefoucauld

Dullness is a misdemeanor.
—Ethel Wilson

Over-excitement and boredom are states of mind which I equally shun.
—E.V. Knox

Passions are less mischievous than boredom, for passions tend to diminish and boredom increase.
—Barbey d'Aurevilly

It is better to be happy for the moment and be burned up with beauty than to live a long time and be bored all the while.
—Don Marquis

Boredom: the desire for desires.
—Leo Tolstoy

The only menace is inertia.
—Saint John Perse

Boredom is useful to me when I notice it and think: Oh I'm bored; there must be something else I want to be doing ... boredom acts as an initiator of originality by pushing me into new activities or new thoughts.
—Hugh Prather

Boredom, like necessity, is very often the mother of invention. —Anon.

One of man's finest qualities is described by the simple word "guts"—the ability to take it. If you have the discipline to stand fast when your body wants to run, if you can control your temper and remain cheerful in the face of monotony or disappointments, you have "guts" in the soldiering sense.
—Colonel John S. Roosman

Life is as tedious as a twice-told tale, vexing the dull ear of a drowsy man.
—William Shakespeare

An enthusiast may bore others, but he has never a dull moment himself.
—John Kieran

Three-quarters of a soldier's life is spent in aimlessly waiting about.
—Eugene Rosenstock-Huessy

DIFFICULT DAYS

DIFFICULT DAYS

Everyone gets their rough day. No
one gets a free ride. Today so far, I
had a good day. I got a dial tone.
—Rodney Dangerfield

Thy fate is the common fate of all,
Into each life some rain must fall,
Some days must be dark and dreary.
—Henry Wadsworth Longfellow

Some days you tame the tiger. And
some days the tiger has you for
lunch.   —Tug McGraw

Some days the dragon wins.
—Anon.

EVERYTHING CHANGES

If matters go badly now, they will
not always be so.   —Horace

The one law that does not change is
that everything changes, and the
hardship I was bearing today was
only a breath away from the pleasures I would have tomorrow, and
those pleasures would be all the richer because of the memories of this I
was enduring.   —Louis L'Amour

Experience cold or heat, pleasure or
pain. These experiences are fleeting;
they come and go. Bear them
patiently.
—Sri Krishna (Bhagavad Gita)

To everything there is a season,
A time for every purpose under
    heaven....
A time to weep, and a time to laugh,
A time to mourn, and a time to
    dance.
—Eccl. 3:1, 4

Let nothing disturb thee,
Let nothing affright thee,
All things are passing,
God changeth never.
—Saint Teresa of Avila

This, too, shall pass.
—William Shakespeare

The present will not long endure.
—Pindar

We do not live an equal life, but one
of contrasts and patchwork; now a
little joy, then a sorrow, now a sin,
then a generous or brave action.
—Ralph Waldo Emerson

I feel successful when the writing goes well. This lasts five minutes. Once, when I was number one on the bestseller list, I also felt success-ful. That lasted three minutes.
—Jacqueline Briskin

To those who shall sit here rejoicing, and to those who shall sit here lamenting, greetings and sympathy. So have we done in our time.
—Bench inscription,
Cornell University

Sadness and gladness succeed each other. —Anon.

Sadness flies away on the wings of time. —Jean de La Fontaine

I don't think that ... one gets a flash of happiness once, and never again; it is there within you, and it will come as certainly as death....
—Isak Dinesen

Life comes in clusters, clusters of solitude, then clusters when there is hardly time to breathe.
—May Sarton

THE CONDITIONS OF OUR LIVES CHANGE LIKE NATURE'S SEASONS

If winter comes, can spring be far behind? —Percy Bysshe Shelley

Human misery must somewhere have a stop; there is no wind that always blows a storm. —Euripides

No winter lasts forever; no spring skips its turn. —Hal Borland

There are trees that seem to die at the end of autumn. There are also the evergreens. —Gilbert Maxwell

Our Lord has written the promise of resurrection, not in books alone, but in every leaf in springtime.
—Martin Luther

For, lo, the winter is past, the rain is over and gone; the flowers appear on the earth.
—Song 2:11–12

Sitting quietly, doing nothing, Spring comes, and the grass grows by itself.
—*The Gospel According to Zen*

There ain't no cloud so thick that the sun ain't shinin' on t'other side.
—Rattlesnake,
an 1870s mountain man

PAIN AND SUFFERING

Pain is never permanent.
—Saint Teresa of Avila

You will suffer and you will hurt. You will have joy and you will have peace. —Alison Cheek

Pain is part of being alive, and we need to learn that. Pain does not last forever, nor is it necessarily unbear-able, and we need to be taught that.
—Rabbi Harold Kushner

Pain is hard to bear.... But with patience, day by day, Even this shall pass away.
—Theodore Tilton

Everything in life that we really accept undergoes a change. So suf-fering must become love. That is the mystery. —Katherine Mansfield

FAILURE AND FINANCIAL PROBLEMS

I've been failing for, like, ten or eleven years. When it turns, it'll turn.

Right now I'm just tryin' to squeeze through a very tight financial period, get the movie out, and put my things in order.   —Francis Ford Coppola

I've never been poor, only broke. Being poor is a frame of mind. Being broke is a temporary situation.
                    —Mike Todd

GOOD THINGS OFTEN RESULT FROM DIFFICULT THINGS

In the darkest hour the soul is replenished and given strength to continue and endure.
                    —Heart Warrior Chosa

He that can't endure the bad will not live to see the good.
                    —Yiddish proverb

Our toil is sweet with thankfulness,
Our burden is our boon;
The curse of earth's gray morning is
The blessing of its noon.
                    —John Greenleaf Whittier

Were it possible for us to see further than our knowledge reaches, perhaps we would endure our sadnesses with greater confidence than our joys. For they are moments when something new has entered into us, something unknown.   —Rainer Maria Rilke

ENDINGS ARE ALSO BEGINNINGS

What we call the beginning is often an end. And to make an end is to make a beginning. The end is where we start from.   —T.S. Eliot

When one door of happiness closes, another opens; but often we look so long at the closed door that we do not see the one which has been opened for us.   —Helen Keller

The world is round, and the place which may seem like the end may also be only the beginning.
                    —Ivy Baker Priest

SOMEDAY, WE'LL LOOK BACK AND THINGS WON'T SEEM AS DIFFICULT AS THEY DO NOW

Perhaps someday it will be pleasant to remember even this.   —Virgil

One day in retrospect the years of struggle will strike you as the most beautiful.   —Sigmund Freud

The crisis of today is the joke of tomorrow.   —H.G. Wells

Sometimes I found that in my happy moments I could not believe that I had ever been miserable.
                    —Joanna Field

Sadness flies away on the wings of time.   —Jean de La Fontaine

IT JUST TAKES TIME

Time, in the turning-over of days, works change, for better or worse.
                    —Pindar

Time brings all things to pass.
                    —Aeschylus

Time is like a river of fleeting events, and its current is strong; as soon as something comes into sight, it is swept past us, and something else takes its place, and that too will be swept away.   —Marcus Aurelius

Time cools, time clarifies; no mood can be maintained quite unaltered through the course of hours.
                    —Thomas Mann

Time bears away all things. —Virgil

Come what come may, time and the hour runs through the roughest day.
—William Shakespeare

We undo ourselves by impatience. Misfortunes have their life and their limits, their sickness and their health.
—Michel de Montaigne

The future is something which everyone reaches at the rate of sixty minutes an hour, whatever he does, whoever he is. —C.S. Lewis

That's the advantage of having lived sixty-five years. You don't feel the need to be impatient any longer.
—Thornton Wilder

Your three best doctors are faith, time, and patience.
—From a fortune cookie

PATIENCE IS A KEY TO SUCCESS, TO VICTORY

Who longest waits most surely wins.
—Helen Hunt Jackson

Patience is a bitter plant, but it has sweet fruit. —German proverb

He that can have patience can have what he will. —Benjamin Franklin

Adopt the pace of nature, her secret is patience. —Ralph Waldo Emerson

Everything comes if a man will only wait. —Benjamin Disraeli

How poor are they that have not patience? What wound did ever heal but by degrees?
—William Shakespeare

All things come round to him who will but wait.
—Henry Wadsworth Longfellow

And he shall reign a goodly king
And sway his hand o'er every clime
With peace writ on his signet ring,
Who bides his time.
—James Whitcomb Riley

It takes time to succeed because success is merely the natural reward of taking time to do anything well.
—Joseph Ross

Patience and fortitude conquer all things. —Ralph Waldo Emerson

Be not afraid of growing slowly, be afraid only of standing still.
—Chinese proverb

Wisely and slow. They stumble that run fast. —William Shakespeare

No great thing is created suddenly, any more than a bunch of grapes or a fig. If you tell me that you desire a fig, I answer you that there must be time. Let it first blossom, then bear fruit, then ripen. —Epictetus

Time deals gently only with those who take it gently. —Anatole France

Hold on; hold fast; hold out. Patience is genius.
—Georges de Buffon

Genius is nothing but a greater aptitude for patience.
—Benjamin Franklin

All human wisdom is summed up in two words: wait and hope.
—Alexandre Dumas

257

Genius is eternal patience.
—Michelangelo

Serene I fold my hands and wait.
—John Burroughs

The race is not to the swift, nor the battle to the strong.
—Eccl. 9:11

BEING PRODUCTIVE WHILE WE'RE BEING PATIENT

Everything comes to him who hustles while he waits.   —Thomas A. Edison

The secret of patience ... to do something else in the meantime.
—Anon.

Have patience with all things, but chiefly have patience with yourself. Do not lose courage in considering your own imperfections, but instantly set about remedying them—every day begin the task anew.
—Saint Francis de Sales

Let us then be up and doing,
With a heart for any fate,
Still achieving, still pursuing,
Learn to labor and to wait.
—Henry Wadsworth Longfellow

GENERAL QUOTATIONS ABOUT DIFFICULT DAYS

God will wait as long as it takes for us.   —Reverend R. Walters

Waiting is not mere empty hoping. It has the inner certainty of reaching the goal.   —I Ching

All things come to him who waits—provided he knows what he is waiting for.   —Woodrow Wilson

Hope and patience are two sovereign remedies for all, the surest reposals, the softest cushions to lean on in adversity.   —Robert Burton

The strongest of all warriors are these two—Time and Patience.
—Leo Tolstoy

Who bides his time tastes the sweet
Of honey in the saltiest tear;
And though he fares with slowest feet
Joy runs to meet him drawing near.
—James Whitcomb Riley

Better is the end of a thing than the beginning thereof: and the patient in spirit is better than the proud in spirit.   —Eccl. 7:8

There is nothing so bitter that a patient mind cannot find some solace for it.
—Marcus Annaeus Seneca

Patience is the best remedy for every trouble.   —Plautus

For ye have need of patience....
—Heb. 10:36

God grant us patience!
—William Shakespeare

They are ill discoverers that think there is no land, when they see nothing but sea.   —Francis Bacon

PART 3

Preparing for Success

POSITIVE THINKING, AND SELF-FULFILLING PROPHESIES AND ACTIONS

OUR FAITH AND BELIEF CREATE OUR REALITY

Man is what he believes.
—Anton Chekhov

Believe that life is worth living, and your belief will help create that fact.
—William James

Dream lofty dreams, and as you dream, so shall you become. Your vision is the promise of what you shall at last unveil.   —John Ruskin

Our belief at the beginning of a doubtful undertaking is the one thing that ensures the successful outcome of our venture.
—William James

If you constantly think of illness, you eventually become ill; if you believe yourself to be beautiful, you become so.   —Shakti Gawain

You have to believe in happiness, or happiness never comes.
—Douglas Malloch

We are what we believe we are.
—Benjamin N. Cardozo

If you keep on saying things are going to be bad, you have a good chance of being a prophet.
—Isaac Bashevis Singer

What one believes to be true either is true or becomes true within limits to be found experientially and experimentally. These limits are beliefs to be transcended.   —John Lilly

The thing always happens that you really believe in; and the belief in a thing makes it happen.
—Frank Lloyd Wright

OUR ATTITUDES CREATE OUR LIVES

When you look at the world in a narrow way, how narrow it seems! When you look at it in a mean way, how mean it is! When you look at it selfishly, how selfish it is! But when you look at it in a broad, generous, friendly spirit, what wonderful people you find in it. —Horace Rutledge

Each of us makes his own weather, determines the color of the skies in the emotional universe which he inhabits.   —Fulton J. Sheen

260

Man's rise or fall, success or failure, happiness or unhappiness depends on his attitude ... a man's attitude will create the situation he imagines.
—James Lane Allen

The greatest discovery of my generation is that man can alter his life simply by altering his attitude of mind.
—William James

Immense power is acquired by assuring yourself in your secret reveries that you were born to control affairs. —Andrew Carnegie

Man's real life is happy, chiefly because he is ever expecting that it soon will be so. —Edgar Allan Poe

'Tis very certain the desire of life prolongs it. —Lord Byron

Could we change our attitude, we should not only see life differently, but life itself would come to be different. Life would undergo a change of appearance because we ourselves had undergone a change in attitude.
—Katherine Mansfield

The words "I am ..." are potent words; be careful what you hitch them to. The thing you're claiming has a way of reaching back and claiming you. —A.L. Kitselman

Self-image sets the boundaries of individual accomplishment.
—Maxwell Maltz

Nothing can stop the man with the right mental attitude from achieving his goal; nothing on earth can help the man with the wrong mental attitude. —W.W. Ziege

If you expect nothing, you're apt to be surprised. You'll get it.
—Malcolm Forbes

Since the human body tends to move in the direction of its expectations—plus or minus—it is important to know that attitudes of confidence and determination are no less a part of the treatment program than medical science and technology.
—Norman Cousins

They can because they think they can. —Virgil

To the timid and hesitating everything is impossible because it seems so. —Sir Walter Scott

We Find What We Look For

What we see depends mainly on what we look for. —John Lubbock

People only see what they are prepared to see.
—Ralph Waldo Emerson

Look for the ridiculous in everything and you find it. —Jules Renard

The more wary you are of danger, the more likely you are to meet it.
—Jean de La Fontaine

He that seeks trouble always finds it.
—English proverb

We are always paid for our suspicion by finding what we suspect.
—Henry David Thoreau

The unthankful heart ... discovers no mercies; but the thankful heart ... will find, in every hour, some heavenly blessings. —Henry Ward Beecher

If you are possessed by an idea, you find it expressed everywhere, you even *smell* it.　　—Thomas Mann

All seems infected that the infected spy, as all looks yellow to the jaundiced eye.　　—Alexander Pope

The faultfinder will find faults even in paradise. —Henry David Thoreau

Those see nothing but faults that seek for nothing else.
　　—Thomas Fuller

LIFE IS LIKE A MIRROR

Life is a mirror and will reflect back to the thinker what he thinks into it.
　　—Ernest Holmes

The world is a looking glass and gives back to every man the reflection of his own face. Frown at it and it will in turn look sourly upon you; laugh at it and with it, and it is a jolly, kind companion.
　　—William Makepeace Thackeray

The world is a great mirror. It reflects back to you what you are. If you are loving, if you are friendly, if you are helpful, the world will prove loving and friendly and helpful to you. The world is what you are.
　　—Thomas Dreier

The world is like a mirror; frown at it, and it frowns at you. Smile and it smiles, too.　　—Herbert Samuels

OUR THOUGHTS DETERMINE OUR LIVES

Our minds can shape the way a thing will be because we act according to our expectations.
　　—Federico Fellini

The way a man's mind runs is the way he is sure to go.
　　—Henry B. Wilson

The happiness of your life depends upon the quality of your thoughts ... take care that you entertain no notions unsuitable to virtue and reasonable nature.　　—Marcus Aurelius

All that a man does outwardly is but the expression and completion of his inward thought. To work effectively, he must think clearly; to act nobly, he must think nobly.
　　—William Ellery Channing

You cannot escape the results of your thoughts.... Whatever your present environment may be, you will fall, remain or rise with your thoughts, your vision, your ideal. You will become as small as your controlling desire, as great as your dominant aspiration.
　　—James Lane Allen

The life each of us lives is the life within the limits of our own thinking. To have life more abundant, we must think in limitless terms of abundance.　　—Thomas Dreier

Before a painter puts a brush to his canvas he sees his picture mentally.... If you think of yourself in terms of a painting, what do you see?... Is the picture one you think worth painting?... You create yourself in the image you hold in your mind.
　　—Thomas Dreier

All that we are is the result of what we have thought. The mind is everything. What we think, we become.
　　—Buddha

I believe that if you think about disaster, you will get it. Brood about death and you hasten your demise. Think positively and masterfully with confidence and faith, and life becomes more secure, more fraught with action, richer in achievement and experience.
—Eddie Rickenbacker

Think you can, think you can't; either way, you'll be right.
—Henry Ford

Our destiny changes with our thoughts; we shall become what we wish to become, do what we wish to do, when our habitual thoughts correspond with our desires.
—Orison Swett Marden

Our best friends and our worst enemies are our thoughts. A thought can do us more good than a doctor or a banker or a faithful friend. It can also do us more harm than a brick. —Dr. Frank Crane

A man's life is what his thoughts make it. —Marcus Aurelius

A man is literally what he thinks.
—James Lane Allen

A man is what he thinks about all day long. —Ralph Waldo Emerson

Nothing befalls us that is not of the nature of ourselves. There comes no adventure but wears to our soul the shape of our everyday thoughts.
—Maurice Maeterlinck

The mere apprehension of a coming evil has put many into a situation of the utmost danger. —Lucan

The soul contains the event that shall befall it, for the event is only the actualization of its thoughts, and what we pray to ourselves for is always granted.
—Ralph Waldo Emerson

If you think it's going to rain, it will.
—Clint Eastwood

As you think, you travel, and as you love, you attract. You are today where your thoughts have brought you; you will be tomorrow where your thoughts take you.
—James Lane Allen

God will help you if you try, and you can if you think you can.
—Anna Delaney Peale

To expect defeat is nine-tenths of defeat itself.
—Francis Marion Crawford

The quality of our expectations determines the quality of our action.
—André Godin

What a man thinks of himself, that is what determines, or rather indicates, his fate. —Henry David Thoreau

Man, being made reasonable, and so a thinking creature, there is nothing more worthy of his being than the right direction and employment of his thoughts; since upon this depends both his usefulness to the public, and his own present and future benefit in all respects. —William Penn

Great men are they who see that the spiritual is stronger than any material force, that thoughts rule the world. —Ralph Waldo Emerson

Never think any oldish thoughts. It's oldish thoughts that make a person old.   —James A. Farley

They can because they think they can.   —Virgil

As a man thinketh, so is he, and as a man chooseth, so is he.   —Bible

Thoughts lead on to purposes; purposes go forth in action; actions form habits; habits decide character; and character fixes our destiny.
                —Tyron Edwards

Keep your thoughts right, for as you think, so are you. Therefore, think only those things that will make the world better, and you unashamed.
                —Henry H. Buckley

Every man is free to rise as far as he's able or willing, but the degree to which he thinks determines the degree to which he'll rise.
                    —Ayn Rand

What you think means more than anything else in your life.
            —George Matthew Adams

Change your thoughts and you change your world.
            —Norman Vincent Peale

Baseball is 90 percent mental. The other half is physical.   —Yogi Berra

The way in which we think of ourselves has everything to do with how our world sees us.   —Arlene Raven

Be careful of your thoughts; they may become words at any moment.
                    —Ira Gassen

The wisdom of all ages and cultures emphasizes the tremendous power our thoughts have over our character and circumstances.   —Liane Cordes

There comes no adventure but wears to our soul the shape of our every-day thoughts.
            —Maurice Maeterlinck

OUR THOUGHTS DETERMINE OUR HAPPINESS

We exaggerate misfortune and happiness alike. We are never either so wretched or so happy as we say we are.   —Honore de Balzac

We are never so happy or so unhappy as we think.
        —Francois de La Rochefoucauld

Man is only miserable so far as he thinks himself so.   —Sannazare

A man's as miserable as he thinks he is.   —Marcus Annaeus Seneca

The most unhappy of all men is he who believes himself to be so.
                    —David Hume

The mind is its own place, and in itself can make a heaven of hell, a hell of heaven.   —John Milton

All happiness is in the mind.
                    —Anon.

Happiness is not a matter of events, it depends upon the tides of the mind.   —Alice Meynell

The greater part of our happiness or misery depends on our dispositions, and not our circumstances.
                —Martha Washington

I am happy and content because I think I am.　　—Alain-Rene Lesage

A happy life consists in tranquility of mind.　　　　　　　　—Cicero

The happiest person is the person who thinks the most interesting thoughts.　　—William Lyon Phelps

Unhappiness indicates wrong thinking, just as ill health indicates a bad regimen.　　　　　—Paul Bourge

Happiness does not depend on outward things, but on the way we see them.　　　　　　—Leo Tolstoy

Happiness will never be any greater than the idea we have of it.
　　　　　—Maurice Maeterlinck

He is happy that knoweth not himself to be otherwise.
　　　　　　　—Thomas Fuller

Misery is almost always the result of thinking.　　　—Joseph Joubert

A great obstacle to happiness is to expect too much happiness.
　　　　　—Bernard de Fontenelle

It isn't our position, but our disposition, that makes us happy.
　　　　　　　　　　—Anon.

OUR THOUGHTS AFFECT OUR BODIES AND OUR HEALTH

Some patients I see are actually draining into their bodies the diseased thoughts of their minds.
　　—Zachary T. Bercovitz, M.D.

The body manifests what the mind harbors.　　　—Jerry Augustine

Since the human body tends to move in the direction of its expectations—plus or minus—it is important to know that attitudes of confidence and determination are no less a part of the treatment program than medical science and technology.
　　　　　　—Norman Cousins

When people asked, I used to tell them how sick I was. The more I talked about being sick, the worse I got. Finally, I started saying, "I'm getting better." It took a while, but then I started to feel better, too.
—Michael Hirsch, person with AIDS

You can promote your healing by your thinking.　—James E. Sweeney

Most of the time we think we're sick it's all in the mind.　—Thomas Wolfe

NEGATIVE, CYNICAL, PESSIMISTIC THINKING IS DANGEROUS

The pessimist is half-licked before he starts.　　　—Thomas A. Buckner

No one can defeat us unless we first defeat ourselves.
　　　　　—Dwight D. Eisenhower

You can't be pessimistic, because there are so many things that go wrong every day that if you were to be negative or pessimistic, you'd go out of business.　—John DePasquale

You can't pay attention to your mistakes. I made a mistake today, I made a mistake yesterday. I think it's ... very important to ignore the negative.　　　　　　—Jerry Rubin

I don't believe in pessimism.
　　　　　　　—Clint Eastwood

We can destroy ourselves by cynicism and disillusion, just as affectively as by bombs. —Kenneth Clark

One of the most devastating experiences in human life is disillusionment. —Art Sisson

The pessimist sees the difficulty in every opportunity; the optimist sees the opportunity in every difficulty.
—L.P. Jacks

No pessimist ever discovered the secrets of the stars, or sailed to an uncharted land, or opened a new heaven to the human spirit.
—Helen Keller

There are people who have an appetite for grief; pleasure is not strong enough and they crave pain. They have mithridatic stomachs which must be fed on poisoned bread, natures so doomed that no prosperity can sooth their ragged and dishevelled desolation.
—Ralph Waldo Emerson

Cynicism is intellectual dandyism.
—George Meredith

When one door of happiness closes, another opens; but often we look so long at the closed door that we do not see the one which has been opened for us. —Helen Keller

Do not sit long with a sad friend. When you go to a garden do you look at the weeds? Spend more time with the roses and jasmines.
—Jelaluddin Rumi

WE ARE RESPONSIBLE FOR OUR THOUGHTS

If we are not responsible for the thoughts that pass our doors, we are at least responsible for those we admit and entertain.
—Charles B. Newcomb

Optimism is an intellectual choice.
—Diana Schneider

Think of only three things: your God, your family and the Green Bay Packers—in that order.
—Vince Lombardi, to his team

We must dare to think unthinkable thoughts. —James W. Fulbright

Politeness is the art of choosing among one's real thoughts.
—Abel Stevens

Your imagination has much to do with your life.... It is for you to decide how you want your imagination to serve you. —Philip Conley

A vacant mind invites dangerous inmates, as a deserted mansion tempts wandering outcasts to enter and take up their abode in its desolate apartments. —Hilliard

Great things are not something accidental, but must certainly be willed.
—Vincent van Gogh

THE IMPORTANCE AND VALUE OF POSITIVE THINKING

Optimism is essential to achievement and is also the foundation of courage and of true progress.
—Nicholas Murray Butler

If I were to wish for anything, I should not wish for wealth and power, but for the passionate sense of the potential, for the eye which, ever young and ardent, sees the possible ... what wine is so sparkling, so fragrant, so intoxicating, as possibility! —Søren Kierkegaard

What after all has maintained the human race on this old globe, despite all the calamities of nature and all the tragic failings of mankind, if not the faith in new possibilities and the courage to advocate them? —Jane Adams

The basic success orientation is having an optimistic attitude.
—John DePasquale

Think positively and masterfully, with confidence and faith, and life becomes more secure, more fraught with action, richer in achievement and experience.
—Eddie Rickenbacker

The biggest quality in successful people, I think, is an impatience with negative thinking ... my feeling was, even if it's as bad as I think it is, we'll make it work.
—Edward McCabe

Optimism and humor are the grease and glue of life. Without both of them we would never have survived our captivity. —Philip Butler, Vietnam POW

Optimism is the faith that leads to achievement. Nothing can be done without hope and confidence.
—Helen Keller

Positive thinking is the key to success in business, education, pro football, anything that you can mention. I go out there thinking that I am going to complete every pass. —Ron Jaworski

POSITIVE THINKING IS PRACTICAL

There is in the worst of fortune the best of chances for a happy change.
—Euripides

It doesn't hurt to be optimistic. You can always cry later.
—Lucimar Santos de Lima

I cannot discover that anyone knows enough to say definitely what is and what is not possible. —Henry Ford

I have learned to use the word *impossible* with the greatest caution.
—Wernher von Braun

The Wright brothers flew right through the smoke screen of impossibility. —Charles Franklin Kettering

On the human chessboard, all moves are possible. —Miriam Schiff

Every noble work is at first impossible. —Thomas Carlyle

In the long run, the pessimist may be proved to be right, but the optimist has a better time on the trip.
—Daniel L. Reardon

All things are possible until they are proved impossible—and even the impossible may only be so as of now. —Pearl S. Buck

267

But Positive Thinking Alone Isn't Enough

Optimism, unaccompanied by personal effort, is merely a state of mind and not fruitful. —Edward L. Curtis

I believe that ... all that can be, will be, if man helps.   —André Gide

We Create Our Own Situations and Circumstances

Like begets like; honesty begets honesty; trust, trust; and so on.
                    —James F. Bell

Honor begets honor; trust begets trust; faith begets faith; and hope is the mainspring of life.
                    —Henry L. Stimson

Events, circumstances, etc. have their origin in ourselves. They spring from seeds which we have sown.
                    —Henry David Thoreau

Hope is like a road in the country; there was never a road, but when many people walk on it, the road comes into existence.
                    —Lin Yutang

If fear is cultivated it will become stronger, if faith is cultivated it will achieve mastery.   —John Paul Jones

A human being fashions his consequences as surely as he fashions his goods or his dwelling. Nothing that he says, thinks or does is without consequences.   —Norman Cousins

We create our fate every day ... most of the ills we suffer from are directly traceable to our own behavior.
                    —Henry Miller

It seems to me probably that any one who has a series of intolerable positions to put up with must have been responsible for them to some extent ... they have contributed to it by impatience or intolerance, or brusqueness—or some provocation.
                    —Robert Hugh Benson

If we live good lives, the times are also good. As we are, such are the times.   —Saint Augustine

Opportunities multiply as they are seized; they die when neglected. Life is a long line of opportunities.
                    —John Wicker

I have found that if you love life, life will love you back.
                    —Arthur Rubinstein

A man is a method, a progressive arrangement; a selecting principle, gathering his like unto him wherever he goes. What you are comes to you.
                    —Ralph Waldo Emerson

Thousands upon thousands are yearly brought into a state of real poverty by their great anxiety not to be thought poor.   —William Cobbett

The world has a way of giving what is demanded of it. If you are frightened and look for failure and poverty, you will get them, no matter how hard you may try to succeed. Lack of faith in yourself, in what life will do for you, cuts you off from the good things of the world. Expect victory and you make victory. Nowhere is this truer than in business that is, where bravery and faith bring both material and spiritual rewards.
                    —Preston Bradley

We are made kind by being kind.
—Eric Hoffer

Kindness gives birth to kindness.
—Sophocles

In Many Cases, We Determine What Will Happen to Us

We choose our joys and sorrows long before we experience them.
—Kahlil Gibran

Man does not simply exist, but always decides what his existence will be, what he will become in the next moment.   —Viktor Frankel

The principle of life is that life responds by corresponding; your life becomes the thing you have decided it shall be.
—Raymond Charles Barker

If we choose to be no more than clods of clay, then we shall be used as clods of clay for braver feet to tread on.   —Marie Corelli

What We Prepare for Often Happens

Preparing for the worst is an activity I have taken up since I turned thirty-five, and the worst actually began to happen.   —Delia Ephron

If you prepare for old age, old age comes sooner.   —Anon.

What we prepare for is what we shall get. —William Graham Sumner

If one asks for success and prepares for failure, he will get the situation he has prepared for.
—Florence Scovel Shinn

The world has a way of giving what is demanded of it. If you are frightened and look for failure and poverty, you will get them, no matter how hard you may try to succeed. Lack of faith in yourself, in what life will do for you, cuts you off from the good things of the world. Expect victory and you make victory. Nowhere is this truer than in business life, where bravery and faith bring both material and spiritual rewards.
—Preston Bradley

Whoso diggeth a pit shall fall therein.   —Prv. 26:27

Debt is a trap which man sets and baits himself, and then deliberately gets into.   —Josh Billings

Self-image sets the boundaries of individual accomplishment.
—Maxwell Maltz

If you expect nothing, you're apt to be surprised. You'll get it.
—Malcolm Forbes

What We Talk about Often Occurs

Persistent prophecy is a familiar way of assuring the event.
—George R. Gissing

The words "I am ..." are potent words; be careful what you hitch them to. The thing you're claiming has a way of reaching back and claiming you.   —A.L. Kitselman

If you keep saying things are going to be bad, you have a good chance of being a prophet.
—Isaac Bashevis Singer

269

When people asked, I used to tell them how sick I was. The more I talked about being sick, the worse I got. Finally, I started saying, "I'm getting better." It took a while, but then I started to feel better, too.
—Michael Hirsch, person with AIDS

WE GET OUT OF LIFE WHAT WE PUT INTO IT

Men will get no more out of life than they put into it.
—William J.H. Boetcker

Whatsoever a man soweth, that shall he also reap. —Gal. 6:7

There is a very real relationship, both quantitatively and qualitatively, between what you contribute and what you get out of this world.
—Oscar Hammerstein II

If a man plants melons he will reap melons; if he sows beans, he will reap beans. —Chinese proverb

He who sows courtesy reaps friendship, and he who plants kindness gathers love. —Saint Basil

Give to the world the best you have and the best will come back to you.
—Madeline Bridges

WE DETERMINE HOW OTHER PEOPLE RELATE TO US

Trust men and they will be true to you; treat them greatly and they will show themselves great.
—Ralph Waldo Emerson

We awaken in others the same attitude of mind we hold toward them.
—Elbert Hubbard

Any man will usually get from other men just what he is expecting of them. If he is looking for friendship he will likely receive it. If his attitude is that of indifference, it will beget indifference. And if a man is looking for a fight, he will in all likelihood be accommodated in that.
—John Richelsen

He who has not faith in others shall find no faith in them. —Lao-tzu

To make the world a friendly place, one must show it a friendly face.
—James Whitcomb Riley

If you would be loved, love and be lovable. —Benjamin Franklin

People are not going to love you unless you love them. —Pat Carroll

Getting people to like you is merely the other side of liking them.
—Norman Vincent Peale

People, by and large, will relate to the image you project. —Chyatee

The confidence which we have in ourselves gives birth to much of that which we have in others.
—Francois de La Rochefoucauld

SELF-DOUBT WILL CREATE THE VERY FAILURE WE FEAR

He who fears he shall suffer, already suffers what he fears.
—Michel de Montaigne

Fear to let fall a drop and you spill a lot. —Malay proverb

The thing we fear we bring to pass.
—Elbert Hubbard

A person who doubts himself is like a man who would enlist in the ranks of his enemies and bear arms against himself. He makes his failure certain by himself being the first person to be convinced of it.
—Alexandre Dumas

To be ambitious for wealth, and yet always expecting to be poor; to be always doubting your ability to get what you long for, is like trying to reach east by travelling west. There is no philosophy which will help a man to succeed when he is always doubting his ability to do so, and thus attracting failure. No matter how hard you work for success, if your thought is saturated with the fear of failure, it will kill your efforts, neutralize your endeavors and make success impossible.
—Charles Baudouin

He who fears being conquered is sure of defeat.
—Napoleon Bonaparte

Dangers by being despised grow great.
—Edmund Burke

If one asks for success and prepares for failure, he will get the situation he has prepared for.
—Florence Scovel Shinn

Doubt breeds doubt.
—Franz Grillparzer

Doubt indulged soon becomes doubt realized. —Francis Ridley Havergal

Proust has pointed out that the predisposition to love creates its own objects; is this not also true of fear?
—Elizabeth Bowen

Those who foresee the future and recognize it as tragic are often seized by a madness which forces them to commit the very acts which makes it certain that what they dread shall happen. —Dame Rebecca West

There are certain people who so ardently and passionately desire a thing, that from dread of losing it they leave nothing undone to make them lose it. —Jean de La Bruyere

Fear breeds fear. —Byron Janis

PEOPLE OFTEN BECOME WHAT IS EXPECTED OF THEM

A great manager has a knack for making ballplayers think they are better than they think they are. He forces you to have a good opinion of yourself. He lets you know he believes in you. He makes you get more out of yourself. And once you learn how good you really are, you never settle for playing anything less than your very best.
—Reggie Jackson

The only way to make a man trust-worthy is to trust him.
—Henry L. Stimson

Children are likely to live up to what you believe of them.
—Lady Bird Johnson

However much we guard against it, we tend to shape ourselves in the image others have of us.
—Eric Hoffer

If you want your children to improve, let them overhear the nice things you say about them to others.
—Haim Ginott

It is the nature of man to rise to greatness if greatness is expected of him.　　　　—John Steinbeck

I dare you to be the strongest boy in this class.
　　—William H. Danforth's teacher

Men have a trick of coming up to what is expected of them, good or bad.　　　　　　—Jacob Riis

Treat people as if they were what they should be, and you help them become what they are capable of becoming.　　—Johann von Goethe

Where much is expected from an individual, he may rise to the level of events and make the dream come true.　　　　　—Elbert Hubbard

People have a way of becoming what you encourage them to be—not what you nag them to be.　—S.N. Parker

Our self-image, strongly held, essentially determines what we become.
　　　　　　—Maxwell Maltz

Act so as to elicit the best in others and thereby in thyself.　—Felix Adler

ACT "AS IF"

If you act like you're rich, you'll get rich.　　　—Adnan Koashoggi

To keep our faces toward change, and behave like free spirits in the presence of fate, is strength undefeatable.　　　　　—Helen Keller

We planted flowers last year, and I didn't know if I'd be alive to see them come up.
　—Neal McHugh, person with AIDS

Act as if it were impossible to fail.
　　　　　—Dorothea Brande

If you want a quality, act as if you already had it.　—William James

If you would be powerful, pretend to be powerful.　　　—Horne Tooke

Assume a virtue, if you have it not.
　　　　—William Shakespeare

We must laugh before we are happy, for fear of dying without having laughed at all.　—Jean de La Bruyere

If you want to be a big company tomorrow, you have to start acting like one today.　　—Thomas Watson

If one advances confidently in the direction of his dreams, and endeavors to live the life which he has imagined, he will meet with a success unexpected in common hours.
　　　—Henry David Thoreau

We are what we pretend to be, so we must be careful about what we pretend to be.　　　—Kurt Vonnegut

Act as if you were already happy, and that will tend to make you happy.　　　　—Dale Carnegie

Always imitate the behavior of the winner when you lose.　　—Anon.

I couldn't hit a wall with a sixgun, but I can twirl one. It looks good.
　　　　　　—John Wayne

It is good to act as if. It is even better to grow to the point where it is no longer an act.
　　　—Charles Caleb Colton

Practice being excited. —Bill Foster

It is easy enough to be pleasant, when life flows by like a song. But the man worthwhile is one who will smile, when everything goes dead wrong. —Ella Wheeler Wilcox

Attempt easy tasks as if they were difficult, and difficult as if they were easy; in the one case that confidence may not fall asleep, in the other that it may not be dismayed.
—Baltasar Gracian

It is best to act with confidence, no matter how little right you have to it.
—Lillian Hellman

If you've got it, flaunt it. If you do not, pretend. —Wally Phillips

If you wish to live a life free from sorrow, think of what is going to happen as if it had already happened. —Epictetus

To establish oneself in the world, one has to do all one can to appear established.
—Francois de La Rochefoucauld

To believe in God is to yearn for His existence, and furthermore, it is to act as if He did exist.
—Miguel de Unamuno

To find oneself jilted is a blow to one's pride. One must do one's best to forget it and if one doesn't succeed, at least one must pretend to.
—Moliere

Our deeds determine us, as much as we determine our deeds.
—George Eliot

Illusory joy is often worth more than genuine sorrow. —Rene Descartes

Live as if you like yourself, and it may happen. —Marge Piercy

If I had a party to attend and didn't want to be there, I would play the part of someone who was having a lovely time. —Shirley MacLaine

Fake feeling good.... You're going to have to learn to fake cheerfulness. Believe it or not, eventually that effort will pay off: you'll actually start feeling happier. —Jean Bach

I long to accomplish a great and noble task, but it is my chief duty to accomplish small tasks as if they were great and noble.
—Helen Keller

We become just by performing just actions, temperate by performing temperate actions, brave by performing brave actions. —Aristotle

Make your judgement trustworthy by trusting it. —Grenville Kleiser

SOME INCREDIBLY POSITIVE APPROACHES

They've got us surrounded again, the poor bastards.
—General Creighton W. Abrams

I'll just hit the dry side of the ball.
—Stan Musial,
on how to handle a spitball

My disease is one of the best things that has happened to me; it has pulled me out of a quietly desperate life toward one full of love and hope.
—Tom O'Connor, person with ARC

Retreat? We're coming out of here as a Marine division. We're bringing our equipment ... our wounded ... our dead. Retreat, hell! We're just advancing in another direction.
—General Oliver Prince Smith

I'm in a wonderful position: I'm unknown, I'm underrated, and there's nowhere to go but up.
—Pierre S. DuPont IV

My center is giving way, my right is in retreat: situation excellent. I am attacking.
—Marshal Ferdinand Foch

I've never been poor, only broke. Being poor is a frame of mind. Being broke is a temporary situation.
—Mike Todd

I am dying, but otherwise I am quite well.   —Edith Sitwell, when asked how she felt

I can't say I was ever lost, but I was bewildered once for three days.
—Daniel Boone

Anyone can have an off decade.
—Larry Cole

Sunshine is delicious, rain is refreshing, wind braces us up, snow is exhilarating; there is really no such thing as bad weather, only different kinds of good weather.
—John Ruskin

We are so outnumbered there's only one thing to do. We must attack.
—Sir Andrew Cunningham

If they do kill me, I shall never die another death.   —Abraham Lincoln

Circumstances—what are circumstances? I make circumstances.
—Napoleon Bonaparte

Focus is important. Focus on those parts of yourself that are working. Look at yourself as someone whose body is in the process of healing. Concentrate on the positive parts.
—Will Garcia, person with AIDS

Disease can be seen as a call for personal transformation through metamorphosis. It is a transition from the death of your old self into the birth of your new.
—Tom O'Connor, person with ARC

I never lost a game. I just ran out of time.   —Bobby Layne

I'm not overweight, I'm just nine inches too short.   —Shelley Winters

GENERAL QUOTATIONS ABOUT POSITIVE THINKING, AND SELF-FULFILLING PROPHESIES AND ACTIONS

The person who says it cannot be done should not interrupt the person doing it.   —Chinese proverb

Being an optimist after you've got everything you want doesn't count.
—Kin Hubbard

There are more defects in temperament than in the mind.
—Francois de La Rochefoucauld

Knock the "t" off the "can't."
—George Reeves

I make the most of all that comes and the least of all that goes.
—Sara Teasdale

Clear your mind of "can't."
—Samuel Johnson

Rosiness is not a worse windowpane than gloomy gray when viewing the world.
—Grace Paley

It is never too late to be what you might have been.
—George Eliot

I will say this about being an optimist: even when things don't turn out well, you are certain they will get better.
—Frank Hughes

We have a problem. "Congratulations." But it's a tough problem. "Then double congratulations."
—W. Clement Stone

One should ... be able to see things as hopeless and yet be determined to make them otherwise.
—F. Scott Fitzgerald

Isn't it splendid to think of all the things there are to find out about? It just makes me feel glad to be alive— it's such an interesting world.
—Lucy Montgomery

To every disadvantage there is a corresponding advantage.
—W. Clement Stone

I learned really to practice mustard seed faith, and positive thinking, and remarkable things happened.
—Sir John Walton

Failure is impossible.
—Susan B. Anthony

The only prison we need to escape from is the prison of our own minds.
—Anon.

Whatever the ups and downs of detail within our limited experience, the larger whole is primarily beautiful.
—Gregory Bateson

He was a "how" thinker, not an "if" thinker.
—Anon.

No man can think clearly when his fists are clenched.
—George Jean Nathan

We think in generalities, but we live in detail.
—Alfred North Whitehead

Some folks think they are thinking when they are only rearranging their prejudices.
—Anon.

How things look on the outside of us depends on how things are on the inside of us.
—Park Cousins

This I conceive to be the chemical function of humor: to change the character of our thought.
—Lin Yutang

Think like a man of action, act like a man of thought.
—Henri Bergson

As is our confidence, so is our capacity.
—William Hazlitt

The more we do, the more we can do; the more busy we are, the more leisure we have.
—William Hazlitt

The young do not know enough to be prudent, and therefore they attempt the impossible—and achieve it, generation after generation.
—Pearl S. Buck

What we love, we shall grow to resemble.
—Bernard of Clairvaux

How much shall I be changed,
before I am changed!
—John Donnell

It is by sitting down to write every
morning that he becomes a writer.
Those who do not do this remain
amateurs.　　　　—Gerald Brenan

There is no miraculous change that
takes place in a boy that makes him
a man. He becomes a man by being
a man.　　　　—Louis L'Amour

Skill to do comes of doing.
—Ralph Waldo Emerson

In the end, the love you take is equal
to the love you make.
—Song lyric, "Abbey Road,"
Paul McCartney

The quality of our expectations
determines the quality of our
actions.　　　　—André Godin

Success produces success, just as
money produces money.
—Nicolas de Chamfort

Once you begin to believe there is
help "out there," you will know it to
be true.　　　　—Saint Bartholomew

ENTHUSIASM

ENTHUSIASM IS ONE OF THE MOST IMPORTANT THINGS IN LIFE

Enthusiasm *is* life.　—Paul Scofield

Enthusiasm is the most important thing in life.　—Tennessee Williams

Enthusiasm signifies God in us.
　—Madame de Stael

Life is enthusiasm, zest.
　—Sir Lawrence Oliver

There is nothing greater than enthusiasm.　—Henry Moore

Enthusiasm is the most beautiful word on earth.
　—Christian Morgenstern

Exuberance is beauty.
　—William Blake

A man can be short and dumpy and getting bald but if he has fire, women will like him.　—Mae West

What a man knows only through feeling can be explained only through enthusiasm.
　—Joseph Joubert

My enthusiasms ... constitute my reserves, my unexploited resources, perhaps my future.　—E.M. Cioran

Enthusiasm moves the world.
　—J. Balfour

Nothing is so contagious as enthusiasm; it moves stones, it charms brutes. Enthusiasm is the genius of sincerity, and truth accomplishes no victories without it.
　—Edward Bulwer-Lytton

What counts is not necessarily the size of the dog in the fight, but the size of the fight in the dog.
　—Dwight D. Eisenhower

Most great men and women are not perfectly rounded in their personalties, but are instead people whose one driving enthusiasm is so great it makes their faults seem insignificant.
　—Charles A. Cerami

Winning isn't everything. *Wanting* to win is.　—Catfish Hunter

Vitality! That's the pursuit of life, isn't it?　—Katharine Hepburn

All we need to make us really happy is something to be enthusiastic about. —Charles Kingsley

In things pertaining to enthusiasm, no man is sane who does not know how to be insane on proper occasions. —Henry Ward Beecher

The great man is he who does not lose his childlike heart. —Mencius

Zest is the secret of all beauty. There is no beauty that is attractive without zest. —Christian Dior

What hunger is in relation to food, zest is in relation to life.
—Bertrand Russell

Wake up with a smile and go after life.... Live it, enjoy it, taste it, smell it, feel it. —Joe Knapp

What one has, one ought to use; and whatever he does, he should do with all his might. —Cicero

Let us go singing as far as we go; the road will be less tedious. —Virgil

And whatsoever ye do, do it heartily.
—Col. 3:23

You will do foolish things, but do them with enthusiasm. —Colette

Whatever you attempt, go at it with spirit. Put some in!
—David Starr Jordan

Passion Is a Vital Force

Every man without passions has within him no principle of action, nor motive to act.
—Claude Helvetius

What is man but his passion?
—Robert Penn Warren

Only passions, great passions, can elevate the soul to great things.
—Denis Diderot

Nothing great in the world has been accomplished without passion.
—George Hegel

Human nature, if it healthy, demands excitement; and if it does not obtain its thrilling excitement in the right way, it will seek it in the wrong. God never makes bloodless stoics; He makes no passionless saints. —Oswald Chambers

All passions exaggerate; it is because they do that they are passions.
—Nicolas de Chamfort

If we resist our passions, it is more from their weakness than from our strength.
—Francois de La Rochefoucauld

Without passion man is a mere latent force and possibility, like the flint which awaits the shock of the iron before it can give forth its spark. —Henri Frederic Amiel

Be still when you have nothing to say; when genuine passion moves you, say what you've got to say, and say it *hot*. —D.H. Lawrence

The passions are the only orators which always persuade.
—Francois de La Rochefoucauld

Passion, though a bad regulator, is a powerful spring.
—Ralph Waldo Emerson

Our passions are ourselves.
—Anatole France

People who never get carried away should be. —Malcolm Forbes

BUT ENTHUSIASM MUST BE CHANNELED

This, indeed, is one of the eternal paradoxes of both life and literature—that without passion little gets done; yet, without control of that passion, its effects are largely ill or null. —F.L. Lucas

The world belongs to the enthusiast who keeps cool. —William McFee

Optimism, unaccompanied by personal effort, is merely a state of mind and not fruitful. —Edward L. Curtis

When enthusiasm is inspired by reason; controlled by caution; sound in theory; practical in application; reflects confidence; spreads good cheer; raises morale; inspires associates; arouses loyalty; and laughs at adversity, it is beyond price.
—Coleman Cox

ENTHUSIASM AND WORK

If you aren't fired with enthusiasm, you will be fired with enthusiasm.
—Vince Lombardi

When his enthusiasm goes, he's through as a player. —Pete Rose

Every production of genius must be the production of enthusiasm.
—Benjamin Disraeli

Give me a man who sings at his work. —Thomas Carlyle

ENTHUSIASM AND SUCCESS

A man can succeed at almost anything for which he has unlimited enthusiasm. —Charles M. Schwab

Flaming enthusiasm, backed up by horse sense and persistence, is the quality that most frequently makes for success. —Dale Carnegie

The world belongs to the energetic.
—Ralph Waldo Emerson

The real difference between men is energy. —Thomas Fuller

Success is going from failure to failure without loss of enthusiasm.
—Sir Winston Churchill

There is a passion for perfection which you rarely see fully developed, but ... in successful lives it is never wholly lacking. —Bliss Carman

Sometimes success is due less to ability than to zeal. —Charles Buxton

Many of the most successful men I have known have never grown up. They have retained bubbling-over boyishness. They have relished wit, they have indulged in humor. They have not allowed "dignity" to depress them into moroseness. Youthfulness of spirit is the twin brother of optimism, and optimism is the stuff of which American business success is fashioned. Resist growing up! —B.C. Forbes

If you have the will to win, you have achieved half your success; if you don't, you have achieved half your failure. —David V.A. Ambrose

Someone's always saying, "It's not whether you win or lose," but if you feel that way, you're as good as dead. —James Caan

To bring one's self to a frame of mind and to the proper energy to accomplish things that require plain hard work continuously is the one big battle that everyone has. When this battle is won for all time, then everything is easy.
—Thomas A. Buckner

We would accomplish many more things if we did not think of them as impossible. —C. Malesherbez

Faith that the thing can be done is essential to any great achievement.
—Thomas N. Carruther

We can accomplish almost anything within our ability if we but think that we can!
—George Matthew Adams

Optimism is essential to achievement and it is also the foundation of courage and of true progress.
—Nicholas Murray Butler

Morale is the greatest single factor in successful wars.
—Dwight D. Eisenhower

The will to conquer is the first condition of victory.
—Marshal Ferdinand Foch

The real secret of success is enthusiasm. Yes, more than enthusiasm, I would say excitement. I like to see men get excited. When they get excited they make a success of their lives. —Walter Chrysler

Always bear in mind that your own resolution to success is more important than any other one thing.
—Abraham Lincoln

It is fatal to enter any war without the will to win it.
—General Douglas MacArthur

The measure of an enthusiasm must be taken between interesting events. It is between bites that the lukewarm angler loses heart.
—Edwin Way Teale

Enthusiasm for one's goal to lessens the disagreeableness of working toward it. —Thomas Eakins

To burn always with this hard gem-like flame. To maintain this ecstasy, is success in life. —Walter Pater

Every man is enthusiastic at times. One man has enthusiasm for thirty minutes, another man has it for thirty days. But it is the man who has it for thirty years who makes a success in life. —Edward B. Butler

Man never rises to great truths without enthusiasm. —Vauvenargues

Success is due less to ability than to zeal. —Charles Buxton

I rate enthusiasm even above professional skill. —Sir Edward Appleton

He did it with all his heart, and prospered. —2 Chr. 31:21

A strong passion for any object will ensure success, for the desire of the end will point out the means.
—William Hazlitt

Nothing great was ever achieved
without enthusiasm.
—Ralph Waldo Emerson

What a man accomplishes in a day
depends upon the way in which he
approaches his tasks. When we
accept tough jobs as a challenge to
our ability and wade into them with
joy and enthusiasm, miracles can
happen. When we do our work with
a dynamic, conquering spirit, we get
things done.   —Arland Gilbert

If you're not happy every morning
when you get up, leave for work, or
start to work at home—if you're not
enthusiastic about doing that, you're
not going to be successful.
—Donald M. Kendall

The method of the enterprising is to
plan with audacity and execute with
vigor.   —Christian Bovee

Do it big or stay in bed.
—Larry Kelly

ENTHUSIASM AND KNOWLEDGE

Zeal will do more than knowledge.
—William Hazlitt

Let a man in a garret burn with
enough intensity, and he will set fire
to the world.
—Antoine de Saint-Exupery

Knowledge is power, but enthusiasm
pulls the switch.   —Ivern Ball

Through zeal, knowledge is gotten;
through lack of zeal, knowledge is
lost.   —Buddha

I prefer the errors of enthusiasm to
the indifference of wisdom.
—Anatole France

ENTHUSIASM AND ENERGY

It is energy, the central element of
which is will, that produces the miracles of enthusiasm in all ages. It is
the mainspring of what is called
force of character and the sustaining
power of all great action.
—Samuel Smiles

The difference between one man and
another is not mere ability ... it is
energy.   —Thomas Arnold

You see me in my most virile
moment when you see me doing
what I do. When I am directing, a
special energy comes upon me.... It is
only when I am doing my work that
I feel truly alive. It is like having sex.
—Federico Fellini

Energy, even like the Biblical grain
of mustard-seed, will move mountains.   —Hosea Ballou

Energy and persistence conquer all
things.   —Benjamin Franklin

Energy will do anything that can be
done in this world.
—Johann von Goethe

The only thing that keeps a man
going is energy. And what is energy
but liking life?   —Louis Auchincloss

ENTHUSIASM AND AGE

No one grows old by living, only by
losing interest in living.
—Marie Beynon Ray

None are so old as those who have
outlived enthusiasm.
—Henry David Thoreau

281

Years wrinkle the face, but to give up enthusiasm wrinkles the soul.
—Watterson Lowe

ENTHUSIASM AND WARFARE

He fights with spirit as well as with the sword.   —Latin proverb

It is fatal to enter any war without the will to win it.
—General Douglas MacArthur

Morale is the greatest single factor in successful wars.
—Dwight D. Eisenhower

The will to conquer is the first condition of victory.
—Marshal Ferdinand Foch

The aim of military training is not just to prepare men for battle, but to make them long for it.
—Louis Simpson

Wars may be fought with weapons, but they are won by men. It is the spirit of men who follow and of the man who leads that gains the victory.   —General George S. Patton

PRIMARY SOURCES OF ENTHUSIASM

Enthusiasm can only be aroused by two things: first, an ideal which takes the imagination by storm, and second, a definite, intelligible plan for carrying that ideal into practice.
—Arnold Toynbee

No one keeps up his enthusiasm automatically. Enthusiasm must be nourished with new actions, new aspirations, new efforts, new vision. Compete with yourself; set your teeth and dive into the job of breaking your own record. It is one's own fault if his enthusiasm is gone; he has failed to feed it.   —*Papyrus*

The same reason makes a man a religious enthusiast that makes a man an enthusiast in any other way ... an uncomfortable mind in an uncomfortable body.   —William Hazlitt

The great composer does not set to work because he is inspired, but becomes inspired because he is working. Beethoven, Wagner, Bach and Mozart settled down day after day to the job in hand with as much regularity as an accountant settles down each day to his figures. They didn't waste time waiting for inspiration.   —Ernest Newman

Opposition inflames the enthusiast, never converts him.
—J.C.F. von Schiller

Whatever course you have chosen for yourself, it will not be a chore but an adventure if you bring to it a sense of the glory of striving, if your sights are set far above the merely secure and mediocre.
—David Sarnoff

Earnestness and sincereness are synonymous.   —Corita Kent

Enthusiasm is nothing more or less than faith in action.
—Henry Chester

Vigor is contagious, and whatever makes us either think or feel strongly adds to our power and enlarges our field of action.
—Ralph Waldo Emerson

Practice being excited.   —Bill Foster

It is the greatest shot of adrenaline to be doing what you've wanted to do so badly. You almost feel like you could fly without the plane.

—Charles Lindbergh

Reason alone is insufficient to make us enthusiastic in any matter.

—Francois de La Rochefoucauld

HOPE

THE IMPORTANCE AND VALUE OF HOPE

If it were not for hopes, the heart would break. —Thomas Fuller

None are completely wretched but those who are without hope, and few are reduced so low as that.
—William Hazlitt

To all the living there is hope, for a living dog is better than a dead lion.
—Eccl. 9:4

Everybody lives for something better to come. —Anon.

Hope is itself a species of happiness, and, perhaps, the chief happiness which this world affords.
—Samuel Johnson

At first we hope too much; later on, not enough. —Joseph Roux

Lord save us all from ... a hope tree that has lost the faculty of putting out blossoms. —Mark Twain

He who does not hope to win has already lost. —José Joaquin Olmedo

We should not let our fears hold us back from pursuing our hopes.
—John F. Kennedy

Man needs, for his happiness, not only the enjoyment of this or that, but hope and enterprise and change.
—Bertrand Russell

In all pleasure hope is a considerable part. —Samuel Johnson

Without hope men are only half alive. With hope they dream and think and work. —Charles Sawyer

They say a person needs just three things to be truly happy in this world. Someone to love, something to do, and something to hope for.
—Tom Bodett

Great hopes make great men.
—Thomas Fuller

Hope is one of those things in life you cannot do without.
—LeRoy Douglas

A leader is a dealer in hope.
—Napoleon Bonaparte

The important thing is not that we can live on hope alone, but that life is not worth living without it.
—Harvey Milk

Hope and patience are two sovereign remedies for all, the surest reposals, the softest cushions to lean on in adversity.   —Robert Burton

It has never been, and never will be, easy work! But the road that is built in hope is more pleasant to the traveler than the road built in despair, even though they both lead to the same destination.
—Marian Zimmer Bradley

Optimism is the faith that leads to achievement. Nothing can be done without hope or confidence.
—Helen Keller

We want to create hope for the person ... we must give hope, always hope.   —Mother Teresa, on AIDS

Take hope from the heart of man and you make him a beast of prey.
—Ouida

And thou shalt be secure because there is hope.   —Jb. 11:18

Hope! Of all the ills that men endure, the only cheap and universal cure.   —Abraham Cowley

Our greatest good, and what we least can spare, is hope.
—John Armstrong

WITHOUT HOPE WE DIE

Hope is the last thing that dies in man.
—Francois de La Rochefoucauld

Hope is the major weapon against the suicide impulse.
—Dr. Karl Menninger

Refusal to hope is nothing more than a decision to die.
—Bernie S. Siegel, M.D.

We must have hope or starve to death.   —Pearl S. Buck

Man can live about forty days without food, about three days without water, about eight minutes without air ... but only for one second without hope.   —Hal Lindsey

To eat bread without hope is still slowly to starve to death.
—Pearl S. Buck

Strong hope is a much greater stimulant of life than any single realized joy could be.   —Friedrich Nietzsche

Hope is the last thing ever lost.
—Italian proverb

HOPE, FAITH, AND BELIEF

Now the God of hope fills you with all joy and peace in believing, that ye may abound in hope.
—Rom. 15:13

Hope is putting faith to work when doubting would be easier.
—Anon.

Hope is the belief, more or less strong, that joy will come; desire is the wish it may come.
—Sydney Smith

There is nothing that fear or hope does not make men believe.
—Vauvenargues

Hope is the parent of faith.

—C.A. Bartol

Hope is faith holding out its hand in the dark. —George Iles

HOPE IS A GREAT MOTIVATOR

No hope, no action. —Peter Levi

Hope is one of the principal springs that keep mankind in motion.

—Thomas Fuller

Hope arouses, as nothing else can arouse, a passion for the possible.

—William Sloan Coffin, Jr.

Hope is the first thing to take some sort of action. —John Armstrong

Hope is the anchor of the soul, the stimulus to action, and the incentive to achievement. —Anon.

Hope is a vigorous principle ... it sets the head and heart to work, and animates a man to do his utmost.

—Jeremy Collier

It is the around-the-corner brand of hope that prompts people to action, while the distant hope acts as an opiate. —Eric Hoffer

HOPE AS A DREAM

Hope is the pillar that holds up the world. Hope is the dream of a waking man. —Pliny, the Elder

Hope is a waking dream. —Aristotle

Hope is but the dream of those that wake. —Matthew Prior

Hope is not a dream, but a way of making dreams become reality.

—L.J. Cardina Suenens

HOPE AND HAPPINESS

Hope is grief's best music.

—Anon.

Hope is the last thing to abandon the unhappy. —Anon.

The miserable have no medicine but hope. —William Shakespeare

Hope is the second soul of the unhappy. —Johann von Goethe

HOPE AND THE FUTURE

Hope is the positive mode of awaiting the future. —Emil Brunner

If we were logical, the future would be bleak indeed. But we are more than logical. We are human beings, and we have faith, and we have hope, and we can work.

—Jacques Cousteau

If winter comes, can spring be far behind? —Percy Bysshe Shelley

There is no medicine like hope, no incentive so great, and no tonic so powerful as expectation of something tomorrow.

—Orison Swett Marden

"Wait'll next year!" is the favorite cry of baseball fans, football fans, hockey fans, and gardeners.

—Robert Orben

HOPE AND PATIENCE

Hope and patience are two sovereign remedies for all, the surest reposals, the softest cushions to lean on in adversity. —Robert Burton

Patience is the art of hoping.

—Vauvenargues

Hope is patience with the lamp lit.
—Tertullian

All human wisdom is summed up in two words—wait and hope.
—Alexandre Dumas

HOPE AND FEAR

Hope is some extraordinary spiritual grace that God gives us to control our fears, not to oust them.
—Vincent NcNabb

Where no hope is left, is left no fear.
—John Milton

There is no hope unmingled with fear, and no fear unmingled with hope.
—Baruch Spinoza

I steer my bark with hope in my heart, leaving fear astern.
—Thomas Jefferson

HOPELESSNESS

When you say a situation or a person is hopeless, you are slamming the door in the face of God.
—Charles L. Allen

Hell is the place where one has ceased to hope.
—A.J. Cronin

There are no hopeless situations; there are only men who have grown hopeless about them.
—Clare Boothe Luce

Hope never abandons you, you abandon it.
—George Weinberg

Other men see only a hopeless end, but the Christian rejoices in an endless hope.
—Gilbert M. Beeken

Never despair.
—Horace

One should ... be able to see things as hopeless and yet be determined to make them otherwise.
—F. Scott Fitzgerald

PRIMARY SOURCES OF HOPE

Extreme hopes are born of extreme misery.
—Bertrand Russell

Hope is brightest when it dawns from fears.
—Sir Walter Scott

Hope is like a road in the country; there was never a road, but when many people walk on it, the road comes into existence.
—Lin Yutang

Hope works in these ways: it looks for the good in people instead of harping on the worst; it discovers what can be done instead of grumbling about what cannot; it regards problems, large or small, as opportunities; it pushes ahead when it would be easy to quit; it "lights the candle" instead of "cursing the darkness."
—Anon.

While there's life, there's hope.
—Terence

When you're depressed, the whole body is depressed, and it translates to the cellular level. The first objective is to get your energy up, and you can do it through play. It's one of the most powerful ways of breaking up hopelessness and bringing energy into the situation.
—O. Carl Simonton

Every area of trouble gives out a ray of hope, and the one unchangeable certainty is that nothing is certain or unchangeable.
—John F. Kennedy

287

OTHER DEFINITIONS OF HOPE

Hope is the poor man's bread.
—Gary Herbert

Oh, what a valiant faculty is hope.
—Michel de Montaigne

Hope is necessary in every condition. The miseries of poverty, sickness and captivity would, without this comfort, be insupportable.
—Samuel Johnson

Hope is a risk that must be run.
—Georges Bernanos

Hope is an adventure, a going forward, a confident search for a rewarding life. —Dr. Karl Menninger

Appetite, with an opinion of attaining, is called hope; the same, without such opinion, despair.
—Thomas Hobbes

Hope is a satisfaction unto itself, and need not be fulfilled to be appreciated. —Dr. Fred O. Henker

Hope is desire and expectation rolled into one. —Ambrose Bierce

To hope is to enjoy.
—Jacques Delille

Hope, that star of life's tremulous ocean. —Paul Moon James

Hope is the word which God has written on the brow of every man.
—Victor Hugo

Hope is the thing with feathers that perches in the soul and sings the tune without words and never stops at all.
—Emily Dickinson

Hope is not the conviction that something will turn out well but the certainty that something makes sense, regardless of how it turns out.
—Vaclav Havel

Hope is a light diet, but very stimulating. —Honore de Balzac

Hope is the power of being cheerful in circumstances which we know to be desperate. —G.K. Chesterton

Honor begets honor, trust begets trust, faith begets faith, and hope is the mainspring of life.
—Henry L. Stimson

GENERAL QUOTATIONS ABOUT HOPE

Hope, like the gleaming taper's light, adorns and cheers our way;
And still, as darker grows the night, emits a lighter ray.
—Oliver Goldsmith

Hope springs eternal in the human breast. —Alexander Pope

Just as dumb creatures are snared by food, human beings would not be caught unless they had a nibble of hope. —Petronius

True hope is swift and flies with
swallow's wings;
Kings it makes Gods, and meaner
creatures kings.
—William Shakespeare

Ten thousand men possess ten thousand hopes. —Euripides

Hope has as many lives as a cat or a king.
—Henry Wadsworth Longfellow

288

Have hope. Though clouds environs now,
And gladness hides her face in scorn,
Put thou the shadow from thy brow—
No night but hath its morn.
                    —J.C.F. von Schiller

In time of trouble avert not thy face from hope, for the soft marrow abideth in the hard bone.   —Hafez

Faith, hope, and charity—if we had more of the first two, we'd need less of the last.   —Anon.

In the face of uncertainty, there is nothing wrong with hope.
                    —O. Carl Simonton

Hope is the only bee that makes honey without flowers.
                    —Robert G. Ingersoll

They sailed. They sailed. Then spoke the mate:
"This mad sea shows its teeth tonight
He curls his lip, he lies in wait,
With lifted teeth, as if to bite!
Brave admiral, say but one good word:
What shall we do when hope is gone?"
The words leapt like a leaping sword: "Sail on! sail on! and on!"   —Joaquin Miller

Hope is a very unruly emotion.
                    —Gloria Steinem

The hopeful man sees success where others see failure, sunshine where others see shadows and storm.
                    —Orison Swett Marden

The wind was cold off the mountains and I was a naked man with enemies behind me, and nothing before me but hope.
                    —Louis L'Amour

Hope sees the invisible, feels the intangible and achieves the impossible.   —Anon.

I always entertain great hopes.
                    —Robert Frost

To hope is not to demand.
                    —Anon.

Hold your head high, stick your chest out. You can make it. It gets dark sometimes but morning comes....
Keep hope alive.   —Jesse Jackson

Forgiving means to pardon the unpardonable,
Faith means believing the unbelievable,
And hoping means to hope when things are hopeless.
                    —G.K. Chesterton

The gift we can offer others is so simple a thing as hope.
                    —Daniel Berrigan

Even the cry from the depths is an affirmation: why cry if there is no hint of hope of hearing?
                    —Martin Marty

It's never too late—in fiction or in life—to revise.   —Nancy Thayer

In the night of death, hope sees a star, and listening love can hear the rustle of a wing.
                    —Robert G. Ingersoll

VISUALIZATION

VISION DOESN'T DEPEND ON OUR EYES

Vision is the art of seeing things invisible. —Jonathan Swift

You can't depend on your eyes when your imagination is out of focus.
—Mark Twain

Just because a man lacks the use of his eyes doesn't mean he lacks vision. —Stevie Wonder

True vision is always twofold. It involves emotional comprehensions as well as physical perception.
—Ross Parmenter

WE DON'T ALL VISUALIZE THE SAME THINGS

We all live under the same sky, but we don't all have the same horizon.
—Konrad Adenauer

A genius is one who shoots at something no one else can see—and hits it. —Anon.

A fool sees not the same tree that a wise man sees. —William Blake

Who is the wise man? He who sees what's going to be born.
—Solomon

A feeble man can see the farms that are fenced and tilled, the houses that are built. The strong man sees the possible houses and farms. His eye makes estates as fast as the sun breeds clouds.
—Ralph Waldo Emerson

Guido the plumber and Michelangelo obtained their marble from the same quarry, but what each saw in the marble made the difference between a nobleman's sink and a brilliant sculpture. —Bob Kall

WE MUST VISUALIZE BEFORE WE ACT OR CREATE

All acts performed in the world begin in the imagination.
—Barbara Grizzuti Harrison

A rock pile ceases to be a rock pile the moment a single man contemplates it, bearing within him the image of a cathedral.
—Antoine de Saint-Exupery

290

Man can only become what he is able to consciously imagine, or to "image forth."   —Dane Rudhyar

VISUALIZING GOALS

Before you begin a thing remind yourself that difficulties and delays quite impossible to foresee are ahead.... You can only see one thing clearly, and that is your goal. Form a mental vision of that and cling to it through thick and thin.
    —Kathleen Norris

Man can only receive what he sees himself receiving.
    —Florence Scovel Shinn

A person can grow only as much as his horizon allows.   —John Powell

VISUALIZATION AND DREAMS

Nothing happens unless first a dream.   —Carl Sandburg

The moment of enlightenment is when a person's dreams of possibilities become images of probabilities.
    —Vic Braden

Reach high, for stars lie hidden in your soul. Dream deep, for every dream precedes the goal.
    —Pamela Vaull Starr

When we can't dream any longer, we die.   —Emma Goldman

Hold fast to dreams, for if dreams die, life is a broken-winged bird that cannot fly.   —Langston Hughes

Dream lofty dreams, and as you dream, so shall you become. Your vision is the promise of what you shall at last unveil.   —John Ruskin

It may be that those who do most, dream most.   —Stephen Leacock

GENERAL QUOTATIONS ABOUT VISION

Imagination has always had powers of resurrection that no science can match.   —Ingrid Bengis

A couple of times a day I sit quietly and visualize my body fighting the AIDS virus. It's the same as me sitting and seeing myself hit the perfect serve. I did that often when I was an athlete.   —Arthur Ashe

Is life so wretched? Isn't it rather your hands which are too small, your vision which is muddled? You are the one who must grow up.
    —Dag Hammarskjold

The artist doesn't see things as they are, but as he is.   —Anon.

Five minutes, just before going to sleep, given to a bit of directed imagination regarding achievement possibilities of the morrow, will steadily and increasingly bear fruit, particularly if all ideas of difficulty, worry or fear are resolutely ruled out and replaced by those of accomplishment and smiling courage.
    —Frederick Pierce

You can vitally influence your life from within by auto-suggestion. The first thing each morning, and the last thing each night, suggest to yourself specific ideas that you wish to embody in your character and personality. Address such suggestions to yourself, silently or aloud, until they are deeply impressed upon your mind.   —Grenville Kleiser

Leaders are visionaries with a poorly developed sense of fear and no concept of the odds against them. They make the impossible happen.
　　　　　—Dr. Robert Jarvik

When there is no vision, people perish.　　　—Ralph Waldo Emerson

ROLE MODELS

THE RIGHT ROLE MODEL CAN BE VERY INSPIRATIONAL

Nothing arouses ambition so much as the trumpet clang of another's fame.   —Baltasar Gracian

I studied the lives of great men and famous women, and I found that the men and women who got to the top were those who did the jobs they had in hand, with everything they had of energy and enthusiasm and hard work.   —Harry S. Truman

People never improve unless they look to some standard or example higher and better than themselves.
          —Tyron Edwards

Without heroes, we are all plain people, and don't know how far we can go.   —Bernard Malamud

That some should be rich shows that others may become rich, and hence is just encouragement to industry and enterprise.   —Abraham Lincoln

The best teachers of humanity are the lives of great men.
          —Charles H. Fowler

As it is our nature to be more moved by hope than fear, the example of one we see abundantly rewarded cheers and encourages us far more than the sight of many who have not been well treated disquiets us.
          —Francesco Guicciardini

Keep away from people who try to belittle your ambitions. Small people always do that, but the really great make you feel that you, too, can become great.   —Mark Twain

To be ignorant of the lives of the most celebrated men of antiquity is to continue in a state of childhood.
          —Plutarch

People seldom improve when they have no other model but themselves to copy.   —Oliver Goldsmith

As you get older it is harder to have heroes, but it is sort of necessary.
          —Ernest Hemingway

The most important single influence in the life of a person is another person ... who is worthy of emulation.
          —Paul D. Shafer

Lives of great men all remind us we
can make our lives sublime; and,
departing, leave behind us, footprints on the sands of time.
—Henry Wadsworth Longfellow

Very few men are wise by their own
counsel, or learned by their own
teaching. For he that was only
taught by himself had a fool for his
master. —Ben Johnson

Call the roll in your memory of conspicuously successful business giants
and ... you will be struck by the fact
that almost every one of them
encountered inordinate difficulties
sufficient to crush all but the gamest
of spirits. Edison went hungry many
times before he became famous.
—B.C. Forbes

WE ALL NEED GOOD EXAMPLES

A good example is the best sermon.
—Anon.

Example has more followers than
reason. —Christian Bovee

Example is the school of mankind,
and they will learn at no other.
—Burke

Example is not the main thing in
influencing others. It is the only
thing. —Albert Schweitzer

Judgement can be acquired only by
acute observation, by actual experience in the school of life, by ceaseless
alertness to learn from others, by
study of the activities of men who
have made notable marks, by striving to analyze the everyday play of
causes and effects, by constant study
of human nature. —B.C. Forbes

Example moves the world more than
doctrine. —Henry Miller

Nothing is so infectious as example.
—Francois de La Rochefoucauld

One filled with joy preaches without
preaching. —Mother Teresa

IMITATION

There is a difference between imitating a good man and counterfeiting
him. —Benjamin Franklin

Each of us is in fact what he is
almost exclusively by virtue of his
imitativeness. —William James

Imitation is a necessity of human
nature. —Oliver Wendell Holmes, Jr.

When people are free to do as they
please, they usually imitate each
other. —Eric Hoffer

Emulation is a noble and just passion, full of appreciation.
—J.C.F. von Schiller

Emulation admires and strives to
imitate great actions; envy is only
moved to malice.
—Honore de Balzac

'Tis no shame to follow the better
precedent. —Ben Johnson

Imitation can acquire pretty much
everything but the power which created the thing imitated.
—Henry S. Haskins

Almost all absurdity of conduct arises from the imitation of those whom
we cannot resemble.
—Samuel Johnson

LEARNING FROM OTHERS' MISTAKES

From the errors of others, a wise man corrects his own.
> —Publilius Syrus

Learn from the mistakes of others—you can't live long enough to make them all yourself.   —Martin Vanbee

Wise men learn by other men's mistakes, fools by their own.
> —H.G. Bohn

A man is fortunate if he encounters living examples of vice, as well as of virtue, to inspire him.
> —Brendan Francis

Learn to see in another's calamity the ills which you should avoid.
> —Publilius Syrus

Don't use the conduct of a fool as a precedent.   —Talmud

A prudent person profits from personal experience, a wise one from the experience of others.
> —Dr. Joseph Collins

Is there anyone so wise as to learn by the experience of others?   —Voltaire

If ... you can't be a good example, then you'll just have to be a horrible warning.   —Catherine Aird

PART 4

Knowing What to Do

CHANGE

CHANGE IS INEVITABLE

Everything passes; everything wears out; everything breaks.
—French proverb

Always! That is the dreadful word ... it is a meaningless word, too.
—Oscar Wilde

What is actual is actual only for one time, and only for one place.
—T.S. Eliot

Our days are a kaleidoscope. Every instant a change takes place.... New harmonies, new contrasts, new combinations of every sort.... The most familiar people stand each moment in some new relation to each other, to their work, to surrounding objects. —Henry Ward Beecher

Just when I think I have learned the way to live, life changes.
—Hugh Prather

Everything changes but change itself.
—John F. Kennedy

We change, whether we like it or not. —Ralph Waldo Emerson

The one unchangeable certainty is that nothing is certain or unchangeable. —John F. Kennedy

All things must change to something new, to something strange.
—Henry Wadsworth Longfellow

Because things are the way they are, things will not stay the way they are.
—Bertolt Brecht

The moral world is as little exempt as the physical world from the law of ceaseless change, of perpetual flux. —Sir James Frazer

Wherever we are, it is but a stage on the way to somewhere else, and whatever we do, however well we do it, it is only a preparation to do something else that shall be different.
—Robert Louis Stevenson

All is change; all yields its place and goes. —Euripides

O visionary world, condition strange,
Where naught abiding is but only change. —James Russell Lowell

Things alter for the worse spontaneously, if they be not altered for the
better designedly.   —Francis Bacon

For good and evil, man is a free creative spirit. This produces the very
queer world we live in, a world in
continuous creation and therefore
continuous change and insecurity.
                              —Joyce Cary

All things change, nothing is extinguished.   —Ovid

Life is always at some turning point.
                           —Irwin Edman

Everything flows, nothing stays still.
                            —Heraclitus

Nothing in this world is permanent.
                       —German proverb

There are no permanent changes
because change itself is permanent.
                        —Ralph L. Woods

Nothing is permanent but change.
                            —Heraclitus

Time, in the turning-over of days,
works change for better or worse.
                              —Pindar

CHANGE IS LIFE ITSELF

Would that life were like the shadow
cast by a wall or a tree, but it is like
the shadow of a bird in flight.
                             —Talmud

Change is the law of life.
                       —John F. Kennedy

To live is to change, and to be perfect is to change often.
          —John Henry Cardinal Newman

One must never lose time in vainly
regretting the past or in complaining
against the changes which cause us
discomfort, for change is the essence
of life.   —Anatole France

A living thing is distinguished from a
dead thing by the multiplicity of the
changes at any moment taking place
in it.   —Herbert Spencer

When you're through changing,
you're through.   —Bruce Barton

Change is the only evidence of life.
                          —Evelyn Waugh

To exist is to change, to change is to
mature, to mature is to go on creating oneself endlessly.
                          —Henri Bergson

Life belongs to the living, and he
who lives must be prepared for
changes.   —Johann von Goethe

Someday change will be accepted as
life itself.   —Shirley MacLaine

What is more enthralling to the
human mind than this splendid,
boundless, colored mutability!—Life
in the making?   —David Grayson

The basic fact of today is the tremendous.   —Jawaharlal Nehru

Each new season grows from the
leftovers from the past. That is the
essence of change, and change is the
basic law.   —Hal Borland

Arriving at one goal is the starting
point to another.   —John Dewey

All that is not eternal is eternally out
of date.   —C.S. Lewis

Why We Should Welcome Change

When people shake their heads because we are living in a restless age, ask them how they would like to life in a stationary one, and do without change.
—George Bernard Shaw

The healthy being craves an occasional wildness, a jolt from normality, a sharpening of the edge of appetite, his own little festival of the Saturnalia, a brief excursion from his way of life. —Robert MacIver

In embracing change, entrepreneurs ensure social and economic stability.
—George Gilder

There is a certain relief in change, even though it be from bad to worse; as I have found in traveling in a stagecoach, it is often a comfort to shift one's position and be bruised in a new place. —Washington Irving

None of us knows what the next change is going to be, what unexpected opportunity is just around the corner, waiting to change all the tenor of our lives. —Kathleen Norris

The art of living does not consist in preserving and clinging to a particular mood of happiness, but in allowing happiness to change its form ... happiness, like a child, must be allowed to grow up.
—Charles L. Morgan

Change does not change tradition. It strengthens it. Change is a challenge and an opportunity, not a threat.
—Prince Phillip of England

It is in changing that things find purpose. —Heraclitus

Turbulence is a life force. It is opportunity. Let's love turbulence and use it for change. —Ramsay Clark

In all change, well looked into, the germinal good out-vails the apparent ill. —Francis Thompson

The time is ripe, and rotten-ripe, for change; then let it come. —Lowell

Society can only pursue its normal course by means of a certain progression of changes.
—John, Viscount Morley of Blackburn

Continuity in everything is unpleasant. —Blaise Pascal

We emphasize that we believe in change because we were born of it, we have lived by it, we prospered and grew great by it. So the status quo has never been our god, and we ask no one else to bow down before it. —Carl T. Rowan

If you do what you've always done, you'll get what you've always gotten.
—Anon.

Man needs, for his happiness, not only the enjoyment of this or that, but hope and enterprise and change.
—Bertrand Russell

To remain young one must change.
—Alexander Chase

Where the old tracks are lost, new country is revealed with its wonders.
—Rabindranath Tagore

Weep not that the world changes—
did it keep a stable, changeless state,
it were a cause indeed to weep.
—William Cullen Bryant

Only in growth, reform, and change,
paradoxically enough, is true security to be found.
—Anne Morrow Lindbergh

CHANGE AND PROGRESS

Change is inevitable in a progressive
society. Change is constant.
—Benjamin Disraeli

Progress is impossible without
change, and those who cannot
change their minds cannot change
anything. —George Bernard Shaw

Why do we shrink from change?
What can come into being save by
change? —Marcus Aurelius

The world hates change, yet it is the
only thing that has brought progress.
—Charles F. Kettering

The art of progress is to preserve
order amid change, and to preserve
change amid order.
—Alfred North Whitehead

Change is the watchword of progression. When we tire of well-worn
ways, we seek for new. This restless
craving in the souls of men spurs
them to climb, and to seek the mountain view. —Ella Wheeler Wilcox

He that will not apply new remedies
must expect new evils.
—Francis Bacon

In a moving world readaptation is
the price of longevity.
—George Santayana

PEOPLE CHANGE

Every saint has a past, and every sin-
ner has a future. —Oscar Wilde

We must always change, renew, reju-
venate ourselves; otherwise we hard-
en. —Johann von Goethe

On the human chessboard, all moves
are possible. —Miriam Schiff

There is nobody who totally lacks
the courage to change. —Rollo May

I've never met a person, I don't care
what his condition, in whom I could
not see possibilities. I don't care how
much a man may consider himself a
failure, I believe in him, for he can
change the thing that is wrong in his
life anytime he is prepared and ready
to do it. Whenever he develops the
desire, he can take away from his life
the thing that is defeating it. The
capacity for reformation and change
lies within. —Preston Bradley

There is change in all things. You
yourself are subject to continual
change and some decay, and this is
common to the entire universe.
—Marcus Aurelius

Readjusting is a painful process, but
most of us need it at one time or
another.
—Arthur Christopher Benson

For many men, the acquisition of
wealth does not end their troubles, it
only changes them.
—Marcus Annaeus Seneca

Our being is continually undergoing
and entering upon changes.... We
must, strictly speaking, at every

301

moment give each other up and let each other go and not hold each other back.   —Rainer Maria Rilke

Change the fabric of your own soul and your own visions, and you change all.   —Vachel Lindsay

A person needs at intervals to separate himself from family and companions and go to new places. He must go without his familiars in order to be open to influence, to change.
        —Katharine Butler Hathaway

There are people who not only strive to remain static themselves, but strive to keep everything else so ... their position is almost laughably hopeless.   —Odell Shepard

The curious paradox is that when I accept myself just as I am, then I can change.   —Carl Rogers

Very often a change of self is needed more than a change of scene.
        —Arthur Christopher Benson

There is not a single ill-doer who could not be turned to some good.
        —Jean-Jacques Rousseau

Things do not change; we change.
        —Henry David Thoreau

We do not succeed in changing things according to our desire, but gradually our desire changes.
        —Marcel Proust

The old woman I shall become will be quite different from the woman I am now. Another I is beginning.
        —George Sand

The absurd man is he who never changes.   —Auguste Barthelemy

Man would be "otherwise." That's the essence of the specifically human.
        —Antonio Machado

CREATING POSITIVE CHANGE

The reality is that changes are coming.... They must come. You must share in bringing them.
        —John Hersey

One must change one's tactics every ten years if one wishes to maintain one's superiority.
        —Napoleon Bonaparte

After you've done a thing the same way for two years, look it over carefully. After five years, look at it with suspicion. And after ten years, throw it away and start all over.
        —Alfred Edward Perlman

All that philosophers have done is interpret the world in different ways. It is our job to change it.
        —Karl Marx

Christians are supposed not merely to endure change, nor even to profit by it, but to cause it.
        —Harry Emerson Fosdick

Changes are not predictable; but to deny them is to be an accomplice to one's own unnecessary vegetation.
        —Gail Sheehy

We must learn to view change as a natural phenomenon—to anticipate it and to plan for it. The future is ours to channel in the direction we want to go ... we must continually ask ourselves, "What will happen if...?" or better still, "How can we make it happen?" —Lisa Taylor

If you have no will to change it, you have no right to criticize it.
—Anon.

WE MUST OFTEN GIVE UP SOMETHING TO GET SOMETHING BETTER

The important thing is this: to be able at any moment to sacrifice what we are for what we could become.
—Charles Du Bos

When patterns are broken, new worlds emerge. —Tuli Kupferberg

One must lose one's life in order to find it. —Anne Morrow Lindbergh

This Mouse must give up one of his Mouse ways of seeing things in order that he may grow.
—Hyemeyohsts Storm

Every one should keep a mental wastepaper basket and the older he grows the more things he will consign to it—torn up to irrecoverable tatters. —Samuel Butler

Unless one says goodbye to what one loves, and unless one travels to completely new territories, one can expect merely a long wearing away of oneself and an eventual extinction. —Jean Dubuffet

WE SHOULD CHANGE COURSE AS SOON AS WE REALIZE IT'S WRONG FOR US

No matter how far you have gone on a wrong road, turn back.
—Turkish proverb

It is only an error in judgement to make a mistake, but it shows infirmity of character to adhere to it when discovered. —Christian Bovee

If you board the wrong train, it is no use running along the corridor in the other direction.
—Dietrich Bonhoeffer

It's never too late—in fiction or in life—to revise. —Nancy Thayer

Any path is only a path, and there is no affront, to oneself or to others, in dropping it if that is what your heart tells you. —Carlos Castaneda

SOMETIMES WE MUST MAKE CHANGES BEFORE WE KNOW WHAT TO DO NEXT

There is a time for departure even when there's no certain place to go.
—Tennessee Williams

Just as we outgrow a pair of trousers, we outgrow acquaintances, libraries, principles, etc., at times before they're worn out and times—and this is the worst of all—before we have new ones.
—Georg Christoph Lichtenberg

BUT DON'T MAKE CHANGES JUST FOR THE SAKE OF MAKING CHANGES

Have no fear of change as such and, on the other hand, no liking for it merely for its own sake.
—Robert Moses

The main dangers in this life are the people who want to change everything ... or nothing. —Lady Astor

303

Our fathers valued change for the sake of its results; we value it in the act. —Alice Meynell

We must beware of needless innovations, especially when guided by logic. —Sir Winston Churchill

All change is not growth, as all movement is not forward. —Ellen Glasgow

Just because everything is different doesn't mean anything has changed. —Irene Peter

None are happy but by the anticipation of change. The change itself is nothing; when we have made it, the next wish is to change again. —Samuel Johnson

We accept the verdict of the past until the need for change cries out loudly enough to force upon us a choice between the comforts of further inertia and the irksomeness of action. —Learned Hand

To some will come a time when change itself is beauty, if not heaven. —Edwin Arlington Robinson

To change and to improve are two different things. —German proverb

IT'S OFTEN MORE IMPORTANT TO CHANGE OUR MINDS AND OPINIONS THAN TO STICK WITH THEM

Today is not yesterday; how can our works and thoughts, if they are always to be the fittest, continue always the same? Change, indeed, is painful, yet ever needful. —Thomas Carlyle

Security can only be achieved through constant change, through discarding old ideas that have outlived their usefulness and adapting others to current facts. —William O. Douglas

You had better be ready to change your mind when needed. —Henry B. Wilson

Loyalty to petrified opinion never yet broke a chain or freed a human soul. —Mark Twain

We are chameleons, and our partialities and prejudices change place with an easy and blessed facility. —Mark Twain

Our firmest convictions are apt to be the most suspect; they mark our limitations and our bounds. Life is a petty thing unless it is moved by the indomitable urge to extend its boundaries. —José Ortega y Gasset

It often takes more courage to change one's opinion than to stick to it. —Georg Christoph Lichtenberg

All our final resolutions are made in a state of mind which is not going to last. —Marcel Proust

It's an ill plan that cannot be changed. —Latin proverb

The death of dogma is the birth of reality. —Immanuel Kant

If anyone accuses me of contradicting myself, I reply: Because I have been wrong once, or oftener, I do not aspire to be always wrong. —Vauvenargues

He who cannot change the very fabric of his thought will never be able to change reality. —Anwar Sadat

It is in the uncompromisingness with which dogma is held, and not in the dogma or want of dogma, that the danger lies. —Samuel Butler

I wish to say what I think and feel today, with the proviso that tomorrow perhaps I shall contradict it all.
—Ralph Waldo Emerson

Progress is impossible without change, and those who cannot change their minds cannot change anything. —George Bernard Shaw

The most significant change in a person's life is a change of attitude. Right attitudes produce right actions. —William J. Johnston

You had better be ready to change your mind when needed, or your mind will change you.
—Henry B. Wilson

The most fatal illusion is the settled point of view. Since life is growth and motion, a fixed point of view kills anybody who has one.
—Brooks Atkinson

The world does not have to change.... The only thing that has to change is our attitude. —Gerald Jampolsky

Oh, would that my mind could let fall its dead ideas, as the tree does its withered leaves! —André Gide

Convictions are more dangerous enemies of truth than lies.
—Friedrich Nietzsche

A foolish consistency is the hobgoblin of little minds, adored by little statesmen and philosophers and divines. —Ralph Waldo Emerson

A man should never be ashamed to own that he has been in the wrong, which is but saying ... that he is wiser today than yesterday.
—Jonathan Swift

We have to live today by what truth we can get today and be ready tomorrow to call it falsehood.
—William James

It is well for people who think to change their minds occasionally in order to keep them clean. For those who do not think, it is best at least to rearrange their prejudices once in a while. —Luther Burbank

New opinions are always suspected, and usually opposed, without any other reason but because they are not already common. —John Locke

Do I contradict myself? Very well then, I contradict myself (I am large, I contain multitudes).
—Walt Whitman

I shall try to correct errors when shown to be errors, and I shall adopt new views so fast as they shall appear to be new views.
—Abraham Lincoln

Contradiction is not a sign of falsity, nor the lack of contradiction a sign of truth. —Blaise Pascal

My opinion is a view I hold until ... well, until I find something that changes it. —Luigi Pirandello

He that never changes his opinions, and never corrects his mistakes, will never be wiser on the morrow than he is today. —Tyron Edwards

CONSISTENCY

Inconsistency is the only thing in which men are consistent.
—Horatio Smith

There is nothing in this world constant but inconstancy.
—Jonathan Swift

Consistency is only suitable for ridicule. —Moliere

The world's a scene of changes, and to be constant, in nature, is inconstancy. —Abraham Cowley

We cannot remain consistent with the world save by growing inconsistent with our past selves.
—Havelock Ellis

Consistency is the last refuge of the unimaginative. —Oscar Wilde

The world is quite right. It does not have to be consistent.
—Charlotte Perkins Gilman

True consistency, that of the prudent and the wise, is to act in conformity with circumstances, and not to act always the same way under a change of circumstances. —John C. Calhoun

Consistency is a paste jewel that only cheap men cherish.
—William Allen White

Consistency requires you to be as ignorant today as you were a year ago. —Bernard Berenson

Consistency is contrary to nature, contrary to life. The only completely consistent people are the dead.
—Aldous Huxley

There are those who would misteach us that to stick in a rut is consistency, and a virtue, and that to climb out of the rut is inconsistency, and a vice. —Mark Twain

To be honest, one must be inconsistent. —H.G. Wells

Too much consistency is as bad for the mind as for the body.
—Aldous Huxley

With consistency a great soul has simply nothing to do.... Speak what you think today in words as hard as cannon balls, and tomorrow speak what tomorrow thinks in hard words again, though it contradicts everything you said today.
—Ralph Waldo Emerson

People who honestly mean to be true really contradict themselves much more rarely than those who try to be "consistent."
—Oliver Wendell Holmes

WHAT NOT CHANGING OUR OPINIONS MAY INDICATE

The only man who can't change his mind is a man who hasn't got one.
—Edward Noyes Westcott

Like all weak men, he laid an exaggerated stress on not changing one's mind. —W. Somerset Maugham

The foolish and the dead alone never change their opinion.
—James Russell Lowell

A fanatic is one who can't change his mind and won't change the subject.
—Sir Winston Churchill

The circumstances of the world are so variable that an irrevocable purpose or opinion is almost synonymous with a foolish one.
—William H. Seward

If in the last few years you haven't discarded a major opinion or acquired a new one, check your pulse. You may be dead.
—Gelett Burgess

A stiff attitude is one of the phenomena of rigor mortis.
—Henry S. Haskins

Those who never retract their opinions love themselves more than they love truth.   —Joseph Joubert

It's the most unhappy people who most fear change.
—Mignon McLaughlin

Obstinacy and heat in sticking to one's opinions is the surest proof of stupidity. Is there anything so cocksure, so immovable, so disdainful, so contemplative, so solemn and serious as an ass?   —Michel de Montaigne

The man who never alters his opinion is like standing water, and breeds reptiles of the mind. —William Blake

When people are least sure, they are often most dogmatic.
—John Kenneth Galbraith

A conclusion is a place where you got tired of thinking.
—*Fischer's Law*

Only fools and dead men don't change their minds. Fools won't. Dead men can't.
—John H. Patterson

The consistent thinker ... is either a walking mummy or else, if he has not succeeded in stifling all his vitality, a fanatical monomaniac.
—Aldous Huxley

Life is not a static thing. The only people who do not change their minds are incompetents in asylums, and those in cemeteries.
—Everett M. Dirksen

To hold the same views at forty as we held at twenty is to have been stupefied for a score of years and to take rank, not as a prophet, but as an unteachable brat, well birched and none the wiser.
—Robert Louis Stevenson

WHY CHANGE IS HARD

To do things today exactly the way you did them yesterday saves thinking.   —Woodrow Wilson

Any change, even a change for the better, is always accompanied by drawbacks and discomforts.
—Arnold Bennett

Every new adjustment is a crisis in self-esteem.   —Eric Hoffer

Even in slight things the experience of the new is rarely without some stirring of foreboding.
—Eric Hoffer

Change is not made without inconvenience, even from worse to better.
—Richard Hooker

All changes, even the most longed for, have their melancholy, for what we leave behind us is a part of ourselves; we must die to one life before we can enter into another.
— Anatole France

How to Make Change Easier

Since changes are going on anyway, the great thing is to learn enough about them so that we will be able to lay hold of them and turn them in the direction of our desires. Conditions and events are neither to be fled from nor passively acquiesced in; they are to be utilized and directed.
— John Dewey

He that has energy enough to root out a vice should go further, and try to plant a virtue in its place.
— Charles Caleb Colton

To change skins, evolve into new cycles, I feel one has to learn to discard. If one changes internally, one should not continue to live with the same objects. They reflect one's mind and psyche of yesterday. I throw away what has no dynamic, living use.
— Anaïs Nin

We must therefore take account of this changeable nature of things and of human institutions, and prepare for them with enlightened foresight.
— Pope Pius XI

Today changes must come fast; and we must adjust our mental habits, so that we can accept comfortably the idea of stopping one thing and beginning another overnight.... We must assume that there is probably a better way to do almost everything. We must stop assuming that a thing which has never been done before probably cannot be done at all.
— Donald M. Nelson

The first step toward change is acceptance. Once you accept yourself, you open the door to change. That's all you have to do. Change is not something you do, it's something you allow.
— Will Garcia, person with AIDS

Still, Some Things Don't Change

The more things change, the more they remain the same.
— Alphonse Karr

Change lays her hand not upon the truth.
— Algernon Swinburne

The spectacle has changed, but our eyes remain the same.
— Joseph Joubert

Other Definitions of Change

Change is what people fear most.
— Fyodor Dostoyevsky

Change means the unknown.
— Eleanor Roosevelt

Nature's mighty law is change.
— Robert Burns

General Quotations about Change

The old order changeth yielding place to new, and God fulfills himself in many ways.
— Alfred, Lord Tennyson

Everybody thinks of changing humanity and nobody thinks of changing himself.
— Leo Tolstoy

The mill wheel turns, it turns forever, though what is uppermost remains not so.　　—Bertolt Brecht

Such is the state of life that none are happy but by the anticipation of change. The change itself is nothing. When we have made it, the next wish is to change again.
　　　　　　—Samuel Johnson

The hearts of great men can be changed.　　　　　—Homer

It's a bad plan that can't be changed.
　　　　　　—Publilius Syrus

You cannot step twice into the same river, for other waters are continually flowing on.　　　—Heraclitus

A man's fortune must first be changed from within.
　　　　　　—Chinese proverb

One change always leaves the way open for the establishment of others.
　　　　　—Niccolo Machiavelli

There is danger in reckless change; but greater danger in blind conservatism.　　　—Henry George

Everything in life that we really accept undergoes a change.
　　　　　—Katherine Mansfield

The moment of change is the only poem.　　　—Adrienne Rich

I have accepted fear as a part of life—specifically the fear of change.... I have gone ahead despite the pounding in the heart that says: turn back....　　　—Erica Jong

As we learn we always change, and so our perception. This changed perception then becomes a new Teacher inside each of us.
　　　　　—Hyemeyohsts Storm

We are restless because of incessant change, but we would be frightened if change were stopped.
　　　　　—Lyman Lloyd Bryson

One must be thrust out of a finished cycle in life, and that leap is the most difficult to make—to part with one's faith, one's love, when one would prefer to renew the faith and recreate the passion.　　　—Anaïs Nin

When one door of happiness closes, another opens; but often we look so long at the closed door that we do not see the one which has been opened for us.　　—Helen Keller

If you want to make enemies, try to change something.
　　　　　—Woodrow Wilson

God, grant me the serenity to accept the things I cannot change, the courage to change the things I can, and the wisdom to know the difference.　　—Reinhold Niebuhr

DECISIONS

WE MUST ALL MAKE DECISIONS

Men and women everywhere must exercise deliberate selection to live wisely.   —Robert Grant

Decision and determination are the engineer and fireman of our train to opportunity and success.
                    —Burt Lawlor

AIDS presents me with a choice: the choice either to be a hopeless victim and die of AIDS, or to make my life right now what it always ought to have been.
        —Graham, person with AIDS

The last of the human freedoms: to choose one's attitude in any given set of circumstances, to choose one's own way.   —Viktor Frankel

You are the one who must choose your place.   —James Lane Allen

Choice of attention ... is to the inner life what choice of action is to the outer. In both cases, a man is responsible for his choice and must accept the consequences, whatever they may be.   —W.H. Auden

Man does not simply exist, but always decides what his existence will be, what he will become in the next moment.   —Viktor Frankel

Full maturity ... is achieved by realizing that you have choices to make.
        —Angela Barron McBride

Wherever you see a successful business, someone once made a courageous decision.   —Peter Drucker

DECISIONS ARE LIFE ITSELF

Life is just a series of trying to make up your mind.   —Timothy Fuller

Life is just an endless chain of judgements.... The more imperfect our judgement, the less perfect our success.   —B.C. Forbes

To know just what has do be done, then to do it, comprises the whole philosophy of practical life.
        —Sir William Osler

Life is like a game of cards. The hand that is dealt you represents determinism; the way you play it is free will.   —Jawaharlal Nehru

Somehow we learn who we really are and then live with that decision.
—Eleanor Roosevelt

Living is a constant process of deciding what we are going to do.
—José Ortega y Gasset

Life is the sum of all your choices.
—Albert Camus

Life is the art of drawing sufficient conclusions from insufficient premises.
—Samuel Butler

The difficulty of life is in the choice.
—George Moore

The strongest principle of growth lies in human choice. —George Eliot

As a man thinketh, so is he, and as a man chooseth, so is he. —Bible

Decisions determine destiny.
—Frederick Speakman

Choices are the hinges of destiny.
—Edwin Markham

Many of life's circumstances are created by three basic choices: the disciplines you choose to keep, the people you chose to be with, and the laws you choose to obey.
—Charles Millhuff

You don't get to choose how you're going to die. Or when. You can only decide how you're going to live. Now. —Joan Baez

SOME GOOD WAYS TO MAKE DECISIONS

Look for your choices, pick the best one, then go with it. —Pat Riley

Form the habit of making decisions when your spirit is fresh ... to let dark moods lead is like choosing cowards to command armies.
—Charles Horton Cooley

Decide which is the line of conduct that presents the fewest drawbacks and then follow it out as being the best one, because one never finds anything perfectly pure and unmixed, or exempt from danger.
—Niccolo Machiavelli

We must make the choices that enable us to fulfill the deepest capacities of our real selves.
—Thomas Merton

Choose always the way that seems the best, however rough it may be; custom will soon render it easy and agreeable. —Pythagoras

In forty hours I shall be in battle, with little information, and on the spur of the moment will have to make the most momentous decisions. But I believe that one's spirit enlarges with responsibility and that, with God's help, I shall make them, and make them right.
—General George S. Patton

Once the "what" is decided, the "how" always follows. We must not make the "how" an excuse for not facing and accepting the "what."
—Pearl Buck

In each action we must look beyond the action at our past, present and future state, and at others whom it affects, and see the relation of all those things. And then we shall be very cautious. —Blaise Pascal

311

One's mind has a way of making itself up in the background, and it suddenly becomes clear what one means to do.

—Arthur Christopher Benson

Not all of your decisions will be correct. None of us is perfect. But if you get into the habit of making decisions, experience will develop your judgment to a point where more and more of your decisions will be right. After all, it is better to be right 51 percent of the time and get something done, than it is to get nothing done because you fear to reach a decision.   —H.W. Andrews

Continually one faces the horrible matter of making decisions. The solution ... is, as far as possible, to avoid conscious rational decisions and choices; simply to do what you find yourself doing; to float in the great current of life with as little friction as possible; to allow things to settle themselves, as indeed they do with the most infallible certainty.

—Christopher Morley

When making a decision of minor importance, I have always found it advantageous to consider all the pros and cons. In vital matters, however, such as the choice of a mate or a profession, the decision should come from the unconscious, from somewhere within ourselves. In the important decisions of personal life, we should be governed, I think, by the deep inner needs of our nature.

—Sigmund Freud

Pick battles big enough to matter, small enough to win.

—Jonathan Kozel

Wisdom consists in being able to distinguish among dangers and make a choice of the least harmful.

—Niccolo Machiavelli

People "died" all the time.... Parts of them died when they made the wrong kinds of decisions—decisions against life. Sometimes they died bit by bit until finally they were just living corpses walking around. If you were perceptive you could see it in their eyes; the fire had gone out ... you always knew when you made a decision against life.... The door clicked and you were safe inside— safe and dead.

—Anne Morrow Lindbergh

I think we should follow a simple rule: if we can take the worst, take the risk.   —Dr. Joyce Brothers

Human foresight often leaves its proudest possessor only a choice of evils.   —Charles Caleb Colton

The best we can do is size up the chances, calculate the risks involved, estimate our ability to deal with them, and then make our plans with confidence.   —Henry Ford

In case of doubt, decide in favor of what is correct.   —Karl Kraus

Each man must for himself alone decide what is right and what is wrong, which course is patriotic and which isn't. You cannot shirk this and be a man. To decide against your conviction is to be an unqualified and inexcusable traitor, both to yourself and to your country, let men label you as they may.

—Mark Twain

When one bases his life on principle, 99 percent of his decisions are already made.   —Anon.

Decide on what you think is right, and stick to it.   —George Eliot

What I emphasize is for people to make choices based not on fear, but on what really gives them a sense of fulfillment.   —Pauline Rose Chance

We lose the fear of making decisions, great and small, as we realize that should our choice prove wrong we can, if we will, learn from the experience.   —Bill W.

WE MUST OFTEN DECIDE AND DO IMPORTANT THINGS WITH VERY LITTLE KNOWLEDGE OR EXPERIENCE

The Pilgrims didn't have any experience when they landed here. Hell, if experience was that important, we'd never have anybody walking on the moon.   —Doug Rader

There is no data on the future.
            —Laurel Cutler

The most important fact about Spaceship Earth: an instruction book didn't come with it.
            —R. Buckminster Fuller

Life is the only art that we are required to practice without preparation, and without being allowed the preliminary trials, the failures and botches, that are essential for the training of a mere beginner.
            —Lewis Mumford

I learn by going where I have to go.
            —Theodore Roethke

Life is like playing a violin in public and learning the instrument as one goes on.   —Samuel Butler

We don't have enough time to premeditate all our actions.
            —Vauvenargues

Every year, if not every day, we have to wager our salvation upon some prophecy based upon imperfect knowledge.
            —Oliver Wendell Holmes, Jr.

Faith ... acts promptly and boldly on the occasion, on slender evidence.
            —John Henry Cardinal Newman

A decision is an action you must take when you have information so incomplete that the answer does not suggest itself.   —Arthur Radford

WE CAN'T RELY ON JUST LOGIC AND REASON AND STATISTICS

How far would Moses have gone if he had taken a poll in Egypt?
            —Harry S. Truman

In the three years I played ball, we won six, lost seventeen and tied two. Some statistician ... calculated that we won 75 percent of the games we didn't lose.   —Roger M. Blough

Many persons of high intelligence have notoriously poor judgement.
            —Sydney J. Harris

How dangerous can false reasoning prove!   —Sophocles

The tendency of modern science is to reduce proof to absurdity by continually reducing absurdity to proof.
            —Samuel Butler

Say you were standing with one foot in the oven and one foot in an ice bucket. According to the percentage people, you would be perfectly comfortable. —Bobby Bragan

Logic is the art of going wrong with confidence. —Joseph Wood Krutch

Reason, with most people, means their own opinions.
—William Hazlitt

Logic pervades the world; the limits of the world are also the limits of logic. —Ludwig Wittgenstein

Man is a reasoning, rather than a reasonable, animal.
—Alexander Hamilton

False conclusions which have been reasoned out are infinitely worse than blind impulse. —Horace Mann

If you do everything you should do, and do not do anything you should not do, you will, according to the best available statistics, live exactly eighteen hours longer than you would otherwise.
—Dr. Logain Clendening, in 1944

Decisions, particularly important ones, have always made me sleepy, perhaps because I know that I will have to make them by instinct, and thinking things out is only what other people tell me I should do.
—Lillian Hellman

Statistics are no substitute for judgement. —Henry Clay

It is the heart always that sees before the head can see. —Thomas Carlyle

Facts are stubborn things, but statistics are more pliable.
—Laurence J. Peter

A true history of human events would show that a far larger proportion of our acts are the result of sudden impulse and accident than of that reason of which we so much boast. —Peter Cooper

It is always thus, impaled by a state of mind which is destined not to last, that we make our irrevocable decisions. —Marcel Proust

A power greater than any human being helped make this decision.
—Herbert J. Steifel

DON'T DELIBERATE TOO LONG

He who reflects too much will achieve little. —J.C.F. von Schiller

The opportunity is often lost by deliberating. —Publilius Syrus

The percentage of mistakes in quick decisions is no greater than in long-drawn-out vacillations, and the effect of decisiveness itself "makes things go" and creates confidence.
—Anne O'Hare McCormick

Deliberation often loses a good chance. —Latin proverb

The mania of thinking renders one unfit for every activity.
—Anatole France

When possible make the decisions now, even if action is in the future. A revised decision usually is better than one reached at the last moment.
—William B. Given, Jr.

314

We spend our days in deliberating, and we end them without coming to any resolve. —L'Estrange

If you think too long, you think wrong. —Jim Kaat

You decide you'll wait for your pitch. Then as the ball starts toward the plate, you think about your stance. And then you think about your swing. And then you realize that the ball that went past you for a strike was your pitch.
—Bobby Mercer

The soul of dispatch is decision.
—William Hazlitt

The moment a question comes to your mind, see yourself mentally taking hold of it and disposing of it. In that moment ... you learn to become the decider and not the vacillator. Thus you build character.
—H. Van Anderson

So what do we do? Anything. Something. So long as we just don't sit there. If we screw it up, start over. Try something else. If we wait until we've satisfied all the uncertainties, it may be too late.
—Lee Iacocca

Often greater risk is involved in postponement than in making a wrong decision. —Harry A. Hopf

Some persons are very decisive when it comes to avoiding decisions.
—Brendan Francis

Do not wait for ideal circumstances, nor the best opportunities; they will never come. —Janet Erskine Stuart

There comes a time when you've got to say, "Let's get off our asses and go...." I have always found that if I move with 75 percent or more of the facts I usually never regret it. It's the guys who wait to have everything perfect that drive you crazy.
—Lee Iacocca

Conditions are never just right. People who delay action until all factors are favorable do nothing.
—William Feather

Common sense does not ask an impossible chessboard, but takes the one before it and plays the game.
—Wendell Phillips

He who postpones the hour of living is like the rustic who waits for the river to run out before he crosses.
—Horace

If you wait for inspiration you'll be standing on the corner after the parade is a mile down the street.
—Ben Nicholas

Nothing at all will be attempted if all possible objections must first be overcome. —Samuel Johnson

ALTERNATIVES

It is the characteristic excellence of the strong man that he can bring momentous issues to the fore and make a decision about them. The weak are always forced to decide between alternatives they have not chosen themselves.
—Dietrich Bonhoeffer

Alternatives, and particularly desirable alternatives, grow only on imaginary trees. —Saul Bellow

Our danger is not too few, but too many options ... to be puzzled by innumerable alternatives.
—Sir Richard Livingstone

The absence of alternatives clears the mind marvelously. —Henry Kissinger

If decisions were a choice between alternatives, decisions would come easy. Decision is the selection and formulation of alternatives.
—Kenneth Burke

WHEN WE'RE DOWN TO TWO CHOICES ...

You cannot have your cake and eat it. —Anon.

You cannot sell the cow and sup the milk. —Anon.

A door must either be shut or open.
—Anon.

You cannot serve God and Mammon. —Mt. 6:24

Between two stools one sits on the ground. —French proverb

When you cannot make up your mind between two evenly balanced courses of action, choose the bolder.
—W.J. Slim

When confronted with two courses of action I jot down on a piece of paper all the arguments in favor of each one, then on the opposite side I write the arguments against each one. Then by weighing the arguments pro and con and cancelling them out, one against the other, I take the course indicated by what remains. —Benjamin Franklin

You cannot have it both ways.
—Anon.

I would sort out all the arguments and see which belonged to fear and which to creativeness. Other things being equal, I would make the decision which had the larger number of creative reasons on its side.
—Katharine Butler Hathaway

Of two evils, choose the less.
—Anon.

Of two evils, choose the prettier.
—Carolyn Wells

Where bad's the best, bad must be the choice. —Anon.

Both choices are painful, but only one is therapeutic.
—Albert M. Wells, Jr.

God offers to every mind its choice between truth and repose. Take which you please—you can never have both. —Ralph Waldo Emerson

Necessity relieves us from the embarrassment of choice. —Vauvenargues

WHAT NOT DECIDING MAY MEAN

When you have to make a choice and don't make it, that is in itself a choice. —William James

A man without decision can never be said to belong to himself; he is as a wave of the sea, or a feather in the air which every breeze blows about.
—John Foster

Nothing is so exhausting as indecision, and nothing is so futile.
—Bertrand Russell

316

Not to decide is to decide.
—Harvey Cox

Decision is a sharp knife that cuts clean and straight; indecision, a dull one that hacks and tears and leaves ragged edges behind it.
—Gordon Graham

There is no more miserable human being than one in whom nothing is habitual but indecision.
—William James

In not making the decision, you've made one. Not doing something is the same as doing it. —Ivan Bloch

There is a time when we must firmly choose the course we will follow, or the relentless drift of events will make the decision for us.
—Herbert B. Prochnow

DECISIONS CAN'T BE EVALUATED UNTIL THEY ARE IMPLEMENTED

You can only predict things after they've happened. —Eugene Ionesco

It is the mark of a good action that it appears inevitable, in retrospect.
—Robert Louis Stevenson

No one knows what he can to do until he tries. —Publilius Syrus

GENERAL QUOTATIONS ABOUT DECISIONS

Of all paths a man could strike into, there is, at any given moment, a best path which, here and now, it were of all things wisest for him to do. To find this path, and walk in it, is the one thing needful for him.
—Thomas Carlyle

After a battle is over people talk a lot about how decisions were methodically reached, but actually there's always a hell of a lot of groping around.
—Admiral Frank Jack Fletcher

No man who has not sat in the assemblies of men can know the light, odd and uncertain ways in which decisions are often arrived at.
—Sir Arthur Helps

No trumpets sound when the important decisions of our life are made. Destiny is made known silently.
—Agnes de Mille

A man must be able to cut a knot, for everything cannot be untied.
—Henri Frederic Amiel

Once to every man and nation comes the moment to decide....
And the choice goes by forever t'wixt that darkness and that light. —James Russell Lowell

Necessity is not an established fact, but an interpretation.
—Friedrich Nietzsche

We are not permitted to choose the frame of our destiny. But what we put into it is ours.
—Dag Hammarskjold

There is a point at which everything becomes simple and there is no longer any question of choice, because all you have staked will be lost if you look back. Life's point of no return. —Dag Hammarskjold

Optimism is an intellectual choice.
—Diana Schneider

The lame man who keeps the right road outstrips the runner who takes a wrong one ... the more active and swift the latter is, the further he will go astray. —Francis Bacon

Nothing is more difficult, and therefore more precious, than to be able to decide. —Napoleon Bonaparte

He who has a choice has trouble.
—Dutch proverb

There is one quality more important than know-how.... This is know-how by which we determine not only how to accomplish our purposes, but what our purposes are to be.
—Norbert Weiner

Destiny is not a matter of chance, it is a matter of choice; it is not a thing to be waited for, it is a thing to be achieved. —William Jennings Bryan

What must be, shall be; and that which is a necessity to him that struggles is little more than choice to him that is willing.
—Marcus Annaeus Seneca

A wiser rule would be to make up your mind soberly what you want, peace or war, and then to get ready for what you want; for what we prepare for is what we shall get.
—William Graham Sumner

We have resolved to endure the unendurable and suffer what is insufferable. —Emperor Hirohito, after the Hiroshima bombing

Choose your rut carefully; you'll be in it for the next ten miles.
—Road sign in Upstate New York

Once a decision was made, I did not worry about it afterward.
—Harry S. Truman

No country can act wisely simultaneously in every part of the globe at every moment of time.
—Henry Kissinger

The last, if not the greatest, of the human freedoms: to choose their own attitude in any given circumstance. —Bruno Bettelheim

INSTINCTS

WE MUST TRUST OUR INSTINCTS

Trust your own instinct. Your mistakes might as well be your own, instead of someone else's.
—Billy Wilder

Some of the finest moral intuitions come to quite humble people. The visiting of lofty ideas doesn't depend on formal schooling. Think of those Galilean peasants.
—Alfred North Whitehead

All I can do is act according to my deepest instinct, and be whatever I must be—crazy or ribald or sad or compassionate or loving or indifferent. That is all anybody can do.
—Katharine Butler Hathaway

Instinct is untaught ability.   —Bain

It is our business to go as we are impelled.   —D.H. Lawrence

Intuition ... appears to be the extrasensory perception of reality.
—Dr. Alexis Carrel

Common sense is instinct. Enough of it is genius. —George Bernard Shaw

A goose flies by a chart which the Royal Geographical Society could not improve.   —Holmes

I go by instinct.... I don't worry about experience.
—Barbra Streisand

Unconsciousness, spontaneity, instinct ... hold us to the earth and dictate the relatively good and useful.   —Henri Frederic Amiel

Every time you don't follow your inner guidance, you feel a loss of energy, loss of power, a sense of spiritual deadness. —Shakti Gawain

Every time a resolve or fine glow of feeling evaporates without bearing fruit, it is worse than a chance lost; it works to hinder future emotions from taking the normal path of discharge.   —William James

It is only by following your deepest instinct that you can lead a rich life.
—Katharine Butler Hathaway

Instinct is the nose of the mind.
—Madame De Girardin

319

One of the reasons why so few of us ever act, instead of react, is because we are continually stifling our deepest impulses.   —Henry Miller

A man should not strive to eliminate his complexes but to get into accord with them, for they are legitimately what directs his conduct in the world.   —Sigmund Freud

If you let your fear of consequence prevent you from following your deepest instinct, your life will be safe, expedient and thin.
            —Katharine Butler Hathaway

Everyone was searching for a formula for survival ... and the only formula that worked was no formula. Instinct ... that's all you had to go on.   —Carolyn Kenmore

I feel there are two people inside me—me and my intuition. If I go against her, she'll screw me every time, and if I follow her, we get along quite nicely.   —Kim Basinger

To be faithful to your instincts and the impulses that carry you in the direction of the excellence you most desire and value ... surely that is to lead the noble life.
            —George E. Woodberry

We each need to let our intuition guide us, and then be willing to follow that guidance directly and fearlessly.   —Shakti Gawain

By learning to contact, listen to, and act on our intuition, we can directly connect to the higher power of the universe and allow it to become our guiding force.   —Shakti Gawain

The struggle to learn to listen to and respect our own intuitive, inner promptings is the greatest challenge of all.   —Herb Goldberg

Once you get rid of the idea that you must please other people before you please yourself, and you begin to follow your own instincts—only then can you be successful. You become more satisfied, and when you are, other people tend to be satisfied by what you do.   —Raquel Welch

If you do not express your own original ideas, if you do not listen to your own being, you will have betrayed yourself.   —Rollo May

Every human being has, like Socrates, an attendant spirit; and wise are they who obey its signals. If it does not always tell us what to do, it always cautions us what not to do.
            —Lydia M. Child

Trust the instinct to the end, though you can render no reason.
            —Ralph Waldo Emerson

The truth of a thing is the feel of it, not the think of it.
            —Stanley Kubrick

Spend time every day listening to what your muse is trying to tell you.
            —Saint Bartholomew

Spontaneity

When I do things without any explanation, but just with spontaneity ... I can be sure that I am right.
            —Federico Fellini

Analysis kills spontaneity. The grain once ground into flour germinates no more.   —Henri Frederic Amiel

Spontaneity is the quality of being able to do something just because you feel like it at the moment, of trusting your instincts, of taking yourself by surprise and snatching from the clutches of your well-organized routine a bit of unscheduled pleasure.   —Richard Iannelli

INSTINCTS, FACTS, AND STATISTICS

I never believe facts; Canning said nothing was so fallacious as facts, except figures.   —Sydney Smith

Facts are not truths; they are not conclusions; they are not even premisses, but in the nature and parts of premisses.
                —Samuel Taylor Coleridge

Statistics are no substitute for judgement.   —Henry Clay

THE RELATIONSHIP BETWEEN INSTINCT AND REASON

We should chiefly depend not upon that department of the soul which is most superficial and fallible (our reason), but upon that department that is deep and sure, which is instinct.
                —Charles Sanders Peirce

I make all my decisions on intuition. I throw a spear into the darkness. That is intuition. Then I must send an army into the darkness to find the spear. That is intellect.
                —Ingmar Bergman

Instinct is intelligence incapable of self-consciousness.   —John Sterling

Impulse without reason is not enough, and reason without impulse is a poor makeshift.
                —William James

The shrewd guess, the fertile hypothesis, the courageous leap to a tentative conclusion—these are the most valuable coin of the thinker at work.
                —Jerome S. Bruner

A trembling in the bones may carry a more convincing testimony than the dry, documented deductions of the brain.   —Llewelyn Powers

Calculation never made a hero.
    —John Henry Cardinal Newman

We are so clothed in rationalization and dissemblance that we can recognize but dimly the deep primal impulses that motivate us.
                —James Ramsey Ullman

All our reasoning ends in surrender to feeling.   —Blaise Pascal

Reason, ruling alone, is a force confining; and passion, unattended, is a flame that burns to its own destruction.   —Kahlil Gibran

Modern man's besetting temptation is to sacrifice his direct perceptions and spontaneous feelings to his reasoned reflections; to prefer in all circumstances the verdict of his intellect to that of his immediate intuitions.
                —Aldous Huxley

Decisions, particularly important ones, have always made me sleepy, perhaps because I know that I will have to make them by instinct, and thinking things out is only what other people tell me I should do.
                —Lillian Hellman

Systems die; instincts remain.
    —Oliver Wendell Holmes, Jr.

I do not believe that the deeper problems of living can ever be answered by the process of thought. I believe that life itself teaches us either patience with regard to them, or reveals to us possible solutions when our hearts are pressed close against duties and sorrows and experiences of all kinds.
—Hamilton Wright Mabie

Life is one long struggle between conclusions based on abstract ways of conceiving cases, and opposite conclusions prompted by our instinctive perception of them.
—William James

Nothing reaches the intellect before making its appearance in the senses.
—Latin proverb

Instinct guides the animal better than the man. In the animal it is pure, in man it is led astray by his reason and intelligence. —Denis Diderot

Ideas pull the trigger, but instinct loads the gun. —Don Marquis

Well-bred instinct meets reason halfway. —George Santayana

Good instincts usually tell you what to do long before your head has figured it out. —Michael Burke

Pure logic is the ruin of the spirit.
—Antoine de Saint-Exupery

When a man begins to reason, he ceases to feel. —French proverb

A mind all logic is like a knife all blade. It makes the hand bleed that uses it. —Rabindranath Tagore

The mind can assert anything, and pretend it has proved it. My beliefs I test on my body, on my intuitional consciousness, and when I get a response there, then I accept.
—D.H. Lawrence

People who lean on logic and philosophy and rational exposition end by starving the best part of the mind.
—William Butler Yeats

Imagination is more important than knowledge. —Albert Einstein

Some other faculty than the intellect is necessary for the apprehension of reality. —Henri Bergson

Command by instinct is swifter, subtler, deeper, more accurate, more in touch with reality than command by conscious mind. The discovery takes one's breath away.
—Michael Novak

No one is more liable to make mistakes than the man who acts only on reflection. —Vauvenargues

Nothing is impossible when we follow our inner guidance, even when its direction may threaten us by reversing our usual logic.
—Gerald Jampolsky

A true history of human events would show that a far larger proportion of our acts are the results of sudden impulses and accident than of that reason of which we so much boast. —Peter Cooper

INSTINCTS AND THE HEART
It is wisdom to believe the heart.
—George Santayana

I follow my heart, for I can trust it.
—J.C.F. von Schiller

The intellect is always fooled by the heart.
—Francois de La Rochefoucauld

Man becomes man only by his intelligence, but he is man only by his heart.   —Henri Frederic Amiel

It is the heart always that sees, before the head can see.
—Thomas Carlyle

There are no rules. Just follow your heart.   —Robin Williams

It is only with the heart that one can see rightly; what is essential is invisible to the eye.
—Antoine de Saint-Exupery

Great thoughts always come from the heart.   —Vauvenargues

It is the heart which experiences God, not the reason.   —Blaise Pascal

The heart has reasons which reason cannot understand.   —Blaise Pascal

In making our decisions, we must use the brains that God has given us. But we must also use our hearts, which He also gave us.
—Fulton Oursler

Just be what you are and speak from your guts and heart—it's all a man has.   —Hubert H. Humphrey

INSTINCTS AND LOVE

When love is not madness, it is not love.   —Pedro Calderon de la Barca

To live is like to love: all reason is against it, and all healthy instinct is for it.   —Samuel Butler

The thinker philosophizes as the lover loves. Even were the consequences not only useless but harmful, he must obey his impulse.
—William James

Falling in love is one of the activities forbidden that tiresome person, the consistently reasonable man.
—Sir Arthur Eddington

INSTINCTS, DESIRES, AND PASSIONS

Our real duty is always found running in the direction of our worthiest desires.   —Randolph Bourne

What you intuitively desire, that is possible to you.   —D.H. Lawrence

Passion and prejudice govern the world, only under the name of reason.   —John Wesley

The conclusions of passion are the only reliable ones.
—Søren Kierkegaard

Man is a passion which brings a will into play, which works an intelligence.   —Henri Frederic Amiel

Life is not governed by will or intention. Life is a question of nerves, and fibers, and slowly built-up cells in which thought hides itself, and passion has its dreams.   —Oscar Wilde

We do not wish ardently for what we desire only through reason.
—Francois de La Rochefoucauld

INSTINCTS DON'T JUST OCCUR— THEY RESULT FROM OTHER INFLUENCES

Trust your hunches. They're usually based on facts filed away just below the conscious level.
—Dr. Joyce Brothers

Inspiration does not come like a bolt, nor is it kinetic energy striving, but it comes to us slowly and quietly and all the time.   —Brenda Euland

Intuition is given only to him who has undergone long preparation to receive it.   —Louis Pasteur

You have first an instinct, then an opinion, then a knowledge, as the plant has root, bud and fruit. Trust the instinct to the end, though you can render no reason.
—Ralph Waldo Emerson

GENERAL QUOTATIONS ABOUT INSTINCTS

A hunch is creativity trying to tell you something.   —Anon.

I write out of instinct.
—Jerome Weidman

Cherish your emotions and never undervalue them.   —Robert Henri

But are not this struggle and even the mistakes one may make better, and do they not develop us more, than if we kept systematically away from emotions?   —Vincent van Gogh

Many a man gets weary of clamping down on his rough impulses, which if given occasional release would encourage the living of life with salt in it, in place of dust.
—Henry S. Haskins

We shall keep our horizon perfectly, absolutely, crystallinely open, ready every day for the scouring gales of impulse.   —John Mistletoe

Intuition is a spiritual faculty and does not explain, but simply points the way.   —Florence Scovel Shinn

Every time I've done something that doesn't feel right, it's ended up not being right.   —Mario Cuomo

None of us can estimate what we do when we do it from instinct.
—Luigi Pirandello

Doing What's Right for Us

We Must Do What's Right for Us

Men can starve from a lack of self-realization as much as they can from a lack of bread.   —Richard Wright

Every man has his own destiny; the only imperative is to follow it, to accept it, no matter where it leads him.   —Henry Miller

You don't get to choose how you're going to die. Or when. You can only decide how you're going to live.
—Joan Baez

Ya gotta do what ya gotta do.
—Sylvester Stallone

Personality, too, is destiny.
—Erik Erikson

A man should not strive to eliminate his complexes but to get into accord with them, for they are legitimately what directs his conduct in the world.   —Sigmund Freud

Live as you will wish to have lived when you are dying.
—Christian Furchtegott Gellert

There is just one life for each of us: our own.   —Euripides

People are ridiculous only when they try or seem to be that which they are not.   —Giacomo Leopardi

Men are created different; they lose their social freedom and their individual autonomy in seeking to become like each other.
—David Riesman

Of all the paths a man could strike into, there is, at any given moment, a best path ... a thing which, here and now, it were of all things wisest for him to do ... to find this path, and walk in it, is the one thing needful for him.   —Thomas Carlyle

In my clinical experience, the greatest block to a person's development is his having to take on a way of life which is not rooted in his own powers.   —Rollo May

This is the chief thing: be not perturbed, for all things are according to the nature of the universal.
—Marcus Aurelius

325

What's a joy to the one is a nightmare to the other.   —Bertolt Brecht

Nothing is good for everyone, but
only relatively to some people.
                          —André Gide

What's important is finding out
what works for you. —Henry Moore

Everyone has a right to his own
course of action.   —Moliere

Freedom and constraint are two
aspects of the same necessity, the
necessity of being the man you are,
and not another. You are free to be
that man, but not free to be another.
          —Antoine de Saint-Exupery

[A] rose is a rose is a rose.
                      —Gertrude Stein

To feel that one has a place in life
solves half the problem of contentment.   —George E. Woodberry

What one man does, another fails to
do; what's fit for me may not be fit
for you.   —Anon.

Let them know a real man, who lives
as he was meant to live.
                      —Marcus Aurelius

There's no right way of writing.
There's only your way.
                      —Milton Lomask

Every man must get to heaven his
own way.   —Frederick the Great

There are as many ways to live and
grow as there are people. Our own
ways are the only ways that should
matter to us.   —Evelyn Mandel

Only he who keeps his eye fixed on
the far horizon will find his right
road.   —Dag Hammarskjold

Those who love a cause are those
who love the life which has to be led
in order to serve it.   —Simone Weil

If you always do what interests you,
at least one person is pleased.
              —Katharine Hepburn's mother

Why not be oneself? That is the
whole secret of a successful appearance. If one is a greyhound, why try
to look like a Pekingese?
                      —Edith Sitwell

Do you know that disease and death
must needs overtake us, no matter
what we are doing? ... What do you
wish to be doing when it overtakes
you? ... If you have anything better
to be doing when you are so overtaken, get to work on that.
                      —Epictetus

I'll walk where my own nature
would be leading; it vexes me to
choose another guide.
                      —Emily Brontë

If you go to heaven without being
naturally qualified for it, you will
not enjoy it there.
                  —George Bernard Shaw

He who walks in another's tracks
leaves no footprints.
                      —Joan L. Brannon

To be what we are, and to become
what we are capable of becoming, is
the only end of life.
                  —Robert Louis Stevenson

Follow your bliss. Find where it is
and don't be afraid to follow it.
—Joseph Campbell

To have no set purpose in one's life
is harlotry of the will.
—Stephen McKenna

BEING TRUE TO OURSELVES

Somehow we learn who we really
are and then live with that decision.
—Eleanor Roosevelt

Seek out that particular mental attitude which makes you feel most
deeply and vitally alive, along with
which comes the inner voice which
says, "This is the real me," and
when you have found that attitude,
follow it. —William James

There is always a certain peace in
being what one is, in being that completely. The condemned man has
that joy. —Ugo Betti

Be what you are. This is the first step
toward becoming better than you
are. —Julius Charles Hare

Keep your promises to yourself.
—David Harold Fink

I believe there's an inner power that
makes winners or losers. And the
winners are the ones who really listen to the truth of their hearts.
—Sylvester Stallone

No matter how ill we may be, nor
how low we may have fallen, we
should not change identity with any
other person. —Samuel Butler

Here I stand. I can do no other. God
help me. Amen. —Martin Luther

Nobody is so miserable as he who
longs to be somebody other than the
person he is. —Angelo Patri

To be nobody-but-yourself—in a
world which is doing its best, night
and day, to make you everybody
else—means to fight the hardest battle which any human being can fight;
and never stop fighting.
—e.e. cummings

To aim at the best and to remain
essentially ourselves is one and the
same thing. —Janet Erskine Stuart

We had as lief not be, as not be ourselves. —William Hazlitt

No man can produce great things
who is not thoroughly sincere in
dealing with himself.
—James Russell Lowell

The most exhausting thing in life is
being insincere.
—Anne Morrow Lindbergh

Misfortunes occur only when a man
is false.... Events, circumstances, etc.,
have their origin in ourselves. They
spring from seeds which we have
sown. —Henry David Thoreau

Every human being is intended to
have a character of his own; to be
what no others are, and to do what
no other can do.
—William Ellery Channing

Do not wish to be anything but what
you are. —Saint Francis de Sales

It is necessary to the happiness of
man that he be mentally faithful to
himself. —Thomas Paine

327

Integrity simply means a willingness not to violate one's identity.
—Erich Fromm

Don't compromise yourself. You are all you've got   —Janis Joplin

The greatest thing in the world is to know how to be one's own self
—Michel de Montaigne

To know what you prefer, instead of humbly saying "Amen" to what the world tells you you ought to prefer, is to keep your soul alive.
—Robert Louis Stevenson

Do what thy manhood bids thee do.
—Sir Richard Burton

We live counterfeit lives in order to resemble the idea we first had of ourselves.   —André Gide

The moment that any life, however good, stifles you, you may be sure it isn't your real life.
—Arthur Christopher Benson

All is disgust when one leaves his own nature and does things that misfit it.   —Sophocles

What does reason demand of a man? A very easy thing—to live in accord with his own nature.
—Marcus Annaeus Seneca

We are sure to be losers when we quarrel with ourselves; it is civil war.
—Charles Caleb Colton

With begging and scrambling we find very little, but with being true to ourselves we find a great deal more.
—Rabindranath Tagore

While you cannot resolve what you are, at last you will be nothing.
—Martial

The highest courage is to dare to appear to be what one is.
—John Lancaster Spalding

Choose always the way that seems the best, however rough it may be; custom will soon render it easy and agreeable.   —Pythagoras

Our whole life is an attempt to discover when our spontaneity is whimsical, sentimental irresponsibility and when it is a valid expression of our deepest desires and values.
—Helen Merrell Lynd

Until you know that life is interesting, and find it so, you haven't found your soul.   —Geoffrey Fisher

It is better to be hated for what you are than loved for what you are not.
—André Gide

Learn what you are, and be such.
—Pindar

We are betrayed by what is false within.   —George Meredith

If I trim myself to suit others I will soon whittle myself away.
—Anon.

This above all: to thine own self be true.   —William Shakespeare

In the world to come they will not ask me, "Why were you not Moses?" They will ask me, "Why were you not Zusya?"
—Zusya of Hanipoli

A man must be obedient to the promptings of his innermost heart.
—Robertson Davies

All life is the struggle, the effort to be itself.   —José Ortega y Gasset

What's a man's first duty? The answer is brief: To be himself.
—Henrik Ibsen

Any path is only a path, and there is no affront, to oneself or to others, in dropping it if that is what your heart tells you.   —Carlos Castaneda

It is possible to be different and still be all right.   —Anne Wilson Schaef

Let me listen to me and not to them.
—Gertrude Stein

She lacks confidence, she craves admiration insatiably. She lives on the reflections of herself in the eyes of others. She does not dare to be herself.   —Anaïs Nin

I will not cut my conscience to fit this year's fashions.
—Lillian Hellman

The crow that mimics a cormorant gets drowned.   —Japanese proverb

Let the world know you as you are, not as you think you should be, because sooner or later, if you are posing, you will forget the pose, and then where are you?   —Fanny Brice

I was raised to sense what someone wanted me to be and be that kind of person. It took me a long time not to judge myself through someone else's eyes.   —Sally Field

Education should be the process of helping everyone to discover his uniqueness.   —Leo Buscaglia

Philosophy is a purely personal matter. A genuine philosopher's credo is the outcome of a single complex personality; it cannot be transferred. No two persons, if sincere, can have the same philosophy.   —Havelock Ellis

Remember always that you have not only the right to be an individual, you have an obligation to be one.
—Eleanor Roosevelt

WE CAN'T BE HAPPY IF WE'RE NOT BEING OURSELVES

It is the chiefest point of happiness that a man is willing to be what he is.   —Erasmus

All the discontented people I know are trying to be something they are not, to do something they cannot do.
—David Graydon

Resolve to be thyself ... he who finds himself loses his misery!
—Matthew Arnold

Happiness, that grand mistress of the ceremonies in the dance of life, impels us through all its mazes and meanderings, but leads none of us by the same route.
—Charles Caleb Colton

A happy life is one which is in accordance with its own nature.
—Marcus Annaeus Seneca

Different men seek after happiness in different ways and by different means, and so make for themselves different modes of life.   —Aristotle

All men have happiness as their object: there is no exception. However different the means they employ, they aim at the same end. —Blaise Pascal

Your readiest desire is your path to joy ... even if it destroys you. —Holbrook Jackson

Be not imitator; freshly act thy part;
Through this world be thou an independent ranger;
Better is the faith that springeth from thy heart
Than a better faith belonging to a stranger. —Persian proverb

There is always a certain peace in being what one is, in being that completely. —Ugo Betti

Posterity weaves no garlands for imitators. —J.C.F. von Schiller

Why feignest thou thyself to be another? —1 Kgs. 14:6

'Tis a gift to be simple, 'tis a gift to be free.
'Tis a gift to come round to where we ought to be.
And when we find a place that feels just right,
We will be in the valley of love and delight. —Appalachian folk song

You have to deal with the fact that your life is your life. —Alex Hailey

I is who I is. —Tom Peterson

There are as many ways to live and grow as there are people. Our own ways are the only ways that should matter to us. —Evelyn Mandel

The white light streams down to be broken up by those human prisms into all the colors of the rainbow. Take your own color in the pattern and be just that. —Charles R. Brown

The search for a new personality is futile; what is fruitful is the human interest the old personality can take in new activities. —Cesare Pavese

We would have to settle for the elegant goal of becoming ourselves. —William Stryon

Our concern must be to live while we're alive ... to release our inner selves from the spiritual death that comes with living behind a facade designed to conform to external definitions of who and what we are. —Elizabeth Kubler-Ross

I searched through rebellion, drugs, diets, mysticism, religions, intellectualism and much more, only to begin to find ... that truth is basically simple—and feels good, clean and right. —Chick Corea

If you're gonna be a failure, at least be one at something you enjoy. —Sylvester Stallone

That suit is best that best suits me. —John Clark

The self is not something that one finds. It is something one creates. —Thomas Szasz

WE FEEL GOOD WHEN WE DO WHAT'S RIGHT FOR US

I'm uncomfortable when I'm comfortable ... I can't help it, it's my personality. —Jay Chiat

I look at ordinary people in their suits, them with no scars, and I'm different. I don't fit with them. I'm where everybody's got scar tissue on their eyes and got noses like saddles. I go to conventions of old fighters like me and I see the scar tissue and all them flat noses and it's beautiful.... They talk like me, like they got rocks in their throats. Beautiful!
—Willie Pastrano

I have the feeling when I write poetry that I'm doing what I'm supposed to do. You don't think about whether you're going to get money or fame, you just do it.
—Doris Lund

A door that seems to stand open must be of a man's size, or it is not the door that providence means for him.
—Henry Ward Beecher

I have the true feeling of myself only when I am unbearably unhappy.
—Franz Kafka

Mountains should be climbed with as little effort as possible and without desire. The reality of your own nature should determine the speed. If you become restless, speed up. If you become winded, slow down. You climb the mountain in an equilibrium between restlessness and exhaustion. Then, when you're no longer thinking ahead, each footstep isn't just a means to an end, but a unique event in itself.
—Robert M. Pirsig

It is the soul's duty to be loyal to its own desires.   —Rebecca West

FINDING WORK THAT WILL USE OUR ABILITIES AND TALENTS

Each of us has some unique capability waiting for realization. Every person is valuable in his own existence, for himself alone ... each of us can bring to fruition these innate, God-given abilities.   —George H. Bender

All of us attain the greatest success and happiness possible in this life whenever we use our native capacities to their fullest extent.... And every life must be chalked up at least a partial failure when it does not succeed in reaching its inherent destiny.   —Smiley M. Blanton

The same man cannot be skilled in everything; each has his special excellence.   —Euripides

Skills vary with the man. We must ... strive by that which is born in us.
—Pindar

People are always neglecting something they can do in trying to do something they can't do.
—Edgar Watson Howe

A man like Verdi must write like Verdi.   —Verdi

I write lustily and humorously. It isn't calculated; it's the way I think. I've invented a writing style that expresses who I am.   —Erica Jong

Each citizen should play his part in the community according to his individual gifts.   —Plato

Genius does what it must, talent does what it can.
—Edward Bulwer-Lytton

Everything keeps its best nature only
by being put to its best use.
—Phillips Brooks

We don't see many fat men walking
on stilts.　　　　　—Bud Miller

I was playing it like Willie Wilson,
but I forgot that I'm in Clint
Hurdle's body.　　—Clint Hurdle

We succeed in enterprises which
demand the positive qualities we
possess, but we excel in those which
can also make use of our defects.
—Alexis de Tocqueville

I wrote because I had to. I couldn't
stop. There wasn't anything else I
could do. If no one ever bought anything, anything I ever did, I'd still be
writing. It's beyond a compulsion.
—Tennessee Williams

To every man according to his ability.
—Mt. 25:4

If a man is called to be a streetsweeper, he should sweep streets even as
Michelangelo painted, or Beethoven
composed music, or Shakespeare
wrote poetry. He should sweep streets
so well that all the hosts of heaven
and earth will pause to say, here lived
a great streetsweeper who did his job
well.　　—Martin Luther King, Jr.

Men whose trade is rat-catching,
love to catch rats; the bug destroyer
seizes on his bug with delight; and
the suppressor is gratified by finding
his vice.　　　　—Sydney Smith

Brutes find out where their talents
lie; a bear will not attempt to fly.
—Jonathan Swift

We may fail of our happiness, strive
we ever so bravely; but we are less
likely to fail if we measure with
judgment our chances and our capabilities.　　　　—Agnes Repplier

The greatest achievement of the
human spirit is to live up to one's
opportunities and make the most of
one's resources.　　—Vauvenargues

The test of a vocation is the love of
the drudgery it involves.
—Logan Pearsall Smith

Are you doing the kind of work you
were built for, so that you can
expect to be able to do very large
amounts of that kind and thrive
under it? Or are you doing a kind of
which you can do comparatively little?　　　　　　—B.C. Forbes

Starting out to make money is the
greatest mistake in life. Do what you
feel you have a flair for doing, and if
you are good enough at it, the
money will come.　　—Greer Garson

Whenever it is possible, a boy should
choose some occupation which he
should do even if he did not need the
money.　　—William Lyon Phelps

The fun of being alive is realizing
you have a talent and you can use it
every day so it grows stronger....
And if you're in an atmosphere
where this talent is appreciated
instead of just tolerated, why, it's
just as good as sex.　—Lou Centlivre

Never desert your own line of talent.
Be what nature intended you for,
and you will succeed.
—Sydney Smith

332

It is only when I am doing my work that I feel truly alive. It is like having sex. —Federico Fellini

If a man has a talent and cannot use it, he has failed. If he has a talent and uses only half of it, he has partly failed. If he has a talent and learns somehow to use the whole of it, he has gloriously succeeded, and won a satisfaction and a triumph few men ever know. —Thomas Wolfe

The high prize of life, the crowning fortune of a man, is to be born with a bias to some pursuit which finds him in employment and happiness. —Ralph Waldo Emerson

Everybody undertakes what he sees another successful in, whether he has the aptitude for it or not. —Johann von Goethe

To find out what one is fitted to do, and to secure an opportunity to do it, is the key to happiness. —John Dewey

The road to happiness lies in two simple principles: find what interests you and that you can do well, and put your whole soul into it—every bit of energy and ambition and natural ability you have. —John D. Rockefeller III

One should stick to the sort of thing for which one was made; I tried to be an herbalist, whereas I should keep to the butcher's trade. —Jean de La Fontaine

If you have to support yourself, you had bloody well better find some way that is going to be interesting. —Katharine Hepburn

When men are rightfully occupied, then their amusement grows out of their work as the color petals out of a fruitful garden. —John Ruskin

A musician must make music, an artist must paint, a poet must write, if he to be at peace with himself. What a man can be, he must be. —Abraham Maslow

We do not write as we want but as we can. —W. Somerset Maugham

Nature arms each man with some faculty which enables him to do easily some feat impossible to any other. —Ralph Waldo Emerson

It is not a dreamlike state, but the somehow insulated state, that a great musician achieves in a great performance. He's aware of where he is and what he's doing, but his mind is on the playing of his instrument with an internal sense of *rightness*—it is not merely mechanical, it is not only spiritual; it is something of both, on a different plane and a more remote one. —Arnold Palmer

We will discover the nature of our particular genius when we stop trying to conform to our own or to other people's models, learn to be ourselves, and allow our natural channel to open. —Shakti Gawain

It requires a certain kind of mind to see beauty in a hamburger bun. Yet, is it any more unusual to find grace in the texture and softly curved silhouette of a bun than to reflect lovingly on ... the arrangement of textures and colors in a butterfly's wing? —Ray Kroc

The question "Who ought to be boss" is like asking "Who ought to be tenor in the quartet?" Obviously, the man who can sing tenor.
—Henry Ford

I'm a salami writer. I try to write good salami, but salami is salami.
—Stephen King

I'd rather be a failure at something I enjoy than a success at something I hate.
—George Burns

WE CAN ONLY DO WHAT WE'RE CAPABLE OF DOING

I cannot do everything, but still I can do something; and because I cannot do everything, I will not refuse to do the something that I can do.
—Edward Everett Hale

Man is not born to solve the problems of the universe, but to find out what he has to do ... within the limits of his comprehension.
—Johann von Goethe

The weakest among us has a gift, however seemingly trivial, which is peculiar to him and which worthily used will be a gift also to his race.
—John Ruskin

Every person is responsible for all the good within the scope of his abilities, and for no more.
—Gail Hamilton

Me, I'm just a hack. I'm just a schlepper. I just do what I can do.
—Bette Midler

The great law of culture: Let each become all that he was created capable of being.
—Thomas Carlyle

Don't bother just to be better than your contemporaries or predecessors. Try to be better than yourself.
—William Faulkner

God requires a faithful fulfillment of the merest trifle given us to do, rather than the most ardent aspiration to things to which we are not called.
—Saint Francis de Sales

When I was young, I said to God, "God, tell me the mystery of the universe." But God answered, "That knowledge is reserved for me alone." So I said, "God, tell me the mystery of the peanut." Then God said, "Well George, that's more nearly your size." And he told me.
—George Washington Carver

I long to accomplish a great and noble task, but it is my chief duty to accomplish small tasks as if they were great and noble.
—Helen Keller

We may fail of our happiness, strive we ever so bravely; but we are less likely to fail if we measure with judgment our chances and our capabilities.
—Agnes Repplier

No amount of study or learning will make a man a leader unless he has the natural qualities of one.
—Sir Archibald Wavell

Choose a subject equal to your abilities; think carefully what your shoulders may refuse, and what they are capable of bearing.
—Horace

In efforts to soar above our nature, we invariably fall below it.
—Edgar Allan Poe

If you could once make up your mind never to undertake more work ... than you can carry on calmly, quietly, without hurry or flurry ... and if the instant you feel yourself growing nervous and ... out of breath, you would stop and take breath, you would find this simple common-sense rule doing for you what no prayers or tears could ever accomplish.   —Elizabeth Prentiss

The driver knows how much the ox can carry, and keeps the ox from being overloaded. You know your way and your state of mind. Do not carry too much.   —Zen saying

The deepest personal defeat suffered by human beings is constituted by the difference between what one was capable of becoming, and what one has in fact become.
                    —Ashley Montagu

SUCCESS IS DOING WHAT'S RIGHT FOR US

There is only one success—to be able to spend your life in your own way.
                    —Christopher Morley

The only success worth one's powder was success in the line of one's idiosyncrasy ... what was talent but the art of being completely whatever one happened to be? —Henry James

Success based on anything but internal fulfillment is bound to be empty.
                    —Dr. Martha Friedman

We succeed in enterprises which demand the positive qualities we possess, but we excel in those which can also make use of our defects.
                    —Alexis de Tocqueville

All I would tell people is to hold on to what was individual about themselves, not to allow their ambition for success to cause them to try to imitate the success of others. You've got to find in on your own terms.
                    —Harrison Ford

For me, writing is the only thing that passes the three tests of *metier*: (1) when I'm doing it, I don't feel that I should be doing something else instead; (2) it produces a sense of accomplishment and, once in a while, pride; and (3) it's frightening.
                    —Gloria Steinem

One can never consent to creep when one feels an impulse to soar.
                    —Helen Keller

My mother said to me, "If you become a soldier, you'll be a general, if you become a monk you'll end up as the pope." Instead, I became a painter and wound up as Picasso.
                    —Pablo Picasso

We only do well the things we like doing.   —Colette

Abasement, degradation is simply the manner of life of the man who has refused to be what it is his duty to be.   —José Ortega y Gasset

Different people have different duties assigned to them by Nature; Nature has given one the power or the desire to do this, the other that. Each bird must sing with his own throat.
                    —Anon.

A first rate soup is better than a second rate painting.
                    —Abraham Maslow

We can't all be heroes, because someone has to sit on the curb and clap as they go by.   —Will Rogers

Nature magically suits a man to his fortunes, by making them the fruit of his character.
—Ralph Waldo Emerson

I'd rather be a lamppost in Chicago than a millionaire in any other city.
—William A. Hulbert

Whatever you are by nature, keep to it; never desert your own line of talent. Be what nature intended you for, and you will succeed; be anything else and you will be ten thousand times worse than nothing.
—Sydney Smith

Ask yourself the secret of your success. Listen to your answer, and practice it.   —Richard Bach

I am only one, but still I am one. I cannot do everything, but still I can do something; and because I cannot do everything, I will not refuse to do something I can do.
—Edward Everett Hale

Starting out to make money is the greatest mistake in life. Do what you feel you have a flair for doing, and if you are good enough at it, the money will come.   —Greer Garson

If a man has a talent and cannot use it, he has failed. If he has a talent and uses only half of it, he has partly failed. If he has a talent and learns somehow to use the whole of it, he has gloriously succeeded, and won a satisfaction and a triumph few men ever know.   —Thomas Wolfe

A man can do only what he can do. But if he does that each day he can sleep at night and do it again the next day.   —Albert Schweitzer

Don't take anyone else's definition of success as your own. (This is easier said than done.) —Jacqueline Briskin

General Quotations about Doing What's Right For Us

You must be holy in the way God asks you to be holy. God does not ask you to be a Trappist monk or a hermit. He wills that you sanctify your everyday life.
—Saint Vincent Pallotti

Bloom where you are planted.
—Anon.

The great enemy of clear language is insincerity. When there is a gap between one's real and one's declared aims, one turns, as it were, instinctively to long words and exhausted idioms, like a cuttlefish squirting out ink.   —George Orwell

If Heaven made him, earth can find some use for him. —Chinese proverb

The hole and the patch should be commensurate.   —Thomas Jefferson

If all misfortunes were laid in one common heap whence everyone must take an equal portion, most people would be contented to take their own and depart.   —Socrates

Every true man, sir, who is a little above the level of the beasts and plants, lives so as to give a meaning and a value to his own life.
—Luigi Pirandello

MOTIVATION

THE IMPORTANCE AND VALUE OF MOTIVATION

What makes life dreary is want of motive. —George Eliot

As long as I have a want, I have a reason for living. Satisfaction is death. —George Bernard Shaw

One must not lose desires. They are mighty stimulants to creativeness, to love and to long life.
—Alexander A. Bogomoletz

Take away the cause, and the effect ceases. —Miguel de Cervantes

Every true man, sir, who is a little above the level of the beasts and plants, lives so as to give a meaning and a value to his own life.
—Luigi Pirandello

The secret of discipline is motivation. When a man is sufficiently motivated, discipline will take care of itself. —Sir Alexander Paterson

Where the willingness is great, the difficulties cannot be great.
—Niccolo Machiavelli

Talent isn't enough. You need motivation—and persistence, too: what Steinbeck called a blend of faith and arrogance. When you're young, plain old poverty can be enough, along with an insatiable hunger for recognition. You have to have that feeling of "I'll show them." If you don't have it, don't become a writer.
—Leon Uris

Never let go of that fiery sadness called desire. —Patti Smith

Winning isn't everything. *Wanting* to win is. —Catfish Hunter

It seems to me we can never give up longing and wishing while we are alive. There are certain things we feel to be beautiful and good, and we must hunger for them.
—George Eliot

One man with a dream, at pleasure,
Shall go forth and conquer a crown,
And three with a new song's measure,
Can trample an empire down.
—Arthur O'Shaughnessy

337

We can do whatever we wish to do provided our wish is strong enough.... What do you want most to do? That's what I have to keep asking myself, in the face of difficulties.
—Katherine Mansfield

DIFFERENT PEOPLE ARE MOTIVATED BY DIFFERENT THINGS

For every man there exists a bait which he cannot resist swallowing.
—Friedrich Nietzsche

Football linemen are motivated by a more complicated, self-determining series of factors than the simple fear of humiliation in the public gaze, which is the emotion that galvanizes the backs and receivers.
—Merlin Olsen

I tried to treat them like me, and some of them weren't.
—Coach Bill Russell, on why he had difficulty with some of his players

To be what we are, and to become what we are capable of becoming, is the only end of life.
—Baruch Spinoza

Every man is said to have his peculiar ambition.   —Abraham Lincoln

The moment somebody says to me, "This is very risky," is the moment it becomes attractive to me.
—Kate Capshaw

Some people are molded by their admirations, others by their hostilities.   —Elizabeth Bowen

A man will fight harder for his interests than for his rights.
—Napoleon Bonaparte

All I want out of life is that when I walk down the street, folks will say, "There goes the greatest hitter who ever lived."   —Ted Williams

Your distress about life might mean you have been living for the wrong reason, not that you have no reason for living.
—Tom O'Connor, person with ARC

Great men undertake great things because they are great; fools, because they think them easy.
—Vauvenargues

There are only two stimulants to one's best efforts: the fear of punishment, and the hope of reward.
—John M. Wilson

When you get hungry enough, you find yourself speaking Spanish pretty well.   —Josh Gibson,
on playing baseball in Cuba

Love teaches even asses to dance.
—French proverb

Discontent is the first step in progress. No one knows what is in him till he tries, and many would never try if they were not forced to.
—Basil W. Maturin

I never work better than when I am inspired by anger; when I am angry, I can write, pray, and preach well, for then my whole temperament is quickened, my understanding sharpened, and all mundane vexations and temptations depart. —Martin Luther

It is for the superfluous things of life that men sweat.
—Marcus Annaeus Seneca

Happiness is in the taste, and not in the things themselves; we are happy from possessing what we like, not from possessing what others like.
—Francois de La Rochefoucauld

We must each find our separate meaning in the persuasion of our days until we meet in the meaning of the world. —Christopher Fry

Don't let other people tell you what you want. —Pat Riley

COMMON MOTIVATORS

Men are more often bribed by their loyalties and ambitions than by money. —Robert H. Jackson

All progress is based upon a universal, innate desire on the part of every living organism to live beyond its income. —Samuel Butler

Everyone expects to go further than his father went; everyone expects to be better than he was born and every generation has one big impulse in its heart—to exceed all the other generations of the past in all the things that make life worth living.
—William Allen White

To sink a six-foot putt with thirty million people looking over your shoulder, convince yourself that, if you miss it, you will be embarrassed and poor. —Jack Nicklaus

Fear, desire, hope still push us on toward the future.
—Michel de Montaigne

Human behavior flows from three main sources: desire, emotion, and knowledge. —Plato

Lust and force are the source of all our actions; lust causes voluntary actions, force involuntary ones.
—Blaise Pascal

I want to do it because I want to do it. —Amelia Earhart

I wish it, I command it. Let my *will* take the place of a reason. —Juvenal

I don't make deals for the money. I've got enough, much more than I'll never need. I do it to do it. Other people paint beautifully on canvas or write wonderful poetry. I like making deals, preferably big deals. That's how I get my kicks.
—Donald Trump

Wealth ... and poverty: the one is the parent of luxury and indolence, and the other of meanness and viciousness, and both of discontent.
—Plato

Anxiety and conscience are a powerful pair of dynamos. Between them, they have ensured that I shall work hard, but they cannot ensure that one shall work at anything worthwhile. —Arnold J. Toynbee

It is the spur of ignorance, the consciousness of not understanding, and the curiosity about that which lies beyond that are essential to our progress. —John Pierce

We all live with the objective of being happy; our lives are all different, and yet the same.
—Anne Frank

Love teaches even asses to dance.
—French proverb

Money and women. They're the two strongest things in the world. There are things you do for a woman you wouldn't do for anything else. Same with money. —Satchel Paige

It is for the superfluous things of life that men sweat.
　　　—Marcus Annaeus Seneca

It is not merely cruelty that leads men to love war, it is excitement.
　　　—Henry Ward Beecher

I am not sending messages with my feet. All I ever wanted was not to come up empty. I did it for the dough, and the old applause.
　　　—Fred Astaire

My advice about acting? Speak clearly, don't bump into people, and if you must have motivation, think of your pay packet on Friday.
　　　—Noel Coward

I take it that what all men are really after is some form of, perhaps only some formula of, peace.
　　　—Joseph Conrad

It is the north wind that lashes men into Vikings; it is the soft, luscious south wind which lulls them to lotus dreams. —Ouida

One starts an action simply because one must do *something*. —T.S. Eliot

Action springs not from thought, but from a readiness for responsibility.
　　　—Dietrich Bonhoeffer

The breakfast of champions is not cereal, it's the opposition.
　　　—Nick Seitz

There's only one good reason to be a writer—we can't help it! We'd all like to be successful, rich and famous, but if those are our *goals,* we're off on the wrong foot.... I just wanted to earn enough money so I could work at home on my writing.
　　　—Phyllis Whitney

NECESSITY AND DISCONTENT ARE BASIC MOTIVATORS

Necessity, who is the mother of our invention. —Plato

Urgent necessity prompts many to do things. —Miguel de Cervantes

Discontent is the first step in the progress of a man or a nation.
　　　—Oscar Wilde

To have a grievance is to have a purpose in life. —Eric Hoffer

What you are must always displease you, if you would attain to that which you are not.
　　　—Saint Augustine

We accept the verdict of the past until the need for change cries out loudly enough to force upon us a choice between the comforts of further inertia and the irksomeness of action. —Louis L'Amour

I can't concentrate on golf or bowling. Those bowling pins aren't going to hurt me. I can concentrate in the ring because someone is trying to kill me. —Carmen Basilio

I happened on the idea of fitting an engine to a bicycle simply because I did not want to ride crowded trains and buses. —Soichire Honda

Always in a moment of extreme danger things can be done which had previously been thought impossible.
—General Erwin Rommel

Acting was a way out at first. A way out of not knowing what to do, a way of focusing ambitions. And the ambition wasn't for fame. The ambition was to do an interesting job.
—Harrison Ford

A loafer never works except when there is a fire; then he will carry out more furniture than anybody.
—Edgar Watson Howe

Necessity is the mother of taking chances.
—Mark Twain

Hardships, poverty and want are the best incentives, and the best foundation, for the success of man.
—Bradford Merrill

Poverty, Frost, Famine, Rain, Disease, are the beadles and guardsmen that hold us to Common Sense.
—Ralph Waldo Emerson

Praise and Recognition Are Common Motivators

If each of us were to confess his most secret desire, the one that inspires all his plans, all his actions, he would say: "I want to be praised."
—E.M. Cioran

We are all motivated by a keen desire for praise, and the better a man is, the more he is inspired by glory.
—Cicero

Applause is the spur of noble minds, the end and aim of weak ones.
—Charles Caleb Colton

We do not content ourselves with the life we have in ourselves; we desire to live an imaginary life in the minds of others, and for this purpose we endeavor to shine.
—Blaise Pascal

The greatest efforts of the race have always been traceable to the love of praise, as the greatest catastrophes to the love of pleasure.
—John Ruskin

Our Interests Are Powerful Motivators

We talk on principle, but we act on interest.
—Walter Savage Landor

A man will fight harder for his interests than for his rights.
—Napoleon Bonaparte

The virtues and the vices are all put in motion by interest.
—Francois de La Rochefoucauld

Interest speaks all sorts of tongues, and plays all sorts of parts, even that of disinterestedness.
—Francois de La Rochefoucauld

Fear Is a Fundamental Motivator

Men's actions depend to a great extent upon fear. We do things either because we enjoy doing them or because we are afraid not to do them.
—John F. Milburn

There are only two forces that unite men—fear and interest.
—Napoleon Bonaparte

The passion to get ahead is sometimes born of the fear lest we be left behind.
—Eric Hoffer

There are only two stimulants to one's best efforts: the fear of punishment, and the hope of reward.
—John M. Wilson

A man who is afraid will do anything. —Jawaharlal Nehru

Fear of losing is what makes competitors so great. Show me a gracious loser and I'll show you a permanent loser. —O.J. Simpson

GENERAL QUOTATIONS ABOUT MOTIVATION

A team that has character doesn't need stimulation. —Tom Landry

Because it's there. —G.H.L. Mallory, on why he wanted to climb Mt. Everest

Men are not against you; they are merely for themselves.
—Gene Fowler

When the flag is unfurled, all reason is in the trumpet.
—Ukrainian proverb

Realistic Expectations

We Need to Have Realistic Expectations about Other People and Life

No one has ever loved anyone the way everyone wants to be loved.
—Mignon McLaughlin

If you expect perfection from other people, your whole life is a series of disappointments, grumbling and complaints. If, on the contrary, you pitch your expectations low, taking folks as the inefficient creatures which they are, you are frequently surprised by having them perform better than you had hoped.
—Bruce Barton

He that will have a perfect brother must resign himself to remaining brotherless.   —Italian proverb

Who ever is adequate? We all create situations which others can't live up to, then break our hearts at them because they don't.
—Elizabeth Bowen

It is a rough road that leads to the heights of greatness.
—Lucius Annaeus Seneca

Friendships aren't perfect, and yet they are very precious. For me, not expecting perfection all in one place was a great release.
—Letty Cottin Pogrebin

Life is not a spectacle or a feast; it is a predicament.   —George Santayana

To expect too much is to have a sentimental view of life, and this is a softness that ends in bitterness.
—Flannery O'Connor

Because you're not what I would have you be, I blind myself to who, in truth, you are.
—Madeline L'Engle

No one from the beginning of time has had security.
—Eleanor Roosevelt

No one is happy all his life long.
—Euripides

Vex not thy spirit at the course of things; they heed not thy vexation. How ludicrous and outlandish is astonishment at anything that may happen in life.   —Marcus Aurelius

343

There are philosophies which are unendurable not because men are cowards, but because they are men.
—Ludwig Lewisohn

When I decided to go into politics I weighed the cost: I would get criticism. But I went ahead. So when the virulent criticism came I wasn't surprised. I was better able to handle it.
—Herbert Hoover

If you want a place in the sun, you've got to put up with a few blisters.
—Abigail van Buren

Never let life's hardships disturb you ... no one can avoid problems, not even saints or sages.
—Nichiren Daishonen

Life is made up of sobs, sniffles, and smiles, with sniffles predominating.
—O. Henry

Expecting the world to treat you fairly because you are a good person is a little like expecting the bull not to attack you because you're a vegetarian.
—Dennis Wholey

When nobody around you seems to measure up, it's time to check your yardstick.
—Bill Lemley

Life to the great majority is only a constant struggle for mere existence, with the certainty of losing it at last.
—Arthur Schopenhauer

Marriage is not just spiritual communion and passionate embraces; marriage is also three meals a day, sharing the workload and remembering to carry out the trash.
—Dr. Joyce Brothers

We [Americans] cheerfully assume that in some mystic way love conquers all, that good outweighs evil in the just balances of the universe and that at the eleventh hour something gloriously triumphant will prevent the worst before it happens.
—Brooks Atkinson

The mass of men lead lives of quiet desperation. —Henry David Thoreau

Free man is by necessity insecure; thinking man is by necessity uncertain.
—Erich Fromm

There is no such thing as something for nothing. —Napoleon Hill

It is arrogance to expect that life will always be music.... Harmony, like a following breeze at sea, is the exception. In a world where most things wind up broken or lost, our lot is to tack and tune. —Harvey Oxenhorn

Being unready and ill-equipped is what you have to expect in life. It is the universal predicament. It is your lot as a human being to lack what it takes. Circumstances are seldom right. You never have the capacities, the strength, the wisdom, the virtue you ought to have. You must always do with less than you need in a situation vastly different from what you would have chosen as appropriate for your special endowments.
—Charlton Ogburn, Jr.

In nature there are neither rewards or punishments—there are consequences. —Robert G. Ingersoll

Hope for a miracle. But don't depend on one. —Talmud

344

Life guarantees a chance—not a fair shake.   —Anon.

Life is a perilous voyage.   —Palladas

HAVING REALISTIC EXPECTATIONS OF OURSELVES

We expect more of ourselves than we have any right to.
—Oliver Wendell Holmes, Jr.

Try as hard as we may for perfection, the net result of our labors is an amazing variety of imperfectness. We are surprised at our own versatility in being able to fail in so many different ways.
—Samuel McChord Crothers

Do not lose courage in considering your own imperfections.
—Saint Francis de Sales

We set up harsh and unkind rules against ourselves. No one is born without faults. That man is best who has fewest.   —Horace

One must not hope to be more than one can be.   —Nicolas de Chamfort

I can't write a book commensurate with Shakespeare, but I can write a book by me.   —Sir Walter Raleigh

I have done what I could do in life, and if I could not do better, I did not deserve it. In vain I have tried to step beyond what bound me.
—Maurice Maeterlinck

Shall a man go and hang himself because he belongs to the race of pygmies, and not be the biggest pygmy that he can?
—Henry David Thoreau

The man with insight enough to admit his limitations comes nearest to perfection.   —Johann von Goethe

The one important thing I have learned over the years is the difference between taking one's work seriously and taking one's self seriously. The first is imperative, and the second is disastrous. —Margaret Fontey

Growth begins when we start to accept our own weakness.
—Jean Vanier

To dream of the person you would like to be is to waste the person you are.   —Anon.

Of all the young men in America, only a few hundred can get into major league baseball, and of these only a handful in a decade can get into the Hall of Fame. So it goes in all human activity.... Some become multimillionaires and chairmen of the board, and some of us must be content to play baseball at company picnics or manage a credit union without pay.   —William Feather

At thirty a man should know himself like the palm of his hand, know the exact number of his defects and qualities.... And, above all, accept these things.   —Albert Camus

You can't make the Duchess of Windsor into Rebecca of Sunnybrook Farm. The facts of life are very stubborn things.
—Cleveland Amory

Sometimes it is more important to discover what one cannot do, than what one can do.   —Lin Yutang

Learn to ... be what you are, and learn to resign with a good grace all that you are not.
—Henri Frederic Amiel

We cannot all be masters.
—William Shakespeare

No man can climb out beyond the limitations of his own character.
—John Morley

To do all that one is able to do is to be a man; to do all that one would like to do is to be a god.
—Napoleon Bonaparte

No one is expected to achieve the impossible.
—French proverb

A hero is a man who does what he can.
—Romain Rolland

It is only fools who keep straining at high C all their lives.
—Charles Dudley Warner

May God ... let me strive for attainable things.
—Pindar

Despair is the price one pays for setting himself an impossible aim.
—Graham Greene

We would have to settle for the elegant goal of becoming ourselves.
—William Styron

A great obstacle to happiness is to expect too much happiness.
—Bernard de Fontenelle

There is a proper balance between not asking enough of oneself and asking or expecting too much.
—May Sarton

I hope to work, support my children and die quietly without pain.
—Sean Connery

As we advance in life, we learn the limits of our abilities.   —J.A. Froud

Striving for excellence motivates you; striving for perfection is demoralizing.   —Dr. Harriet Braiker

It is enough that I am of value to somebody today.   —Hugh Prather

A tomb now suffices him for whom the whole world was not sufficient.
—Epitaph of Alexander the Great

To wish to act like angels while we are still in this world is nothing but folly.   —Saint Teresa of Avila

It isn't important to come out on top; what matters is to be the one who comes out alive.
—Bertolt Brecht

I long to accomplish a great and noble task, but it is my chief duty to accomplish small tasks as if they were great and noble.
—Helen Keller

I cannot do everything, but still I can do something; and because I cannot do everything, I will not refuse to do something I can do.
—Edward Everett Hale

WE MUST ACCEPT THE SPREAD BETWEEN OUR WISHES AND LIFE'S REALITIES

Happy the man who early learns the wide chasm that lies between his wishes and his powers.
—Johann von Goethe

Real life is, to most men ... a perpetual compromise between the ideal and the possible. —Bertrand Russell

People are lucky and unlucky ... according to the ratio between what they get and what they have been led to expect.   —Samuel Butler

He who cannot do what he wants must make do with what he can.
                    —Terence

What has always made a hell on earth has been that man has tried to make it his heaven.
            —Friedrich Holderlin

Good is not good, where better is expected.   —Thomas Fuller

Nobody has things just as he would like them. The thing to do is to make a success with what material I have. It is a sheer waste of time and soul-power to imagine what I would do if things were different. They are not different.   —Dr. Frank Crane

We must like what we have when we don't have what we like.
            —Roger De Bussy-Rabutin

Better is the enemy of the good.
                    —Voltaire

If you aspire to the highest place, it is no disgrace to stop at the second, or even the third, place.   —Cicero

Genius does what it must, talent does what it can.
            —Edward Bulwer-Lytton

A hero is a man who does what he can.   —Romain Rolland

Nature is what you may do. There is much you may not do.
            —Ralph Waldo Emerson

Results are what you expect; consequences are what you get.
                    —Anon.

The resistance to the unpleasant situation is the root of suffering.
            —Ram Dass and Paul Gorman

To expect life to be tailored to our specifications is to invite frustration.
                    —Anon.

Each of us does, in effect, strike a series of "deals," or compromises, between the wants and longings of the inner self, and an outer environment that offers certain possibilities and sets certain limitations.
                    —Maggie Scarf

Man is the only animal that laughs and weeps, for he is the only animal that is struck with the difference between what things are, and what they might have been.
                    —William Hazlitt

We do not write as we want, but as we can.   —W. Somerset Maugham

Every creator painfully experiences the chasm between his inner vision and its ultimate expression. The chasm is never completely bridged. We all have the conviction, perhaps illusory, that we have much more to say than appears on the paper.
            —Isaac Bashevis Singer

A body shouldn't heed what might be. He's got to do with what is.
                    —Louis L'Amour

The chief pang of most trials is not so much the actual suffering itself as our own spirit of resistance to it.
—Jean Nicholas Grou

The greatest and most important problems in life are all in a certain sense insoluble. They can never be solved, but only outgrown.
—Carl Jung

The art of living lies less in eliminating our troubles than in growing with them. —Bernard M. Baruch

DOING WHAT'S RIGHT WON'T GUARANTEE HAPPINESS OR SUCCESS

Life has not taught me to expect nothing, but she has taught me not to expect success to be the inevitable result of my endeavors.
—Alan Paton

Doing what's right is no guarantee against misfortune.
—William McFee

WE HAVE TO DEAL WITH WHAT'S POSSIBLE

Knowledge of what is possible is the beginning of happiness.
—George Santayana

If I were to wish for anything, I should not wish for wealth and power, but for the passionate sense of the potential, for the eye which, ever young and ardent, sees the possible ... what wine is so sparkling, so fragrant, so intoxicating, as possibility! —Søren Kierkegaard

To seek fulfillment is to invite frustration. —Jiddu Krishnamurti

Half the unhappiness in the world is due to the failure of plans which were never reasonable, and often impossible. —Edgar Watson Howe

There is an illusion that has much to do with ... most of our unhappiness.... We expect too much.
—Joseph Farrell

A fool or idiot is one who expects things to happen that never can happen. —George Eliot

Shall a man go and hang himself because he belongs to the race of pygmies, and not be the biggest pygmy that he can?
—Henry David Thoreau

Life is a compromise of what your ego wants to do, what experience tells you to do, and what your nerves let you do. —Bruce Crampton

We almost made it, but we wanted it all. —From the song "We Wanted It All," Burt Bachrach and Carole Bayer Sager

No, Doctor, I don't want to grow young again. I just want to keep on growing old.
—Madame de Rothschild

What we call reality is an agreement that people have arrived at to make life more livable. —Louise Nevelson

There is no such thing as pure pleasure; some anxiety always goes with it. —Ovid

When somebody tells you nothing is impossible, ask him to dribble a football. —Anon.

No country can act wisely simultaneously in every part of the globe at every moment of time.

—Henry Kissinger

The most important thing in marriage is not happiness, but stability.

—Gabriel Garcia Marquez

So often we search out the impossible, and then throw ourselves into trying to do it.   —Anon.

ANTICIPATION IS OFTEN MORE ENJOYABLE THAN REALIZATION

Nothing is so good as it seems beforehand.   —George Eliot

Prospect is often better than possession.   —Thomas Fuller

The hours we pass with happy prospects in view are more pleasing than those crowned with fruition.

—Oliver Goldsmith

'Tis expectation makes a blessing dear; heaven were not heaven if we knew what it were.

—Sir John Suckling

Life is so constructed that the event does not, cannot, will not, match the expectation.   —Charlotte Brontë

There is no greater enemy to those who would please than expectation.

—Michel de Montaigne

To dream too much of the person you would like to be is to waste the person you are.   —Anon.

Too many people miss the silver lining because they're expecting gold.

—Maurice Setter

For people who live on expectations, to face up to their realization is something of an ordeal.

—Elizabeth Bowen

My expectations—which I extended whenever I came close to accomplishing my goals—made it impossible ever to feel satisfied with my success.   —Ellen Sue Stern

REALITY AND WARFARE

Every attempt to make war easy and safe will result in humiliation and disaster. —General William Sherman

I sincerely wish war was a pleasanter and easier business than it is, but it does not admit of holidays.

—Abraham Lincoln

There is many a boy here today who looks on war as all glory, but boys, it is all hell.

—General William T. Sherman

Moderation in war is imbecility.

—Admiral John Fisher

War is not an adventure. It is a disease. It is like typhus.

—Antoine de Saint-Exupery

In combat, life is short, nasty and brutish. The issues of national policy which brought him into war are irrelevant to the combat soldier; he is concerned with his literal life chances.   —Charles E. Moskos, Jr.

In war, more than anywhere else in the world, things happen differently from what we had expected, and look differently when near from what they did at a distance.

—Karl Von Clausewitz

In spite of all of the training you get and the precautions you take to keep yourself alive, it's largely a matter of luck that decides whether or not you get killed. —James Jones

General Quotations about Realistic Expectations

When one's expectations are reduced to zero, one really appreciates everything one does have.
—Stephen Hawking

Life didn't promise to be wonderful.
—Teddy Pendergrass

We never enjoy perfect happiness; our most fortunate successes are mingled with sadness; some anxieties always perplex the reality of our satisfaction. —Pierre Corneille

Do not commit the error, common among the young, of assuming that if you cannot save the whole of mankind you have failed.
—Jan de Hartog

The art of living lies less in eliminating our troubles than in growing with them. —Bernard M. Baruch

If one considered life as a simple loan, one would perhaps be less exacting. —Eugene Delacroix

Why are we surprised when fig trees bear figs? —Margaret Titzel

Those who aim at great deeds must also suffer greatly. —Plutarch

I have nothing to offer but blood, toil, tears, and sweat.
—Sir Winston Churchill

There's no map, there's no master plan, there's just people. —Stingray

Every writer I know has trouble writing. —Joseph Heller

Men expect too much, do too little.
—Allen Tate

GOALS

IT'S TREMENDOUSLY IMPORTANT TO HAVE GOOD GOALS

An aim in life is the only fortune worth finding.
—Jacqueline Kennedy Onassis

You have to have a dream so you can get up in the morning.
—Billy Wilder

The tragedy of life doesn't lie in not reaching your goal. The tragedy lies in having no goal to reach.
—Benjamin Mays

The poor man is not he who is without a cent, but he who is without a dream.
—Harry Kemp

He is conscious of touching the highest pinnacle of fulfillment ... when he is consumed in the service of an idea, in the conquest of the goal pursued.
—R. Briffault

He who has a *why* to live for can bear almost any *how*.
—Friedrich Nietzsche

Purpose is what gives life a meaning.
—C.H. Parkhurst

The great and glorious masterpiece of man is to know how to live to purpose.
—Michel de Montaigne

Great minds have purposes, others have wishes.
—Washington Irving

Unless you give yourself to some great cause, you haven't even begun to live.
—William P. Merrill

Be a life long or short, its completeness depends on what it was lived for.
—David Starr Jordan

To live means to have ... a mission to fulfill—and in the measure in which we avoid setting our life to something, we make it empty.
—José Ortega y Gasset

To seek one's goals and to drive toward it, steeling one's heart, is most uplifting!
—Henrik Ibsen

The true worth of a man is to be measured by the objects he pursues.
—Marcus Aurelius

A useless life is an early death.
—Johann von Goethe

My father used to play with my brother and me in the yard. Mother would come out and say, "You're tearing up the grass." "We're not raising grass," Dad would reply. "We're raising boys."
—Harmon Killebrew

Without a purpose, nothing should be done.   —Marcus Aurelius

Our plans miscarry because they have no aim. When a man does not know what harbor he is making for, no wind is the right wind.
—Marcus Annaeus Seneca

Every true man, sir, who is a little above the level of the beasts and plants, lives so as to give a meaning and a value to his own life.
—Luigi Pirandello

Men cannot for long live hopefully unless they are embarked upon some great unifying enterprise, one for which they may pledge their lives, their fortunes and their honor.
—C.A. Dykstra

No pleasure philosophy, no sensuality, no place nor power, no material success can for a moment give such inner satisfaction as the sense of living for good purpose.
—Minot Simons

Many are stubborn in pursuit of the path they have chosen, few in pursuit of the goal.
—Friedrich Nietzsche

There is one thing which gives radiance to everything. It is the idea of something around the corner.
—G.K. Chesterton

Lack of something to feel important about is almost the greatest tragedy a man may have. —Charles C. Noble

There are three ingredients in the good life: learning, earning and yearning.   —Christopher Morely

To grow and know what one is growing towards—that is the source of all strength and confidence in life.
—James Baillie

If you cry "Forward," you must make plain in what direction to go.
—Anton Chekov

Men, like nails, lose their usefulness when they lose direction and begin to bend.   —Walter Savage Landor

In everything one must consider the end.   —Jean de La Fontaine

A novelist must know what his last chapter is going to say and one way or another work toward that last chapter.... To me it is utterly basic, yet it seems like it's a great secret.
—Leon Uris

The purpose of life is a life of purpose.   —Robert Byrne

Life has a value only when it has something valuable as its object.
—George Hegel

Obstacles are those frightful things you see when you take your eyes off the goal.   —Hannah More

You must have long-range goals to keep you from being frustrated by short-range failures.
—Charles C. Noble

352

The world stands aside to let anyone pass who knows where he is going.
—David Starr Jordan

This is true joy of life—the being used for a purpose that is recognized by yourself as a right one, instead of being a feverish, selfish little clod of ailments and grievances, complaining that the world will not devote itself to making you happy.
—George Bernard Shaw

It is when things go hardest, when life becomes most trying, that there is greatest need for having a fixed goal. When few comforts come from without, it is all the more necessary to have a fount to draw on from within.
—B.C. Forbes

A straight path never leads anywhere except to the objective.
—André Gide

There's some end at last for the man who follows a path; mere rambling is interminable.
—Marcus Annaeus Seneca

Having a goal is a state of happiness.
—E.J. Bartek

Not only must we be good, but we must also be good for something.
—Henry David Thoreau

The American people can have anything they want; the trouble is, they don't know what they want.
—Eugene V. Debs

Life has a meaning only if one barters it day by day for something other than itself.
—Antoine de Saint-Exupery

To have a reason to get up in the morning, it is necessary to possess a guiding principle. A belief of some kind. A bumper sticker, if you will.
—Judith Guest

An aspiration is a joy forever, a possession as solid as a landed estate, a fortune which we can never exhaust and which gives us year by year a revenue of pleasurable activity.
—Robert Louis Stevenson

The soul that has no established aim loses itself.   —Michel de Montaigne

He turns not back who is bound to a star.   —Leonardo da Vinci

He might never really do what he said, but at least he had it in mind. He had somewhere to go.
—Louis L'Amour

The great and glorious masterpiece of man is how to live with a purpose.   —Michel de Montaigne

What most counts is not to live, but to live aright.   —Socrates

Choosing a goal and sticking to it changes everything.   —Scott Reed

No wind serves him who addresses his voyage to no certain port.
—Michel de Montaigne

Laboring toward distant aims sets the mind in a higher key, and puts us at our best.   —C.H. Parkhurst

Everything's in the mind. That's where it all starts. Knowing what you want is the first step toward getting it.   —Mae West

Set short term goals and you'll win games. Set long term goals and you'll win championships!   —Anon.

We act as though comfort and luxury were the chief requirements of life, when all that we need to make us really happy is something to be enthusiastic about.
                    —Charles Kingsley

Unhappiness is in not knowing what we want and killing ourselves to get it.   —Don Herold

The purpose of life is life.
                    —Karl Lagerfeld

Having a dream isn't stupid.... It's not having a dream that's stupid.
                    —Anon.

Happiness is the overcoming of not unknown obstacles toward a known goal.   —L. Ron Hubbard

To have no set purpose in one's life is the harlotry of the will.
                    —Stephen McKenna

There is no happiness except in the realization that we have accomplished something.   —Henry Ford

Strong lives are motivated by dynamic purposes.
                    —Kenneth Hildebrand

One of the sources of pride in being a human being is the ability to bear present frustrations in the interests of longer purposes.
                    —Helen Merrell Lynd

Aim at nothing and you'll succeed.
                    —Anon.

Only he who can see the invisible can do the impossible.
                    —Frank Gaines

If you don't know where you are going, how can you expect to get there?   —Basil S. Walsh

The only people who attain power are those who crave for it.
                    —Erich Kastner

In this life we get only those things for which we hunt, for which we strive, and for which we are willing to sacrifice.
                    —George Matthew Adams

You seldom get what you go after unless you know in advance what you want.   —Maurice Switzer

Destiny is not a matter of chance, it is a matter of choice; it is not a thing to be waited for, it is a thing to be achieved.   —William Jennings Bryan

Where no plan is laid, where the disposal of time is surrendered merely to the chance of incident, chaos will soon reign.   —Victor Hugo

A life that hasn't a definite plan is likely to become driftwood.
                    —David Sarnoff

Only he who keeps his eye fixed on the far horizon will find his right road.   —Dag Hammarskjold

Fortunate is the person who has developed the self-control to steer a straight course toward his objective in life, without being swayed from his purpose by either commendation or condemnation.   —Napoleon Hill

Nothing is more terrible than activity without insight. —Thomas Carlyle

If we would only give, just once, the same amount of reflection to what we want to get out of life that we give to the question of what to do with a two weeks' vacation, we would be startled at our false standards and the aimless procession of our busy days.
—Dorothy Canfield Fisher

WE EACH HAVE OUR OWN GOALS

Every man is said to have his peculiar ambition.   —Abraham Lincoln

We all live with the objective of being happy; our lives are all different, and yet the same.   —Anne Frank

Follow your bliss. Find where it is and don't be afraid to follow it.
—Joseph Campbell

I am not sending messages with my feet. All I ever wanted was not to come up empty. I did it for the dough, and the old applause.
—Fred Astaire

First say to yourself what you would be, and then do what you have to do.   —Epictetus

We can do whatever we wish to do provided our wish is strong enough.... What do you want most to do? That's what I have to keep asking myself, in the face of difficulties.
—Katherine Mansfield

To be what we are, and to become what we are capable of becoming, is the only end of life.
—Baruch Spinoza

Ambition means longing and striving to attain some purpose. Therefore, there are as many brands of ambition as there are human aspirations.
—B.C. Forbes

The aim of life is self-development, to realize one's nature perfectly.
—Oscar Wilde

Concentrate on finding your goal, then concentrate on reaching it.
—Colonel Michael Friedman

Enthusiasm for one's goal lessens the disagreeableness of working toward it.   —Thomas Eakins

WE CAN HAVE TOO MANY GOALS

He who wants to do everything will never do anything. —André Maurois

As you emphasize your life, you must localize and define it ... you cannot do everything.
—Phillips Brooks

There are people who want to be everywhere at once, and they get nowhere.   —Carl Sandburg

A windmill is eternally at work to accomplish one end, although it shifts with every variation of the weathercock, and assumes ten different positions in a day.
—Charles Caleb Colton

People can have many different kinds of pleasure. The real one is that for which they will forsake the others.   —Marcel Proust

Nations, like individuals, have to limit their objectives or take the consequences.   —James Reston

One of the most important factors, not only in military matters but in life as a whole, is ... the ability to direct one's whole energies towards the fulfillment of a particular task.
—Field Marshal Erwin Rommel

It is in self-limitation that a master first shows himself.
—Johann von Goethe

One cannot manage too many affairs: like pumpkins in the water, one pops up while you try to hold down the other.   —Chinese proverb

One principle reason why men are so often useless is that they ... divide and shift their attention among a multitude of objects and pursuits.
—Nathaniel Emmons

I can tell you how to get what you want: You've just got to keep a thing in view and go for it and never let your eyes wander to right or left or up or down. And looking back is fatal.   —William J. Lock

He who begins many things finishes but few.   —Italian proverb

Who begins too much accomplishes little.   —German proverb

Never try to catch two frogs with one hand.   —Chinese proverb

If you run after two hares, you will catch neither.   —Thomas Fuller

The greyhound that starts many hares kills none.   —Spanish proverb

A bull does not enjoy fame in two herds.   —Rhodesian proverb

The man who seeks one thing in life, and but one
May hope to achieve it before life be done.
But he who seeks all things wherever he goes
Only reaps from the hopes which around him he sows
A harvest of barren regrets.
—Owen Meredith

No man can serve two masters: for either he will hate the one, and love the other; or else he will hold to the one, and despise the other.
— Mt. 6:24

He who serves two masters has to lie to one.   —Portuguese proverb

Those who attain any excellence commonly spend life in one pursuit; for excellence is not often granted upon easier terms.
—Samuel Johnson

He who wishes to fulfill his mission in the world must be a man of one idea, one great overmastering purpose, overshadowing all his aims, and guiding and controlling his entire life.   —Bate

Firmness of purpose is one of the most necessary sinews of character and one of the best instruments of success. Without it, genius wastes its efforts in a maze of inconsistencies.
—Lord Chesterfield

A double-minded man is unstable in all his ways.... A determinate purpose in life, and a steady adhesion to it through all disadvantages, are indispensable conditions of success.
—William M. Punshion

He who hunts two hares leaves one and loses the other.
—Japanese proverb

If you would be Pope, you must think of nothing else.
—Spanish proverb

One should want only one thing and want it constantly. Then one is sure of getting it. But I desire everything, and consequently get nothing.
—André Gide

I care not what your education is, elaborate or nothing, what your mental calibre is, great or small, that man who concentrates all his energies of body, mind and soul in one direction is a tremendous man.
—T. DeWitt Talmage

MAKE THE ENJOYMENT OF LIFE A PRIMARY GOAL

All animals except man know that the ultimate of life is to enjoy it.
—Samuel Butler

Let us live, while we are alive!
—Johann von Goethe

Since we must all die sooner or later, let us enjoy life while we can!
—Otoma no Tabito

Life is an end in itself, and the only question as to whether it is worth living is whether you have had enough of it.
—Oliver Wendell Holmes, Jr.

I take it as a prime cause of the present confusion of society that it is too sickly and too doubtful to use pleasure as a test of value.
—Rebecca West

There is no cure for birth and death save to enjoy the interval.
—George Santayana

Life is about enjoying yourself and having a good time.
—Cher

All men seek one goal: success or happiness.
—Aristotle

What I'm out for is a good time. All the rest is propaganda.
—*Saturday Night and Sunday Morning*

The goal of all civilization, all religious thought, and all that sort of thing is simply to have a good time. But man gets so solemn over the process that he forgets the end.
—Don Marquis

The business of life is to enjoy oneself; everything else is a mockery.
—Norman Douglas

The true object of human life is play.
—G.K. Chesterton

Use your health, even to the point of wearing it out. That is what it is for. Spend all you have before you die; do not outlive yourself.
—George Bernard Shaw

Pleasure is the object, duty and the goal of all rational creatures.
—Voltaire

Pleasure is the only thing to live for. Nothing ages like happiness.
—Oscar Wilde

I finally figured out the only reason to be alive is to enjoy it.
—Rita Mae Brown

Life exists for the love of music or beautiful things.   —G.K. Chesterton

There is only one meaning of life: the act of living itself.   —Erich Fromm

The main obligation is to amuse yourself.   —S.J. Perelman

GOALS AND PEACE OF MIND

From his cradle to the grave, a man never does a single thing which has any first and foremost object save one—to secure peace of mind, spiritual comfort, for himself.
—Mark Twain

I take it that what all men are really after is some form of, perhaps only some formula of, peace.
—James Conrad

ALWAYS AIM HIGH

Why should I deem myself to be a chisel, when I could be the artist?
—J.C.F. von Schiller

Aim at the sun, and you may not reach it; but your arrow will fly far higher than if aimed at an object on a level with yourself.   —J. Hawes

If you would hit the mark, you must aim a little above it; every arrow that flies feels the attraction of earth.
—Henry Wadsworth Longfellow

Man's reach should exceed his grasp, or what's a heaven for?
—Robert Browning

In the long run men hit only what they aim at. Therefore, though they should fall immediately, they had better aim at something high.
—Henry David Thoreau

The tragedy of life doesn't lie in not reaching your goal. The tragedy lies in having no goal to reach. It isn't a calamity to die with dreams unfulfilled, but it is a calamity not to dream. It is not disgrace to reach the stars, but it is a disgrace to have no stars to reach for. Not failure, but low aim, is a sin.   —Benjamin Mays

The most absurd and reckless aspirations have sometimes led to extraordinary success.   —Vauvenargues

When you reach for the stars, you may not quite get one, but you won't come up with a handful of mud, either.   —Leo Burnett

Unless in one thing or another we are straining toward perfection, we have forfeited our manhood.
—Stephen McKenna

Too low they build, who build beneath the stars.   —Edward Young

Whatever course you have chosen for yourself, it will not be a chore but an adventure if you bring to it a sense of the glory of striving, if your sights are set far above the merely secure and mediocre.
—David Sarnoff

Once you say you're going to settle for second, that's what happens to you.   —John F. Kennedy

Aim at heaven and you get earth thrown in; aim at earth and you get neither.   —C.S. Lewis

We are all in the gutter, but some of us are looking at the stars.
—Oscar Wilde

Aim at perfection in everything, though in most things it is unattainable. However they who aim at it, and persevere, will come much nearer to it than those whose laziness and despondency make them give it up as unattainable.

—Lord Chesterfield

One may miss the mark by aiming too high, as too low.

—Thomas Fuller

Shoot for the moon. Even if you miss it, you will land among the stars.

—Les Brown

We aim above the mark to hit the mark. Every act hath some falsehood or exaggeration in it.

—Ralph Waldo Emerson

Life is a petty thing unless it is moved by the indomitable urge to extend its boundaries.

—José Ortega y Gasset

Far away in the sunshine are my highest inspirations. I many not reach them, but I can look up and see the beauty, believe in them and try to follow where they lead.

—Louisa May Alcott

A man's worth is no greater than the worth of his ambitions.

—Marcus Aurelius

Not failure, but low aim, is crime.

—James Russell Lowell

Great is the road I climb, but ... the garland offered by an easier effort is not worth the gathering.

—Propertius

I never took a position we were going to be a good ball club. I took the position we were going to be a *winning* ball club.   —Red Auerbach

WE MUST VISUALIZE OUR GOALS

Before you begin a thing, remind yourself that difficulties and delays quite impossible to foresee are ahead.... You can only see one thing clearly and that is your goal. Form a mental vision of that and cling to it through thick and thin.

—Kathleen Norris

Man can only receive what he sees himself receiving.

—Florence Scovel Shinn

A person can grow only as much as his horizon allows.   —John Powell

GOALS AND HAPPINESS

Enjoyment is not a goal, it is a feeling that accompanies important ongoing activity.   —Paul Goodman

What our deepest self craves is not mere enjoyment, but some supreme purpose that will enlist all our powers and give unity and direction to our life.   —Henry J. Golding

The very first condition of lasting happiness is that a life should be full of purpose, aiming at something outside self.   —Hugh Black

The only true happiness comes from squandering ourselves for a purpose.

—John Mason Brown

There is more to life than just existing and having a pleasant time.

—J.C.F. von Schiller

359

Happiness is not the end of life; character is. —Henry Ward Beecher

Many persons have a wrong idea of what constitutes true happiness. It is not attained through self-gratification, but through fidelity to a worthy purpose. —Helen Keller

Doing Our Duty and Pursuing Goals Leads to Happiness

This is true joy of life—being used for a purpose that is recognized by yourself as a mighty one ... instead of being a feverish, selfish little clod of ailments and grievances, complaining that the world will not devote itself to making you happy.
—George Bernard Shaw

Never mind your happiness; do your duty. —Will Durant

Human happiness and moral duty are inseparably connected.
—George Washington

When we ... devote ourselves to the strict and unsparing performance of duty, then happiness comes of itself.
—Wilhelm von Humboldt

Seek happiness for its own sake, and you will not find it; seek for duty, and happiness will follow, as the shadow comes with the sunshine.
—Tyron Edwards

True happiness ... is not attained through self-gratification, but through fidelity to a worthy purpose.
—Helen Keller

The only true happiness comes from squandering ourselves for a purpose.
—William Cowper

True happiness, we are told, consists in getting out of one's self, but the point is not only to get out; you must stay out, and to stay out, you must have some absorbing errand.
—Henry James

Happiness is the natural flower of duty. —Phillips Brooks

The happiest excitement in life is to be convinced that one is fighting for all one is worth on behalf of some clearly seen and deeply felt good.
—Ruth Benedict

The secret of living is to find ... the pivot of a concept on which you can make your stand. —Luigi Pirandello

The only ones among you who will be really happy are those who will have sought and found how to serve.
—Albert Schweitzer

He who never sacrificed a present to a future good, or a personal to a general one, can speak of happiness only as the blind speak of color.
—Horace Mann

There is no happiness except in the realization that we have accomplished something. —Henry Ford

The full-grown modern human being ... is conscious of touching the highest pinnacle of fulfillment ... when he is consumed in the service of an idea, in the conquest of the goal pursued.
—R. Briffault

Happiness is essentially a state of going somewhere, wholeheartedly, one-directionally, without regret or reservation. —William H. Sheldon

360

A man's happiness: to do the things proper to man. —Marcus Aurelius

Happy the man who knows his duties!—Christian Furchtegott Gellert

I believe half the unhappiness in life comes from people being afraid to go straight at things.
—William J. Locke

Happiness is the overcoming of not unknown obstacles toward a known goal. —L. Ron Hubbard

Give a man health and a course to steer, and he'll never stop to trouble about whether he's happy or not.
—George Bernard Shaw

Having a goal is a state of happiness.
—E.J. Bartek

Happiness lies in the joy of achievement and the thrill of creative effort.
—Franklin Delano Roosevelt

Without duty, life is soft and boneless. —Joseph Joubert

SUCCESS

The man who succeeds above his fellows is the one who early in life discerns his object and toward that object habitually directs his powers. Even genius itself is but fine observation strengthened by fixity of purpose. —Edward Bulwer-Lytton

If one advances confidently in the direction of his dreams, and endeavors to live the life which he has imagined, he will meet with a success unexpected in common hours.
—Henry David Thoreau

A determinate purpose of life, and steady adhesion to it through all disadvantages, are indispensable conditions of success.
—William M. Punshon

The secret of success is constancy to purpose. —Benjamin Franklin

The man who fails because he aims astray, or because he does not aim at all, is to be found everywhere.
—Frank Swinnerton

Life has ... taught me not to expect success to be the inevitable result of my endeavors. She taught me to seek sustenance from the endeavor itself, but to leave the result to God.
—Alan Paton

GOALS AND WARFARE

The object of war is not to die for your country, but to make the other bastard die for his.
—General George S. Patton

The object of war is to survive it.
—John Irving

ULTIMATE GOALS

Much pleasure and little grief is every man's desire.
—Spanish proverb

I think the purpose of life is to be useful, to be responsible, to be honorable, to be compassionate. It is, after all, to matter: to count, to stand for something, to have made some difference that you lived at all.
—Leo C. Rosten

The great business of life is to be, to do, to do without, and to depart.
—John Morley

The proper function of man is to live—not to exist. —Jack London

Life's objective is life itself.
　　　　　—Johann von Goethe

I seek the utmost pleasure and the least pain. —Plautus

There are two things to aim at in life: first, to get what you want, and after that to enjoy it. Only the wisest of mankind achieve the second.
　　　　　—Logan Pearsall Smith

I am searching for that which every man seeks—peace and rest.
　　　　　—Dante Alighieri

Reach high, for stars lie hidden in your soul. Dream deep, for every dream precedes the goal.
　　　　　—Pamela Vaull Starr

Never undertake anything for which you wouldn't have the courage to ask the blessings of heaven.
　　　　　—Georg Christoph Lichtenberg

The one thing worth living for is to keep one's soul pure.
　　　　　—Marcus Aurelius

The greatest use of life is to spend it for something that will outlast it.
　　　　　—William James

PART 5

Overcoming Negatives and Uncertainties

FEAR

ALL LIVING CREATURES FEAR SOMETHING

The horse does abominate the camel; the mighty elephant is afraid of a mouse; and they say that the lion, which scorneth to turn his back upon the stoutest animal, will tremble at the crowing of a cock.
—Increase Mather

The flocks fear the wolf, the crops the storm, and the trees the wind.
—Virgil

We all choke, and the man who says he doesn't choke is lying like hell.
—Lee Trevino

A man who says he has never been scared is either lying or else he's never been any place or done anything.
—Louis L'Amour

This is the century of fear.
—Albert Camus

All men are afraid in battle. The coward is the one who lets his fear overcome his sense of duty. Duty is the essence of manhood.
—General George S. Patton

Only the self-deceived will claim perfect freedom from fear.
—Bill W.

Every day I wake up a little afraid. Only a fool is never afraid.
—Ron Meyer

FEAR IS ONE OF THE MOST TERRIBLE THINGS IN LIFE

There is perhaps nothing so bad and so dangerous in life as fear.
—Jawaharlal Nehru

Fear, true fear, is a savage frenzy. Of all the insanities of which we are capable, it is surely the most cruel.
—Georges Bernanos

A man's doubts and fears are his worst enemies. —William Wrigley, Jr.

Fear is the most devastating of all human emotions. Man has no trouble like the paralyzing effects of fear.
—Paul Parker

Neither a man nor a crowd nor a nation can be trusted to act humanely or to think sanely under the influence of a great fear.
—Bertrand Russell

The worst sorrows in life are not in its losses and misfortunes, but its fears. —Arthur Christopher Benson

No passion so effectually robs the mind of all its powers of acting and reasoning as fear. —Edmund Burke

The thing I fear most is fear.
—Michel de Montaigne

Nothing is so much to be feared as fear. —Henry David Thoreau

Nothing is terrible except fear itself.
—Francis Bacon

The only thing we have to fear is fear itself—nameless, unreasoning, unjustified terror which paralyzes needed efforts to convert retreat into advance.
—Franklin Delano Roosevelt

It is better by noble boldness to run the risk of being subject to half the evils we anticipate than to remain in cowardly listlessness for fear of what might happen. —Herodotus

There is no devil but fear.
—Elbert Hubbard

Men who look young, act young, and everlastingly harp on the fact that they are young—but who nevertheless think and act with a degree of caution what would be excessive in their grandfathers—are the curses of the world. —Robertson Davies

There's nothing I'm afraid of like scared people. —Robert Frost

God! Is there anything uglier than a frightened man! —Jean Anouilh

The only thing I am afraid of is fear.
—Arthur Wellesley,
Duke of Wellington

THE HORRIBLE EFFECTS OF FEAR

Of all the passions, fear weakens judgment most. —Cardinal De Retz

All forms of fear produce fatigue.
—Bertrand Russell

Power does not corrupt. Fear corrupts, perhaps the fear of a loss of power. —John Steinbeck

When men are ruled by fear, they strive to prevent the very changes that will abate it. —Alan Paton

Fear, if allowed free rein, would reduce all of us to trembling shadows of men, for whom only death could bring release.
—John M. Wilson

If we let things terrify us, life will not be worth living.
—Marcus Annaeus Seneca

When fear is excessive it can make many a man despair.
—Saint Thomas Aquinas

Fear makes the wolf bigger than he is. —German proverb

One of the effects of fear is to disturb the senses and cause things to appear other than what they are.
—Miguel de Cervantes

What begins in fear usually ends in folly. —Samuel Taylor Coleridge

In doubt, fear is the worst of prophets. —Statius

Fear is the most damnable, damaging thing to human personality in the whole world.   —William Faulkner

Fear is the main source of superstition, and one of the main sources of cruelty.   —Bertrand Russell

Fear is like fire. If controlled it will help you; if uncontrolled, it will rise up and destroy you. Men's actions depend to a great extent upon fear. We do things either because we enjoy doing them or because we are afraid not to do them.
—John F. Milburn

To hate and to fear is to be psychologically ill ... it is, in fact, the consuming illness of our time.
—Harry A. Overstreet

Fear is an acid which is pumped into one's atmosphere. It causes mental, moral and spiritual asphyxiation, and sometimes death; death to energy and all growth. —Horace Fletcher

Fear is the proof of a degenerate mind.   —Virgil

Fear is an insidious virus. Given a breeding place in our minds ... it will eat away our spirit and block the forward path of our endeavors.
—James F. Bell

A man who is afraid will do anything.   —Jawaharlal Nehru

Excessive fear is always powerless.
—Aeschylus

Fear makes strangers of people who should be friends.
—Shirley MacLaine

O, how vain and vile a passion is this fear! What base, uncomely things it makes men do.
—Samuel Johnson

The unknown is what it is. And to be frightened of it is what sends everybody scurrying around chasing dreams, illusions, wars, peace, love, hate, all that. Unknown is what it is. Accept that it's unknown, and it's plain sailing.   —John Lennon

No passion so effectively robs the mind of its powers of acting and reasoning as fear.   —Edmund Burke

As many people die from an excess of timidity as from bravery.
—Norman Mailer

If a man harbors any sort of fear, it percolates through all his thinking, damages his personality, makes him landlord to a ghost.
—Lloyd C. Douglas

If you let fear of consequence prevent you from following your deepest instinct, then your life will be safe, expedient and thin.
—Katharine Butler Hathaway

There is nothing that fear or hope does not make men believe.
—Vauvenargues

All fear is bondage.   —Anon.

Fear is the prison of the heart.
—Anon.

I have come to realize that all my trouble with living has come from fear and smallness within me.
—Angela L. Wozniak

He who fears something gives it power over him. —Moorish proverb

How very little can be done under the spirit of fear.
—Florence Nightingale

We promise according to our hopes, and perform according to our fears.
—Francois de La Rochefoucauld

There seemed to be endless obstacles ... it seemed that the root cause of them all was fear. —Joanna Field

No power is strong enough to be lasting if it labors under the weight of fear. —Cicero

Where fear is, happiness is not.
—Marcus Annaeus Seneca

Primary Sources of Fear

Many fears are born of fatigue and loneliness. —Max Ehrmann

Fear always springs from ignorance.
—Ralph Waldo Emerson

The craven's fear is but selfishness, like his merriment.
—John Greenleaf Whittier

When did reason ever direct our desires or our fears? —Juvenal

Fear is secured by a dread of punishment. —Niccolo Machiavelli

We are largely the playthings of our fears. To one, fear of the dark; to another, of physical pain; to a third, of public ridicule; to a fourth, of poverty; to a fifth, of loneliness ... for all of us, our particular creature waits in ambush. —Horace Walpole

If your desires be endless, your cares and fears will be so, too.
—Thomas Fuller

We fear the thing we want the most.
—Dr. Robert Anthony

We are more often frightened than hurt; and we suffer more from imagination than from reality.
—Marcus Annaeus Seneca

Fear, born of that stern matron, Responsibility. —William McFee

Only your mind can produce fear.
—A Course in Miracles

Fear follows crime, and is its punishment. —Voltaire

All infractions of love and equity in our social relations are ... punished by fear. —Ralph Waldo Emerson

The only thing we have to fear on this planet is man. —Carl Jung

Uncertainty Can Fill People with Fear

I can stand what I know. It's what I don't know that frightens me.
—Frances Newton

Fear comes from uncertainty. When we are absolutely certain, whether of our worth or worthlessness, we are almost impervious to fear.
—William Congreve

We all fear what we don't know— it's natural. —Leo Buscaglia

Anxiety about the Future

He that fears not the future may enjoy the present. —Thomas Fuller

To tremble before anticipated evils is to bemoan what thou hast never lost. —Johann von Goethe

He who foresees calamities suffers them twice over. —Beilby Porteous

He who fears he shall suffer already suffers what he fears.
—Michel de Montaigne

Nothing in life is more remarkable than the unnecessary anxiety which we endure, and generally create ourselves. —Benjamin Disraeli

Do not think of all your anxieties, you will only make yourself ill.
—Shih King

Only man clogs his happiness with care, destroying what is with thoughts of what may be.
—John Dryden

If you are afraid for your future, you don't have a present.
—James Petersen

Cowards die many times before their deaths; the valiant never taste of death but once.
—William Shakespeare

Every man, through fear, mugs his aspirations a dozen times a day.
—Brendan Francis

The mind that is anxious about the future is miserable.
—Marcus Annaeus Seneca

I am not afraid of tomorrow, for I have seen yesterday and I love today.
—William Allen White

We are more disturbed by a calamity which threatens us than by one which has befallen us.
—John Lancaster Spalding

It is never safe to look into the future with eyes of fear. —E.H. Harriman

The future is called "perhaps," which is the only possible thing to call the future. And the important thing is not to allow that to scare you. —Tennessee Williams

Grief has limits, whereas apprehension has none. For we grieve only for what we know has happened, but we fear all that possibly may happen.
—Pliny, the Younger

Cowardice ... is almost always simply a lack of ability to suspend the functioning of the imagination.
—Ernest Hemingway

We need not be afraid of the future, for the future will be in our own hands. —Thomas E. Dewey

Anxiety is a thin stream of fear trickling through the mind. If encouraged, it cuts a channel into which all other thoughts are drained.
—Arthur Somers Roche

Most of the fear that spoils our life comes from attacking difficulties before we get to them.
—Dr. Frank Crane

Fear is created not by the world around us, but in the mind, by what we think is going to happen.
—Elizabeth Gawain

FEAR CAN BE A SELF-FULFILLING PROPHECY

Proust has pointed out that the predisposition to love creates it's own objects: is this not also true of fear?
—Elizabeth Bowen

Fear to let fall a drop and you spill a lot.
—Malay proverb

Be not afraid of life. Believe that life is worth living, and your belief will help create the fact. —William James

We are terrified by the idea of being terrified.
—Friedrich Nietzsche

He who fears being conquered is sure of defeat.
—Napoleon Bonaparte

What we fear comes to pass more speedily than what we hope.
—Publilius Syrus

The greatest mistake you can make is to be continually fearing you will make one.
—Elbert Hubbard

The mere apprehension of a coming evil has put many into a situation of the utmost danger.
—Lucan

The thing we fear we bring to pass.
—Elbert Hubbard

How often the fear of one evil leads into a worse.
—Nicolas Bouleau-Despreaux

Fear breeds fear.
—Byron Janis

FEARS CAN BE UNLEARNED

Fears are educated into us, and can, if we wish, be educated out.
—Dr. Karl Menninger

Human beings are born with just two basic fears. One is the fear of loud noises. The other is the fear of falling. All other fears must be learned.
—Ronald Rood

Needless fear and panic over disease or misfortune that seldom materialize are simply bad habits. By proper ventilation and illumination of the mind it is possible to cultivate tolerance, poise and real courage.
—Elie Metchnikoff

Nothing in life is to be feared. It is only to be understood.
—Marie Curie

We have to start teaching ourselves not to be afraid. —William Faulkner

Victory over fear is the first spiritual duty of man.
—Nicholas Berdyaev

I am not afraid of storms, for I am learning how to sail my ship.
—Louisa May Alcott

WE CAN'T FEAR EITHER FAILURE OR SUCCESS

True success is overcoming the fear of being unsuccessful.
—Paul Sweeney

Most people are afraid of failing. I think there's nothing wrong in failing.
—Mark N. Cohen

He is much to be dreaded who stands in dread of poverty.
—Publilius Syrus

There are those who are so scrupulously afraid of doing wrong that they seldom venture to do anything.
—Vauvenargues

To be ambitious for wealth, and yet always expecting to be poor, to be always doubting your ability to get what you long for, is like trying to reach east by traveling west.... No matter how hard you work for success, if your thought is saturated with the fear of failure, it will kill your efforts, neutralize your endeavors and make success impossible.
—Charles Baudouin

Studies by Medical Corps psychiatrists of combat fatigue cases ... found that fear of killing, rather than fear of being killed, was the most common cause of battle failure, and that fear of failure ran a strong second.
—S.L.A. Marshall

Half the things that people do not succeed in are through fear of making the attempt.   —James Northcote

A champion is afraid of losing. Everyone else is afraid of winning.
—Billie Jean King

We fear our highest possibility (as well as our lowest one). We are generally afraid to become that which we can glimpse in our most perfect moments.   —Abraham Maslow

We fear the thing we want the most.
—Dr. Robert Anthony

We should not let our fears hold us back from pursuing our hopes.
—John F. Kennedy

The ambitious climb high and perilous stairs, and never care how to come down; the desire of rising hath swallowed up their fear of a fall.
—Thomas Adams

WE CAN'T FEAR EITHER DYING OR LIVING

It is not death that a man should fear, he should fear never beginning to live.   —Marcus Aurelius

Some people are so afraid to die that they never begin to live.
—Henry Van Dyke

The worst of all fears is the fear of living.   —Theodore Roosevelt

Those who fear life are already three parts dead.   —Bertrand Russell

Fear not that thy life shall come to an end, but rather that it shall never have a beginning.
—John Henry Cardinal Newman

People living deeply have no fear of death.   —Anaïs Nin

The fear of life is the favorite disease of the twentieth century.
—William Lyon Phelps

Too many people are thinking of security instead of opportunity. They are more afraid of life than death.
—James F. Byrnes

Fear of life in one form or another is the great thing to exorcise.
—William James

If we let things terrify us, life will not be worth living.
—Marcus Annaeus Seneca

A good life fears not life, nor death.
—Thomas Fuller

He who fears death cannot enjoy life.   —Spanish proverb

Healthy children will not fear life if their elders have integrity enough not to fear death.

—Erik H. Erikson

To live your life in the fear of losing it is to lose the point of life.

—Malcolm Forbes

It is not death we fear, but the thought of it.

—Marcus Annaeus Seneca

Fear of death is worse than dying.

—J.C.F. von Schiller

It is not death or pain that is to be dreaded, but the fear of pain or death.

—Epictetus

Death is not the enemy, living in constant fear of it is.

—Norman Cousins

WE MUST GO ON DESPITE OUR FEAR

We must act in spite of fear ... not because of it.

—Anon.

I have accepted fear as a part of life—specifically the fear of change.... I have gone ahead despite the pounding in the heart that says: turn back....

—Erica Jong

Go forth to meet the shadowy Future without fear and with a manly heart.

—Henry Wadsworth Longfellow

The fishermen know that the sea is dangerous and the storm terrible, but they have never found these dangers sufficient reason for remaining ashore.

—Vincent van Gogh

SUCCESS AND HAPPINESS DEPEND ON FACING OUR FEARS DIRECTLY

You gain strength, courage and confidence by every experience in which you really stop to look fear in the face.... You must do the thing you think you cannot do.

—Eleanor Roosevelt

I believe that anyone can conquer fear by doing the things he fears to do, provided he keeps doing them until he gets a record of successful experiences behind him.

—Eleanor Roosevelt

When in fear, it is safest to force the attack.

—Marcus Annaeus Seneca

The way to develop self-confidence is to do the thing you fear, and get a record of successful experiences behind you.

—William Jennings Bryan

He that fleeth from the fear shall fall into the pit.

—Jeremiah

To live with fear and not be afraid is the final test of maturity.

—Edward Weeks

Constant exposure to dangers will breed contempt for them.

—Marcus Annaeus Seneca

To do anything in this world worth doing, we must not stand back shivering and thinking of the cold and danger, but jump in and scramble through as well as we can.

—Sydney Smith

Do the thing you fear, and the death of fear is certain.

—Ralph Waldo Emerson

You cannot run away from a weakness. You must sometimes fight it out or perish; and if that be so, why not now, and where you stand?
—Robert Louis Stevenson

Often I have found that the one thing that can save is the thing which appears most to threaten ... one has to go down into what one most fears and in that process ... comes a saving flicker of light and energy that, even if it does not produce the courage of a hero, at any rate enables a trembling mortal to take one step further.
—Laurens Van Der Post

I was afraid to write *Fear of Flying;* ergo, I had to write it. I have lived my life according to this principle: If I'm afraid of it, then I must do it.
—Erica Jong

One ought never to turn one's back on a threatened danger and try to run away from it. If you do that, you will double the danger. But if you meet it promptly and without flinching, you will reduce the danger by half. Never run away from anything. Never!
—Sir Winston Churchill

I wanted to be scared again ... I wanted to feel unsure again. That's the only way I learn, the only way I feel challenged.
—Connie Chung

Being "brave" means doing or facing something frightening ... Being "fearless" means being without fear.
—Penelope Leach

From a distance it is something, and nearby it is nothing.
—Jean de La Fontaine

What you are afraid to do is a clear indicator of the next thing you need to do.
—Anon.

He that is afraid to shake the dice will never throw a six.
—Chinese proverb

ACTION IS A GREAT ANTIDOTE TO FEAR

The most drastic, and usually the most effective, remedy for fear is direct action.
—William Burnham

To be busy with material affairs is the best preservative against reflection, fears, doubts.... I suppose a fellow proposing to cut his throat would experience a sort of relief while occupied in stropping his razor carefully.
—Joseph Conrad

Many of our fears are tissuepaper-thin, and a single courageous step would carry us clear through them.
—Brendan Francis

The habit of doing one's duty drives away fear.
—Charles Baudelaire

Become so wrapped up in something that you forget to be afraid.
—Lady Bird Johnson

Things done well and with care exempt themselves from fear.
—William Shakespeare

One had to take some action against fear when once it laid hold of one.
—Rainer Maria Rilke

Too busy with the crowded hour to fear to live or die.
—Ralph Waldo Emerson

When thinking won't cure fear,
action will.   —W. Clement Stone

A life of action and danger moderates the dread of death. It not only gives us fortitude to bear pain, but teaches us at every step the precarious tenure on which we hold our present being.   —William Hazlitt

If you want to conquer fear, don't sit at home and think about it. Go out and get busy.   —Dale Carnegie

MOST FEARS ARE USELESS

Half our fears are baseless, the other half discreditable.
        —Christian Bovee

We poison our lives with fear of burglary and shipwreck and ... the house is never burgled, and the ship never goes down.   —Jean Anouilh

To relinquish a present good through apprehension of a future evil is in most instances unwise ... from a fear which may afterwards turn out groundless, you lost the good that lay within your grasp.
        —Francesco Guicciardini

Envy and fear are the only passions to which no pleasure is attached.
        —John Churton Collins

There is often less danger in the things we fear than in the things we desire.   —John Churton Collins

Needless fear and panic over disease or misfortune that seldom materialize are simply bad habits. By proper ventilation and illumination of the mind it is possible to cultivate tolerance, poise and real courage.
        —Elie Metchnikoff

There are very few monsters who warrant the fear we have of them.
        —André Gide

THE COMPETITION IS AFRAID, TOO

General Grant had a simple, childlike recipe for meeting life ... "I am terribly afraid, but the other fellow is afraid, too."   —Sherwood Anderson

Above all things, never be afraid. The enemy who forces you to retreat is himself afraid of you at that very moment.   —André Maurois

Every great batter works on the theory that the pitcher is more afraid of him than he is of the pitcher.
        —Ty Cobb

The superpowers often behave like two heavily armed blind men feeling their way around a room, each believing himself in mortal peril from the other, whom he assumes to have perfect vision.
        —Henry Kissinger

If you knew how cowardly your enemy is, you would slap him. Bravery is knowledge of the cowardice in the enemy.
        —Edgar Watson Howe

FAITH IS ESSENTIAL TO OVERCOMING FEAR

Fear is faithlessness.
        —George MacDonald

There is much in the world to make us afraid. There is much more in our faith to make us unafraid.
        —Frederick W. Cropp

Deep faith eliminates fear.
        —Lech Walesa

Fear knocked at the door. Faith answered. And lo, no one was there.
—Anon.

A perfect faith would lift us absolutely above fear.
—George MacDonald

If fear is cultivated it will become stronger. If faith is cultivated it will achieve the mastery ... faith is the stronger emotion because it is positive, whereas fear is negative.
—John Paul Jones

Fear imprisons, faith liberates; fear paralyzes, faith empowers; fear disheartens, faith encourages; fear sickens, faith heals; fear makes useless, faith makes serviceable.
—Harry Emerson Fosdick

Fear is faith that it won't work out.
—Sister Mary Tricky

Fear is the absence of faith.
—Paul Tillich

Faith in yourself and faith in God are the key to mastery of fear.
—Harold Sherman

God is our refuge and strength, a very present help in trouble. Therefore we will not fear.
—Ps. 36:1–2

I will not fear, for you are ever with me, and you will never leave me to face my perils alone.
—Thomas Merton

OTHER WAYS TO OVERCOME FEAR

If you wish to fear nothing, consider that everything is to be feared.
—Marcus Annaeus Seneca

How does one kill fear?... How do you shoot a specter through the heart, slash off its spectral head, take it by its spectral throat?
—Joseph Conrad

Perhaps the most important thing we can undertake toward the reduction of fear is to make it easier for people to accept themselves; to like themselves.
—Bonaro Overstreet

We will not be driven by fear ... if we remember that we are not descended from fearful men.
—Edward R. Murrow

When we are afraid we ought not to occupy ourselves with endeavoring to prove that there is no danger, but in strengthening ourselves to go on in spite of the danger.
—Mark Rutherford

Every time I start a picture ... I feel the same fear, the same self-doubts ... and I have only one source on which I can draw, because it comes from within me.
—Federico Fellini

Fear is met and destroyed with courage.
—James F. Bell

A cheerful frame of mind, reinforced by relaxation, which in itself banishes fatigue, is the medicine that puts all ghosts of fear on the run.
—George Matthew Adams

To hell with pleasure that's haunted by fear!
—Jean de La Fontaine

What I emphasize is for people to make choices based not on fear, but on what really gives them a sense of fulfillment.
—Pauline Rose Chance

I steer my bark with hope in my heart, leaving fear astern.
—Thomas Jefferson

Why should a man fear, since chance is all in all for him, and he can clearly fore-know nothing? Best to live lightly as one can, unthinking.
—Sophocles

I sought the Lord, and He heard me, and delivered me from all my fears.
—Ps. 34:4

Any device whatever by which one frees himself from fear is a natural good.
—Epicurus

Joking about death—or anything else that oppresses us—makes it less frightening.
—Allen Klein

Humor acts to relieve fear.
—Dr. William F. Fry, Jr.

GOOD THINGS TO BE GAINED FROM FEAR

Fear is a kind of bell, or gong, which rings the mind into quick life and avoidance upon the approach of danger. It is the soul's signal for rallying.
—Henry Ward Beecher

Fear is the single strongest motivating force in our lives ... The more frightened you become, the better your chances of achieving success.
—Lois Korey

We only really face up to ourselves when we are afraid.
—Thomas Bernhard

If you're never scared or embarrassed or hurt, it means you never take any chances.
—Julia Sorel

Fear makes us feel our humanity.
—Benjamin Disraeli

A coward's fear can make a coward valiant.
—Thomas Fuller

Fear drives you and makes you better.
—Donna E. Shalala

Fear is an instructor of great sagacity, and the herald of all revolutions.
—Ralph Waldo Emerson

Just as courage imperils life, fear protects it.
—Leonardo da Vinci

There are times when fear is good. It must keep its watchful place at the heart's controls.
—Aeschylus

A danger foreseen is half avoided.
—Thomas Fuller

A good scare is worth more to a man than good advice.
—Edgar Watson Howe

Fear is a fine spur.
—Irish proverb

Men who fear God face life fearlessly. Men who do not fear God end up fearing everything.
—Richard Halverson

It is only the fear of God that can deliver us from the fear of men.
—John Witherspoon

Being scared can keep a man from getting killed, and often makes a better fighter of him.
—Louis L'Amour

Nerves provide me with energy.... It's when I don't have them, when I feel at ease, that I get worried.
—Mike Nichols

Fear is an emotion indispensable for survival. —Hannah Arendt

Fear gives sudden instincts of skill.
—Samuel Taylor Coleridge

I quit being afraid when my first venture failed and the sky didn't fall down. —Allen H. Neuharth

Fear of losing is what makes competitors so great. Show me a gracious loser and I'll show you a permanent loser. —O.J. Simpson

Fear is the father of courage and the mother of safety.
—Henry H. Tweedy

OTHER DEFINITIONS OF FEAR

Fear is the needle that pierces us, that it may carry a thread to bind us to heaven. —James Hastings

Fear is the thought of admitted inferiority. —Elbert Hubbard

Fear is nature's warning signal to get busy. —Henry Link

Fear is an uneasiness of the mind, upon the thought of a future evil likely to befall us. —John Locke

Fear is a cloak which old men huddle about their love, as if to keep it warm. —William Wordsworth

Fear is the tax that conscience pays to guilt. —Anon.

Fear is pain arising from the anticipation of evil. —Aristotle

Fear is the soul's signal for rallying.
—Henry Ward Beecher

Fear is an instructor of great sagacity, and the herald of all revolutions.
—Ralph Waldo Emerson

Fear is static that prevents me from hearing myself. —Samuel Butler

FEAR: False Evidence Appearing Real. —Anon.

Fear is the main source of superstition, and one of the main sources of cruelty. —Bertrand A. Russell

Fear is a slinking cat I find beneath the lilacs of my mind.
—Sophie Tunnell

Fear is the start of wisdom.
—Miguel de Unamuno

Fear is the lengthened shadow of ignorance. —Arnold Glasow

Fear is the highest fence.
—Dudley Nichols

Fear is uncertainty. —Eric Hoffer

Fear is sand in the machinery of life.
—E. Stanley Jones

Fear is the dark room in which negatives are developed. —Anon.

GENERAL QUOTATIONS
ABOUT FEAR

Nothing is more despicable than respect based on fear.
—Albert Camus

Fear betrays unworthy souls.
—Virgil

Fear could never make a virtue.
—Voltaire

Considering how dangerous everything is, nothing is really very frightening. —Gertrude Stein

Were the diver to think on the jaws
of the shark, he would never lay
hands on the precious pearl.
—Sa'Di

Fear is stronger than arms.
—Aeschylus

Fear is sharp-sighted, and can see
things under ground, and much
more in the skies.
—Miguel de Cervantes

It is better to have a right destroyed
than to abandon it because of fear.
—Phillip Mann

Better a fearful end than fear without end. —Anon.

A great philosophy is not a philosophy without reproach; it is philosophy without fear. —Charles Peguy

There is a time to take counsel of
your fears, and there is a time to
never listen to any fear.
—General George S. Patton

I, a stranger and afraid, in a world I
never made. —A.E. Housman

While we wait in silence for that
final luxury of fearlessness, the
weight of that silence will choke us.
—Audre Lorde

All we are asked to bear we can
bear. That is a law of the spiritual
life. The only hindrance to the working of this law, as of all benign laws,
is fear. —Elizabeth Goudge

"But" is a fence over which few leap.
—German proverb

There are always two voices sounding in our ears—the voice of fear and
the voice of confidence. One is the
clamor of the senses, the other is the
whispering of the higher self.
—Charles B. Newcomb

Fear nothing, for every renewed
effort raises all former failures into
lessons, all sins into experience.
—Katherine Tingley

Better hazard once than always be in
fear. —Thomas Fuller

Pitching is the art of instilling fear by
making a man flinch.
—Sandy Koufax

Fear has a large shadow, but he himself is small. —J. Ruth Gendler

Stripped of all their masquerades,
the fears of men are quite identical:
the fear of loneliness, rejection, inferiority, unmanageable anger, illness
and death. —Joshua Loth Liebman

What is there to be afraid of? The
worst thing that can happen is you
fail. So what? I failed at a lot of
things. My first record was horrible.
—John Mellencamp

There is no hope unmingled with
fear, and no fear unmingled with
hope. —Baruch Spinoza

Leaders are visionaries with a poorly
developed sense of fear and no concept of the odds against them. They
make the impossible happen.
—Dr. Robert Jarvik

Those who love to be feared, fear to be loved. Some fear them, but they fear everyone.　—Jean Pierre Camus

Keep your fears to yourself, but share your courage with others.
　　　　　—Robert Louis Stevenson

There is a courageous wisdom; there is also a false reptile prudence, the result, not of caution, but of fear.
　　　　　—Edmund Burke

The man who fears nothing is as powerful as he who is feared by everybody.　　—J.C.F. von Schiller

To conquer fear is the beginning of wisdom.　　—Bertrand Russell

Who is more foolish, the child afraid of the dark, or the man afraid of the light?　　—Maurice Freehill

The one permanent emotion of the inferior man is fear—fear of the unknown, the complex, the inexplicable. What he wants beyond everything else is safety.　—H.L. Mencken

Fear is only an illusion. It is the illusion that creates the feeling of separateness—the false sense of isolation that exists only in your imagination.
　　　　　—Jeraldine Saunders

A fool without fear is sometimes wiser than an angel with fear.
　　　　　—Nancy Astor

Fear can be headier than whiskey, once man has acquired a taste for it.
　　　　　—Donald Dowes

The first and great commandment is, don't let them scare you.
　　　　　—Elmer Davis

WORRY

SOME NEGATIVE, HARMFUL EFFECTS OF WORRY

Worry affects the circulation, the heart, the glands, the whole nervous system, and profoundly affects the health. You have never known a man who died from overwork, but many who died from doubt.
—Charles W. Mayo, M.D.

Worry is a god, invisible but omnipotent. It steals the bloom from the cheek and lightness from the pulse; it takes away the appetite, and turns the hair gray.
—Benjamin Disraeli

Worry often gives a small thing a big shadow. —Swedish proverb

If your eyes are blinded with your worries, you cannot see the beauty of the sunset. —Krishnamurti

If you worry about what might be, and wonder what might have been, you will ignore what is. —Anon.

Bacteria and other microorganisms find it easier to infect people who worry and fret. —Leo Rangell

WORRY IS USELESS AND WASTEFUL

Worry is a funky luxury when a lot has to be done. —Melvin Peebles

There is nothing so wretched or foolish as to anticipate misfortunes. What madness is it in expecting evil before it arrives?
—Marcus Annaeus Seneca

Worry is evidence of an ill-controlled brain; it is merely a stupid waste of time in unpleasantness.
—Arnold Bennett

When speculation has done its worst, two and two still make four.
—Samuel Johnson

Anxiety never yet successfully bridged any chasm. —Ruffini

Anxiety is the poison of human life, the parent of many sins and of more miseries.... Can it alter the cause, or unravel the mystery of human events? —Paxton Blair

It only seems as if you are doing something when you're worrying.
—Lucy Maud Montgomery

A hundredload of worry will not pay an ounce of debt.   —George Herbert

Worry is a futile thing, it's somewhat like a rocking chair,
Although is keeps you occupied, it doesn't get you anywhere.
—Anon.

Worry never climbed a hill, worry never paid a bill,
Worry never dried a tear, worry never calmed a fear,
Worry never darned a heel, worry never cooked a meal,
It never led a horse to water, nor ever did a thing it "oughter."
—Anon.

I am reminded of the advice of my neighbor. "Never worry about your heart 'til it stops beating."
—E.B. White

Worry is as useless as a handle on a snowball.   —Mitzi Chandler

When you worry, you go over the same ground endlessly and come out the same place you started. Thinking, on the other hand, makes progress from one place to another.... The problem of life is to change worry into thinking, and anxiety into creative action.
—Harold B. Walker

Which of you by being anxious can add one cubit unto his stature?
—Mt. 6:27

I think these difficult times have helped me to understand better than before how infinitely rich and beautiful life is in every way, and that so many things that one goes around worrying about are of no importance whatsoever.   —Isak Dinesen

You always get negative reactions. If you worry about that, you would never do anything.
—Tom Monaghan

WORRY AND TOMORROW

Cast away care; he that loves sorrow lengthens not a day, nor can he buy tomorrow.   —Thomas Dekker

Worry doesn't help tomorrow's troubles, but it does ruin today's happiness.   —Anon.

There are two days in the week about which and upon which I never worry.... One of these days is Yesterday ... And the other day I do not worry about is Tomorrow.
—Robert Jones Burdette

Worry never robs tomorrow of its sorrow, but only saps today of its strength.   —A.J. Cronin

Be, therefore, not anxious about tomorrow; for tomorrow will be anxious for the things of itself.
—Mt. 6:34

WORRY AND WORK

Never despair, but if you do, work on in despair.   —Edmund Burke

If you are doing your best, you will not have time to worry about failure.
—Robert Hillyer

It is not work that kills men, it is worry. Work is healthy; you can hardly put more upon a man that he can bear. Worry is rust upon the blade.   —Henry Ward Hughes

No good work is ever done while the heart is hot and anxious and fretted.
—Olive Schreiner

A day of worry is more exhausting than a day of work. —John Lubbock

The reason why worry kills more people than work is that more people worry than work. —Robert Frost

WORRY AND FEAR

Worry is a form of fear.
—Bertrand A. Russell

Worry is a complete cycle of inefficient thought revolving about a pivotal fear. —Anon.

Worry is a state of mind based on fear. —Napoleon Hill

Worry is a thin stream of fear trickling through the mind. If encouraged, it cuts a channel into which all other thoughts are drained.
—Arthur Somers Roche

BASIC WAYS TO EASE YOUR WORRIES

If we would keep filling our minds with the picture of happy things ahead, many worries and anxieties, and perhaps ill health, would naturally melt away.... Always expect the best. Then if you have to hurdle a few tough problems, you will have generated the strength and courage to do so. —George Matthew Adams

Turn resolutely to work, to recreation, or in any case to physical exercise till you are so tired you can't help going to sleep, and when you wake up you won't want to worry. —B.C. Forbes

A great many worries can be diminished by realizing the unimportance of the matter which is causing anxiety. —Bernard Russell

A problem not worth praying about is not worth worrying about.
—Anon.

We can always get along better by reason and love of truth than by worry of conscience and remorse. Harmful are these, and evil.
—Baruch Spinoza

As a cure for worrying, work is better than whiskey.
—Thomas A. Edison

Every morning I spend fifteen minutes filling my mind full of God, and so there's no room left for worry thoughts.
—Howard Chandler Christy

Worry compounds the futility of being trapped on a dead-end street. Thinking opens new avenues.
—Cullen Hightower

Rule No. 1 is, don't sweat the small stuff. Rule No. 2 is, it's all small stuff. —Robert Eliot

If only the people who worry about their liabilities would think about the riches they do possess, they would stop worrying. Would you sell both your eyes for a million dollars ... or your two legs ... or your hands ... or your hearing? Add up what you do have, and you'll find that you won't sell them for all the gold in the world. The best things in life are yours, if you can appreciate yourself. —Dale Carnegie

Accept the Worst That Can Happen

You'll break the worry habit the day you decide you can meet and master the worse that can happen to you.
—Arnold Glasow

Peace of mind is that mental condition in which you have accepted the worst.
—Lin Yutang

The worst is not so long as we can say, "This is the worst."
—William Shakespeare

What is there to be afraid of? The worst thing that can happen is you fail. So what? I failed at a lot of things. My first record was horrible.
—John Mellencamp

When you first learn to love hell, you will be in heaven.
—Thaddeus Golas

Accept that all of us can be hurt, that all of us can—and surely will at times—fail. Other vulnerabilities, like being embarrassed or risking love, can be terrifying, too. I think we should follow a simple rule: if we can take the worst, take the risk.
—Dr. Joyce Brothers

A wise man fights to win, but he is twice a fool who has no plan for possible defeat.   —Louis L'Amour

Most Things We Worry about Never Happen

There are people who are always anticipating trouble, and in this way they manage to enjoy many sorrows that never really happen.
—Josh Billings

Our worst misfortunes never happen, and most miseries lie in anticipation.   —Honore de Balzac

Some men storm imaginary Alps all their lives, and die in the foothills cursing difficulties which do not exist.   —Edgar Watson Howe

How much pain they have cost us, the evils which have never happened.
—Thomas Jefferson

The misfortunes hardest to bear are those which never happen.
—James Russell Lowell

What torments of grief you endured, from evils that never arrived.
—Ralph Waldo Emerson

We poison our lives with fear of burglary and shipwreck, and the house is never burgled, and the ship never goes down.   —Jean Anouilh

Do we not all spend the greater part of our lives under the shadow of an event that has not yet come to pass?
—Maurice Maeterlinck

This was a great year for preventive worrying. Seldom in recent history have so many people worried about so many things that didn't happen in the end.   —James Reston

Worry is a morbid anticipation of events which never happen.
—Russell Green

I remember the story of the old man who said on his deathbed that he had had a lot of trouble in his life, most of which never happened.
—Sir Winston Churchill

Needless fear and panic over disease or misfortune that seldom materialize are simply bad habits. By proper ventilation and illumination of the mind it is possible to cultivate tolerance, poise and real courage.
—Elie Metchnikoff

Some of your hurts you have cured,
And the sharpest you still have survived,
But what torments of grief you endured
From the evil which never arrived.
—Ralph Waldo Emerson

I am an old man and have known a great many troubles, but most of them never happened.
—Mark Twain

My life has been full of terrible misfortunes, most of which never happened.
—Michel de Montaigne

Though life is made up of mere bubbles
'Tis better than many have,
For while we've a whole lot of troubles
The most of them never occur.
—Nixon Waterman

If you see ten troubles coming down the road, you can be sure that nine will run into the ditch before they reach you.
—Calvin Coolidge

The crisis you have to worry about most is the one you don't see coming.
—Mike Mansfield

OTHER DEFINITIONS OF WORRY

Anxiety is the great modern plague. But faith can cure it.
—Smiley Blanton, M.D.

Worry is the sin we're not afraid to commit.
—Anon.

Worry is the only insupportable misfortune of life.
—Henry Saint John

Worry is the cross which we make for ourselves by overanxiety.
—Francois de Fenelon

Worry is interest paid on trouble before it comes due.
—William Ralph Inge

GENERAL QUOTATIONS ABOUT WORRY

That man is blest
Who does his best
And leaves the rest,
Then—do not worry.
—Charles F. Deems

Happy the man who has broken the chains which hurt the mind, and has given up worrying, once and for all.
—Ovid

It is the little things that fret and worry us; you can dodge an elephant, but not a fly.
—Josh Billings

To be rich is not the end, but only a change, of worries.
—Epicurus

Don't hurry, don't worry. You're only here for a short visit. So be sure to stop and smell the flowers.
—Walter Hagen

Every faculty and virtue I possess can be used as an instrument with which to worry myself.
—Mark Rutherford

What worries you, masters you.
—Haddon W. Robinson

Worry is most apt to ride you ragged not when you are in action, but when the day's work is done. Your imagination can run riot then ... your mind is like a motor operating without its load.

—James L. Muresell

"Worry" is a word that I don't allow myself to use.

—Dwight D. Eisenhower

Real difficulties can be overcome, it is only the imaginary ones that are unconquerable.   —Theodore N. Vail

Doubts and Uncertainties

Uncertainty Is Part of Life

Unrest and uncertainty are our lot.
—Johann von Goethe

If we insist on being as sure as is conceivable ... we must be content to creep along the ground, and can never soar.
—John Henry Cardinal Newman

Our lives are never certain, even for an hour. —Ferrant Sanchez Calavera

Throughout this life, you can never be certain of living long enough to take another breath. —Huang Po

The longing for certainty ... is in every human mind. But certainty is generally illusion.
—Oliver Wendell Holmes

No great deed is done by falterers who ask for certainty.
—George Eliot

Every year, if not every day, we have to wager our salvation upon some prophecy based upon imperfect knowledge.
—Oliver Wendell Holmes, Jr.

All business proceeds on beliefs, or judgment of probabilities, and not on certainties. —Charles W. Eliot

The man who insists upon seeing with perfect clearness before he decides, never decides.
—Henri Frederic Amiel

There is nothing certain in a man's life but that he must lose it.
—Owen Meredith

Ah, what a dusty answer gets the soul when hot for certainties in this, our life! —George Meredith

When I was young I was sure of everything; in a few years, having been mistaken a thousand times, I was not half so sure of most things as I was before; at present, I am hardly sure of anything but what God has revealed. —John Wesley

We can be absolutely certain only about things we do not understand.
—Eric Hoffer

You are all you will ever have for certain. —June Havoc

Certitude is not the test of certainty. We have been cock-sure of many things that were not so.
—Oliver Wendell Holmes, Jr.

A reasonable probability is the only certainty.　—Edgar Watson Howe

Doubt is not a pleasant state, but certainty is a ridiculous one.
—Voltaire

Being unready and ill-equipped is what you have to expect in life. It is the universal predicament. It is your lot as a human being to lack what it takes. Circumstances are seldom right. You never have the capacities, the strength, the wisdom, the virtue you ought to have. You must always do with less than you need in a situation vastly different from what you would have chosen.
—Charlton Ogburn, Jr.

To be absolutely certain about something, one must know everything, or nothing, about it.　—Olin Miller

Free man is by necessity insecure, thinking man by necessity uncertain.
—Erich Fromm

We are not certain, we are never certain.　—Albert Camus

We sail within a vast sphere, ever drifting in uncertainty, driven from end to end.　—Blaise Pascal

Something must be left to chance; nothing is sure in a sea fight.
—Horatio Nelson

There is nothing certain about war except that one side won't win.
—Sir Ian Hamilton

UNCERTAINTY IS THE ONLY CERTAINTY

There is only one thing about which I am certain, and this is that there is very little about which one can be certain.　—W. Somerset Maugham

The only certainty is that nothing is certain.　—Pliny, the Elder

There is one thing certain, namely, that we can have nothing certain; therefore it is not certain that we can have nothing certain.
—Samuel Butler

Every area of trouble gives out a ray of hope, and the one unchangeable certainty is that nothing is certain or unchangeable.　—John F. Kennedy

NEEDING CERTAINTY CAN BE COWARDICE

Any coward can fight a battle when he's sure of winning.
—George Eliot

The demand is for certainty is a sign of weakness.　—Mark Rutherford

The unknown is what it is. And to be frightened of it is what sends everybody scurrying around chasing dreams, illusions, wars, peace, love, hate, all that.... Accept that it's unknown, and it's plain sailing.
—John Lennon

Only a weak mind seeks ultimate answers.　—Agnes Thornton

DEMANDING CERTAINTY CAN BE PARALYZING

He who forecasts all perils will never sail the sea.　—Anon.

There is a time for departure, even when there's no certain place to go.
—Tennessee Williams

One doesn't discover new lands without consenting to lose sight of shore for a very long time.
—André Gide

To teach how to live with uncertainty, yet without being paralyzed by hesitation, is perhaps the chief thing that philosophy can do.
—Bertrand Russell

Faith ... acts promptly and boldly on the occasion, on slender evidence.
—John Henry Cardinal Newman

If we wait until we've satisfied all the uncertainties, it may be too late.
—Lee Iacocca

The successful man is he who, when he sees that no further certainty is attainable, promptly decides on the most probable side, as if he were completely sure it was right.
—Mark Rutherford

WE SHOULDN'T WORRY IF WE CAN'T SEE THE FINAL RESULT

There is no advancement to him who stands trembling because he cannot see the end from the beginning.
—E.J. Klemme

To end with certainty, we must begin with doubting. —Stanislaus

In the face of uncertainty, there is nothing wrong with hope.
—Bernie S. Siegel, M.D.

Maturity of mind is the capacity to endure uncertainty. —John H. Finley

If a man will begin with certainties, he shall end in doubts, but if he will content to begin with doubts, he shall end in certainties.
—Francis Bacon

UNCERTAINTY AND THE FUTURE

Nobody can really guarantee the future. The best we can do is size up the chances, calculate the risks involved, estimate our ability to deal with them and make our plans with confidence. —Henry Ford II

The future is no more uncertain than the present. —Walt Whitman

Many live in dread of what is coming. Why should we? The unknown puts adventure into life.... The unexpected around the corner gives a sense of anticipation and surprise. Thank God for the unknown future.
—E. Stanley Jones

WE CAN'T BE INTIMIDATED BY DOUBTS

Action will remove the doubts that theory cannot solve. —Tehyi Hsieh

Soon after a heart-wrung decision, something inevitably occurs to cast doubt on your choice. Holding steady against that doubt usually proves your decision.
—R.I. Fitzhenry

Doubt breeds doubt.
—Franz Grillparzer

In doubt, fear is the worst of prophets. —Statius

Doubt is a pain too lonely to know that faith is his twin brother.
—Kahlil Gibran

When in doubt, do it.
—Oliver Wendell Holmes, Jr.

Doubts and mistrust are the mere panic of timid imagination, which the steadfast heart will conquer, and the large mind transcend.
—Helen Keller

Doubt indulged soon becomes doubt realized.   —Francis Ridley Havergal

When one devotes oneself to meditation, mental burdens, unnecessary worries, and wandering thoughts drop off one by one; life seems to run smoothly and pleasantly. A student may now depend on intuition to make decisions. As one acts on intuition, second thought, with its dualism, doubt and hesitation, does not arise.   —Nyogen Senzaki

The only limit to our realization of tomorrow will be our doubts of today. Let us move forward with strong and active faith.
—Franklin Delano Roosevelt

In case of doubt, decide in favor of what is correct.   —Karl Kraus

Faith and doubt both are needed, not as antagonists, but working side by side to take us around the unknown curve.   —Lillian Smith

Our doubts are traitors, and make us lose the good we often might win, by fearing to attempt.
—William Shakespeare

A man's doubts and fears are his worst enemies.
—William Wrigley, Jr.

WE MUSTN'T DOUBT OURSELVES

A person who doubts himself is like a man who would enlist in the ranks of his enemies and bear arms against himself.   —Alexandre Dumas

To be ambitious for wealth, and yet always expecting to be poor; to be always doubting your ability to get what you long for, is like trying to reach east by traveling west. There is no philosophy which will help a man to succeed when he is always doubting his ability to do so, and thus attracting failure. No matter how hard you work for success, if your thought is saturated with the fear of failure, it will kill your efforts, neutralize your endeavors and make success impossible. —Charles Baudouin

Doubt whom you will, but never yourself.   —Christian Bovee

Self distrust is the cause of most of our failures. In the assurance of strength, there is strength, and they are the weakest, however strong, who have no faith in themselves or their own powers. —Christian Bovee

FOCUS ON THE POSITIVE ASPECTS OF UNCERTAINTY

Uncertainty and expectation are the joys of life. Security is an insipid thing.   —William Congreve

When nothing is sure, everything is possible.   —Margaret Drabble

Uncertainty and mystery are energies of life. Don't let them scare you unduly, for they keep boredom at bay and spark creativity.
—R.I. Fitzhenry

The quest for certainty blocks the search for meaning. Uncertainty is the very condition to impel man to unfold his powers.   —Erich Fromm

All uncertainly is fruitful ... so long as it is accompanied by the wish to understand.   —Antonio Machado

I'm delighted that the future is unsure. That's the way it should be.
—William Sloane Coffin

When we are not sure, we are alive.
—Graham Greene

Freedom is nothing else but a chance to be better, whereas enslavement is a certainty of the worst.
—Albert Camus

The only thing that makes life possible is permanent, intolerable uncertainty, not knowing what comes next.   —Ursula K. LeGuin

In the face of uncertainty, there is nothing wrong with hope.
—Bernie S. Siegel, M.D.

SECURITY

SECURITY DOESN'T EXIST

Security is mostly superstition. It does not exist in nature.... Avoiding danger is no safer in the long run than outright exposure. The fearful are caught as often as the bold.
—Helen Keller

Security is a false god; begin making sacrifices to it and you are lost.
—Paul Bowles

God Himself is not secure, having given man dominion over His works.
—Helen Keller

The man who looks for security, even in the mind, is like a man who would chop off his limbs in order to have artificial ones which will give him no pain or trouble.
—Henry Miller

If you want total security, go to prison. There you're fed, clothed, given medical care and so on. The only thing lacking ... is freedom.
—Dwight D. Eisenhower

Happiness, greatness, pride—nothing is secure, nothing keeps.
—Euripides

There is no security on this earth. Only opportunity.
—General Douglas MacArthur

SAFETY ISN'T SECURITY

It is the risk element which ensures security. Risk brings out the ingenuity and resourcefulness which insure success.
—Robert Rawls

The way to be safe is never to be secure.
—Benjamin Franklin

We are never more in danger than when we think ourselves most secure, nor in reality more secure than when we seem to be most in danger.
—William Cowper

It is when we all play safe that we create a world of utmost insecurity.
—Dag Hammarskjold

To keep oneself safe does not mean to bury oneself.
—Marcus Annaeus Seneca

"Safety first" has been the motto of the human race for half a million years; but it has never been the motto of leaders.
—Anon.

Security and Money

If money is your hope for independence you will never have it. The only real security that a man can have in this world is a reserve of knowledge, experience and ability.
—Henry Ford

Our greatest illusion is reliance upon the security and permanence of material possessions. We must search for some other coin.
—John Cudahy

Solvency is entirely a matter of temperament, not of income.
—Logan Pearsall Smith

Security depends not so much upon how much you have, as upon how much you can do without.
—Joseph Wood Krutch

Other Sources of Security

Security can only be achieved through constant change, through discarding old ideas that have outlived their usefulness and adapting others to current facts.
—William O. Douglas

The only peace, the only security, is in fulfillment.
—Henry Miller

Only in growth, reform, and change, paradoxically enough, is true security to be found.
—Anne Morrow Lindbergh

Security is not the absence of danger, but the presence of God, no matter what the danger.
—Anon.

I'm in love with the potential of miracles. For me, the safest place is out on a limb.
—Shirley MacLaine

We Are Our Own Security

Man's security comes from within himself.
—Manly Hall

You are all you will ever have for certain.
—June Havoc

Your real security is yourself. You know you can do it, and they can't ever take that away from you.
—Mae West

Only those means of security are good, are certain, are lasting, that depend on yourself and your own vigor.
—Niccolo Machiavelli

No one can build her security upon the nobleness of another person.
—Willa Cather

Lack of Security Can Be a Positive Force

Uncertainty and expectation are the joys of life. Security is an insipid thing.
—William Congreve

To be on the alert is to live; to be lulled into security is to die.
—Oscar Wilde

Prudence keeps life safe, but does not often make it happy.
—Samuel Johnson

Whatever course you have chosen for yourself, it will not be a chore but an adventure if you bring to it a sense of the glory of striving ... if your sights are set far above the merely secure and mediocre.
—David Sarnoff

Security is a kind of death.
—Tennessee Williams

Without danger we cannot get beyond danger.... Each one of us requires the spur of insecurity to force us to do our best.
—Dr. Harold W. Dodds

Nerves provide me with energy.... It's when I don't have them, when I feel at ease, that I get worried.
—Mike Nichols

Protection and security are only valuable if they do not cramp life excessively.   —Carl Jung

GENERAL QUOTATIONS ABOUT SECURITY

Too many people are thinking of security instead of opportunity; they seem more afraid of life than of death.   —James F. Byrnes

The one permanent emotion of the inferior man is fear—fear of the unknown, the complex, the inexplicable. What he wants beyond everything else is safety.   —H.L. Mencken

We spend our time searching for security and hate it when we get it.
—John Steinbeck

Be like the bird that, passing on her flight awhile on boughs too slight, feels them give way beneath her, and yet sings, knowing that she hath wings.   —Victor Hugo

We hear of a silent generation, more concerned with security than integrity, with conforming than performing, with imitating than creating.
—Thomas J. Watson

RISKS

RISKS ARE PART OF LIFE

Life is a risk.
　　　　—Diane Von Furstenberg

You risk just as much in being credulous as in being suspicious.
　　　　—Denis Diderot

Any life truly lived is a risky business, and if one puts up too many fences against the risks one ends by shutting out life itself.
　　　　—Kenneth S. Davis

However well organized the foundations of life may be, life must always be full of risks.　　—Havelock Ellis

Do not be too timid and squeamish.... All life is an experiment. The more experiments you make, the better.　　—Ralph Waldo Emerson

This nation was built by men who took risks—pioneers who were not afraid of the wilderness, business men who were not afraid of failure, scientists who were not afraid of the truth, thinkers who were not afraid of progress, dreamers who were not afraid of action.　—Brooks Atkinson

To be alive at all involves some risk.
　　　　—Harold MacMillan

To laugh is to risk appearing the fool.
To weep is to risk appearing sentimental.
To reach for another is to risk involvement.
To expose your ideas, your dreams, before a crowd, is to risk their loss.
To love is to risk not being loved in return.
To live is to risk dying.
To believe is to risk failure.
But risks must be taken, because the greatest hazard in life is to risk nothing.
The people who risk nothing do nothing, have nothing, are nothing.
They may avoid suffering and sorrow, but they cannot learn, feel, change, grow, love, live.
Chained by their attitudes, they are slaves; they have forfeited their freedom.
Only a person who risks is free.
　　　　—Poem quoted in
　　　　　"Dear Abby"

393

All life is a chance. So take it! The person who goes furthest is the one who is willing to do and dare.
—Dale Carnegie

I postpone death by living, by suffering, by error, by risking, by giving, by losing.　　　　—Anaïs Nin

If you don't take chances, you can't do anything in life. —Michael Spinks

Only those who dare, truly live.
—Ruth P. Freedman

If your life is ever going to get better, you'll have to take risks. There is simply no way you can grow without taking chances.　—David Viscot

You've got to keep fighting—you've got to risk your life every six months to stay alive.　　　—Elia Kazan

It takes courage to lead a life. Any life.　　　　　—Erica Jong

There's no such thing as a sure thing. That's why they call it gambling.
—Neil Simon

It is only by risking ... that we live at all.　　　　—William James

DANGER IS PART OF LIFE

It is the business of the future to be dangerous.
—Alfred North Whitehead

To achieve anything, you must be prepared to dabble on the boundary of disaster.　　—Stirling Moss

He that will not sail till all dangers are over must never put to sea.
—Thomas Fuller

The fishermen know that the sea is dangerous and the storm terrible, but they have never found these dangers sufficient reason for remaining ashore.　　—Vincent van Gogh

If we are intended for great ends, we are called to great hazards.
—John Henry Cardinal Newman

Liberty is always dangerous, but it is the safest thing we have.
—Harry Emerson Fosdick

As soon as there is life, there is danger.　　　—Ralph Waldo Emerson

One never finds anything perfectly pure and ... exempt from danger.
—Niccolo Machiavelli

He that is not in the war is not out of danger.　　　　—Anon.

WE MUST FACE RISKS AND DANGERS DIRECTLY

Danger itself is the best remedy for danger.　　　　—Anon.

Without danger we cannot get beyond danger.　　　—Anon.

Constant exposure to dangers will breed contempt for them.
—Marcus Annaeus Seneca

Avoiding danger is no safer in the long run than outright exposure. The fearful are caught as often as the bold.　　　—Helen Keller

It is not manly to turn one's back on fortune.　—Marcus Annaeus Seneca

Be bold, and mighty forces will come to your aid.　　—Basil King

A leader must face danger. He must take the risk and the blame, and the brunt of the storm.
—Herbert N. Casson

Fortune and love befriend the bold.
—Ovid

Our safety is not in blindness, but in facing our danger.
—J.C.F. von Schiller

Of course people are afraid. But honestly facing that fear, seeing it for what it is, is the only way of putting it to rest. —Harvey Fierstein

Unless you enter the tiger's den, you cannot take the cubs.
—Japanese proverb

All work of man is as the swimmer's: a vast ocean threatens to devour him; if he front it not bravely, it will keep its word. —Thomas Carlyle

They are surely to be esteemed the bravest spirits who, having the clearest sense of both the pains and pleasures of life, do not on that account shrink from danger. —Thucydides

PUTTING RISKS INTO PERSPECTIVE

If one is forever cautious, can one remain a human being?
—Aleksandr Solzhenitsyn

An individual dies ... when, instead of taking risks and hurling himself toward being, he cowers within, and takes refuge there. —E.M. Cioran

Few are they who have never had a chance to achieve happiness—and fewer those who have taken that chance. —André Maurois

You have all eternity to be cautious in when you're dead. —Lois Platford

Without risk, faith is an impossibility. —Søren Kierkegaard

Who dares nothing, need hope for nothing. —J.C.F. von Schiller

If you're never scared or embarrassed or hurt, it means you never take any chances. —Julia Sorel

It is not because things are difficult that we do not dare, it is because we do not dare that they are difficult.
—Marcus Annaeus Seneca

Only those who will risk going too far can possibly find out how far one can go. —T.S. Eliot

In order to find the edge, you must risk going over the edge.
—Dennis Dugan

Make voyages. Attempt them. There's nothing else.
—Tennessee Williams

The faster you go, the more chance there is of stubbing your toe, but the more chance you have of getting somewhere. —Charles F. Kettering

Taking risks gives me energy.
—Jay Chiat

The torment of precautions often exceeds the dangers to be avoided. It is sometimes better to abandon one's self to destiny.
—Napoleon Bonaparte

What is necessary is never a risk.
—Cardinal de Retz

To render ourselves insensible to pain we must forfeit also the possibilities of happiness.
—John Lubbock

Take risks: if you win, you will be happy; if you lose, you will be wise.
—Anon.

WE CAN'T SUCCEED WITHOUT TAKING RISKS

The men who have done big things are those who were not afraid to attempt big things, who were not afraid to risk failure in order to gain success.
—B.C. Forbes

If the risk-reward ratio is right, you can make big money buying trouble.
—Anon.

What isn't tried won't work.
—Claude McDonald

All great reforms require one to dare a lot to win a little.
—William L. O'Neill

If you limit your actions in life to things that nobody can possibly find fault with, you will not do much.
—Charles Lutwidge Dodgson

The ambitious climb high and perilous stairs, and never care how to come down; the desire of rising hath swallowed up their fear of a fall.
—Thomas Adams

He that would have fruit must climb the tree.
—Thomas Fuller

Every noble acquisition is attended with its risks; he who fears to encounter the one must not expect to obtain the other. —Pietro Metastasio

To get profit without risk, experience without danger and reward without work is as impossible as it is to live without being born.
—A.P. Gouthey

The method of the enterprising is to plan with audacity and execute with vigor.
—Christian Bovee

Great deeds are usually wrought at great risks.
—Herodotus

Only those who dare to fail greatly can ever achieve greatly.
—Robert F. Kennedy

He that is overcautious will accomplish little.
—J.C.F. von Schiller

No one reaches a high position without daring.
—Publilius Syrus

Cadillacs are down at the end of the bat.
—Ralph Kiner, when asked why he didn't choke up and hit "for average"

It is impossible to win the great prizes of life without running risks.
—Theodore Roosevelt

You can't expect to hit the jackpot if you don't put a few nickels in the machine.
—Flip Wilson

Who dares nothing, need hope for nothing.
—J.C.F. von Schiller

Progress always involves risks. You can't steal second base and keep your foot on first.
—Frederick B. Wilcox

You can't catch trout with dry breeches.
—Spanish proverb

I don't think about risks much. I just do what I want to do. If you gotta go, you gotta go.
—Miss Lillian Carter

Behold the turtle. He makes progress only when he sticks his neck out.
—James Bryant Conant

Nothing ventured, nothing gained.
—Anon.

Don't be afraid to take a big step if one is indicated. You can't cross a chasm in two small steps.
—David Lloyd George

Take Smart— Not Crazy—Risks

Take calculated risks. That is quite different from being rash.
—General George S. Patton

Courage is rarely reckless or foolish ... courage usually involves a highly realistic estimate of the odds that must be faced.   —Margaret Truman

Valour lies just halfway between rashness and cowardice.
—Miguel de Cervantes

I compensate for big risks by always doing my homework and being well-prepared. I can take on larger risks by reducing the overall risk.
—Donna E. Shalala

Accept that all of us can be hurt, that all of us can—and surely will at times—fail. Other vulnerabilities, like being embarrassed or risking love, can be terrifying, too. I think we should follow a simple rule: if we can take the worst, take the risk.
—Dr. Joyce Brothers

Every man has the right to risk his own life in order to preserve it. Has it ever been said that a man who throws himself out the window to escape a fire is guilty of suicide?
—Jean-Jacques Rousseau

Paradox: Risks Can Provide Safety

It is the risk element which ensures security. Risk brings out the ingenuity and resourcefulness which ensure success.   —Robert Rawls

Entrepreneurs, in accepting risk, achieve security for all. In embracing change, they ensure social and economic stability.   —George Gilder

Those who cling to life die, and those who defy death live.
—Uyesugi Kenshin

And the trouble is, if you don't risk anything, you risk even more.
—Erica Jong

Danger can never by overcome without taking risks.   —Latin proverb

Taking Risks Can Be Sweet

Every minute of life I take a risk; it's part of the enjoyment.
—Otto Preminger

Everything is sweetened by risk.
—Alexander Smith

We may by our excessive prudence squeeze out of the life we are guarding so anxiously all the adventurous quality that makes it worth living.
—Randolph Bourne

Danger and delight grow on one stalk.   —English proverb

Life has no romance without risk.
—Sarah Doherty, the first one-legged
person to scale Mt. McKinley

The moment somebody says "this is very risky" is the moment it becomes attractive to me. —Kate Capshaw

One can never consent to creep when one feels an impulse to soar.
—Helen Keller

Prudence keeps life safe, but does not often make it happy.
—Samuel Johnson

WORTHY VICTORIES

The greater the difficulty, the more glory in surmounting it. —Epicurus

Victories that are cheap are cheap. Those only are worth having which come as the result of hard fighting.
—Henry Ward Beecher

The greater the obstacle, the more glory in overcoming it. —Moliere

The harder the conflict, the more glorious the triumph. What we obtain too cheaply, we esteem too lightly; 'tis dearness only that gives everything its value. —Thomas Paine

The fiery trials through which we pass will light us down in honor or dishonor to the last generation.
—Abraham Lincoln

To conquer without risk is to triumph without glory.
—Pierre Corneille

There could be no honor in a sure success, but much might be wrested from a sure defeat. —T.E. Lawrence
(Lawrence of Arabia)

ABOUT THE RISKS WE DON'T TAKE ...

The follies which a man regrets most in his life are those which he didn't commit when he had the opportunity. —Helen Rowland

There is no memory with less satisfaction than the memory of some temptation we resisted.
—James Branch Cabell

The only things one never regrets are one's mistakes. —Oscar Wilde

The only things you regret are the things you don't do.
—Michael Curtiz

For of all sad words of tongues or pen the saddest are these: It might have been.
—John Greenleaf Whittier

Calculation never made a hero.
—John Henry Cardinal Newman

To play it safe is not to play.
—Robert Altman

Better hazard once than always be in fear. —Thomas Fuller

SOMETIMES WE MUST RISK EVERYTHING

No one would have crossed the ocean if he could have gotten off the ship in the storm.
—Charles F. Kettering

Nine times out of ten the best thing that can happen to a young man is to be tossed overboard and compelled to sink or swim.
—James A. Garfield

Why not go out on a limb? Isn't that where the fruit is?   —Frank Scully

You might as well fall flat on your face as lean over too far backward.
                —James Thurber

Defensive strategy never has produced ultimate victory.
    —General Douglas MacArthur

We fail far more often by timidity than by over-daring.
                —David Grayson

Nothing can resist a will which will stake even existence upon its fulfillment.   —Benjamin Disraeli

He gets a good hold on the paintbrush, then confidently has the ladder removed.   —Roger Vaughan,
            speaking of Ted Turner

No guts, no glory.   —Anon.

The important thing is this: to be able at any moment to sacrifice what we are for what we could *become*.
                —Charles Du Bos

Better that we should die fighting than be outraged and dishonored. Better to die than to live in slavery.
            —Emmeline Pankhurst

The fixed determination to have acquired the warrior soul, to either conquer or perish with honor, is the secret of victory.
        —General George S. Patton

If man is not ready to risk his life, where is his dignity?
                —André Malraux

GENERAL QUOTATIONS
ABOUT RISKS

All serious daring starts from within.
                —Eudora Welty

To avoid an occasion for our virtues is a worse degree of failure than to push forward pluckily and make a fall.   —Robert Louis Stevenson

Risk! Risk anything!... Do the hardest thing on earth for you. Act for yourself. Face the truth.
            —Katherine Mansfield

Living at risk is jumping off the cliff and building your wings on the way down.   —Ray Bradbury

I prefer liberty with danger to peace with slavery.
            —The Palatine of Posnan

Be wary of the man who urges an action in which he himself incurs no risk.   —Joaquin Setanti

Necessity is the mother of taking chances.   —Mark Twain

Something must be left to chance; nothing is sure in a sea fight beyond all others.   —Horatio Nelson

We must dare, and dare again, and go on daring.
            —Georges Jacques Danton

Dare to be naive.
            —R. Buckminster Fuller

COURAGE

COURAGE IS THE FOUNDATION OF ALL OUR VIRTUES

Courage is the first of the human qualities because it is the quality which guarantees all the others.
—Sir Winston Churchill

Without courage, all other virtues lose their meaning.
—Sir Winston Churchill

Success is never found. Failure is never fatal. Courage is the only thing. —Sir Winston Churchill

Courage is the most important of all virtues, because without it we can't practice any other virtue with consistency. —Maya Angelou

Courage is not simply one of the virtues, but the form of every virtue at the testing point. —C.S. Lewis

Courage is the ladder on which all other virtues mount.
—Clare Boothe Luce

Courage is the basic virtue for everyone so long as he continues to grow, to move ahead. —Rollo May

Courage is the greatest of all the virtues. Because if you haven't courage, you may not have an opportunity to use any of the others.
—Samuel Johnson

The courage of life is often a less dramatic spectacle than the courage of a final moment, but it is no less a magnificent mixture of triumph and tragedy. A man does what he must— in spite of personal consequences, in spite of obstacles and dangers and pressures—and that is the basis of all morality. —John F. Kennedy

Nothing but courage can guide life.
—Vauvenargues

Wealth lost—something lost; Honor lost—much lost; Courage lost—all lost. —Old German proverb

BOLDNESS AND BRAVERY ARE VITAL QUALITIES

Why not go out on a limb? Isn't that where the fruit is? —Frank Scully

In difficult situations, when hope seems feeble, the boldest plans are safest. —Livy

Courage is the best slayer—courage which attacketh, for in every attack there is the sound of triumph.
—Friedrich Nietzsche

He who finds Fortune on his side should go briskly ahead, for she is wont to favor the bold.
—Baltasar Gracian

It is better by noble boldness to run the risk of being subject to half of the evils we anticipate than to remain in cowardly listlessness for fear of what might happen.
—Herodotus

A decent boldness ever meets with friends.   —Homer

In times of stress, be bold and valiant.   —Horace

It is the bold man who every time does best, at home or abroad.
—Homer

Attacking is the only secret. Dare and the world always yields; or if it beats you sometimes, dare it again, and it will succumb.
—William Makepeace Thackeray

You don't learn to hold your own in the world by standing on guard, but by attacking, and getting well-hammered yourself.
—George Bernard Shaw

The brave venture anything.
—Anon.

Fortune helps the brave.   —Virgil

Audacity augments courage; hesitation, fear.   —Publilius Syrus

Fortune reveres the brave, and overwhelms the cowardly.
—Marcus Annaeus Seneca

God helps the brave.
—J.C.F. von Schiller

Fortune befriends the bold.
—John Dryden

Fortune and love favor the brave.
—Ovid

Fortune favors the audacious.
—Erasmus

Audacity has made kings.
—Crebillion

Audacity, more audacity, always audacity. —Georges Jacques Danton

With audacity one can undertake anything.   —Napoleon Bonaparte

Bravery and faith bring both material and spiritual rewards.
—Preston Bradley

He who loses wealth loses much; he who loses a friend loses more; but he who loses his courage loses all.
—Miguel de Cervantes

True miracles are created by men when they use the courage and intelligence that God gave them.
—Jean Anouilh

THE COURAGE TO FACE LIFE DIRECTLY

Tender-handed stroke a nettle, and it stings you for your pains;
Grasp it like a man of mettle, and it soft as silk remains.
—Thomas Fuller

401

Life is the acceptance of responsibilities, or their evasion; it is a business of meeting obligations, or avoiding them.   —Ben Ames Williams

Facing it—always facing it—that's the way to get through. Face it!
                    —Joseph Conrad

He shall fare well who confronts circumstances aright.   —Plutarch

He that handles a nettle tenderly is soonest stung.   —Thomas Fuller

He who is afraid of every nettle should not piss in the grass.
                    —Thomas Fuller

Let us be brave in the face of adversity.   —Marcus Annaeus Seneca

Only one feat is possible: not to have run away.   —Dag Hammarskjold

There is something healthy and invigorating about direct action.
                    —Henry Miller

Confidence ... is directness and courage in meeting the facts of life.
                    —John Dewey

The superior man makes the difficulty to be overcome his first interest; success comes only later.
                    —Confucius

The man who most vividly realizes a difficulty is the man most likely to overcome it.   —Joseph Farrell

I believe half the unhappiness in life comes from people being afraid to go straight at things.
                    —William J. Lock

No man will succeed unless he is ready to face and overcome difficulties, and is prepared to assume responsibilities.
                    —William J.H. Boetcher

The fly that doesn't want to be swatted is most secure when it lights on the fly-swatter.
                    —Georg Christoph Lichtenberg

The fly ought to be used as the symbol of impertinence and audacity, for whilst all other animals shun man more than anything else, and run away even before he comes near them, the fly lights upon his very nose.   —Arthur Schopenhauer

All problems become smaller if you don't dodge them, but confront them.   —William F. Halsey

The best way out of a problem is through it.   —Anon.

We cannot solve life's problems except by solving them.
                    —M. Scott Peck

A great man is one who seizes the vital issue in a complex question, what we might call the jugular vein of the whole organism, and spends his energies upon that.
                    —Joseph Rickaby

Have the courage to face a difficulty lest it kick you harder than you bargain for.   —Stanislaus

It is often wonderful how putting down on paper a clear statement of a case helps one to see, not perhaps the way out, but the way *in*.
                    —Arthur Christopher Benson

As a rule, what is out of sight disturbs men's minds more seriously
than what they see.   —Julius Caesar

Every difficulty slurred over will be a
ghost to disturb your repose later on.
　　　　　　　　—Frédéric Chopin

Life is a battle in which we fall from
wounds we receive in running away.
　　　　　　　　—William L. Sullivan

Fools, through false shame, conceal
their open wounds.　　　—Horace

The truth will set you free, but first
it will make you miserable.
　　　　　　　　—James A. Garfield

Let us not look back in anger, nor
forward in fear, but around us in
awareness.　　　—James Thurber

It takes courage to know when you
ought to be afraid.
　　　　　　　　—James A. Michener

However mean your life is, meet it
and live it; do not shun it and call it
hard names. It is not so bad as you
are.　　　—Henry David Thoreau

Genius is an infinite capacity for taking life by the scruff of the neck.
　　　　　　　　—Katharine Hepburn

If you suppress grief too much, it can
well redouble.　　　—Moliere

Bad weather always looks worse
through a window.　　　—Anon.

The frontiers are not east or west,
north or south, but wherever a man
fronts a fact.
　　　　　　　　—Henry David Thoreau

Should I, after tea and cakes and
ices, have the strength to force the
moment to its crisis?　　　—T.S. Eliot

Whatever you are trying to avoid
won't go away until you confront it.
　　　　　　　　—Anon.

None are so blind as those who will
not see.　　　—Anon.

You don't change the course of history by turning the faces of portraits
to the wall.　　　—Jawaharlal Nehru

Soldiers, strike the foe in the face!
　　　　　　　　—Florus

Get in front of the ball, you won't
get hurt. That's what you've got a
chest for, young man.
　　　　　　　　—John McGraw

Knowledge of sin is the beginning of
salvation. —Marcus Annaeus Seneca

Courage is a quietness, not martial
　music made
Born of facing up to life, even when
　afraid.
　　　　　　　　—Emily Sargent Councilman

The great virtue in life is real
courage that knows how to face
facts and live beyond them.
　　　　　　　　—D.H. Lawrence

Risk! Risk anything!... Do the hardest thing on earth for you. Act for
yourself. Face the truth.
　　　　　　　　—Katherine Mansfield

The first rule is to keep an untroubled spirit. The second is to look
things in the face and know them for
what they are.　　　—Marcus Aurelius

403

It is courage, courage, courage, that raises the blood of life to crimson splendor. Live bravely and present a brave front to adversity!   —Horace

It is easy to be brave from a safe distance.   —Aesop

THE COURAGE TO FACE THE TRUTH ABOUT OURSELVES

You can't expect to win unless you know why you lose.
—Benjamin Lipson

We run away all the time to avoid coming face to face with ourselves.
—Anon.

Awakening begins when a man realizes that he is going nowhere, and does not know where to go.
—Georges Gurdjieff

The man with insight enough to admit his limitations comes nearest to perfection.   —Johann von Goethe

You're only as sick as your secrets.
—Anon.

The confession of evil works is the first beginning of good works.
—Saint Augustine

Admitting errors clears the score and proves you wiser than before.
—Arthur Guiterman

An excuse is a lie guarded.
—Jonathan Swift

Honesty is the first chapter of the book of wisdom. —Thomas Jefferson

The real gift of love is self disclosure.
—John Powell

We only really face up to ourselves when we are afraid.
—Thomas Bernhard

EMOTIONAL, SPIRITUAL, AND MENTAL COURAGE

It takes a lot of courage to show your dreams to someone else.
—Erma Bombeck

It takes more courage to reveal insecurities than to hide them, more strength to relate to people than to dominate them, more "manhood" to abide by thought-out principles rather than blind reflex. Toughness is in the soul and spirit, not in muscles and an immature mind.
—Alex Karras

I have often though morality may perhaps consist solely in the courage of making a choice.   —Leon Blum

The highest courage is to dare to appear to be what one is.
—John Lancaster Spalding

True courage is not the brutal force of vulgar heroes, but the firm resolve of virtue and reason.
—Alfred North Whitehead

Greatness, in the last analysis, is largely bravery—courage in escaping from old ideas and old standards.
—James Harvey Robinson

The highest courage is not to be found in the instinctive acts of men who risk their lives to save a friend or slay a foe; the physical fearlessness of a moment or an hour is not to be compared with immolation of months or years for the sake of wisdom or art.   —Joseph H. Odell

I have met brave women who are exploring the outer edge of human possibility, with no history to guide them, and with a courage to make themselves vulnerable that I find moving beyond words.

—Gloria Steinem

Valour is nobleness of the mind.

—Anon.

Courage ... is nothing less than the power to overcome danger, misfortune, fear, injustice, while continuing to affirm inwardly that life, with all its sorrows, is good; that everything is meaningful, even if in a sense beyond our understanding; and that there is always tomorrow.

—Dorothy Thompson

This is the art of courage: to see things as they are and still believe that the victory lies not with those who avoid the bad, but those who taste, in living awareness, every drop of the good.　　　—Victoria Lincoln

God grant me the courage not to give up what I think is right, even though I think it is hopeless.

—Admiral Chester W. Nimitz

The great virtue in life is real courage that knows how to face facts and live beyond them.　　　—D.H. Lawrence

Physical courage, which despises all danger, will make a man brave in one way; and moral courage, which despises all opinion, will make a man brave in another. The former would seem most necessary for the camp; the latter for the council; but to constitute a great man, both are necessary.　　—Charles Caleb Colton

Courage is the power to let go of the familiar.　　　—Raymond Lindquist

Valor is stability, not of legs and arms, but of courage and the soul.

—Michel de Montaigne

One of man's finest qualities is described by the simple word "guts"—the ability to take it. If you have the discipline to stand fast when your body wants to run, if you can control your temper and remain cheerful in the face of monotony or disappointment, you have "guts" in the soldiering sense.

—Colonel John S. Roosman

Whatever course you decide upon, there is always someone to tell you that you are wrong. There are always difficulties arising which tempt you to believe that your critics are right. To map out a course of action and follow it to an end requires ... courage.

—Ralph Waldo Emerson

COURAGE AND CONVICTION

Courage is more than standing for a firm conviction. It includes the risk of questioning that conviction.

—Julian Weber Gordon

Courage is what it takes to stand up and speak; courage is also what it takes to sit down and listen.

—Anon.

The hallmark of courage in our age of conformity is the capacity to stand on one's convictions—not obstinately or defiantly (these are gestures of defensiveness, not courage) nor as a gesture of retaliation, but simply because these are what one believes.　　—Rollo May

Reacting to Difficult Situations

The greatest test of courage on earth is to bear defeat without losing heart. —Robert G. Ingersoll

Courage is to take hard knocks like a man when occasion calls. —Plautus

This is courage ... to bear unflinchingly what heaven sends. —Euripides

Courage, in the final analysis, is nothing but an affirmative answer to the shocks of existence. —Dr. Kurt Goldstein

Courage is a perfect sensibility of the measure of danger, and a mental willingness to endure it. —General William T. Sherman

To have courage for whatever comes in life—everything lies in that. —Saint Teresa of Avila

To accept whatever comes, regardless of the consequences, is to be unafraid. —John Cage

The Courage of the Minority

The test of courage comes when we are in the minority. —Ralph W. Sockman

One man with courage makes a majority. —Andrew Jackson

Courage and Happiness

Many women miss their greatest chance of happiness through a want of courage in a decisive moment. —Winifred Gordon

We must have the courage to be happy. —Henri Frederic Amiel

There is a courage of happiness as well as a courage of sorrow. —Maurice Maeterlinck

Happy the man who ventures boldly to defend what he holds dear. —Ovid

All happiness depends on courage and work. —Honore de Balzac

There is nothing in the world so much admired as a man who knows how to bear unhappiness with courage. —Marcus Annaeus Seneca

We must have courage to bet on our ideas, on the calculated risk, and to act. Everyday living requires courage if life is to be effective and bring happiness. —Maxwell Maltz

Courage and Love

Faint heart never won fair lady. —Miguel de Cervantes

The last thing a woman will consent to discover in a man whom she loves, or on whom she simply depends, is want of courage. —Joseph Conrad

None but the brave deserve the fair. —John Dryden

Fortune and love favor the brave. —Ovid

The bravest are the tenderest. The loving are the daring. —Henry Wadsworth Longfellow

COURAGE AND WARFARE

The weapon of the brave is in his heart. —Anon.

The guts carry the feet, not the feet the guts. —Miguel de Cervantes

War is fear cloaked in courage.
—General William Westmoreland

A bold heart is half the battle.
—Anon.

Courage in danger is half the battle.
—Plautus

A man of courage never wants weapons. —Anon.

A brave arm makes a short sword long. —Anon.

Courage which goes against military expediency is stupidity, or, if it is insisted upon by a commander, irresponsibility.
—General Erwin Rommel

LIVING CAN TAKE MORE COURAGE THAN DYING

There is, in addition to a courage with which men die, a courage by which men must live.
—John F. Kennedy

Have the courage to live. Anyone can die. —Robert Cody

Where life is more terrible than death, it is the truest valor to dare to live. —Sir Thomas Browne

The courage we desire and prize is not the courage to die decently, but to live manfully. —Thomas Carlyle

Often the test of courage is not to die, but to live.
—Conte Vittorio Alfieri

He who has the courage to laugh is almost as much the master of the world as he who is ready to die.
—Giacomo Leopardi

Sometimes even to live is an act of courage. —Marcus Annaeus Seneca

Life shrinks or expands in proportion to one's courage. —Anaïs Nin

Only those are fit to live who are not afraid to die.
—General Douglas MacArthur

To say yes, you have to sweat and roll up your sleeves and plunge both hands into life up to the elbows. It is easy to say no, even if saying no means death. —Jean Anouilh

WE CAN'T SUCCEED WITHOUT COURAGE

Because a fellow has failed once or twice or a dozen times, you don't want to set him down as a failure till he's dead or loses his courage—and that's the same thing.
—George Horace Lorimer

What is more mortifying than to feel that you have missed the plum for want of courage to shake the tree?
—Logan Pearsall Smith

To persevere, trusting in what hopes he has, is courage. The coward despairs. —Euripides

It takes vision and courage to create—it takes faith and courage to prove. —Owen D. Young

407

Whatever you do, you need courage.... To map out a course of action and follow it to an end requires some of the same courage which a soldier needs. —Ralph Waldo Emerson

Who dares nothing, need hope for nothing. —J.C.F. von Schiller

Have the courage of your desire. —George R. Gissing

To see what is right, and not do it, is want of courage. —Confucius

No great thing comes to any man unless he has courage. —Cardinal James Gibbons

Great things are done more through courage than through wisdom. —German proverb

Courage permits the caliber of performance to continue at its peak, until the finish line is crossed. —Stuart Walker

Failure is only postponed success as long as courage "coaches" ambition. The habit of persistence is the habit of victory. —Herbert Kaufman

Courage and perseverance have a magical talisman, before which difficulties disappear, and obstacles vanish into air. —John Quincy Adams

There are a lot of fellas with all the ability it takes to play in the major leagues, but ... they always get stuck in the minor leagues because they haven't got the guts to make the climb. —Cookie Lavagetto

You will never do anything in this world without courage. —James Lane Allen

Where there is a brave man, in the thickest of the fight, there is the post of honor. —Henry David Thoreau

It takes as much courage to have tried and failed as it does to have tried and succeeded. —Anne Morrow Lindbergh

Whenever you see a successful business, someone once made a courageous decision. —Peter Drucker

Courage to start and willingness to keep everlasting at it are the requisites for success. —Alonzo Newton Benn

One of the biggest factors in success is the courage to undertake something. —James A. Worsham

WITHOUT COURAGE, ABILITY AND TALENT WON'T BE ENOUGH

Everyone has a talent. What is rare is the courage to follow that talent to the dark place where it leads. —Erica Jong

The world is not perishing for the want of clever or talented or well-meaning men. It is perishing for the want of men of courage and resolution. —Robert J. McCracken

Knowledge without courage is sterile. —Baltasar Gracian

Courage is the thing. All goes if courage goes. —Sir James M. Barrie

We Must Have the Courage to Begin

It's weak and despicable to go on wanting things and not trying to get them. —Joanna Field

How many feasible projects have miscarried through despondency, and been strangled in their birth by a cowardly imagination? —Jeremy Collier

One of the biggest factors in success is the courage to undertake something. —James A. Worsham

When it comes to betting on yourself ... you're a chicken-livered coward if you hesitate. —B.C. Forbes

What would life be if we had no courage to attempt anything? —Vincent van Gogh

Be courageous!... I have seen many depressions in business. Always America has come out stronger and more prosperous. Be as brave as your fathers before you. Have faith! Go forward. —Thomas A. Edison

Dare to begin! He who postpones living rightly is like the rustic who waits for the river to run out before he crosses. —Horace

Nothing ventured, nothing gained. —Anon.

The brave venture anything. —Anon.

The difference between getting somewhere and nowhere is the courage to make an early start. —Charles M. Schwab

Life is to be entered upon with courage. —Alexis de Tocqueville

We ought to face our destiny with courage. —Friedrich Nietzsche

You can surmount the obstacles in your path if you are determined, courageous and hardworking.... Do not fear to pioneer, to venture down new paths of endeavor. —Ralph J. Bunche

The great man is the man who does a thing for the first time. —Alexander Smith

Imposing limitations on yourself is cowardly because it protects you from having to try, and perhaps failing. —Vladimir Zworykin

What you can do, or dream you can do, begin it; boldness has genius, power and magic in it. —Johann von Goethe

We need the courage to start and continue what we should do, and courage to stop what we shouldn't do. —Richard L. Evans

Caution, Prudence, Safety

Prudence which degenerates into timidity is very seldom the path to safety. —Viscount Cecil

He that is overcautious will accomplish little. —J.C.F. von Schiller

We can easily become as much slaves to precaution as we can to fear. —Randolph Bourne

To the timid and hesitating everything is impossible because it seems so. —Sir Walter Scott

409

Do not be too timid and squeamish.... All life is an experiment. The more experiments you make, the better.   —Ralph Waldo Emerson

Courage is rarely reckless or foolish ... courage usually involves a highly realistic estimate of the odds that must be faced.   —Margaret Truman

Valour lies just halfway between rashness and cowardice.
          —Miguel de Cervantes

COURAGE AND FEAR

When you're my size in the pros, fear is a sign that you're not stupid.
          —Jerry Levias

Keep your fears to yourself, but share your courage with others.
          —Robert Louis Stevenson

Courage leads starward, fear toward death.   —Marcus Annaeus Seneca

Go forth to meet the shadowy Future without fear and with a manly heart.
          —Henry Wadsworth Longfellow

Fate loves the fearless.
          —James Russell Lowell

There is no such thing as bravery, only degrees of fear.
          —John Wainwright

Courage is a peculiar kind of fear.
          —Charles Kennedy

Courage is fear that has said its prayers.   —Dorothy Bernard

Courage is fear holding on a minute longer.   —General George S. Patton

Courage is the ability to solve problems realistically in the presence of fear.   —Stuart Walker

Courage is resistance to fear, mastery of fear—not absence of fear.
          —Mark Twain

Courage is ... the knowledge of how to fear what ought to be feared and how not to fear what ought not to be feared.   —David Ben-Gurion

Courage is knowing what not to fear.   —Plato

Courage is the right disposition toward fear.   —Anon.

Courage is a scorner of things which inspire fear.
          —Marcus Annaeus Seneca

We must constantly build dykes of courage to hold back the flood of fear.   —Martin Luther King, Jr.

Courage is never letting your actions be influenced by your fears.
          —Arthur Koestler

COWARDICE

Cowards cannot see that their greatest safety lies in dauntless courage.
          —Johann Kaspar Lavater

A coward turns away, but a brave man's choice is danger.   —Euripides

Cowardice is the mother of cruelty.
          —Michel de Montaigne

Cowards die many times before their deaths; the valiant never taste of death but once.
          —William Shakespeare

Optimism and self-pity are the positive and negative poles of modern cowardice. —Cyril Connolly

To say a person is a coward has no more meaning than to say he is lazy: It simply tells us that some vital potentiality is unrealized or blocked. —Rollo May

There are at least two kinds of cowards. One kind always lives with himself, afraid to face the world. The other kind lives with the world, afraid to face himself. —Roscoe Snowden

There is a time when to avoid trouble is to store up trouble, and when to seek for a lazy and a cowardly peace is to court a still greater danger. —William Barclay

To know what is right and not do it is the worst cowardice. —Confucius

Spiritual cowardice is not only weakness but wickedness. —J.B. Gambrell

The most mortifying infirmity in human nature ... is, perhaps, cowardice. —Charles Lamb

Men perish by the sword, cowards by disease. —Phillippus

Between cowardice and despair, valour is gendered. —John Donne

If you knew how cowardly your enemy is, you would slap him. —Edgar Watson Howe

Bravery is the knowledge of the cowardice in the enemy. —Edgar Watson Howe

Any coward can fight a battle when he's sure of winning. —George Eliot

The coward despairs. —Euripides

Cowardice, as distinguished from panic, is almost always simply a lack of ability to suspend the functioning of the imagination. —Ernest Hemingway

The only cowards are sinners; fighting the fight is all. —John G. Neihardt

All men would be cowards if they durst. —John Wilmot, Earl of Rochester

That cowardice is incorrigible which the love of power cannot overcome. —Charles Caleb Colton

WE CAN'T BE BRAVE IF WE'RE NOT AFRAID

Courage is doing what you're afraid to do. There can be no courage unless you're scared. —Eddie Rickenbacker

You look at a guy who's being brave. He's afraid, or he wouldn't be brave. If he isn't afraid, he's stupid. —Joe Torre

To fight a bull when you are not scared is nothing. And to *not* fight a bull when you are scared is nothing. But to fight a bull when you are scared is something. —Anon.

Being "brave" means doing or facing something frightening.... Being "fearless" means being without fear. —Penelope Leach

It takes courage to know when you ought to be afraid.
—James A. Michener

Courage is being scared to death ... and saddling up anyway.
—John Wayne

Bravery is being the only one who knows you're afraid.
—Franklin P. Jones

Perfect courage means doing unwitnessed what we would be capable of with the world looking on.
—Francois de La Rochefoucauld

Bravery is the capacity to perform properly even when scared half to death.   —General Omar N. Bradley

COURAGE CAN COME FROM NECESSITY

Necessity makes even the timid brave.   —Sallust

Necessity does the work of courage.
—Nicholas Murray Butler

When it comes to the pinch, human beings are heroic.   —George Orwell

Many become brave when brought to bag.   —Norwegian proverb

Courage mounteth with occasion.
—William Shakespeare

When you have no choice, mobilize the spirit of courage.
—Jewish proverb

DREAMS FUEL COURAGE

Courage is sustained by calling up anew the vision of the goal.
—A.G. Sertillanges

Optimism is the foundation of courage.   —Nicholas Murray Butler

Courage is like love, it must have hope for nourishment.
—Napoleon Bonaparte

COWARDICE CAN CREATE COURAGE

I would often be a coward, but for the shame of it.   —Ralph Connor

At the bottom of a good deal of bravery ... lurks a miserable cowardice. Men will face powder and steel because they cannot face public opinion.   —Edwin H. Chapin

We would be cowards, if we had courage enough.   —Thomas Fuller

A coward's fear can make a coward valiant.   —Thomas Fuller

OTHER SOURCES OF COURAGE

Courage is as often the outcome of despair as of hope; in the one case we have nothing to lose, in the other everything to gain.
—Diane De Pottiers

Despair gives courage to a coward.
—Anon.

No one has yet computed how many imaginary triumphs are silently celebrated by people each year to keep up their courage.
—Henry S. Haskins

If we survive danger, it steels our courage more than anything else.
—Reinhold Niebuhr

Courage is the fear of being thought a coward.   —Horace Smith

How, then, find the courage for action? By slipping a little into unconsciousness, spontaneity, instinct which holds one to the earth and dictates the relatively good and useful.... By accepting the human condition more simply, and candidly, by dreading troubles less, calculating less, hoping more.
—Henri Frederic Amiel

It takes courage to live —courage and strength and hope and humor. And courage and strength and hope and humor have to be bought and paid for with pain and work and prayers and tears.
—Jerome P. Fleishman

Courage that grows from constitution often forsakes a man ... courage which arises from a sense of duty acts in a uniform manner.
—Joseph Addison

He who knows how to suffer everything can dare everything.
—Vauvenargues

Courage does not always march to airs blown by a bugle, it is not always wrought out of the fabric ostentation wears.
—Frances Rodman

The paradox of courage is that a man must be a little careless of his life in order to keep it.
—G.K. Chesterton

All men are afraid in battle. The coward is the one who lets his fear overcome his sense of duty. Duty is the essence of manhood.
—General George S. Patton

We learn courageous action by going forward whenever fear urges us back. —David Seabury

OTHER DEFINITIONS OF COURAGE

Courage is required not only in a person's occasional crucial decision for his own freedom, but in the little hour-to-hour decisions which place the bricks in the structure of his building of himself into a person who acts with freedom and responsibility. —Rollo May

Courage does not consist in calculation, but in fighting against chances.
—John Henry Cardinal Newman

Courage is its own reward.
—Plautus

Courage is the price that life exacts for granting peace. —Amelia Earhart

Courage is a kind of salvation.
—Plato

Courage is grace under pressure.
—Ernest Hemingway

Courage is the lovely virtue—the rib of Himself that God sent down to His children. —Sir James M. Barrie

Courage is the integrating strength that causes one to overcome tragedy.
—Eugene E. Brussell

Courage is almost a contradiction in terms. It means a strong desire to live taking the form of readiness to die. —G.K. Chesterton

Courage is the virtue which champions the cause of right. —Cicero

413

Courage is generosity of the highest order, for the brave are prodigal of the most precious things.
—Charles Caleb Colton

Courage is clearly a readiness to risk self-humiliation.   —Nigel Dennis

Courage is fire, and bullying is smoke.   —Benjamin Disraeli

Courage consists of the power of self-recovery.
—Ralph Waldo Emerson

Courage is a virtue only so far as it is directed by prudence.
—Francois de Fenelon

Courage is a quality so necessary for maintaining virtue that it is always respected even when it is associated with vice.   —Samuel Johnson

Courage is the footstool of the Virtues, upon which they stand.
—Robert Louis Stevenson

Courage is to feel the daily daggers of relentless steel and keep on living.
—Douglas Malloch

Courage is a peculiar kind of fear.
—Charles Kennedy

Courage is what preserves our liberty, safety, life, and our homes and parents, our country and children. Courage comprises all things.
—Plautus

GENERAL QUOTATIONS ABOUT COURAGE

There is plenty of courage among us for the abstract, but not for the concrete.   —Helen Keller

Every man has his own courage, and is betrayed because he seeks in himself the courage of other persons.
—Ralph Waldo Emerson

Valor is a gift. Those having it never know for sure if they have it till the test comes. And those having it in one test never know for sure if they will have it when the next test comes.   —Carl Sandburg

Until the day of his death, no man can be sure of his courage.
—Jean Anouilh

Among wellborn spirits courage does not depend on age.
—Pierre Corneille

Courage easily finds its own eloquence.   —Plautus

But screw your courage to the sticking place and we'll not fail.
—William Shakespeare

Courage is always the surest wisdom.   —Sir Wilfred Grenfell

On many of the great issues of our time, men have lacked wisdom because they have lacked courage.
—William Benton

If you are scared to go to the brink, you are lost.   —John Foster Dulles

It takes courage to lead a life. Any life.   —Erica Jong

Nothing is as valuable to a man as courage.   —Terence

I'd rather give my life than be afraid to give it.   —Lyndon B. Johnson

The only courage that matters is the kind that gets you from one moment to the next. —Mignon McLaughlin

Courage ought to have eyes as well as arms. —H.G. Bohn

We'll Get Whatever We Need to Handle Whatever Life Demands of Us

God Matches Our Problems to Our Capabilities

Sorrow is a fruit. God does not allow it to grow on a branch that is too weak to bear it.　—Victor Hugo

The will of God will not take you where the grace of God cannot keep you.　　　　　—Anon.

So when the crisis is upon you, remember that God, like a trainer of wrestlers, has matched you with a tough and stalwart antagonist ... that you may prove a victor at the Great Games.　　　　　—Epictetus

What God expects us to attempt, He also enables us to achieve.
　　　　　—Stephen Olford

The Bible tells us that a sparrow does not fall without God's notice. I know he will help us meet our responsibilities through his guidance.
　　　　　—Michael Cardone, Sr.

God gives us always strength enough, and sense enough, for everything He wants us to do.
　　　　　—John Ruskin

With them I gladly shared my all and learned the great truth that where God guides, He provides.
　　　　　—Frank N.D. Buchman

God gave burdens, also shoulders.
　　　　　—Yiddish proverb

Our Abilities Will Always Be Equal to Our Challenges

Nothing befalls a man except what is in his nature to endure.
　　　　　—Marcus Aurelius

Life only demands from you the strength you possess.
　　　　　—Dag Hammarskjold

Everyone will be taxed according to his means.　—J.C.F. von Schiller

The burden is equal to the horse's strength.　　　　　—Talmud

All we are asked to bear we can bear. That is a law of the spiritual life. The only hindrance to the working of this law, as of all benign laws, is fear.　　　—Elizabeth Goudge

When it comes to the pinch, human beings are heroic.　—George Orwell

WE CAN DO WHATEVER WE HAVE TO DO

The human spirit is stronger than anything that can happen to it.
—George. C. Scott

What one has to do usually can be done.
—Eleanor Roosevelt

Man performs and engenders so much more than he can or should have to bear. That's how he finds that he can bear anything.
—William Faulkner

The peril of the hour moved the British to tremendous exertions, just as always in a moment of extreme danger things can be done which had previously been thought impossible. Mortal danger is an effective antidote for fixed ideas.
—General Erwin Rommel

WHAT WE NEED IS ALREADY WITHIN US

Within us all there are wells of thought and dynamos of energy which are not suspected until emergencies arise. Then oftentimes we find that it is comparatively simple to double or triple our former capacities and to amaze ourselves by the results achieved.
—Thomas J. Watson

We all carry it within us: supreme strength, the fullness of wisdom, unquenchable joy. It is never thwarted, and cannot be destroyed.
—Huston Smith

We have what we seek. It is there all the time, and if we give it time, it will make itself known to us.
—Thomas Merton

Truth is not introduced into the individual from without, but was within him all the time.
—Søren Kierkegaard

Nature arms each man with some faculty which enables him to do easily some feat impossible to any other.
—Ralph Waldo Emerson

OUR PROBLEMS THEMSELVES CONTAIN THE RESOURCES TO OVERCOME THEM

Nature reacts not only to physical disease, but also to moral weakness; when the danger increases, she gives us greater courage.
—Johann von Goethe

Our energy is in proportion to the resistance it meets. We attempt nothing great but from a sense of the difficulties we have to encounter; we persevere in nothing great but from a pride in overcoming them.
—William Hazlitt

We shall draw from the heart of suffering itself the means of inspiration and survival.
—Sir Winston Churchill

Courage mounteth with occasion.
—William Shakespeare

Trouble creates a capacity to handle it.
—Oliver Wendell Holmes, Jr.

In the darkest hour the soul is replenished and given strength to continue and endure.
—Heart Warrior Chosa

Exigencies create the necessary ability to meet and conquer them.
—Wendell Philips

417

The moment one definitely commits oneself, then Providence moves too. All sorts of things occur to help that would never otherwise have occurred. A stream of events issues from the decision, raising unforeseen incidents and meetings and material assistance, which no man could have dreamt would have come his way.

—W.H. Murray

In forty hours I shall be in battle, with little information, and on the spur of the moment will have to make the most momentous decisions. But I believe that one's spirit enlarges with responsibility and that, with God's help, I shall make them, and make them right.

—General George S. Patton

"Ignorance"

Not Knowing That Something Is "Impossible" Can Be a Blessing

Progress results only from the fact that there are some men and women who refuse to believe that what they know to be right cannot be done.
—Russell W. Davenport

The good thing about being young is that you are not experienced enough to know you cannot possibly do the things you are doing. —Gene Brown

The young do not know enough to be prudent, and therefore they attempt the impossible—and achieve it, generation after generation.
—Pearl S. Buck

Sometimes it proves the highest understanding not to understand.
—Baltasar Gracian

Lack of understanding is a great power. Sometimes it enables men to conquer the world. —Anatole France

An impossibility does not disturb us until its accomplishment shows what fools we were. —Henry S. Haskins

God may have been waiting for centuries for somebody ignorant enough of the impossible to do that thing.
—Dr. J.A. Holmes

The greatest wisdom often consists in ignorance. —Baltasar Gracian

Great things are accomplished by those who do not feel the impotence of man. This ... is a precious gift.
—Valery

It is our duty as men and women to proceed as though limits to our abilities do not exist.
—Pierre Teilhard de Chardin

Men are always averse to enterprises in which they foresee difficulties.
—Niccolo Machiavelli

Not Knowing How to Do Something Can Be a Gift

Painting is easy when you don't know how, but very difficult when you do. —Edgar Degas

To measure up to all that is demanded of him, a man must overestimate his capacities. —Johann von Goethe

419

Every true genius is bound to be naive. —J.C.F. von Schiller

To write a good love letter you ought to begin without knowing what you mean to say, and to finish without knowing what you have written. —Jean-Jacques Rousseau

When we are not sure, we are alive. —Graham Greene

FAMOUS PEOPLE WHO ADMITTED THEY SOMETIMES DIDN'T KNOW WHAT THEY WERE DOING

Basic research is what I'm doing when I don't know what I'm doing. —Wernher von Braun

I don't know what I'm doing. I don't know what actors do. —Geraldine Page

In baseball, you don't know nothing. —Yogi Berra

I know it was wonderful, but I don't know how I did it. —Sir Lawrence Oliver, after a brilliant performance

What makes a good pinch hitter? I wish the hell I knew. —Bobby Mercer

We couldn't possibly know where it would lead, but we knew it had to be done. —Betty Friedan, on the Women's Movement

People think the Beatles know what's going on. We don't. We're just doing it. —John Lennon

I don't know what humor is. —Will Rogers

Unprovided with original learning, unformed in the habits of thinking, unskilled in the arts of composition, I resolved to write a book. —Edward Gibbon

When Columbus started out he didn't know where he was going, when he got there he didn't know where he was, and when he got back he didn't know where he had been. —Anon.

All I know about humor is that I don't know anything about it. —Fred Allen

It is a sign of strength, not of weakness, to admit that you don't know all the answers. —John P. Loughrane

WE LEARN AS WE GO ALONG

I learn by going where I have to go. —Theodore Roethke

One learns by doing the thing; for though you think you know it, you have no certainty until you try. —Sophocles

No one knows what he can do until he tries. —Publilius Syrus

Education is learning what you didn't even know you didn't know. —Daniel Boorstin

The true test of character is ... how we behave when we don't know what to do. —John Holt

Nothing in this world can one imagine beforehand, not the least thing. Everything is made up of so many unique particulars that cannot be foreseen. —Rainer Maria Rilke

420

The work will teach you how to do it. —Estonian proverb

Where there is an unknowable, there is a promise. —Thornton Wilder

Dare to be naive.
—R. Buckminster Fuller

Living is a form of not being sure, not knowing what next or how. The moment you know how, you begin to die a little. The artist never entirely knows. We guess. We may be wrong, but we take leap after leap in the dark. —Agnes de Mille

GETTING GOING

WE MUSTN'T HESITATE

Act decidedly and take the consequences. No good is ever done by hesitation. —Thomas Henry Huxley

To know what has to be done, then do it, comprises the whole philosophy of practical life.
—Sir William Osler

If you want to do something, do it!
—Plautus

Something must happen!
—Heinrich Böll

Putting off an easy thing makes it hard. Putting off a hard thing makes it impossible.
—George Claude Lorimer

Delay always breeds danger, and to protract a great design is often to ruin it. —Miguel de Cervantes

The wise man does at once what the fool does finally. —Baltasar Gracian

In putting off what one has to do, one runs the risk of never being able to do it. —Charles Baudelaire

Getting an idea should be like sitting down on a pin; it should make you jump up and do something.
—E.L. Simpson

Procrastination is opportunity's assassin. —Victor Kiam

To do anything in this world worth doing, we must not stand back shivering and thinking of the cold and danger, but jump in and scramble through as well as we can.
—Sydney Smith

The man who will not execute his resolutions when they are fresh upon him can have no hope from them afterwards; they will be dissipated, lost and perish in the hurry and scurry of the world, or sunk in the slough of indolence.
—Marie Edgeworth

Why always, "not yet"? Do flowers in spring say, "not yet"?
—Norman Douglas

We are very near to greatness: one step and we are safe; can we not take the leap? —Ralph Waldo Emerson

The keen spirit seizes the prompt occasion. —Hannah Moore

The hour is ripe, and yonder lies the way. —Virgil

Delay not to seize the hour! —Aeschylus

I was seldom able to see an opportunity until it had ceased to be one. —Mark Twain

This one makes a net, this one stands and wishes.
Would you like to make a bet which one gets the fishes? —Chinese rhyme

Inspirations never go in for long engagements; they demand immediate marriage to action. —Brendan Francis

If we really want to live, we'd better start at once to try. —W.H. Auden

The rewards in business go to the man who *does something* with an idea. —William Benton

The important thing is somehow to begin. —Henry Moore

Eighty percent of success is showing up. —Woody Allen

As long as you can start, you are all right. The juice will come. —Ernest Hemingway

The way to get ahead is to start *now*. —William Feather

Begin doing what you want to do *now*. —Marie Beynon Ray

It is no good hearing an inner voice or getting an inner prompting if you do not immediately act on that inner prompting. —David Spangler

Even if you're on the right track, you'll get run over if you just sit there. —Will Rogers

THE FIRST STEP

The first step is the hardest. —Anon.

Every beginning is hard. —Anon.

A journey of a thousand miles must begin with a single step. —Chinese proverb

If you miss the first buttonhole, you will not succeed in buttoning up your coat. —Johann von Goethe

If you don't place your foot on the rope, you'll never cross the chasm. —Anon.

He who is outside the door has already a good part of his journey behind him. —Dutch proverb

The beginning is half of every action. —Greek proverb

The man who removes a mountain begins by carrying away small stones. —Chinese proverb

WE MUST BEGIN WHEREVER WE ARE

Everyone who got where he is had to begin where he was. —Robert Louis Stevenson

The most important thing about getting somewhere is starting right where we are. —Bruce Barton

Sometimes we look so intently toward the pinnacle that we stumble over the steps leading to it. Development begins just where you are.
—Mrs. Herman Stanley

We Must Begin, Even If We're Not Exactly Sure Where We're Going

Few begin with anything like a clear view of what they want to do, and the fortune they seek may come in a very different form from that which they have kept in view.
—The Independent

Beginnings are apt to be shadowy.
—Rachel Carson

We will not know unless we begin.
—Howard Zinn

Let us watch well our beginnings, and results will manage themselves.
—Alexander Clark

To Get What We Want, We Must Take Action

"Mean to" don't pick no cotton.
—Anon.

To always be intending to live a new life, but never to find time to set about it; this is as if a man should put off eating and drinking and sleeping from one day and night to another, till he is starved and destroyed.
—Tillotson

Knowing is not enough, we must apply. Willing is not enough, we must do.
—Johann von Goethe

Do noble things, do not dream them all day long.
—Charles Kingsley

That is the principal thing: not to remain with the dream, with the intention, with the being in the mood, but always forcibly to convert it into all things.
—Rainer Maria Rilke

The individual activity of one man with backbone will do more than a thousand men with a mere wishbone.
—William J.H. Boetcker

With mere good intentions hell is proverbially paved.
—William James

All the beautiful sentiments in the world weigh less than a single lovely action.
—James Russell Lowell

You can't steal second base and keep one foot on first.
—Frederick B. Wilson

You cannot dream yourself into a character; you must hammer and forge one for yourself.
—James A. Froude

What the Puritans gave the world was not thought, but action.
—Wendell Phillips

Stagnation is something worse than death. It is corruption, also.
—Simms

I myself must mix with action, lest I wither by despair.
—Alfred, Lord Tennyson

Psychology is action, not thinking about oneself.
—Albert Camus

The great end of life is not knowledge, but action.
—Thomas Henry Huxley

The biggest sin is sitting on your ass.
—Florynce Kennedy

This is a world of action, and not for moping and droning in.
—Charles Dickens

Honors and rewards fall to those who show their good qualities in action.
—Aristotle

Share the passion and action of your time, at peril of being judged not to have lived.
—Oliver Wendell Holmes Jr.

Action is eloquence.
—William Shakespeare

The end of man is action.
—Thomas Carlyle

Optimism, unaccompanied by personal effort, is merely a state of mind, and not fruitful.
—Edward L. Curtis

To attain happiness in another world we need only to believe something, while to secure it in this world, we must do something.
—Charlotte Perkins Gilman

The only menace is inertia.
—Saint John Perse

One of the reasons why so few of us ever act, instead of react, is because we are continually stifling our deepest impulses.
—Henry Miller

If a man wants his dreams to come true, he must wake them up.
—Anon.

Men expect too much, do too little.
—Allen Tate

Action may not always bring happiness, but there is no happiness without action.
—William James

The shortest answer is doing.
—English proverb

Things don't turn up in this world until somebody turns them up.
—James A. Garfield

Act—act in the living present!
—Henry Wadsworth Longfellow

Life is essentially a series of events to be lived through rather than intellectual riddles to be played with and solved.
—George A. Buttrick

THE RISKS OF TAKING ACTION CAN BE LESS THAN THE RISKS OF INACTION

There are risks and costs to a program of action. But they are far less than the long-range risks and costs of comfortable inaction.
—John F. Kennedy

He that is overcautious will accomplish little.
—J.C.F. von Schiller

Often greater risk is involved in postponement than in making a wrong decision.
—Harry A. Hopf

The only things you regret are the things you didn't do.
—Michael Curtiz

Above all, try something.
—Franklin Delano Roosevelt

To avoid an occasion for our virtues is a worse degree of failure than to push forward pluckily and make a fall.
—Robert Louis Stevenson

Indifference and inaction must always pay a penalty.
—William Feather

Shun idleness. It is a rust that attaches itself to the most brilliant metals.
—Voltaire

I do not believe in a fate that falls on men however they act, but I do believe in a fate that falls on men *unless* they act. —G.K. Chesterton

WE CAN'T LET TALKING GET IN THE WAY OF ACTION

Deeds, not words.
—Motto of the McRarie family

Words are mere bubbles of water, but deeds are drops of gold.
—Chinese proverb

A man of words and not of deeds is like a garden full of weeds.
—Anon.

Life is worth being lived, but not worth being discussed all the time.
—Isabelle Adfani

Action, not words, are the true criterion of the attachment of friends.
—George Washington

Words without actions are the assassins of idealism. —Herbert Hoover

If you have something to do that is worthwhile doing, don't talk about it ... do it. —George W. Biount

If deeds are wanting, all words appear mere vanity and emptiness.
—Greek proverb

Talking is easy, action difficult.
—Spanish proverb

One's feelings waste themselves in words; they ought all to be distilled into action ... which bring results.
—Florence Nightingale

Boast not of what thou would'st have done, but *do*. —John Milton

When I talked, no one listened to me. But as soon as I acted I became persuasive, and I no longer find anyone incredulous. —Giosue Borsi

If you can talk brilliantly about a problem, it can create the consoling illusion that it has been mastered.
—Stanley Kubrick

Words gain credibility by deed.
—Terence

Men are alike in their promises. It is only in their deeds that they differ.
—Moliere

An acre of performance is worth a whole world of promise.
—W.D. Howells

Well done is better than well said.
—Benjamin Franklin

Our chief defect is that we are more given to talking about things than to doing them. —Jawaharlal Nehru

We have too many sounding words and too few actions that correspond with them. —Abigail Adams

WE CAN'T LET PLANNING GET IN THE WAY OF ACTION

Activity in back of a very small idea will produce more than inactivity and the planning of a genius.
—James A. Worsham

Get good counsel before you begin; and when you have decided, act promptly. —Sallust

All worthwhile men have good thoughts, good ideas and good intentions, but precious few of them ever translate those into action.
—John Hancock Field

A thought which does not result in an action is nothing much, and an action which does not proceed from a thought is nothing at all.
—Georges Bernanos

To think is easy. To act is difficult. To act as one thinks is the most difficult of all. —Johann von Goethe

Unless a capacity for thinking be accompanied by a capacity for action, a superior mind exists in torture. —Benedetto Croce

Contemplation often makes life miserable. We should act more, think less, and stop watching ourselves live. —Nicolas de Chamfort

What you theoretically know, vividly realize. —Francis Thompson

We must not waste life in devising means. It is better to plan less and do more. —William Ellery Channing

Ideas are one thing, and what happens is another. —John Cage

The best way to prepare for life is to begin to live. —Elbert Hubbard

We are always getting ready to live, but never living.
—Ralph Waldo Emerson

Action will remove the doubt that theory cannot solve. —Tehyi Hsieh

It is a common observation that those who dwell continually upon their expectations are apt to become oblivious to the requirements of their actual situation.
—Charles Sanders Peirce

He who deliberates fully before taking a step will spend his entire life on one leg. —Chinese proverb

We don't have enough time to premeditate all our actions.
—Vauvenargues

The opportunity is often lost by deliberating. —Publilius Syrus

To think too long about doing a thing often becomes its undoing.
—Eva Young

WE CAN'T WAIT TOO LONG FOR "THE RIGHT CIRCUMSTANCES," OR FOR INSPIRATION

Do not wait for ideal circumstances, nor the best opportunities; they will never come.
—Janet Erskine Stuart

Do what you can, with what you have, where you are.
—Theodore Roosevelt

Common sense does not ask an impossible chessboard, but takes the one before it and plays the game.
—Wendell Phillips

He who postpones the hour of living is like the rustic who waits for the river to run out before he crosses.
—Horace

427

Being unready and ill-equipped is what you have to expect in life. It is the universal predicament. It is your lot as a human being to lack what it takes. Circumstances are seldom right. You never have the capacities, the strength, the wisdom, the virtue you ought to have. You must always do with less than you need in a situation vastly different from what you would have chosen.
—Charlton Ogburn, Jr.

You decide you'll wait for your pitch. Then as the ball starts toward the plate, you think about your stance. And then you think about your swing. And then you realize that the ball that went past you for a strike was your pitch.
—Bobby Murcer

Conditions are never just right. People who delay action until all factors are favorable do nothing.
—William Feather

So what do we do? Anything. Something. So long as we just don't sit there. If we screw it up, start over. Try something else. If we wait until we've satisfied all the uncertainties, it may be too late.
—Lee Iacocca

Nothing at all will be attempted if all possible objections must first be overcome.   —Samuel Johnson

No age or time of life, no position or circumstance, has a monopoly on success. Any age is the right age to start doing!   —Anon.

Everyone must row with the oars he has.   —English proverb

The question for each man is not what he would do if he had the means, time, influence and educational advantages, but what he will do with the things he *has*.
—Frank Hamilton

How many opportunities come along? If you wait for the right one, that's wrong, because it may never be right, and what have you got to lose? Even if it's a disaster, you've tried, you've learned something, you've had an adventure. And that doesn't mean you can't do it again.
—Edward McCabe

We should be taught not to wait for inspiration to start a thing. Action always generates inspiration. Inspiration seldom generates action.
—Frank Tibolt

If you wait for inspiration you'll be standing on the corner after the parade is a mile down the street.
—Ben Nicholas

The best place to succeed is where you are with what you have.
—Charles M. Schwab

One of these days is none of these days.   —H.G. Bohn

And now, Lord, what wait I for?
—Psalms

Who waits until the wind shall silent keep
Will never find the ready hour to sow.   —Helen Hunt Jackson

Begin somewhere; you cannot build a reputation on what you *intend* to do.   —Liz Smith

If you wait for the perfect moment when all is safe and assured, it may never arrive. Mountains will not be climbed, races won, or lasting happiness achieved.   —Maurice Chevalier

There is nothing to be gained by waiting for a better situation. You see where you are and you do what you can with that.

—Jacob K. Javits

WE ARE OUR ACTIONS

It is in your act that you exist, not in your body. Your act is yourself, and there is no other you.

—Antoine de Saint-Exupery

The test of any man lies in action.

—Pindar

By his deeds we know a man.

—African proverb

A human being has no discernible character until he acts.

—Constantine Nash and
Virginia Oakley

To do is to be.   —Socrates

To be is to do.   —Plato

The way to do is to be.   —Lao-tzu

The ordinary man is involved in action, the hero acts. An immense difference.   —Henry Miller

We judge ourselves by what we feel capable of doing, while others judge us by what we have already done.

—Henry Wadsworth Longfellow

Our deeds determine us, as much as we determine our deeds.

—George Eliot

WE FEEL BETTER WHEN WE TAKE ACTION

Performance releases pressure.

—Fisher

The emotions are not always subject to reason ... but they are always subject to action. When thoughts do not neutralize an undesirable emotion, action will.   —William James

He who desires but acts not breeds pestilence.   —William Blake

When I am idle and shiftless, my affairs become confused; when I work, I get results ... not great results, but enough to encourage me.

—Edgar Watson Howe

To be busy with material affairs is the best preservative against reflection, fears, doubts ... all these things which stand in the way of achievement. I suppose a fellow proposing to cut his throat would experience a sort of relief while occupied in stropping his razor carefully.

—Joseph Conrad

Acting can work a peculiar magic on the actor ... it can cure you (at least for the length of a performance) of a whole variety of ailments. Migraine headaches, miserable colds or toothaches will suddenly disappear as you're up there going through your paces.   —Barbara Harris

It is only when I dally with what I am about, look back and aside instead of keeping my eyes straight forward, that I feel these cold sinkings of the heart. But the first broadside puts all to rights.

—Sir Walter Scott

429

Action is the antidote to despair.
　　　　　　　　　　　—Joan Baez

Action is the only reality; not only reality, but morality as well.
　　　　　　　　　—Abbie Hoffman

ACTION AND WEALTH

Wishing does not make a poor man rich.　　　　　　—Arab proverb

You can't get rich sitting on the bench.　　　　　　　—Phil Linz

Action makes more fortunes than caution.　　　　　—Vauvenargues

HOW TO GET GOING

For purposes of action, nothing is more useful than narrowness of thought combined with energy of will.　　　　—Henri Frederic Amiel

How, then, find the courage for action?... By accepting the human condition more simply and candidly, by dreading troubles less, calculating less, hoping more.
　　　　—Henri Frederic Amiel

One starts an action simply because one must do *something*. —T.S. Eliot

We couldn't possibly know where it would lead, but we knew it had to be done.　　　　—Betty Friedan,
　speaking of the Women's Movement

Action springs not from thought, but from a readiness for responsibility.
　　　　　—Dietrich Bohoeffer

Necessity of action takes away the fear of the act.　—Francis Quarles

COURAGE IS ESSENTIAL TO BEGINNING

What you can do, or dream you can do, begin it; boldness has genius, power and magic in it.
　　　　　　—Johann von Goethe

The difference between getting somewhere and nowhere is the courage to make an early start.
　　　　　　—Charles M. Schwab

How many feasible projects have miscarried through despondency, and been strangled in their birth by a cowardly imagination?
　　　　　　　—Jeremy Collier

All glory comes from daring to begin.　　　　　　　—Anon.

More powerful than the will to win is the courage to begin.　—Anon.

Courage to start and willingness to keep everlasting at it are the requisites for success.
　　　　　—Alonzo Newton Benn

There is no such thing as a long piece of work, except one that you dare not start.
　　　　　　—Charles Baudelaire

To the timid and hesitating everything is impossible because it seems so.　　　　—Sir Walter Scott

He who begun has half done. Dare to be wise; begin.　　　—Horace

It's weak and despicable to go on wanting things and not trying to get them.　　　　　—Joanna Field

430

When it comes to betting on yourself ... you're a chicken-livered coward if you hesitate. —B.C. Forbes

Imposing limitations on yourself is cowardly because it protects you from having to try, and perhaps failing. —Vladimir Zworykin

All know the way, few actually walk it. —Bodhidharma

The distance doesn't matter, only the first step is difficult.
—Madame Marquise du Deffand

GENERAL QUOTATIONS ABOUT GETTING GOING

Seize opportunity by the beard, for it is bald behind. —Bulgarian proverb

Procrastination usually results in sorrowful regret. Today's duties put off until tomorrow give us a double burden to bear; the best way is to do them in their proper time.
—Ida Scott Taylor

If you dam a river it stagnates. Running water is beautiful water.
—English proverb

Never mistake motion for action.
—Ernest Hemingway

Procrastination is the thief of time.
—Edward Young

If a man would move the world, he must first move himself. —Socrates

Who hesitate and falter life away, and lose tomorrow the ground won today. —Matthew Arnold

Now or never was the time.
—Laurence Sterne

Can anything be sadder than work unfinished? Yes; work never begun.
—Christina Rossetti

Fear not that thy life shall come to an end, but rather that it shall never have a beginning.
—John Henry Cardinal Newman

Go ahead with your life, your plans.... Don't waste time by stopping before the interruptions have started.
—Richard L. Evans

A hard beginning makes a good ending. —John Heywood

We may our ends by our beginnings know. —Sir John Denham

The only joy in the world is to begin.
—Cesare Pavese

Every artist was first an amateur.
—Ralph Waldo Emerson

The best way to prepare for life is to begin to live. —Elbert Hubbard

431

PART 6

Making Dreams Come True

SUCCESS

BASIC SUCCESS TECHNIQUES

The successful person is the individual who forms the habit of doing what the failing person doesn't like to do. —Donald Riggs

The secret of every man who has ever been successful lies in the fact that he formed the bait of doing those things that failures don't like to do. —A. Jackson King

Nature gave men two ends—one to sit on, and one to think with. Ever since then man's success or failure has been dependent on the one he used most.
—George R. Kirkpatrick

Make yourself indispensable and you'll be moved up. Act as if you're indispensable and you'll be moved out. —Anon.

What is the recipe for successful achievement? To my mind there are just four essential ingredients: Choose a career you love.... Give it the best there is in you.... Seize your opportunities.... And be a member of the team. —Benjamin F. Fairless

Vacillating people seldom succeed. They seldom win the solid respect of their fellows. Successful men and women are very careful in reaching decisions, and very persistent and determined in action thereafter.
—L.G. Elliott

Many people have the ambition to succeed; they may even have a special aptitude for their job. And yet they do not move ahead. Why? Perhaps they think that since they can master the job, there is no need to master themselves.
—John Stevenson

I've been polite and I've always shown up. Somebody asked me if I had any advice for young people entering the business. I said: "Yeah, show up." —Tom T. Hall

The wise man puts all his eggs in one basket and watches the basket.
—Andrew Carnegie

I know the price of success: dedication, hard work and an unremitting devotion to the things you want to see happen. —Frank Lloyd Wright

434

Success is that old ABC—Ability, Breaks and Courage.
—Charles Luckman

The secret of success in life is for a man to be ready for his opportunity when it comes. —Benjamin Disraeli

If one advances confidently in the direction of his dreams, and endeavors to live the life which he has imaged, he will meet with success unexpected in common hours.
—Henry David Thoreau

Before everything else, getting ready is the secret of success.
—Henry Ford

To be ambitious for wealth, and yet always expecting to be poor; to be always doubting your ability to get what you long for, is like trying to reach east by traveling west. There is no philosophy which will help man to succeed when he is always doubting his ability to do so, and thus attracting failure. No matter how hard you work for success, if your thought is saturated with the fear of failure, it will kill your efforts, neutralize your endeavors and make success impossible. —Charles Baudouin

We may fail of our happiness, strive we ever so bravely, but we are less likely to fail if we measure with judgement our chances and our capabilities.   —Agnes Repplier

A double-minded man is unstable in all his ways.... A determinate purpose in life and a steady adhesion to it through all disadvantages are indispensable conditions of success.
—William M. Punshion

The conditions of conquest are always easy. We have but to toil awhile, endure awhile, believe always, and never turn back.
—Marcus Annaeus Seneca

I cannot give you the formula for success, but I can give you the formula for failure, which is—try to please everybody.
—Herbert Bayard Swope

The very first step towards success in any occupation is to become interested in it.   —Sir William Osler

I studied the lives of great men and famous women; and I found that the men and women who got to the top were those who did the jobs they had in hand, with everything they had of energy and enthusiasm and hard work.   —Harry S. Truman

Without ambition one starts nothing. Without work one finishes nothing. The prize will not be sent to you. As to methods there may be a million and then some, but the principles are few. The man who grasps principles can successfully select his own methods. The man who tries methods, ignoring principles, is sure to have trouble.
—Ralph Waldo Emerson

Success is blocked by concentrating on it and planning for it.... Success is shy—it won't come out while you're watching.   —Tennessee Williams

Three outstanding qualities make for success: judgement, industry, health. And the greatest of these is judgement.   —William Maxwell Aitken, Lord Beaverbrook

There are no secrets to success. It is the result of preparation, hard work, learning from failure.
—General Colin L. Powell

Thirteen virtues necessary for true success: temperance, silence, order, resolution, frugality, industry, sincerity, justice, moderation, cleanliness, tranquility, chastity, and humility.
—Benjamin Franklin

Find a need and fill it.
—Ruth Stafford Peale

Put your heart, mind, intellect and soul even to your smallest acts. This is the secret of success.
—Swami Sivananda

Four steps to achievement: plan purposefully, prepare prayerfully, proceed positively, pursue persistently.
—William A. Ward

Success follows doing what you want to do. There is no other way to be successful.   —Malcolm Forbes

Always aim for achievement, and forget about success.
—Helen Hayes

Success, which is something so simple in the end, is made up of thousands of things, we never fully know what.   —Rainer Maria Rilke

Self-trust is the first secret of success.
—Ralph Waldo Emerson

The man who will use his skill and constructive imagination to see how much he can give for a dollar, instead of how little he can give for a dollar, is bound to succeed.
—Henry Ford

THE IMPORTANCE OF INTERPERSONAL RELATIONS

The most important single ingredient in the formula of success is knowing how to get along with people.
—Theodore Roosevelt

The art of dealing with people is the foremost secret of successful men. A man's success in handling people is the very yardstick by which the outcome of his whole life's work is measured.   —Paul C. Packe

The ability to form friendships, to make people believe in you and trust you is one of the few absolutely fundamental qualities of success. Selling, buying, negotiating are so much smoother and easier when the parties enjoy each other's confidence. The young man who can make friends quickly will find that he will glide, instead of stumble, through life.
—John J. McGuirk

No matter how much a man can do, no matter how engaging his personality may be, he will not advance far in business if he cannot work through others.   —John Craig

The way to rise is to obey and please.   —Ben Johnson

Skill is fine, and genius is splendid, but the right contacts are more valuable than either.
—Sir Archibald McIndoe

Whatever your grade or position, if you know how and when to speak, and when to remain silent, your chances of real success are proportionately increased.
—Ralph C. Smedley

The Importance of Desire, Enthusiasm, Zeal, Optimism, and Energy

A man can succeed at almost anything for which he has unlimited enthusiasm. —Charles M. Schwab

Flaming enthusiasm, backed up by horse sense and persistence, is the quality that most frequently makes for success. —Dale Carnegie

The world belongs to the energetic. —Ralph Waldo Emerson

There is a passion for perfection which you rarely see fully developed; but you may note this fact, that in successful lives it is never wholly lacking. —Bliss Carman

Sometimes success is due less to ability than to zeal. —Charles Buxton

Many of the most successful men I have known have never grown up. They have retained bubbling-over boyishness. They have relished wit, they have indulged in humor. They have not allowed "dignity" to depress them into moroseness. Youthfulness of spirit is the twin brother of optimism, and optimism is the stuff of which American business success is fashioned. Resist growing up! —B.C. Forbes

If you have the will to win, you have achieved half your success; if you don't, you have achieved half your failure. —David V.A. Ambrose

Someone's always saying, "It's not whether you win or lose," but if you feel that way, you're as good as dead. —James Caan

The real difference between men is energy. —Fuller

Success is going from failure to failure without loss of enthusiasm. —Sir Winston Churchill

To bring one's self to a frame of mind and to the proper energy to accomplish things that require plain hard work continuously is the one big battle that everyone has. When this battle is won for all time, then everything is easy. —Thomas A. Buckner

We would accomplish many more things if we did not think of them as impossible. —C. Malesherbez

Faith that the thing can be done is essential to any great achievement. —Thomas N. Carruther

We can accomplish almost anything within our ability if we but think that we can! —George Matthew Adams

Optimism is essential to achievement and it is also the foundation of courage and of true progress. —Nicholas Murray Butler

Morale is the greatest single factor in successful wars. —Dwight D. Eisenhower

The will to conquer is the first condition of victory. —Marshal Ferdinand Foch

Always bear in mind that your own resolution to success is more important than any other one thing. —Abraham Lincoln

The real secret of success is enthusiasm. Yes, more than enthusiasm, I would say excitement. I like to see men get excited. When they get excited, they make a success of their lives.   —Walter Chrysler

It is fatal to enter any war without the will to win it.
          —General Douglas MacArthur

The measure of an enthusiasm must be taken between interesting events. It is between bites that the lukewarm angler loses heart.
          —Edwin Way Teale

Enthusiasm for one's goal lessens the disagreeableness of working toward it.   —Thomas Eakins

To burn always with this hard gem-like flame, to maintain this ecstasy, is success in life.   —Walter Pater

Every man is enthusiastic at times. One man has enthusiasm for thirty minutes, another man has it for thirty days. But it is the man who has it for thirty years who makes a success in life.   —Edward B. Butler

Man never rises to great truths without enthusiasm.   —Vauvenargues

Success is due less to ability than to zeal.   —Charles Buxton

I rate enthusiasm even above professional skill.   —Sir Edward Appleton

He did it with all his heart, and prospered.   —2 Chr. 31:21

Do it big or stay in bed.
          —Larry Kelly

Nothing great was ever achieved without enthusiasm.
          —Ralph Waldo Emerson

What a man accomplishes in a day depends upon the way in which he approaches his tasks. When we accept tough jobs as a challenge to our ability and wade into them with joy and enthusiasm, miracles can happen. When we do our work with a dynamic conquering spirit, we get things done.   —Arland Gilbert

If you're not happy every morning when you get up, leave for work, or start to work at home, if you're not enthusiastic about doing that, you're not going to be successful.
          —Donald M. Kendall

A strong passion for any object will ensure success, for the desire of the end will point out the means.
          —William Hazlitt

The method of the enterprising is to plan with audacity and execute with vigor.   —Christian Bovee

SELF-RELIANCE AND SUCCESS

If you want to succeed, you must make your own opportunities as you go.   —John B. Gough

Every man is the architect of his own fortune.   —Sallust

A wise man will make more opportunities than he finds.
          —Francis Bacon

No man will succeed unless he is ready to face and overcome difficulties and prepared to assume responsibilities.   —William J.H. Boetcker

Man is still responsible.... His success lies not with the stars, but with himself. He must carry on the fight of self-correction and discipline.
—Frank Curtis Williams

No one can help you in holding a good job except Old Man You.
—Edgar Watson Howe

Under normal periods, any man's success hinges about five percent on what others do for him and 95 percent on what he does.
—James A. Worsham

If, after all, men cannot always make history have a meaning, they can always act so that their own lives have one.   —Albert Camus

The brave man carves out his fortune, and every man is the sum of his own works.   —Miguel de Cervantes

If a man wants his dreams to come true, he must wake up.   —Anon.

Pa, he always said a man had to look spry for himself, because nobody would do it for him; your opportunities didn't come knocking around, you had to hunt them down and hog-tie them.   —Louis L'Amour

Men at some time are masters of their fates.   —William Shakespeare

Destiny is not a matter of chance, it is a matter of choice; it is not a thing to be waited for, it is a thing to be achieved.   —William J. Bryan

The people who get on in this world are the people who get up and look for the circumstances they want,

and, if they can't find them, make them.   —George Bernard Shaw

WE MUST TAKE RISKS TO SUCCEED

The men who have done big things are those who were not afraid to attempt big things, who were not afraid to risk failure in order to gain success.   —B.C. Forbes

If the risk-reward ratio is right, you can make big money buying trouble.
—Anon.

What isn't tried won't work.
—Claude McDonald

All great reforms require one to dare a lot to win a little.
—William L. O'Neill

If you limit your actions in life to things that nobody can possibly find fault with, you will not do much.
—Charles Lutwidge Dodgson

The ambitious climbs high and perilous stairs and never cares how to come down; the desire of rising hath swallowed up his fear of a fall.
—Thomas Adams

He that would have fruit must climb the tree.   —Thomas Fuller

To get profit without risk, experience without danger and reward without work is as impossible as it is to live without being born.
—A.P. Gouthey

Every noble acquisition is attended with its risks; he who fears to encounter the one must not expect to obtain the other. —Pietro Metastasio

439

The method of the enterprising is to plan with audacity and execute with vigor. —Christian Bovee

Great deeds are usually wrought at great risks. —Herodotus

Only those who dare to fail greatly can ever achieve greatly.
—Robert F. Kennedy

He that is overcautious will accomplish little. —J.C.F. von Schiller

No one reaches a high position without daring. —Publilius Syrus

Cadillacs are down at the end of the bat. —Ralph Kiner, when asked why he didn't choke up and hit for average

It is impossible to win the great prizes of life without running risks.
—Theodore Roosevelt

You can't expect to hit the jackpot if you don't put a few nickels in the machine. —Flip Wilson

Who dares nothing, need hope for nothing. —J.C.F. von Schiller

Progress always involves risks. You can't steal second base and keep your foot on first.
—Frederick B. Wilcox

I don't think about risks much. I just do what I want to do. If you gotta go, you gotta go.
—Miss Lillian Carter

Behold the turtle. He makes progress only when he sticks his neck out.
—James Bryant Conant

Nothing ventured, nothing gained.
—Anon.

You can't catch trout with dry breeches. —Spanish proverb

Don't be afraid to take a big step if one is indicated. You can't cross a chasm in two small jumps.
—David Lloyd George

WE CAN'T SUCCEED WITHOUT COURAGE

Because a fellow has failed once or twice or a dozen times, you don't want to set him down as a failure till he's dead or loses his courage—and that's the same thing.
—George Horace Lorimer

What is more mortifying than to feel that you have missed the plum for want of courage to shake the tree?
—Logan Pearsall Smith

To persevere, trusting in what hopes he has, is courage. The coward despairs. —Euripides

Whatever you do, you need courage.... To map out a course of action and follow it to an end requires some of the same courage which a soldier needs. —Ralph Waldo Emerson

Who dares nothing, need hope for nothing. —J.C.F. von Schiller

Have the courage of your desire.
—George R. Gissing

To see what is right, and not do it, is want of courage. —Confucius

It takes vision and courage to create—it takes faith and courage to prove. —Owen D. Young

No great thing comes to any man
unless he has courage.
—Cardinal James Gibbons

Great things are done more through
courage than through wisdom.
—German proverb

Courage permits the caliber of performance to continue at its peak,
until the finish line is crossed.
—Stuart Walker

Failure is only postponed success as
long as courage "coaches" ambition.
The habit of persistence is the habit
of victory.   —Herbert Kaufman

Courage and perseverance have a
magical talisman, before which difficulties disappear, and obstacles vanish into air.   —John Quincy Adams

You will never do anything in this
world without courage.
—James Lane Allen

It takes as much courage to have
tried and failed as it does to have
tried and succeeded.
—Anne Morrow Lindbergh

Where there is a brave man, in the
thickest of the fight, there is the post
of honor.   —Henry David Thoreau

Whenever you see a successful business, someone once made a courageous decision.   —Peter Drucker

There are a lot of fellas with all the
ability it takes to play in the major
leagues, but they never make it, they
always get stuck in the minor leagues
because they haven't got the guts to
make the climb. —Cookie Lavagetto

Courage to start and willingness to
keep everlasting at it are the requisites for success.
—Alonzo Newton Benn

One of the biggest factors in success
is the courage to undertake something.   —James A. Worsham

It is weak and despicable to go on
wanting things and not trying to get
them.   —Joanna Field

WORK AND SUCCESS

Nothing worthwhile comes easily.
Half effort does not produce half
results. It produces no results. Work,
continuous work and hard work, is
the only way to accomplish results
that last.   —Hamilton Holt

If a man wakes up famous he hasn't
been sleeping.   —Wes Izzard

Success is dependent on effort.
—Sophocles

Success comes before work only in
the dictionary.   —Anon.

Striving for success without hard
work is like trying to harvest where
you haven't planted.   —David Bly

Sweat plus sacrifice equals success.
—Charles O. Finley

Success usually comes to those who
are too busy to be looking for it.
—Henry David Thoreau

In all human affairs there are *efforts*,
and there are *results*, and the
strength of the effort is the measure
of the result.   —James Lane Allen

WE MUST WORK ON THE RIGHT THINGS

It is no use saying "we are doing our best." You have got to succeed in doing what is necessary.
—Sir Winston Churchill

Many people who wonder why they don't amount to more than they do have good stuff in them, and are energetic, persevering, and have ample opportunities. It is all a case of trimming the useless branches and throwing the whole force of power into the development of something that counts.   —Walter J. Johnston

Will you be satisfied with the fruit of your life's work? Will the efforts you are making now bring you satisfaction when the things of time are receding, and eternity looms ahead?
—Raymond L. Cox

SUCCESS AND CHARACTER

Character is the real foundation of all worthwhile success.
—John Hays Hammond

Some men succeed by what they know; some by what they do; and a few by what they are.
—Elbert Hubbard

Try not to become a man of success, but rather a man of value.
—Albert Einstein

It is abundantly clear that success tends to negate humility.
—Landrum P. Leavell

Success seems to be that which forms the distinction between confidence and conceit. —Charles Caleb Colton

The common idea that success spoils people by making them vain, egotistic, and self-complacent is erroneous; on the contrary, it makes them, for the most part, humble, tolerant, and kind. Failure makes people cruel and bitter.   —W. Somerset Maugham

Character cannot be developed in ease and quiet. Only through experience of trial and suffering can the soul be strengthened, vision cleared, ambition inspired, and success achieved.   —Helen Keller

If a man be self-controlled, truthful, wise, and resolute, is there aught that can stay out of reach of such a man?   —The Panchatantra

TO SUCCEED, WE MUST LEARN TO ADMIT AND ACCEPT FAILURE

One of the first businesses of a sensible man is to know when he is beaten, and to leave off fighting at once.
—Samuel Butler

If you can't accept losing, you can't win.   —Vince Lombardi

You can't have any successes unless you can accept failure.
—George Cukor

We have fought this fight as long, and as well, as we know how. We have been defeated ... there is now but one course to pursue. We must accept the situation. —Robert E. Lee

The most considerable difference I note among men is not in their readiness to fall into error, but in their readiness to acknowledge these inevitable lapses.
—Thomas Henry Huxley

An error gracefully acknowledged is a victory won.

—Caroline L. Gascoigne

The man who can own up to his error is greater than he who merely knows how to avoid making it.

—Cardinal De Retz

I have made mistakes, but I have never made the mistake of claiming that I never made one.

—James Gordon Bennett

WE MUST PERSEVERE TO BE SUCCESSFUL

I am not the smartest or most talented person in the world, but I succeeded because I keep going, and going, and going.—Sylvester Stallone

I know the price of success: dedication, hard work and an unremitting devotion to the things you want to see happen.   —Frank Lloyd Wright

Victory belongs to the most persevering.   —Napoleon Bonaparte

Success generally depends upon knowing how long it takes to succeed.   —Charles de Montesquieu

Success seems to be largely a matter of hanging on after others have let go.   —William Feather

Call the roll in your memory of conspicuously successful business giants and ... you will be struck by the fact that almost every one of them encountered inordinate difficulties sufficient to crush all but the gamest of spirits. Edison went hungry many times before he became famous.

—B.C. Forbes

If you wish success in life, make perseverance your bosom friend.

—Joseph Addison

They who are the most persistent, and work in the true spirit, will invariably be the most successful.

—Samuel Smiles

If at first you don't succeed, try, try, try again.   —W.E. Hickson

If at first you don't succeed, you're running about average.

—M.H. Alderson

The only way to the top is by persistent, intelligent, hard work.

—A.T. Mercier

The heights by great men reached
  and kept
Were not attained by sudden flight,
But they, while their companions
  slept
Were toiling upward in the night.
      —Henry Wadsworth Longfellow

I realized early on that success was tied to not giving up. Most people in this business gave up and went on to other things. If you simply didn't give up, you would outlast the people who came in on the bus with you.   —Harrison Ford

Perseverance is a great element of success. If you only knock long enough and loud enough at the gate, you are sure to wake up somebody.

—Henry Wadsworth Longfellow

Four steps to achievement: plan purposefully, prepare prayerfully, proceed positively, pursue persistently.

—William A. Ward

443

The secret of success is constancy of purpose. —Benjamin Disraeli

I'm hardnosed about luck. I think it sucks. Yeah, if you spend seven years looking for a job as a copywriter, and then one day somebody gives you a job, you can say, "Gee, I was lucky I happened to go up there today." But dammit, I was going to go up there sooner or later in the next seventy years.... If you're persistent in trying and doing and working, you almost make your own fortune. —Jerry Della Femina

Flaming enthusiasm, backed up by horse sense and persistence, is the quality that most frequently makes for success. —Dale Carnegie

It's the plugging away that will win
  you the day
So don't be a piker, old pard!
Just draw on your grit, it's so easy to
  quit—
It's the keeping your chin up that's
  hard. —Robert W. Service

No one succeeds without effort....
Those who succeed owe their success to their perseverance.
  —Ramana Maharshi

Big shots are only little shots who keep shooting.
  —Christopher Morley

Entrepreneurs average 3.8 failures before final success. What sets the successful ones apart is their amazing persistence. There are a lot of people out there with good and marketable ideas, but pure entrepreneurial types almost never accept defeat.
  —Lisa M. Amos

Be of good cheer. Do not think of today's failures, but of the success that may come tomorrow. You have set yourselves a difficult task, but you will succeed if you persevere; and you will find a joy in overcoming obstacles. Remember, no effort that we make to attain something beautiful is ever lost. —Helen Keller

The way to succeed is never quit. That's it. But really be humble about it.... You start out lowly and humble and you carefully try to learn an accretion of little things that help you get there. —Alex Hailey

There are no shortcuts to any place worth going. —Beverly Sills

Continuous effort—not strength or intelligence—is the key to unlocking our potential.
  —Sir Winston Churchill

Plodding wins the race. —Aesop

The difficulties and struggles of today are but the price we must pay for the accomplishments and victories of tomorrow.
  —William J.H. Boetcker

Let me tell you the secret that has led me to my goal. My strength lies solely in my tenacity. —Louis Pasteur

A winner never quits, and a quitter never wins. —Anon.

It isn't hard to be good from time to time in sports. What's tough is being good every day. —Willie Mays

If you start to take Vienna, take Vienna. —Napoleon Bonaparte

444

Men who have attained things worth having in this world have worked while others idled, have persevered when others gave up in despair, have practiced early in life the valuable habits of self-denial, industry, and singleness of purpose. As a result, they enjoy in later life the success so often erroneously attributed to good luck.　　—Grenvill Kleiser

In the realm of ideas, everything depends on enthusiasm; in the real world, all rests on perseverance.
　　—Johann von Goethe

There's such a thin line between winning and losing.　　—John R. Tunis

SUCCESS TAKES TIME

It takes time to be a success.
　　—Anon.

Actually, I'm an overnight success. But it took twenty years.
　　—Monty Hall

It takes time to succeed because success is merely the natural reward for taking time to do anything well.
　　—Joseph Ross

Success generally depends upon knowing how long it takes to succeed.　　—Charles de Montesquieu

It takes twenty years to make an overnight success.　　—Eddie Cantor

SUCCESS IS RELATIVE

Our business in life is not to get ahead of others but to get ahead of ourselves—to break our own records, to outstrip our yesterdays by our today, to do our work with more force than ever before.
　　—Steward B. Johnson

Success is to be measured not so much by the position that one has reached in life as by the obstacles which he has overcome.
　　—Booker T. Washington

Success has always been easy to measure. It is the distance between one's origins and one's final achievement.
　　—Michael Korda

How can they say my life is not a success? Have I not for more than sixty years got enough to eat and escaped being eaten?
　　—Logan Pearsall Smith

Survival is triumph enough.
　　—Harry Crews

Success is peace of mind, which is a direct result of knowing you did your best to become the best that you are capable of becoming.
　　—John Wooden

Success is relative: It is what we can make of the mess we have made of things.　　—T.S. Eliot

The conventional army loses if it does not win. The guerrilla wins if he does not lose.　　—Henry Kissinger

The man who has done his level best, and who is conscious that he has done his best, is a success, even though the world may write him down a failure.　　—B.C. Forbes

My success is measured by my willingness to keep trying.　　—Anon.

If you've had a good time playing the game, you're a winner even if you lose.　　—Malcolm Forbes

Success is living up to your potential. That's all. Wake up with a smile and go after life.... Live it, enjoy it, taste it, smell it, feel it.   —Joe Kapp

I have fought a good fight, I have finished my course, I have kept the faith.   —2 Tm. 4:7

On earth we have nothing to do with success or results, but only with being true to God, and for God. Defeat in doing right is nevertheless victory.   —Frederick W. Robertson

The reward of a thing well done is to have done it.
      —Ralph Waldo Emerson

I'd rather be a lamppost in Chicago than a millionaire in any other city.
      —William A. Hulbert

A successful man is he who receives a great deal from his fellow men, usually incomparably more than corresponds to his service to them. The value of a man, however, should be seen in what he gives, and not in what he is able to receive.
      —Albert Einstein

SUCCESS IS DOING WHAT'S RIGHT FOR US

There is only one success—to be able to spend your life in your own way.
      —Christopher Morley

The only success worth one's powder was success in the line of one's idiosyncrasy ... what was talent but the art of being completely whatever one happened to be? —Henry James

We only do well the things we like doing.   —Colette

Success based on anything but internal fulfillment is bound to be empty.
      —Dr. Martha Friedman

All I would tell people is to hold on to what was individual about themselves, not to allow their ambition for success to cause them to try to imitate the success of others. You've got to find it on your own terms.
      —Harrison Ford

For me, writing is the only thing that passes the three tests of *metier:* (1) when I'm doing it, I don't feel that I should be doing something else instead; (2) it produces a sense of accomplishment and, once in a while, pride; and (3) it's frightening.
      —Gloria Steinem

One can never consent to creep when one feels an impulse to soar.
      —Helen Keller

My mother said to me, "If you become a soldier, you'll be a general, if you become a monk you'll end up as the pope." Instead, I became a painter and wound up as Picasso.
      —Pablo Picasso

Abasement, degradation is simply the manner of life of the man who has refused to be what it is his duty to be.   —José Ortega y Gasset

Different people have different duties assigned to them by Nature; Nature has given one the power or the desire to do this, the other that. Each bird must sing with his own throat.
      —Henrik Ibsen

A first rate soup is better than a second rate painting.
      —Abraham Maslow

We can't all be heroes because someone has to sit on the curb and clap as
they go by.   —Will Rogers

Nature magically suits a man to his
fortunes, by making them the fruit of
his character.
          —Ralph Waldo Emerson

I'd rather be a lamppost in Chicago
than a millionaire in any other city.
          —William A. Hulbert

We succeed in enterprises which
demand the positive qualities we
possess, but we excel in those which
can also make use of our defects.
          —Alexis de Tocqueville

A man can do only what he can do.
But if he does that each day he can
sleep at night and do it again the
next day.   —Albert Schweitzer

Don't take anyone else's definition
of success as your own. (This is easier said than done.)
          —Jacqueline Briskin

Whatever you are by nature, keep to
it; never desert your own line of talent. Be what nature intended you
for, and you will succeed; be anything else and you will be ten thousand times worse than nothing.
          —Sydney Smith

Ask yourself the secret of *your* success. Listen to your answer, and
practice it.   —Richard Bach

I cannot do everything, but still I can
do something; and because I cannot
do everything I will not refuse to do
something that I can do.
          —Edward Everett Hale

Starting out to make money is the
greatest mistake in life. Do what you
feel you have a flair for doing, and if
you are good enough at it, the
money will come.   —Greer Garson

If a man has a talent and cannot use
it, he has failed. If he has a talent
and uses only half of it, he has partly
failed. If he has a talent and learns
somehow to use the whole of it, he
has gloriously succeeded, and won a
satisfaction and a triumph few men
ever know.   —Thomas Wolfe

BEFORE WE CAN SUCCEED, WE HAVE TO NOT FAIL

Most ball games are lost, not won.
          —Casey Stengel

Before you can win a game, you
have to not lose it.   —Chuck Noll

Football games aren't won, they're
lost.   —Fielding Yost

THE JOURNEY IS MORE IMPORTANT THAN ARRIVING

Success is a journey, not a destination.   —Ben Sweetland

To travel hopefully is a better thing
than to arrive, and the true success is
to labor.   —Robert Louis Stevenson

Despite the success cult, men are
most deeply moved not by the reaching of the goal, but by the grandness
of effort involved in getting there—
or failing to get there.   —Max Lerner

To live only for some future goal is
shallow. It's the sides of the mountain that sustain life, not the top.
          —Robert M. Pirsig

The reward of the general is not a bigger tent, but command.
—Oliver Wendell Holmes, Jr.

It is good to have an end to journey toward; but it is the journey that matters, in the end.
—Ursula K. LeGuin

We're still not where we're going, but we're not where we were.
—Natash Jasefowitz

'Tis the motive exalts the action, 'Tis the doing, and not the deed.
—Margaret Junkin Preston

Arriving at one goal is the starting point to another.   —John Dewey

I think that wherever your journey takes you, there are new gods waiting there, with divine patience—and laughter.   —Susan M. Watkins

It has never been, and never will be, easy work! But the road that is built in hope is more pleasant to the traveler than the road built in despair, even though they both lead to the same destination.
—Marian Zimmer Bradley

In the long run, the pessimist may be proved to be right, but the optimist has a better time on the trip.
—Daniel L. Reardon

The excursion is the same when you go looking for your sorrow as when you go looking for your joy.
—Eudora Welty

The reward of a thing well done is to have done it.
—Ralph Waldo Emerson

The problem is not that you cannot have what you think you want. The problem is that when you get what you think you want, it won't satisfy.
—Anon.

The struggle alone pleases us, not the victory.   —Blaise Pascal

We should scarcely desire things ardently if we were perfectly acquainted with what we desire.
—Francois de La Rochefoucauld

With the catching ends the pleasures of the chase.   —Abraham Lincoln

To have realized your dream makes you feel lost.   —Oriana Fallaci

Need and struggle are what excite and inspire us; our hour of triumph is what brings the void.
—William James

We spend our time searching for security, and hate it when we get it.
—John Steinbeck

Happiness is not a station to arrive at, but a manner of traveling.
—Margaret Lee Runbeck

Happiness is to be found along the way, not at the end of the road, for then the journey is over and it is too late.   —Robert R. Updegraff

The really happy man is one who can enjoy the scenery on a detour.
—Anon.

You wear yourself out in the pursuit of wealth or love or freedom, you do everything to gain some right, and once it's gained you take no pleasure in it.   —Oriana Fallaci

Success Isn't the Total Answer

Success is counted sweetest by those who ne'er succeed.
—Emily Dickinson

Granting our wish is one of Fate's saddest jokes.
—James Russell Lowell

Now that I'm here, where am I?
—Janis Joplin

Success is not greedy, as people think, but insignificant. That's why it satisfies nobody.
—Marcus Annaeus Seneca

Is there anything in life so disenchanting as attainment?
—Robert Louis Stevenson

Nothing fails like success; nothing is so defeated as yesterday's triumphant cause.   —Phyllis McGinley

There are two tragedies in life. One is to lose your heart's desire. The other is to gain it.
—George Bernard Shaw

Success has ruined many a man.
—Benjamin Franklin

Fame always brings loneliness. Success is as ice cold and lonely as the North Pole.   —Vicki Baum

Success has killed more men than bullets.   —Texas Guinan

Achievement: The death of an endeavor, and the birth of disgust.
—Ambrose Bierce

Success and failure are equally disastrous.   —Tennessee Williams

The problems of victory are more agreeable than those of defeat, but they are no less difficult.
—Sir Winston Churchill

We are never further from our wishes than when we imagine that we possess what we have desired.
—Johann von Goethe

Some aspects of success seem rather silly as death approaches.
—Donald A. Miller

Unless a man has been taught what to do with success after getting it, the achievement of it must inevitably leave him a prey to boredom.
—Bertrand Russell

If I had known what it would be like to have it all, I might have been willing to settle for less.   —Lily Tomlin

Success and failure are both difficult to endure. Along with success come drugs, divorce, fornication, bullying, travel, meditation, medication, depression, neurosis and suicide. With failure comes failure.
—Joseph Heller

The two hardest things to handle in life are failure and success.
—Anon.

The best thing that can come with success is the knowledge that it is nothing to long for.   —Liv Ullmann

The closer one gets to the top, the more one finds there is no "top."
—Nancy Barcus

Oh, how quickly the world's glory passes away.   —Thomas a'Kempis

The minute you think you've got it made, disaster is just around the corner. —Joe Paterno

Creating success is tough. But keeping it is tougher. You have to keep producing, you can't ever stop. —Pete Rose

Out of every fruition of success, no matter what, comes forth something to make a new effort necessary. —Walt Whitman

The toughest thing about success is that you've got to keep on being a success. Talent is only a starting point in business. You've got to keep working that talent. —Irving Berlin

We would often be sorry if our wishes were gratified. —Aesop

Nothing except a battle lost can be half so melancholy as a battle won. —Arthur Wellesley, Duke of Wellington

Being frustrated is disagreeable, but the real disasters of life begin when you get what you want. —Irving Kristol

We grow weary of those things (and perhaps soonest) which we most desire. —Samuel Butler

Our desires always increase with our possessions. The knowledge that something remains yet unenjoyed impairs our enjoyment of the good before us. —Samuel Johnson

Oddly enough, success over a period of time is more expensive than failure. —Grant Tinker

There must be more to life than having everything! —Maurice Sendak

It's not that I'm not grateful for all this attention. It's just that fame and fortune ought to add up to more than fame and fortune. —Robert Fulghum

If you live long enough, you'll see that every victory turns into a defeat. —Simone de Beauvoir

One more such victory and we are undone. —Pyrrhus

Pray that success will not come any faster than you are able to endure it. —Elbert Hubbard

The prospect of success in achieving our most cherished dream is not without its terrors. Who is more deprived and alone than the man who has achieved his dream? —Brendan Francis

Success can also cause misery. The trick is not to be surprised when you discover it doesn't bring you all the happiness and answers you thought it would. —Prince

Adversity is sometimes hard upon a man, but for one man who can stand prosperity, there are a hundred that will stand adversity. —Thomas Carlyle

OTHER DEFINITIONS OF SUCCESS
Success is getting what you want; happiness is wanting what you get. —Anon.

Life is a succession of moments. To live each one is to succeed. —Corita Kent

450

To laugh often and much;
To win the respect of intelligent people, and the affection of children;
To earn the appreciation of honest critics, and endure the betrayal of false friends;
To appreciate beauty;
To find the best in others;
To leave the world a bit better, whether by a healthy child, a garden patch, or a redeemed social condition;
To know that even one life has breathed easier because you lived.
This is to have succeeded.
—Ralph Waldo Emerson

Success has nothing to do with what you gain in life or accomplish for yourself. It's what you do for others.
—Danny Thomas

If you have a good name, if you are right more often than you are wrong, if your children respect you, if your grandchildren are glad to see you, if your friends can count on you and you can count on them in time of trouble, if you can face your God and say "I have done my best," then you are a success.   —Ann Landers

You have reached the pinnacle of success as soon as you become uninterested in money, compliments, or publicity.   —Thomas Wolfe

GENERAL QUOTATIONS ABOUT SUCCESS

Marconi invented radio, but Ted Husing knew what to do with it.
—Ralph Edwards

Success produces success, just as money produces money.
—Nicolas de Chamfort

God may allow His servant to succeed when He has disciplined him to a point where he does not need to succeed to be happy. The man who is elated by success and is cast down by failure is still a carnal man. At best his fruit will have a worm in it.
—A.W. Tozer

There is no business in the world so troublesome as the pursuit of fame: life is over before you have hardly begun your work.
—Jean de La Bruyere

Nothing fails like success because we don't learn from it. We learn only from failure.   —Kenneth Boudling

Success makes men rigid and they tend to exalt stability over all the other virtues; tired of the effort of willing, they become fanatics about conservatism.   —Walter Lippman

All outward success, when it has value, is but the inevitable result of an inward success of full living, full play and enjoyment of one's faculties.   —Robert Henri

There are three types of baseball players—those who make it happen, those who watch it happen, and those who wonder what happened.
—Tommy Lasorda

The exclusive worship of the bitch-goddess Success is our national disease.   —William James

Success causes us to be more praised than known.   —Joseph Roux

Along with success comes a reputation for wisdom.   —Euripides

Great men have not been concerned with fame. The joy of achievement that comes from finding something new in the universe is by far their greatest joy.   —William P. King

Out of the strain of the Doing, into the peace of the Done.
                    —Julia Louise Woodruff

Success is like a liberation, or the first phase of a love affair.
                    —Jeanne Moreau

There is always room at the top.
                    —Daniel Webster

An act of love that fails is just as much a part of the divine life as an act of love that succeeds, for love is measured by its own fullness, not by its reception.   —Harold Loukes

The best place to succeed is where you are with what you have.
                    —Charles M. Schwab

Success covers a multitude of blunders.   —George Bernard Shaw

How to succeed: try hard enough. How to fail: Try too hard.
                    —Malcolm Forbes

I have found that it is much easier to make a success in life than to make a success of one's life.   —G.W. Follin

There could be no honor in a sure success, but much might be wrested from a sure defeat.   —T.E. Lawrence
                    (Lawrence of Arabia)

Bad will be the day for every man when he becomes absolutely contented with the life he is living, when there is not forever beating at the doors of his soul some great desire to do something larger.
                    —Phillips Brooks

When there is no feeling of accomplishment, children fail to develop properly and old people rapidly decline.   —Joseph Whitney

Those who have easy, cheerful attitudes tend to be happier than those with less pleasant temperaments, regardless of money, "making it," or success.   —Dr. Joyce Brothers

Theirs is not to reason why, theirs is but to do or die.
                    —Alfred, Lord Tennyson

Victory at all costs, victory in spite of all terror, victory however long and hard the hard may be; for without victory there is no survival.
                    —Sir Winston Churchill

In war there is no second prize for the runner-up.
                    —General Omar N. Bradley

LUCK

LUCK CAN BE VERY IMPORTANT

Luck is everything.... My good luck in life was to be a really frightened person. I'm fortunate to be a coward, to have a low threshold of fear, because a hero couldn't make a good suspense film. —Alfred Hitchcock

I would rather have a lucky general than a smart general.... They win battles, and they make me lucky.
—Dwight D. Eisenhower

Everything in life is luck.
—Donald Trump

'Tis man's to fight, but Heaven's to give success. —Homer

I am persuaded that luck and timing have, in my case, been very important. —Mike Wallace

I have been extraordinarily lucky. Anyone who pretends that some kind of luck isn't involved in his success is deluding himself.
—Arthur Hailey

'Tis better to be fortunate than wise.
—John Webster

I wish I could tell you that the Children's Television Workshop and Sesame Street were thanks to my genius, but it really was a lucky break. —Joan Ganz Cooney

In the queer mess of human destiny, the determining factor is luck.
—William E. Woodward

Much of my good fortune was a matter of nothing more clever on my part than luck. —James Fixx

Though men pride themselves on their great actions, often they are not the result of any great design, but of chance.
—Francois de La Rochefoucauld

No writer should minimize the factor that affects everyone, but is beyond control: luck. —John Jakes

Everything that happened to me happened by mistake. I don't believe in fate. It's luck, timing and accident.
—Merv Griffin

Name the greatest of all inventors: Accident. —Mark Twain

Still, We Can't Depend Too Heavily on Luck

Luck always seems to be against the man who depends on it. —Anon.

Good luck is often with the man who doesn't include it in his plans.
—Anon.

Depend on the rabbit's foot if you will, but it didn't work for the rabbit!
—Anon.

Destiny is the invention of the cowardly, and the resigned.
—Ignazio Silone

They who await no gifts from chance have conquered fate.
—Matthew Arnold

The worst cynicism, a belief in luck.
—Joyce Carol Oates

To believe in luck ... is skepticism.
—Ralph Waldo Emerson

Shallow men believe in luck, wise and strong men in cause and effect.
—Ralph Waldo Emerson

Those who trust to chance must abide by the results of chance.
—Calvin Coolidge

Luck is what a capricious man believes in.
—Benjamin Disraeli

Luck serves ... as rationalization for every people that is not master of its own destiny.
—Hannah Arendt

It is a madness to make fortune the mistress of events, because in herself she is nothing, but is ruled by prudence.
—John Dryden

Luck is a word devoid of sense; nothing can exist without a cause.
—Voltaire

Woe to him who would ascribe something like reason to Chance, and make a religion of surrendering to it.
—Johann von Goethe

Fortune is the rod of the weak, and the staff of the brave.
—James Russell Lowell

The man who is intent on making the most of his opportunities is too busy to bother about luck.
—B.C. Forbes

Luck implies an absolute absence of any principle.
—Chuang-tzu

We Must Create Our Own Luck

I'm hardnosed about luck. I think it sucks. Yeah, if you spend seven years looking for a job as a copywriter, and then one day somebody gives you a job, you can say, "Gee, I was lucky I happened to go up there today." But dammit, I was going to go up there sooner or later in the next seventy years.... If you're persistent in trying and doing and working, you almost make your own fortune.
—Jerry Della Femina

It is a great piece of skill to know how to guide your luck, even while waiting for it.
—Baltasar Gracian

I was thinking of my patients, and how the worst moment for them was when they discovered they were masters of bad or good luck. When they could no longer blame fate, they were in despair.
—Anaïs Nin

Some are satisfied to stand politely before the portals of Fortune and to await her bidding; better those who push forward, who employ their enterprise, who on the wings of their worth and valor seek to embrace luck, and to effectively gain her favor. —Baltasar Gracian

The champion makes his own luck. —Red Blaik

Chance never helps those who do not help themselves. —Sophocles

Failure and success seem to have been allotted to men by their stars. But they retain the power of wriggling, of fighting with their star or against it, and in the whole universe the only really interesting movement is this wriggle. —E.M. Forster

If fate means you to lose, give him a good fight anyhow. —William McFee

Go and wake up your luck. —Persian proverb

People make their own luck. —David Liederman

We create our fate every day ... most of the ills we suffer from are directly traceable to our own behavior. —Henry Miller

Of course, fortune has its part in human affairs, but conduct is really much more important. —Jeanne Detourbey

You don't just luck into things.... You build step by step, whether it's friendships or opportunities. —Barbara Bush

We must master our good fortune, or it will master us. —Publilius Syrus

GOOD LUCK COMES FROM HARD WORK

I'm a great believer in luck, and I find the harder I work, the more I have of it. —Thomas Jefferson

Luck means the hardships and privations which you have not hesitated to endure, the long nights you have devoted to work. Luck means the appointments you have never failed to keep, the trains you have never failed to catch. —Max O'Relling

Luck is what you have left over after you give 100 percent. —Langston Coleman

Luck is not chance, it's toil; fortune's expensive smile is earned. —Emily Dickinson

The lucky fellow is the plucky fellow who has been burning midnight oil and taking defeat after defeat with a smile. —James B. Hill

I find I'm luckier when I work harder. —Dr. Denton Cooley

Men who have attained things worth having in this world have worked while others idled, have persevered when others gave up in despair, have practiced early in life the valuable habits of self-denial, industry, and singleness of purpose. As a result, they enjoy in later life the success so often erroneously attributed to good luck. —Grenville Kleiser

Luck is the by-product of busting your fanny. —Don Sutton

455

When you work seven days a week, fourteen hours a day, you get lucky.
—Armand Hammer

No man ever wetted clay and then left it, as if there would be bricks by chance and fortune.   —Plutarch

It's hard to detect good luck—it looks so much like something you've earned.   —Frank A. Clark

Chance favors those in motion.
—Dr. James H. Austin

Work and acquire, and thou hast chained the wheel of Chance.
—Ralph Waldo Emerson

Superiority to fate is difficult to gain, 'tis not conferred of any, but possible to earn.   —Emily Dickinson

Some folk want their luck buttered.
—Thomas Hardy

Diligence is the mother of good luck, and God gives all things to industry.
—Benjamin Franklin

Fortune is ever seen accompanying industry.   —Oliver Goldsmith

BOLDNESS AND COURAGE CAN HELP CREATE LUCK

Fortune favours the bold. —Terence

A stout heart breaks bad luck.
—Miguel de Cervantes

Fortune reveres the brave, and overwhelms the cowardly.
—Marcus Annaeus Seneca

Fortune sides with him who dares.
—Virgil

WE MUST PREPARE TO RECEIVE OUR LUCK

Chance favors the prepared mind.
—Louis Pasteur

You have to be eligible for luck to strike, and I think that's a matter of education and preparation, and character and all the other solid attributes that sometimes people laugh at.   —James A. Michener

Get as much experience as you can, so that you're ready when luck works. That's the luck.
—Henry Fonda

You've got to be in a position for luck to happen. Luck doesn't go around looking for a stumblebum.
—Darrell Royal

Luck is the residue of design.
—Branch Rickey

Luck affects everything. Let your hook be always cast. In the stream where you least expect it, there will be fish.   —Ovid

Chance does nothing that has not been prepared beforehand.
—Alexis de Tocqueville

Luck is being ready for the chance.
—J. Frank Dobie

Chance usually favors the prudent man.   —Joseph Joubert

Combine common sense and the Golden Rule, and you will have very little bad luck.   —Anon.

Thorough preparation makes its own luck.   —Joe Poyer

Luck is a matter of preparation meeting opportunity.
—Oprah Winfrey

WE MUST RECOGNIZE AND MAXIMIZE OUR LUCK

There are so many people with all kinds of lucky things happening to them, and they don't know how to use it.
—Rocky Aoki

Probably any successful career has "X" number of breaks in it, and maybe the difference between successful people and those who aren't superachievers is taking advantage of those breaks.
—Joan Ganz Cooney

You must always be open to your luck. You cannot force it, but you can recognize it.
—Henry Moore

Luck ... taps, once in a lifetime, at everybody's door, but if industry does not open it, luck goes away.
—Charles Haddon Spurgeon

When something bad happens to me, I think I'm able to deal with it in a pretty good way. That makes me lucky. Some people fall apart at the first little thing that happens.
—Christie Brinkley

A wise man turns chance into good fortune.
—Thomas Fuller

It's funny, but ... you're sort of a moving target for fortune, and you never know when it will befall you.
—Thomas McGuane

OTHER SOURCES OF LUCK

Lady Luck generally woos those who earnestly, enthusiastically, unremittingly woo her.
—B.C. Forbes

Luck is good planning, carefully executed.
—Anon.

What helps luck is a habit of watching for opportunities, of having a patient, but restless mind, of sacrificing one's ease or vanity, of uniting a love of detail to foresight, and of passing through hard times bravely and cheerfully.
—Charles Victor Cherbuliez

Luck is believing you're lucky.
—Tennessee Williams

I think that one can have luck if one tries to create an atmosphere of spontaneity.
—Federico Fellini

Each man's character shapes his fortunes.
—Latin proverb

Chance works for us when we are good captains.
—George Meredith

Motivation triggers luck.
—Mike Wallace

Good and bad luck is a synonym, in the great majority of instances, for good and bad judgment.
—John Chatfield

Luck is a combination of confidence and getting the breaks.
—Christy Mathewson

I was born lucky, and I have lived lucky. What I had was used. What I still have is being used. Lucky.
—Katharine Hepburn

Luck is largely a matter of paying attention.
—Susan M. Dodd

Your luck is how you treat people.
—Bridget O'Donnell

LUCK CHANGES

The only sure thing about luck is
that it will change.   —Bret Harte

The man who glories in his luck may
be overthrown by destiny.
                    —Euripides

There is in the worst of fortune the
best of chances for a happy change.
                    —Euripides

It is more easy to get a favor from
fortune than to keep it.
                —Publilius Syrus

Since luck's a nine days' wonder,
wait their end.   —Euripides
Fortune is with you for an hour, and
against you for ten!   —Arab proverb

Breaks balance out. The sun don't
shine on the same old dog's rear end
every day.   —Darrell Royal

What the reason of the ant labori-
ously drags into a heap, the wind of
accident will collect in one breath.
                —J.C.F. von Schiller

Fortune is like the market, where
many times, if you can stay a little,
the price will fall.   —Francis Bacon

The profits of good luck are perish-
able; if you build on fortune, you
build on sand; the more advancement you achieve, the more dangers
you run.   —Marquis de Racan

Every possession and every happiness is but lent by chance for an
uncertain time, and may therefore be
demanded back the next hour.
                —Arthur Schopenhauer

Life is full of chances and changes,
and the most prosperous of men may
... meet with great misfortunes.
                    —Aristotle

OPPORTUNITY

LIFE IS FULL OF OPPORTUNITIES, BUT WE OFTEN MISS THEM

Great opportunities come to all, but many do not know they have met them. The only preparation to take advantage of them is simple fidelity to watch what each day brings.
—Albert E. Dunning

The world is all gates, all opportunities, strings of tension waiting to be struck.   —Ralph Waldo Emerson

No great man ever complains of want of opportunity.
—Ralph Waldo Emerson

Men do with opportunities as children do at the seashore; they fill their little hands with sand, and then let the grains fall through, one by one, till all are gone.   —T. Jones

Do not wait for ideal circumstances, nor for the best opportunities; they will never come.
—Janet Erskine Stuart

Nothing is so often irretrievably missed as a daily opportunity.
—Marie von Ebner-Eschenbach

If a man looks sharply and attentively, he shall see fortune; for though she be blind, yet she is not invisible.
—Francis Bacon

Know thine opportunity.   —Pittacus

In great affairs we ought to apply ourselves less to creating chances than to profiting from those that are offered.
—Francois de La Rochefoucauld

Opportunity is as scarce as oxygen; men fairly breathe it and do not know it.   —Doc Sane

Opportunities do not come with their values stamped upon them.... To face every opportunity of life thoughtfully, and ask its meaning bravely and earnestly, is the only way to meet supreme opportunities when they come, whether open-faced or disguised.   —Maltbie D. Babcock

We are told that talent creates its own opportunities. But it sometimes seems that intense desire creates not only its own opportunities, but its own talents.   —Eric Hoffer

How many opportunities present themselves to a man without his noticing them?   —Arab proverb

Luck affects everything. Let your hook be always cast. In the stream where you least expect it, there will be a fish.   —Ovid

The opportunity that God sends does not wake up him who is asleep.
   —Senegalese proverb

Present opportunities are neglected, and attainable good is slighted, by minds busied in extensive ranges and intent upon future advantages.
   —Samuel Johnson

Opportunities multiply as they are seized; they die when neglected. Life is a long line of opportunities.
   —John Wicker

I think luck is the sense to recognize an opportunity and the ability to take advantage of it. Everyone has bad breaks, but everyone also has opportunities. The man who can smile at his breaks and grab his chances gets on.   —Samuel Goldwyn

To improve the golden moment of opportunity, and catch the good that is within our reach, is the great art of life.   —Samuel Johnson

The greatest achievement of the human spirit is to live up to one's opportunities, and make the most of one's resources.   —Vauvenargues

It is often hard to distinguish between the hard knocks in life and those of opportunity.
   —Frederick Phillips

When one door closes, another opens. But we often look so long and so regretfully upon the closed door that we do not see the one which has opened for us.   —Helen Keller

The opportunities for enjoyment in your life are limitless. If you feel you are not experiencing enough joy, you have only yourself to blame.
   —David E. Bresler

Opportunities are often things you haven't noticed the first time around.
   —Catherine Deneuve

The successful man is one who had the chance and took it.
   —Roger Babson

Vigilance in watching opportunity; tact and daring in seizing upon opportunity; force and persistence in crowding opportunity to its utmost possible achievement—these are the martial virtues which must command success.   —Austin Phelps

To avoid an occasion for our virtues is a worse degree of failure than to push forward pluckily and make a fall.   —Robert Louis Stevenson

Opportunity knocks but once.
   —Anon.

I was seldom able to see an opportunity until it had ceased to be one.
   —Mark Twain

If Fortune calls, offer him a seat.
   —Yiddish proverb

What the student calls a tragedy, the master calls a butterfly.
   —Richard Bach

Opportunity is missed by most people because it is dressed in overalls, and looks like work.

—Thomas A. Edison

OPPORTUNITIES ARE OFTEN FOUND IN TOUGH SITUATIONS

Times of stress and difficulty are seasons of opportunity when the seeds of progress are sown.

—Thomas F. Woodlock

We must look for the opportunity in every difficulty instead of being paralyzed at the thought of the difficulty in every opportunity.

—Walter E. Cole

WE MUST PREPARE FOR OUR OPPORTUNITIES

Opportunity can benefit no man who has not fitted himself to seize it and use it. Opportunity woos the worthy, shuns the unworthy. Prepare yourself to grasp opportunity, and opportunity is likely to come your way. It is not so fickle, capricious and unreasoning as some complain.

—B.C. Forbes

Opportunity rarely knocks until you are ready. And few people have ever been really ready without receiving opportunity's call.

—Channing Pollock

The secret to success in life is for a man to be ready for his opportunity when it comes. —Benjamin Disraeli

I think the young actor who really wants to act will find a way ... to keep at it and seize every opportunity that comes along.

—Sir John Gielgud

Unless a man has trained himself for his chance, the chance will only make him ridiculous.

—William Matthews

WE MUST ALSO CREATE OUR OWN OPPORTUNITIES

Capacity never lacks opportunity. It cannot remain undiscovered because it is sought by too many anxious to use it. —Cochran

A wise man will make more opportunities than he finds.

—Francis Bacon

If you want to succeed in the world, you must make your own opportunities. —John B. Gough

Mediocre men wait for opportunity to come to them. Strong, able, alert men go after opportunity.

—B.C. Forbes

A filly who wants to run will always find a rider. —Jacques Audiberti

Many things are lost for want of asking. —English proverb

You don't just luck into things ... you build step by step, whether it's friendships or opportunities.

—Barbara Bush

Every man is the architect of his own fortune. —Sallust

He that waits upon fortune is never sure of a dinner.

—Benjamin Franklin

OPPORTUNITY AND SECURITY

There is no security on this earth. Only opportunity.

—General Douglas MacArthur

461

Too many people are thinking of security instead of opportunity; they seem more afraid of life than of death. —James F. Byrnes

Freedom is nothing else but a chance to be better, whereas enslavement is a certainty of the worst.
—Albert Camus

We Often Lose Opportunities By Overdeliberation

The opportunity is often lost by deliberating. —Publilius Syrus

You decide you'll wait for your pitch. Then as the ball starts toward the plate, you think about your stance. And then you think about your swing. And then you realize that the ball that went past you for a strike was your pitch.
—Bobby Murcer

General Quotations about Opportunity

Small opportunities are often the beginning of great enterprises.
—Demosthenes

Ability is of little account without opportunity. —Napoleon Bonaparte

Our opportunities to do good are our talents. —Cotton Mather

Opportunity knocks at every man's door once. On some men's door it hammers till it breaks down the door and then it goes in and wakes him up if he's asleep, and ever afterward it works for him as a night watch-man. —Finley Peter Dunne

It is less important to redistribute wealth than it is to redistribute opportunity. —Arthur Vandenberg

A door that seems to stand open must be a man's size, or it is not the door that Providence means for him.
—Henry Ward Beecher

Next to knowing when to seize an opportunity, the most important thing in life is to know when to forgo an advantage.
—Benjamin Disraeli

The follies which a man regrets most in his life are those which he didn't commit when he had the opportuni-ty. —Helen Rowland

It is not manly to turn one's back on fortune. —Marcus Annaeus Seneca

462

COMMITMENT

TO LIVE FULLY AND SUCCESSFULLY, WE MUST COMMIT TO SOMETHING

If you don't make a total commitment to whatever you're doing, then you start looking to bail out the first time the boat starts leaking. It's tough enough getting that boat to shore with everybody rowing, let alone when a guy stands up and starts putting his life jacket on.
—Lou Holtz

If a man hasn't discovered something that he will die for, he isn't fit to live.
—Martin Luther King, Jr.

Winners are men who have dedicated their whole lives to winning.
—Woody Hayes

Unless you can find some sort of loyalty, you cannot find unity and peace in your active living.
—Josiah Royce

Sometimes success is due less to ability than zeal. The winner is he who gives himself to his work body and soul.
—Charles Buxton

Now I am steel-set: I follow the call to the clear radiance and glow of the heights.
—Henrik Ibsen

Love me, please, I love you; I can bear to be your friend. So ask of me anything ... I am not a tentative person. Whatever I do, I give up my whole self to it.
—Edna Saint Vincent Millay

I don't care a damn for your loyal service when you think I am right; when I really want it most is when you think I am wrong.
—General Sir John Monash

One's lifework, I have learned, grows with the working and the living. Do it as if your life depended on it, and first thing you know, you'll have made a life out of it. A good life, too.
—Theresa Helburn

If you don't stand for something, you'll fall for anything.
—Michael Evans

If you deny yourself commitment, what can you do with your life?
—Harvey Fierstein

463

The person who makes a success of living is the one who sees his goal steadily and aims for it unswervingly. That is dedication.
—Cecil B. DeMille

Theirs is not to reason why, theirs is but to do or die.
—Alfred, Lord Tennyson

Either do not attempt at all, or go through with it. —Ovid

If you start to take Vienna, take Vienna. —Napoleon Bonaparte

If you aren't going all the way, why go at all? —Joe Namath

You can be an ordinary athlete by getting away with less than your best. But if you want to be a great, you have to give it all you've got—your everything.
—Duke P. Kahanamoku

Put your heart, mind, intellect and soul even to your smallest acts. This is the secret of success.
—Swami Sivananda

Moderation in war is imbecility.
—Admiral John Fisher

It is fatal to enter any war without the will to win it.
—General Douglas MacArthur

Men, like snails, lose their usefulness when they lose direction and begin to bend. —Walter Savage Landor

It is by losing himself in the objective, in inquiry, creation, and craft, that a man becomes something.
—Paul Goodman

The height of your accomplishments will equal the depth of your convictions. —William F. Scolavino

The dedicated life is the life worth living. —Annie Dillard

The secret of living is to find a pivot, the pivot of a concept on which you can make your stand.
—Luigi Pirandello

THE PERILS OF THE MIDDLE OF THE ROAD

There's nothing in the middle of the road but yellow stripes and dead armadillos. —Jim Hightower

Standing in the middle of the road is very dangerous; you get knocked down by traffic from both sides.
—Margaret Thatcher

He who walks in the middle of the road gets hit from both sides.
—George P. Schultz

I never liked the middle ground—the most boring place in the world.
—Louise Nevelson

The hottest places in hell are reserved for those who, in a period of moral crisis, maintain their neutrality. —Dante Alighieri

The man who sees both sides of an issue is very likely on the fence or up a tree. —Anon.

The principle of neutrality ... has increasingly become an obsolete conception, and, except under very special circumstances, it is an immoral and shortsighted conception.
—John Foster Dulles

We know what happens to people who stay in the middle of the road. They get run over. —Aneurin Bevan

The middle of the road is where the white line is, and that's the worst place to drive. —Robert Frost

Show me a person who is not an extremist about some things, who is a "middle-of-the-roader" in everything, and I will show you someone who is insecure. —G. Aiken Taylor

INDIFFERENCE

There is nothing harder than the softness of indifference.
—Juan Montalvo

The opposite of love is not hate, it's indifference.
The opposite of art is not ugliness, it's indifference.
The opposite of faith is not heresy, it's indifference.
And the opposite of life is not death, it's indifference. —Elie Wiesel

COMMITMENT AND THE HEART

The only place you can win a football game is on the field. The only place you can lose it is in your heart.
—Darrell Royal

I am seeking, I am striving, I am in it with all my heart.
—Vincent van Gogh

He did it with all his heart, and prospered. —2 Chr. 31:21

Wars may be fought with weapons, but they are won by men. It is the spirit of the men who follow, and of the man who leads, that gains the victory. —General George S. Patton

It was my tongue that swore; my heart is unsworn. —Euripides

Morale is the greatest single factor in successful wars.
—Dwight D. Eisenhower

COMMITMENT AND WILLPOWER

Nothing can resist a will which will stake even existence upon its fulfillment. —Benjamin Disraeli

Nothing is difficult to those who have the will.
—Motto of the Dutch Poets' Society

Our future and our fate lie in our wills more than in our hands, for our hands are but the instruments of our wills. —B.C. Forbes

Nothing is so common as unsuccessful men with talent. They lack only determination. —Charles Swindoll

The will to conquer is the first condition of victory.
—Marshal Ferdinand Foch

Strength is a matter of the made-up mind. —John Beecher

Your own resolution to success is more important than any other one thing. —Abraham Lincoln

COMMITMENT AND BELIEF

What distinguishes the majority of men from the few is their ability to act accordingly to their beliefs.
—Henry Miller

When you have decided what you believe, what you feel must be done, have the courage to stand alone and be counted. —Eleanor Roosevelt

What a man believes, he will die for.
What a man merely thinks, he will
change his mind about.   —Anon.

The eloquent man is he who is no
beautiful speaker, but who is
inwardly and desperately drunk with
a certain belief.
                    —Ralph Waldo Emerson

A belief which does not spring from
a conviction in the emotions is no
belief at all.   —Evelyn Scott

Whether you are really right or not
doesn't matter, it's the belief that
counts.   —Robertson Davies

SOMETIMES WE MUST BURN OUR BRIDGES BEHIND US

Many a man has walked up to the
opportunity for which he has long
been preparing himself, looked it full
in the face, and then begun to get
cold feet ... when it comes to betting
on yourself and your power to do
the thing you know you must do or
write yourself down a failure, you're
a chicken-livered coward if you hesitate.   —B.C. Forbes

The wise man puts all his eggs in one
basket and watches the basket.
                    —Andrew Carnegie

Poverty is uncomfortable, as I can
testify: but nine times out of ten the
best thing that can happen to a
young man is to be tossed overboard
and compelled to sink or swim for
himself.   —James A. Garfield

Anytime you play golf for whatever
you've got, that's pressure. I'd like to
see H.L. Hunt go out there and play
for $3 billion.   —Lee Trevino

There is a point at which everything
becomes simple and there is no
longer any question of choice,
because all you have staked will be
lost if you look back. Life's point of
no return.   —Dag Hammarskjold

Even now we can draw back. But
once we cross that little bridge, we
must settle things by the sword.
                    —Julius Caesar, to his troops
                        as they prepared to cross
                            the Rubicon River

So will I go in unto the king ... and if
I perish, I perish.
                    —Est. 4:16

You don't know what pressure is
until you play for $5 with only $2 in
your pocket.   —Lee Trevino

The fixed determination to have
acquired the warrior soul, to either
conquer or perish with honor, is the
secret of victory.
                    —General George S. Patton

COMMITMENT AND WARFARE

In war there is no substitute for victory.   —Dwight D. Eisenhower

Victory at all costs, victory in spite
of all terror, victory however long
and hard the road may be; for without victory there is no survival.
                    —Sir Winston Churchill

Better that we should die fighting
than be outraged and dishonored.
Better to die than to live in slavery.
                    —Emmeline Pankhurst

I sincerely wish war was a pleasanter
and easier business than it is, but it
does not admit of holidays.
                    —Abraham Lincoln

Every attempt to make war easy and safe will result in humiliation and disaster. —General William T. Sherman

If you start to take Vienna, take Vienna. —Napoleon Bonaparte

General Quotations about Commitment

The worth of every conviction consists precisely in the steadfastness with which it is held. —Jane Adams

The moment one definitely commits oneself, the Providence moves, too. All sorts of things occur to help that would never otherwise have occurred. A stream of events issues from the decision, raising unforeseen incidents and meetings and material assistance, which no man could have dreamt would have come his way. —W.H. Murray

We can do whatever we wish to do provided our wish is strong enough. But the tremendous effort needed— one doesn't always want to make it—does one?... But what else can be done? What's the alternative? What do you want most to do? That's what I have to keep asking myself, in the face of difficulties. —Katherine Mansfield

There is no strong performance without a little fanaticism in the performer. —Ralph Waldo Emerson

If you don't wake up with something in your stomach every day that makes you think, "I want to make this movie," it'll never get made. —Sherry Lansing

Perform without fail what you resolve. —Benjamin Franklin

To say yes, you have to sweat and roll up your sleeves and plunge both hands into life up to the elbows. It is easy to say no, even if saying no means death. —Jean Anouilh

What one has, one ought to use; and whatever he does, he should do with all his might. —Cicero

Whatsoever thy hand findeth to do, do it with thy might. —Eccl. 9:10

He that rides his hobby gently must always give way to him that rides his hobby hard. —Ralph Waldo Emerson

Nothing of worthy or weight can be achieved with half a mind, with a faint heart, and with a lame endeavor. —Isaac Barrow

Firmness of purpose is one of the most necessary sinews of character, and one of the best instruments of success. Without it, genius wastes its efforts in a maze of inconsistencies. —Lord Chesterfield

My face is set, my gait is fast, my goal is Heaven, my road is narrow, my way is rough, my companions are few, my guide is reliable, my mission is clear. I cannot be bought, compromised, detoured, lured away, turned back, diluted, or delayed. I will not flinch in the face of sacrifice, hesitate in the presence of adversity, negotiate ... at the table of the enemy, ponder at the pool of popularity, or meander in a maze of mediocrity. I won't give up, shut up, let up, or slow up. —Robert Moorehead

To have no loyalty is to have no dignity, and in the end, no manhood.
— Peter Taylor Forsyth

If you are ashamed to stand by your colors, you had better seek another flag.
— Anon.

Great minds have purposes, others have wishes.
— Washington Irving

I don't want people who want to dance, I want people who *have* to dance.
— George Balanchine

What a man wants to do he generally can do, if he wants to badly enough.
— Louis L'Amour

Never grow a wishbone, daughter, where your backbone ought to be.
— Clementine Paddleford

Happy are those who dream dreams and are ready to pay the price to make them come true.
— L.J. Cardinal Suenens

He turns not back who is bound to a star.
— Leonardo da Vinci

One advantage of marriage, it seems to me, is that when you fall out of love with him, or he falls out of love with you, it keeps you together until you maybe fall in love again.
— Judith Viorst

You can't *try* to do things; you simply must *do* them.
— Ray Bradbury

I am in earnest; I will not equivocate; I will not excuse; I will not retreat a single inch; and I *will* be heard.
— William Lloyd Garrison

CONCENTRATION

THE IMPORTANCE OF CONCENTRATION

The ability to concentrate and to use your time well is everything.
—Lee Iacocca

It is only when I dally with what I am about, look back and aside, instead of keeping my eyes straight forward, that I feel these cold sinkings of the heart. —Sir Walter Scott

A straight path never leads anywhere except to the objective.
—André Gide

Nothing interferes with my concentration. You could put on an orgy in my office and I wouldn't look up. Well, maybe once. —Isaac Asimov

To be able to concentrate for a considerable time is essential to difficult achievement. —Bertrand Russell

If there is anything that can be called genius, it consists chiefly in the ability to give that attention to a subject which keeps it steadily in the mind, till we have surveyed it accurately on all sides. —Thomas Reid

If you don't concentrate, you'll end up on your rear. —Tai Babilonia

If I have ever made any valuable discoveries, it has been owing more to patient attention than to any other talent. —Isaac Newton

For him who has no concentration, there is no tranquility.
—Bhagaved Gita

The secret to success in any human endeavor is total concentration.
—Kurt Vonnegut

The secret of concentration is the secret of self-discovery. You reach inside yourself to discover your personal resources, and what it takes to match them to the challenge.
—Arnold Palmer

DON'T TRY TO DO TOO MANY THINGS

Beware of dissipating your powers; strive constantly to concentrate them. —Johann von Goethe

One arrow does not bring down two birds. —Turkish proverb

No horse gets anywhere until he is harnessed. No steam or gas ever drives anything until it is confined. No Niagara is ever turned into light and power until it is tunneled. No life ever grows great until it is focused, dedicated, disciplined.
—Harry Emerson Fosdick

A man may be so much of everything that he is nothing of everything.
—Samuel Johnson

Concentrate your energies, your thoughts and your capital.... The wise man puts all his eggs in one basket and watches the basket.
—Andrew Carnegie

One man; two loves. No good ever comes of that.
—Euripides

One cannot both feast and become rich.
—Ashanti proverb

The perplexity of life arises from there being too many interesting things in it for us to be interested properly in any of them.
—G.K. Chesterton

No country can act wisely simultaneously in every part of the globe at every moment of time.
—Henry Kissinger

CONCENTRATE ON ONE THING

The field of consciousness is tiny. It accepts only one problem at a time.
—Antoine de Saint-Exupery

To do two things at once is to do neither.
—Publilius Syrus

Successful minds work like a gimlet, to a single point.
—Christian Bovee

A bird can roost but on one branch. A mouse can drink no more than its fill from a river.
—Chinese proverb

Each man is capable of doing one thing well. If he attempts several, he will fail to achieve distinction in any.
—Plato

This one thing I do ... I press toward the mark.
—Phil. 3:13–14

All good is gained by those whose thought and life are kept pointed close to one main thing, not scattered abroad upon a thousand.
—Stephen McKenna

The first law of success ... is concentration: to bend all the energies to one point, and to go directly to that point, looking neither to the right nor the left.
—William Matthews

Give me a man who says this one thing I do, and not these fifty things I dabble in.
—Dwight L. Moody

A single idea, if it is right, saves us the labor of an infinity of experiences.
—Jacques Maritain

One thought driven home is better than three left on base.
—James Liter

Purity of heart is to will one thing.
—Søren Kierkegaard

ELIMINATE THE NON-ESSENTIAL

A man should remove not only unnecessary acts, but also unnecessary thoughts, for then superfluous activity will not follow.
—Marcus Aurelius

No man will swim ashore and take his baggage with him.
—Marcus Annaeus Seneca

Many people who wonder why they don't amount to more than they do have good stuff in them, and are energetic, persevering, and have ample opportunities. It is all a case of trimming the useless branches and throwing the whole force of power into the development of something that counts. —Walter J. Johnston

A great man is one who seizes the vital issue in a complex question, what we might call the jugular vein of the whole organism, and spends his energies upon that.
—Joseph Rickaby

ALWAYS FOCUS ON THE IMMEDIATE TASK

While the work or play is on ... don't constantly feel you ought to be doing the other. —Franklin P. Adams

When one is learning, one should not think of play; and when one is at play, one should not think of learning. —Lord Chesterfield

The immature mind hops from one thing to another; the mature mind seeks to follow through.
—Harry A. Overstreet

If you want to hit a bird on the wing you must have all your will in focus, you must not be thinking about yourself and, equally, you must not be thinking about your neighbor: you must be living in your eye on that bird. Every achievement is a bird on the wing.
—Oliver Wendell Holmes, Jr.

When walking, walk. When eating, eat. —Zen Maxim

The difference in men does not lie in the size of their hands, nor in the perfection of their bodies, but in this one sublime ability of concentration: to throw the weight with the blow, to live an eternity in an hour.
—Elbert Hubbard

I go at what I am about as if there was nothing else in the world for the time being. —Charles Lingsley

Choice of attention, to pay attention to this and ignore that, is to the inner life what choice of action is to the outer. —W.H. Auden

Concentration is everything. On the day I'm performing, I don't hear anything anyone says to me.
—Luciano Pavarotti

The real essence of work is concentrated energy. —Walter Begehot

I've learned ruthless concentration. I can write under any circumstances ... street noises, loud talk, music, you name it. —Sylvia Porter

Do whatever you do intensely.
—Robert Henri

The effectiveness of work increases according to geometrical progression if there are no interruptions.
—André Maurois

Other people's interruptions of your work are relatively insignificant compared with the countless times you interrupt yourself.
—Brendan Francis

471

If you direct your whole thought to work itself, none of the things which invade eyes or ears will reach the mind. —Quintilian

A full mind is an empty baseball bat. —Branch Rickey

There is time enough for everything in the course of the day if you do but one thing at once; but there is not time enough in the year if you will do two things at a time. —Lord Chesterfield

You can't ring the bells and, at the same time, walk in the procession. —Spanish proverb

OTHER SOURCES OF CONCENTRATION

If you direct your whole thought to work itself, none of the things which invade eyes or ears will reach the mind. —Quintilian

Become so wrapped up in something that you forget to be afraid. —Lady Bird Johnson

Attention to a subject depends upon our interest in it. —Tyron Edwards

I can't concentrate on golf or bowling. Those bowling pins aren't going to hurt me. I can concentrate in the ring because someone is trying to kill me. —Carmen Basilio

When I come into a game in the bottom of the ninth, bases loaded, no one out and a one-run lead ... it takes people off my mind. —Tug McGraw

Concentrate on finding your goal, then concentrate on reaching it. —Colonel Michael Friedsman

Those who set out to serve both God and Mammon soon discover that there is no God. —Logan Pearsall Smith

When a man knows he is to be hanged in a fortnight, it concentrates his mind wonderfully. —Samuel Johnson

WORK

WORK IS ESSENTIAL TO MOST PEOPLE'S HAPPINESS

The road to happiness lies in two simple principles: find what it is that interests you and that you can do well, and when you find it, put your whole soul into it—every bit of energy and ambition and natural ability you have.   —John D. Rockefeller III

The happy people are those who are producing something.
—William Ralph Inge

Congenial labor is essence of happiness.   —Arthur Christopher Benson

Employment is nature's physician, and is essential to human happiness.
—Galen

When I stop [working], the rest of the day is posthumous. I'm only really alive when I'm working.
—Tennessee Williams

Continuity of purpose is one of the most essential ingredients of happiness in the long run, and for most men this comes chiefly through their work.   —Bertrand Russell

It is only when I am doing my work that I feel truly alive. It is like having sex.   —Federico Fellini

After fifty years of living, it occurs to me that the most significant thing that people do is go to work, whether it is to go to work on their novel or at the assembly plant or fixing somebody's teeth.
—Thomas McGuane

He who labors diligently need never despair, for all things are accomplished by diligence and labor.
—Menander

The fun of being alive is realizing that you have a talent and you can use it every day, so it grows stronger.... And if you're in an atmosphere where this talent is appreciated instead of just tolerated, why, it's just as good as sex.   —Lou Centlivre

Work! Thank God for the swing of it, for the clamoring, hammering ring of it.   —Anon.

There are certain natures to whom work is nothing, the act of work everything.   —Arthur Symons

473

ALL WORK HAS DIGNITY

There's no labor a man can do that's undignified, if he does it right.
—Bill Cosby

If a man is called to be a streetsweeper, he should sweep streets even as Michelangelo painted, or Beethoven composed music or Shakespeare wrote poetry. He should sweep streets so well that all the hosts of heaven and earth will pause to say, here lived a great streetsweeper who did his job well.
—Martin Luther King, Jr.

The work praises the man.
—Irish proverb

Originality and the feeling of one's own dignity are achieved only through work and struggle.
—Fyodor Dostoyevsky

There is a kind of victory in good work, no matter how humble.
—Jack Kemp

Labor disgraces no man; unfortunately, you occasionally find men who disgrace labor.
—Ulysses S. Grant

Honest labor bears a lovely face.
—Thomas Dekker

I have friends in overalls whose friendship I would not swap for the favor of the kings of the world.
—Thomas A. Edison

The world is moved not only by the mighty shoves of the heroes, but also by the aggregate of the tiny pushes of each honest worker.
—Helen Keller

A professional is someone who can do his best work when he doesn't feel like it.
—Alistair Cooke

The highest reward for man's toil is not what he gets for it, but what he becomes by it.
—John Ruskin

THE IMPORTANCE OF FINDING THE WORK WE WERE MEANT TO DO

Starting out to make money is the greatest mistake in life. Do what you feel you have a flair for doing, and if you are good enough at it, the money will come.
—Greer Garson

Never desert your own line of talent. Be what nature intended you for, and you will succeed.
—Sydney Smith

Everybody undertakes what he sees another successful in, whether he has the aptitude for it or not.
—Johann von Goethe

Men take only their needs into consideration, never their abilities.
—Napoleon Bonaparte

One should stick to the sort of thing for which one was made; I tried to be an herbalist, whereas I should keep to the butcher's trade.
—Jean de La Fontaine

One principal reason why men are so often useless is that they neglect their own profession or calling, and divide and shift their attention among a multitude of objects and pursuits.
—Nathaniel Emmons

Some people are born to lift heavy weights, some are born to juggle golden balls.
—Max Beerbohm

Men whose trade is rat-catching love to catch rats; the bug destroyer seizes on his bug with delight; the suppressor is gratified by finding his vice.
—Sydney Smith

Life is to be lived. If you have to support yourself, you had bloody well better find some way that is going to be interesting. And you don't do that by sitting around wondering about yourself. —Katharine Hepburn

To find out what one is fitted to do, and to secure an opportunity to do it, is the key to happiness.
—John Dewey

The high prize of life, the crowning fortune of man, is to be born with a bias to some pursuit which finds him in employment and happiness.
—Ralph Waldo Emerson

They are happy men whose natures sort with their vocations.
—Francis Bacon

WORK YOU LOVE ISN'T WORK

The test of a vocation is the love of the drudgery it involves.
—Logan Pearsall Smith

Whenever it is possible, a boy should choose some occupation which he should do even if he did not need the money. —William Lyon Phelps

I love Mickey Mouse more than any woman I've ever known.
—Walt Disney

Only he is successful in his business who makes that pursuit which affords him the highest pleasure sustain him. —Henry David Thoreau

Give me a man who sings at his work. —Thomas Carlyle

To love what you do and feel that it matters—how could anything be more fun? —Katharine Graham

When men are rightly occupied, their amusement grows out of their work, as the color-petals out of a fruitful flower. —John Ruskin

When love and skill work together, expect a masterpiece.
—John Ruskin

Work consists of whatever a body is obliged to do, and play consists of whatever a body is not obliged to do. —Mark Twain

Work and play are words used to describe the same thing under differing conditions. —Mark Twain

The more I want to get something done, the less I call it work.
—Richard Bach

WORK AND SUCCESS

Nothing worthwhile comes easily. Half effort does not produce half results, it produces no results. Work, continuous work and hard work, is the only way to accomplish results that last. —Hamilton Holt

If a man wakes up famous, he hasn't been sleeping. —Wes Izzard

Success is dependent on effort.
—Sophocles

Striving for success without hard work is like trying to harvest where you haven't planted. —David Bly

Success comes before work only in the dictionary. —Anon.

Sweat plus sacrifice equals success.
—Charles O. Finley

Success usually comes to those who are too busy to be looking for it.
—Henry David Thoreau

In all human affairs there are *efforts,* there are *results,* and the strength of the effort is the measure of the result. —James Lane Allen

WORK PAYS DIVIDENDS

Diligence is the mother of good luck, and God gives all things to industry.
—Benjamin Franklin

To industry, nothing is impossible.
—Latin proverb

God sells us all things at the price of labor. —Leonardo da Vinci

Fortune is ever seen accompanying industry. —Oliver Goldsmith

Manual labor to my father was not only good and decent for its own sake, but as he was given to saying, it straightened out one's thoughts.
—Mary Ellen Chase

I get satisfaction of three kinds. One is creating something, one is being paid for it and one is the feeling that I haven't just been sitting on my ass all afternoon. —William F. Buckley

GENERAL QUOTATIONS
ABOUT WORK

There is no more dreadful punishment than futile and hopeless labor.
—Albert Camus

Any man who has had the job I've had and didn't have a sense of humor wouldn't still be here.
—Harry S. Truman

The heights by great men reached
   and kept
Were not attained by sudden flight,
But they, while their companions
   slept,
Were toiling upward in the night.
—Henry Wadsworth Longfellow

Opportunity is missed by most people because it is dressed in overalls, and looks like work.
—Thomas A. Edison

Be strong!
We are not here to play, to dream, to
   drift;
We have hard work to do and loads
   to lift;
Shun not the struggle—face it; 'tis
   God's gift. —Maltbie D. Babcock

If you could once make up your mind never to undertake more work ... than you can carry on calmly, quietly, without hurry or flurry ... and if the instant you feel yourself growing nervous and ... out of breath, you would stop and take a breath, you would find this simple common-sense rule doing for you what no prayers or tears could ever accomplish. —Elizabeth Prentiss

It is better to have no emotion when it is work. Do what needs to be done, and do it coolly.
—Louis L'Amour

A man's work is from sun to sun, but a mother's work is never done.
—Anon.

476

What a man accomplishes in a day depends upon the way in which he approaches his tasks. When we accept tough jobs as a challenge to our ability and wade into them with joy and enthusiasm, miracles can happen. When we do our work with a dynamic, conquering spirit, we get things done. —Arland Gilbert

The one important thing I have learned over the years is the difference between taking one's work seriously, and taking one's self seriously. The first is imperative, and the second is disastrous. —Margot Fonteyn

Work is the best method devised for killing time. —William Feather

Industry is a better horse to ride than genius. —Walter Lippman

Elbow grease is the best polish. —English proverb

Never despair, but if you do, work on in despair. —Edmund Burke

Laziness is a secret ingredient that goes into failure. But it's only kept a secret from the person who fails. —Robert Half

PERFECTION

NOTHING IS PERFECT

Perfection does not exist. To understand this is the triumph of human intelligence; to expect to possess it is the most dangerous kind of madness.
—Alfred de Musset

The essence of man is imperfection.
—Norman Cousins

The essence of being human is that one does not seek perfection.
—George Orwell

There is no perfection in humanity.
—Samuel Montagne

Perfection never exists in reality, but only in our dreams.
—Dr. Rudolf Dreikurs

He is lifeless that is faultless.
—English proverb

Perfection is out of the question.
—Anne Archer

Angels can do no better.
—K. Panuthos

His only fault is that he has no fault.
—Pliny, the Younger

If you're looking for perfection, look in the mirror. If you find it there, expect it elsewhere.
—Malcolm Forbes

A perfect poem is impossible. Once it has been written, the world would end.   —Robert Graves

It is the function of perfection to make one know one's imperfection.
—Saint Augustine

The man with insight enough to admit his limitations comes nearest to perfection.   —Johann von Goethe

A man would do nothing if he waited until he could do it so well that no one could find fault.
—John Henry Cardinal Newman

Nothing you write, if you hope to be any good, will ever come out as you first hoped.   —Lillian Hellman

All of us failed to match our dreams of perfection.   —William Faulkner

What, after all, is a halo? It's only one more thing to keep clean.
—Christopher Fry

We Don't Need to Be Perfect

To talk about the need for perfection in man is to talk about the need for another species.   —Norman Cousins

Striving for perfection is the greatest stopper there is. You'll be afraid you can't achieve it.... It's your excuse to yourself for not doing anything. Instead, strive for excellence, doing your best.   —Sir Laurence Olivier

The "C" students run the world.
    —Harry S. Truman

You know what they call the guy who finishes last in medical school? They call him Doctor!
    —Abe Lemons

Perfection is no more a requisite to art than to heroes.   —Ned Rorem

A good garden may have some weeds.   —Thomas Fuller

At times failure is very necessary for the artist. It reminds him that failure is not the ultimate disaster. And this reminder liberates him from the mean fussing of perfectionism.
    —John Berger

People Don't Expect or Want Perfection

Living with a saint is more grueling than being one.   —Robert Neville

He is all fault who hath no fault at all. For who loves me must have a touch of earth.
    —Alfred, Lord Tennyson

You're only human, you're supposed to make mistakes.   —Billy Joel

I don't like a man to be too efficient. He's likely to be not human enough.
    —Felix Frankfurter

Sainthood is acceptable only in saints.   —Pamela Hansford Johnson

I like a man with faults, especially when he knows it. To err is human—I'm uncomfortable around gods.   —Hugh Prather

If the best man's faults were written on his forehead, it would make him pull his hat over his eyes.
    —Gaelic proverb

Friendships aren't perfect, and yet they are very precious. For me, not expecting perfection all in one place was a great release.
    —Letty Cottin Pogrebin

It Isn't Healthy to Seek Perfection

A concern with the perfectibility of mankind is always a symptom of thwarted or perverted development.
    —Hugh Kingsmill

When everything has to be right, something isn't.   —Stanislaw Lec

The maxim "Nothing avails but perfection" may be spelled "Paralysis."
    —Sir Winston Churchill

Perfectionism is a dangerous state of mind in an imperfect world.
    —Robert Hillyer

Perfectionism is slow death.
    —Hugh Prather

Perfect order is the forerunner of perfect horror.   —Carlos Fuentes

The more a human being feels himself a self, tries to intensify this self and reach a never-attainable perfection, the more drastically he steps out of the center of being.
—Eugene Herrigel

The man who makes no mistakes lacks boldness and the spirit of adventure. He never tries anything new. He is a brake on the wheels of progress.
—M.W. Larmour

WE JUST NEED TO DO THE BEST WE CAN

I only have to stop the puck, not beat it to death.
—Don Beaupre, hockey goalie

Even a clock that is not going is right twice a day.
—Polish proverb

Have patience with all things, but chiefly have patience with yourself. Do not lose courage in considering your own imperfections, but instantly set about remedying them—every day begin the task anew.
—Saint Francis de Sales

We're the best team in baseball. But not by much.
—Sparky Anderson, after winning the World Series

Use what talents you have; the woods would have little music if no birds sang their song except those who sang best.
—Reverend Oliver G. Wilson

I'll take any way to get into the Hall of Fame. If they want a batboy, I'll go in as a batboy.
—Phil Rizzuto

GENERAL QUOTATIONS ABOUT PERFECTION

One must not hold one's self so divine as to be unwilling occasionally to make improvements in one's creations.
—Ludwig van Beethoven

The artist who aims at perfection in everything achieves it in nothing.
—Eugene Delacroix

You just have to learn not to care about the dust mites under the beds.
—Margaret Mead

Just Do the Footwork, Then Let It Go

ACTION

Having the world's best idea will do you no good unless you act on it. People who want milk shouldn't sit on a stool in the middle of a field in hopes that a cow will back up to them. —Curtis Grant

Ideas are powerful things, requiring not a studious contemplation but an action, even if it is only an inner action. —Midge Dector

Life happens at the level of events, not words. —Alfred Adler

The only way to get positive feelings about yourself is to take positive actions. Man does not live as he thinks, he thinks as he lives. —Reverend Vaughan Quinn, O.M.I.

The only measure of what you believe is what you do. If you want to know what people believe, don't read what they write, don't ask them what they believe, just observe what they do. —Ashley Montagu

Our nature consists in motion; complete rest is death. —Blaise Pascal

Who can separate his faith from his actions, or his belief from his occupations? —Kahlil Gibran

The prayer of the chicken hawk does not get him the chicken. —Swahili proverb

The superior man is modest in his speech, but excels in his actions. —Confucius

There is no genius in life like the genius of energy and activity. —Donald G. Mitchell

An ounce of action is worth a ton of theory. —Friedrich Engels

Action is the only reality, not only reality but morality, as well. —Abbie Hoffman

Let us work as if success depended upon ourselves alone, but with heartfelt conviction that we are doing nothing, and God everything. —Saint Ignatius Loyola

Right action is the key to good living. —*Twelve Steps and Twelve Traditions*

481

Even if you're on the right track, you'll get run over if you just sit there.   —Will Rogers

If faith without works is dead, willingness without action is fantasy.
                                    —Anon.

Inspirations never go in for long engagements; they demand immediate marriage to action.
                      —Brendan Francis

The door of opportunity won't open unless you do some pushing.
                                    —Anon.

The life of the spirit is centrally and essentially a life of action. Spirituality is something done, not merely something believed, or known or experienced.
                —Mary McDermott Shideler

It is a great piece of skill to know how to guide your luck, even while waiting for it.   —Baltasar Gracian

The man who has done nothing but wait for his ship to come in has already missed the boat.   —Anon.

God doesn't make orange juice, God makes oranges.   —Jesse Jackson

WE'RE RESPONSIBLE FOR THE EFFORT—NOT THE OUTCOME

Learn to do thy part and leave the rest to Heaven.
        —John Henry Cardinal Newman

Trust in God and *do* something.
                                —Mary Lyon

God helps them that helps themselves.   —Benjamin Franklin

He will hew the line of right, let the chips fall where they may.
                            —Roscoe Conklin

Let me win, but if I cannot win, let me be brave in the attempt.
              —Motto of the Special Olympics

We cannot merely pray to You, O
    God, to end war;
For we know that You have made
    the world in a way
That man must find his own path to
    peace
Within himself, and with his neighbor.   —Jack Riemer

Oh Lord, thou givest us everything, at the price of an effort.
                      —Leonardo da Vinci

On God for all events depend;
You cannot want when God's your
    friend.
Weigh well your part and do your
    best;
Leave to your Maker all the rest.
                      —Nathaniel Cotton

You, yourself, must make the effort. The buddhas are only teachers.
                        —Buddhist proverb

There is a time for all things; a time to preach and a time to pray, but those times have passed away; there is a time to fight, *and that time has come!*   —General Peter Muhlenberg

Doing what's right is no guarantee against misfortune.
                            —William McFee

It is not yours to finish the task, but neither are you free to take no part in it.   —Anon.

Life has ... taught me not to expect success to be the inevitable result of my endeavors. She taught me to seek sustenance from the endeavor itself, but to leave the result to God.
—Alan Paton

'Tis man's to fight, but Heaven's to give success.　　—Homer

That man is blest who does his best and leaves the rest; do not worry.
—Charles F. Deems

If people are suffering, then they must look within themselves.... Happiness is not something ready-made [Buddha] can give you. It comes from your own actions.
—The Dalai Lama

I am not bound to win, but
I am bound to be true.
I am not bound to succeed, but
I am bound to live up to what light I
　have.　　—Abraham Lincoln

No way exists in the present to accurately determine the future effect of the least of our actions.
—Gerald Jampolsky

In vain our labours are, whatsoe'er they be, unless God gives the Benediction.　　—Robert Herrick

God alone can finish. —John Ruskin

In all human affairs there are *efforts,* and there are results, and the strength of the effort is the measure of the result.　　—James Lane Allen

God hasn't called me to be successful. He's called me to be faithful.
—Mother Teresa

An act of love that fails is just as much a part of the divine life as an act of love that succeeds, for love is measured by its own fullness, not by its reception.　　—Harold Loukes

Happy people plan actions, they don't plan results.
—Dennis Wholey

On earth we have nothing to do with success or results, but only with being true to God, and for God. Defeat in doing right is nevertheless victory.　—Frederick W. Robertson

The man who has done his level best, and who is conscious that he has done his best, is a success, even though the world may write him down a failure.　　—B.C. Forbes

To create is to boggle the mind and alter the mood. Once the urge has surged, it maintains its own momentum. We may go along for the ride, but when we attempt to steer the course, the momentum dies.
—Sue Atchley Ebaugh

Try first thyself, and after call in
　God,
For to the worker God himself lends
　aid.　　—Euripides

If thou workest at that which is before thee ... expecting nothing, fearing nothing, but satisfied with thy present activity according to Nature, and with heroic truth in every word and sound which thou utterest, thou wilt live happy. And there is no man who is able to prevent this.　　—Marcus Aurelius

483

WE CAN'T—AND DON'T NEED TO—CONTROL THINGS

You have striven so hard, and so long, to *compel* life. Can't you now slowly change, and let life slowly drift into you ... let the invisible life steal into you and slowly possess you. —D.H. Lawrence

I began to have an idea of my life, not as the slow shaping of achievement to fit my preconceived purposes, but as the gradual discovery and growth of a purpose which I did not know. —Joanna Field

A guru might say that spiritual deepening involves a journey toward the unselfconscious living of life as it unfolds, rather than toward a willful determination to make it happen. —John Fortunato

Somehow, when we no longer feel in control, we become available to deeper aliveness. —Richard Moss

Relinquishing control is the ultimate challenge of the Spiritual Warrior. —*The Book of Runes*

The bird of paradise alights only upon the hand that does not grasp. —John Berry

Living upon a basis of unsatisfied demands, we were in a state of continual disturbance and frustration. Therefore, no peace was to be had unless we could find a means of reducing these demands. —*Twelve Steps and Twelve Traditions*

You have freedom when you're easy in your harness. —Robert Frost

Life is made up of desires that seem big and vital one minute, and little and absurd the next. I guess we get what's best for us in the end. —Alice Caldwell Rice

As the soft yield of water cleaves obstinate stone,
So to yield with life solves the insolvable:
To yield, I have learned, is to come back again. —Lao-tzu

As your faith is strengthened, you will find that there is no longer the need to have a sense of control, that things will flow as they will, and that you will flow with them, to your great delight and benefit. —Emmanuel

For peace of mind, resign as general manager of the universe. —Anon.

Eventually I lost interest in trying to control my life, to make things happen in a way that I thought I wanted them to be. I began to practice surrendering to the universe and finding out what "it" wanted me to do. —Shakti Gawain

It had been my repeated experience that when you said to life calmly and firmly (but very firmly!), "I trust you; do what you must," life had an uncanny way of responding to your need. —Olga Ilyin

Men never cling to their dreams with such tenacity as at the moment when they are losing faith in them, and know it, but do not dare yet to confess it to themselves. —William Graham Sumner

So often we try to alter circumstances to suit ourselves, instead of letting them alter us.
—Mother Maribel

Willfulness must give way to willingness and surrender. Mastery must yield to mystery.   —Gerald G. May

The worst thing you can do is to try to cling to something that's gone, or to recreate it.   —Johnette Napolitano

I claim not to have controlled events, but confess plainly that events have controlled me.   —Abraham Lincoln

Letting people be okay without us is how we get to be okay without them.   —Merrit Malloy

WE ARE INSTRUMENTS OF GOD

We are the wire, God is the current. Our only power is to let the current pass through us.   —Carlo Carretto

I am like a little pencil in God's hand. He does the writing. The pencil has nothing to do with it.
—Mother Teresa

There are two kinds of people: those who say to God, "Thy will be done," and those to whom God says, "All right, then, have it your way."
—C.S. Lewis

Here am I; send me.

—Is. 6:8

'Tis God gives skill, but not without men's hands: he could not make Antonio Stradivarius violins without Antonio.   —George Eliot

WE MUST TRUST OUR HIGHER POWER

Life is God's novel. Let him write it.
—Isaac Bashevis Singer

To character and success, two things, contradictory as they may seem, must go together—humble dependence and manly independence: humble dependence on God, and manly reliance on self.
—William Wordsworth

Whate'er we leave to God, God does and blesses us.
—Henry David Thoreau

God will help you if you try, and you can if you think you can.
—Anna Delaney Peale

Doing what is right isn't the problem; it's *knowing* what is right.
—Lyndon B. Johnson

Let each look to himself and see what God wants of him and attend to this, leaving all else alone.
—Henry Suso

God tests His real friends more severely than the lukewarm ones.
—Katheryn Hulme

In vain our labours are, whatsoe'er they be, unless God gives the Benediction.   —Robert Herrick

Much that I sought, I could not find; much that I found, I could not bind; much that I bound, I could not free; much that I freed, returned to me.
—Lee Wilson Dodd

If you can't help it, don't think
about it. —Carmel Myers

Wanna fly, you got to give up the
shit that weighs you down.
—Toni Morrison

Do not inflict your will.
Just give love.
The soul will take that love and put
it where it can best be used.
—Emmanuel

God alone can finish. —John Ruskin

Be God or let God. —Anon.

With us is the Lord our God, to help
us and to fight our battles.
—2 Chr.

It is better to trust in the Lord than
to put confidence in man.
—Ps. 118:8

Cast thy burden on the Lord, and he
shall sustain thee.
—Ps. 55:22

But I trusted in thee, O Lord; I said,
Thou art my God. My times are in
thy hand. —Psalms

God's will is not an itinerary, but an
attitude. —Andrew Dhuse

Trust in the Lord with all thine
heart, and lean not unto thine own
understanding; in all thy ways
acknowledge Him, and He shall
direct thy paths. —Prv. 3:5

Casting all your care upon Him, for
He careth for you.
—1 Pt. 5:7

My life is ... a mystery which I do
not attempt to really understand, as
though I were led by the hand in a
night where I see nothing, but can
fully depend on the love and protection of Him who guides me.
—Thomas Merton

Be like the bird that, passing on her
flight awhile on boughs too slight,
feels them give way beneath her, and
yet sings, knowing that she hath
wings. —Victor Hugo

I come to the office each morning
and stay for long hours doing what
has to be done to the best of my ability. And when you've done the best
you can, you can't do any better. So
when I go to sleep I turn everything
over to the Lord and forget it.
—Harry S. Truman

Even now I am full of hope, but the
end lies in God. —Pindar

TAKE ONE STEP AT A TIME

BIG THINGS ARE ACCOMPLISHED ONE STEP AT A TIME

When you have a great and difficult task, something perhaps almost impossible, if you only work a little at a time, every day a little, suddenly the work will finish itself.

—Isak Dinesen

Nothing is particularly hard if you divide it into small jobs.

—Henry Ford

Look at a stone cutter hammering away at his rock, perhaps a hundred times without as much as a crack showing in it. Yet at the hundred-and-first blow it will split in two, and I know it was not the last blow that did it, but all that had gone before.

—Jacob A. Riis

Not to go back is somewhat to advance. And men must walk, at least, before they dance.

—Alexander Pope

Great things are not done by impulse, but by a series of small things brought together.

—Vincent van Gogh

Well-being is attained little by little, and is no little thing itself.

—Zeno of Citium

Bigness comes from doing many small things well.... Individually, they are not very dramatic transactions. Together, though, they add up.

—Edward S. Finkelstein

If you only keep adding little by little, it will soon become a big heap.

—Hesiod

He who would learn to fly one day must first learn to stand and walk and run and climb and dance; one cannot fly into flying.

—Friedrich Nietzsche

All that I have accomplished ... has been by that plodding, patient, persevering process of accretion which builds the ant heap particle by particle, thought by thought, fact by fact.

—Elihu Burritt

Many things which cannot be overcome when they are together, yield themselves up when taken little by little.

—Plutarch

True worth is doing each day some little good, not dreaming of great things to do by and by.   —Anon.

Little by little does the trick.
                                          —Aesop

It is by attempting to reach the top at a single leap that so much misery is caused in the world.
                              —William Cobbett

Yesterday I dared to struggle. Today I dare to win.   —Bernadette Devlin

I think and think for months, for years. Ninety-nine times the conclusion is false. The hundredth time I am right.   —Albert Einstein

Many strokes overthrow the tallest oaks.   —John Luly

Much rain wears the marble.
                          —William Shakespeare

Little drops of water, little grains of
     sand,
Make the mighty ocean, and the
     pleasant land:
So the little minutes, humble though
     they be,
Make the mighty ages of eternity.
Little deeds of kindness, little words
     of love,
Help to make earth happy, like
     Heaven up above. —Julia Carney

It is a mistake to look too far ahead. Only one link in the chain of destiny can be handled at a time.
                          —Sir Winston Churchill

One thing at a time, all things in succession. That which grows slowly endures.   —J.G. Hubbard

A successful individual typically sets his next goal somewhat, but not too much, above his last achievement.
                                  —Kurt Lewin

SMALL STEPS ARE BIG DEALS

One sits down first; one thinks afterwards.   —Jean Cocteau

Many strokes, though with a little axe, hew down and fell the hardest-timber'd oak. —William Shakespeare

Progress is the sum of small victories won by individual human beings.
                              —Bruce Catton

What saves a man is to take a step. Then another step.
                    —Antoine de Saint-Exupery

The waters wear the stones.
                                  —Jb. 14:19

One step and then another, and the
     longest walk is ended.
One stitch and then another, and the
     longest rent is mended.
One brick upon another, and the
     tallest wall is made.
One flake and then another, and the
     deepest snow is laid.   —Anon.

You don't just luck into things....
You build step by step, whether it's friendships or opportunities.
                              —Barbara Bush

The way a chihuahua goes about eating a dead elephant is to take a bite and be very present with that bite. In spiritual growth, the definitive act is to take one step and let tomorrow's step take care of itself!
                          —William H. Houff

INCHES ADD UP

Victory is won not in miles, but in inches. Win a little now, hold your ground, and later win a little more.
—Louis L'Amour

Inches make a champion.
—Vince Lombardi

If we take care of the inches, we will not have to worry about the miles.
—Hartley Coleridge

Yard by yard, it's very hard. But inch by inch, it's a cinch.
—Anon.

When Ty Cobb got on first base he had an apparently nervous habit of kicking the bag.... By kicking the bag hard enough Cobb could move it a full two inches closer to second base. He figured that this improved his chances for a steal, or for reaching second base safely on a hit.
—Norman Vincent Peale

LITTLE THINGS ARE BIG THINGS

Most people would succeed in small things if they were not troubled with great ambitions.
—Henry Wadsworth Longfellow

Life is made up of little things. It is very rarely that an occasion is offered for doing a great deal at once. True greatness consists in being great in little things.
—Charles Simmons

Life is a great bundle of little things.
—Oliver Wendell Holmes

Nothing can be done except little by little.
—Charles Baudelaire

Practice yourself in little things, and thence proceed to greater.
—Epictetus

Those people work more wisely who seek to achieve good in their own small corner of the world ... than those who are forever thinking that life is in vain, unless one can ... do big things.
—Herbert Butterfield

I recommend you to take care of the minutes, for the hours will take care of themselves.
—Lord Chesterfield

You've got to think about "big things" while you're doing small things, so that all the small things go in the right direction.
—Alvin Toffler

Little strokes fell great oaks.
—Benjamin Franklin

Take your needle, my child, and work at your pattern; it will come out a rose by and by. Life is like that; one stitch at a time taken patiently, and the pattern will come out all right, like embroidery.
—Oliver Wendell Holmes

Most of us miss out on life's big prizes. The Pulitzer. The Nobel. Oscars. Tonys. Emmys. But we're all eligible for life's small pleasures. A pat on the back. A kiss behind the ear. A four-pound bass. A full moon. An empty parking space. A crackling fire. A great meal. A glorious sunset. Hot Soup. Cold beer. Don't fret about copping life's grand awards. Enjoy its tiny delights. There are plenty for all of us.
—United Technologies Corporation advertisement

Why not learn to enjoy the little things—there are so many of them.
—Anon.

The mere sense of living is joy enough.   —Emily Dickinson

Human felicity is produced not so much by great pieces of good fortune that seldom happen as by little advantages that occur every day.
—Benjamin Franklin

Trifles make up the happiness or the misery of mortal life.
—Alexander Smith

Even a small star shines in the darkness.   —Finnish proverb

How far that little candle throws his beams! So shines a good deed in a naughty world.
—William Shakespeare

It is better to light a candle than to curse the darkness.
—Chinese proverb

If you don't enjoy getting up and working and finishing your work and sitting down to a meal with family or friends, then the chances are you're not going to be happy. If someone bases his happiness or unhappiness on major events like a great new job, huge amounts of money, a flawlessly happy marriage or a trip to Paris, that person isn't going to be happy much of the time. If, on the other hand, happiness depends on a good breakfast, flowers in the yard, a drink or a nap, then we are more likely to live with quite a bit of happiness.
—Andy Rooney

The big things that come our way are ... the fruit of seeds planted in the daily routine of our work.
—William Feather

The little things are infinitely the most important. —Sir Arthur Conan Doyle

Enjoy the little things, for one day you may look back and realize they were the big things.
—Robert Brault

It is in trifles, and when he is off his guard, that a man best shows his character.   —Arthur Schopenhauer

Life is denied by lack of attention, whether it be to cleaning windows or trying to write a masterpiece.
—Nadia Boulanger

It was only a sunny smile,
But it scattered the night
And little it cost in the giving;
Like morning light,
And made the day worth living.
—Anon.

Sometimes the littlest things in life are the hardest to take. You can sit on a mountain more comfortably than on a tack.   —Anon.

Put your heart, mind, intellect, and soul even to your smallest acts. This is the secret of success.
—Swami Sivananda

The smallest effort is not lost,
Each wavelet on the ocean tost
Aids in the ebb-tide or the flow;
Each rain-drop makes some floweret blow;
Each struggle lessens human woe.
—Charles Mackay

490

In life's small things be resolute and
   great
To keep thy muscle trained;
Know'st thou when Fate
Thy measure takes, or when she'll
   say to thee,
"I find thee worthy; do this deed for
   me?"   —James Russell Lowell

He that is faithful in that which is
least is faithful also in much; and he
that is unjust in the least is unjust
also in much.   —Lk. 16:10

We think in generalities, but we live
in detail. —Alfred North Whitehead

JUST DOING WHATEVER WE
CAN IS ENOUGH

I cannot do everything, but still I can
do something; and because I cannot
do everything, I will not refuse to do
something that I can do.
              —Edward Everett Hale

We cannot do everything at once,
but we can do something at once.
              —Calvin Coolidge

Nobody makes a greater mistake
than he who did nothing because he
could only do a little.
              —Edmund Burke

We must not ... ignore the small
daily differences we can make which,
over time, add up to big differences
that we often cannot foresee.
              —Marian Write Edelman

God requires a faithful fulfillment of
the merest trifle given us to do,
rather than the most ardent aspiration to things to which we are not
called.   —Saint Francis de Sales

MODEST BEGINNINGS CAN LEAD
TO GREAT RESULTS

Large streams from little mountains
flow, tall oaks from little acorns
grow.   —David Everett

The man who removes a mountain
begins by carrying away small
stones.   —Chinese proverb

A journey of a thousand miles must
begin with a single step.
                    —Chinese proverb

The distance doesn't matter; only the
first step is difficult.
              —Madame Marquise du Deffand

A terrace nine stories high begins
with a pile of earth.   —Lao-tzu

Though thy beginning was small, yet
thy latter end should greatly
increase.   —Jb. 8:7

Almost everything comes from
almost nothing.
              —Henri Frederic Amiel

The greatest masterpieces were once
only pigments on a palette.
              —Henry S. Haskins

From a little spark may burst a
mighty flame.   —Dante Alighieri

Start by doing what's necessary, then
what's possible, and suddenly you
are doing the impossible.
              —Saint Francis of Assisi

If you wish to reach the highest,
begin at the lowest. —Publilius Syrus

Great issues develop from small
beginnings. —Norman Vincent Peale

Events of great consequence often spring from trifling circumstances.
—Livy

No matter how big and tough a problem may be, get rid of confusion by taking one little step toward solution. Do *something*.
—George F. Nordenholt

Most of the critical things in life, which become the starting points of human destiny, are little things.
—R. Smith

Sow an act, reap a habit; sow a habit, reap a character; sow a character, reap a destiny.
—G.D. Boardman

The way to succeed is never quit. That's it. But really be humble about it.... You start out lowly and humble and you carefully try to learn an accretion of little things that help you get there. —Alex Hailey

GENERAL QUOTATIONS ABOUT TAKING ONE STEP AT A TIME

A little neglect may breed great mischief.... For want of a nail, the shoe was lost; for want of a shoe, the horse was lost; for want of a horse, the battle was lost; for want of the battle, the war was lost.
—Benjamin Franklin

Inspiration does not come like a blot, nor is it kinetic energy striving, but it comes to us slowly and quietly all the time. —Brenda Euland

There is time enough for everything in the course of the day if you do but one thing once; but there is not time enough in the year if you will do two things at a time. —Lord Chesterfield

Think not because no man sees, such things will remain unseen.
—Henry Wadsworth Longfellow

I long to accomplish a great and noble task, but it is my chief duty to accomplish small tasks as if they were great and noble. —Helen Keller

Let us then be up and doing, With a heart for any fate, Still achieving, still pursuing, Learn to labor and to wait.
—Henry Wadsworth Longfellow

If, after all, men cannot always make history have a meaning, they can always act so that their own lives have one. —Albert Camus

Every worthwhile accomplishment, big or little, has its stages of drudgery and triumph; a beginning, a struggle, and a victory.
—Anon.

The world is moved not only by the mighty shoves of the heroes, but also by the aggregate of the tiny pushes of each honest worker.
—Helen Keller

In great matters men show themselves as they wish to be seen; in small matters, as they are.
—Gamaliel Bradford

PERSEVERANCE

THE IMPORTANCE AND VALUE OF PERSEVERANCE

There's nothing in this world that comes easy. There are a lot of people who aren't going to bother to win. We learn in football to get up and go once more. —Woody Hayes

You can do what you want to do, accomplish what you want to accomplish, attain any reasonable objective ... if you want it, if you will to do it, if you work to do it, over a sufficiently long period of time.
—William E. Holler

To persevere, trusting in what hopes he has, is courage in a man. The coward despairs. —Euripides

There are but two roads that lead to an important goal and to the doing of great things: strength and perseverance. Strength is the lot of but a few privileged men; but austere perseverance, harsh and continuous, may be employed by the smallest of us and rarely fails of its purpose, for its silent power grows irresistibly greater with time.
—Johann von Goethe

We conquer by continuing.
—George Matheson

When it goes wrong, you feel like cutting your throat, but you go on. You don't let anything get you down so much that it beats you or stops you. —George Cukor

Great works are performed not by strength, but by perseverance.
—Samuel Johnson

Any man can work when every stroke of his hands brings down the fruit rattling from the tree ... but to labor in season and out of season, under every discouragement ... that requires a heroism which is transcendent. —Henry Ward Beecher

Be like a postage stamp—stick to one thing until you get there.
—Josh Billings

Keep on going, and the chances are that you will stumble on something, perhaps when you are least expecting it. I never heard of anyone ever stumbling on something sitting down. —Charles F. Kettering

493

With ordinary talent and extraordinary perseverance, all things are attainable.

—Sir Thomas Foxwell Buxton

For me, at least, there came moments when faith wavered. But there is the great lesson and the great triumph: keep the fire burning until, by and by, out of the mass of sordid details there comes some result.

—Oliver Wendell Holmes, Jr.

Nothing in the world can take place of persistence. Talent will not; nothing is more common than unsuccessful individuals with talent. Genius will not; unrewarded genius is almost a proverb. Education will not; the world is full of educated derelicts. Persistence and determination alone are omnipotent.

—Calvin Coolidge

Let me tell you the secret that has led me to my goal: my strength lies solely in my tenacity.　—Louis Pasteur

In the game of life nothing is less important than the score at half time.　—Anon.

In the realm of ideas everything depends on enthusiasm; in the real world, all rests on perseverance.

—Johann von Goethe

Without perseverance talent is a barren bed.　—Welsh proverb

Don't be discouraged. It's often the last key in the bunch that opens the lock.　—Anon.

Diamonds are only lumps of coal that stuck to their jobs.

—B.C. Forbes

Persistence is the master virtue. Without it, there is no other.

—Anon.

WE MUST PERSEVERE TO BE SUCCESSFUL

I am not the smartest or most talented person in the world, but I succeeded because I keep going, and going, and going.

—Sylvester Stallone

I know the price of success: dedication, hard work and an unremitting devotion to the things you want to see happen.　—Frank Lloyd Wright

Victory belongs to the most persevering.　—Napoleon Bonaparte

Success generally depends upon knowing how long it takes to succeed.　—Charles de Montesquieu

Success seems to be largely a matter of hanging on after others have let go.　—William Feather

If you wish success in life, make perseverance your bosom friend.

—Joseph Addison

They who are the most persistent, and work in the true spirit, will invariably be the most successful.

—Samuel Smiles

If at first you don't succeed, try, try, try again.　—W.E. Hickson

If at first you don't succeed, you're running about average.

—M.H. Alderson

The secret of success is constancy of purpose.　—Benjamin Disraeli

494

The only way to the top is by persistent, intelligent, hard work.
—A.T. Mercier

The heights by great men reached
    and kept
Were not attained by sudden flight,
But they, while their companions
    slept
Were toiling upward in the night.
—Henry Wadsworth Longfellow

I realized early on that success was tied to not giving up. Most people in this business gave up and went on to other things. If you simply didn't give up, you would outlast the people who came in on the bus with you.
—Harrison Ford

Call the roll in your memory of conspicuously successful [business] giants and, if you know anything about their careers, you will be struck by the fact that almost every one of them encountered inordinate difficulties sufficient to crush all but the gamest of spirits. Edison went hungry many times before he became famous.
—B.C. Forbes

Perseverance is a great element of success. If you only knock long enough and loud enough at the gate, you are sure to wake up somebody.
—Henry Wadsworth Longfellow

Four steps to achievement: plan purposefully, prepare prayerfully, proceed positively, pursue persistently.
—William A. Ward

Flaming enthusiasm, backed up by horse sense and persistence, is the quality that most frequently makes for success.
—Dale Carnegie

I'm hardnosed about luck. I think it sucks. Yeah, if you spend seven years looking for a job as a copywriter, and then one day somebody gives you a job, you can say, "Gee, I was lucky I happened to go up there today." But dammit, I was going to go up there sooner or later in the next seventy years.... If you're persistent in trying and doing and working, you almost make your own fortune.
—Jerry Della Femina

It's the plugging away that will win
    you the day
So don't be a piker old pard!
Just draw on your grit; it's so easy to
    quit—
It's the keeping your chin up that's
    hard.
—Robert W. Service

No one succeeds without effort....
Those who succeed owe their success to their perseverance.
—Ramana Maharshi

Big shots are only little shots who keep shooting.
—Christopher Morley

Be of good cheer. Do not think of today's failures, but of the success that may come tomorrow. You have set yourselves a difficult task, but you will succeed if you persevere; and you will find a joy in overcoming obstacles. Remember, no effort that we make to attain something beautiful is ever lost.
—Helen Keller

The way to succeed is never quit. That's it. But really be humble about it.... You start out lowly and humble and you carefully try to learn an accretion of little things that help you get there.
—Alex Hailey

There are no shortcuts to any place worth going. —Beverly Sills

Continuous efforts—not strength or intelligence—is the key to unlocking our potential.
—Sir Winston Churchill

Plodding wins the race. —Aesop

The difficulties and struggles of today are but the price we must pay for the accomplishments and victories of tomorrow.
—William J.H. Boetcker

Let me tell you the secret that has led me to my goal: my strength lies solely in my tenacity. —Louis Pasteur

A winner never quits and a quitter never wins. —Anon.

It isn't hard to be good from time to time.... What's tough is being good every day. —Willie Mays

Men who have attained things worth having in this world have worked while others idled, have persevered when others gave up in despair, have practiced early in life the valuable habits of self-denial, industry, and singleness of purpose. As a result, they enjoy in later life the success so often erroneously attributed to good luck. —Grenville Kleiser

In the realm of ideas, everything depends on enthusiasm; in the real world, all rests on perseverance.
—Johann von Goethe

There's such a thin line between winning and losing. —John R. Tunis

WE MUST FINISH WHAT WE START

The great majority of men are bundles of beginnings.
—Ralph Waldo Emerson

It is easier to begin well than to finish well. —Plautus

Great is the art of beginning, but greater is the art of ending.
—Henry Wadsworth Longfellow

We rate ability in men by what they finish, not by what they begin.
—Anon.

Everyone has his superstitions. One of mine has always been when I started to go anywhere, or to do anything, never to turn back or to stop until the thing intended was accomplished. —Ulysses S. Grant

I just kept on doing what everyone starts out doing. The real question is, why did other people stop?
—William Stafford

Men perish because they cannot join the beginning with the end.
—Alcmaeon

Business is full of brilliant men who started out with a spurt and lacked the stamina to finish. Their places were taken by patient and unshowy plodders who never knew when to quit. —J.R. Todd

I can remember walking as a child. It was not customary to say you were fatigued. It was customary to complete the goal of the expedition.
—Katharine Hepburn

He that has cut the claws of the lion will not feel quite secure until he has also drawn his teeth.
—Charles Caleb Colton

Courage to start and willingness to keep everlasting at it are the requisites for success.
—Alonzo Newton Benn

I went for years not finishing anything. Because, of course, when you finish something you can be judged.... I had poems which were rewritten so many times I suspect it was just a way of avoiding sending them out.
—Erica Jong

Let no one 'til his death be called
  unhappy.
Measure not the work
Until the day's out, and the labor
  done:
Then bring your gauges.
—Elizabeth Barrett Browning

All is well that ends well.
—John Heywood

Either do not attempt at all, or go through with it.   —Ovid

In soloing—as in other activities—it is far easier to start something than it is to finish it.   —Amelia Earhart

It is a matter first of beginning—and then following through.
—Richard L. Evans

Genius begins great works, labor alone finishes it.   —Joseph Joubert

There is but an inch of difference between the cushioned chamber and the padded cell.   —G.K. Chesterton

SMALL, CONSTANT EFFORTS PAY OFF

The drops of rain make a hole in the stone not by violence, but by oft falling.   —Lucretius

I work every day—or at least I force myself into my office or room. I may get nothing done, but you don't earn bonuses without putting in time. Nothing may come for three months, but you don't earn the fourth without it.   —Mordecai Richler

When nothing seems to help, I go and look at a stonecutter hammering away at his rock perhaps a hundred times without as much as a crack showing in it. Yet at the hundred and first blow it will split in two, and I know it was not that blow that did it, but all that had gone before.
—Jacob Riis

PERSEVERANCE IS MORE IMPORTANT THAN SPEED

It does not matter how slowly you go, so long as you do not stop.
—Confucius

The great thing in this world is not so much where we are, but in what direction we are moving.
—Oliver Wendell Holmes

The race is not always to the swift, but to those who keep on running.
—Anon.

By perseverance the snail reached the Ark.   —Charles Haddon Spurgeon

The race is not to the swift, nor the battle to the strong.
—Eccl. 9:11

If we are facing in the right direction, all we have to do is keep on walking.

—Ancient Buddhist proverb

It's the steady, constant driving to the goal for which you're striving, not the speed with which you travel, that will make your victory sure.

—Anon.

I'm a slow walker, but I never walk back.

—Abraham Lincoln

Slow and steady wins the race.

—Robert Lloyd

Character is built into the spiritual fabric of personality hour by hour, day by day, year by year in much the same deliberate way that physical health is built into the body.

—E. Lamar Kincaid

No great thing is created suddenly.

—Epictetus

Be content to grow a little each day. If the improvement is the sort of thing which is very slow, do not measure it too often. Do a self-comparison every two weeks, or every six months, whatever is appropriate.

—Lewis F. Presnall

Pray that success will not come any faster than you are able to endure it.

—Elbert Hubbard

Wisely and slow. They stumble that run fast.

—William Shakespeare

Plodding wins the race.

—Aesop

The way of progress is neither swift nor easy.

—Marie Curie

One thing at a time, all things in succession. That which grows slowly endures.

—J.G. Holland

Make haste slowly.

—Augustus

Slow motion gets you there faster.

—Hoagy Carmichael

I'm not there yet, but I'm closer than I was yesterday.

—Anon.

SOMETIMES WE JUST HAVE TO GET OVER THE HUMP

Life begins on the other side of despair.

—Jean-Paul Sartre

The lowest ebb is the turn of the tide.

—Henry Wadsworth Longfellow

You give 100 percent in the first half of the game, and if that isn't enough, in the second half you give what's left.

—Yogi Berra

One can go a long way after one is tired.

—French proverb

The great thing, and the hard thing, is to stick to things when you have outlived the first interest, and not yet got the second, which comes with a sort of mastery.

—Janet Erskine Stuart

If something is boring after two minutes, try it for four. If still boring, try for eight, sixteen, thirty-two, and so on. Eventually, one discovers that it is not boring, but very interesting.

—Anon.

Effort only fully releases its reward after a person refuses to quit.

—Napoleon Hill

No one ever did anything worth doing unless he was prepared to go on with it long after it became something of a bore.   —Douglas V. Steere

I've been failing for like, ten or eleven years. When it turns, it'll turn. Right now I'm just tryin' to squeeze through a very tight financial period, get the movie out, and put my things in order.   —Francis Ford Coppola

In our day, when a pitcher got into trouble in a game, instead of taking him out, our manager would leave him in and tell him to pitch his way out of trouble.   —Cy Young

KEEP GOING,
JUST A LITTLE LONGER

I'm a little wounded, but I am not slain; I will lay me down to bleed a while. Then I'll rise and fight again.
—John Dryden

The tragedy of life is not that man loses, but that he almost wins.
—Heywood Broun

A hero is no braver than an ordinary man, but he is brave five minutes longer.   —Ralph Waldo Emerson

Courage is fear holding on a minute longer.   —General George S. Patton

The line between failure and success is so fine that we ... are often on the line and do not know it. How many a man has thrown up his hands at a time when a little more effort, a little more patience, would have achieved success. A little more persistence, a little more effort, and what seemed hopeless failure may turn to glorious success.   —Elbert Hubbard

When you get to the end of your rope, tie a knot and hang on.
—Franklin Delano Roosevelt

Saints are sinners who kept on going.   —Robert Louis Stevenson

When you get into a tight place and everything goes against you, 'til it seems as though you could not hold on a minute longer, never give up then, for that is just the place and time that the tide will turn.
—Harriet Beecher Stowe

We can do anything we want to do if we stick to it long enough.
—Helen Keller

Men do not fail, they stop trying.
—Elihu Root

It ain't over 'til it's over.
—Yogi Berra

Triumph often is nearest when defeat seems inescapable.
—B.C. Forbes

Don't bother about genius. Don't worry about being clever. Trust to hard work, perseverance and determination. And the best motto for a long march is, "Don't grumble. Plug on!"   —Sir Frederick Treves

Some men give up their designs when they have almost reached the goal; while others, on the contrary, obtain a victory by exerting, at the last moment, more vigorous efforts than before.   —Polybius

Never stop. One always stops as soon as something is about to happen.   —Peter Brook

Many of life's failures are men who did not realize how close they were to success when they gave up.

—Thomas A. Edison

Fight one more round. When your feet are so tired you have to shuffle back to the center of the ring, fight one more round. —James J. Corbett

Don't leave before the miracle happens! —Anon.

If something doesn't come up the way you want, you have to forge ahead. —Clint Eastwood

Fortune is like the market, where many times, if you can stay a little, the price will fall. —Francis Bacon

Sometimes It Pays Not to Know We're "Beaten"

This man Wellington is so stupid he does not know when he is beaten, and goes on fighting.

—Napoleon Bonaparte

He never knew when he was whipped ... so he never was.

—Louis L'Amour

Never Admit Defeat

Entrepreneurs average 3.8 failures before a final success. What sets the successful ones apart is their amazing persistence. There are a lot of people out there with good and marketable ideas, but pure entrepreneurial types almost never accept defeat.

—Lisa M. Amos

As long as a person doesn't admit he is defeated, he is not defeated—he's just a little behind, and isn't through fighting. —Darrell Royal

Defeat never comes to any man until he admits it. —Josephus Daniels

Never give in! Never give in! Never, never, never, never.... In nothing great or small, large or petty, never give in except to convictions or honor and good sense!

—Sir Winston Churchill

First there are those who are winners, and know they are winners. Then there are the losers who know they are losers. Then there are those who are not winners, but don't know it. They're the ones for me. They never quit trying. They're the soul of our game. —Bear Bryant

Never admit defeat!

—Arthur Rimbaud

We shall go on to the end. We shall fight in France, we shall fight with growing confidence and growing strength in the air, we shall defend our island, whatever the cost may be. We shall fight on the beaches, we shall fight on the landing grounds, we shall fight in the fields, and in the streets, we shall fight in the halls. We shall never surrender.

—Sir Winston Churchill

Endurance Is Critical

He conquers who endures.

—Anon.

Emotional maturity is the ability to stick to a job and to struggle through until it is finished, to endure unpleasantness, discomfort and frustration.

—Edward A. Strecker

To bear is to conquer our fate.

—Thomas Campbell

The first and final thing you have to do in this world is to last in it, and not be smashed by it.

—Ernest Hemingway

The first need of being is endurance; to endure with gladness if we can, with fortitude in any event.

—Bliss Carman

I bend, but I do not break.

—Jean de La Fontaine

He that endureth to the end shall be saved.   —Mt. 10:22

Whatever necessity lays upon thee, endure; whatever she commands, do.

—Johann von Goethe

To be somebody you must last.

—Ruth Gordon

In the clutch of circumstance, I have not winced or cried aloud;
Under the bludgeoning of chance, my head is bloody, but unbowed.

—William E. Henley

We shall live to fight again, and to strike another blow.

—Alfred, Lord Tennyson

Giving up is the ultimate tragedy.

—Robert J. Donovan

God Almighty hates a quitter.

—Samuel Fessenden

Endurance is one of the most difficult disciplines, but it is to the one who endures that the final victory comes.   —Buddha

Endure, and preserve yourselves for better things.   —Virgil

Every kind of fortune is to be overcome by bearing it.   —Virgil

When we see ourselves in a situation which must be endured and gone through, it is best to make up our minds to meet it with firmness, and accommodate everything to it in the best way practical. This lessons the evil, while fretting and fuming only serve to increase your own torments.

—Thomas Jefferson

If you want to see the sun shine, you have to weather the storm.

—Frank Lane

If you want the rainbow, you gotta put up with the rain.

—Dolly Parton

He that can't endure the bad will not live to see the good.

—Yiddish proverb

To struggle when hope is banished.
To live when life's salt is gone!
To dwell in a dream that's vanished—
To endure, and go calmly on!

—Ben Johnson

A high heart ought to bear calamities and not flee them, since in bearing them appears the grandeur of the mind, and in fleeing them the cowardice of the heart.   —Pietro Aretino

Endurance is nobler than strength, and patience than beauty.

—John Ruskin

They merit more praise who know how to suffer misery than those who temper themselves with contentment.

—Pietro Aretino

What cannot be altered must be borne, not blamed.
—Thomas Fuller

We must endure what fortune sends.
—Greek proverb

People can bear anything.
—Philip Slater

We must learn from life how to suffer it.
—French proverb

This is courage in a man: to bear unflinchingly what heaven sends.
—Euripides

To be unable to bear an ill is itself a great ill.
—Bion

Man never made any material as resilient as the human spirit.
—Bern Williams

Obstacles cannot crush me, every obstacle yields to stern resolve.
—Leonardo da Vinci

And let us not be weary in well doing; for in due season we shall reap, if we faint not.
—Gal. 6:9

Hold on with a bulldog grip, and chew and choke as much as possible.
—Abraham Lincoln

There remain times when one can only endure. One lives on, one doesn't die, and the only thing that one can do is to fill one's mind and time as far as possible with the concerns of other people. It doesn't bring immediate peace, but it brings the dawn nearer.
—Arthur Christopher Benson

WE MUST KEEP GETTING UP

Our greatest glory consists not in never falling, but in rising every time we fall.
—Ralph Waldo Emerson

Success consists of getting up just one more time than you fall.
—Oliver Goldsmith

If I don't get off the mat, I'll lose the fight.
—Archie Moore

For a just man falleth seven times, and riseth up again.
—Prv. 24:16

WE MUST KEEP STARTING OVER

Persistent people begin their success where others end in failure.
—Edward Eggleston

Vitality shows not only in the ability to persist, but in the ability to start over.
—F. Scott Fitzgerald

To be happy, drop the words "if only" and substitute instead the words "next time."
—Smiley Blanton, M.D.

WE MUST KEEP AT IT UNTIL WE LEARN WHAT WE NEED TO KNOW

Life is a maze in which we take the wrong turning before we learn to walk.
—Cyril Connolly

Education is hanging around until you've caught on.
—Robert Frost

You go back to the gym and you just do it again and again until you get it right.
—Arnold Schwarzenegger

As long as one keeps searching, the answers come.
—Joan Baez

How many years you have to keep on doing, until you know what to do and how to do!
—Johann von Goethe

Tolerate the ... process of coming to knowledge or certainty or clarity through sometimes apparently hopeless thickets of confusion or bewilderment. Learn not to be surprised or disheartened by the muddle you inhabit, and not to press too soon for a superficial reprieve.
—Joe David Bellamy

What can any of us do with his talent but try to develop his vision, so that through frequent failures we may learn better what we have missed in the past.
—William Carlos Williams

SOME THINGS THAT STIMULATE AND SUSTAIN PERSEVERANCE

All effort is in the last analysis sustained by faith that it is worth making.
—Ordway Tead

Life has no smooth road for any of us; and in the bracing atmosphere of a high aim the very roughness stimulates the climber to steadier steps till the legend, "over steep ways to the stars," fulfills itself.
—W.C. Doane

If I had refused to institute a negotiation or had not persevered in it, I would have been degraded in my own estimation as a man of honor.
—John Adams

I read my own books sometimes to cheer me when it is hard to write, and then I remember that it was always difficult, and how nearly impossible it was sometimes.
—Ernest Hemingway

The difference between perseverance and obstinacy is that one comes from a strong will, and the other from a strong won't.
—Henry Ward Beecher

When you're a professional, you come back no matter what happened the day before.
—Billy Martin

We can do whatever we wish to do provided our wish is strong enough.... What do you want most to do? That's what I have to keep asking myself, in the face of difficulties.
—Katherine Mansfield

Desire and hope will push us on toward the future.
—Michel de Montaigne

The champ may have lost his stuff temporarily or permanently, he can't be sure. When he can no longer throw his high hard one, he throws his heart instead. He throws something. He just doesn't walk off the mound and weep.
—Raymond Chandler

We attempt nothing great but from a sense of the difficulties we have to encounter; we persevere in nothing great but from a pride in overcoming them.
—William Hazlitt

He turns not back who is bound to a star.
—Leonardo da Vinci

What helps me go forward is that I stay receptive, I feel that anything can happen.
—Anouk Aimee

There was a Texas Ranger one time who said that there's no stopping a man who knows he's in the right and keeps a-coming.
—Louis L'Amour

Whatever course you decide upon, there is always someone to tell you that you are wrong. There are always difficulties arising which tempt you to believe that your critics are right. To map out a course of action and follow it to an end requires ... courage.

—Ralph Waldo Emerson

I have accepted fear as a part of life—specifically the fear of change.... I have gone ahead despite the pounding in the heart that says: turn back....　　　—Erica Jong

Tribulation produces perseverance; and perseverance, character; and character, hope.

—Romans

"Brave admiral, say but one good
　　word:
What shall we do when hope is
　　gone?"
The words leapt like a leaping
　　sword:
"Sail on! sail on! and on!"

—Joaquin Miller

We must dare, and dare again, and go on daring.

—Georges Jacques Danton

Austere perseverance, harsh and continuous, may be employed by the least of us and rarely fails of its purpose, for its silent power grows irresistibly greater with time.

—Johann von Goethe

Grant me the courage not to give up, even though I think it is hopeless.

—Admiral Chester W. Nimitz

I have often been adrift, but I have always stayed afloat.　—David Berry

God helps those who persevere.

—Koran

Gnaw your own bone; gnaw at it, bury it, unearth it, gnaw it still.

—Henry David Thoreau

Like ships, men flounder time and time again.　　　—Henry Miller

To strive, to seek, to find, and not to yield.　　—Alfred, Lord Tennyson

To keep a lamp burning we have to keep putting oil in it.

—Mother Teresa

If you stop struggling, then you stop life.　　　—Huey Newton

One thing we learned. To make a start and keep plugging. When I had fights at school, the little while I went, I just bowed my neck and kept swinging until something hit the dirt. Sometimes it was me, but I always got up.　　　—Louis L'Amour

You may have to fight a battle more than once to win it.

—Margaret Thatcher

Jesus taught that perseverance is the essential element of prayer. Men must be in earnest when they kneel at God's footstool. Too often we get faint-hearted and quit praying at the point when we ought to begin. We let go at the very point where we should hold on strongest. Our prayers are weak because they are not impassioned by an unfailing and resistless will.　　—E.M. Bounds

Be strong!
It matters not how deep entrenched
　　the wrong
How hard the battle goes, the day
　　how long
Faint not—fight on!
Tomorrow comes the song.
　　　　　　　—Maltbie D. Babcock

Never grow a wishbone, daughter,
where your backbone ought to be.
　　　　　　　—Clementime Paddleford

Good people are good because
they've come to wisdom through
failure.　　　　　—William Saroyan

Problems

Everyone Has Problems

None of us can be free of conflict and woe. Even the greatest men have had to accept disappointments as their daily bread.
—Bernard M. Baruch

There is no man in any rank who is always at liberty to act as he would incline. In some quarter or other he is limited by circumstances. —Blair

Life has no smooth road for any of us; and in the bracing atmosphere of a high aim the very roughness stimulates the climber to steadier steps till the legend, "over steep ways to the stars," fulfills itself. —W.C. Doane

Every path has its puddle.
—English proverb

If all our misfortunes were laid in one common heap, whence everyone must take an equal portion, most people would be content to take their own and depart. —Socrates

Identifying Real Problems

A problem well stated is a problem half solved. —Charles F. Kettering

It isn't that they can't see the solution, it's that they can't see the problem. —G.K. Chesterton

If we can really understand the problem, the answer will come out of it, because the answer is not separate from the problem.
—Jiddu Krishnamurti

The man who most vividly realizes a difficulty is the man most likely to overcome it. —Joseph Farrell

A good problem statement often includes: (a) what is known, (b) what is unknown, and (c) what is sought. —Edward Hodnett

Several Ways to Solve Problems

You often get a better hold upon a problem by going away from it for a time and dismissing it from your mind altogether. —Dr. Frank Crane

When I feel difficulty coming on, I switch to another book I'm writing. When I get back to the problem, my unconscious has solved it.
—Isaac Asimov

You can surmount the obstacles in your path if you are determined, courageous and hard-working. Never be fainthearted. Be resolute, but never bitter.... Permit no one to dissuade you from pursuing the goals you set for yourselves. Do not fear to pioneer, to venture down new paths of endeavor.—Ralph J. Bunche

Any concern too small to be turned into a prayer is too small to be made into a burden.   —Corrie ten Bloom

When you approach a problem, strip yourself of preconceived opinions and prejudice, assemble and learn the facts of the situation, make the decision which seems to you to be the most honest, and then stick to it.
—Chester Bowles

No matter how big and tough a problem may be, get rid of confusion by taking one little step towards solution. Do something. Then try again. At the worst, so long as you don't do it the same way twice, you will eventually use up all the wrong ways of doing it and thus the next try will be the right one.
—George F. Nordenholt

The greatest and most important problems of life are all in a certain sense insoluble. They can never be solved, but only outgrown.
—Carl Jung

The art of living lies less in eliminating our troubles than in growing with them.   —Bernard M. Baruch

You can overcome anything if you don't bellyache.
—Bernard M. Baruch

There is no other solution to a man's problems but the day's honest work, the day's honest decisions, the day's generous utterance, and the day's good deed.   —Clare Boothe Luce

Every problem contains the seeds of its own solution.   —Stanley Arnold

When you can't solve the problem, manage it. —Dr. Robert H. Schuller

WHEN TRYING TO SOLVE A PROBLEM, FOCUS ON ITS POSITIVE ASPECTS

The block of granite, which was an obstacle in the path of the weak, becomes a stepping stone in the path of the strong.   —Thomas Carlyle

Many a man curses the rain that falls upon his head, and knows not that it brings abundance to drive away hunger.   —Saint Basil

Times of general calamity and confusion have ever been productive of the greatest minds. The purest ore is produced from the hottest furnace, and the brightest thunderbolt is elicited from the darkest storms.
—Charles Caleb Colton

What is difficulty? Only a word indicating the degree of strength requisite for accomplishing particular objects; a mere notice of the necessity for exertion ... a mere stimulus to men.   —Samuel Warren

Problems are only opportunities in work clothes.   —Henry J. Kaiser

Real difficulties can be overcome, it is only the imaginary ones that are unconquerable. —Theodore N. Vail

We must look for the opportunity in every difficulty, instead of being paralyzed at the thought of the difficulty in every opportunity.
—Walter E. Cole

IT'S USUALLY BEST TO FACE PROBLEMS DIRECTLY

Half the unhappiness in life comes from people being afraid to go straight at things. —William J. Lock

All work of man is as the swimmer's: a vast ocean threatens to devour him; if he front it not bravely, it will keep its word. —Thomas Carlyle

All problems become smaller if you don't dodge them, but confront them. —William F. Halsey

The best way out of a problem is through it. —Anon.

A great man is one who seizes the vital issue in a complex question, what we might call the jugular vein of the whole organism, and spends his energies upon that.
—Joseph Rickaby

Only one feat is possible: not to have run away. —Dag Hammarskjold

We only really face up to ourselves when we are afraid.
—Thomas Bernhard

Life is the acceptance of responsibilities or their evasion; it is a business of meeting obligations or avoiding them. To every man the choice is continually being offered, and by the manner of his choosing you may fairly measure him.
—Ben Ames Williams

The superior man makes the difficulty to be overcome his first interest; success comes only later.
—Confucius

No man will succeed unless he is ready to face and overcome difficulties and is prepared to assume responsibilities.
—William J.H. Boetcher

IT'S A WONDERFUL THING TO OVERCOME PROBLEMS

The harder the conflict, the more glorious the triumph. What we obtain too cheap, we esteem too lightly; 'tis dearness only that gives everything it's value.
—Thomas Paine

The greater the difficulty, the more glory in surmounting it. —Epicurus

Life affords no higher pleasure than that of surmounting difficulties.
—Samuel Johnson

Can it be that man is essentially a being who loves to conquer difficulties, a creature whose function is to solve problems? —Gorham Munson

Conquering any difficulty always gives one a secret joy, for it means pushing back a boundary-line and adding to one's liberty.
—Henri Frederic Amiel

To overcome difficulties is to experience the full delight of existence.
—Arthur Schopenhauer

Success is to be measured not so much by the position that one has reached in life as by the obstacles he has overcome trying to succeed.
—Booker T. Washington

508

Happiness is the overcoming of not unknown obstacles toward a known goal.   —L. Ron Hubbard

Difficulties exist to be surmounted.
                    —Ralph Waldo Emerson

Failures and Mistakes

Everyone Makes Mistakes and Has Failures

Imagine a congress of eminent celebrities such as More, Bacon, Grotius, Pascal, Cromwell, Bossuet, Montesquieu, Jefferson, Napoleon, Pitt, etc. They would be an Encyclopedia of Errors.

—Lord Acton

Flops are a part of life's menu, and I've never been a girl to miss out on any of the courses.

—Rosalind Russell

Every man's got to figure to get beat sometime. —Joe Louis

Man errs as long as he struggles.
—Johann von Goethe

The best brewer sometimes makes bad beer. —German proverb

We must somehow get comfortable with the reality of periodic failure.... Like a trip to the dentist, the thought of occasional reverses may not make us tingle with joyful anticipation, but then again, it's not the end of the world. —Sam Collins

The progress of rivers to the ocean is not so rapid as that of man to error.
—Voltaire

All men are liable to error; and most men are ... by passion or interest, under temptation to it. —John Locke

To err is human, to forgive divine.
—Alexander Pope

He only is exempt from failures who makes no effort. —Richard Whately

Only he who does nothing makes no mistakes. —French proverb

The only man who makes no mistakes is the man who never does anything. —Eleanor Roosevelt

Life is not life unless you make mistakes. —Joan Collins

We all choke, and the man who says he doesn't choke is lying like hell. We all leak oil. —Lee Trevino

He who has never failed somewhere, that man cannot be great.
—Herman Melville

510

He is always right who suspects that he makes mistakes. —Spanish proverb

The man who makes no mistakes does not usually make anything. —Bishop W.C. Magee

A good marksman may miss. —Thomas Fuller

He that has much to do will do something wrong. —Samuel Johnson

For a just man falleth seven times, and riseth up again. —Prv. 24:16

To make no mistake is not in the power of man; but from their errors and mistakes the wise and good learn wisdom for the future. —Plutarch

The greatest mistake you can make in life is to be continually fearing you will make one. —Elbert Hubbard

The fellow who never makes a mistake takes his orders from one who does. —Herbert B. Prochnow

Accept that all of us can be hurt, that all of us can—and surely will at times—fail. Other vulnerabilities, like being embarrassed or risking love, can be terrifying, too. I think we should follow a simple rule: if we can take the worst, take the risk. —Dr. Joyce Brothers

All of us failed to match our dreams of perfection. —William Faulkner

WINNERS JUST MAKE THE FEWEST MISTAKES

The greatest general is he who makes the fewest mistakes. —Napoleon Bonaparte

War is a series of catastrophes that results in victory. —Georges Clemenceau

Victory goes to the player who makes the next-to-last mistake. —Savielly Grigorievitch Tartakower

A man finds he has been wrong at every stage of his career, only to deduce the astonishing conclusion that he is at last entirely right. —Robert Louis Stevenson

One loss is good for the soul. Too many losses are not good for the coach. —Knute Rockne

In the game of life it's a good idea to have a few early losses, which relieves you of the pressure of trying to maintain an undefeated season. —Bill Vaughan

In all science, error precedes the truth, and it is better it should go first than last. —Hugh Walpole

Virtually nothing comes out right the first time. Failures, *repeated* failures, are finger posts on the road to achievement. The only time you don't want to fail is the last time you try something.... One fails forward toward success. —Charles F. Kettering

BIG MISTAKES

A clever man commits no minor blunders. —Johann von Goethe

Any man whose errors take ten years to correct is quite a man.
—J. Robert Oppenheimer, speaking of Albert Einstein

Sometimes a noble failure serves the world as faithfully as a distinguished success.　　　　　　—Dowden

No man ever progressed to greatness and goodness but through great mistakes.　　　—Frederick W. Robertson

The credit belongs to the man who is actually in the arena; whose face is marred by dust and sweat and blood; who strives valiantly; who errs and comes short again and again; who knows the great enthusiasms, the great devotions, and spends himself in a worthy cause; who, at the best, knows in the end the triumph of high achievement; and who, at the worst, if he fails, at least fails while daring greatly, so that his place shall never be with those cold and timid souls who know neither victory nor defeat.
—Theodore Roosevelt

The errors of great men are venerable because they are more fruitful than the truths of little men.
—Friedrich Nietzsche

There is something distinguished about even his failures; they sink not trivially, but with a certain air of majesty, like a great ship, its flags flying, full of holes.
—George Jean Nathan

If all else fails, immortality can always be assured by spectacular error.　　—John Kenneth Galbraith

CORRECTING MISTAKES

Life, like war, is a series of mistakes, and he is best who wins the most splendid victories by the retrieval of mistakes.　—Frederick W. Robertson

A man who has committed a mistake and doesn't correct it is committing another mistake.　　　—Confucius

The great virtue of man lies in his ability to correct his mistakes and to continually make a new man of himself.　　　—Wang Yang-Ming

It is only error in judgement to make a mistake, but it shows infirmity of character to adhere to it when discovered.　　　—Christian Bovee

It is human to err, but it is devilish to remain willfully in error.
—Saint Augustine

Intelligence is not to make no mistakes, but quickly to see how to make them good.　—Bertolt Brecht

Our mistakes won't irreparably damage our lives unless we let them.
—James E. Sweaney

WE MUST ACCEPT RESPONSIBILITY FOR OUR ERRORS AND MISTAKES

We have not passed that subtle line between childhood and adulthood until ... we have stopped saying "It got lost," and say, "I lost it."
—Sydney J. Harris

A chief is a man who assumes responsibility. He does not say "My men were beaten," he says, "I was beaten." —Antoine de Saint-Exupery

The most considerable difference I note among men is not in their readiness to fall into error, but in their readiness to acknowledge these inevitable lapses.
—Thomas Henry Huxley

Do not blame anybody for your mistakes and failures.
—Bernard M. Baruch

The fault, dear Brutus, is not in our stars, but in ourselves.
—William Shakespeare

Mistakes fail in their mission of helping the person who blames them on the other fellow.
—Henry S. Haskins

I have known men who could see through the motivations of others with the skill of a clairvoyant; only to prove blind to their own mistakes. I have been one of those men.
—Bernard M. Baruch

Admitting error clears the score, and proves you wiser than before.
—Arthur Guiterman

I have made mistakes, but I have never made the mistake of claiming that I never made one.
—James Gordon Bennett

The man who can own up to his error is greater than he who merely knows how to avoid making it.
—Cardinal De Retz

A man may fall many times, but he won't be a failure until he says that someone pushed him.
—Elmer G. Letterman

JUST DON'T MAKE THE SAME MISTAKE TWICE

Do not be afraid of mistakes, providing you do not make the same one twice.
—Eleanor Roosevelt

To stumble twice against the same stone is a proverbial disgrace.
—Cicero

Fool me once, shame on you; fool me twice, shame on me.
—Chinese proverb

He who is shipwrecked twice is foolish to blame the sea.
—Publilius Syrus

He who is shipwrecked the second time cannot lay the blame on Neptune.
—English proverb

He that's cheated twice by the same man is an accomplice with the cheater.
—Thomas Fuller

If you would not have affliction visit you twice, listen at once to what it teaches.
—James Burgh

You can beat the Bear once, but never the same way twice.
—John McKay

Any man can make mistakes, but only an idiot persists in his error.
—Cicero

There is nothing wrong with making mistakes. Just don't respond with encores.
—Anon.

The road to wisdom? Well, it's plain and simple to express: Err, and err, and err again. But less, and less, and less.
—Piet Hein

Never Be Negative about Mistakes and Failures

The biggest quality in successful people I think is an impatience with negative thinking.... How many opportunities come along? If you wait for the right one, that's wrong, because it may never be right, and what have you got to lose? Even if it's a disaster, you've tried, you've learned something, you've had an adventure. And that doesn't mean you can't do it again.   —Edward McCabe

I made a mistake today, I made a mistake yesterday. I think it's ... very important to ignore the negative.
                    —Jerry Rubin

When we can begin to take our failures non-seriously, it means we are ceasing to be afraid of them. It is of immense importance to learn to laugh at ourselves.
               —Katherine Mansfield

If I lose, I'll walk away and never feel bad.... Because I did all I could, there was nothing more to do.
                    —Joe Frazier

A man must learn to forgive himself.
          —Arthur Davison Ficke

Forget mistakes. Forget failure. Forget everything except what you're going to do now and do it. Today is your lucky day.   —Will Durant

"Failure" Is Just a Detour, a Delay

Failure is delay, but not defeat. It is a temporary detour, not a dead-end street.   —William Arthur Ward

Failure really isn't terrible if you can say to yourself, hey, I know I'm gonna be successful at what I want to do someday. Failure doesn't become a big hangup then because it's only temporary. If failure is absolute, then it would be a disaster, but as long as it's only temporary you can just go and achieve almost anything.   —Jerry Della Femina

Failure is an event, never a person.
          —William D. Brown

I've never met a person, I don't care what his condition, in whom I could not see possibilities. I don't care how much a man may consider himself a failure, I believe in him, for he can change the thing that is wrong in his life anytime he is prepared and ready to do it. Whenever he develops the desire, he can take away from his life the thing that is defeating it. The capacity for reformation and change lies within.   —Preston Bradley

I think and think for months, for years. Ninety-nine times the conclusion is false. The hundredth time I am right.   —Albert Einstein

When it goes wrong, you feel like cutting your throat, but you go on. You don't let anything get you down so much that it beats you or stops you.   —George Cukor

You must have long-range goals to keep you from being frustrated by short-range failures.
          —Charles C. Noble

Life is a series of relapses and recoveries.   —George Ade

We learn courageous action by going forward whenever fear urges us back. A little boy was asked how he learned to skate. "By getting up every time I fell down," he answered. —David Seabury

Failure is only postponed success as long as courage 'coaches' ambition. The habit of persistence is the habit of victory. —Herbert Kaufman

Entrepreneurs average 3.8 failures before final success. What sets the successful ones apart is their amazing persistence. There are a lot of people out there with good and marketable ideas, but pure entrepreneurial types almost never accept defeat. —Lisa M. Amos

Success is going from failure to failure without loss of enthusiasm. —Sir Winston Churchill

I don't accept defeat as final. Only death is final—and even then I hope for a reprieve. —Phil Gramm

Never confuse a single defeat with a final defeat. —F. Scott Fitzgerald

Men's best successes come after their disappointments. —Henry Ward Beecher

I've been failing for, like, ten or eleven years. When it turns, it'll turn. Right now I'm just tryin' to squeeze through a very tight financial period, get the movie out, and put my things in order. —Francis Ford Coppola

Don't let a kick in the ass stop you. It's how you cope that says what you are. —George Cukor

What is to be got at to make the air sweet, the ground good under the feet, can only be got at by failure, trial, again and again and again failure. —Sherwood Anderson

They say President Wilson has blundered. Perhaps he has, but I notice he usually blunders forward. —Thomas A. Edison

Some "Failures" Aren't Failures

Not all who seem to fail have failed indeed. Not all who fail have therefore worked in vain. There is no failure for the good and brave. —Archbishop Trench

Defeat in doing right is nevertheless victory. —Frederick W. Robertson

There are defeats more triumphant than victories. —Michel de Montaigne

An error gracefully acknowledged is a victory won. —Caroline L. Gascoigne

We're Not a Failure Until ...

Because a fellow has failed once or twice, or a dozen times, you don't want to set him down as a failure until he's dead or loses his courage— and that's the same thing. —George Horace Lorimer

No man is a failure who is enjoying life. —William Feather

You are beaten to earth? Well, well, what's that? Come up with a smiling face, it's nothing against you to fall down flat, but to lie there—that's disgrace. —Edmund Vance Cooke

515

He alone fails who gives up and lies down. —Ralph Waldo Trine

Never give a man up until he has failed at something he likes.
—Lewis E. Lawes

They were never defeated, they were only killed. —Said of the French Foreign Legion

Failure is not in losing, but in no longer believing that winning is worthwhile. —Anon.

He's no failure. He's not dead yet.
—W.L. George

Inside of a ring or out, ain't nothing wrong with going down. It's staying down that's wrong.
—Muhammad Ali

It ain't no disgrace for a man to fall, but to lie there and grunt is.
—Josh Billings

If you have made mistakes, even serious ones, there is always another chance for you. What we call failure is not the falling down, but the staying down. —Mary Pickford

SOME OF THE MOST IMPORTANT KINDS OF "FAILURE"

If a man has a talent and cannot use it, he has failed. If he has a talent and uses only half of it, he has partly failed. If he has a talent and learns somehow to use the whole of it, he has gloriously succeeded, and won a satisfaction and a triumph few men ever know. —Thomas Wolfe

Not failure, but low aim, is a crime.
—Ernest Holmes

There is only one real failure in life that is possible, and that is not to be true to the best one knows.
—Frederic W. Farrar

Perhaps the only real failure is that implying waste, a conscious and flagrant non-use or misuse of ability.
—Joseph H. Odell

There are two kinds of failures: The man who will do nothing he is told, and the man who will do nothing else. —Dr. Perle Thompson

The only failure a man ought to fear is failure in cleaving to the purpose he sees to be best. —George Eliot

TRUE FAILURE IS IN NOT TRYING

There is no failure except in no longer trying. —Elbert Hubbard

Men do not fail; they stop trying.
—Elihu Root

Men must try and try again.
—Lawson Purdy

The only failure which lacks dignity is the failure to try.
—Malcolm F. MacNeil

A mistake is not a failure, but evidence that someone tried to do something. —Anon.

Man must strive, and in striving, he must err. —Johann von Goethe

If you're not failing, you're not trying anything. —Woody Allen

Those who try and fail are much wiser than those who never try for fear of failure. —André Bustanoby

A man's life is interesting primarily when he has failed—I well know. For it's a sign that he tried to surpass himself.   —Georges Clemenceau

To avoid an occasion for our virtues is a worse degree of failure than to push forward pluckily and fall.
    —Robert Louis Stevenson

They fail, and they alone, who have not striven. —Thomas Bailey Aldrich

You may be disappointed if you fail, but you are doomed if you don't try.
    —Beverly Sills

It takes as much courage to have tried and failed as it does to have tried and succeeded.
    —Anne Morrow Lindbergh

Failure is something made only by those who fail to dare, not by those who dare to fail.   —Louis Binstock

The man who has done his level best, and who is conscious that he has done his best, is a success, even though the world may write him down a failure.   —B.C. Forbes

Many a man never fails because he never tries.   —Norman MacEwan

MISTAKES CAN BE ENORMOUSLY VALUABLE

Good judgment comes from experience, and experience comes from poor judgment.   —Anon.

Life is very interesting, if you make mistakes.   —Georges Carpentier

When I have listened to my mistakes, I have grown.   —Hugh Prather

Mistakes and errors are the discipline through which we advance.
    —Channing

A stumble may prevent a fall.
    —Thomas Fuller

A life spent making mistakes is not only more honorable but more useful than a life spent doing nothing.
    —George Bernard Shaw

VALUABLE THINGS WE CAN GET FROM DEFEAT

It is defeat that turns bone to flint; it is defeat that turns gristle to muscle; it is defeat that makes men invincible. Do not then be afraid of defeat. You are never so near to victory as when defeated in a good cause.
    —Henry Ward Beecher

Defeat should never be a source of discouragement, but rather a fresh stimulus.   —South

Besides the practical knowledge which defeat offers, there are important personality profits to be taken. Defeat strips away false values and makes you realize what you really want. It stops you from chasing butterflies and puts you to work digging gold.   —William M. Marston

No experiment is ever a complete failure. It can always be used as a bad example.   —Paul Dickson

Failure is the foundation of success, and the means by which it is achieved.   —Lao-tzu

There is much to be said for failure. It is more interesting than success.
    —Max Beerbohm

517

Failure sometimes enlarges the spirit. You have to fall back upon humanity and God.
—Charles Horton Cooley

It is often the failure who is the pioneer in new lands, new undertakings, and new forms of expression.
—Eric Hoffer

Let us not be needlessly bitter; certain failures are sometimes fruitful.
—E.M. Cioran

If I win several tournaments in a row, I get so confident I'm in a cloud. A loss gets me eager again.
—Chris Evert Lloyd

There's nothing that cleanses your soul like getting the hell kicked out of you.   —Woody Hayes

Failure is only an opportunity to begin again more intelligently.
—Henry Ford

Disappointments are to the soul what the thunder-storm is to the air.
—J.C.F. von Schiller

The wisest person is not the one who has the fewest failures, but the one who turns failures to best account.
—Richard R. Grant

One of the advantages of defeat in life—maybe the main advantage—is that it provides an excuse for change. Defeat ... invariably leads to new adventures.   —James Reston

Failure is God's own tool for carving some of the finest outlines in the character of his children.
—Thomas Hodgkin

I quit being afraid when my first venture failed and the sky didn't fall down.   —Allen H. Neuharth

FAILURE IS EDUCATIONAL

What is defeat? Nothing but education, nothing but the first step to something better. —Wendell Phillips

From their errors and mistakes the wise and good learn wisdom for the future.   —Plutarch

Having harvested all the knowledge and wisdom we can from our mistakes and failures, we should put them behind us and go ahead.
—Edith Johnson

Nothing is a waste of time if you use the experience wisely.
—Auguste Rodin

To lose is to learn.   —Anon.

It is the true nature of mankind to learn from mistakes, not from example.   —Fred Hoyle

The psychotherapist learns little or nothing from his successes. They mainly confirm him in his mistakes, while his failures, on the other hand, are priceless experiences in that they not only open up the way to a deeper truth, but force him to change his views and methods.   —Carl Jung

Failure ... is, in a sense, the highway to success, inasmuch as every discovery of what is false leads us to seek earnestly after what is true, and every fresh experience points out some form of error which we shall afterward carefully avoid.
—John Keats

518

We need to teach a highly educated person that it is not a disgrace to fail and that he must analyze every failure to find its cause. He must learn how to fail intelligently, for failing is one of the greatest arts of the world.
—Charles F. Kettering

When a man is pushed, tormented, defeated, he has a chance to learn something; he has been put on his wits; on his manhood; he has gained the facts; learned his ignorance; is cured of the insanity of conceit; has got moderation and real skill.
—Ralph Waldo Emerson

There are no mistakes. The events we bring upon ourselves, no matter how unpleasant, are necessary in order to learn what we need to learn; whatever steps we take, they're necessary to reach the places we've chosen to go.   —Richard Bach

Failure is instructive. The person who really thinks learns quite as much from his failures as from his successes.   —John Dewey

Failure is a school in which the truth always grows strong.
—Henry Ward Beecher

The important thing is to learn a lesson every time you lose.
—John McEnroe

It's good to fail now and again—you learn a lot more out of failure than you do out of success.   —Ian Hunter

One of the reasons mature people stop learning is that they become less and less willing to risk failure.
—John W. Gardner

Through failure, we learn a lesson in humility which is probably needed, painful though it is.   —Bill W.

A failure is a man who has blundered, but is not able to cash in the experience.   —Elbert Hubbard

Like success, failure is many things to many people. With Positive Mental Attitude, failure is a learning experience, a rung on the ladder, a plateau at which to get your thoughts in order and prepare to try again.   —W. Clement Stone

Disappointment is the nurse of wisdom.   —Sir Bayle Roche

When you make a mistake, don't look back at it long. Take the reason of the thing into your mind, and then look forward. Mistakes are lessons of wisdom. The past cannot be changed. The future is yet in your power.   —Hugh White

What can any of us do with his talent but try to develop his vision, so that through frequent failures we may learn better what we have missed in the past.
—William Carlos Williams

WE SHOULD LEARN FROM OTHERS' MISTAKES

From the errors of others, a wise man corrects his own.
—Publilius Syrus

Learn from the mistakes of others— you can't live long enough to make them all yourself.   —Martin Vanbee

Don't use the conduct of a fool as a precedent.   —Talmud

Wise men learn by other men's mistakes, fools by their own.

—H.G. Bohn

Learn to see in another's calamity the ills which you should avoid.

—Publilius Syrus

A man is fortunate if he encounters living examples of vice, as well as of virtue, to inspire him.

—Brendan Francis

WE'RE OFTEN CLOSER TO SUCCESS THAN WE THINK

The line between failure and success is so fine that we scarcely know when we pass it; so fine that we are often on the line and do not know it.

—Elbert Hubbard

Failure is that early morning hour of darkness which precedes the dawning of the day of success.

—Leigh Mitchell Hodges

SOME REASONS PEOPLE FAIL

The causes of mistakes are "I didn't know"; "I didn't think"; and "I didn't care."

—Henry H. Buckley

Failures are divided into two classes: those who thought and never did, and those who did and never thought.

—John Charles Salak

A failure establishes only this, that our determination to succeed was not strong enough.

—Christian Bovee

Self-distrust is the cause of most of our failures. They are the weakest, however strong, who have no faith in themselves or their own powers.

—Christian Bovee

Defeat is a thing of weariness, of incoherence, of boredom.

—Antoine de Saint-Exupery

Failure at a task may be the result of having tackled it at the wrong time.

—Brendan Francis

Failure is more frequently from want of energy than want of capital.

—Daniel Webster

Lack of will power has caused more failures than lack of intelligence or ability.

—Flower A. Newhouse

Losers have tons of variety. Champions take pride in just learning to hit the same old boring winners.

—Vic Braden

The word fate ... is the refuge of every self-confessed failure.

—Andrew Soutar

Half the things that people do not succeed in are through fear of making the attempt.

—James Northcote

The man who fails because he aims astray, or because he does not aim at all, is to be found everywhere.

—Frank Swinnerton

Half the failures in life come from pulling one's horse in when he is leaping.

—A.W. Hare

I cannot give you the formula for success, but I can give you the formula for failure: try to please everybody.

—Herbert Bayard Swope

If your project doesn't work, look for the part that you didn't think was important.

—Arther Bloch

We fail more often by timidity than by over-daring. —David Grayson

Ninety-nine percent of the failures come from people who have the habit of making excuses.
—George Washington Carver

One who fears failure limits his activities. —Henry Ford

The difference between failure and success is doing a thing nearly right and doing a thing exactly right.
—Edward Simmons

We have forty million reasons for failure, but not a single excuse.
—Rudyard Kipling

The greatest mistake you can make in life is to be continually fearing you will make one.
—Elbert Hubbard

How to succeed: Try hard enough. How to fail: Try too hard.
—Malcolm Forbes

Most men fail, not through lack of education, but from lack of dogged determination, from lack of dauntless will. —Orison Swett Marden

Failure comes only when we forget our ideals and objects and principles.
—Jawaharlal Nehru

An error is simply a failure to adjust immediately from a preconception to an actuality. —John Cage

We are less likely to fail if we measure with judgement our chances and our capabilities. —Agnes Repplier

Laziness is a secret ingredient that goes into failure. But it's only kept a secret from the person who fails.
—Robert Half

Failure is usually the line of least persistence. —Wilfred Beaver

You can't expect to win unless you know why you lose.
—Benjamin Lipson

Most people don't plan to fail, they fail to plan. —John L. Beckley

General Quotations about Mistakes and Failures

Failure is not sweet, but it need not be bitter. —Anon.

Losses are comparative, imagination only makes them of any moment.
—Blaise Pascal

I would prefer even to fail with honor than win by cheating.
—Sophocles

And what if I did run my ship aground; oh, still it was splendid to sail it! —Henrik Ibsen

If you're gonna be a failure, at least be one at something you enjoy.
—Sylvester Stallone

Who would not rather flounder in the fight than not have known the glory of the fray? —Richard Hovey

The probability that we may fail in the struggle ought not to deter us from the support of a cause we believe to be just.
—Abraham Lincoln

THE ADVANTAGES OF ADVERSITY

DIFFICULTIES CAN STIMULATE US TO OUR GREATEST ACHIEVEMENTS

A wounded deer leaps the highest.
　　　　　—Emily Dickinson

The difficulties which I meet with in order to realize my existence are precisely what awaken and mobilize my activities, my capacities.
　　　　—José Ortega y Gasset

I have always been pushed by the negative.... The apparent failure of a play sends me back to my typewriter that very night, before the reviews are out. I am more compelled to get back to work than if I had a success.
　　　　—Tennessee Williams

To be thrown upon one's own resources is to be cast into the very lap of fortune, for our faculties then undergo a development and display an energy of which they were previously unsusceptible.
　　　　—Benjamin Franklin

Every failure made me more confident. Because I wanted even more to achieve things, as revenge. To show that I could.　　—Roman Polanski

Adversity is, to me at least, a tonic and a bracer.　　—Sir Walter Scott

Difficulties should act as a tonic. They should spur us to greater exertion.　　　　—B.C. Forbes

There are times in everyone's life when something constructive is born out of adversity ... when things seem so bad that you've got to grab your fate by the shoulders and shake it.
　　　　　　　　—Anon.

Brave men rejoice in adversity, just as brave soldiers triumph in war.
　　　—Marcus Annaeus Seneca

Some minds seem almost to create themselves, springing up under every disadvantage and working their solitary but irresistible way through a thousand obstacles.
　　　　—Washington Irving

Every calamity is a spur and valuable hint.　　—Ralph Waldo Emerson

Treasure the memories of past misfortunes; they constitute our bank of fortitude.　　　　—Eric Hoffer

If you will call your troubles experiences, and remember that every experience develops some latent force within you, you will grow vigorous and happy, however adverse your circumstances may seem to be.
—John R. Miller

Necessity is often the spur to genius.
—Honore de Balzac

Necessity is the mother of "taking chances."
—Mark Twain

Necessity makes even the timid brave.
—Sallust

People wish to be settled; only as far as they are unsettled is there any hope for them.
—Ralph Waldo Emerson

Difficulties are meant to rouse, not discourage. The human spirit is to grow strong by conflict.
—William Ellery Channing

Adversity causes some men to break, others to break records.
—William A. Ward

OPPOSITION CAN INSPIRE AND IMPROVE US

Opposition inflames the enthusiast, never converts him.
—J.C.F. von Schiller

A certain amount of opposition is a great help to a man; it is what he wants and must have to be good for anything. Hardship and opposition are the native soil of manhood and self-reliance.
—John Neal

When the going gets tough, the tough get going.
—Frank Leahy

The effects of opposition are wonderful. There are men who rise refreshed on hearing of a threat, men to whom a crises, which intimidates and paralyzes the majority, comes as graceful and beloved as a bride!
—Ralph Waldo Emerson

He that wrestles with us strengthens our nerves and sharpens our skills. Our antagonist is our helper.
—Edmund Burke

The block of granite which was an obstacle in the path of the weak becomes a steppingstone in the path of the strong.
—Thomas Carlyle

Strong people are made by opposition, like kites that go up against the wind.
—Frank Harris

You'll never find a better sparring partner than adversity.
—Walt Schmidt

Enemies can be an incentive to survive and become someone in spite of them. Enemies can keep you alert and aware.
—Louis L'Amour

Problems are the cutting edge that distinguishes between success and failure. Problems ... create our courage and wisdom.
—M. Scott Peck

Men strive for peace, but it is their enemies that give them strength, and I think if man no longer had enemies, he would have to invent them, for his strength only grows from struggle.
—Louis L'Amour

The English nation is never so great as in adversity.
—Benjamin Disraeli

There's Tremendous Value in Hitting Bottom

It is often better to have a great deal of harm happen to one than a little; a great deal may rouse you to remove what a little will only accustom you to endure.
—Grenville Kleiser

When things come to the worse, they generally mend.   —Susanna Moodie

Things have got to be wrong in order that they may be deplored.
—Whitney Griswold

Remorse begets reform.
—William Cowper

Life begins on the other side of despair.   —Jean-Paul Sartre

In order to change, we must be sick and tired of being sick and tired.
—Anon.

I didn't know I'd have to be torn down before I could be built up.
—Anon.

Suffering Also Has Its Benefits

Suffering!... We owe to it all that is good in us, all that gives value to life; we owe to it pity, we owe to it courage, we owe to it all the virtues.
—Anatole France

Much of your pain is the bitter potion by which the physician within you heals your sick self.
—Kahlil Gibran

Man cannot remake himself without suffering, for he is both the marble and the sculptor. —Dr. Alexis Carrel

Out of suffering have emerged the strongest souls; the most massive characters are seared with scars.
—Edwin H. Chapin

There is no coming to consciousness without pain.   —Carl Jung

Suffering is the sole origin of consciousness.   —Fyodor Dostoyevsky

Pain makes man think. Thought makes man wise. Wisdom makes life endurable.   —John Patrick

If you suffer, thank God! It is a sure sign that you are alive.
—Elbert Hubbard

Suffering is also one of the ways of knowing you're alive.
—Jessamyn West

Don't look forward to the day when you stop suffering. Because when it comes, you'll know you're dead.
—Tennessee Williams

How sublime a thing it is to suffer and be strong.
—Henry Wadsworth Longfellow

He disposes Doom who hath suffered him.   —Emily Dickinson

They merit more praise who know how to suffer misery than those who temper themselves in contentment.
—Pietro Aretino

Character cannot be developed in ease and quiet. Only through experience of trial and suffering can the soul be strengthened, vision cleared, ambition inspired, and success achieved.   —Helen Keller

524

Never to suffer would have been never to have been blessed.
—Edgar Allan Poe

We are healed of a suffering only by experiencing it to the full.
—Marcel Proust

TOUGH TIMES AND ADVERSITY CAN GENERATE OPPORTUNITY AND PROGRESS

From the discontent of man, the world's best progress springs.
—Ella Wheeler Wilcox

The difficulties and struggles of today are but the price we must pay for the accomplishments and victories of tomorrow.
—William J.H. Boetcker

Problems are the price of progress. Don't bring me anything but trouble.
—Charles F. Kettering

Trouble is the thing that strong men grow by. Met in the right way, it is a sure-fire means of putting iron into the victim's will and making him a tougher man to down forever after.
—H. Bertram Lewis

Discontent is the first step in the progress of a man or a nation.
—Oscar Wilde

Restlessness is discontent, and discontent is the first necessity of progress.
—Thomas A. Edison

Noble discontent is the path to heaven.
—Thomas Higginson

No pain, no palm; no thorns, no throne; no gall, no glory; no cross, no crown.
—William Penn

Times of stress and difficulty are seasons of opportunity when the seeds of progress are sown.
—Thomas F. Woodlock

The gem cannot be polished without friction, nor man perfected without trials.
—Confucius

As there is no worldly gain without some loss, so there is no worldly loss without some gain.... Set the allowance against the loss, and thou shalt find no loss great.
—Francis Quarles

Never complain about your troubles; they are responsible for more than half of your income.
—Robert R. Updegraff

Emergencies have always been necessary to progress. It was darkness which produced the lamp. It was fog that produced the compass. It was hunger that drove us to exploration. And it took a depression to teach us the real value of a job.
—Victor Hugo

Many men owe the grandeur of their lives to their tremendous difficulties.
—Charles Haddon Spurgeon

It is often hard to distinguish between the hard knocks in life and those of opportunity.
—Frederick Phillips

A problem is a chance for you to do your best.
—Duke Ellington

ADVERSITY AS A TEST

Fire is the test of gold, adversity of strong men.
—Marcus Annaeus Seneca

Calamity is the test of integrity.
—Richardson

The fiery trials through which we pass will light us down in honor or dishonor to the last generation.
—Abraham Lincoln

Our trials are tests; our sorrows pave the way for a fuller life when we have earned it.
—Jerome P. Fleishman

LIKE OTHER ELEMENTS, PEOPLE DEVELOP THROUGH PRESSURE

Times of general calamity and confusion have ever been productive of the greatest minds. The purist ore is produced from the hottest furnace, and the brightest thunderbolt is elicited from the darkest storms.
—Charles Caleb Colton

A diamond is a chunk of coal that made good under pressure.
—Anon.

A clay pot sitting in the sun will always be a clay pot. It has to go through the white heat of the furnace to become porcelain.
—Mildred W. Struven

Men habitually use only a small part of the powers which they possess and which they might use under appropriate circumstances.
—William James

It is the north wind that lashes men into Vikings; it is the soft, luscious south wind which lulls them to lotus dreams.
—Ouida

It is the surmounting of difficulties that makes heroes.
—Kossuth

It is grief that develops the powers of the mind.
—Marcel Proust

Unless a man has been kicked around a little, you can't really depend upon him to amount to anything.
—William Feather

Adversity is another way to measure the greatness of individuals. I never had a crisis that didn't make me stronger.
—Lou Holtz

It is not in the still calm of life, or the repose of a pacific station, that great characters are formed.... Great necessities call out great virtues.
—Abigail Adams

THE VALUE OF ADVERSITY IN YOUTH

My luck was my father not striking oil ... we'd have been rich. I'd never have set out for Hollywood with my camera, and I'd have had a lot less interesting life.
—King Vidor

When I was very young, I tried selling used cars. It didn't last long. I guess that was my good luck too, that I didn't show more promise at it, or I might have been an automobile dealer.
—King Vidor

I was lucky I wasn't a better boxer, or that's what I'd be now—a punchy ex-pug.
—Bob Hope

I'm very grateful that I was too poor to get to art school until I was 21.... I was old enough when I got there to know how to get something out of it.
—Henry Moore

Of all the advantages which come to any young man ... poverty is the greatest.
—Josiah G. Holland

In my youth, poverty enriched me, but now I can afford wealth.
—Marc Chagall

The most valuable gift I ever received was ... the gift of insecurity ... my father left us. My mother's love might not have prepared me for life the way my father's departure did. He forced us out on the road, where we had to earn our bread.
—Lillian Gish

Americans are like a rich father who wishes he knew how to give his sons the hardships that made him rich.
—Robert Frost

I would never have amounted to anything were it not for adversity. I was forced to come up the hard way.
—J.C. Penney

ADVERSITY HELPS US LEARN ABOUT OURSELVES

Adversity introduces a man to himself.
—Anon.

I thank God for my handicaps for, through them, I have found myself, my work, and my God.
—Helen Keller

Adversity has ever been considered as the state in which a man most easily becomes acquainted with himself, being free from flatterers.
—Samuel Johnson

He knows not his own strength who hath not met adversity.
—Samuel Johnson

Adversity leads us to think properly of our state, and so is most beneficial to us.
—Samuel Johnson

In the depth of winter, I finally learned that there was in me an invincible summer.
—Albert Camus

Who hath not known ill fortune, never knew himself, or his own virtue.
—Mallett

Adversity is the trial of principle. Without it a man hardly knows whether he is honest or not.
—Henry Fielding

I think the years I have spent in prison have been the most formative and important in my life because of the discipline, the sensations, but chiefly the opportunity to think clearly, to try to understand things.
—Jawaharial Nehru

We only really face up to ourselves when we are afraid.
—Thomas Bernhard

Difficulties are things that show what men are.
—Epictetus

Even if misfortune is only good for bringing a fool to his senses, it would still be just to deem it good for something.
—Jean de La Fontaine

Never does a man know the force that is in him till some mighty affection or grief has humanized the soul.
—Frederick W. Robertson

Disappointment is the nurse of wisdom.
—Sir Bayle Roche

Challenges make you discover things about yourself that you never really knew. They're what make the instrument stretch, what make you go beyond the norm.
—Cicely Tyson

A woman is like a tea bag: you never know her strength until you drop her in hot water.   —Nancy Reagan

TOUGH TIMES ARE GREAT TEACHERS

Trouble brings experience, and experience brings wisdom.   —Anon.

Adversity is a severe instructor.... He that wrestles with us strengthens our nerves and sharpens our skill. Our antagonist is our helper.
                    —Edmund Burke

Forget the times of your distress, but never forget what they taught you.
                    —Herbert Gasser

You can learn little from victory. You can learn everything from defeat.   —Christy Mathewson

Adversity has the effect of eliciting talents, which, in prosperous circumstances, would have lain dormant.
                    —Horace

A smooth sea never made a skillful mariner.   —English proverb

When a man is pushed, tormented, defeated, he has a chance to learn something; he has been put on his wits ... he has gained facts, learned his ignorance, is cured of the insanity of conceit, has got moderation and real skill.   —Ralph Waldo Emerson

From their errors and mistakes, the wise and good learn wisdom for the future.   —Plutarch

By becoming more unhappy, we sometimes learn how to be less so.
                    —Madame Swetchine

Every experience, however bitter, has its lesson, and to focus one's attention on the lesson helps one overcome the bitterness.
                    —Edward Howard Griggs

It is from the level of calamities ... that we learn impressive and useful lessons.
                    —William Makepeace Thackeray

A good scare is worth more to a man than good advice.
                    —Edgar Watson Howe

When I have listened to my mistakes, I have grown.   —Hugh Prather

We only think when we are confronted with a problem.
                    —John Dewey

Adversity comes with instruction in its hand.   —Anon.

There is no education like adversity.
                    —Benjamin Disraeli

Mistakes are often the best teachers.
                    —James A. Froude

Pain, indolence, sterility, endless ennui have also their lesson for you.
                    —Ralph Waldo Emerson

Prosperity is a great teacher; adversity is a greater. Possession pampers the mind; privation trains and strengthens it.   —William Hazlitt

Wisdom comes by disillusionment.
                    —George Santayana

You have learned something. That always feels at first as if you had lost something.   —George Bernard Shaw

528

I have always grown from my problems and challenges, from the things that don't work out. That's when I've really learned.   —Carol Burnett

Those things that hurt, instruct.
                    —Benjamin Franklin

Pain is the root of knowledge.
                    —Simone Weil

Life can be real tough ... you can either learn from your problems, or keep repeating them over and over.
                    —Marie Osmond

Bad times have a scientific value. These are occasions a good learner would not miss.
                    —Ralph Waldo Emerson

ADVERSITY AND PROSPERITY

Prosperity is not without many fears and distastes, and adversity is not without comforts and hopes.
                    —Francis Bacon

The good things that belong to prosperity are to be wished, but the good things that belong to adversity are to be admired.
                    —Marcus Annaeus Seneca

One who was adored by all in prosperity is abhorred by all in adversity.
                    —Baltasar Gracian

The human race has had long experience and a fine tradition in surviving adversity. But we now face a task for which we have little experience, the task of surviving prosperity.
                    —Alan Gregg

Adversity reveals genius, prosperity conceals it.   —Horace

The virtue of prosperity is temperance; the virtue of adversity is fortitude.   —Francis Bacon

In the day of prosperity be joyful, but in the day of adversity consider.
                    —Eccl. 9:11

In victory even the cowardly like to boast, while in adverse times even the brave are discredited.   —Sallust

Adversity is sometimes hard upon a man; but for one man who can stand prosperity, there are a hundred that will stand adversity.
                    —Thomas Carlyle

DARKNESS AND LIGHT

When it is dark enough, you can see the stars.   —Charles A. Beard

There is not enough darkness in all the world to put out the light of even one small candle.   —Robert Alden

Flowers grow out of dark moments.
                    —Corita Kent

SOME SPIRITUAL ADVANTAGES AND ASPECTS OF ADVERSITY

All sorts of spiritual gifts come through privations, if they are accepted.   —Janet Erskine Stuart

There is nothing the body suffers which the soul may not profit by.
                    —George Meredith

God will not look you over for medals, degrees or diplomas, but for scars.   —Anon.

There are three modes of bearing the ills of life: by indifference, by philosophy, and by religion.
                    —Charles Caleb Colton

The same reason makes a man a religious enthusiast that makes a man an enthusiast in any other way: an uncomfortable mind in an uncomfortable body.   —William Hazlitt

WORTHY VICTORIES

Victories that are cheap are cheap. Those only are worth having which come as the result of hard fighting.
                —Henry Ward Beecher

The greater the difficulty, the more glory in surmounting it.   —Epicurus

The greater the obstacle, the more glory in overcoming it.   —Moliere

The harder the conflict, the more glorious the triumph. What we obtain too cheaply, we esteem too lightly; 'tis dearness only that gives everything its value. —Thomas Paine

The fiery trials through which we pass will light us down in honor or dishonor to the last generation.
                —Abraham Lincoln

To conquer without risk is to triumph without glory.
                —Pierre Corneille

There could be no honor in a sure success, but much might be wrested from a sure defeat. —T.E. Lawrence
                (Lawrence of Arabia)

TO REALLY APPRECIATE GOOD THINGS, WE MUST KNOW THE NOT-SO-GOOD THINGS

In order to have great happiness, you have to have great pain and unhappiness—otherwise how would you know when you're happy?
                —Leslie Caron

To really enjoy the better things in life, one must first have experienced the things they are better than.
                —Oscar Homoka

Misfortunes tell us what fortune is.
                —Thomas Fuller

A man is insensible to the relish of prosperity till he has tasted adversity.   —Sa'Di

Who has never tasted what is bitter does not know what is sweet.
                —German proverb

Victory is sweetest when you've known defeat.   —Malcolm Forbes

No man better knows what good is than he who has endured evil.
                —Anon.

He that has never suffered extreme adversity knows not the full extent of his own depravation.
                —Charles Caleb Colton

Sleep, riches and health, to be truly enjoyed, must be interrupted.
                —Jean Paul Fichter

If there were no tribulation, there would be no rest; if there were no winter, there would be no summer.
                —Saint John Chrysostom

If you want the rainbow, you gotta put up with the rain. —Dolly Parton

If you want to see the sun shine, you have to weather the storm.
                —Frank Lane

He that can't endure the bad will not live to see the good.
                —Yiddish proverb

I have lived long enough to be battered by the realities of life, and not too long to be downed by them.

—John Mason Brown

EVERY SITUATION HAS POSITIVE ASPECTS; WE MUST FIND AND FOCUS ON THEM

If you will call your troubles experiences, and remember that every experience develops some latent force within you, you will grow vigorous and happy, however adverse your circumstances may seem to be.

—J.R. Miller

If your house is on fire, warm yourself by it. —Spanish proverb

Anything other than death is a minor injury. —Bill Muncey

When written in Chinese, the word "crisis" is composed of two characters. One represents danger, and the other represents opportunity.

—John F. Kennedy

From a fallen tree, make kindling.

—Spanish proverb

Our real blessings often appear to us in the shape of pains, losses and disappointments; but let us have patience, and we soon shall see them in their proper figures.

—Joseph Addison

To every disadvantage there is a corresponding advantage.

—W. Clement Stone

The same wind that extinguishes a light can set a brazier on fire.

—Pierre de Beaumarchais

OTHER DEFINITIONS OF ADVERSITY

Adversity is the touchstone of virtue.

—Anon.

Adversity is the first path to truth.

—Lord Byron

GENERAL QUOTATIONS ABOUT ADVERSITY

Diseases can be our spiritual flat tires—disruptions in our lives that seem to be disasters at the time, but end by redirecting our lives in a meaningful way.

—Bernie S. Siegel, M.D.

What the student calls a tragedy, the master calls a butterfly.

—Richard Bach

Failure is, in a sense, the highway to success, inasmuch as every discovery of what is false leads us to seek earnestly after what is true, and very fresh experience points out some form of error which we shall afterward carefully avoid. —John Keats

There is in the worst of fortune the best of chances for a happy change.

—Euripides

Let us not be needlessly bitter: certain failures are sometimes fruitful.

—E.M. Cioran

Sweet are the uses of adversity.

—William Shakespeare

Strength does not come from winning. Your struggles develop your strengths. When you go through hardships and decide not to surrender, that is strength.

—Arnold Schwarzenegger

The ultimate measure of a man is not where he stands in moments of comfort and convenience, but where he stands at times of challenge and controversy.
—Martin Luther King, Jr.

Do not free a camel of the burden of his hump; you may be freeing him from being a camel.
—G.K. Chesterton

I walk firmer and more secure up hill than down.   —Michel de Montaigne

Adversity is like the period of the rain ... cold, comfortless, unfriendly to man and to animal; yet from that season have their birth the flower, the fruit, the date, the rose and the pomegranate.   —Sir Walter Scott

In adversity, remember to keep an even mind.   —Horace

If we survive danger, it steels our courage more than anything else.
—Reinhold Niebuhr

The virtue of adversity is fortitude, which in mortals is the heroical virtue.   —Francis Bacon

To turn an obstacle to one's advantage is a great step towards victory.
—French proverb

Great occasions do not make heroes or cowards; they simply unveil them to the eyes of men ... crisis shows us what we have become.
—Bishop Westcott

Strong men greet war, tempest, hard times. They wish, as Pindar said, to tread the floors of hell, with necessities as hard as iron.
—Ralph Waldo Emerson

REACTING TO EVENTS

HOW WE REACT TO EVENTS IS VERY IMPORTANT

All that is necessary is to accept the unacceptable, do without the indispensable, and bear the unbearable.
—Kathleen Norris

The great difference between one person and another is how he takes hold and uses his first chance, and how he takes his fall if it scored against him   —Thomas Hughes

The prizes go to those who meet emergencies successfully. And the way to meet emergencies is to do each daily task the best we can.
—William Feather

Mishaps are like knives that either serve us or cut us as we grasp them by the blade or the handle.
—James Russell Lowell

Fortune does not change men; it unmasks them.   —Madame Necker

I love the man that can smile in trouble, that can gather strength from distress, and grow brave by reflection.   —Thomas Paine

Wise men ne'er sit and wail their loss, but cheerily seek how to redress their harms.   —William Shakespeare

Trouble has no necessary connection with discouragement; discouragement has a germ of its own, as different from trouble as arthritis is different from a stiff joint.
—F. Scott Fitzgerald

Life is a grindstone, and whether it grinds a man down or polishes him up depends on the stuff he's made of.   —Josh Billings

When we accept tough jobs as a challenge and wade into them with joy and enthusiasm, miracles can happen.   —Arland Gilbert

He who, having lost one ideal, refuses to give his heart and soul to another and nobler, is like a man who declines to build a house on rock because the wind and rain ruined his house on the sand.
—Constance Naden

Whenever you fall, pick something up.   —Oswald Avery

533

I have seen boys on my baseball team go into slumps and never come out of them, and I have seen others snap right out and come back better than ever. I guess more players lick themselves than are ever licked by an opposing team. The first thing any man has to know is how to handle himself. —Connie Mack

Consider how much more you often suffer from your anger and grief than from those very things for which you are angry and grieved.
—Marcus Aurelius

We must never despair; our situation has been compromising before, and it has changed for the better; so I trust it will again. If difficulties arise, we must put forth new exertion and proportion our efforts to the exigencies of the times.
—George Washington

What counts in making a happy marriage is not so much how compatible you are, but how you deal with incompatibility.
—George Levinger

Noble souls, through dust and heat, rise from disaster and defeat the stronger.
—Henry Wadsworth Longfellow

Let no feeling of discouragement prey upon you, and in the end you are sure to succeed.
—Abraham Lincoln

I'm not happy, I'm cheerful. There's a difference. A happy woman has no cares at all. A cheerful woman has cares but has learned how to deal with them. —Beverly Sills

Our mistakes won't irreparably damage our lives unless we let them.
—James E. Sweaney

Oh, a trouble's a ton, or a trouble's an ounce,
Or a trouble is what you make it,
And it isn't the fact that you're hurt that counts,
But only how you take it.
—Edmund Vance Cooke

When the rock is hard, we get harder than the rock. When the job is tough, we get tougher than the job.
—George Cullum, Sr.

To be happy, drop the words "if only" and substitute instead the words "next time."
—Smiley Blanton, M.D.

Always take an emergency leisurely.
—Chinese proverb

Keep strong if possible; in any case, keep cool. —Sir Basil Liddell Hart

When something bad happens to me, I think I'm able to deal with it in a pretty good way. That makes me lucky. Some people fall apart at the first little thing that happens.
—Christie Brinkley

Concern should drive us into action, not into a depression.
—Karen Horney

Happiness is not the absence of conflict, but the ability to cope with it.
—Anon.

A man has no more character than he can command in a time of crisis.
—Ralph W. Sockman

Results? Why, man, I have gotten a lot of results. I know several thousand things that won't work.
—Thomas Alva Edison

The tragedy is not that things are broken. The tragedy is that they are not mended again.　　—Anon.

Don't curse the darkness—light a candle.　　　—Chinese proverb

Any man can shoot a gun, and with practice he can draw fast and shoot accurately, but that makes no difference. What counts is how you stand up when somebody is shooting back at you.　　—Louis L'Amour

We are troubled on every side, yet not distressed; we are perplexed, but not in despair.
—2 Cor. 4:8

Anyone can hold the helm when the sea is calm.　　—Publilius Syrus

An error is simply a failure to adjust immediately from a preconception to an actuality.　　—John Cage

What the caterpillar calls a tragedy, the Master calls a butterfly.
—Richard Bach

You are beaten to earth? Well, well, what's that?
Come up with a smiling face,
It's nothing against you to fall down flat
But to lie there—that's a disgrace.
—Edmund Vance Cooke

The longer we dwell on our misfortunes, the greater is their power to harm us.　　—Voltaire

When the going gets tough, the tough get going.　　—Frank Leahy

The difficulties of life are intended to make us better, not bitter.
—Anon.

Acceptance of what has happened is the first step to overcoming the consequences of any misfortune.
—William James

We can either change the complexities of life ... or develop ways that enable us to cope more effectively.
—Herbert Benson

It is arrogance to expect that life will always be music.... Harmony, like a following breeze at sea, is the exception. In a world where most things wind up broken or lost, our lot is to tack and tune.　—Harvey Oxenhorn

The winds and waves are always on the side of the ablest navigators.
—Edward Gibbon

REACTING TO DIFFICULT SITUATIONS

No matter what has happened, always behave as if nothing had happened.　　—Arnold Bennett

When things go wrong, don't go with them.　　—Anon.

Nothing is so bad that you have to sit down and go crazy.—John Telgen

In adversity, remember to keep an even mind.　　—Horace

Do not lose your inward peace for anything whatsoever, even if your whole world seems upset.
—Saint Francis de Sales

OUR PERCEPTIONS AND THOUGHTS ABOUT WHAT HAPPENS ARE WHAT COUNT

We are not troubled by things, but by the opinion which we have of things. —Epictetus

Things are in their essence what we choose to make them. A thing is, according to the mode in which one looks at it. —Oscar Wilde

We are never so happy or so unhappy as we think.
—Francois de La Rochefoucauld

We exaggerate misfortune and happiness alike. We are never either so wretched or so happy as we say we are. —Honore de Balzac

The most unhappy of all men is he who believes himself to be so.
—David Hume

Happiness does not depend on outward things, but on the way we see them. —Leo Tolstoy

The mind is its own place, and in itself can make a heaven of hell, a hell of heaven. —John Milton

Almost all our misfortunes in life come from the wrong notions we have about the things that happen to us. —Stendhal

Riches, like glory or health, have no more beauty or pleasure than their possessor is pleased to lend them.
—Michel de Montaigne

Losses are comparative, imagination only makes them of any moment.
—Blaise Pascal

Man is only miserable so far as he thinks himself so. —Sannazare

The art of life consists in taking each event which befalls us with a contented mind, confident of good.... With this method ... rejoice always, though in the midst of sorrows, and possess all things, though destitute of everything. —James Fretman Clarke

So long as one does not despair, so long as one doesn't look upon life bitterly, things work out fairly well in the end. —George Moore

The meaning of things lies not in the things themselves, but in our attitude towards them.
—Antoine de Saint-Exupery

Pain is inevitable. Suffering is optional. —Anon.

If you are distressed by anything external, the pain is not due to the thing itself but to your own estimate of it; and this you have the power to revoke at any moment.
—Marcus Aurelius

Little things affect little minds.
—Benjamin Disraeli

Do not weep; do not wax indignant. Understand. —Baruch Spinoza

No emotional crisis is wholly the product of outward circumstances. These may precipitate it. But what turns an objective situation into a subjectively critical one is the interpretation the individual puts upon it—the meaning it has in his emotional economy; the way it affects his self-image. —Bonaro Overstreet

There is nothing either good or bad,
but thinking makes it so.
—William Shakespeare

Men are not influenced by things,
but by their thoughts about things.
—Epictetus

Nothing is miserable unless you
think it so. —Boethius

I can complain because rose bushes
have thorns, or rejoice because thorn
bushes have roses. It's all how you
look at it. —J. Kenfield Morley

MAKE THE BEST OF WHATEVER HAPPENS

I make the most of all that comes
and the least of all that goes.
—Sara Teasdale

We must make the best of those ills
which cannot be avoided.
—Alexander Hamilton

If you have to be in a soap opera, try
not to get the worst role.
—Boy George

True contentment is the power of
getting of any situation all that there
is in it. —G.K. Chesterton

On the occasion of every accident
that befalls you ... inquire what
power you have for turning it to use.
—Epictetus

Things turn out best for people who
make the best of the way things turn
out. —Anon.

Experience is not what happens to
you; it is what you do with what
happens to you. —Aldous Huxley

Whatever evil befalls us, we ought to
ask ourselves ... how we can turn it
into good. So shall we take occasion,
from one bitter root, to raise perhaps
many flowers. —Leigh Hunt

There are no accidents so unlucky
from which clever people are not
able to reap some advantage, and
none so lucky that the foolish are
not able to turn them to their own
disadvantage.
—Francois de La Rochefoucauld

A wise man turns chance into good
fortune. —Thomas Fuller

Losses are comparative, only imagination makes them of any moment.
—Blaise Pascal

Your living is determined not so
much by what life brings to you as
by the attitude you bring to life; not
so much by what happens to you as
by the way your mind looks at what
happens. —John Homer Miller

Riches, like glory or health, have no
more beauty or pleasure than their
possessor is pleased to lend them.
—Michel de Montaigne

Trouble is the thing that strong men
grow by. Met in the right way, it is a
sure-fire means of putting iron into
the victim's will and making him a
tougher man to down forever after.
—H. Bertram Lewis

When fate hands you a lemon, make
lemonade. —Dale Carnegie

To a brave man, good and bad luck
are like his right and left hand. He
uses both. —Saint Catherine of Siena

There are two ways of meeting difficulties. You alter the difficulties or you alter yourself to meet them.
—Phyllis Bottome

Turn your stumbling blocks into stepping stones. —Anon.

One cannot get through life without pain.... What we can do is choose how to use the pain life presents to us. —Bernie S. Siegel, M.D.

Never despair, but if you do, work on in despair. —Edmund Burke

Groan and forget it.
—Jessamyn West

Let us not be needlessly bitter: certain failures are sometimes fruitful.
—E.M. Cioran

The most important thing in life is not to capitalize on your gains. Any fool can do that. The really important thing is to profit from your losses. —William Bolitho

Disease can be seen as a call for personal transformation through metamorphosis. It is a transition from the death of your old self into the birth of your new. —Tom O'Connor, person with ARC

Find the grain of truth in criticism—chew it and swallow it.—Don Sutton

LIFE IS LIKE A GAME OF CARDS
You gotta play the hand that's dealt you. There may be pain in that hand, but you play it. —James Brady

Boys, this is only game. But it's like life in that you will be dealt some bad hands. Take each hand, good or bad, and don't whine and complain, but play it out. If you're men enough to do that, God will help and you will come out well.
—Dwight D. Eisenhower's mother

Life is like a game of cards. The hand that is dealt you represents determination; the way you play it is free will. —Jawaharlal Nehru

Life consists not in holding good cards, but in playing those you do hold well. —Josh Billings

The game of life is not so much in holding a good hand as playing a poor hand well. —H.T. Leslie

All I can do is play the game the way the cards fall. —James A. Michener

True luck consists not in holding the best cards at the table; luckiest he who knows just when to rise and go home. —John Hay

COURAGE IS CRITICAL
The greatest test of courage on earth is to bear defeat without losing heart. —Robert G. Ingersoll

Courage is to take hard knocks like a man when occasion calls.
—Plautus

This is courage ... to bear unflinchingly what heaven sends. —Euripides

To accept whatever comes, regardless of the consequences, is to be unafraid. —John Cage

Let us be brave in the face of adversity. —Marcus Annaeus Seneca

538

Courage, in the final analysis, is nothing but an affirmative answer to the shocks of existence.
—Dr. Kurt Goldstein

Courage is a perfect sensibility of the measure of danger, and a mental willingness to endure it.
—General William T. Sherman

To have courage for whatever comes in life—everything lies in that.
—Saint Teresa of Avila

HUMOR HELPS

There is no defense against adverse fortune which is so effectual as an habitual sense of humor.
—Thomas W. Higginson

When we begin to take our failures non-seriously, it means we are ceasing to be afraid of them. It is of immense importance to learn to laugh at ourselves.
—Katherine Mansfield

Humor prevents one from becoming a tragic figure even though he/she is involved in tragic events.
—E.T. "Cy" Eberhart

Humor is my sword and my shield. It protects me. You can open a door with humor and drive a truck right through. —Alan Simpson

A sense of humor can help you overlook the unattractive, tolerate the unpleasant, cope with the unexpected, and smile through the unbearable. —Moshe Waldoks

Humor is an affirmation of dignity, a declaration of man's superiority to all that befalls him. —Roman Gary

Humor is the instinct for taking pain playfully. —Max Eastman

Humor is a means of obtaining pleasure in spite of the distressing effects that interface with it.
—Sigmund Freud

Humor is the healthy way of feeling "distance" between one's self and the problem, a way of standing off and looking at one's problems with perspective. —Rollo May

A person without a sense of humor is like a wagon without springs, jolted by every pebble in the road.
—Henry Ward Beecher

Total absence of humor renders life impossible. —Colette

If I had no sense of humor, I should long ago have committed suicide.
—Mahatma Gandhi

A sense of humor judges one's actions and the actions of others from a wider reference ... it pardons shortcomings; it consoles failure. It recommends moderation.
—Thornton Wilder

Were it not for my little jokes, I could not bear the burdens of this office. —Abraham Lincoln

Any man who has had the job I've had and didn't have a sense of humor wouldn't still be here.
—Harry S. Truman

Humor is an attitude. It's a way of looking at life and of telling others how you feel about what's happening around you. —Gene Perret

Humor is just another defense
against the universe.　　—Mel Brooks

Optimism and humor are the grease
and glue of life. Without both of
them we would never have survived
our captivity.
　　　　—Philip Butler, Vietnam POW

GENERAL QUOTATIONS ABOUT REACTING TO EVENTS

Good people are good because
they've come to wisdom through
failure.　　　　—William Saroyan

Everyday ... life confronts us with
new problems to be solved which
force us to adjust our old programs
accordingly.　　　—Dr. Ann Faraday

What can any of us do with his talent but try to develop his vision, so
that through frequent failures we
may learn better what we have
missed in the past.
　　　　—William Carlos Williams

There are more serious problems in
life than financial ones, and I've had
a lot of those. I've been broke
before, and will be again.
Heartbroke? That's serious. Lose a
few bucks? That's not.
　　　　—Willie Nelson

A life of reaction is a life of slavery,
intellectually and spiritually. One
must fight for a life of action, not
reaction.　　　—Rita Mae Brown

SELF-PITY

IT'S HUMAN TO BE TEMPTED BY SELF-PITY

Self-pity comes so naturally to all of us.   —André Maurois

Every man supposes himself not to be fully understood or appreciated.
—Ralph Waldo Emerson

SOME DISASTROUS EFFECTS OF SELF-PITY

Self-pity is our worst enemy and if we yield to it, we can never do anything wise in this world.
—Helen Keller

What poison is to food, self-pity is to life.   —Oliver C. Wilson

Being sorry for myself is a luxury I can't afford.
—Stephen King and Peter Straub

To feel sorry for oneself is one of the most disintegrating things the individual can do to himself.
—Winifred Rhoades

Self-pity is one of the most dangerous forms of self-centeredness. It fogs our vision.   —Anon.

Self-pity is one of the most unhappy and consuming defects that we know. It is a bar to all spiritual progress and can cut off all effective communication with our fellows because of its inordinate demands for attention and sympathy. It is a maudlin form of martyrdom, which we can ill afford.   —As Bill Sees It

Grumbling is the death of love.
—Marlene Dietrich

To hear complaints is wearisome to the wretched and the happy alike.
—Samuel Johnson

WE MUST BANISH SELF-PITY

Sympathy is never wasted except when you give it to yourself.
—John W. Raper

The opposite of having faith is having self-pity.   —Og Guinness

Optimism and self-pity are the positive and negative poles of modern cowardice.   —Cyril Connolly

He who complains, sins.
—Saint Francis de Sales

This life is not for complaint, but for satisfaction. —Henry David Thoreau

How to Get Past Self-Pity

Is life so wretched? Isn't it rather your hands which are too small, your vision which is muddled? You are the one who must grow up.
—Dag Hammarskjold

Suffering isn't ennobling, recovery is.
—Christian N. Barnard

You can overcome anything if you don't bellyache.
—Bernard M. Baruch

There is only one way to end a self-pity cycle: stop comparing yourself to others, and simply follow Christ.
—Linda Harry

Do not weep; do not wax indignant. Understand.   —Baruch Spinoza

When any fit of gloominess, or perversion of mind, lays hold upon you, make it a rule not to publish it by complaints.   —Samuel Johnson

Taking Action Is a Great Way to Overcome Self-Pity

The secret of being miserable is to have leisure to bother about whether you are happy or not. The cure for it is occupation.
—George Bernard Shaw

The cure for grief is motion.
—Elbert Hubbard

I got the blues thinking of the future, so I left off and made some marmalade. It's amazing how it cheers one up to shred oranges or scrub the floor.   —D.H. Lawrence

When you find yourself overpowered, as it were, by melancholy, the best way is to go out and do something.   —John Keble

The best mask for demoralization is daring.   —Lucan

We Choose to Indulge in Self-Pity

Self-pity is a death that has no resurrection, a sinkhole from which no rescuing hand can drag you because you have *chosen* to sink.
—Elizabeth Elliot

Pain is inevitable. Suffering is optional.   —Anon.

I am convinced, the longer I live, that life and its blessings are not so entirely unjustly distributed as when we are suffering greatly we are inclined to suppose.
—Mary Todd Lincoln

Despair is the absolute extreme of self-love. It is reached when a man deliberately turns his back on all help from anyone else in order to taste the rotten luxury of knowing himself to be lost. —Thomas Merton

General Quotations about Self-Pity

Sometimes I go about pitying myself, and all the time I am being carried on great winds across the sky.
—Ojibway Dream Song

Others may argue about whether the world ends with a bang or a whimper. I just want to make sure mine doesn't end with a whine.
—Barbara Gordon

I never saw a wild thing sorry for
itself.
A small bird will drop frozen dead
from a bough
Without ever having felt sorry for
itself.   —D.H. Lawrence

Every message of despair is the statement of a situation from which
everybody must freely try to find a
way out.   —Eugene Ionesco

A man's as miserable as he thinks he
is.   —Marcus Annaeus Seneca

Your distress about life might mean
you have been living for the wrong
reason, not that you have no reason
for living.   —Tom O'Connor,
                              person with ARC

Sadness is almost never anything but
a form of fatigue.   —André Gide

The human mind can bear plenty of
reality, but not too much unintermit-
tent gloom.   —Margaret Drabble

He's simply got the instinct for being
unhappy highly developed.
                    —Saki (H.H. Munro)

Misery is a communicable disease.
                    —Martha Graham

Never give way to melancholy; resist
it steadily, for the habit will
encroach.   —Sydney Smith

Despair is criminal.
                    —Samuel Johnson

Even the cry from the depths is an
affirmation: Why cry if there is no
hint or hope of hearing?
                    —Martin Marty

INDEX

552

553

Hickson, W.E., 443, 494
Higginson, Thomas Wentworth, 57, 525, 539
Higher Power, 112–17
Hightower, Cullen, 123, 381
Hightower, Jim, 464
Hildebrand, Kenneth, 354
Hill, James B., 455
Hill, Napoleon, 344, 354, 381, 498
Hillel, 175
Hilliard, 266
Hillis, Burton, 223
Hillyer, Robert, 380, 479
Hindu proverb, 21, 85, 87, 107, 126
Hippocrates, 151
Hippolytus, 99
Hirohito, Emperor, 318
Hirsch, Michael, person with AIDS, 265, 270
Hiscox, E.T., 121
Hitchcock, Alfred, 196, 453
Hobbes, John Oliver, 60, 75, 219
Hobbes, Thomas, 123, 288
Hodges, Leigh Mitchell, 238, 520
Hodgkin, Thomas, 518
Hodgson, Ralph, 118
Hodnett, Edward, 506
Hoffer, Eric, 44, 80, 123, 187, 190, 233, 251, 269, 271, 286, 294, 307, 340, 341, 376, 385, 459, 518, 522
Hoffman, Abbie, 225, 430, 481
Hoffman, Dustin, 74
Hofmann, Hans, 195
Holdcroft, L. Thomas, 3, 223, 245
Holderlin, Friedrich, 38, 347
Holland, J.G., 498
Holland, Josiah, 151, 191, 526
Holler, William E., 90, 493
Holmes, 319
Holmes, Carol, 18
Holmes, Dr. J.A., 419
Holmes, Ernest, 113, 262, 516
Holmes, John Andrew, 79, 85
Holmes, Oliver Wendell, 8, 53, 58, 94, 97, 103, 115, 122, 124, 200, 202, 210, 220, 306, 489, 497
Holmes, Oliver Wendell, Jr., 171, 209, 294, 313, 321, 345, 357, 385, 386, 388, 417, 425, 448, 471, 494
Holt, Hamilton, 441, 475
Holt, John, 420
Holtby, Winifred, epitaph of, 147
Holtz, Lou, 463, 526
Homer, 63, 101, 109, 209, 309, 401, 453, 483, 537
Homoka, Oscar, 530
Honda, Soichire, 340
Hood, Thomas, 244
Hooker, Richard, 307
Hoover, Herbert, 42, 54, 344, 426

Hoover, J. Edgar, 160
Hope, 284–89
Hope, Bob, 526
Hope, Laurence, 42
Hopf, Harry A., 315, 425
Hopi Indian saying, 118
Horace, 26, 43, 44, 48, 57, 63, 64, 69, 71, 72, 74, 171, 201, 225, 232, 246, 254, 287, 315, 334, 345, 360, 401, 403, 404, 409, 427, 430, 528, 529, 532, 535
Horban, Donald, 64
Horne, 158, 272
Horney, Karen, 534
Houff, William H., 488
Housman, A.E., 84, 239, 377
Hovey, Richard, 521
Howe, Edgar Watson, 93, 96, 97, 102, 189, 239, 244, 331, 341, 348, 373, 375, 382, 386, 411, 429, 439, 528
Howe, John, 200
Howells, W.D., 426
Hoyle, Fred, 518
Hsieh, Tehyi, 107, 387, 427
Huang Po, 385
Hubbard, Elbert, 23, 49, 56, 83, 87, 109, 119, 186, 195, 209, 216, 224, 233, 240, 270, 272, 365, 369, 376, 427, 431, 442, 450, 471, 498, 499, 511, 516, 519, 520, 521, 524, 542
Hubbard, J.G., 488
Hubbard, Kin, 24, 47, 64, 274
Hubbard, L. Ron, 18, 354, 361, 509
Hube, R.M., 74
Huerta, Dolores, 50
Hughes, Frank, 275
Hughes, Henry Ward, 380
Hughes, Langston, 291
Hughes, Thomas, 92, 533
Hugo, Victor, 26, 85, 120, 133, 203, 241, 288, 354, 392, 416, 486, 525
Hulbert, William A., 336, 446, 447
Hulme, Katheryn, 485
Hulst, Maurice, 86
Humboldt, Wilhelm von, 17, 35, 360
Hume, David, 16, 36, 264, 536
Hummell, Charles, 229
Humphrey, Hubert H., 62, 222, 323
Humphreys, Harry E., Jr., 92
Hungarian proverb, 77
Hunt, Earl G., Jr., 133, 156
Hunt, Leigh, 244, 537
Hunter, Catfish, 277, 337
Hunter, Ian, 519
Hurdle, Clint, 332
Huvelin, Abbé Henri, 124
Huxley, Aldous, 15, 54, 69, 108, 125, 177, 185, 194, 219, 244, 306, 307, 321, 537

Huxley, Thomas Henry, 422, 424, 442, 513

I Ching, 258
Iacocca, Lee, 204, 315, 387, 428, 469
Iannelli, Richard, 321
Ibsen, Henrik, 6, 329, 351, 446, 463, 521
Ignorance, 419–21
Iles, George, 286
Independent, The, 424
Indian proverb, 151
Inge, William Ralph, 13, 22, 63, 115, 124, 251, 252, 383, 473
Ingelow, Jean, 158
Ingenieros, José, 223
Ingersoll, Robert G., 25, 289, 344, 406, 538
inn located in Lancaster, England, written on, 147
Instincts, 319–24
International Standard Bible Encyclopedia, 161
Ionesco, Eugene, 317, 543
Irish proverb, 83, 170, 183, 375, 474
Iron, Mary Jean, 53, 250
Irving, John, 196, 361
Irving, Washington, 300, 351, 468, 522
Irwin, Ben, 201
Irwin, William A., 206
Isidore of Seville, 231
Italian proverb, 285, 343, 356
Ivener, Goldie, 230
Izzard, Wes, 441, 475

Jacks, L.P., 266
Jackson, Andrew, 406
Jackson, Delma, 128
Jackson, Dr. Bill, 171
Jackson, Helen Hunt, 224, 257, 428
Jackson, Holbrook, 6, 13, 330
Jackson, Jesse, 237, 289, 482
Jackson, LaToya, 76
Jackson, Reggie, 271
Jackson, Robert H., 339
Jacobi, Friedrich, 116
Jacobs, Joseph, 51
Jakes, John, 453
James, Henry, 5, 17, 80, 335, 360, 446
James, Paul Moon, 288
James, William, 15, 43, 92, 94, 110, 113, 125, 155, 174, 251, 260, 261, 272, 294, 305, 316, 317, 319, 321, 322, 323, 327, 362, 369, 370, 394, 424, 425, 429, 448, 451, 526, 535
Jameson, Storm, 9, 11, 195, 226, 235
Jampolsky, Gerald, 47, 49, 50, 239, 305, 322, 483
Janis, Byron, 271, 369
Japanese proverb, 66, 67, 221,

557